THE CONFESSIONS

SAINT AUGUSTINE OF HIPPO

THE CONFESSIONS

With an Introduction and
Contemporary Criticism

Edited by DAVID VINCENT MECONI, S.J.

Ignatius Critical Editions Editor
JOSEPH PEARCE

IGNATIUS PRESS   SAN FRANCISCO

This translation was first published in the United States by New City Press,
Hyde Park, N.Y. as part of the series *The Works of Saint Augustine:*
A Translation for the 21st Century
© 1997 by the Augustinian Heritage Institute, Villanova, Pa.
Used with permission from New City Press.

Cover art:
Saint Augustine in His Study
by Sandro Botticelli (1444–1510)
Uffizi Gallery, Florence, Italy.
Photograph by Scala/Art Resource, N.Y.

Cover design by John Herreid

© 2012 by Ignatius Press, San Francisco
ISBN 978-1-58617-683-9
Library of Congress Control Number 2011940926
Printed in India ∞

CONTENTS

INTRODUCTION

David Vincent Meconi, S.J.

Carthage, 371

Dear Mom,

School is a blast! I am sorry for not having written earlier, but things here are quite challenging. You're right, I have made some good friends and have taken to the big city world rather well. I must admit that this has helped to ease the initial homesickness I was suffering earlier. Mom, I wish you could meet my new girlfriend. We may come from very different places, but we have taught each other some important lessons. We have been staying together for a year or so now, and want you to know that you are soon going to meet your grandson! Don't worry, all will be well, as I shall soon be ready to take on some students of my own in order to pay the bills. Yet I am wondering if I really want to pursue law. More and more the study of words simply to effect some rhetorical flare seems so empty. What would you say if I changed my major and became a philosopher instead? Ha, I know it wouldn't lead to much, but I have read some great books here and am coming to see that there must be something more behind words than just allure, there must be some substance that attracts and moves others to truth. But I don't know, living without insisting on truth is a lot easier.

You should, however, be happy that this new investigation into "truth" (whatever that is) has me going back to church most weeks. That is what you wanted for me, after all, isn't it? The only problem may be—and please don't get upset—that I am not going to the Church of Rome you know, but to a group of believers called the Manicheans. As far as I can tell, Mani the great prophet is the only one able to make real sense of the scriptures and of the problem of evil and why there is pain

vii

and destruction in this world. I think you and your friends have
been reading the scriptures wrongly for a long time: the god of
the Old Testament is really the god of destruction and decay.
Just look at all the wars and all the instances of deceit and
impiety in those books. Compare that with the god of the New
Testament, Mom. Isn't that where you always exhorted me and
my siblings when we were growing up? There is where I see
the goodness of god, a god of true light and not of this world.
The Manicheans here have helped me see that this world is at
war because god is at war with another all-powerful deity. Good
and evil are in constant conflict, and once I came to see that,
so much in this world made sense and I began feeling a lot
better about my own inadequacies, that's for sure! Anyway, I
have to go and shall write more later. Send *pecunia*! Your loving son,

   Augustine

A perennial search gives way to a perennial figure: no different than most young people of each age, Augustine of
Hippo is known best for his "restless heart", seeking rightly
and wrongly after so many pleasures. Begun in the year 397,
these searches, both futile and fertile, are recorded in the
Confessions, a work whose overall unity and purpose continue
to amaze and attract. From Saint Patrick's *Confession*
in the fifth century to Rousseau's in the eighteenth century,
writers have seen in Augustine's memoirs a template for self-
disclosure as well as a tool for helping readers come to
a better understanding of their own motives, their own life's
story. This was no doubt what drove Saint Teresa of Ávila and
Saint Ignatius of Loyola to compose their own *Autobiography* in the sixteenth century, while Margery Kempe
(ca. 1373–ca. 1438) produced the first story of the self in
English, as she chronicled her pilgrimages to various holy places
and what God was then doing in her wayfaring soul. While
this genre of the personal memoir was not unique to Christianity (e.g., Isocrates attempts the same sort of self-disclosure
as far back as the late fourth century B.C.), those who followed Jesus relied on revealing their souls in a special way

because they knew it was in their *confessio* that God hearkened and spoke.

A New Bishop in an Old Land

But what prompted Augustine to commit his past life's search to the written page? Why did he think it important to memorialize his restlessness? The first and most immediate reason Augustine composed his *Confessions* is to defend himself from lingering suspicions over the authenticity of his Catholic conversion, attempting to placate the Punic Primate who was obviously uncomfortable with two bishops in the relatively insignificant backwater town of Hippo Regius—that is, Augustine put to print the details of his life leading up to his baptism so as to defend not mainly himself but his bishop Valerius' decision to consecrate the young Augustine a coadjutor, an auxiliary bishop within his Diocese of Hippo Regius.

As we shall see, Augustine's sordid youth back in those North African cities and plains must have been quite memorable. While his adolescent antics were not known internationally and while his vices were not extraordinary when compared with the dalliances of his fourth-century contemporaries, the fact that he was a well-known member of the anti-Catholic, new age cult, the Manichees or Manichaeans, as well as an imperial mouthpiece acting on behalf of an anti-Catholic Arian ruler, gave pause to Megalius, the Primate of Numidia (and thus the one responsible for approving Augustine's ordination). Two bishops in one diocese was not only unheard of in North Africa; it was directly opposed to the eighth canon of the Council of Nicaea, which suggested that two bishops in any one city was not at all desirable. Moreover, according to the same set of conciliar canons (cf. §6), any episcopal consecration had to be first approved by the Metropolitan of that area.

Nevertheless, the aging Valerius was in dire need of help. Hippo was a relatively small town—about thirty thousand inhabitants—and Catholics there were in the minority, and

Valerius' command of the local Punic dialect left him struggling to connect with the locals. The Donatists, those ecclesial purists who demanded the perfection of clergy and member
alike, outnumbered the Roman Catholics in most cities in
the dusty Maurentanias and Numidian plains. In Augustine,
Valerius saw a capable orator, one whose conversion he trusted
and whose talents to understand and elucidate the true Spirit
of God he sought, not only to make him known to the rest
of the Church; he presumably also sought to keep him in
Hippo. Handing the episcopacy to Augustine was the most
sure way of securing his stay. Yet, Megalius, the Bishop of
Carthage and overall Primate of Numidia, was right to question Valerius' desire to consecrate a coadjutor, not to mention one of Augustine's status. Two bishops in one diocese
was then a very uncommon custom; yet notwithstanding ecclesiastical tradition, the man in question was known "in these
parts" as a former Manichee, a ne'er-do-well, and a blasphemer.
Augustine himself many years later makes reference to the
letter Megalius wrote to Valerius laying out his concerns, and
Augustine himself responds in turn. For the *Confessions* is his
first work after his episcopal consecration and no doubt his
first public attempt to defend his Catholic conversion as
authentic and fruitful.

Another important reason Augustine composed the *Confessions* was to provide Paulinus of Nola (ca. 353–431, ordained
Bishop of Nola, Italy, in 408) with an account of the Church
in North Africa in general and a bit of the life of his corre-
spondent Alypius in particular. It seems that late in 395, Alypius (then Bishop of Thagaste) writes to the wealthy and
aristocratic Paulinus (*Letter* 4) to introduce himself and possibly to secure some assets for works within his own Diocese
of Thagaste. Paulinus replied and requested an account from
Alypius addressing how he too had come to the faith, how he
was made bishop, and what interest he shared in the ascetical
life. Here unfortunately the paper trail ends, and we possess
neither Alypius' response nor how Augustine came to this information. What most scholars argue, however, is that the many

pages of the *Confessions* dedicated to the life of Alypius are in fact in response to this exchange, a sign of Augustine's respect for both his friend Alypius and his peer Paulinus.

According to recent scholarship, Paulinus sensed that Augustine would prove a better exegetical guide in understanding the Scriptures than the irascible and far-off (in the Holy Land) Jerome. Four letters from Paulinus and eight from Augustine remain; yet internal evidence suggests at least twenty-six more missives were exchanged between these two giants, averaging at least one exchange of letters a year for the rest of their lives. According to Augustine, in *Letter* 27, Paulinus did in fact request an account of the life of the new Bishop of Thagaste, Augustine's childhood friend Alypius, but never received it from his own hand. It is likely that out of respect for both Paulinus' request and Alypius' perhaps-forgotten promise, Augustine involved elements of Alypius' life that would have otherwise been omitted.

God Speaks to the Self

Augustine's *Confessions* internalized the phenomenon of allowing the experiences of one's life to speak the power of God more successfully than any other work before it (and, in my estimation, since!), and such theology is included already in the very telling title. From the Latin verb *fateor*, "to speak" or "to disclose", "fessio" refers to the act of relating truths, of divulging what would otherwise remain unknown (e.g., the *fates* are those who reveal what is to come). The prefix "con-" comes from the Latin *cum-*, meaning "along with" or "besides". As such, the *Confessions* are thus primarily conversation, a dialogue, an exchange. Throughout, Augustine is never alone, for this is the recording of incessant human and divine interaction. To confess, then, is primarily to pray, an oration between creature and Creator, while only secondarily is it to be understood in the usual sense today of "going to confession". While the recording of sins is a part of Augustine's story, the *Confessions* are not simply about that type of examination of

conscience. Rather, the life we here encounter has been written down not to record the author's own sinfulness, but in
order to praise God for *his* goodness and fidelity.

The division of the *Confessions* into thirteen books comes
from Augustine's own hand. Within the earliest manuscripts,
only these thirteen divisions exist; there are no titles, no sub-
headings, and no section numbers. Sometime in the fifteenth
century chapter numbers began to appear in the various manuscripts around Europe, in order to make referring to particular
passages within the *Confessions* easier; in their 1679 edition,
the Maurist Benedictines in France even went on to insert
paragraph numbers. This division into book, section, and paragraph is what we still use today (see note 2, p. 465). Such
precise referencing has proven necessary for the author who
has left us more writings than anyone else in the ancient world,
almost 5.4 million words. Moreover, such a massive corpus will
obviously show variant readings and different versions as the
Latin was copied from generation to generation. However, the
Confessions as we now have them enjoy a rather uniform trans-
mission, and we can rest assured that the fine English translation provided here by Maria Boulding, O.S.B. (d. 2009), is a
faithful reproduction. Augustine's three main works all capture the drama of the Christian narrative: whereas the *Confessions* detail the drama of the human soul as it must daily
choose between self and God, the massive *City of God* (written over the years 413–427) registers this battle on a more
cosmic scale, the clash between the "City of Man" and the
"City of God", while *On the Trinity* (composed over a long
span, 399–422/426) captures the very life of Father, Son, and
Holy Spirit as beautifully as any creature could. Yet, it has been
the *Confessions* that has proven the best known of Augustine's
works, the most translated, and the most widely read.

Exactly what are the *Confessions*? We understand them best
when we see how the Bishop of Hippo came to realize how
biography could be a powerful witness to the grace of God,
thus setting out to lay down not a story of his life but a story
of every soul's journey. What we have before us is thus not

simply an autobiography but an omnibiography, as it sets out to explain every human soul's journey from and back to its loving and ever-forgiving Creator. This is surely why the *Confessions* is so stingy with names, places, and particular dates. But this is not Augustine's story—it is ours; it is everyone's.

The opening line of the *Confessions* is highly significant for what lies ahead: "Great are you, O Lord, and exceedingly worthy of praise". This gambit alone should prove that this is no autobiography in the normal sense. Whereas you or I would most likely begin with the subject "I", as in "I was born in ...", we thereby limit our story to the most private and exclusive agent possible: our own selves. Augustine, however, situates his confession in the person of the living God, the most public and inclusive being possible. Of course, what follows next is the dramatic line of this whole story: "[Y]ou have made us and drawn us to yourself, and our heart is unquiet until it rests in you."[1] One God, one heart, one search, one rest— this is the story of collective humanity, of every human soul if it only had the wherewithal to perceive reality rightly. What follows is thus an omnibiography, the story of Everyman, of every restless creature. Book I covers the years from Augustine's birth in 354 to roughly his sixteenth year. The opening book is thus dedicated to the movements of human infancy. Why so? Whereas *con-fessio* means "to speak with", *in-fans* means "the inability to speak", and Augustine rightly begins by asking how one can even begin to attempt to speak with God. Must we not first know God before we can call out to him, but must we not be able to call on him if we are going to come to know him?

The great orator stumbles, toddles, to know how to speak to God, and in Book II (covering 370) this unsteady wobbling is translated into the antics of youth, memorialized by the stealing of the pears. Far from being a compulsive, scrupulous worrier,

---

[1] Saint Augustine, *The Confessions*, ed. David Vincent Meconi, S.J., Ignatius Critical Editions (San Francisco: Ignatius Press, 2012), I.1.1. Subsequent quotations from this edition will be cited in the text. References are to book, section, and paragraph.

Augustine recalls this event from his childhood because stealing simply out of the forbiddance of it enthralls him: he did it for no other reason than it was prohibited (see *Conf.* II.4.9). This is about as close to the abyss of nothingness that a moral agent can get. Yet in the pear tree, three important images are conjured: (1) the Tree of Eden, (2) the prodigal son's feeding of unclean swine, and (3) the Manichean abhorrence of a fruit containing the good god. But the story continues because Augustine now knows that while evil may unfortunately play a part in human living, it is neither the first nor the last word. We therefore confess both good and evil, both Christ's grace as well as our own sins, because this is the only way to wholeness, to understanding who we are really.

Books III–VI (covering the years 371–385/386) bring the reader into the plans of a young man beginning to make his way in the world: first as a student in Carthage struggling with his own fallen desires, then as a young father, and finally as one who is searching for meaning in his life. Seemingly unable to find satisfying answers in the Christian faith he knew through his mother, Augustine joins a Gnostic religious sect then in vogue, Manichaeism. Their founder was a Persian mystic, Mani (d. A.D. 276), whose cosmic dualism taught that all of reality was the unfortunate mixture of a good god and a malicious god eternally at war. Such a dualistic worldview not only provided an easy answer to Augustine's nagging question why there was evil in the world, but it also excused his "real" self from sinning, as wrongdoing and destruction were simply inescapable realities. He lived this life as a Manichean "hearer" for nine years but was eventually dismayed by the utter ignorance of the sect's leaders. By this time Augustine has moved to Rome and then to Milan (in the autumn of 384), now the seat of the western Roman Empire (moved there by the emperor Diocletian in 293), where he was made the imperially appointed professor of rhetoric. He had achieved everything any Roman Empire orator could ever desire. Aurelius Augustine of Hippo was thriving, but the Lord, as all would soon discover, had other plans.

The contours of Books VII–IX are a bit more subtle, the movement here being less geographical and much more intellectual. In Milan Augustine encounters the beauty of human reason, as exemplified in Neoplatonic philosophy (most probably during the summer of 386), as well as the intelligibility of the Christian faith, as personified in the Bishop of Milan, Ambrose. The philosophy Augustine now read was mainly the works of Plotinus (d. A.D. 270), the father of Neoplatonism, an Egyptian who once in Rome reworked the major insights of Plato, developing a philosophical worldview many early Church Fathers found to be very helpful in elucidating the truths of Christianity. The tenets of Neoplatonism introduced Augustine, for example, to the existence of immaterial reality, the eternal nature of the soul, as well as evil as the privation of being. That is, by reading these "books by the Platonists" (see *Conf.* VII.9.13), translated into Latin by Marius Victorinus, Augustine learned how the Manichees were wrong to posit a substantial evil, for if evil is a parasite of the good, anything substantially or essentially evil would in fact be nothing. Evil is therefore not a substance to which one could point, but a parasite that can be explained only as the "absence" of being in an essentially good creature.

In Bishop Ambrose, Augustine met an intelligent orator like himself, someone, however, who sacrificed his very successful and powerful career as a Roman governor, the prefect of Liguria and Emilia, when called upon by the Catholics in their dispute with the Arians intent on taking their property. Augustine quickly perceived how Ambrose's training in classical rhetoric equipped him in preaching, but he also, and much more importantly, knew that this was no mere word play. Ambrose had something to say—something important, eternally important. He was struck by how deeply Ambrose understood the Christian scriptures, but also by how he lived a life of rigorous asceticism and was willing to serve all who came to him. In the fall of 386, after months of listening to Ambrose, Augustine resigned his post of rhetoric and (along with his mother, Monica; his son, Adeodatus; his brother, Navigius; as well as five other friends) he and his intellectual cohort left the city to make a long retreat out in the countryside so as to prepare for entry into the Church.

In the rural hamlet of Cassiciacum, just northeast of Milan (today's Cassiago di Brianza, Italy), Augustine began to write his early dialogues, treatises dedicated to order, education, knowledge, and happiness. On Holy Saturday, April 24, 387, he presented himself in the Milanese Cathedral, and Ambrose lovingly brought him into the Body of Christ, making him a Christian in the regenerative waters of holy baptism. With a new mother, the Church, Augustine spends the rest of Book IX telling us about his earthly mother, whose faith and example helped make this very moment possible. Together Augustine, his mother, his son, friends, and former students pray, talk, and worship. Sometime in the autumn of 387, Monica fell asleep in Christ at the port town of Ostia while waiting their return to North Africa.

With Book X our author transforms the *Confessions* and opens up his narrative now to the dynamics that make any recalling of one's life and God's fidelity possible. In particular, we are no longer taken through the salient moments of Augustine's Christian pilgrimage, but now we come to a treatise dedicated to the theme of human memory. While some earlier scholars in the twentieth century argued that with Book X comes only later afterthoughts, mere attachments our author did not know where else to put (some editions even went so far as to sell the *Confessions* as only Books I–IX), memory is not some awkward postscript but is the very instrument that made the recalling of Augustine's story hitherto possible.

And through what does memory traverse? Time. Book XI accordingly analyzes the need to understand that past and future exist only in the memory, in the mind as recall and as anticipation. There is no time save for the now, and when the human person can begin to live this way, he begins to live like God, who dwells antecedent to time, who lives forever in an eternal now. This is one of the most insightful and prescient books of the *Confessions*; it is also one of the most difficult. Augustine anticipated many later theories of time by stressing how the only objective reality is the present "now", while the "past" exists only cognitively in the memory, the "future" existing only in the soul's anticipation of what will (sooner or later) be the present. Only God dwells in an eternal now, all times present before him. Created time, on the other hand, tends toward the opposite of God, nonbeing, but in so doing also points us to the eternal from which it comes. Book XI on time therefore acts to show the reader how temporal creatures can enjoy stability and permanence only when united with the timeless. The soul united with God thus rises above the fluctuations of fallen time and dwells in eternity.

Books XII–XIII fittingly bring us all the way back to the genesis of this dazzling story: to the moment of God's good creation in which he brought all things about. Here Augustine begins by dissecting the manifold ways to understand how in the beginning God created heaven and earth. But more importantly, we come to see how the Church is the apex of God's good creation, that all else is brought into existence for the sake of unified and collective praise—the Body of Christ constituted by all the faithful, all the good angels, and all of God's saints. This is the end toward which Augustine's life, every life, must tend. In this way we see how the story of a soul sanctified is never one of loneliness and separation, but one of community and intimate union. The Church gathers all those willing to enter her to join them into one living body, one voice of eternal praise and worship. In one way these last books are really lengthy expositions on the opening lines of the book of Genesis: out of utter nothingness, God from his eternity has risked bringing into existence a formed heaven and earth, a new dramatic order of being that can now choose itself over its Creator, or can return to God with love and proper praise. This is why the *Confessions* end ecclesiologically, the Church emerging as the last character of our story. For only within Christ's Church does a human life enjoy an authentic narrative, a story of event and of integrity; for only here united to Christ is a life not swept away by the distention of decay.

In good Platonic fashion, only the immutable is really real and only that which has form and permanence can be communicated. Augustine discovers that his life's narrative makes sense only when understood as the life of a saint, as the fulfillment of that divine image and likeness imprinted in every human soul. In contrast to a Manichean view where two warring selves are never reconciled, Augustine's woundedness now finds wholeness in the side of Christ's body.

What is about to unfold in the pages ahead is the story of the creature in God. As with any newborn, steps come slowly and stumbles inevitably occur, but as one wakes up to the many-layered beauty and love in the world, one's steps grow more intentional and surer. Augustine's aim here is therefore not to place God in the experiences of his life but to place his life in God, to understand himself not with God as one more agent in his life's story but as the only one in whom human living makes sense. In order to be intelligible, all human experience must be placed within God, placed within him as the standard and measure of all truth and reality: "Or should I say, rather, that I should not exist if I were not in you, from whom are all things, through whom are all things, in whom are all things" (see *Conf.* I.2.2, p. 5). In this way the divine life is not merely one more encounter, one more character within Augustine's story, but precisely that which makes Augustine's story intelligible and able to be narrated.

God, not Augustine, emerges from these pages as the principle of coherence, identity, and sanity. Throughout this ancient story, God is no mere external agent waiting to meet Augustine as he makes his way back home. God is his home. As every human wanderer realizes as he comes home, Augustine sees that he has all along been God's sole concern, God's obsession. The Father does not stand aloof watching Augustine's story; he is Augustine's story—at times ignored, at other times embraced, but never absent from the pilgrim soul. Our author thus comes to realize that it is not until he can tell his story from God's perspective that he actually has a story to tell. In composing the *Confessions* and in structuring them as they now come to us, Augustine argues that by means of memory through the gift of time, the children of Adam and Eve can finally come to understand how the one love they sought their entire lives has been theirs all along.

The *Confessions* is ultimately a story about the particularities of such a love. No beloved wants to think that he is not wholly and uniquely special in the eyes of the other. Each wants to know that only he shares that one particular glance, that special sobriquet, an otherwise unfrequented restaurant or unplayed song. No one remains content being loved as just a member of a larger group, say, carnally as a member of the opposite sex, or even spiritually as a member of the Church. We all want to be loved personally and exclusively. We want to be loved for who we are, with *all* of our past experiences and anticipated desires. The God Augustine recognizes to be more present to his innermost self than he himself has ever been (see *Conf.* III.6.11) writes a love story with the experiences of Augustine's life that no one else could ever know or claim. As we continue our earthly pilgrimage, then, the following pages were written to help us see that the life each of us has lived has been perhaps never easy and was probably not always enjoyable, but it is the very life God uses to convey his singular and unequaled love for each restless heart.

TEXTUAL NOTE

Historically *The City of God* and *On The Trinity* have drawn more scholarly attention than any other work of Augustine's legacy. Yet with the twentieth century's new emphasis on the role of the subject and the power of personal narrative, a robust interest in his *Confessions* arose. This naturally inspired more modern vernacular translations, and the English-speaking world did not suffer a shortage of many fine editions. While translations exist from such towering figures as the apologist and wit Frank Sheed (1942), the Catholic University of America philosopher Monsignor John K. Ryan (1959), as well as the unmatchable Oxford professor of ecclesiastical history Henry Chadwick (1991), Benedictine Sister Maria Boulding's translation combines the linguistic accuracy demanded by fourth-century Latin with the poetic power aimed at by Augustine, not as discernable in previous translations.

Born Mary in Liverpool on May 7, 1929, Maria Boulding, O.S.B. was always linguistically gifted and theologically astute. Turning down a full scholarship to Oxford, she joined the enclosed Benedictine nuns at Stanbrook Abbey in September of 1947, where she unceasingly labored for sixty-two years. She spent much of her later life translating Augustine, and her works are now available through the Focolare Movement's publishing house, New City Press in Hyde Park, New York. Her translations of the Bishop of Hippo's *Confessions* as well as his *Expositions of the Psalms* will prove standards for unforeseeable generations. Sister Boulding died on November 11, 2009. Once the sole woman at a patristic convocation, Sister was reading a section of her paper where a lengthy quotation from Augustine landed, and at the end of her paragraph, she looked coyly up and said, "That bit's Augustine, not me." Her male colleagues, chuckling, responded, "We know you're marvelous, Maria, but we can tell the difference." Yes, Sister Maria, you are that marvelous, and we thank you, New City Press, and all who labor to close the difference between Augustine and our world.

SAINT AUGUSTINE CHRONOLOGY

November 13, 354: Born Aurelius Augustinus to Patricius and Monica in Thagaste (Numidia) into a family of at least one older brother named Navigius as well as at least two (unnamed) sisters

365–369: First studies away from home in Madaura (most often left in the Latin *Madauros*, modern-day M'Daourouch, Algeria; see *Conf.* I.9.14)

369–370: Year back at home in order to save money for further education (see *Conf.* II.3.5); Patricius dies sometime in 370 or 371

371–373: Studies in Carthage (see *Conf.* III.1.1), the birth of Adeodatus (in 372; see *Conf.* IV.2.2), and the joining of the Manichean sect (in 373; see *Conf.* III.6.10)

374–376: Operates his own school back in Thagaste

376–383: Returns to Carthage to many successful achievements: prizes for rhetoric, teaching accolades, and publications (see *Conf.* IV.2.2); in 382 Augustine meets Faustus, the Manichean bishop (see *Conf.* V.6.10), and is greatly disillusioned

383: Off to Rome to begin a new teaching career (see *Conf.* V.8.14)

384: Called to Milan to serve as the imperial rhetor; finally leaves the Manichees (see *Conf.* V.13.23)

385: Monica arrives in Milan (see *Conf.* VI.1.1) to orchestrate further success for her Augustine

386: In early winter he discovers the truths of Neoplatonic philosophy (see *Conf.* VII.9.13), begins to understand the Christian scriptures rightly, experiences God's voice in the garden (see *Conf.* VIII.12.29), and consequently resigns from office (see *Conf.* IX.2.2) to prepare for baptism in Cassiciacum with like-minded catechumens (see *Conf.* IX.4.7)

April 24, 387: Baptized by Bishop Ambrose at Easter Vigil (see *Conf.* IX.6.14); later that spring Monica dies awaiting voyage in Ostia (see *Conf.* IX.11.27–28)

388: Returns to Thagaste with Adeodatus (who dies sometime soon thereafter, 389/390) to start a quasimonastic community of prayer, study, and manual labor

391: End of monastic life, as Augustine is ordained a priest for the Diocese of Hippo Regius

392: Begins to preach on the Psalms, resulting in *Expositions of the Psalms* (completed in 422)

395: Consecrated auxiliary bishop alongside with Valerius

397–401: Composition of *Confessions*; busy with many other theological treatises as well, especially against the Manichees

399: Begins the groundbreaking *On the Trinity* (completed between 422 and 426)

403–412: The Donatist schism becomes the focus of many writings

410: The fall of Rome to Alaric and his army and the subsequent flood of Italian Christians into North Africa; the rumblings of the *The City of God* begin (413–426) as well as awareness of the monk Pelagius' criticisms of Augustine's theology

411: Council of Carthage, at which Augustine successfully debates and defeats the Donatist bishops, leading to the imperial decree in 412, condemning all forms of Donatism

415: A synod in Diospolis, Palestine, declares Pelagius to be orthodox and worthy of emulation, setting Augustine arduously to work

417: Pelagius condemned at a synod in Rome as an enemy to public peace and orthodox faith

418: The Council of Carthage under Bishop Augustine declares Pelagius an enemy of the faith, and following the ban of Pelagians from Rome a year earlier exiles all Pelagius' followers

September 26, 426: The aging Augustine assembles his clergy in the Basilica Pacis to name the priest Eraclius as his episcopal successor

428: Augustine sits down with his faithful secretary Possidius to compose his *Retractions*, or *Reconsiderations*, which chronicle and summarize all his written works

429: Geneseric and his Vandal army (most being Arian Christians in their religious belief) invade North Africa from Spain, now moving eastward, arrive at the outskirts of Hippo the following year

August 28, 430: At seventy-six years old, and with a psalm on his lips, Augustine dies from fever

The Text of

THE CONFESSIONS

Book I

Infancy and Boyhood

Chapter 1

Opening prayer and meditation

1. Great are you, O Lord, and exceedingly worthy of praise;[1] your power is immense, and your wisdom beyond reckoning.[2] And so we humans, who are a due part of your creation, long to praise you—we who carry our mortality about with us,[3] carry the evidence of our sin and with it the proof that you thwart the proud.[4] Yet these humans, due part of your creation as they are, still do long to praise you. You stir us so that praising you may bring us joy, because you have made us and drawn us to yourself, and our heart is unquiet until it rests in you.[5]

---

[1] *Great are you, O Lord . . . worthy of praise*: See Psalm 47:2(48:1); 95(96):4; 144(145):3. As mentioned in the Introduction, notice how Augustine roots his story in God's greatness. What is about to unfold is no normal "autobiography" but the story of every soul as it draws near to God, thereby recognizing his power and wisdom. By situating his own life's story in the Creator of all, Augustine very cleverly invites his readers to see their own selves herein as well.

[2] *your power . . . beyond reckoning*: See Psalm 146(147):5.

[3] *And so we humans . . . who carry our mortality about with us*: See 2 Corinthians 4:10.

[4] *carry the evidence . . . thwart the proud*: See 1 Peter 5:5. For Augustine, all creatures teeter between the fullness of God and the nothingness from which God made them. After the Fall, therefore, human persons bear witness both to their innate desire to praise their Maker as well as the mortality inherited by sinful Adam.

[5] *our heart is unquiet until it rests in you*: This, of course, is the most famous celebrated line in all the *Confessions*, establishing Saint Augustine as the theologian of the heart, of recognizing the human need for God and how all of life's experiences are shadowy attempts to find him. Often the phrase is rendered "restless heart" but the Latin here is *inquietum*, the unquiet that comes from being away from God.

Grant me to know and understand, Lord, which comes first: to call upon you or to praise you? To know you or to call upon you? Must we know you before we can call upon you? Anyone who invokes what is still unknown may be making a mistake. Or should you be invoked first, so that we may then come to know you? But how can people call upon someone in whom they do not yet believe? And how can they believe without a preacher?[6] But scripture tells us that those who seek the Lord will praise him,[7] for as they seek they find him,[8] and on finding him they will praise him. Let me seek you, then, Lord, even while I am calling upon you, and call upon you even as I believe in you; for to us you have indeed been preached. My faith calls upon you, Lord, this faith which is your gift to me, which you have breathed into me through the humanity of your Son and the ministry of your preacher.[9]

Chapter 2

2. How shall I call upon my God, my God and my Lord, when by the very act of calling upon him I would be calling him into myself? Is there any place within me into which my God might come? How should the God who made heaven and earth come into me?[10] Is there any room in me for you, Lord, my

[6] *how can they believe without a preacher*: See Romans 10:14.

[7] *those who seek . . . praise him*: See Psalm 21:27 (22:26).

[8] *as they seek they find him*: See Matthew 7:7–8; Luke 11:10.

[9] *your gift to me . . . ministry of your preacher*: Augustine will more often than not speak of God as a Trinity, and here one notices how it is the Lord, the Father, who gives the gift of the Holy Spirit through the humanity of Jesus the Son. Such Trinitarian references are imbedded throughout these reflections. Augustine began his famous On the Trinity (De Trinitate) just two years after finishing the Confessions (not finishing it until 426), a work that revolutionized how early theologians began to envision the life of the Triune God, now seeing how the Spirit is the living bond of Love between the Lover, the Father, and the Beloved, the Son, and how this triad marked the soul as the Trinity's "image and likeness", the human person's remembering (memory), knowing (intellect), and desiring (will) God.

[10] *God . . . come into me*: See Genesis 1:1. One of Augustine's lasting contributions to all of Western thought is this notion of interiority. Some scholars argue that he actually invented the concept of the inner self, representing the

God? Even heaven and earth, which you have made and in which you have made me—can even they contain you? Since nothing that exists would exist without you, does it follow that whatever exists does in some way contain you? But if this is so, how can I, who am one of these existing things, ask you to come into me, when I would not exist at all unless you were already in me? Not yet am I in hell, after all, but even if I were, you would be there too; for if I descend to the underworld, you are there.[11] No, my God, I would not exist, I would not be at all, were you not in me. Or should I say, rather, that I should not exist if I were not in you, from whom are all things, through whom are all things, in whom are all things?[12] Yes, Lord, that is the truth, that is indeed the truth. To what place can I invite you, then, since I am in you? Or where could you come from, in order to come into me? To what place outside heaven and earth could I travel, so that my God could come to me there, the God who said, *I fill heaven and earth*?[13]

Chapter 3

3. So then, if you fill heaven and earth, does that mean that heaven and earth contain you? Or, since clearly they cannot hold you, is there something of you left over when you have filled them? Once heaven and earth are full, where would that remaining part of you overflow? Or perhaps you have no need to be contained by anything, but rather contain everything yourself, because whatever you fill you contain, even as you

---

created soul as the place where God primarily encounters and engages the human person. For a priest and bishop who celebrated the Mass daily in his basilica in Hippo Regius, this was, of course, not to deny the need for the Church and her sacraments, but to stress how God longs to dwell deeply within every human soul, thus calling and leading each from within.

[11] *Not yet . . . you are there*: See Psalm 138(139):8.

[12] *I should not exist . . . in whom are all things*: See Romans 11:36; 1 Corinthians 8:6. Here lies the whole point of the *Confessions*: Augustine is seeking to place his entire life within the life of God, for only here can his self and his experiences have any permanence, any real meaning.

[13] *I fill heaven and earth*: Jeremiah 23:24.

fill it? The vessels which are full of you do not lend you stability, because even if they break, you will not be spilt. And when you pour yourself out over us,[14] you do not lie there spilt but raise us up; you are not scattered, but gather us together.[15] Yet all those things which you fill, you fill with the whole of yourself. Should we suppose, then, that because all things are incapable of containing the whole of you, they hold only a part of you, and all of them the same part? Or does each thing hold a different part, greater things larger parts, and lesser things smaller parts? Does it even make sense to speak of larger or smaller parts of you? Are you not everywhere in your whole being, while there is nothing whatever that can hold you entirely?

Chapter 4

4. What are you, then, my God? What are you, I ask, but the Lord God? For who else is lord except the Lord, or who is god if not our God?[16] You are most high, excellent, most powerful, omnipotent, supremely merciful and supremely just, most hidden yet intimately present, infinitely beautiful and infinitely strong, steadfast yet elusive, unchanging yourself though you control the change in all things, never new, never old, renewing all things[17] yet wearing down the proud though they know it not;[18] ever active, ever at rest, gathering while knowing no need, supporting and filling and guarding, creating and nurturing and perfecting, seeking although you lack nothing. You love without frenzy, you are jealous yet secure, you regret without sadness,[19] you grow angry yet remain tranquil, you alter your works but never your plan; you take back what you

[14] *you pour yourself out over us*: See Joel 2:28–29; Acts 2:17–18.

[15] *you do not lie there . . . gather us together*: A constant theme in early Christian theology is how goodness unifies and how evil scatters (diabolical, for example, means literally to throw apart, to break apart), and this is really what Augustine is out to show: a life in God has coherence and integrity, while a life of sin is never focused, never stable, never at rest.

[16] *who else is lord . . . if not our God*: See Psalm 17:32(18:31).

[17] *You are most high . . . renewing all things*: See Wisdom 7:27.

[18] *yet wearing down . . . know it not*: See Job 9:5.

[19] *You love . . . without sadness*: See Genesis 6:6–7.

find although you never lost it; you are never in need yet you rejoice in your gains, never avaricious yet you demand profits.[20] You allow us to pay you more than you demand, and so you become our debtor, yet which of us possesses anything that does not already belong to you? You owe us nothing, yet you pay your debts; you write off our debts to you, yet you lose nothing thereby.

After saying all that, what have we said, my God, my life, my holy sweetness? What does anyone who speaks of you really say? Yet woe betide those who fail to speak, while the chatterboxes go on saying nothing.[21]

Chapter 5

5. Who will grant me to find peace in you? Who will grant me this grace, that you would come into my heart and inebriate it, enabling me to forget the evils that beset me[22] and embrace you, my only good? What are you to me? Have mercy on me, so that I may tell.[23] What indeed am I to you, that you should command me to love you, and grow angry with me if I do not, and threaten me with enormous woes? Is not the

[20] *you grow angry . . . demand profits*: See Matthew 25:27.

[21] *those who fail to speak . . . chatterboxes go on saying nothing*: Augustine begins by trying to understand how one can name and thereby call upon God. Language is one of the first lenses through which we come to understand the divine. While Augustine knows that no created language can capture God fully, he does know that some ways of describing God are nonetheless correct (albeit insufficient) and thus better than other terms and images. We therefore see Augustine's insistence that if we are going to love God properly, we must be able to call upon him rightly, and the religious language we use therefore is ultimately a matter of worship and praise.

[22] *forget the evils that beset me*: See Jeremiah 44:9.

[23] *Have mercy . . . may tell*: This is a good example of the linguistic properties our author is trying to lay out in this opening book: God's grace allows us to speak about God aright; that is, Christianity is more than simply having the right "data" about God and speaking the right words. It is a matter of being transformed by God's action upon the soul, and when the Lord of all life draws near, only then do we begin to act and speak and see differently. This is why we can hear in just a couple of lines later that it is Augustine's "heart" that is listening, as encountering God is always both a matter of external senses as well as internal renewal.

failure to love you woe enough in itself? Alas for me! Through your own merciful dealings with me, O Lord my God, tell me what you are to me. Say to my soul, *I am your salvation*.[24] Say it so that I can hear it. My heart is listening, Lord; open the ears of my heart and say to my soul, *I am your salvation*. Let me run toward this voice and seize hold of you. Do not hide your face from me:[25] let me die so that I may see it, for not to see it would be death to me indeed.[26]

6. The house of my soul is too small for you to enter: make it more spacious by your coming. It lies in ruins: rebuild it. Some things are to be found there which will offend your gaze; I confess this to be so and know it well. But who will clean my house?[27] To whom but yourself can I cry, *Cleanse me of my hidden sins, O Lord, and for those incurred through others pardon your servant?*[28] I believe, and so I will speak.[29] You know everything, Lord.[30] Have I not laid my own transgressions bare before you to my own condemnation, my God, and have you not forgiven the wickedness of my heart?[31] I do not argue my case

---

[24] I am your salvation: Psalm 34(35):3.

[25] *Do not hide your face from me*: See Deuteronomy 32:20.

[26] *let me die . . . death to me indeed*: See Exodus 33:23.

[27] *who will clean my house*: Of all the early Christian thinkers he studied, C. S. Lewis drew most often from Saint Augustine without always acknowledging such. Take for example his image of God coming to rebuild the soul into a personal dwelling, possibly prompted by this passage in the *Confessions*: "Imagine yourself as a living house. God comes in to rebuild that house. At first, perhaps, you can understand what He is doing. He is getting the drains right and stopping the leaks in the roof and so on; you knew that those jobs needed doing and so you are not surprised. But presently He starts knocking the house about in a way that hurts abominably and does not seem to make any sense. What on earth is He up to? The explanation is that He is building quite a different house from the one you thought of—throwing out a new wing here, putting on an extra floor there, running up towers, making courtyards. You thought you were being made into a decent little cottage: but He is building a palace. He intends to come and live in it Himself" (C. S. Lewis, *Mere Christianity* [San Francisco: HarperCollins, (1952) 2001], p. 205.).

[28] Cleanse me . . . your servant: Psalm 18(19):13.

[29] *I believe, and so I will speak*: See Psalm 115(116):10; 2 Corinthians 4:13.

[30] *You know everything, Lord*: See John 21:17.

[31] *Have I not laid my own transgressions . . . wickedness of my heart*: See Psalm 31(32):5.

against you,[32] for you are truth itself; nor do I wish to deceive myself, lest my iniquity be caught in its own lies.[33] No, I do not argue the case with you, because *if you, Lord, keep the score of our iniquities, then who, Lord, can bear it?*[34]

Chapter 6

Infancy[35]

7. Yet allow me to speak, though I am but dust and ashes,[36] allow me to speak in your merciful presence, for it is to your mercy that I address myself, not to some man who would mock me. Perhaps you too are laughing at me,[37] but still you will turn mercifully toward me;[38] for what is it that I am trying to say, Lord, except that I do not know whence I came into this life that is but a dying, or rather, this dying state that leads to life? I do not know where I came from. But this I know, that I was welcomed by the tender care your mercy provided for me, for so I have been told by the parents who gave me life according to the flesh, those parents through whose begetting and bearing you formed me within time, although I do not remember it myself. The comforts of human milk were waiting for me, but my mother and my nurses did not fill their own breasts; rather you gave me an infant's nourishment through them in accordance with your plan, from the riches deeply hidden in creation. You restrained me from craving more than you provided, and inspired in those who nurtured me

[32] *I do not argue . . . against you:* See Job 9:2–3.

[33] *you are truth . . . in its own lies:* See Psalm 26(27):12.

[34] *if you, Lord, keep the score of our iniquities, then who, Lord, can bear it?* Psalm 129(130):3.

[35] Infancy: Ironically, whereas *con-fession* means "to speak with", *in-fancy* means "unable to speak", and this is precisely Augustine's point: just as we begin our biological life not knowing how to express ourselves properly, every life of grace likewise stumbles about trying to understand and speak to God correctly.

[36] *I am but dust and ashes:* See Genesis 18:27; Job 42:6.

[37] *you too are laughing at me:* See Psalm 2:4; 36(37):13; Wisdom 4:18.

[38] *you will turn mercifully toward me:* See Jeremiah 12:15.

the will to give me what you were giving them, for their love for me was patterned on your law, and so they wanted to pass on to me the overflowing gift they received from you. It was a bounty for them, and a bounty for me from them; or, rather, not from them but only through them, for in truth all good things are from you, O God. Everything I need for health and salvation flows from my God. This I learned later as you cried the truth aloud to me through all you give me, both within and without. At that time I knew only how to suck and be deliciously comforted, and how to cry when anything hurt my body, but no more.

8. After this I began to smile, at first only in my sleep and then when I was awake. So I have been told, and I believe it on the strength of what we see other babies doing, for I do not remember doing it myself. Little by little I began to notice where I was, and I would try to make my wishes known to those who might satisfy them; but I was frustrated in this, because my desires were inside me, while other people were outside and could by no effort of understanding enter my mind.[39] So I tossed about and screamed, sending signals meant to indicate what I wanted, those few signs that were the best I could manage, though they did not really express my desires. Often I did not get my way, either because people did not understand or because what I demanded might have harmed me, and then I would throw a tantrum because my elders were not subject to me, nor free people willing to be my slaves; so I would take revenge on them by bursting into tears. I have learned that babies behave like this from those I have been able to watch, and they without knowing it have taught me more surely what I was like myself than did my nurses who knew me well.

9. My infancy has been so long dead now, whereas I am alive. But you, O Lord, are ever living and in you nothing

---

[39] *my desires were inside . . . by no effort of understanding enter my mind*: This is part of the restless heart for all creatures: no one but God can see fully the internal movements of the soul and of one's every joy and fear. Regardless how intimately close one might be to his beloved, a creature will always be "outside" of one's heart, a "space" reserved for God alone.

dies, for you exist before the dawn of the ages, before anything that can be called "before"; you are God and Lord of
everything that you have created. In you stand firm the causes
of all unstable things; in you the unchangeable origins of all
changeable things abide; in you live the eternal ideas of all
irrational and transient creatures. Tell me, I beg you, tell your
miserable suppliant, O merciful God, whether my infancy was
itself the sequel to some earlier age, now dead and gone. Was
there nothing before it, except the life I lived in my mother's
womb? Some information about that has been given me, and
I have myself seen pregnant women. But then, my God, my
sweetness, what came before that? Was I somewhere else? Was
I even someone? I have nobody to tell me: neither father nor
mother could enlighten me, nor the experience of others, nor
any memory of my own. Are you laughing at me for asking
you these questions,[40] and are you perhaps commanding me
to praise you and confess to you simply about what I do know?

10. Confess to you I will, Lord of heaven and earth,[41] and
praise you for my earliest days and my infancy, which I do not
remember. You allow a person to infer by observing others what
his own beginnings were like; we can learn much about ourselves even from the reports of womenfolk. Already I had existence and life, and as my unspeaking stage drew to a close I
began to look for signs whereby I might communicate my ideas
to others. Where could a living creature like this have come
from, if not from you, Lord? Are any of us skillful enough to
fashion ourselves? Could there be some channel hollowed out
from some other source through which existence and life might

----

[40] *whether my infancy . . . asking you these questions:* See Psalm 2:4; 36(37):13;
Wisdom 4:18. Augustine admits that he really never settled on an answer to
how the human soul was created and transmitted into the womb. Throughout
his life, he wavered between four possible positions: (1) that the individual soul
comes from the one human soul God created in the beginning (traducianism);
(2) that the soul is created individually within the womb (creationism); (3) that
God sends human souls already in existence to matter upon conception; (4)
that these preexistent souls come of their own agency to inhabit bodies (cf. *On
Free Will*, bk. 3, sec. 20, par. 56–57).

[41] *Confess to you I will, Lord of heaven and earth:* See Matthew 11:25.

flow to us, apart from yourself, Lord, who create us? Could we derive existence and life from anywhere other than you, in whom to be and to live are not two different realities, since supreme being and supreme life are one and the same? You are supreme and you do not change,[42] and in you there is no "today" that passes. Yet in you our "today" does pass, inasmuch as all things exist in you, and would have no means even of passing away if you did not contain them.[43] Because your years do not fail,[44] your years are one "Today." How many of our days and our ancestors' days have come and gone in this "Today" of yours, have received from it their manner of being and have existed after their fashion, and how many others will likewise receive theirs, and exist in their own way? Yet you are the selfsame: all our tomorrows and beyond, all our yesterdays and further back, you will make in your Today, you have made in your Today.

What does it matter to me, if someone does not understand this? Let such a person rejoice even to ask the question, "What does this mean?" Yes, let him rejoice in that, and choose to find by not finding rather than by finding fail to find you.

Chapter 7

11. O God, hear me. Alas for the sins of humankind! A human it is who here bewails them, and you treat him mercifully because you made him, though the sin that is in him is not of your making.[45] Who is there to remind me of the sin of my infancy (for sin there was: no one is free from sin in your sight, not even an infant whose span of earthly life is but a single

---

[42] *You are supreme . . . do not change*: See Malachi 3:6.

[43] *in you there is no "today" . . . contain them*: The dynamics of time are important throughout the *Confessions* because it is only in time that we come to know the eternal, and only by uniting ourselves to the eternal do we come to know who we truly are; this is the entire purpose of Book XI below.

[44] *your years do not fail*: See Psalm 101:28(102:27); Hebrews 1:12.

[45] *sin that is in him is not of your making*: In an Augustinian worldview, all goodness is ultimately God's, while the only reality a lone individual can claim as strictly his own is sinfulness.

day);[46] who can remind me of it? Some little mite who is a tiny child now, in whom I might observe conduct I do not remember in myself? What then was my sin at that age? Was it perhaps that I cried so greedily for those breasts? Certainly if I behaved like that now, greedy not for breasts, of course, but for food suitable to my age, I should provoke derision and be very properly rebuked. My behavior then was equally deserving of rebuke, but since I would not have been able to understand anyone who scolded me, neither custom nor common sense allowed any rebuke to be given. After all, we eradicate these habits and throw them off as we grow up. Yes, but I have never seen any sensible person throw away good things when clearing out, so can we suppose that even in an infant such actions were good—the actions of a child who begs tearfully for objects that would harm him if given, gets into a tantrum when free persons, older persons and his parents, will not comply with his whims, and tries to hurt many people who know better by hitting out at them as hard as his strength allows, simply because they will not immediately fall in with his wishes or obey his commands, commands which would damage him if they were carried out?

The only innocent feature in babies is the weakness of their frames; the minds of infants are far from innocent. I have watched and experienced for myself the jealousy of a small child: he could not even speak, yet he glared with livid fury at his fellow-nursling. Everyone has seen this. Mothers and nurses claim to have some means of their own to charm away such behavior. Is this to be regarded as innocence, this refusal to tolerate a rival for a richly abundant fountain of milk, at a time when the other child stands in greatest need of it and depends for its very life on this food alone? Behavior of this kind is cheerfully condoned, however, not because it is trivial or of small account, but because everyone knows that it will fade away as the baby grows up.[47] This is clear from the fact

---

[46] *Who is there . . . but a single day*: See Job 14:4–5.

[47] *The only innocent feature in babies . . . as the baby grows up*: Critics of Augustine often point out how harsh he is toward babies in this early book. His point

that those same actions are by no means calmly tolerated if detected in anyone of more mature years.

12. Your will is that I should praise you, O Lord my God, who gave life and a body to that infant; you will me to praise you who equipped him with faculties, built up his limbs, and adorned him with a distinctive shape, as we can see. You implanted in him all the urges proper to a living creature to ensure his coherence and safety; and now you command me to praise you for those gifts, and to confess to you and sing to your name, O Most High,[48] because you are God, almighty and good, and would be so even if you had wrought no other works than these, since none but yourself, the only God, can bring them into existence. From you derives all manner of being, O God most beautiful, who endow all things with their beautiful form and by your governance direct them in their due order.[49]

But it irks me, Lord, to link that phase of my existence with my present life, the life I live now in this world; I do not remember passing through it, I have to rely on the reports of others concerning it, and I can only infer from my observation of other infants that I went through it too, though certainly this inference is well founded. As far as the dark blank in my memory is concerned, that period of infancy is on a par with the

---

here, however, is not to condemn children for their seemingly selfish behavior when hungry or tired, but simply to point out that while we may not want to admit it, we are born wholly "I-centered" with only our own interests in mind. In a very mundane way, this now shows the noxious effects of the concupiscence Adam brought about when he turned himself and all his descendents away from God. This is why we must learn to "speak" anew, to come to God with desires and intentions not turned in on self but on him.

[48] *You implanted in him . . . O Most High*: See Psalm 91:2(92:1).

[49] *you are God . . . in their due order*: Trinitarian expressions abound all over Augustine's works: here, for example, we see the Father, who imparts existence, all "manner of being"; the Son, who endows creatures with their nature, the "beautiful form" that makes them what they are; and the Holy Spirit, who governs all the cosmos by placing each creature in its proper place within the hierarchy of being. Aligning such tasks with each Person of the Trinity is common for Augustine: the Father brings all into existence, the Son shapes all things into what they essentially are, and the Spirit orders them rightly.

time I spent in my mother's womb. And if I was even conceived in iniquity, and with sin my mother nourished me in
her womb,[50] where, I beg of you, my God, where was I, your
servant, ever innocent? Where, Lord, and when?

So I will leave that period aside. What does it matter to me
now, since it has vanished without trace from my memory?

Chapter 8

Learning to speak

13. Did I make my way from that infant stage into boyhood?
Or should I rather say that boyhood caught up with me and
took over from infancy? Yet infancy did not depart, so what
happened to it? It did not stay with me, for I was no longer an
infant who lacked the faculty of speech, but a boy who could
talk. I remember this, and later I turned my attention to the
way in which I had learned to speak. It was not that older
people taught me by offering me words by way of formal instruction, as was the case soon afterward with reading. No, I taught
myself, using the mind you gave me, O my God, because I was
unable to express the thoughts of my heart by cries and inarticulate sounds and gestures in such a way as to gain what I
wanted or make my entire meaning clear to everyone as I
wished; so I grasped at words with my memory; when people
called an object by some name, and while saying the word
pointed to that thing, I watched and remembered that they
used that sound when they wanted to indicate that thing. Their
intention was clear, for they used bodily gestures, those natural words which are common to all races, such as facial expressions or glances of the eyes or movements of other parts of the
body, or a tone of voice that suggested some particular attitude to things they sought and wished to hold on to, or rejected
and shunned altogether.

[50] *And if I was even conceived . . . nourished me in her womb*: See Psalm
50:7 (51:5).

In this way I gradually built up a collection of words, observing them as they were used in their proper places in different sentences and hearing them frequently. I came to understand which things they signified, and by schooling my own mouth to utter them I declared my wishes by using the same signs. Thus I learned to express my needs to the people among whom I lived, and they made their wishes known to me; and I waded deeper into the stormy world of human life, although I was still subject to the authority of my parents and the guidance of my elders.

Chapter 9

Augustine goes to school

14. Ah, God, my God, what wretchedness I suffered in that world, and how I was trifled with! The program for right living presented to me as a boy was that I must obey my mentors, so that I might get on in this world and excel in the skills of the tongue, skills which lead to high repute and deceitful riches. To this end I was sent to school to learn my letters, though I, poor wretch, could see no point in them.[51] All the same, I would be beaten whenever I was lazy about learning. This punishment was taken for granted by grown-up people and many a pupil had undergone it before we did, laying down those rough roadways along which we were now being driven, as we bore our part in the heavy labor and pain allotted to the sons of Adam.[52]

We did, however, meet at school some people who prayed to you, Lord, and we learned from them, imagining you as best we could in the guise of some great personage who, while not

---

[51] *I was sent to school . . . no point in them:* The year is now 365 and Augustine receives his first taste of a formal education in Madaura, Algeria (birthplace of the famous Latin satirist Apuleius), about fifteen miles from Thagaste, where Augustine was born. Augustine will remain here for four years.

[52] *we bore our part . . . sons of Adam:* See Genesis 3:16; Sirach 40:1.

evident to our senses, was yet able to hear and help us.[53] So it
came about that even then in boyhood I began to pray to you,
my aid and refuge.[54] By calling upon you I untied the knots of
my tongue and begged you, in my little-boy way but with no
little earnestness, not to let me be beaten at school. You did
not hear my prayer, lest by hearing it you might have consigned me to a fool's fate; so my stripes were laughed at by my
elders and even my parents, who would not have wished anything bad to happen to me. But bad it was, and very dreadful
for me.

15. Is it possible, Lord, that there exists anyone so courageous, so united to you by intense love, that he could make
light of rack, hooks and similar torments, from which other
people the world over pray to you to be delivered? Is there
any such person who could rise above them through devout
union with you, rather than out of mere cloddish insensibility
that counterfeits courage? But if this person loved others who
are terrified of such tortures, could he still make light of them,
as did our parents, who laughed at the torments we boys suffered? We were just as terrified of punishment as other people
of torture, and our prayers to you were no whit less heartfelt
as we begged that we might escape.

All the same, we were blameworthy, because we were less
assiduous in reading, writing and concentrating on our studies
than was expected of us. It was not that we lacked intelligence or ability, Lord, for you had endowed us with these in a
measure appropriate to our age; it was simply that we loved to
play, and we were punished by adults who nonetheless did the
same themselves.[55] But whereas the frivolous pursuits of

[53] *We did, however, meet . . . hear and help us*: Augustine obviously found the
Christianity he knew as a boy very unrefined and thus unable to attract him in
any real way.

[54] *my aid and refuge*: See Psalm 93(94):22; 17:3(18:2).

[55] *we were punished . . . same themselves*: An ugly truth is here revealed when
Augustine wonders why children are punished for finding diversions more enjoyable than the work they are asked to do, when most adults spend their years
acting the same way, chasing after frivolities and playthings instead of devoting
themselves wholeheartedly to their respective vocations in life.

grown-up people are called "business," children are punished for behaving in the same fashion, and no one is sorry for either the children or the adults; so are we to assume that any sound judge of the matter would think it right for me to be beaten because I played ball as a boy, and was hindered by my game from more rapid progress in studies which would only equip me to play an uglier game later? Moreover, was the master who flogged me any better himself? If he had been worsted by a fellow scholar in some pedantic dispute, would he not have been racked by even more bitter jealousy than I was when my opponent in a game of ball got the better of me?

Chapter 10

16. O Lord God, you are the disposer and creator of everything in nature, but of our sins the disposer only; and I did sin at that time, Lord my God, by disobeying the instructions of my parents and teachers, for I was later able to make good use of the lessons my relatives wanted me to learn, whatever may have been their intention in so directing me. I sinned because I disobeyed them not in order to choose something more worthwhile, but simply because I loved games. I hankered to win myself glory in our contests, and to have my ears tickled by tall stories which only made them itch more hotly;[56] and all the while that same curiosity more and more inflamed my eyes with lust for the public shows which are the games of grownups. The people who provide these entertainments enjoy such celebrity and public esteem that nearly all of them hope their children will follow their example; and yet they are quite prepared to see those children beaten for watching similar shows to the detriment of their study, study which, as their parents hope, will bring them to a position in which they in turn will provide the shows![57]

---

[56] *my ears tickled . . . itch more hotly*: See 2 Timothy 4:3–4.

[57] *people who provide these entertainments . . . provide the shows*: While not all shared this view, many of the first Christians were suspicious of how secular shows and other forms of entertainment, especially gladiatorial games, acted upon

Look with mercy on these follies, Lord, and set us free who already call upon you. Set free those also who do not yet call upon you, so that they may invoke you and you may give them freedom.

Chapter 11

His baptism is deferred

17. While still a boy I had heard about the eternal life promised to us through the humility of our Lord and God, who stooped even to our pride; and I was regularly signed with the cross and given his salt even from the womb of my mother, who firmly trusted in you. You saw, Lord, how one day in my boyhood I was suddenly seized by stomach pains and, as my fever mounted, came near to death. You saw, my God, because even then you were guarding me, with what distress and what faith I earnestly begged to be baptized into your Christ, who is my God and my Lord;[58] you saw how I pleaded with my loving, kindly mother and with the mother of us all, your Church. She who had given me life according to the flesh was very anxious, because in her pure heart, through her faith in you and with a love still more tender, she was bringing my eternal salvation to birth. She would have hastened to ensure that I was initiated into the saving sacraments and washed clean by confessing you, Lord Jesus, for the forgiveness of my sins, had I not rapidly recovered.[59]

---

the soul, inducing in it lust and oftentimes misplaced sorrow or elation. There are many early Christian treatises against such spectacles; e.g., the two best known are both named *De Spectaculis* (*On the Games*) by Tertullian in A.D. 197 and by Novatian in ca. A.D. 251.

[58] *my God and my Lord*: See John 20:28.

[59] *She would have hastened . . . had I not rapidly recovered*: Deferring baptism until one was close to death was not uncommon in the early Church. The "first Christian emperor", Constantine, for example, was not baptized until he was on his deathbed. The theology behind this practice may have been misplaced but, as Augustine alludes to in the next sentence, it stressed the hope to leave this world with an unsullied soul, with *all* of one's sins remitted.

My cleansing was therefore deferred on the pretext that if I lived I would inevitably soil myself again, for it was held that the guilt of sinful defilement incurred after the laver of baptism was graver and more perilous. I was already a believer, as were my mother and all the household, with the sole exception of my father.[60] He, however, did not overrule the influence my mother's piety exercised over me, by making any attempt to stop me believing in Christ, in whom he did not at that time believe himself. My mother did all she could to see that you, my God, should be more truly my father than he was, and in this endeavor you helped her to win the argument against a husband to whom she, though a better person, was ordinarily subject, for in taking this course she was in fact subjecting herself to you, who so commanded her.

18. My God, I beg you to tell me—for I would very much like to know, if it is your will—to what purpose my baptism was postponed, and whether it was for my good that the restraints against sinning were in some degree slackened for me; it is true, is it not, that they were slackened? Why is it that we still hear nowadays people saying on all sides of many another person, "Let him be, let him do as he likes, he is not baptized yet"? Where bodily health is at stake we do not say, "Let him be, let him go on injuring himself, he is not cured yet." How much better it would have been if I had been healed at once, and if everything had been done by my own efforts and those of my family to ensure that the good health my soul had received should be kept safe in the care of you who had given it. Yes, how much better it would have been! But many towering waves of temptation seemed to be looming in the period beyond boyhood. My mother already anticipated them and thought it better to risk in them the clay from which I would later be molded than the new-formed man himself.

[60] *exception of my father*: Augustine's relationship with his father was strained at best. Patricius was not a Christian as Augustine grew and was not, as we shall see, much help in raising his children in truly virtuous ways; yet shortly before his death in 372 Patricius accepted the Catholic faith and was baptized.

Chapter 12

19. Yet even during that time of my boyhood, when it was supposed that I was safer than I would be in adolescence, I was not fond of study, and hated being driven to it. Driven I was, though, and that did me good, though my own attitude was far from good, because I learned only under compulsion, and no one is doing right who acts unwillingly, even if what he does is good in itself. The people who forced me on were not acting well either, but good accrued to me all the same from you, my God. They did not foresee to what use I would put the lessons they made me learn: they thought only of sating man's insatiable appetite for a poverty tricked out as wealth and a fame that is but infamy. But you, who have even kept count of our hairs,[61] turned to my profit the misguided views of those who stood over me and made me learn, just as you also turned to my profit my own perverse unwillingness to learn by using it to punish me, for I certainly deserved punishment, being a great sinner for such a tiny boy. In this way you turned to my good the actions of those who were doing no good, and gave me my just deserts by means of my sin itself. Matters are so arranged at your command that every disordered soul is its own punishment.

Chapter 13

Latin and Greek studies

20. Even to this day I have been unable to make up my mind why I hated the Greek that was dinned into me in early boyhood. Latin studies, on the contrary, I loved, not the elementary kind under my first teachers, but the lessons taught by masters of literature; for the early lessons in reading, writing and arithmetic had been no less burdensome and boring to me than all the elements of Greek.[62] What other reason could

---

[61] *you, who have even kept count of our hairs*: See Matthew 10:30.
[62] *Latin studies . . . elements of Greek*: In Augustine's day, a learned Westerner conducted his daily affairs in Latin but was also expected to possess a working

there be for this than the sinful, inane pride in my life, flesh as I was, a passing breath that comes not again?[63] Those early lessons in literacy were unquestionably more profitable because more dependable; by means of them I was gradually being given a power which became mine and still remains with me: the power to read any piece of writing I come across and to write anything I have a mind to myself. Far more useful, then, were those studies than others in which I was forced to memorize the wanderings of some fellow called Aeneas, while forgetting my own waywardness, and to weep over Dido, who killed herself for love, when all the while in my intense misery I put up with myself with never a tear, as I died away from you, O God, who are my life.

21. What indeed is more pitiful than a piteous person who has no pity for himself? I could weep over the death Dido brought upon herself out of love for Aeneas, yet I shed no tears over the death I brought upon myself by not loving you. O God, you are the light of my heart, bread for the inward mouth of my soul, the virtue wedded to my mind and the innermost recesses of my thought; yet I did not love you, and breaking my troth I strayed away from you.[64] Even in this troth-breaking the approval of people all around me rang in my ears: "Fine! Well done!"[65] To pander to this world is to fornicate against you, but so loudly do they shout, "Well done!" that one feels ashamed to fall short of their expectations. For these things I did not weep, yet I wept for Dido, "slain as she

---

knowledge of Greek, similar to how French fluency marked an erudite person throughout much of early modernity.

[63] *flesh as I was, a passing breath that comes not again*: See Psalm 77(78):39.

[64] *I could weep over the death Dido brought . . . away from you*: See Psalm 72(73):27. Here we read of a very concrete way pagan spectacles or literature stood in the way of Augustine's loving God, feeling more sorrow for Dido's fictional suicide than for the death of his own soul as he continued to run from God by pursuing such learning. Note too how Sister Boulding chooses the Middle English noun *troth* for the pledge or oath planted in Augustine's heart to find rest in God alone.

[65] *people all around me rang in my ears: "Fine! Well done!"* See Psalm 34(35):21; 39:16(40:15); 69:4(70:3).

sought her last end by the sword," while I myself was abandoning you to seek the last dregs of your creation; dust I was, and unto dust returning.[66] If forbidden to read those tales, I was saddened at being prevented from reading what would sadden me. How insane it is to regard these studies as more civilized and rewarding than the elementary lessons in which I learned to read and write!

22. But now let my God cry more loudly in my soul, so that your truth may tell me, "No, that is not the case; it is not true. The primary teaching is better in every respect." I am undoubtedly more ready today to forget the wanderings of Aeneas and so forth than how to write or read. Curtains may well hang at the entrance to schools of literature, but they serve less to signal the prestige of elite instruction than to conceal error. Let not those buyers and sellers of literary studies[67] shout me down, my God, as I confess to you according to my soul's need, and acquiesce as you chide me for those evil ways of mine and bring me to love your good ways; let them not shout me down, for I fear them no longer. If I put to them the question whether the poet spoke truly when he affirmed that Aeneas once came to Carthage, the uneducated will say they do not know, while the more scholarly will admit that it is untrue. If, on the other hand, I ask how to spell the name "Aeneas," everyone who has studied the subject will give me a correct answer in accordance with the settled convention which people have made among themselves in fixing those signs. If I then go further and ask which would be a graver handicap in this life, to forget how to read and write, or to forget those poetic fantasies, can one doubt what answer would be given by anyone in his right mind?

Sin I did, then, in boyhood, by preferring those frivolous tales to much more useful attainments, or rather by loving the

---

[66] *dust I was, and unto dust returning:* See Genesis 3:19.

[67] *buyers and sellers of literary studies:* Ever critical of sophists who study rhetoric only to sound appealing and to win any argument, regardless of their position, even early on in his career, Augustine knew that fine oratory divorced from truthful content misleads and endangers others, especially the orator himself.

one and loathing the other. Already the jingle, "One and one make two, two and two make four," was hateful to me, whereas a wooden horse full of armed men, Troy afire, and the shade of Creusa—these were a spectacle on which I delighted to gaze, and as empty as they were entertaining.[68]

Chapter 14

23. Why was it, then, that I hated studying Greek literature, which had similar songs to sing? Homer was just as skilled at weaving stories, and he too was empty in a thoroughly entertaining way, yet as a boy I found him distasteful. I expect Virgil is equally distasteful to Greek boys, when they are forced to study him as I was Homer. It was so difficult; and the difficulty of thoroughly mastering a foreign language seemed to sprinkle bitterness over those fabulous narratives for all their Greek sweetness, because I knew none of the words, and the threat of savage, terrifying punishments was used to make me learn them. Time was, in my infancy, when I had known no Latin words either, but those I had learned by paying attention, without any fear or pain at all, amid the cuddles of my nurses, and teasing, and playful, happy laughter. So I learned then without the painful pressure of people pestering me, because my own heart prompted me to bring forth its ideas, as it never could have done had I not learned words. Only I learned in infancy not from teachers but from speakers, into whose ears I in my turn was able to give utterance to what I had conceived in my mind. It is evident that the free play of curiosity is a more powerful spur to learning these things than is fear-ridden coercion; yet in accordance with your laws, O

---

[68] *wooden horse . . . as empty as they were entertaining*: Obviously Augustine is referring here to the Trojan Horse, found in Book 2 of Virgil's *Aeneid*, the mainstay of any Latin boy's education. What troubles Augustine here is how the true and serious propositions of math (and apparently other sciences) fail to move him, but he is inordinately aroused by fanciful tales. He is becoming more and more sensitive to the powerful impact that words can have on the soul and on the formation of character, with the overall concern that we become like that which we love.

God, coercion checks the free play of curiosity. By your laws it constrains us, from the beatings meted out by our teachers to the ordeals of the martyrs, for in accord with those laws it prescribes for us bitter draughts of salutary discipline to recall us from the venomous pleasure which led us away from you.

Chapter 15

24. Hear my prayer, Lord.[69] Let not my soul faint under your discipline, nor let me weary as I confess before you those acts of mercy[70] by which you plucked me from all my evil ways.[71] I long for you to grow sweeter to me than all those allurements I was pursuing. You have enabled me to love you with all my strength and with passionate yearning grasp your hand, so that you may rescue me from every temptation until my life's end.[72] See, Lord, you are my king and my God;[73] let every useful thing I learned as a boy be devoted now to your service; let whatever I speak, write, read or count serve you, for even as I was learning such vanities you were schooling me, and you have forgiven the sins of self-indulgence I committed in those frivolous studies. Through them I acquired a great many useful words, though admittedly the same words can be learned just as well from texts which are by no means frivolous, and would make a safer path for children to tread.

Chapter 16

25. Woe, woe to you, you flood of human custom! Who can keep his footing against you? Will you never run dry? How long will you toss the children of Eve into a vast, terrifying sea, which even those afloat on the saving wood can scarcely cross? Did you not give me a story to read in which Jupiter is

---

[69] *Hear my prayer, Lord*: See Psalm 60:2(61:1).
[70] *those acts of mercy*: See Psalm 106(107).
[71] *you plucked me from all my evil ways*: See 2 Kings 17:13.
[72] *you may rescue me . . . until my life's end*: See 1 Corinthians 1:8.
[73] *my king and my God*: See Psalm 5:3(2); 43:5(44:4).

both the Thunderer and an adulterer?[74] He could not possibly be both; yet so he was represented, to the end that his real adultery might seem to establish itself as deserving of imitation because a faked thunderclap acted as go-between. Who among our hooded masters of oratory give sober consideration to the cry of one who was of the same clay as themselves, "Homer invented these stories and attributed human actions to the gods, but I wish he had rather provided us with examples of divine behavior"? It would be truer to say that Homer did indeed make up these tales, and thereby seemed to invest the disgraceful deeds of human beings with an aura of divinity, so that depraved actions should be reckoned depraved no longer, since anyone who behaved so could pretend to be imitating not abandoned humans but the gods above.

26. O hellish river, human children clutching their fees are still pitched into you to learn about these exploits, and general interest is aroused when education is publicly touted in the forum, in view of the law which decrees that a state salary be paid to teachers over and above the pupils' fees. You clash your rocks and set up a great din: "This is the place to acquire literacy; here you will develop the eloquence essential to persuasion and argument." Really? Could we not have learned those useful words elsewhere, words like "shower," "golden," "lap," "trick," "heavenly temples," if Terence had not presented to us a young scoundrel who took Jupiter as a model for his own fornication? This young man looks at a mural painting which shows how Jupiter tricked a woman by sending a golden shower into Danae's lap. Watch the dissolute youth making use of heavenly instruction to work up his lust! "What a god!" he exclaims, "a god who makes the temples of heaven ring with his thunder!" Well, a poor little fellow like me can't do that, but I have imitated him in the other thing, and what fun it was!

---

[74] *story to read in which Jupiter is both the Thunderer and an adulterer*: Behind the poet Virgil, the North African playwright Terence (d. 159 B.C.) would have factored heavily in Augustine's early education; here he is referring to a scene from Terence's *Eunuchus* where Jupiter's deceiving Danae by changing himself into a shower of gold so as to seduce her is held up as exemplary trickery.

It is simply not true that such words are more conveniently learned from obscene stories of this type, though it is all too true that under the influence of the words obscene deeds are the more boldly committed. I am blaming not the words, which are finely-wrought, precious vessels,[75] but the wine of error mixed for us in them by teachers who are drunk themselves. If we as boys refused to drink it, we were caned, and no appeal to a sober judge was open to us. Wretch that I was, I learned these things eagerly and took pleasure in them; and so I was accounted a boy of high promise. But in your presence, my God, I can remember it now and be at peace.[76]

Chapter 17

27. Allow me to say something, my God, about the intelligence which was your gift to me, and the crazy employments in which I frittered it away. An exercise was set for me which was fraught with worrying implications, for I hoped to win praise and honor if I succeeded, but if not, I ran the risk of being caned. I was required to produce a speech made by Juno expressing her anger and grief at being unable to repulse the Trojan king from Italy, but in words which I had never heard Juno use. We were obliged to follow the errant footsteps of poetic fantasies and to express in prose what the poet had said in verse. That boy was adjudged the best speaker who most convincingly suggested emotions of anger and grief and clothed them in apt words, as befitted the dignity of the person represented. What did it profit me, O God, my true life,[77] that my speech was acclaimed above those of my many peers and fellow-students? Was it not all smoke and wind? Was there no other material on which I could have exercised my intelligence and my tongue? Yes, there was: your praise, O Lord; your

---

[75] *words . . . precious vessels*: See Proverbs 20:15.

[76] *Wretch . . . be at peace*: In God, even the confessions of past sins can be salvific: Augustine can recall even the wretched deeds of his past life as an act of praise because he now sees how the Lord was faithful to him even in those times, laboring to bring him to a true life of grace.

[77] *O God, my true life*: See John 11:25; 14:6.

praise in the words of the scriptures would have supported the drooping vine of my soul, and then it would not have yielded a crop of worthless fruit for the birds to carry off. Sacrifice can be offered to those birds of prey, the rebel angels, in more ways than one.

Chapter 18

28. Small wonder, then, that I was swept off helplessly after profitless things and borne away from you, my God. The models proposed to me for imitation were people who would have been caught out and covered with confusion if they had related any of their doings—deeds not wrong in themselves—in a barbaric accent or with grammatical blunders, whereas to relate licentious deeds in correct and well-turned phrases, in ample and elegant style, would have won them praise and honor. You see this, Lord, but you are very patient and look on silently; you are exceedingly merciful and worthy of our trust.[78] Will you always remain silent?[79] From this vast, deep sea you are even now drawing out to safety[80] a soul that seeks you and thirsts to enjoy you,[81] one whose heart pleads with you, *I have sought your face, O Lord, your face will I seek*,[82] for at that time I was far away from your countenance in darkness of spirit. Not with our feet or by traversing great distances do we journey away from you or find our way back. That younger son of yours in the gospel[83] did not hire horses or carriages, nor did he board ships, nor take wing in any visible sense nor put one foot before the other when he journeyed to that far country where he could squander at will the wealth you, his gentle

[78] *Lord, . . . worthy of our trust:* See Psalm 102(103):8; 85(86):15.

[79] *Will you always remain silent?* See Isaiah 42:14. Throughout the *Confessions*, there is constant interplay between Augustine's need for ornate rhetoric and divine silence, between the panache of oratory and the true but often latent power of God.

[80] *From this vast, deep sea . . . drawing out to safety:* See Psalm 85(86):13.

[81] *a soul . . . to enjoy you:* See Psalm 41:3(42:2); 62:2(63:1).

[82] I have sought your face, O Lord, your face will I seek: Psalm 26(27):8.

[83] *younger son of yours in the gospel:* See Luke 15:32.

father, had given him at his departure. Gentle you were then, but gentler still with him when he returned in his need. No, to be estranged in a spirit of lust, and lost in its darkness, that is what it means to be far away from your face.

29. Look upon all this, O Lord God and, as you look, patiently consider how carefully human beings observe those orthographic conventions and syllabic quantities which they have received from earlier orators, while neglecting the eternal rules directed to unending salvation which they have received from you. A speaker who wishes to maintain and teach those long-standing conventions will give greater offense to his fellow-men by pronouncing the word "human" without sounding the "h," in defiance of grammatical discipline, than if he, human as he is, flouts your commands by hating a fellow-human.[84] Does he suppose that another human being who is his enemy can do him more harm than does the very hatred with which he regards that other person, or that anyone can do more serious damage to another by hostile behavior than he does to his own soul by harboring hostile intent? Knowledge of letters lies less deep in us than the law written in our conscience[85] which forbids us to do to another what we would not have done to ourselves.[86]

How hidden you are, dwelling on high[87] in your silence, great and only God, who by your unfaltering law spread the punishment of blindness over unlawful human lusts! A man in persistent search of fame pleads before a merely human judge, with a crowd of other humans standing round, and accuses his

---

[84] *pronouncing the word "human" . . . flouts your commands by hating a fellow-human*: Proper pronunciation was, of course, the mark of a learned individual, and for the young Augustine enamored by the power of polished rhetoric to move others, appearing cultivated was of paramount importance. Here he is making fun of those who go through life changing their speech, piling affectation upon affectation, simply to look more intelligent than they probably are. He most certainly knew of Poem 85 of Catullus (d. 54 B.C.) where the same sort of gibe is made.

[85] *Knowledge of letters . . . written in our conscience*: See Romans 2:15.

[86] *forbids us to . . . not have done to ourselves*: See Tobit 4:16; Matthew 7:12; Luke 6:31.

[87] *dwelling on high*: See Isaiah 33:5.

adversary with savage hatred. He takes the utmost care that no slip of the tongue betrays him into saying, "them fellows …," while caring not a whit that by his rage he is about to remove a fellow-human from human society.

Chapter 19

Childish sins

30. Such were the moral standards of the world at whose threshold I lay, a wretched boy; this was the arena in which I was to struggle. It made me more wary of committing some barbarism in speech than of being jealous of others who did not commit it when I did. I tell you this, my God, and confess to you those efforts for which I was praised; for at that time I believed that living a good life consisted in winning the favor of those who commended me. I failed to recognize the whirlpool of disgraceful conduct into which I had been flung, out of your sight.[88] What could have been fouler in your eyes at that time than myself? I was earning the disapproval even of those same people by the countless lies with which I deceived the slave who took me to school, my teachers and my parents, and all because of my love for play and the absurd anxiety with which I craved to gawk at worthless shows and imitate what I watched.

I stole from my parents' larder too, and their table, either out of gluttony or to get something with which I could bribe other boys to let me join in their games, for they exacted a price even though they enjoyed our play as much as I did. In those games I would often seek to dominate by fraudulent

---

[88] *I failed to recognize … out of your sight*: See Psalm 30:23 (31:22). As we approach the end of Book I, we see what has been at stake all along: character formation begins in the womb, and what one comes to love in life shapes what kind of person he becomes. Augustine now sees how his early loves were terribly distorted because he ran after only the flashy and faddish, craving acceptance from only those who were immersed in the same superficialities; more importantly, however, he now sees how God was gently guiding him in and through all of these experiences so as to show him the true exhilaration and beauty of human living.

means, because I was myself dominated by a vain urge to excel. And what was it that I was so unwilling to excuse, what did I so fiercely condemn if I detected it in others, but the very cheating I practiced myself? If I was caught out and accused of cheating I was more apt to lose my temper than to admit it. Is this boyhood innocence? No, Lord, it is not; hear me, dear God, it is not. These same sins grow worse as we grow older: first it is offenses against pedagogues and teachers, or cheating over nuts and balls and sparrows; then later it is crimes against prefects and kings, and fraud in gold and estates and slaves, just as a schoolboy's canings are succeeded by heavier punishments. It was only the small stature of a child that you mentioned with approval as a symbol of humility, O Lord our king, when you declared that *of such is the kingdom of heaven.*[89]

Chapter 20

Thanksgiving

31. In spite of all this, O Lord our God, I give thanks to you, the most perfect, most good creator and ruler of the universe, and I would still thank you even if you had not willed me to live beyond boyhood. Even then I existed, I lived and I experienced; I took good care to keep myself whole and sound and so preserve the trace in me of your profoundly mysterious unity, from which I came. By means of my inner sense I coordinated my sensible impressions, and in my little thoughts about little things I delighted in truth. I was unwilling to be deceived, I had a lively memory, I was being trained in the use of words, I was comforted by friendship, and I shrank from pain, groveling and ignorance.[90]

[89] of such is the kingdom of heaven: Matthew 19:14.

[90] *being trained in the use of words . . . groveling and ignorance:* One of the more beautiful aspects of the *Confessions* is how Augustine weaves prayer into his prose. Often throughout the books of his story he composes a prayer serving as a way to intensify his confession of God's fidelity and goodness, while also summarizing the major points of his reflections up to that point.

In a living creature such as this
everything is wonderful and worthy of praise,
but all these things are gifts from my God.
I did not endow myself with them,
but they are good, and together they make me what I am.
He who made me is good, and he is my good too;
rejoicing, I thank him for all those good gifts
which made me what I was, even as a boy.
In this lay my sin,
that not in him was I seeking pleasures, distinctions and truth,
but in myself and the rest of his creatures,
and so I fell headlong into pains, confusions and errors.
But I give thanks to you, my sweetness, my honor, my
    confidence;
to you, my God, I give thanks for your gifts.
Do you preserve them for me.
So will you preserve me too,
and what you have given me will grow and reach perfection,
and I will be with you; because this too is your gift to me
—that I exist.

Book II

Adolescence

Chapter 1

Sexual awakening[1]

1. Now I want to call to mind the foul deeds I committed, those sins of the flesh that corrupted my soul, not in order to love them, but to love you, my God. Out of love for loving you I do this, recalling my most wicked ways and thinking over the past with bitterness so that you may grow ever sweeter to me; for you are a sweetness that deceives not, a sweetness blissful and serene. I will try now to give a coherent account of my disintegrated self, for when I turned away from you, the one God, and pursued a multitude of things, I went to pieces.[2] There was a time in adolescence when I was afire to take my fill of hell. I boldly thrust out rank, luxuriant growth in various furtive love affairs; my beauty wasted away and I rotted in your sight, intent on pleasing myself and winning favor in the eyes of men.

---

[1] Sexual awakening: Book II is where Augustine most poignantly wrestles with the fallen desires of his awakening libido. Surely he has the three sins of 1 John 2:14 in mind throughout: concupiscence of the flesh, concupiscence of the eyes, and desire for worldly power. The year is about 370, he is sixteen years old, and he looks back realizing how important both the internal mastery of one's desires and the influence of one's friends are on the type of person one becomes.

[2] *give a coherent account . . . went to pieces*: By providing a "coherent account" of his life's story, Augustine is seeking to place all of who he is and all he has done into God, so as to make his own life ordered and meaningful and thereby leave behind the "disintegrated self" realized when one is immersed in sin and aimless pursuits. Realizing God's infinite knowledge and mercy, Augustine here is showing that even the things one would rather leave unconfessed, unannounced, must be offered as well, as Christ comes not to redeem the strong and self-sufficient but, rather, the feeble and fragile.

Chapter 2

2. What was it that delighted me? Only loving and being loved.[3] But there was no proper restraint, as in the union of mind with mind, where a bright boundary regulates friendship. From the mud of my fleshly desires[4] and my erupting puberty belched out murky clouds that obscured and darkened my heart until I could not distinguish the calm light of love from the fog of lust. The two swirled about together and dragged me, young and weak as I was, over the cliffs of my desires, and engulfed me in a whirlpool of sins. Your anger had grown hot at my doings, yet I did not know. I was deafened by that clanking chain of my mortal state which was the punishment for my soul's pride, and I was wandering away from you, yet you let me go my way. I was flung hither and thither, I poured myself out, frothed and floundered in the tumultuous sea of my fornications; and you were silent.[5] O my joy, how long I took to find you! At that time you kept silence as I continued to wander far from you and sowed more and more sterile seeds to my own grief, abased by my pride and wearied by my restlessness.

3. Who was there to alleviate my distress? No one took thought to arrange a marriage for me, so that my pursuit of fleeting beauties through most ignoble experiences might be diverted into useful channels.[6] Some bounds might have

[3] *Only loving and being loved*: This is quintessentially Augustinian: to love and to be loved (*amare et amari* in Latin) is the essence of personhood (both divine and human) and the sole purpose of the human heart. What he comes to see by reflecting on the movements of his life, however, is that all love must be properly ordered. For when one loves that which is in truth unlovable, one perverts his soul and thereby becomes not loving but lustful.

[4] *fleshly desires*: See 1 John 2:16.

[5] *you were silent*: See Isaiah 42:14.

[6] *arrange a marriage . . . useful channels*: At this time it would have been a young person's parents who would have arranged a marriage for their child. Clearly Augustine looks back seeing how this move may have saved him from some of his dalliances, but now realizes God had different plans for his life. At this stage in adolescence, Augustine seems to see marriage only as a bridle against his sexual seething, but later will provide three main purposes for the institution of

been set to my pleasures if only the stormy surge of my adolescence had flung me up onto the shore of matrimony. Or
again, if I had been unable to find tranquility in that way,
content to use my sexuality to procreate children as your law
enjoins,[7] O Lord (since you propagate the stock of our mortal race by this means, powerfully using your gentle hand to
control the thorns which have no place in your paradise,[8] for
your almighty power is never far from us, even when we are
far from you), if, as I say, I could not have found peace in
marriage, this at all events is certain, that I ought to have
listened more attentively to the voice from your clouds which
proclaimed, *Those who marry will have trials in their married
life; and I would wish to spare you;*[9] and again, *It is a good thing
for a man not to touch a woman;*[10] and, *An unmarried man is
preoccupied with the affairs of God, and with pleasing God; but a
married man is preoccupied with the affairs of the world, and with
pleasing his wife.*[11] Yes, I could have listened more attentively
to those words, and made myself a eunuch for the kingdom
of heaven.[12] In that way I might have waited more contentedly for your embrace.

4. But I was far too impetuous, poor wretch, so I went with
the flood-tide of my nature and abandoned you. I swept across
all your laws,[13] but I did not escape your chastisements, for
what mortal can do that? You were ever present to me, mercifully angry, sprinkling very bitter disappointments over all
my unlawful pleasures so that I might seek a pleasure free from
all disappointment. If only I could have done that, I would

---

marriage: the faithfulness between a man and a woman, the begetting of children, and the sacrament by which such a union manifests Christ's love for his
Church (*fides, proles,* and *sacramentum*).

[7] *procreate children as your law enjoins*: See Genesis 1:28.

[8] *thorns which have no place in your paradise*: See Genesis 3:18.

[9] Those who marry ... wish to spare you: 1 Corinthians 7:28.

[10] It is a good thing ... a woman: 1 Corinthians 7:1.

[11] An unmarried man ... pleasing his wife: 1 Corinthians 7:32–33.

[12] *eunuch for the kingdom of heaven*: See Matthew 19:12.

[13] *your laws*: See Leviticus 10:11.

have found nothing but yourself, Lord, nothing but you yourself who use pain to make your will known to us,[14] and strike only to heal,[15] and even kill us lest we die away from you. Where was I, and how far was I exiled from the joys of your house[16] in that sixteenth year of my bodily age, when the frenzy of lust imposed its rule on me, and I wholeheartedly yielded to it? A lust it was licensed by disgraceful human custom, but illicit before your laws. Yet none of my family made any attempt to avert my ruin by arranging a marriage for me; their only concern was that I should learn to excel in rhetoric and persuasive speech.

Chapter 3

A year at home

5. In that same year, my sixteenth, my studies were interrupted and I was brought back from Madaura, a nearby city where I had been lodging for instruction in literature and rhetoric.[17] The reason for this was that my father was saving up to send me further afield, to Carthage, though it was his shameless ambition that suggested the plan, not his wealth, for he was no more than a fairly obscure town councillor at Thagaste. But to whom am I telling this story? Not to you, my God; rather in your presence I am relating these events to my own kin, the human race, however few of them may chance upon these writings of mine. And why? So that whoever reads

[14] *use pain to make your will known to us*: See Psalm 93(94):20.

[15] *strike only to heal*: See Hosea 6:1–2.

[16] *exiled from the joys of your house*: See Luke 15:13.

[17] *studies . . . in literature and rhetoric*: Augustine studied in Madaura (still very much a pagan populace) from approximately 365–369 and then had to return home to Thagaste because his father had decided to save his money on (what we would call today) a boarding school, so as to be able to send his son to the best possible "high school" then available, in the city of Carthage. As alluded to next, Patricius was a man of modest yet stable means, employed by the Roman Empire as a *curialis*, and a member of the municipality overseeing the daily operations of Thagaste's public services.

them may reflect with me on the depths from which we must cry to you.[18] What finds a readier hearing with you than a heart that confesses to you, a life lived from faith?[19]

At the time I speak of anyone would have heaped praise upon my father, a man prepared to go beyond his means in spending as much money as was needed to send his son away to study, even in a distant city. No such efforts were made on behalf of the children of many other citizens who were far richer; yet all the while this same father of mine was unconcerned about how I would grow up for you, and cared little that I should be chaste, provided I was intellectually cultivated. It would be truer to say that I was left of your cultivation, O God, who are the only true and good owner of your field, my heart.[20]

6. Owing to the state of family finances in this sixteenth year of my life there was an interval of leisure for me, during which, being free from all schooling, I began to spend time in my parents' company. The thorn-bushes of my lust shot up higher than my head, and no hand was there to root them out. Least of all my father's; for when at the baths one day he saw me with unquiet adolescence, my only covering, and noted my ripening sexuality, he began at once to look forward eagerly to grandchildren, and gleefully announced his discovery to my mother.[21] His glee sprang from that intoxication which has blotted you, our creator, out of this world's memory and led it to love the creature instead,[22] as it drinks the unseen wine of

---

[18] *depths from which we must cry to you*: See Psalm 129(130):1.

[19] *life lived from faith*: See Habakkuk 2:4; Romans 1:17; Galatians 3:11; Hebrews 10:38.

[20] *intellectually cultivated . . . your field, my heart*: See Matthew 13:24–30.

[21] *at the baths one day . . . discovery to my mother*: It is very tempting to parallel this scene with Augustine's baptism (see *Conf.* IX.6.14) where another father (Ambrose) would have witnessed him naked plunged into the waters and perhaps too hoped for children (Augustine's adopted children, his future congregations) and thus announces to Mother Church that a new son and father has come of age.

[22] *love the creature instead*: See Romans 1:25. Augustine is critical of his father's worldliness, caring only about temporal power and thereby focusing on creatures instead of their Creator. Upon seeing his son naked in the baths, Patricius' sole

its perverse inclination and is dragged down to the depths. In my mother's soul, however, you had already begun to build your temple and prepare for your holy indwelling,[23] whereas my father was still a catechumen, and a recent one at that. She therefore started up in devout fear and trembling, for she was afraid for me even though I was not yet a Christian. She saw the twisted paths I followed, those paths trodden by people who turn their backs to you, not their faces.[24]

Adolescent lust

7. Alas for me! Do I dare to say that you were silent, my God, when I was straying from you? Were you really silent to me at that time? Whose, then, were the words spoken to me by my mother, your faithful follower? Were they not your words, the song you were constantly singing into my ears? None of it sank down to my heart, though, to induce me to act on it. She urged me to keep clear of fornication, and especially not to commit adultery with any man's wife. I remember in my inmost heart the intense earnestness with which she cautioned me against this; but these warnings seemed to me mere woman's talk, which I would have blushed to heed. In truth they came from you, but I failed to realize that, and assumed that you were silent and she alone was talking.[25] By using her you were

---

concern was not that Augustine would grow to conduct himself as a loving and holy man but only that he was postpubescent and thus able to carry on the family name.

[23] *you had already begun . . . prepare for your holy indwelling*: See 1 Corinthians 3:16–17. We know Patricius converted and was baptized shortly before dying in 370 or 371.

[24] *people who turn their backs to you, not their faces*: See Jeremiah 2:27.

[25] *they came from you . . . she alone was talking*: As one grows in knowing God, one sees how he relies on creatures to make himself known. Here Augustine is able to look back to understand how Monica was God's representative, nudging him ever more closer to Christ and his Church. Perhaps he is here acknowledging some residual chauvinistic paganism as well, still unable to see how God could rely on a "mere woman's talk" to make his own words known. Notice the larger issue here as well: love renders creatures transparent to the

not silent to me at all; and when I scorned her I was scorning
you—I, her son, the son of your handmaid, I your servant![26]
But I was quite reckless; I rushed on headlong in such blindness that when I heard other youths of my own age bragging
about their immoralities I was ashamed to be less depraved
than they. The more disgraceful their deeds, the more credit
they claimed; and so I too became as lustful for the plaudits as
for the lechery itself. What is more to be reviled than vile
debauchery? Afraid of being reviled I grew viler, and when I
had no indecent acts to admit that could put me on a level
with these abandoned youths, I pretended to obscenities I had
not committed, lest I might be thought less courageous for being
more innocent, and be accounted cheaper for being more
chaste.

8. With companions like these I roamed the streets of Babylon and wallowed in its filth as though basking amid cinnamon and precious ointments.[27] My invisible enemy trampled
on me and seduced me in order to fix me still faster in the
center of that city, for I was easy enough to seduce. My natural mother had by this time fled from the center of Babylon,[28] though she still lingered in its suburbs. She warned me
to live chastely, but did not extend her care to restraining within
the bounds of conjugal love (if it could not be cut right back
to the quick) this behavior of mine, of which she had heard
from her husband, even though she judged it to be corrupt
already and likely to be dangerous in the future. Her reluctance

---

divine, allowing us to meet God through his agents on earth, while lust blocks
God working through creatures, imploding them unattractively back on
themselves.

[26] *son of your handmaid, I your servant*: See Psalm 115(116):16.

[27] *Babylon . . . cinnamon and precious ointments*: In Augustine's writings, "Babylon" stands for the "City of Man", the absolute contrast to Jerusalem and to the
"City of God". Whereas the former represents fallen man's "lust for power" (*libido
dominandi*), the latter "city" is constituted by the holy ones' incessant desire to
praise God. Here Babylon and the surrounding images of filth, cinnamon, and
ointments represent the decadence into which the young Augustine has fallen,
as well as his need for human praise to make any (earthly) progress whatsoever.

[28] *fled from the center of Babylon*: See Jeremiah 51:6.

to arrange a marriage for me arose from the fear that if I were encumbered with a wife my hope could be dashed—not hope in you for the world to come, to which she held herself, but my hope of academic success. Both my parents were very keen on my making progress in study: my father, because he thought next to nothing about you and only vain things about me; and my mother, because she regarded the customary course of studies as no hindrance, and even a considerable help, toward my gaining you eventually. So, at least, do I interpret their respective attitudes, as I remember them now as best I can.[29]

The restraints placed upon my amusements were also slackened more than strict discipline would have approved, with the result that I strayed into various disreputable amours. Throughout these experiences a dark fog cut me off from your bright truth, my God, and my sin grew sleek on my excesses.[30]

Chapter 4

He robs a pear tree

9. Beyond question, theft is punished by your law, O Lord,[31] and by the law written in human hearts,[32] which not even sin itself can erase; for does any thief tolerate being robbed by another thief, even if he is rich and the other is driven by want? I was under no compulsion of need, unless a lack of moral sense can count as need, and a loathing for justice, and a greedy, full-fed love of sin. Yet I wanted to steal, and steal I did. I already had plenty of what I stole, and of much better

---

[29] *She warned me to live chastely . . . as best I can*: Even saints must grow in virtue: at this stage, Monica is willing to turn a proverbial blind eye to Augustine's unchasteness, believing that if he were to marry early, he would not be able to advance in his studies, the one hope she held on to as the means to his full conversion to Catholicism. Patricius was simply happy he was excelling in school with quite an eager eye to worldly success.

[30] *my sin grew sleek on my excesses*: See Psalm 72(73):7.

[31] *theft is punished by your law, O Lord*: See Exodus 20:15; Deuteronomy 5:19.

[32] *law written in human hearts*: See Romans 2:14–15.

quality too, and I had no desire to enjoy it when I resolved to steal it. I simply wanted to enjoy the theft for its own sake, and the sin.

Close to our vineyard there was a pear tree laden with fruit. This fruit was not enticing, either in appearance or in flavor. We nasty lads went there to shake down the fruit and carry it off at dead of night, after prolonging our games out of doors until that late hour according to our abominable custom. We took enormous quantities, not to feast on ourselves but perhaps to throw to the pigs; we did eat a few, but that was not our motive: we derived pleasure from the deed simply because it was forbidden.[33]

Look upon my heart, O God, look upon this heart of mine, on which you took pity in its abysmal depths. Enable my heart to tell you now what it was seeking in this action which made me bad for no reason, in which there was no motive for my malice except malice. The malice was loathsome, and I loved it. I was in love with my own ruin, in love with decay: not with the thing for which I was falling into decay but with decay itself, for I was depraved in soul, and I leapt down from your strong support into destruction, hungering not for some advantage to be gained by the foul deed, but for the foulness of it.

---

[33] *derived pleasure . . . was forbidden*: See Luke 15:15–16. This is perhaps the most celebrated scene in the *Confessions*, and scholars have long wondered why such a seemingly innocent act bothered Augustine so many years later. The answer lies in his understanding of reality: God is the fullness of being while evil is the absence of being, a parasite that only eats on goodness. Engaging in an intrinsically evil action (e.g., stealing) without seeking anything beyond the act itself, Augustine now sees that he was choosing about as close to "nothing" as one can. There was here no contentment, no actual savoring of the fruit, nor any ill-gotten booty to be enjoyed later; at least in other immoral actions there are usually pleasures enjoyed, but here what astounds is how the theft of the pears was attractive simply because it was forbidden. At play here too is Augustine's again casting himself as the prodigal son who also found his sustenance with the swine, as well as an anti-Manichean trope—as the Manichees likened their good deity with fruit such as pears (and figs—see *Conf.* III.10.18, p. 69) and for them to read that a former member tossed them to the pigs would certainly have caused outrage.

Chapter 5

Question of motives

10. The beautiful form of material things attracts our eyes, so we are drawn to gold, silver and the like. We are powerfully influenced by the feel of things agreeable to the touch; and each of our other senses finds some quality that appeals to it individually in the variety of material objects. There is the same appeal in worldly rank, and the possibility it offers of commanding and dominating other people: this too holds its attraction, and often provides an opportunity for settling old scores. We may seek all these things, O Lord, but in seeking them we must not deviate from your law. The life we live here is open to temptation by reason of a certain measure and harmony between its own splendor and all these beautiful things of low degree. Again, the friendship which draws human beings together in a tender bond is sweet to us because out of many minds it forges a unity.[34] Sin gains entrance through these and similar good things when we turn to them with immoderate desire, since they are the lowest kind of goods and we thereby turn away from the better and higher: from you yourself, O Lord our God, and your truth and your law. These lowest goods hold delights for us indeed, but no such delights as does my God, who made all things; for in him the just man finds delight, and for upright souls[35] he himself is joy.

---

[34] *friendship . . . forges a unity*: Throughout the *Confessions*, friendship plays an essential role not only in Augustine's life but in how the reader is invited to think about Jesus Christ and his role in our lives. Playing off perhaps Aristotle's definition (see *Nicomachean* Ethics IX.9), but certainly Cicero's (see *On Friendship* §21), Augustine understands a friend to be *another self*, implying that we become like those with whom we spend time, become like those whom we love. A friend for Augustine longs to become one with his beloved, and this is precisely the purpose of the Incarnation: God became like us in Jesus Christ, so that in Christ we may become like God, a God who no longer calls us servants, but friends (see John 15:15).

[35] *just man finds delight, and for upright souls*: See Psalm 63:11(64:10).

11. So then, when people look for the reason why some criminal act has been committed, their account is usually reckoned credible only when it is evident that there may have been greed on the malefactor's part to gain possession of goods belonging to someone else—those goods we have called "lowest"—or fear of losing his own; for these good things truly are beautiful and lovely in their own way, even though base and mean in comparison with the higher goods that bring us true happiness. Suppose someone has committed homicide. Why did he do it? Perhaps he was in love with the victim's wife, or coveted his estate, or wanted to steal from him in order to support himself, or feared to be robbed of the like himself by the other man, or had been injured and burned for revenge. Is it likely that he would kill another person without any motive, simply because he enjoyed killing? Who could believe that? Admittedly it is reported of a certain frenzied and outrageously cruel man that "he preferred being evil and cruel with no provocation", but a motive for his crimes was nonetheless declared: he wished to ensure, the historian tells us, that "neither hand nor mind should atrophy from inaction." We might further ask, "And what else did he intend?" He meant to use crime for the training of his young conspirators, in order eventually to gain control of the city and win honors, power and riches; thus he would be free from fear of the law and from the difficulties in his circumstances arising from "shortage of money and his guilty record." Even Catiline, then, did not love his criminal acts for their own sake, but only the advantages he had in view when committing them.

Chapter 6

12. How does this apply to me, poor wretch? What did I love in you, O my theft, what did I love in you, the nocturnal crime of my sixteenth year? There was nothing beautiful about you, for you were nothing but a theft. Are you really anything at all, for me to be speaking to you like this?

O good God, creator of all things[36] and more beautiful than all of them, those pears we stole did have a certain beauty because they were your creation—yours, O God, who are the highest good and the true good for me. Those pears were beautiful, but they were not what my miserable soul loved. I had plenty of better ones, and I plucked them only for the sake of stealing, for once picked I threw them away. I feasted on the sin, nothing else, and that I relished and enjoyed. Even if some morsel of the pears did enter my mouth, it was only the criminal act that lent it savor.[37] So now, Lord my God, when I ask what it was that gave me pleasure in that theft, I find nothing of fair, seductive form at all. I do not mean simply that it lacked the beauty to be found in justice and prudence, or the beauty of the human mind and intelligence, or that of our senses and bodily life, or the beauty inherent in the stars, so lovely in their appointed places, or in the earth and the sea full of young life born there to replace the things that die. No, I mean more: my theft lacked even the sham, shadowy beauty with which even vice allures us.

13. For in vice there lurks a counterfeit beauty: pride, for instance—even pride apes sublimity, whereas you are the only God, most high above all things. As for ambition, what does it crave but honors and glory, while you are worthy of honor beyond all others, and eternally glorious? The ferocity of powerful men aims to inspire fear; but who is to be feared except the one God? Can anything be snatched from his power or withdrawn from it—when or where or whither or by whom? Flirtatiousness aims to arouse love by its charming wiles, but nothing can hold more charm than your charity, nor could anything be loved to greater profit than your

[36] *God, creator of all things:* See 2 Maccabees 1:24.

[37] *criminal act that lent it savor:* The psychologizing of sinfulness continues: the only sweetness to Augustine's malformed soul in stealing the pears was the "savor" of standing apart from God, and now Augustine sees how he literally came to love nothingness, to relish the lack of goodness. His soul has become perverse, twisted downward onto that which tends toward nonbeing, and this terrifies him greatly, as the intensity of these nine sections attests (cf. *Conf.* II.4.9–9.17).

truth, which outshines all else in its luminous beauty. Curiosity poses as pursuit of knowledge, whereas you know everything to a supreme degree. Even ignorance or stupidity masquerades as simplicity and innocence, but nothing that exists is simpler than yourself; and what could be more innocent than you, who leave the wicked to be hounded by their own sins? Sloth pretends to aspire to rest, but what sure rest is there save the Lord? Lush living likes to be taken for contented abundance, but you are the full and inexhaustible store of a sweetness that never grows stale. Extravagance is a bogus generosity, but you are the infinitely wealthy giver of all good things. Avarice strives to amass possessions, but you own everything. Envy is contentious over rank accorded to another, but what ranks higher than you? Anger seeks revenge, but who ever exacts revenge with greater justice than yourself? Timidity dreads any unforeseen or sudden threat to the things it loves, and takes precautions for their safety; but is anything sudden or unforeseen to you? Who can separate what you love from you?[38] Where is ultimate security to be found, except with you? Sadness pines at the loss of the good things with which greed took its pleasure, because it wants to be like you, from whom nothing can be taken away.

14. A soul that turns away from you therefore lapses into fornication[39] when it seeks apart from you what it can never find in pure and limpid form except by returning to you. All those who wander far away and set themselves up against you are imitating you, but in a perverse way; yet by this very mimicry they proclaim that you are the creator of the whole of nature, and that in consequence there is no place whatever where we can hide from your presence.[40]

---

[38] *Who can separate . . . from you?* See Romans 8:35.

[39] *soul that turns away . . . lapses into fornication*: See Psalm 72(73):27.

[40] *you are the creator of the whole of nature . . . from your presence*: All human activity is, in the end, a search for consummate completion in the one in whose image we are made. Every beat of the heart, every reaching out of our hands, every glance of our eyes, is really after love himself.

With regard to my theft, then: what did I love in it, and in what sense did I imitate my Lord, even if only with vicious perversity? Did the pleasure I sought lie in breaking the law at least in that sneaky way, since I was unable to do so with any show of strength? Was I, in truth a prisoner, trying to simulate a crippled sort of freedom, attempting a shady parody of omnipotence by getting away with something forbidden? How like that servant of yours who fled from his Lord and hid in the shadows! What rottenness, what a misshapen life! Rather a hideous pit of death! To do what was wrong simply because it was wrong—could I have found pleasure in that?

Chapter 7

15. How can I repay the Lord[41] for my ability to recall these things without fear? Let me love you, Lord, and give thanks to you and confess to your name, because you have forgiven my grave sins and wicked deeds. By your sheer grace and mercy you melted my sins away like ice.[42] To your grace also do I ascribe whatever sins I did not commit, for what would I not have been capable of, I who could be enamored even of a wanton crime? I acknowledge that you have forgiven me everything, both the sins I willfully committed by following my own will, and those I avoided through your guidance.

Is there anyone who can take stock of his own weakness and still dare to credit his chastity and innocence to his own

---

[41] *How can I repay the Lord*: See Psalm 115(116):12.

[42] *Let me love you, Lord . . . you have melted my sins away like ice*: See Sirach 3:17. [Augustine's numbering of Sirach differed from ours today; see Sirach 3:15 A modern-day reader of the *Confessions* should be aware that Augustine never saw a Bible as we think of it and was working from, what he called simply, *scripturae*: the Scriptures in individual books or in a collection of select books (e.g., the Gospels or Epistles of Paul). Augustine did not have Jerome's Vulgate but instead read the "Old Latin" collection of Scriptures, reduplicated most accurately in Pierre Sabatier, *Bibliorum Sacrorum Latinae Versiones antiquae seu Vetus Italica*. As such, there are oftentimes scriptural references that appear in the critical edition of the *Confessions* that do not translate easily into a contemporary English version of Scripture. Where these chapter and version numbers do not coincide, it is noted in the footnotes of this edition.]

efforts?[43] And could such a person think to love you less, on the pretext that he has had smaller need of your mercy, that mercy with which you forgive the sins of those who turn back to you? If there is anyone whom you have called, who by responding to your summons has avoided those sins which he finds me remembering and confessing in my own life as he reads this, let him not mock me; for I have been healed by the same doctor who has granted him the grace not to fall ill, or at least to fall ill less seriously. Let such a person therefore love you just as much, or even more, on seeing that the same physician who rescued me from sinful diseases of such gravity has kept him immune.

Chapter 8

16. What fruit did I ever reap from those things which I now blush to remember,[44] and especially from that theft in which I found nothing to love save the theft itself, wretch that I was? It was nothing, and by the very act of committing it I became more wretched still. And yet, as I recall my state of mind at the time, I would not have done it alone;[45] I most certainly would not have done it alone. It follows, then, that I also loved the camaraderie with my fellow-thieves. So it is not true to say that I loved nothing other than the theft? Ah, but it is true, because that gang-mentality too was a nothing. What

---

[43] *Is there anyone . . . his own efforts?* Augustine seems to come to his first understanding of the power of grace to transform through the mastery of his sexual desires. Named the "Doctor of Grace" by the early Church, Augustine knew better than most the necessity of God's indwelling in the human soul if a fallen creature is ever to love rightly. This would be a major battlefield with his decades-long fight against the Pelagians, the group of Christians who believed that since Adam left us only a bad example, those who choose not to follow Adam can live upright (if not perfect) lives. Against this thesis, Augustine understandably turned some of his most pessimistic lines about the goodness of human nature.

[44] *What fruit . . . now blush to remember:* See Romans 6:21.

[45] *I would not have done it alone:* Community matters: since we become like those with whom we spend time, none of us become neither great sinners nor great saints in isolation. For Augustine, we are essentially relational creatures who grow through imitation and appropriation of others' qualities, virtues, and vices.

was it in fact? Who can teach me, except the One who illumines my heart[46] and distinguishes between its shadows? Why has this question come into my mind now, to be examined and discussed and considered? If the object of my love had been the pears I stole, and I simply wanted to enjoy them, I could have done it alone; similarly, if the act of committing the sin had sufficed by itself to yield me the pleasure I sought, I would not have further inflamed my itching desire by the stimulation of conspiracy. But since my pleasure did not lie in the pears, it must have been in the crime as committed in the company of others who shared in the sin.

Chapter 9

17. What kind of attitude was that? An extremely dishonorable one, certainly; alas for me, that I entertained it! Yet what exactly was it? Who understands his faults?[47] The theft gave us a thrill, and we laughed to think we were outwitting people who had no idea what we were doing, and would angrily stop us if they knew. Why could I not have derived the same pleasure from doing it alone? Perhaps because it is not easy to enjoy a joke by oneself? Not easy, to be sure, but it does sometimes happen that people who are entirely alone, with no one else present, are overcome by laughter, if something very funny presents itself to their senses or their thoughts. Possibly ... but I would not have done that deed alone; in no way would I have done it alone. In your presence I declare it, my God, this is my soul's vivid remembrance. On my own I would not have perpetrated that theft in which I felt no desire for what I stole, but only for the act of stealing; to do it alone would have aroused no desire whatever in me, nor would I have done it.

[46] *Who can teach me, except the One who illumines my heart*: See Sirach 2:10. ["Who can teach me, except the one who illumines my heart" reads *inluminabuntur corda uestra* in Augustine's *Old Latin* text, but not in the Greek Septuagint, upon which most English translations are based today.]

[47] *Who understands his faults?* See Psalm 18:13(19:12).

What an exceedingly unfriendly form of friendship that was! It was a seduction of the mind hard to understand, which instilled into me a craving to do harm for sport and fun. I was greedy for another person's loss without any desire on my part to gain anything or to settle a score. Let the others only say, "Come on, let's go and do it!" and I am ashamed to hold back from the shameless act.

Chapter 10

The prodigal's wanderings begin

18. Who can unravel this most snarled, knotty tangle? It is disgusting, and I do not want to look at it or see it. O justice and innocence, fair and lovely, it is on you that I want to gaze with eyes that see purely and find satiety in never being sated. With you is rest and tranquil life. Whoever enters into you enters the joy of his Lord;[48] there he will fear nothing and find his own supreme good in God who is supreme goodness. I slid away from you and wandered away, my God; far from your steadfastness I strayed in adolescence, and I became to myself a land of famine.[49]

[48] *joy of his Lord*: See Matthew 25:21.
[49] *land of famine*: See Luke 15:14.

Book III

Student Years at Carthage

Chapter 1

Student life: sex and shows

1. So I arrived at Carthage, where the din of scandalous love-affairs raged cauldron-like around me.[1] I was not yet in love, but I was enamored with the idea of love, and so deep within me was my need that I hated myself for the sluggishness of my desires. In love with loving, I was casting about for something to love; the security of a way of life free from pitfalls seemed abhorrent to me, because I was inwardly starved of that food which is yourself, O my God. Yet this inner famine created no pangs of hunger in me. I had no desire for the food that does not perish, not because I had my fill of it, but because the more empty I was, the more I turned from it in revulsion. My soul's health was consequently poor. It was covered with sores and flung itself out of doors, longing to soothe its misery by rubbing against sensible things; yet these were soulless, and so could not be truly loved. Loving and being loved were sweet to me, the more so if I could also enjoy a lover's body; so I polluted the stream of friendship with my filthy desires and clouded its purity with hellish lusts; yet all the while, befouled and disgraced though I was, my boundless vanity made me long

---

[1] *Carthage . . . cauldron-like around me*: A famous wordplay opens Book III, as Augustine likens Carthage (*Carthago*) to a boiling cauldron (*sartago*). It is now the fall of 370 and Augustine is just about to turn seventeen, having arrived in one of the largest cities in North Africa (second only to Alexandria in Egypt). While Carthage has some Christian areas, it is for the most part still largely pagan and, as this opening line portents, offers many forms of debauched entertainment.

to appear elegant and sophisticated. I blundered headlong into the love which I hoped would hold me captive, but in your goodness, O my God, my mercy,[2] you sprinkled bitter gall over my sweet pursuits. I was loved, and I secretly entered into an enjoyable liaison, but I was also trammeling myself with fetters of distress, laying myself open to the iron rods and burning scourges of jealousy and suspicion, of fear, anger and quarrels.[3]

Chapter 2

2. I was held spellbound by theatrical shows full of images that mirrored my own wretched plight and further fueled the fire within me. Why is it that one likes being moved to grief at the sight of sad or tragic events on stage, when one would be unwilling to suffer the same things oneself?[4] In the capacity of spectator one welcomes sad feelings; in fact, the sadness itself is the pleasure. What incredible stupidity! The more a person is buffeted by such passions in his own life, the more he is moved by watching similar scenes on stage, although his state of mind is usually called misery when he is undergoing them himself and mercy when he shows compassion for others so afflicted. But how real is the mercy evoked by fictional dramas? The listener is not moved to offer help, but merely invited to feel sorrow; and the more intensely he feels it the more highly he rates the actor in the play. If these tragic human stories—whether referring to events long past or fictional— are played in such a way that they fail to move the spectator to sadness, he walks out in disgust, criticizing the performance;

[2] *my God, my mercy*: See Psalm 58:18(59:17).

[3] *jealousy and suspicion, of fear, anger and quarrels*: See Galatians 5:20.

[4] *Why is it that one likes being moved . . . same things oneself?* This irony plagues Augustine most of his early years and is most evident here in Book III as he is attracted to pagan shows and theatrical performances: Why are we drawn to see and hear what we otherwise work to avoid in our own lives? There is something about the sad song or the tragic play that draws us in but which we would never want to experience for ourselves. In the following sections, he shall offer some possible reasons for why this is.

but if he feels sad, he stays on, keenly attentive, and enjoys a good cry.

3. So it is possible to enjoy sad feelings; yet there can be no doubt that everyone aspires to be happy. Can this be the reason: that no one wants to be miserable, but we do like to think ourselves merciful, and mercy must entail some sorrow? Can it be for this reason alone that sorrowful feelings are welcomed? To be sure, this power of sympathy derives from the stream of friendship. But where does it flow to, whither is it bound? Why does it debouch into a torrent of boiling pitch, into seething passions of monstrous lust, so that it loses itself in them, is diverted and thrown off course, and deviates by its own choice from its heavenly serenity? Is mercy, then, to be rejected? By no means; it is sometimes right to entertain compassionate feelings. But beware of impurity, my soul: under the guardianship of my God, the God of our fathers who is to be praised and most highly exalted for ever,[5] beware of impurity.

Even today I am not devoid of merciful sensibility, but at that time it was different; I rejoiced with lovers on the stage who took sinful pleasure in one another, even though their adventures were only imaginary and part of a dramatic presentation, and when they lost each other I grieved with them, ostensibly merciful; yet in both instances I found pleasure in my emotions.[6] Today I feel greater pity for someone who takes delight in a sinful deed than for someone else who seems to suffer grievously at the loss of pernicious pleasure and the passing of a bliss that was in fact nothing but misery. This is unquestionably a truer mercy, but the sadness it entails holds no

[5] *God . . . highly exalted for ever:* See Daniel 3:52.

[6] *I rejoiced with lovers on the stage . . . found pleasure in my emotions:* It is important to realize the Platonic background here. For Plato (ca. 424–348 B.C.), to be real is to be immutable, and, therefore, nothing in this sensible world of change is ultimately real. This is why in Book X of his *Republic,* Plato condemns most forms of art because they are only imitations of that which is not really real anyway (i.e., the sensible world). Despite this warning, Augustine still finds himself equating reality with entertainment. How many of us are perhaps likewise drawn into the lives and the unfolding drama of many television characters, into lives that are not truly real but where we nonetheless find ourselves invested?

attraction for me. A person who sorrows for someone who is miserable earns approval for the charity he shows, but if he is genuinely merciful he would far rather there were nothing to sorrow about. If such a thing as spiteful benevolence existed (which is impossible, of course, but supposing it did), a genuinely and sincerely merciful person would wish others to be miserable so that he could show them mercy!

We must conclude that, while some sorrow is commendable, no sorrow is to be valued for its own sake. You, Lord God, lover of souls, show mercy far more purely than we can, and in a way free from all taint, because no sorrow can wound you. Which of us is sufficient for this?

4. At that time I was truly miserable, for I loved feeling sad and sought out whatever could cause me sadness. When the theme of a play dealt with other people's tragedies—false and theatrical tragedies—it would please and attract me more powerfully the more it moved me to tears. I was an unhappy beast astray from your flock and resentful of your shepherding, so what wonder was it that I became infected with foul mange? My love for tragic scenes sprang from no inclination to be more deeply wounded by them, for I had no desire to undergo myself the woes I liked to watch. It was simply that when I listened to such doleful tales being told they enabled me superficially to scrape away at my itching self, with the result that these raking nails raised an inflamed swelling, and drew stinking discharge from a festering wound. Was that life I led any life at all, O my God?

Chapter 3

5. Far above me your faithful mercy was hovering. How great were the sins on which I spent all my strength, as I followed my impious curiosity![7] It led me to abandon you and plunge

---

[7] *I followed my impious curiosity*: Curiosity for the ancients was a vice opposed to the virtue of *studiositas*, opposed to the ability to think deeply and purposefully and not simply flitter intellectually about with no goal to the end of one's pursuits. Thomas Aquinas would place this under the deadly sin of sloth or acedia

into treacherous abysses, into depths of unbelief and a delu-
sive allegiance to demons, to whom I was offering my evil deeds
in sacrifice.[8] And in all these sins your scourges beat upon
me. Even within the walls of your church, during the celebration of your sacred mysteries, I once made bold to indulge in
carnal desire and conduct that could yield only a harvest of
death;[9] and for this you struck me with severe punishments,
though none that matched my guilt. O my God, you were
immensely merciful to me, and were my refuge from the terrible dangers amid which I wandered, head held high. I withdrew further and further from you, loving my own ways and
not yours, relishing the freedom of a runaway slave.

The "wreckers"

6. The prestigious course of studies I was following looked as
its goal to the law-courts, in which I was destined to excel
and where I would earn a reputation all the higher in the measure that my performance was the more unscrupulous. So blind
can people be that they glory even in their blindness! Already
I was the ablest student in the school of rhetoric. At this I

(see his *Summa Theologiae* II–II.35.4), literally meaning the inability to care about
one's spiritual perfection. This aimlessness is precisely what Augustine is coming
to terms with at this point in his life's story.

[8] *allegiance to demons . . . in sacrifice*: See Deuteronomy 32:17; 1 Corinthians
10:20.

[9] *within the walls of your church . . . harvest of death*: See Romans 7:5. Scholars
have long debated what detestable act Augustine accuses himself here "within
the walls" of a church, but most have conveniently avoided raising the question.
Piecing it together, we see that his lament concerns "carnal desire", which leads
to a "harvest of death", and so are left thinking that whatever transpired, Augustine is here contrasting his fallen sexual desires with the new life attainable only
in true sacramental worship. The juxtaposition between his own carnality and
God's goodness represents well the disconnect he is experiencing during these
late teenage years. We know from one other admittance (*Sermon* 359B, dated
January 23, 404), that he bemoans the vigil Masses he used to attend, because
Bishop Aurelius had not yet separated the men and women in the congregation,
and in such a tight space, all sorts of suggestive talk (if not touch) and temptations occurred.

was elated and vain and swollen with pride; but as you know, O Lord, I was a good deal quieter than the "wreckers" and kept well clear of their destructive activities. I was ashamed of the sense of shame that held me back from being like these "wreckers," whose perverse and diabolical nickname is almost a badge of good education; I associated with them and sometimes enjoyed friendly contacts, but always recoiled from their acts of violence. They would chase sensitive freshmen relentlessly, taunting and hounding them on no provocation, simply for their own malicious amusement. Nothing is more like demonic activity than this behavior.[10] What apter name could be found for such people than "wreckers"? They are first wrecked and twisted themselves; then the spirits who secretly seduce and deceive them laugh to see them deceiving and laughing at other people.

Chapter 4

The quest for wisdom: Cicero's Hortensius

7. Still young and immature, I began in the company of these people to study treatises on eloquence. This was a discipline in which I longed to excel, though my motive was the damnably proud desire to gratify my human vanity. In the customary course of study I had discovered a book by an author called Cicero, whose language is almost universally admired, though not its inner spring. This book of his is called the *Hortensius* and contains an exhortation to philosophy. The book changed my way of feeling and the character of my prayers to you, O Lord, for under its influence my petitions and desires altered.[11]

---

[10] *quieter than the "wreckers" . . . this behavior*: While Augustine's youth may have been marked for an inordinate need for attention and approval, as well as a weakness in his own sexual self-mastery, he was never given to violence. This is what he found so unattractive in these "wreckers", that they used the strength of their common friendship to gang up on weaker individuals.

[11] *study treatises . . . my petitions and desires altered*: This is the first real intellectual awakening of Augustine: Cicero (d. 43 B.C.) provided Augustine with a

All my hollow hopes suddenly seemed worthless, and with unbelievable intensity my heart burned with longing for the immortality that wisdom seemed to promise. I began to rise up, in order to return to you.[12] My interest in the book was not aroused by its usefulness in the honing of my verbal skills (which was supposed to be the object of the studies I was now pursuing, in my nineteenth year, at my mother's expense, since my father had died two years earlier); no, it was not merely as an instrument for sharpening my tongue that I used that book, for it had won me over not by its style but by what it had to say.

8. How ardently I longed, O my God, how ardently I longed to fly to you away from earthly things! I did not understand then how you were dealing with me. Wisdom resides with you,[13] but love for wisdom is called by the Greek name, "philosophy," and this love it was that the book kindled in me. There are people who lead others astray under the pretense of philosophy, coloring and masking their errors under that great, fair, honorable name. Nearly all who did so in Cicero's own day are mentioned and shown up in his book; and there too one can almost find an exposition of the salutary warning given by your Spirit through your good, devout servant: *Take care that no one deceives you with philosophy and empty, misleading ideas derived from man-made traditions, centered on the elemental spirits of this world and not on Christ; for in him all the fullness of the Godhead dwells in bodily wise.*[14] At the time these words of the apostle were still unknown to me; but you know, O light of my heart, that there was one thing and one only that brought

---

model of a Roman orator who was not only verbally prolix but also profoundly intellectual. In many ways Cicero was the bridge between Greek philosophy and Roman pragmatism, introducing into Latin such terms as "humanity" and "essence". Unfortunately we possess his *Hortensius* only in fragments, but therein Augustine's love for philosophy was ignited, thus changing not simply his mind but (in very Augustinian fashion) primarily his desires. Understanding the world aright allowed Augustine to begin to order his loves properly.

[12] *All my hollow hopes . . . return to you:* See Luke 15:18–20.

[13] *Wisdom resides with you:* See Job 12:13, 16.

[14] Take care . . . Godhead dwells in bodily wise: Colossians 2:8–9.

me joy in the exhortation to wisdom: that by its call I was aroused and kindled and set on fire to love and seek and capture and hold fast and strongly cling not to this or that school, but to wisdom itself, whatever it might be. Only one consideration checked me in my ardent enthusiasm: that the name of Christ did not occur there.[15] Through your mercy, Lord, my tender little heart had drunk in that name, the name of my Savior and your Son, with my mother's milk, and in my deepest heart I still held on to it. No writing from which that name was missing, even if learned, of literary elegance and truthful, could ever captivate me completely.

Chapter 5

Distaste for Scripture

9. Accordingly I turned my attention to the holy scriptures to find out what they were like. What I see in them today is something not accessible to the scrutiny of the proud nor exposed to the gaze of the immature, something lowly as one enters but lofty as one advances further, something veiled in mystery. At that time, though, I was in no state to enter, nor prepared to bow my head and accommodate myself to its ways. My approach then was quite different from the one I am suggesting now: when I studied the Bible and compared it with Cicero's dignified prose, it seemed to me unworthy. My swollen pride recoiled from its style and my intelligence failed to penetrate to its inner meaning. Scripture is a reality that grows along with little children,

[15] *name of Christ did not occur there*: Cicero gave Augustine both a new insight into reality as ordered and purposeful as well as an eager devotion to discovering the truth of things, no longer content with the opinion of the powerful. What the pre-Christian could not, however, give him was the name of Jesus Christ. However, confident that all truth leads to the Truth himself (see John 14:6), Augustine pursues his study of philosophy, and we shall see later in Book VII how this again occurs with the Greek books of the Platonists, wherein Augustine embraced many truths about God's nature, the immortality of the human soul, and the goodness of being, but had to rely on Christian revelation to provide the truths of God's humility and humanity in Jesus Christ.

but I disdained to be a little child[16] and in my high and mighty arrogance regarded myself as grown up.

Chapter 6

He joins the Manichees

10. In reaction to this disappointment I fell among a set of proud madmen, exceedingly carnal and talkative people in whose mouths were diabolical snares[17] and a sticky mess compounded by mixing the syllables of your name, and the names of the Lord Jesus Christ and the Holy Spirit, who is our Paraclete and Consoler. These names were never far from their mouths, but amounted to no more than sound and the clacking of tongues, for their hearts were empty of the truth. They would say, "Truth, truth!" and had plenty to tell me on the subject, but truth had no place in them. They told me lies not only about you, who are truly the Truth, but also about the elements of this world that is your creation. I ought to have gone beyond them and beyond what even truthful philosophers have taught out of love for you, my Father, who are the highest good and the loveliness in all lovely things.

[16] *I disdained to be a little child*: See Matthew 7:27. [This citation of Matthew is more than curious, indicating varied ancient biblical manuscripts; what we would call to mind here today is most probably Matthew 18:4 "whoever humbles himself like this child".]

[17] *I fell among a set of proud madmen . . . were diabolical snares*: See 1 Timothy 3:7; 2 Timothy 2:26. Cicero sparked Augustine's search for and love of truth, but sensing a more explicit need for worship and a religious community, Augustine fell in with the Manichean sect. Mani (c. 216–276) was a Persian religious leader who taught there were two primal deities: one good god and one malicious god whose eternal conflict gave way to this world's divisions between life and death, good and evil, spirit and matter, male and female, and so on. Into this dualism, Mani provided elaborate ritual and secret teaching (gnosis, from where we get the word Gnosticism, a type of privileged "deliverance" out of any dualism). Finding the Christianity he knew too simplistic, Augustine found the exotic and esoteric nature of the Manichees attractive and belonged to them for nine years; relegating truth and charity always to the extraordinary and elusive is a constant temptation for all, remedied only by the Incarnation and God's willingness to be found in the most mundane of encounters.

O Truth, Truth, how the deepest and innermost marrow of my mind ached for you, even then while they prattled your name to me unremittingly and in so many ways, though only in words and in their huge, copious tomes! I was hungering for you, but their teachings were like plates on which they served me not you but the sun and moon, which are your beautiful works, to be sure, but still your works, not yourself, and not even your primary works at that; for your spiritual creations are nobler than material creatures, nobler even than these brilliant heavenly bodies. I was hungering and thirsting for you, not for your creations, not even for your spiritual creations, but for yourself, O Truth, *in whom there is no variation, no play of changing shadow;*[18] and all they set before me were dishes of glittering myths. It would have been more profitable to love the sun in the sky, which at least our eyes perceive truly, than those chimeras offered to a mind that had been led astray through its eyes. Yet I ate those offerings, believing that I was feeding on you; I ate them without appetite, for there was no taste in my mouth of you as you are, since those insubstantial shams were not you. I derived no nourishment from them, but was left the more drained. The food we dream we are eating in our sleep is very like the food we eat when awake, but it does not nourish the dreamers, because they are asleep. Those mythical objects, however, did not even come near to resembling you as you are when you speak to me today, because they were nothing but figments of the imagination invested with bodily form, counterfeit bodies. The material objects we see with our eyes of flesh, in the sky or on earth, are more real than they; what we see in company with the beasts and birds is far more dependable than images of the same things conjured

---

[18] *in whom there is no variation, no play of changing shadow*: James 1:17. Augustine may have found a religious community with the Manichees, but he also knew that their religion could not attain to God himself because the one true God cannot change nor be dragged unwillingly down into the "shadow" of things. This insight stems from either the smatterings of Christianity he received as a child or from some residual Platonism from his study of Cicero: as totally sovereign, the ultimately real will be unchangeable and in need of nothing and at war with nothing.

up in our imagination. Yet even if we do but see these things in our mind's eye, still they are more real than other objects of which we might form some notion from them—greater, supposedly infinite beings which have no reality whatever. On such inanities was I being fed, and unfed I remained.

But you, O my love, for whom I faint with longing that I may be strong, you are not those material objects we can see, in heaven though they are, nor are you the beings which we do not see there, for you have created them and do not even count them as your highest works. How much more distant are you, then, from mere figments of my imagination, fantasy-bodies that have no reality at all! More real are the memory-pictures we form of objects which at least do exist, and more real again than these are the physical beings themselves; yet none of these are you. Better and more certain than the bodies of material creatures is the soul that gives life to their bodies, yet you are not the soul either. You are the life of souls, the life of all lives, the life who are yourself living and unchanging, the life of my own soul.[19]

11. Where were you at that time? How far from me? I was certainly roving far away from you, and debarred even from the pods I was feeding to pigs.[20] The fables of schoolmasters and poets are far better than the snares then being set for me; yes, verses, songs and tales of Medea in flight are undeniably more wholesome than myths about the five elements being metamorphosed to defeat the five caverns of darkness. These

---

[19] *yourself living and unchanging*: While we may use images and pictures to describe God, the divine nature, of course, transcends all created figments. Augustine remains "unfed" because Manichean theology was limited to the anthropomorphic and overly carnal: the good god is attacked, he fights, he gets mixed into the visible order. We shall see that this was the same critique Augustine leveled against the Christianity he knew until he meets Bishop Ambrose in Milan and discovers how to read sacred Scripture allegorically. Finally, notice Augustine's cosmology: the ever-changing body is made real by the immortal (and therefore less mutable) soul, while the soul receives all its life and being from the immutable God, who is the supreme life of all that lives and is.

[20] *debarred even from the pods I was feeding to pigs*: See Luke 15:16. Over and over he sees these years through the lens of the prodigal son's archetypal rebellion against the father.

latter have no truth in them at all and are lethal to anyone who believes them, whereas I can turn verse and song into a means of earning real food. When I sang of Medea in her flying chariot I was not vouching for any of it as fact, nor, when I listened to someone else singing of it, did I believe the story; but I did believe the Manichean lies.[21] All the worse for me! By these stages I was led deeper into hell,[22] laboring and chafing under the scarcity of truth, because I was seeking you, my God, not through that power of the mind by which you have chosen to rank me above the beasts, but only through carnal inclination. To you do I confess this, for you showed mercy to me before ever I could confess it. You were more intimately present to me than my innermost being, and higher than the highest peak of my spirit.

But I stumbled upon that bold woman devoid of prudence in Solomon's allegory; she was sitting outside on her stool and inviting me: *Come and enjoy eating bread in secret, and drink sweet, stolen water.*[23] She seduced me because she found me living outside, in my carnal eyes, and ruminating within myself only on what I had devoured through them.

Chapter 7

12. The trouble was that I knew nothing else; I did not recognize the other, true reality. I was being subtly maneuvered into accepting the views of those stupid deceivers by the questions they constantly asked me about the origin of evil,[24] and

---

[21] *Medea . . . Manichean lies*: The *Medea* is one of Euripides' (d. 406 B.C.) great tragedies on the nature of revenge, and Augustine here queries why he knew such tales were fiction while he still held onto the Manichean fables as true and worthy of his assent.

[22] *led deeper into hell*: See Proverbs 9:18.

[23] *Come and enjoy eating bread . . . stolen water*: Proverbs 9:17.

[24] *they constantly asked me about the origin of evil*: Manichaeism provided Augustine with a long-sought, albeit overly facile, answer to the problem of evil. A question that plagued him for quite some time, Manichean dualism simply taught that evil exists in the world because there was an evil god on par with and just as powerful as the good god. All of reality, then, is an unavoidable admixture of good and evil, of perfection and imperfection. Christianity, on the other hand,

whether God was confined to a material form with hair and nails, and whether people who practiced polygamy, killed human beings and offered animal sacrifices could be considered righteous. Being ignorant of these matters I was very disturbed by the questions, and supposed that I was approaching the truth when I was in fact moving away from it. I did not know that evil is nothing but the diminishment of good to the point where nothing at all is left. How could I see that, I whose power of sight was restricted to seeing material shapes with my eyes and imaginary forms with my mind?

Nor did I know that God is spirit,[25] not a being with limbs stretching far and wide, and having a certain size. The notion of size implies that a body is smaller in a single part than in the whole of itself; so that, if it is infinite, it would somehow be smaller in a spatially defined section than spread out through infinity—rather than present everywhere in its entirety, as a spirit is and as God is. Moreover I had no inkling of what there could be in us which would give grounds for saying that we are made in the image of God, as scripture rightly says we are.[26]

13. I did not know either that true inward righteousness takes as its criterion not custom but the most righteous law of almighty God, by which the morality of countries and times was formed as appropriate to those countries and times, while

---

teaches that all that exists is desired (and therefore brought into being) by God and therefore all that exists is good. But then how does one explain the source and nature of evil? This is where Augustine does not yet have any answers, leaving it to his study of Neoplatonism in a few years to answer. From the "books of the Platonists", he will soon learn to define evil as the privation of the good (see *Conf.* VII.12.18, note 66, p. 182).

[25] *God is spirit*: See John 4:24.

[26] *we are made in the image of God, as scripture rightly says we are*: See Genesis 1:27. As mentioned, and as we shall see later, such false readings of Scripture stemmed from Augustine's inability to read the Bible, especially some of the more overly anthropomorphic sections of the Old Testament, spiritually in terms of allegory and symbol. Thus, for example, to be made in God's "image and likeness" is not to imply that God is corporeal but that we share in his reason and ability to love and to be loved.

God's law itself has remained unchanged everywhere and always, not one thing in one place and something different elsewhere. By this norm Abraham, Isaac, Jacob, Moses, David and all those of whom God spoke approvingly were indeed righteous; they are accounted guilty only by persons of limited experience who judge *by some human day of reckoning*[27] and measure the conduct of the human race at large by the standard that befits their own. They are like someone who knows nothing about armor, or which piece belongs where, and tries to cover his head with the greaves and his feet with the helmet, and then grumbles because they do not fit properly.[28] Or again, they are like a man who on a certain day which is appointed a public holiday from noon onward is indignant because he is not allowed to set out his goods for sale in the afternoon, although this was allowed in the morning; or like a person who in one and the same house sees something being handled by one servant which another one, who serves drinks, is not allowed to touch, or something being done behind the stables which is not properly done at table, and gets angry about this, complaining because, while there is one house and one staff of servants, the same actions are not permitted to everybody in all places. Equally foolish are

[27] *who judge* by some human day of reckoning: See 1 Corinthians 4:3.

[28] *They are like someone who . . . grumbles because they do not fit properly*: The Manichees grumbled against creation because they saw how imperfect some things appeared to them. Whereas a Christian could never rightly argue that a creature should never have been brought into existence, the Manichees found fault with all sorts of things they attributed to the influence of the evil god. In his *Commentary on Genesis Against the Manicheans* (I.16.26), Augustine playfully counters that "if a layman enters a workman's shop, he will see many instruments whose purpose he is ignorant of, and which, if he is more than usually silly, he thinks superfluous. What's more, if he carelessly tumbles into the furnace or cuts himself on a sharp steel instrument when he handles it wrongly, he reckons that there are many pernicious and harmful things there too. However, the master workman, who knows the use of everything there, has a good laugh at his silliness and takes no notice of his inept remarks, and just presses on with the work in hand. . . . I must confess that I have not the slightest idea why mice and frogs were created, and flies and worms; yet I can still see that they are all beautiful in their own specific kind, although because of our sins many of them seem to be against our interests . . . but, after all, God manages it all infinitely better than any one of us is able to manage our own homes."

people who grow indignant on hearing that some practice was allowed to righteous people in earlier ages which is forbidden to the righteous in our own day, and that God laid down one rule for the former and a different one for the latter, as the difference between the two periods of time demands; whereas in fact both sets of people have been subject to the same norm of righteousness.[29] This attitude is just as stupid as being upset because, with regard to a single man or a single day or a single house, one perceives different pieces of armor to be designed for different limbs, and an activity to be lawful until a certain hour but not afterward, and something to be permitted or even ordered in a corner but forbidden and punished elsewhere. Does this mean that justice is fickle and changeable? No, but the epochs over which she rules do not all unfold in the same way, precisely because times change. Human beings live on earth for a brief span only, and they lack the discernment to bring the conditions of earlier ages, of which they have no experience, into the same frame of reference with those they know well; but they can easily perceive in one body or one day or one house what is appropriate for each limb, each period of time and all persons and places. Thus while they may be scandalized by the one, they readily submit to the other.

14. All this was beyond my comprehension at the time and I made no allowance for it; although these truths leapt to the eye, I failed to see them. Yet I was quite accustomed to compose songs in which I was not free to place the metrical foot anywhere I fancied: different meters demanded different placing of the stress, and sometimes even within one line the feet were not uniform throughout. In spite of this, the art of poetry itself, in accordance with which I sang, was not different in different places, but worked always on the same principles. I

---

[29] *God laid down one rule . . . same norm of righteousness:* Still unlearned and lacking any real training in Catholic theology, Augustine at this time did not yet know how to read Scripture rightly and did not understand the relationship between the old and the new covenants, how to read properly therefore the Old Testament in light of the New and how God allowed for Old Testament dispensations so as to assist the unfolding of his kingdom on earth.

lacked the insight to understand that justice, of which good and holy people are the servants, contains in itself, in a far more excellent and sublime way, the principles of all it prescribes, and is unvaryingly self-consistent, yet does not impose all its demands at once, but adjusts and allots to different periods the provisions most apt for them. In my blindness I censured the holy patriarchs, who not only made use of the opportunities available to them in the way ordained and inspired by God, but also prefigured what was to come, as God revealed it through them.

Chapter 8

15. Can we suppose that it is ever or anywhere unjust to love God with one's whole heart, whole soul and whole mind, and to love one's neighbor as oneself?[30] By the same token, vices contrary to nature are everywhere and always to be detested and punished. Such were the sins of the Sodomites. If all nations behaved as the Sodomites did, they too would be held guilty under the divine law, which did not make men to have that kind of relationship with each other. The very fellowship which ought to hold between ourselves and God is violated when our nature is defiled by perverted lust, since our nature is his creation.[31]

---

[30] *love God . . . love one's neighbor as oneself*: See Matthew 22:37, 39; Mark 12:30, 33; Luke 10:27.

[31] *divine law . . . nature is his creation*: Unlike Thomas Aquinas (1225–1274), who dedicates entire treatises on law, Augustine's understanding of the various types of law is found throughout his diverse writings. In the most famous passage, *Against Faustus the Manichean*, he defines the "eternal law" as God's "divine reason" (22.27) and subsumes natural law underneath, as the way things work in the natural order is an expression of God's will. Under natural law appears civil or human law (the "human codes" appearing in the first line of the next paragraph here), those agreed-upon statutes of civilized communities. As this paragraph ends, we encounter Augustine's real interest in law: vices contrary to human nature disfigure the soul; all of nature is God's creation, and thus living in accord with nature can best align the soul to receive God (through grace), while living opposed to one's nature and against the purposefulness of God's good creation defiles and perverts the soul.

Transgressions against human codes are a different matter: they vary in accordance with variable customs; but they are to be avoided all the same, lest an agreement made by citizens or compatriots among themselves, and rendered stable by custom and law, be violated at the whim of any citizen or foreigner; for a part which fails to harmonize with the whole is a source of mischief. If, on the other hand, God commands something which conflicts with the customs or rules of any human society, then it is to be done, even if it has never been done there before; if it has fallen into abeyance, it must be restored, or if not established previously, it must be established now. After all, a king has the right to command that something be done in the state over which he reigns, even if neither he nor any of his predecessors has ever ordered it before. To obey him in such an instance does not undermine that community; indeed, to disobey him would harm it, for a general contract to obey its rulers holds good in human society. How much more, then, are we bound unhesitatingly to serve God, the Ruler over all creation, in any matter where he commands us! As in the hierarchy of human society a more powerful official is placed above one of lesser rank and is to be obeyed, so God stands above all.

16. It is the same with crimes against the person. They may spring from a desire to hurt another person, whether by insulting language or by injury, and in either case may be prompted by a spirit of revenge, as when someone attacks his enemy. Or the motive may be to secure something belonging to another, as when a robber attacks a traveler, or to forestall some evil, when one attacks a person of whom one is afraid. Again, crime may be motivated by envy, as when a person in wretched circumstances envies one more fortunate, or one who is successful in an enterprise jealously injures another because he fears the other will catch up with him, or is chagrined because that person already has. Or it may simply be pleasure in the misfortunes of others that tempts people to crime: this is the pleasure felt by those who watch gladiators, and anyone who laughs and mocks at other people.

These are the chief kinds of sin, which sprout from a craving for domination, or for watching shows, or for sensory pleasure, or from any two of these, or all three together. The consequence is an evil life in opposition to that other "three plus seven," the ten-stringed harp, your decalogue, O God most high and most sweet.

But how can our vices touch you, who are incorruptible? What crimes can be committed against you, who are immune from harm? You avenge them nonetheless by causing the sin to rebound on the sinner, for even when people sin against you, they are maliciously damaging their own souls. Iniquity plays itself false[32] when it corrupts and perverts its own nature, to which you gave life and order, or when it makes intemperate use of lawful things, or again when it burns with desire for other things not permitted, lusting to enjoy them in a way contrary to nature. Or again, the guilt of sinners may lie in rebelling against you in word or intention, thereby kicking against the goad,[33] or in casting off the restraints of human society and defiantly enjoying private alliances and feuds, as dictated by their own likes and dislikes. This is what happens when anyone abandons you, the fountain of life,[34] the One, the true creator and ruler of the universe, and in self-sufficient arrogance chooses to love a part of it only, a bogus "one."

Yet through loving humility we find our way back to you. You purify our evil dispositions; you are merciful toward the sins of those who confess to you; you hear the groans of

---

[32] *Iniquity plays itself false*: See Psalm 26(27):12. An insightful Christian and astute psychologist, Augustine knows that the "fruit" of sin is actually its own punishment. Ironically, and it took him a very long time to understand this, the punishment—the getting caught, the intervention, the moral conviction that haunts the soul—is actually a sign of God's love and mercy. Iniquity is its own falsehood, regardless how "true" or "pleasant" it might feel at the moment. This is exactly why his understanding of "confession" is so necessary for spiritual growth: the doors to our souls open only backward, and so we come to a greater awareness of the type of person we are becoming only in retrospect.

[33] *kicking against the goad*: See Acts 9:5; 26:14.

[34] *fountain of life*: See Jeremiah 2:13.

captives[35] and set us free from the bonds we have forged for
ourselves, provided only we no longer defy you in the arrogance of a spurious freedom, greedy to have more and thereby
incurring the loss of everything, loving some advantage of our
own better than yourself, who are the good of all.

Chapter 9

17. Particularly deserving of mention among vices, crimes and
the many other kinds of iniquity are the sins of those who are
making some progress, sins which in the eyes of people qual-
ified to judge are at the same time blameworthy when measured by ideal standards yet praiseworthy inasmuch as they offer
hope for the future, as green shoots promise the crop. There
are also certain deeds which look like vices or crimes against
others, yet are not really sins, for they offend neither you, our
Lord and God, nor the human community. So, for instance,
someone may accumulate goods for use in ordinary life or to
meet some particular need, yet it is by no means sure that any
avarice was involved; or again, people are punished by someone in authority zealous for their correction, but there it is
not clear whether vindictiveness played any part. It happens,
therefore, that many things are done which to human judgment would seem to merit condemnation, yet are expressly
commended by you, while many actions approved by human
reckoning are by you explicitly condemned, because often there
is a discrepancy between the appearance of an action and the
intention of the agent; and the circumstances of the time, which
may be obscure, make a difference too.

When you suddenly command some unusual, unexpected
course of action, then even if it is something you have hitherto forbidden, even if for the time being you conceal the reason for your behest, and even if it contravenes the accepted
norms of a human society, can we doubt that it is right to
obey, seeing that a human society is just precisely insofar as it

---

[35] *groans of captives*: See Psalm 101:21(102:20).

serves you?[36] Blessed are they who know that you have commanded them. Everything that is done by your servants is done
either to make plain what needs to be revealed at present, or
to foreshadow the future.

Chapter 10

18. I knew nothing of all this, and so I derided your holy servants and prophets. Even as I laughed at them I deserved to
be laughed at by you, for gradually, little by little, I was being
lured into such absurdities as the belief that a fig wept when
plucked, and its mother tree too wept milky tears.[37] Then, I
was told, if one of the saints ate the fig (plucked, of course,
not by any fault on his part but by someone else's), it would
be absorbed by his digestive system and then when he belched
or groaned in prayer he would spew out angels, or even particles of God. These particles of God most high, of the true
God, would have remained trapped in the fruit unless liberated by the teeth and belly of one of the holy elect! I believed,
poor wretch, that it was accordingly a higher duty to show
mercy to the fruits of the earth than to human beings, for whom
they came into existence; for if some hungry person who was
not a Manichee asked for one, it was believed that to give it
to him entailed passing a death-sentence on that morsel.

[36] *When you suddenly command . . . as it serves you?* This is the central thesis
of Augustine's massive *City of God*, composed (413–427) after the Visigoth Alaric's sack of Rome in 410, in order to defend the Christians being accused of
bringing ruin upon the empire for their unwillingness to worship the gods and
goddesses of Rome: true justice demands true worship, and therefore Rome was
never really a just society or commonwealth, because, while it may have proven
an advance over many aspects of barbarism on the human level, it failed to
render proper worship through and to Christ, the true statesman (*rector rei
publicae*).

[37] *belief that a fig . . . wept milky tears:* The Manichean liturgy revolved around
the Bema feast. During this ritualistic eating, the Elect would consume certain
foods, fruits, and vegetables mostly, that theoretically freed the good god back
into heaven away from this world of flesh and decay. The hearers (or auditors)
would be the ones responsible for picking and preparing such foods, feeding them
to the Elect or saints, whose consumption, digestion, and consequent belching
and flatulence thus aided the reunion of cosmic wholeness.

Chapter 11

Monica, grieved, is consoled by a vision

19. You stretched out your hand from on high and pulled my soul[38] out of these murky depths because my mother, who was faithful to you, was weeping for me more bitterly than ever mothers wept for the bodily death of their children. In her faith and in the spiritual discernment she possessed by your gift she regarded me as dead; and you heard her, O Lord, you heard her and did not scorn those tears of hers which gushed forth and watered the ground beneath her eyes wherever she prayed. Yes, you did indeed hear her, for how else can I account for the dream by which you so comforted her that she agreed to live with me and share my table, under the same roof? She had initially been reluctant to do so, repelled by my blasphemous errors, which were loathsome to her. But she dreamt that she was standing on some kind of wooden ruler, and saw a young man of radiant aspect coming toward her; he cheerfully laughed at her, whereas she was sorrowful, overwhelmed with grief. He asked her the reason for her gloom and daily tears, though as usual his question was intended to teach her, not to elicit information for himself. She replied that she was mourning my ruin. He then instructed and admonished her to take good heed and see that where she stood, there also stood I. This was to reassure her. She took heed, and saw me standing close beside her on the same rule.[39]

---

[38] *You stretched out your hand . . . pulled my soul*: See Psalm 143(144):7.

[39] *she dreamt . . . the same rule*: Monica's dream has her standing on a wooden ruler, which most students of the *Confessions* have interpreted as the Church's "rule of faith" (*regula fidei*), a term that appears again below at *Conf.* VIII.12.30. "Rule", or *regula* in Latin, is equivalent to the term *canon* in Greek and thus signifies an accepted measure of truth, of how a community appraises its acceptable readings, practices, and expectations. The "rule of faith" on which Monica here stands is nothing other than the Church's growing canon of not only biblical books but of liturgy, practices, devotions, theological formulas, and all other orthodox expressions of faith. In short, Monica appears on the standard by which

How else could this have happened, if not because your ears were open to the plea of her heart, O good and all-powerful God, who care for each of us as though each were the only one, and for all alike with the same tenderness you show to each?

20. Another telling point was that when she had related the vision to me, and I had launched into an attempt to persuade her that she must not give up hope of some day becoming what I was, she promptly replied, without the slightest hesitation, "No: I was not told, 'Where he is, you will be too,' but, 'Where you are, he will be.'"[40] I confess to you, Lord, that, as my memory serves me—and I have often spoken of this episode—I was more deeply disturbed by this answer that came from you through my sharp-eyed mother than by the dream itself. She was not worried by the false interpretation that had come to me so pat, but saw immediately what needed to be seen, as I had not done until she spoke. The dream foretold, so long in advance, the joy in store for this devout woman many years later, and so gave her comfort in her present anxiety. Nearly nine years were to follow during which I floundered in the mud of the deep[41] and the darkness of deception, often struggling to extricate myself but crashing heavily back again. Yet throughout those years my mother, a chaste, God-fearing, sensible widow of the kind so dear to you, though more eager in her hope was no less assiduous in her weeping and entreaty, never at any time ceasing her plangent prayers to you about me. Her pleas found their way into your presence, but you left me still wrapped around by the fog, and enveloped in it.

Christian truth is measured and sees Augustine one day making his way to her, to his true mother, Christ's one, holy, catholic, and apostolic body.

[40] *Where you are, he will be*: This line comes from the Roman marriage rite during which the bride-to-be vows, "Where you are, there I will be", signifying Augustine's ordination as priest and bridegroom, thereby taking his bride the Church for his own.

[41] *I floundered in the mud of the deep*: See Psalm 68:3 (69:2). Augustine acknowledges being a Manichee for almost nine years, 373–384.

Chapter 12

"A son of tears"

21. Meanwhile you gave another answer, as I recall. (I am, of course, omitting many things, being in a hurry to get to those which more powerfully impel me to praise you; and in any case there are many that I do not remember.) You gave this second answer through a priest of yours, a certain bishop who had been nurtured in the Church and well versed in your scriptures. The woman asked him if he would be so kind as to talk to me, to rebut my errors, disabuse me of my harmful persuasions and teach me good ones; for he was used to doing this, whenever he happened to find anyone apt to profit by it. He refused, however, and very wisely, as I subsequently understood. He replied that I was as yet unteachable; I was puffed up with the novelty of my heresy and had been tormenting plenty of unskilled persons with finicky little questions, as she told him. "Leave him alone," he advised. "Simply pray for him to the Lord. He will find out for himself through his reading how wrong these beliefs are, and how profoundly irreverent." At the same interview he told her how he had himself been handed over to the Manichees as a little boy by his mother, who had also been led astray; he had not only read nearly all their books but had even written some himself, and without anyone having to argue or persuade him it had become clear to him that the sect was something he should flee from. So he had fled.

These assurances did not satisfy her. She pleaded all the more insistently and with free-flowing tears that he would consent to see me and discuss matters with me. A little vexed, he answered, "Go away now; but hold on to this: it is inconceivable that he should perish, a son of tears like yours." In her conversations with me later she often recalled that she had taken these words to be an oracle from heaven.

Book IV

Augustine the Manichee

Chapter 1

Augustine sells rhetorical skills

1. Throughout those nine years, from my nineteenth to my twenty-eighth year, I and others like me were seduced and seducers, deceived ourselves and deceivers of others amid a welter of desires: publicly through the arts reputed "liberal," and secretly under the false name of religion.[1] In the one we were arrogant, in the other superstitious, and in both futile; under the auspices of the former we pursued trumpery, popular acclaim, theatrical plaudits, song-competitions and the contest for ephemeral wreaths, we watched trashy shows and indulged our intemperate lusts; through the latter we sought to be purged of these defilements by providing food for the so-called "elect" or "saints," in the hope that they would turn the food into angels and gods for us in the workshops of their bellies to be the agents of our liberation.[2] These ends I pursued,

---

[1] *Throughout those nine years . . . false name of religion*: Book IV begins with our author's admittance that he has failed on the two fronts of both faith and reason: the natural and the supernatural. His faith life centered around the Manichean religion, and now he sees he found it convenient because it allowed him to indulge his fallen desires while simultaneously providing him with the means to merit the good god's forgiveness by enacting the proper rites. His more natural pursuits, his career and social engagements, he now sees, were really passing pleasures lacking purpose and any real goodness. Now quite sensitive to the importance of friendship and community, he also admits how he scandalized others through bad example, deceiving those around him by joining them (if not leading them) in the empty exploits of temporal success and theatrical shows.

[2] *we pursued . . . agents of our liberation*: For more on the Manichean Bema feast, see *Conf.* III.10.18, note 37, p. 69.

these things I did, in the company of friends who through me and with me were alike deceived.

Let the haughty laugh at me, let them laugh who have never yet been flat on their faces, felled for their own good by you, my God; but let me confess my disgraceful deeds to you, and in confessing praise you. Allow me this, I beg you, and grant me to trace today the twisting arguments that led me astray at that past time, shouting my joy to you as I offer you this sac‑rifice.[3] Without you, what am I to myself but a guide to my own downfall? Or, when things go well with me, what am I but a child suckled on your milk and fed on you, the food that perishes not?[4] What kind of human being is anyone who is human and nothing more?[5] Let the strong and mighty laugh at us, then, but let us weak and needy folk confess to you.

Chapter 2

2. During these years I was teaching the art of rhetoric, selling talkative skills apt to sway others because greed swayed me. Yet I preferred to have good pupils, or such as passed for good, as you know, O Lord; and without any trickery on my part I taught them the tricks of the trade, never such as would secure the condemnation of the innocent, though sometimes such as were calculated to get the guilty acquitted. And you saw from afar, O God, how I was losing my foothold on slippery ground,

[3] *offer you this sacrifice*: See Psalm 26(27):6.

[4] *food that perishes not*: See John 6:27.

[5] *What kind of human . . . nothing more?* Here lies a hint into how Augustine understands the Christian life: living as more than merely human, but living a life in constant union with God, thereby participating in his own perfections. Christianity does not, however, eradicate one's humanity but elevates it and allows it to function at its highest possible level—lovingly, mercifully, truthfully, incor‑ruptibly, immortally. This is what Augustine will at times call "becoming God" or becoming divinely adopted children of the Father; it is in fact what allows him to make such wonderfully bold claims as: "Let us rejoice then and give thanks that we have become not only Christians, but Christ himself" (*Commentary on John* 21.8; quoted in the *Catechism of the Catholic Church*, no. 795). This does not mean that a Christian's human nature is destroyed but is in fact perfected. Made in God's own image and likeness, when humans grow closer to God, they become paradoxically both more like God and more like their truest selves.

but how amid the smoke a spark of integrity still guttered in me; for though I taught students who loved worthless things and sought falsehood,[6] in which pursuits I bore them company, I did try to teach them honestly.

He begins to cohabit with an unnamed girl

At this time too I lived with a girl not bound to me in lawful wedlock but sought out by the roving eye of reckless desire; all the same she was the only girl I had, and I was sexually faithful to her.[7] This experience taught me at first hand what a difference there is between a marriage contracted for the purpose of founding a family, and a relationship of love charged with carnal desire in which children may be born even against the parents' wishes—though once they are born one cannot help loving them.

3. Another thing I remember is that once when I had decided to enter a dramatic poetry contest some sorcerer fellow sent word to me to ask what I was prepared to pay him to ensure that I would win. I replied that I detested and loathed those obscene rites, and would not countenance the killing of a fly to bring me victory, even if the crown to be won were of gold that would last for ever. This fellow was prepared to offer living creatures in sacrifice, and I suspected that he intended by these rites to enlist

[6] *Loved worthless things and sought falsehood*: See Psalm 4:3. [English editions vary widely on this citation, indicating how different Augustine's version of the Psalms was from ours today.]

[7] *I lived with a girl . . . faithful to her*: It was not uncommon for a young man in the Roman Empire to take a concubine as Augustine has; in fact, as it tended to foster (at least temporary) fidelity, it was a respectable alternative for those who were disallowed from marrying under Roman law. Since legal customs prevented slaves from marrying as well as a man and a woman from different social classes, Augustine's *matrona* here was possibly a freed slave or servant woman. Every evidence we have points to how much he must have loved her, and he chooses to save her reputation by never naming her. We simply know that they met in Carthage probably in the year 371, together had one son, Adeodatus (372–389), who died early, and that they are separated after seventeen years together (see *Conf.* VI.15.25). Pious legend has her leaving Augustine to live a life of Christian consecration and seclusion, but, in truth, we do not know whatever became of her.

demonic support for my cause. But it was not out of reverence for your purity that I rejected this evil thing, O God of my heart, for I had not yet learned to love you; all I had learned was to think about brilliant material objects. Is not a soul that sighs for such make-believe gods wantonly forsaking you, trusting in illusions and feeding the winds?[8] Yet while refusing to have sacrifice offered to demons on my behalf I was all the while offering myself in sacrifice to them through my superstition; for what does "feeding the winds" mean but feeding demons, providing pleasure and amusement for them by our errors?

Chapter 3

He investigates astrology

4. I made no move whatever to break off my habit of consulting those charlatans whom people call "mathematicians,"[9] for I took the view that no sacrifice was being offered by them, nor any prayer addressed to spirits in the practice of divination. Nonetheless true Christian piety is consistent with its own principles in rejecting and condemning astrology. It is good to confess to you, O Lord,[10] and to say, *Have mercy on me; heal my soul, for I have sinned against you;*[11] it is good to beware of abusing your forgiveness by regarding it as a license to sin, and good to remember our Lord's warning, *See now, you are healed: sin no more, lest some worse fate befall you.*[12] When people say, "The sky is responsible for your sin, so you cannot avoid

---

[8] *a soul that sighs for such make-believe gods . . . feeding the winds*: See Psalm 72(73):27; Proverbs 10:4; Hosea 12:1. [While Augustine's use of Proverbs 10:4 here raises questions of the edition before him (true for many of his citations to the Wisdom literature), in his mind, each of these scriptural references has to do with mortals' perishing because of their sins, described here as empty illusions and as committing fornication against God, Israel's true lover.]

[9] *mathematicians*: The "mathematicians" in question are not those expert in numbers and sums simply, as we today might imagine, but for Augustine, a *mathematicus* was an astrologer and one who dabbled in the occult.

[10] *It is good to confess to you, O Lord*: See Psalm 91:2(92:1).

[11] *Have mercy on me . . . I have sinned against you*: Psalm 40:5(41:4).

[12] *See now, you are healed . . . worse fate befall you*: John 5:14.

it," or "Venus did this, or Saturn, or Mars," they invalidate our whole salvation. They are suggesting that human beings are guiltless—humans who are flesh and blood and putrid pride!—and that the fault lies with the creator and controller of sky and stars. And who is this? You, our God, sweetness and the fount of justice, who will repay each of us as our actions deserve, and do not disdain a broken and humbled heart.[13]

5. At this time there was a certain man of deep insight, very skilled and highly reputed in the art of medicine, who as proconsul had set his hand on my unsound head, but only to crown me with the wreath won in the contest.[14] No healer's hand did he lay upon me, for you, Lord, were the only healer of my sickness, you who thwart the proud but give grace to the humble.[15] Were you deserting me, or giving up the task of curing my soul? No; even through that old man you were at work. It happened like this. I had become quite well known to him, and listened regularly and attentively to his speeches, for although unpolished in style they were pleasant to the ear and weighty for the vigorous ideas they expressed. Through conversation with me he learned that I was deeply interested in the writings of those who professed to cast birth horoscopes. In kindly and fatherly fashion he advised me to throw them away, and not to waste on such rubbish the care and effort better spent on more useful enterprises. He told me that as a

[13] *who will repay . . . broken and humbled heart*: See Matthew 16:27; Romans 2:6; Psalm 50:19(51:17).

[14] *certain man of deep insight . . . wreath won in the contest*: At *Conf.* VII.6.8 we learn that this is Vindicianus, one of the leading medical doctors of the day and the personal physician of the emperor Valentinian (364–375). For this he was made a proconsul in North Africa, and as part of his civic duties, he would have ruled over various public spectacles, and here it was a rhetoric contest in Carthage where he crowns Augustine the winner in 377. Also known as a caring and wise Christian, perhaps getting to know a young man of such promise as Augustine led Vindicianus to take a special interest in him and to help him see the follies of astrology. Augustine later calls him "the great physician of our times" and goes on to describe his art of healing (*Letter* 138) and remains grateful for being brought to see the emptiness of trying to predict the future through the movement of the sky's stars and orbs.

[15] *you who thwart the proud . . . grace to the humble*: See James 4:6; 1 Peter 5:5.

young man he had learned astrology with such zeal that he had wanted to make it his career and earn his living by it. If he had the intelligence to understand Hippocrates, he pointed out, he was certainly capable of mastering those books. Later, however, he abandoned them and took up medicine, for no other reason than that he had discovered them to be entirely misleading, and as an honorable man he did not want to make his living by deceiving others. "But you," he said, "you can support yourself and maintain your social position by the profession of rhetoric, so you are pursuing this fraudulent study as a hobby, not from any economic necessity. All the more reason, then, for you to believe me when I inform you about this subject in which I was so well versed myself that I meant to make my living by it alone."

I asked him how, in that case, it came about that astrologers could often make predictions which proved true. He gave the best answer available, saying that this was due to chance, a force prevalent throughout nature. Think how frequently it happens, he said, that a person looks for guidance in the pages of some poet who was singing of an unrelated matter and had something quite different in mind, yet a line stands out which is wonderfully apposite to the question in hand; well, then, surely we should not wonder if, in response to some prompting from above, an utterance issues from a human mind unaware of what is happening in it, and this utterance corresponds to the circumstances and actions of the client. This would be chance, not skill.

6. By the answer he gave me, or which you gave me through him, you made provision for my needs and sketched in my memory an outline of the truth I was later to search out for myself. Yet at the time neither he nor my very dear friend, Nebridius,[16] a fine and extremely sensible young man who

[16] *Nebridius*: Nebridius came from a relatively wealthy family, born in Carthage, and became friends with Augustine when both were students there. They were lifelong confidants thereafter, and we still have three of Nebridius' letters to Augustine (*Letters* 5, 6, and 8) and nine of Augustine's to Nebridius. We shall see how Nebridius' clear thinking helped Augustine finally reject

ridiculed the whole business of divination, was able to persuade me to throw those books away, because the authority of
the writers weighed with me too heavily, and because I had as
yet found no certain teaching which could convince me beyond
doubt that any truthful statements delivered by diviners were
due to chance and coincidence, rather than to genuine skill
on the part of stargazers.

Chapter 4

Death of a friend at Thagaste

7. At this same period, when I first began to teach in the town
where I was born, I had a friend who shared my interests and
was exceedingly dear to me.[17] He was the same age as myself
and, like me, now in the flower of young manhood. As a boy
he had grown up with me; we had gone to school together
and played together. He was not then such a friend to me as
he was to become later, though even at the later time of which
I speak our union fell short of true friendship, because friendship is genuine only when you bind fast together people who
cleave to you through the charity poured abroad in our hearts
by the Holy Spirit who is given to us.[18] I did love him very
tenderly, though, and similarity of outlook lent warmth to our

Manichaeism (see *Conf.* VII.2.3) as well as astrology (see *Conf.* VII.6.8). We
know that Nebridius traveled to be with Augustine while he was preparing for
baptism in Milan; Nebridius himself became a Christian at some point (after
having come to terms with the proper way of understanding the Christ's Incarnation) and spent the years until his death before 391 in North Africa witness-
ing to Christ by observing "perfect chastity and continence" (see *Conf.* IX.3.6).

[17] *I first began to teach in the town . . . dear to me*: Augustine and his family
(Adeodatus and his mother) return to his birthplace, the city of Thagaste (about
sixty miles south of Hippo) in 373 to begin a school (staying only two years,
until 375). He has finished his formal education in Carthage and now embarks
on the life of a teacher of rhetoric, attracting students for pay and guiding them
in everything from basic grammar to the art of persuasive speechmaking.

[18] *charity poured abroad . . . Holy Spirit who is given to us*: See Romans 5:5,
Augustine's most often cited biblical verse, attesting to the centrality of divine
charity in his theology. Here, for example, even all friendship is truly worthy of

relationship; for I had lured him from the true faith, which he had held in a thoroughly immature way and without conviction, to the superstitious and baneful fables which my mother deplored in me. Already this man was intellectually astray along with me, and my soul could not bear to be without him. Ah, but you were pursuing close behind us, O God of vengeance,[19] who are the fount of all mercy and turn us back to yourself in wondrous ways. You took him from this life after barely a year's friendship, a friendship sweeter to me than any sweetness I had known in all my life.[20]

8. Who can of himself alone extol your deeds, even those you have wrought in him alone? O my God, what was it that you then did for me? How unfathomable the abyss of your judgments![21] As my friend struggled with fever he lay for a long time unconscious and sweating at death's door; and as hope for his recovery dwindled he was baptized without his knowledge.[22] I cared little for this, since I took it for granted that

---

the name when people are brought together by God's love and not their own natural affection only.

[19] God of vengeance: See Psalm 93(94):1.

[20] You took him ... all my life: This friend remains unnamed but we see why Augustine is the first Christian writer to develop a theory of friendship: he shows a deep appreciation for how the relationships closest to us transform us and determine what we find pleasant, loveable, and worth our time and attention. Augustine saw friendship no longer as mere human harmony, as most of his pagan predecessors defined it, but now as a matter of grace and union in the Spirit and in the sacraments elevating us upward toward God. As he would later write, friendship (amicitia) is "agreement on things human and divine (quoting Cicero) in Christ Jesus, our Lord, our truest peace.... In the first there is agreement on things divine along with good will and love; in the second there is such agreement on things human. If you hold on to these two most firmly along with me, our friendship will be true and everlasting, and it will unite us not only to each other but also to the Lord. In order that this may come about, I urge you to receive now the sacraments of the faithful" (Letter 258.4).

[21] How unfathomable the abyss of your judgments! See Romans 11:33.

[22] at death's door. . . baptized without his knowledge: Delaying baptism until one's deathbed was a common practice up through Augustine's time. As sharing the same "superstitious and baneful fables", obviously this unnamed friend was a fellow Manichee who returned with Augustine from Carthage. Reflecting on this incident of his baptism must have truly upset his Manichean readers, as they scorned the Church's sacraments, baptism especially, as superfluous and irrational.

his mind was more likely to retain what he had received from me, irrespective of any rite performed on his unconscious body. How wrong I was; for he rallied and grew stronger, and immediately, or as soon as I possibly could (which is to say at the first moment that he was fit for it, for I did not leave him, so closely were we dependent on each other), I attempted to chaff him, expecting him to join me in making fun of the baptism he had undergone while entirely absent in mind and unaware of what was happening. But he had already learned that he had received it, and he recoiled from me with a shudder as though I had been his enemy, and with amazing, new-found independence warned me that if I wished to be his friend I had better stop saying such things to him. I stood aghast and troubled, but deferred telling him of my feelings in order to let him get better first, thinking that once he was in normal health again I would be able to do what I liked with him. But he was snatched away from my mad designs, to be kept safe with you for my consolation: a few days later the fever seized him anew and he died. And I was not there.[23]

9. Black grief closed over my heart,[24] and wherever I looked I saw only death. My native land was a torment to me and my father's house unbelievable misery. Everything I had shared with my friend turned into hideous anguish without him. My eyes sought him everywhere, but he was missing; I hated all things because they held him not, and could no more say to me, "Look, here he comes!" as they had been wont to do in his lifetime when he had been away. I had become a great enigma to myself, and I questioned my soul, demanding why it was sorrowful and why it so disquieted me, but it had no answer. If I bade it, "Trust in God," it rightly disobeyed me, for the man it had

[23] *I was not there*: Given the mastery of his prose and his gift to convey many meanings at once, one wonders if Augustine's absence here is much more than geographical. Augustine was "not there" with his friend because through his illness his friend had come to love the Church and savor the sacraments, while such wisdom and appreciation would still prove years away for Augustine.

[24] *grief closed over my heart*: See Lamentations 5:17.

held so dear and lost was more real and more lovable than the fantasy in which it was bidden to trust. Weeping alone brought me solace, and took my friend's place as the only comfort of my soul.

Chapter 5

10. All this is over now, Lord, and my hurt has been assuaged with time. Let me listen now to you who are truth; bring the ear of my heart close to your mouth, that you may tell me why weeping is a relief to the wretched. Can it be that although you are everywhere present you have flung our wretchedness far away from you, abiding unmoved in yourself[25] while we are tossed to and fro amid human trials? Surely not, for if we could not weep into your very ears, no shred of hope would be left to us. How comes it, then, that such sweet fruit is plucked from life's bitterness, the sweetness of groans, tears, sighs and laments? Does the comfort lie in this, that we hope you will hear? This is certainly true of our prayers, for they presuppose a desire to reach you. But is it true of sorrow for what we have lost, and of the grief that overwhelmed me then? No, for I neither hoped that he would come back to life nor made my tears a plea that he should; I simply mourned and wept, for I was beset with misery and bereft of my joy. Or is it that bitter tears match the weariness we feel over what we once enjoyed, but find attractive no more?

Chapter 6

11. But why am I talking thus? This is no time for asking questions, but for confessing to you. I was miserable, and miserable too is everyone whose mind is chained by friendship with mortal things, and is torn apart by their loss, and then becomes aware of the misery that it was in even before it lost them. This was my condition at the time; I wept very bitterly and

---

[25] *you are everywhere present . . . abiding unmoved in yourself*: See Wisdom 7:27.

found repose in the bitterness. Miserable as I was, I held even this miserable life dearer than my friend; for although I might wish to change it, I would have been even less willing to lose it than I was to lose him. I do not even know if I would have been willing to lose it for him, after the manner of Orestes and Pylades, who wanted to die for one another or, failing that, to die together, because for either to live without the other would have been worse than death—or so the story goes, though it may not be true.[26] Some kind of emotion opposed to this had sprung up in me, so that although my weariness with living was intense, so too was my fear of dying. I believe that the more I loved him, the more I hated death, which had taken him from me; I hated it as a hideous enemy, and feared it, and pictured it as ready to devour all human beings, since it had been able to make away with him. Yes, this was my state of mind: I remember it.

Look upon my heart, O my God, look deep within it. See, O my hope, who cleanse me from the uncleanness of such affections, who draw my eyes to yourself and pull my feet free from the snare,[27] see that this is indeed what I remember. I was amazed that other mortals went on living when he was dead whom I had loved as though he would never die, and still more amazed that I could go on living myself when he was dead—I, who had been like another self to him.[28] It was well said that a friend is half one's own soul. I felt that my soul and his had been but one soul in two bodies, and I shrank from life with loathing because I could not bear to be only half alive; and perhaps I was so afraid of death because

---

[26] *Orestes and Pylades . . . may not be true*: Orestes and Pylades were *the* symbol of friendship in the ancient world: sent to live with Pylades and his family in central Greece during the fallout of his mother's (Clytemnestra's) affair with Aegisthus, Orestes returns to avenge his father but only with Pylades' divinelike encouragement. Orestes thus sees in Pylades a bond stronger than family and an inspiration more powerful than mere human piety.

[27] *who draw my eyes . . . feet free from the snare*: See Psalm 24(25):15.

[28] *another self to him*: Augustine would have read in the works he studied that a friend is "another self" (an *alter ipse*), appearing in both Aristotle, *Nicomachean Ethics* IX.4, and Cicero, *On Friendship* 21.80.

I did not want the whole of him to die, whom I had loved so dearly.

Chapter 7

12. Woe to the madness which thinks to cherish human beings as though more than human! How foolish the human heart that anguishes without restraint over human ills, as I did then! Feverishly I thrashed about, sighed, wept and was troubled, and there was no repose for me, nor any counsel. Within me I was carrying a tattered, bleeding soul that did not want me to carry it, yet I could find no place to lay it down. Not in pleasant countryside did it find rest, nor in shows and songs, nor in sweet-scented gardens, nor in elaborate feasts, nor in the pleasures of couch or bed, nor even in books and incantations. All things loured at me,[29] even daylight itself, and everything that was not what he was seemed to me offensive and hateful, except for mourning and tears, in which alone I found some slight relief. Whenever my soul was drawn away from this, it burdened me with a great load of misery. I should have lifted it up to you, Lord,[30] to be healed, but I was neither willing nor able to do so, especially because when I thought about you you did not seem to be anything solid or firm. For what I thought of was not you at all; an empty fantasy and my own error were my god. If I tried to lodge my soul in that, hoping that it might rest there, it would slip through that insubstantial thing and fall back again on me, who had remained to myself an unhappy place where I could not live,

---

[29] *loured at me*: From the Old German *lauern*, "to lurk", here "lour" has the sense of scowling down upon, or menacing Augustine. His lament is the result of his inability to rest in the only unchanging good: God. When that is denied, all human desires prove insatiable and all pursuits prove empty, usually resulting in the false belief that if only one's restless soul could make some change (of place or career, of marriage or religious vows, etc.), one would finally be fulfilled. Here Augustine is accordingly preparing to leave his hometown of Thagaste to return to Carthage, a move back to the more easily found diversions of the bigger city.

[30] *lifted it up to you, Lord*: See Psalm 24(25):1.

but from which I could not escape. Whither could my heart flee to escape itself? Where could I go and leave myself behind? Was there any place of refuge where I would not be followed by my own self? Yet flee I did from my native land, for my eyes were less inclined to look for him where they had not been wont to see him before. So I left Thagaste and came to Carthage.[31]

Chapter 8

Consolation in other friends at Carthage

13. Time does not stand still, nor are the rolling seasons useless to us, for they work wonders in our minds. They came and went from day to day, and by their coming and going implanted in me other hopes and other memories. Little by little they set me up again and turned me toward things that had earlier delighted me, and before these my sorrow began to give ground. Yet its place was taken, not indeed by fresh sorrows, but by the seeds of fresh sorrows; for how had that sorrow been able so easily to pierce my inmost being, if not because I had poured out my soul into the sand by loving a man doomed to death as though he were never to die? What restored and re-created me above all was the consolation of other friends, in whose company I loved what I was loving as a substitute for you. This was a gross fable and a long-sustained lie, and as our minds itched to listen they were corrupted by its adulterous excitation, but the fable did not die for me when any of my friends died.

There were other joys to be found in their company which still more powerfully captivated my mind—the charms of talking and laughing together and kindly giving way to each other's wishes, reading elegantly written books together, sharing jokes

---

[31] *I left Thagaste and came to Carthage*: This would now be sometime in the late summer or autumn of 376, just as Augustine was about to turn twenty-two years old.

and delighting to honor one another, disagreeing occasionally but without rancor, as a person might disagree with himself, and lending piquancy by that rare disagreement to our much more frequent accord. We would teach and learn from each other, sadly missing any who were absent and blithely welcoming them when they returned. Such signs of friendship sprang from the hearts of friends who loved and knew their love returned, signs to be read in smiles, words, glances and a thousand gracious gestures. So were sparks kindled and our minds were fused inseparably, out of many becoming one.

Chapter 9

14. This is what we esteem in our friends, and so highly do we esteem it that our conscience feels guilt if we fail to love someone who responds to us with love, or do not return the love of one who offers love to us, and this without seeking any bodily gratification from the other save signs of his goodwill. From this springs our grief if someone dies, from this come the darkness of sorrow and the heart drenched with tears because sweetness has turned to bitterness, so that as the dying lose their life, life becomes no better than death for those who live on. Blessed is he who loves you, and loves his friend in you and his enemy for your sake.[32] He alone loses no one dear to him, to whom all are dear in the One who is never lost. And who is this but our God, the God who made heaven and earth and fills them, because it was by filling them that he made them? No one loses you unless he tries to get rid of you, and if he does try to do that, where can he go, whither does he flee,[33] but from you in your tranquillity to you in your anger? Does he not encounter your law everywhere, in his own punishment? Your law is truth, as you yourself are truth.[34]

---

[32] *loves you . . . enemy for your sake*: See Matthew 5:44; Luke 6:27.
[33] *whither does he flee*: See Psalm 138(139):7.
[34] *Your law is truth . . . you yourself are truth*: See Psalm 118(119):142; John 14:6.

Chapter 10

Transience of created things

15. Turn us toward yourself, O God of Hosts, show us your face and we shall be saved;[35] for wheresoever a human soul turns, it can but cling to what brings sorrow unless it turns to you, cling though it may to beautiful things outside you and outside itself. Yet were these beautiful things not from you, none of them would be at all. They arise and sink; in their rising they begin to exist and grow toward their perfection, but once perfect they grow old and perish; or, if not all reach old age, yet certainly all perish. So then, even as they arise and stretch out toward existence, the more quickly they grow and strive to be, the more swiftly they are hastening toward extinction. This is the law of their nature. You have endowed them so richly because they belong to a society of things that do not all exist at once, but in their passing away and succession together form a whole, of which the several creatures are parts.[36] So is it with our speaking as it proceeds by audible signs: it will not be a whole utterance unless one word dies away after making its syllables heard, and gives place to another.

Let my soul use these things to praise you,
O God, creator of them all,
but let it not be glued fast to them by sensual love,
for they are going whither they were always destined to go,
toward extinction;
and they rend my soul with death-dealing desires,
for it too longs to be, and loves to rest in what it loves.
But in them it finds no place to rest,

[35] *show us your face . . . shall be saved*: See Psalm 79:8(80:7).
[36] *do not all exist . . . creatures are parts*: In his many writings on the goodness of creation and various commentaries on Genesis, Augustine sees how God brings some things into existence while allowing other creatures to fade out of existence, all the while holding the harmony and beauty of the created order together. Always a rhetorician, he likens this to speaking: some words can appear only after others transpire.

because they do not stand firm;
they are transient, and who can follow them with the senses
  of the body?
Or who can seize them, even near at hand?
Tardy is carnal perception, because it is carnal;
such is the law of its nature.
Sufficient it is for another purpose, for which it was made,
but insufficient to catch the fleeting things
that rush past from their appointed beginning
to their appointed end.
In your Word, through whom they are created,
they hear your command,
"From here begin, and thus far you shall go."

Chapter 11

16. Be not vain, my soul, and take care that the ear of your heart be not deafened by the din of your vanity. You too must listen to the selfsame Word who calls you back, and there find a place of imperturbable quiet, where love is never forsaken unless it chooses to forsake. See, those things go their way that others may succeed them, and that a whole may exist comprised of all its parts, though a lowly whole indeed. "But I," says the Word of God, "shall I depart to any place?" Fix your dwelling there,[37] my soul, lay up there for safe-keeping whatever you have thence received, if only because you are weary of deceits. Entrust to Truth whatever of truth is in you, and you will lose nothing; your rotten flesh will flower anew,[38] all your diseases will be healed,[39] all your labile elements will be restored and bound fast to you; they will not drag you with them in their own collapse, but will stand firm with you and abide, binding you to the ever-stable, abiding God.[40]

[37] *Fix your dwelling there:* See John 14:23.
[38] *Entrust to Truth whatever of truth is in you:* See Psalm 27(28):7.
[39] *your diseases will be healed:* See Matthew 4:23; Psalm 102(103):3.
[40] *ever-stable, abiding God:* See Psalm 101:13(102:12); Hebrews 1:11; 1 Peter 1:23.

17. Why follow your flesh, perverted soul?[41] Rather let it follow you, once you are converted. Whatever you experience through it is partial, and you do not know the whole, of which these experiences are but a part, although they give you pleasure. Were your carnal perception able to grasp the whole, were it not, for your punishment, confined to its due part of the whole, you would long for whatever exists only in the present to pass away, so that you might find greater joy in the totality. When with this same carnal perception you listen to human speech, you do not want to halt the succession of syllables: you want them to fly on their way and make room for others, so that you may hear the whole. So is it always with the constituent elements of a simple object, constituents which do not all exist simultaneously: in their entirety they give us greater pleasure, provided we can perceive them all together, than they do separately. But better still, better by far, is he who made all things. He is our God, who does not pass away, for there is nothing else to supplant him.

Chapter 12

18. If sensuous beauty delights you, praise God for the beauty of corporeal things, and channel the love you feel for them onto their Maker, lest the things that please you lead you to displease him.[42] If kinship with other souls appeals to you, let them be loved in God, because they too are changeable and

---

[41] *perverted soul*: Without loving rightly, God first and all else in God, the soul becomes literally perverted, turned downward. As such, Augustine often depicts the drama of human living as a battle between the soul's perversion and its conversion, choosing whether the Creator or a creature will be at the heart of its desire and devotion.

[42] *If sensuous beauty delights you . . . displease him*: God must once again be at the center of things: Augustine is here not against created beauty but insists that it must be situated in its Creator. The manifold excellences of creation for him must always be understood to be participatory goods in God, and so to delight in creatures means ultimately to thank God. No creature is an end in itself for Augustine, but as each of our life's story closes, all creatures will ultimately prove to have been the first steps into either heaven or hell—i.e., how we live in creation determines how we spend eternity.

gain stability only when fixed in him; otherwise they would go their way and be lost. Let them be loved in him, and carry off to God as many of them as possible with you, and say to them:

> Let us love him, for he made these things and he is not far off,[43] for he did not make them and then go away: they are from him but also in him. You know where he is, because you know where truth tastes sweet. He is most intimately present to the human heart, but the heart has strayed from him. Return to your heart, then, you wrongdoers, and hold fast to him who made you. Stand with him and you will stand firm, rest in him and you will find peace. Where are you going, along your rough paths? Tell me, where are you going? The good which you love derives from him, and insofar as it is referred to him it is truly good and sweet, but anything that comes from him will justly turn bitter if it is unjustly loved by people who forsake him. Why persist in walking difficult and toilsome paths?[44] There is no repose where you are seeking it. Search as you like, it is not where you are looking. You are seeking a happy life in the realm of death, and it will not be found there. How could life be happy, where there is no life at all?

19. He who is our very life came down[45] and took our death upon himself. He slew our death by his abundant life and summoned us in a voice of thunder to return to him in his hidden place, that place from which he set out to come to us when first he entered the Virgin's womb.[46] There a human creature, mortal flesh, was wedded to him that it might not remain mortal for ever; and from there he came forth like a bridegroom from his nuptial chamber, leaping with joy like a giant to run his course.[47] Impatient of delay he ran, shouting by his words, his deeds, his death and his life, his descent to hell and his

[43] *he made these things . . . not far off*: See Psalm 99(100):3; Acts 17:27.

[44] *walking difficult and toilsome paths*: See Wisdom 5:7.

[45] *He who is our very life came down*: See John 6:33.

[46] *He slew our death . . . entered the Virgin's womb*: Lest one passes over such rhetorical flourishes too quickly, notice the contrasting couplets and how Augustine adroitly interweaves such opposites as death and life, booming thunder to hidden places, God's coming out to us by first entering Mary's womb.

[47] *bridegroom . . . giant to run his course*: See Psalm 18:6–7(19:5).

ascension to heaven,[48] shouting his demand that we return to him. Then he withdrew from our sight,[49] so that we might return to our own hearts and find him there. He withdrew, yet look, here he is. It was not his will to remain with us, yet he has not abandoned us either; for he has gone back to that place which he never left, because the world was made through him, and though he was in this world he had made[50] he came into it to save sinners.[51] To him my soul confesses, and he heals this soul that has sinned against him.[52] O mortals, how long will you be heavy-hearted?[53] Life has come down to you, and are you reluctant to ascend and live? But what room is there for you to ascend, you with your high-flown ways and lofty talk?[54] Come down, that you may ascend, ascend even to God, for you have fallen in your attempts to ascend in defiance of God.

This is what you must tell them, to move them to tears in this valley of weeping,[55] and by this means carry them off with you to God, because if you burn with the fire of charity as you speak, you will be saying these things to them by his Spirit.

Chapter 13

What is beauty? He writes a book

20. Being ignorant of all this at the time, and in love with beautiful things below me, I was plunging into the depths. To

---

[48] *his descent to hell . . . ascension to heaven:* See Ephesians 4:8–9.

[49] *he withdrew from our sight:* See Luke 24:51; Acts 1:9.

[50] *world was made through him . . . in this world he had made:* See John 1:10–11.

[51] *he came into it to save sinners:* See 1 Timothy 1:15.

[52] *he heals this soul that has sinned against him:* See Psalm 40:5(41:4).

[53] *O mortals, how long will you be heavy-hearted:* See Psalm 4:3(2).

[54] *Life has come down . . . lofty talk:* See Psalm 72(73):8. This couplet of ascending and descending is one of Augustine's most employed: "He descended for us, let us ascend to him" (*Commentary on John* 12.8), or again, "God is with us in order that we may be with him—he who came down to us in order to be with us is now at work to draw us up to himself" (*Commentary on the Psalms* 145.1).

[55] *valley of weeping:* See Psalm 83:7(84:6).

my friends I would say, "Do we love anything save what is beautiful? And what is beautiful, then? Indeed, what is beauty? What is it that entices and attracts us in the things we love? Surely if beauty and loveliness of form were not present in them, they could not possibly appeal to us." I applied my mind to these questions and it struck me that in material objects there was both a quality inherent in the whole—beauty—and a different quality that was seemly in something that was harmoniously adapted to something else, as a part of the body to the whole, or a sandal to the foot, and other similar things. This realization welled up in my mind from my innermost heart, and I wrote some books entitled *The Beautiful and the Harmonious*, two or three books, I think—you know, O God, but it escapes me, for I no longer have them; they have somehow been lost.[56]

Chapter 14

21. What was it, O Lord my God, that prompted me to dedicate those books to an orator in Rome, Hierius? I did not know him personally, but I had come to esteem him for his splendid reputation for learning; I had also heard him quoted, and liked what I had heard. But what I liked still better was the fact that he found favor with others, people who extolled him highly and marveled that a Syrian, previously formed in Greek eloquence, had reached such eminence as a Latin orator and was at the same time so exceedingly learned in philosophical matters. When a man is praised, then, it is possible to love him, even in his absence: does this mean that love is transmitted from the mouth of the person who praises him to the heart of the listener? Certainly not; but one lover can be set on fire by another. We can truly love a person who is the subject of eulogy as long as we believe that the one who proclaims his merits is not doing so with intent to deceive: that is, that the person spoken of is being praised by one who loves him sincerely.

[56] The Beautiful and the Harmonious ... *lost*: This work entitled *De Pulchro et Apto* was completed by 380 but, as Augustine notes, was quickly misplaced.

22. At that time I admired people simply because they were judged praiseworthy by others, not on the strength of any judgment of yours, O my God, by which no one is deceived. All the same, why was the esteem in which I held Hierius[57] not like that evoked, say, by some noble charioteer, or a gladiator made widely famous by popular enthusiasm, but something far different, more serious, and akin to the commendation I hoped to win myself? I had no wish to be celebrated and loved in the way actors are, even though I myself celebrated and loved them; I would have preferred obscurity to notoriety like theirs, and would rather have been hated than loved in that manner. How can these contrasted and warring loves be carried in a single soul and balanced against each other? How can I love in another what I loathe and ward off from myself, and this when both of us are human? A good horse can be admired by someone who would not want to be a horse himself, even if he could; but the case is different with an actor, for he shares our own nature. Do I then love in another man what I would hate to be myself, when I too am a man? A human being is an immense abyss, but you, Lord, keep count even of his hairs,[58] and not one of them is lost in you; yet even his hairs are easier to number than the affections and movements of his heart.

23. This orator, however, was the sort of man I loved in the sense of wanting to be like him. I was driven off course by my pride and tossed about by every wind,[59] for your guidance of me was very unobtrusive. How do I know, how can I confess to you with such certainty, that I had come to love him more for the love he aroused in those who sang his praises than for the achievements by which he won them? I know it because if, instead of praising him, those same people had recounted his deeds with disparagement and contempt, I would not have

---

[57] *Hierius*: Hierius, to whom Augustine dedicated *De Pulchro et Apto*, was, by most accounts, a Greek-speaking Syrian who moved to Rome and opened a school of rhetoric in Trajan's forum, and who (along with his brother, Domitius) was a member of Symmachus' close circle of intellectuals (see *Conf.* V.13.23, p. 125).

[58] *keep count even of his hairs*: See Matthew 10:30.

[59] *tossed about by every wind*: See Ephesians 4:14.

warmed to him or felt any interest; and yet neither the facts nor the man himself would have been different; the difference would have lain only in the attitude of those who related them. To such weakness is a soul reduced when it is not yet anchored in the solid ground of truth. It is tossed and turned, whirled and spun, by every breath of opinion from the mouths of those who think they know; its light is obscured by clouds and it cannot see the truth. But look! Truth is straight ahead of us.

Accordingly I set great store by bringing my oratory and my research to this man's notice. If he approved them, I would glow with satisfaction, but if he did not, a heart vain and empty for lack of your solid strength would be wounded. But I continued to enjoy turning over in my mind the question of the beautiful and the harmonious about which I had written to him; I considered it with a contemplative eye and admired it, although no one shared my appreciation.

Chapter 15

24. I did not yet see that the whole vast question hinged on your artistry, almighty God, who alone work wonders.[60] My mind scanned material forms, and I defined and distinguished what was beautiful in itself from what was harmonious because fittingly adapted to something else, supporting my distinction with material examples. I turned to the nature of the soul, but here I was balked by the false opinion which I held concerning spiritual entities, and unable to discern the truth.[61] Truth was thrusting itself upon me, staring me in the face, but I averted my trembling thought from incorporeal reality and looked instead toward shapes and colors and distended mass, and, since in the soul I could not see these, concluded that I

[60] *almighty God, who alone work wonders:* See Psalm 71(72):18; 135(136):4. Here God's Providence in ordering the life of those who long for him is beautifully described as a certain type of masterful artistry, evoking images of God's gently guiding our experiences and (what may seem to us) chance encounters.

[61] My *mind scanned material forms . . . discern the truth:* As a Manichee, Augustine is still unable to grasp the concept of immateriality; all reality is corporeal, either fine or heavy.

was not able to see the soul. I loved the peace that accompanied virtue, and hated the discord inseparable from a vicious way of life, and I observed that in the former unity was to be found, but in the latter fragmentation. Hence it appeared to me that unity, in which the rational mind subsisted, was itself the essence of truth and of the supreme good, whereas I believed that in disintegration some indefinable substance of irrational life was to be found, which was the essence of supreme evil. I thought this to be not only a substantial reality but also life in the fullest sense—life not derived from you, my God, from whom are all things.[62] This was my opinion, wretch that I was. I called the unity "Monad," conceiving it as a sexless soul; but the other I called "Dyad," to include the anger that issues in crimes and the self-indulgent cravings that lead to vice.[63] But I did not understand what I was talking about. I did not know, never having learned, that evil is no substance at all, and that our mind is not the supreme, immutable good.

25. When the impetuous power of the soul is viciously inclined, and it swaggers in mutinous, insolent pride, violent crimes are the outcome; when that appetite of the soul which thirsts for carnal pleasures is not moderated, vices are the result; so too, if the rational mind itself is vicious, errors and wrong-headed opinions corrupt our life. Such was the condition of my mind at this time. I did not realize that it needed to be open to the radiance of another light in order to become a partaker in the truth, for it is not itself the essence of truth. Rather it is you, Lord, who will light my lamp: O God, you will illuminate my darkness[64] and from your fullness we have all received.[65] For you are *the true light, which illumines every*

---

[62] *God, from whom are all things*: See Romans 11:36; 1 Corinthians 8:6.

[63] *Monad . . . lead to vice*: Here Augustine uses Pythagorean language to provide an image of how he thought of divine reality at this stage: the good god, who was a "Monad", and the malicious second god, the "Dyad", in whom was found anger and all vice. Again, as a Manichee he still understood evil as a separate, self-sufficient existence and not as the "absence of being" always dependent upon goodness.

[64] *O God, you will illuminate my darkness*: See Psalm 17:29(18:28).

[65] *from your fullness we have all received*: See John 1:16.

human person who comes into this world,[66] and in you *there is no variation, no play of changing shadow.*[67]

26. Instead I was striving to reach you by my own efforts, and you thrust me away to taste death, because you *thwart the proud.*[68] What could be prouder than my outlandish delusion, whereby I laid claim to be by nature what you are? I was subject to change, as was obvious to me from the fact that I was clearly seeking to be wise in order to change for the better, yet I was prepared even to think you changeable rather than admit that I was not what you are. Therefore I was thrust away, and you thwarted my puffed-up obstinacy. I conjured up material forms in my imagination, and I who was flesh disparaged the flesh, for I was *a roving spirit that had not yet returned* to you.[69] I persisted in walking after things that had no existence either in you or in me or in any creature, ideas not created for me by your truth but invented in material shape by my own vanity. To your little ones,[70] faithful Christians and my fellow-citizens, from whom I was unwittingly exiled, I babbled away in my petulant fashion, asking, "If God made the soul, why does it fall into error?" But I did not like to hear in reply, "On your showing, we might ask why God falls into error." I was readier to assert that your immutable substance had been forced into error than to confess that my own mutable substance had gone astray by its own will, and that its error was its punishment.

27. I was about twenty-six or twenty-seven when I wrote those volumes. The materialistic images on which I was speculating set up a din in the ears of my heart, ears which were straining to catch your inner melody, O gentle truth. I was thinking about the beautiful and the harmonious, and longing to stand and hear you, that my joy might be perfect at the

---

[66] the true light ... into this world: John 1:9.

[67] there is no variation, no play of changing shadow: James 1:17.

[68] thwart the proud: James 4:6; 1 Peter 5:5.

[69] a roving spirit that had not yet returned to you: Psalm 77(78):39; see Proverbs 2:19.

[70] your little ones: See Matthew 11:25.

sound of the Bridegroom's voice,[71] but I could not, because I was carried off outside myself by the clamor of my errors, and I fell low, dragged down by the weight of my pride. No joy and gladness from you reached my ears, nor did my bones exult, for they had not yet been humbled.[72]

Chapter 16

He reads Aristotle's Categories

28. When I was about twenty a certain writing of Aristotle had been put into my hands, entitled *The Ten Categories*. What a proud mouthful it was when my rhetoric master at Carthage, and others reputedly learned, rattled off the list of them! At the very name of the book I would hang on his words agape, as though expecting some important divine revelation. Yet I read them in private and understood them, though I wonder now what profit that was to me.[73] When I compared notes with other students, who admitted that they had scarcely understood the *Categories* from the most expert masters—masters who not only gave oral instruction but even drew plenty of diagrams in the dust—I found that they were unable to tell me anything that I had not already grasped from my private reading. The categories seemed clear enough to me as they spoke of substances (a man, for example) and of accidents inhering in them, such as his appearance (what he is like), his stature (how many feet high), his relationship (whose brother), where he is, when he was born, his posture (standing or sitting), whether he is wearing sandals or is armed, whether he is doing anything or whether anything is being done to him;[74]

---

[71] *Bridegroom's voice:* See John 3:29.

[72] *joy and gladness . . . been humbled:* See Psalm 50:10(51:8).

[73] *I wonder now what profit that was to me:* See Ecclesiastes 2:15.

[74] Categories . . . *being done to him:* Aristotle's (d. 322 B.C.) *Categories* was the central work of logic at this time and one of the few works of Aristotle known to the Church Fathers (the rest were lost to antiquity and resurfaced only through the Arab world around A.D. 1100). In the *Categories* Aristotle discusses how to

or spoke of any of the innumerable attributes to be found in any of these nine categories, a few of which I have mentioned by way of example, or in the main genus of substance.

29. What profit had it been to me? Supposing that these ten predicates covered everything that exists, I mistakenly attempted to understand even you, my God, in terms of them, you who are wonderfully simple and changeless, imagining that you were the subject of your greatness and beauty, and that those attributes inhered in you as in their subject, as they might in a material thing. I did not realize that you are yourself identical with your greatness and beauty, whereas a material thing is not great and beautiful simply because it is that thing, because even if it were smaller or less beautiful it would still be the material thing it is. No, the reading had been no profit to me—a hindrance, rather. My conclusions about you were falsehood, not truth, the figments of my misery, not the firmament of your happiness. As you had commanded, so did it befall me: the earth brought forth thorns and thistles for me, and I garnered my bread by much labor.[75]

30. Furthermore, what profit was it to me that I, rascally slave of selfish ambitions that I was, read and understood by myself as many books as I could get concerning the so-called liberal arts? I enjoyed these, not recognizing the source of whatever elements of truth and certainty they contained. I had turned my back to the light and my face to the things it illuminated, and so no light played upon my own face, or on the eyes that perceived them. Whatever I understood of the arts of grammar and rhetoric, of dialectic, geometry, music and arithmetic, without much difficulty or tuition from anyone, I understood because my swift intelligence and keen wits were your

---

predicate various attributes (listed here by Augustine) of any one being; this way we can speak of a being undergoing accidental change (in terms of size, relationship, locale, etc.) while remaining essentially the same. The problem is that such classification fails to capture how one can rightly discuss the divine nature, and in applying these to God, Augustine continues to treat God as one being among many.

[75] *thorns and thistles . . . bread by much labor*: See Genesis 3:18–19.

gift; you know it, O Lord my God. Yet from this gift I offered you no sacrifice. It therefore worked not to my advantage but rather to my harm, because I took care that this excellent part of my substance should be under my own control, and I did not guard my strength by approaching you, but left you and set out for a distant land to squander it there on the quest for meretricious gratifications. What profit was this good gift to me when I failed to use it well? It only made me less able to appreciate how very difficult these liberal arts were for even the most zealous and clever to understand. I found this out only when I tried to expound them to my pupils, among whom only the brightest could follow my explanation without dragging.

31. But what profit was that to me, since I supposed that you, my God, you who are truth, were an immense, luminous body, and that I was a particle of it?[76] What outrageous perversity! But that is what I was like, and I am not ashamed to confess to you your own deeds of mercy toward me and to invoke you, my God, since I was not ashamed then to profess to my human hearers my own blasphemous views and to bay doglike against you. What profit to me then was the ingenuity that nimbly picked its way amid those teachings, and the plethora of intricate books I had unraveled without human tuition to support me, if I was crippled and led astray by sacrilegious depravity where the teachings of true godliness were concerned? On the other hand, what disadvantage was it to your little ones that they were much more slow-minded than I? They did not forsake you, but stayed safely in the nest of your Church[77] to grow their plumage and strengthen the wings of their charity on the wholesome nourishment of the faith.[78]

---

[76] *immense, luminous body . . . particle of it*: Here is another fallacy of Manichaeism, that all bodies are visible particles and thus manifest extensions of the lighter god now dragged into this hostile world.

[77] *nest of your Church*: See Psalm 83:4 (84:3).

[78] *wings . . . nourishment of the faith*: See Job 39:26.

O Lord our God,
grant us to trust in your overshadowing wings:
protect us beneath them and bear us up.
You will carry us as little children,
and even to our grey-headed age you will carry us still.
When you are our strong security, that is strength indeed,
but when our security is in ourselves, that is but weakness.
Our good abides ever in your keeping,
but in diverting our steps from you we have grown perverse.
Let us turn back to you at last, Lord, that we be not
    overturned.
Unspoilt, our good abides with you,
for you are yourself our good.
We need not fear to find no home again
because we have fallen away from it;
while we are absent our home falls not to ruins,
for our home is your eternity.

Book V

Faustus at Carthage, Augustine to Rome and Milan

Chapter 1

1. Accept the sacrifice of my confessions, offered to you by the power of this tongue of mine which you have fashioned and aroused to confess to your name;[1] bring healing to all my bones,[2] and let them exclaim, *Lord, who is like you?*[3] A person who confesses to you is not informing you about what goes on within him, for a closed heart does not shut you out, nor is your hand pushed away by human obduracy; you melt it when you choose, whether by showing mercy or by enforcing your claim, and from your fiery heat no one can hide.[4]

But allow my soul to give you glory that it may love you the more, and let it confess to you your own merciful dealings,[5] that it may give you glory. Your whole creation never wearies of praising you, never falls silent; never a breath from the mouth[6] of one who turns to you but gives you glory, never is praise lacking from the universe of living creatures and corporeal beings as they laud you through the mouths of those who contemplate them. Supported by these things you have made let the human soul rise above its weariness and pass through these creatures to you, who have made them so wonderfully. There it will find refreshment, there is its true strength.

---

[1] *power of this tongue . . . confess to your name*: See Proverbs 18:21.

[2] *bring healing to all my bones*: See Psalm 6:3(2).

[3] *Lord, who is like you?* Psalm 34(35):10.

[4] *A person who confesses . . . heat no one can hide*: See Psalm 18:7(19:6). Obviously the *Confessions* are much more than "informing" another about the events of a life. For Augustine, to confess is to allow the soul to bring itself and all within it freely to God, not that God may learn who the creature is but so the creature may better come to know who God is.

[5] *give you glory . . . merciful dealings*: See Psalm 106(107):8.

[6] *praising you . . . breath from the mouth*: See Psalm 150:7(6).

Chapter 2

2. Wicked, restless folk may go their way and flee from you as they will. You see them, for your eyes pierce their darkness, and how lovely is the whole of which they are part, lovely though they are foul! And how have they harmed you? Have they in any point brought your rule into disrepute, that rule which is just and perfect from highest heaven to the lowest of creatures? Where have they fled, in fleeing from your face? Is there any place where you cannot find them?[7] They have fled all the same, to avoid seeing you who see them, and so in their blindness they have stumbled over you—for you abandon nothing you have made; yes, stumbled over you, these unjust folk, and justly hurt themselves; for they distanced themselves from your gentleness only to trip over your probity and fall upon the rough edges of your anger.[8] Clearly they do not know that you are everywhere, for you are not confined to any place, and you alone are present to those who run far away from you.

Let them turn back, and seek you,
for you do not forsake your creation
as they have forsaken their creator.
Let them only turn back,
see! there you are in their hearts,
in the hearts of all those who confess to you,
who fling themselves into your arms
and weep against your breast after their difficult journey,
while you so easily will wipe away their tears.[9]
At this they weep the more,
yet even their laments are matter for joy,
because you, Lord, are not some human being of flesh and
    blood,
but the Lord who made them,
and now make them anew and comfort them.

---

[7] *Is there any place . . . cannot find them?* See Psalm 138(139):7–8.

[8] *in their blindness . . . your anger:* echoes of Romans 11:7–11.

[9] *wipe away their tears:* See Isaiah 25:8; Revelation 7:17; 21:4.

And what of myself: where was I as I sought you? You were straight ahead of me, but I had roamed away from myself and could not find even myself, let alone you![10]

Chapter 3

Augustine hopes to question Faustus

3. Now, in my God's presence, I will describe my twenty-ninth year.

A certain Manichean bishop, Faustus by name, had lately arrived in Carthage.[11] He was a lethal trap set by the devil. Many people were ensnared by the persuasive sweetness of his eloquence, and I too was ready to admire it, but I was beginning to distinguish it from the truth I hungered to learn. What interested me was not the dainty verbal dish on which he served his offerings, this Faustus of such high renown, but how much

---

[10] *where was I . . . let alone you*: Wandering is a central metaphor in this work: Augustine has, of course, not wandered spatially from the ubiquitous God but refuses to be drawn into God and in this refusal; he loses a sense not only of divine mystery but even of his own self. Made in God's image, every desire and action moves the human person either closer to or further away from God. In the Augustinian tradition—exemplified well in Blaise Pascal's (1623–1662) famous wager (*Pensées* §233) where *not* betting on whether there is a God or not is not an option—there is no "middle ground", no agnosticism, as every movement of our heart unites us just a little bit more with either God or earth: "Always move ahead, always make progress, for where you remain pleasing to yourself you are in fact moving backwards" (*Sermon* 169.18).

[11] *Manichean bishop, Faustus . . . Carthage*: Faustus of Milevis (ca. 340–post-385?) was a pagan convert to Manichaeism who left his wife and children to become a Manichean Elect and eventually bishop. While Augustine admits he was eloquent here, he will soon recognize that he is in fact a man of little learning (see *Conf.* V.6.11). At the end of 382 these two men meet in Carthage, and due to Faustus' lack of intelligence, Augustine begins to rethink the basic tenets of Manichaeism. In his *Against Faustus* (398–400)—Augustine's longest anti-Manichean work—Augustine refutes Faustus' opinion that Christians should not read the Old Testament (a view first found in the heresiarch Marcion but typical of all Gnostic dualisms) and explains the proper way to understand the Incarnation and shows why the Church is indispensable for true salvation. Sensed to be a grave threat to imperial unity, Manichaeism was sporadically but strongly condemned (beginning with Diocletian in 296), and in 385 Faustus was exiled from Carthage and died in oblivion thereafter.

knowledge he could provide for me to eat; for I had been told earlier how extremely well informed he was in all branches of reputable scholarship, and how particularly learned in the liberal arts.

Now, I had read widely in the works of philosophers, committed a good deal to memory and still retained it, and I began to compare certain elements from my reading with the long-winded myths of the Manichees. The philosophers' conclusions seemed to me more probable, since these men had been clever enough to make calculations about the world, even though they were quite unsuccessful in discovering its Lord.[12] For great are you, Lord, and you look kindly on what is humble, but the lofty-minded you regard from afar.[13] Only to those whose hearts are crushed do you draw close.[14] You will not let yourself be found by the proud, nor even by those who in their inquisitive skill count stars or grains of sand, or measure the expanses of heaven, or trace the paths of planets.

Valid observations of the natural world by "philosophers"

4. With their intellect and the intelligence you have given them they investigate these things, and so they have discovered much, and predicted eclipses of the sun's light, or the moon's, many years in advance, indicating precisely the day, the hour, and the extent of the eclipse. And their calculations have been accurate. It has therefore been possible for them to make forecasts and draw up rules from their research. On the basis of these rules, which are still studied today, it can be predicted in which year, in which month, on which day of the month and at what hour an eclipse will occur, and what proportion of its light the sun or moon will lose.[15] And, as forecast,

Astronomy/Science

---

[12] *clever enough . . . discovering its Lord*: See Wisdom 13:8–9; Romans 1:18–25.

[13] *lofty-minded you regard from afar*: See Psalm 137(138):6.

[14] *whose hearts are crushed . . . draw close*: See Psalm 33:19(34:18).

[15] *it can be predicted . . . sun or moon will lose*: Study of the celestial bodies is, of course, one of humanity's oldest natural sciences, and Augustine's disenchantment with Manichaeism is now allowing him to see that while there are some

it happens. People think this wonderful: those who are ignorant of such matters are dumbfounded, while the experts strut
and make merry. In their impious pride they draw away from
you and lose your light, because these scholars who foresee a
future eclipse of the sun long beforehand fail to see their own
in the present, for want of inquiring in a religious spirit from
whom they have received the very intelligence which enables
them to inquire into these phenomena. If they discover that
you have made them, they do not give themselves to you so
that you may preserve what you have made, nor do they slay
in your honor those selves of their own making, nor immolate
their high-flown pride as though it were a sacrifice of birds,
nor make into an offering of fish that curiosity whereby they
walk the secret pathways of the deep, nor sacrifice their self-
indulgent habits like beasts of the field,[16] so that you, O God,
who are a devouring fire,[17] may consume their dead ambitions and re-create the seekers for eternal life.

5. They do not know him who is the Way,[18] your Word
through whom you made[19] those very things they are reckoning, together with themselves who do the reckoning, and
the senses with which they perceive the things they reckon,
and the mind with which they reckon; yet your wisdom is
beyond reckoning.[20] Your only-begotten Son has become our

---

valid and quite profound ways to study the movements of the heavens (astron-
omy), the myths and meanings attached to them by the Manichees and others
(astrology) are in fact pernicious to the soul. Catholicism's censure of such
astrological myths is ancient: Gregory of Nazianzus (d. ca. 390), for example,
sees in the Star of Bethlehem the end of astrology, for here the stars no longer
fix humanity's fate but now a man, the babe Jesus Christ, determined the stars
(see *Dogmatic Poems* V.53–64). Pope Benedict XVI cites this example, beautifully adding: "It is not the elemental spirits of the universe, the laws of matter,
which ultimately govern the world and mankind, but a personal God governs
the stars, that is, the universe; it is not the laws of matter and of evolution that
have the final say, but reason, will, love—a Person" (*Spe Salvi* §5).

[16] *they do not give themselves to you*: See 1 John 2:16.

[17] *devouring fire*: See Deuteronomy 4:24; Hebrews 12:29.

[18] *the Way*: See John 14:6.

[19] *your Word through whom you made*: See John 1:3.

[20] *wisdom is beyond reckoning*: See Psalm 146(147):5.

wisdom, our righteousness and our sanctification,[21] yet he was reckoned as one of us and paid tribute to Caesar. They do not know him as the Way whereby they can climb down from their lofty selves to him, and thus by him ascend to him. Of this Way they know nothing; they think themselves exalted to the stars and brilliant. But they have crashed down to earth[22] and their foolish hearts are darkened.[23] Many true statements do they make about creation, but they do not find the Truth who is artificer of creation because they do not seek him with reverence.[24] Or, if they do find him and recognize God, they do not honor him as God or give him thanks; their reasoning grows unsound as they claim to be wise and arrogate to themselves what is yours. This in turn leads them into an extreme of blind perversity, where they will even ascribe to you what is theirs, blaming you, who are Truth, for their own lies, and changing the glory of the incorruptible God into the likeness of corruptible humans, or birds or four-footed beasts or crawling things. They distort truth into a lie, and they worship and serve the creature instead of the creator.

6. For all that, I kept in mind many true conclusions which they had drawn from creation itself, and I saw that these could be verified by calculation, by observing the succession of the seasons and by the visible evidence of the stars. I then compared them with the assertions of Mani, who had written voluminously (and incoherently) on these subjects. What I read

[21] *Son has become . . . our sanctification*: See 1 Corinthians 1:30.

[22] *they have crashed down to earth*: See Isaiah 14:12–13.

[23] *their foolish hearts are darkened*: See Romans 1:21–25.

[24] *Many true statements . . . reverence*: For Augustine, theology is more than gathering the proper data about God; it is about personal transformation, of becoming evermore united with God as one studies. This is why, he argues, the evil spirits may know who Jesus is but because they attempt to know without love, they remain demons. They may seek out Jesus and even "confess" who he is, but they do so not for union but to bring about distance: "It is one thing to confess Christ so you may cling to him; but it is altogether different to confess Christ so that you may push him away from yourself" (*Homilies on First Epistle of John* 10.1).

there was confirmed neither by any rational account of solstices and equinoxes and eclipses, nor by anything else of this kind that I had learned from books of secular philosophy. I was simply bidden to believe, and what I was required to believe did not correspond to the rational explanations I had worked out and discovered by my own observations; in fact there was a wide discrepancy.[25]

Chapter 4

7. Lord God of truth, it surely cannot be that simply knowing these things renders a person pleasing to you? Unhappy is anyone who knows it all but does not know you, whereas one who knows you is blessed, even if ignorant of all these. Nor is anyone who knows both you and them more blessed for knowing them, but blessed on your account alone, provided that such a person recognizes you as you are, and glorifies you and gives you thanks, and does not drift off into unsound reasoning. Someone who knows enough to become the owner of a tree, and gives thanks to you for the benefits it brings him, is in a better state, even if ignorant of its height in feet and the extent of its spread, than another who measures and counts all its branches but neither owns it nor knows its creator nor loves him. Similarly a person who lives by faith owns the whole world's wealth, for though he may have nothing he possesses all things if he but clings to you,[26] the master of them all: he may have scanty acquaintance with the wheeling paths of the

[25] *compared them with the assertions of Mani, . . . wide discrepancy*: Any authority Manichaeism may still have had over Augustine is quickly crumbling. He is finally comparing the myths and stories upon which the Manichees based their doctrine and rituals with, simply, the reality of what is. Christianity may teach truths that are above reason (supernatural), but it never asks one to put faith in a proposition that offends nature (irrational), and this is precisely what Augustine is realizing.

[26] *owns the whole world's wealth . . . clings to you*: See 2 Corinthians 6:10. Such verbs as "clinging" (here, *inhaerendo*, by inhering) emerge as the images Augustine sees as best defining the sanctified soul's relationship to God—images of unity with, participation in, and becoming as thus abound in his preaching and writings.

Great Bear, yet it would be foolish to doubt that he is better off than a man who measures the sky and numbers the stars and weighs the elements, yet leaves you out of his reckoning, you who have disposed all things according to measure and number and weight.[27]

Chapter 5

Manichean assertions about natural phenomena are astray

8. Who ever thought of asking some fellow called Mani to write on these subjects? People could perfectly well have learned true piety without any such expertise. Your advice to us is, *Reverence for God, that is true wisdom.*[28] Obviously Mani might have been thoroughly conversant with scientific truths, even if a stranger to piety. In fact, however, he was ignorant of them, but still had the effrontery to teach them, and from this it emerges that he knew nothing about piety either; for to profess these theories about the world is a mark of vanity, whereas piety is proved by confession to you. It was providential that this man talked so much about scientific subjects, and got it wrong, because this gave people who had truly studied them the chance to convict him of error; and then by implication his insight into other, more recondite matters could be clearly assessed. Mani was content with no modest evaluation: he tried to persuade his followers that the Holy Spirit, who comforts your faithful people and enriches them with his gifts, was with full authority present in him personally. It followed, therefore, that when he was caught out in untrue statements about the sky and the stars, or the changes in sun or moon, his presumption was plainly revealed as sacrilegious, because although these matters are not directly

---

[27] *you who have disposed all things according to measure and number and weight:* See Wisdom 11:20.

[28] Reverence for God, that is true wisdom: Job 28:28.

relevant to religious doctrine, he was not simply discoursing on things of which he was ignorant, but even, in his insane, pretentious vanity, passing off his erroneous opinions as those of a divine person—himself, no less.

9. When I hear one or other of my fellow-Christians expressing a mistaken opinion arising from his ignorance in these fields, I regard with tolerance the person who entertains the notion. As long as he does not believe anything unseemly about you, O Lord, creator of all things, I do not see that it does him any harm if he chances to be ignorant of the position or characteristics of a material creature. It does harm him, however, if he thinks his view forms an essential part of our doctrine and belief, and presumes to go on obstinately making assertions about what he does not know. Yet when this kind of weakness occurs while faith is in its cradle, our mother, charity, bears with it, looking forward to the day when newly-created humanity will grow to the stature of perfect manhood, and no longer be tossed about by every gust of teaching.[29]

The case was quite different with a man who set himself up as a teacher and writer, and as the leader and principal guide of those to whom he propounded his views, and this so persuasively that his disciples thought they were following no ordinary man but your Holy Spirit. If ever such a man were proved to have spoken untruly, could anyone doubt that he must have been grossly deranged, and that his ideas were abhorrent, and to be rejected outright?

I, however, had not yet clearly determined whether variations in the length of day and night, eclipses of the moon and the sun, and similar phenomena of which I had read in other books could be explained equally well by his account of them. If by chance they could, it would still be possible for me to keep open the question of whether his version or theirs more plausibly represented things as they really were, and thus to prefer his authority as a guide to my faith, on the grounds of his alleged holiness.

---

[29] *newly-created humanity . . . gust of teaching*: See Ephesians 4:24; 4:13–14.

Chapter 6

Augustine is disappointed in Faustus

10. All through that period of about nine years, during which I was spiritually adrift as a hearer among the Manichees,[30] I had been awaiting the arrival of this Faustus with an expectancy that had been at full stretch too long. Whenever I had been in contact with others of the sect, and their replies to the questions I raised on these topics failed to satisfy me, they would put me off with promises about him. Once he had arrived, they assured me, and I had an opportunity to discuss things with him, these points, together with any more serious problems I might raise, would quite easily be sorted out and resolved. When he came, then, he did indeed impress me as a man of pleasant and smooth speech, who chattered on the usual themes much more beguilingly than the rest. A man adept at serving finer wines, then; but what was that to me in my thirst? My ears were sated with such offerings already. The content did not seem better to me for being better presented, nor true because skillfully expressed, nor the man wise of soul because he had a handsome face and a graceful turn of speech. Those who had held out promises to me were not good judges; to them he seemed wise and prudent merely because they enjoyed the way he talked. But I realized that there were people of a different stamp who doubted even the possibility of truth, and were unwilling to trust anything conveyed in elegant and fluent style.

For some time, though, you had been teaching me in wondrous, hidden ways, my God (and I believe what you have taught me because it is true; there is no other teacher of truth except you, though teachers aplenty have made a name for themselves in many a place); so I had already learned under your tuition that nothing should be regarded as true

---

[30] *All through that period . . . Manichees*: beginning from his joining the Manichees in 373 until his meeting Bishop Ambrose of Milan in 384.

because it is eloquently stated, nor false because the words sound clumsy. On the other hand, it is not true for being expressed in uncouth language either, nor false because couched in splendid words. I had come to understand that just as wholesome and rubbishy food may both be served equally well in sophisticated dishes or in others of rustic quality, so too can wisdom and foolishness be proffered in language elegant or plain.[31]

11. After waiting so long and so eagerly for this man, I was certainly delighted with his lively and spirited style in debate, and by his apt choice of words to clothe his thought, words that came to him readily. Yes, I was delighted, and along with others I praised and extolled him; indeed, I was in the forefront of those who did so. But I was annoyed that amid the crowd who went to hear him I was unable to catch his attention or share my anxious questionings with him in intimate conversation and the give and take of discussion.[32] If ever I did succeed in gaining a hearing with him in the company of intimate friends and at a time which was not unsuitable for an exchange of ideas, and I put to him some of the problems that preoccupied me, then, before even coming to anything deeper, what I found was a man ill-educated in the liberal arts, apart from grammar, and even in that schooled only to an average level. He had read a few of Cicero's speeches and one or two books by Seneca, and some volumes fairly well written in Latin for his own sect, and because in addition to this he was accustomed to preach daily, he had acquired a fair command of language, which was rendered the more glib and seductive by his skillful management of what ability he had and a certain natural charm.

[31] *language elegant or plain:* For a successful orator like Augustine, this is a significant step: he no longer equates truth with sophistic style, regardless how alluring. Both Manichaeism in general and Faustus in particular have helped him to see how language apart from truth can only deceive.

[32] *unable to catch his attention . . . give and take of discussion:* contrast with Bishop Ambrose's loving attention to all who ask for his time (see *Conf.* VI.3.3, pp. 133–34).

Is my recollection not accurate, Lord God, judge of my conscience? My heart and my memory of these things lie open before you,[33] who were leading me by your hidden, secret providence, and were already bringing my shameful errors round in front of my face,[34] that I might see and hate them.

Chapter 7

12. Once it had become sufficiently clear to me that he was poorly informed about the very disciplines in which I had believed him to excel, I began to give up hope that he could elucidate and clear up for me the problems with which I was concerned. To be sure, he could have been ignorant about these and still have had a grasp of religious truth, but only on condition of not being a Manichee. Their books are full of interminable myths concerning sky, stars, sun and moon, and it had been my earnest wish that by comparing these with the numerical calculations I had read elsewhere he would demonstrate to me that the phenomena in question could be more plausibly explained by the account given in Mani's books, or at least that an equally valid explanation could be found there; but now I no longer deemed him capable of explaining these things to me with any precision.

I must say, however, that when I raised these points for consideration and discussion he refused courteously enough, reluctant to risk taking on that burden; for he knew that he did not know about these matters, and was not ashamed to admit it. He was not one of the talkative kind, of whom I had suffered many, who tried to teach me but said nothing. His heart was, if not right with you,[35] yet not without discretion. He was not altogether unaware of his own lack of awareness and was unwilling to enter rashly into argument that might leave

---

[33] *memory of these things lie open before you*: See Numbers 10:9.

[34] *leading me . . . bringing my shameful errors round in front of my face*: See Psalm 49(50):21; cf. *Conf.* IV.16.30, p. 98.

[35] *heart was, if not right with you*: See Psalm 77(78):37; Acts 8:21.

him cornered, with no way out and no easy means of retracting. This attitude endeared him to me all the more, for the restraint of a mind that admits its limitations is more beautiful than the beautiful things about which I desired to learn. I found him consistent in this approach to all the more difficult and subtle questions.

13. The keen attention I had directed toward Mani's writings was therefore rebuffed, for I felt more hopeless than ever in respect of their other teachers now that this man, for all his reputation, had turned out to be so incompetent in many of the subjects that mattered to me. I began to spend much time in his company on account of his ardent enthusiasm for the literature that I, as a master of rhetoric, was teaching to the young men of Carthage, and thereafter I fell into the habit of reading with him any works which he had heard of and wished to study, or which were, in my judgment, suited to his ability. Apart from this, all the plans I had formed for advancement in the sect lapsed into oblivion now that I had come to know this man: not that I severed my connection with it entirely, but since I had found nothing better than this sect into which I had more or less blundered, I resolved to be content with it for the time being, unless some preferable option presented itself.

Thus it came about that this Faustus, who was a death-trap for many, unwittingly and without intending it began to spring the trap in which I was caught, for thanks to your hidden providence, O my God, your hands did not let go of my soul. Through my mother's tears the sacrifice of her heart's blood was being offered to you day after day, night after night, for my welfare; and you dealt with me in wondrous ways. You, my God, you it was who dealt so with me; for *our steps are directed by the Lord, and our way is of his choosing.*[36] What other provision is there for our salvation, but your hand that remakes what you have made?

---

[36] our steps ... his choosing: Psalm 36(37):23.

Chapter 8

Indiscipline among his students prompts move to Rome

14. You dealt with me in such a way that I was persuaded to move to Rome, to teach there instead what I had been teaching at Carthage.[37] I must not omit to confess to you the reasons why I was so persuaded, because in them your deep, secret providence was at work, and your ever-present mercy, and these are to be pondered and proclaimed. I did not want to go to Rome because my friends promised me that there I would command higher fees and enjoy greater prestige—though these arguments were not without force for me; the principal and almost the sole reason was that I heard that young men there study more quietly and are controlled by a more systematic regime of strict discipline to prevent them from rushing pell-mell and at random into the school of a teacher with whom they are not enrolled; in fact they are not admitted at all except by his permission. At Carthage things are very different: the unbridled licentiousness of the students is disgusting. Looking almost like madmen they burst in recklessly and disrupt the discipline each master has established to ensure that his pupils make progress. With boorishness that defies belief they commit many acts of violence which would attract legal penalties if custom did not seem to plead in their defense; yet this in itself proves that the perpetrators are the more to be pitied, inasmuch as they do with apparent legality what will never be permitted by your eternal law, and think they are acting so

---

[37] *move to Rome . . . Carthage*: In the autumn of 383 Augustine moves from Carthage to Rome, made possible through strong Manichean connections there. While downplaying this new opportunity, it is in every way a promotion and the kind of advancement a young man of Augustine's caliber sought. In Rome the students were traditionally more serious about their classical studies, and, as mentioned, a more established educational system brought pedagogues a better wage and more prestige. Given Augustine's overall purpose in the *Confessions*, this career move is subordinate to and valued only within God's greater purpose of weaning Augustine off the Manichean fables, out of Carthage and to Rome, where he will encounter seriously minded Catholics and Bishop Ambrose.

with impunity, whereas the very blindness that dictates their behavior is itself their punishment, and they suffer far worse damage themselves than they inflict on others.

Accordingly while teaching these youths I was being forced to endure those very forms of misconduct I had been chary of adopting myself in my student days; and I decided to depart for a place where, by all accounts, such things did not happen.

But in truth it was you, *my hope and my inheritance in the country of the living*,[38] who for my soul's salvation prompted me to change my country, and to this end you provided both the goads at Carthage that dislodged me from there and the allurements at Rome that attracted me; and this you did through the lovers of a life that is no more than death, who on the one hand behaved insanely and on the other held out to me vain promises. To bring my steps back to the straight path you secretly made use of both their perversity and mine; for those who disturbed my tranquility were blinded by disgusting frenzy, while those who invited me elsewhere were wise only in the things of this earthly country,[39] while I, for my part, loathed real misery in the one place and craved spurious happiness in the other.

Monica's opposition; Augustine departs by stealth

15. You knew all along, O God, the real reason why I left to seek a different country, but you did not reveal it either to me or to my mother, who bitterly bewailed my departure and followed me to the seashore. She held on to me with all her strength, attempting either to take me back home with her or to come with me, but I deceived her, pretending that I did not want to take leave of a friend until a favorable wind should arise and enable him to set sail. I lied to my mother, my incomparable mother! But I went free, because in your mercy you forgave me. Full of detestable filth as I was, you kept me safe

---

[38] *my hope and my inheritance in the country of the living:* Psalm 141:6(142:5).
[39] *wise . . . earthly country:* See Philippians 3:18–19.

from the waters of the sea to bring me to the water of your grace; once I was washed in that, the rivers of tears that flowed from my mother's eyes would be dried up, those tears with which day by day she bedewed the ground wherever she prayed to you for me.

At the time, however, she refused to go home, and it was only with difficulty that I persuaded her to spend the night in a place very near our ship, a memorial chapel to Blessed Cyprian.[40] That same night I left by stealth; she did not, but remained behind praying and weeping. And what was she begging of you, my God, with such abundant tears? Surely, that you would not allow me to sail away. But in your deep wisdom you acted in her truest interests: you listened to the real nub of her longing and took no heed of what she was asking at this particular moment, for you meant to make me into what she was asking for all the time. So the wind blew for us and filled our sails, and the shore dropped away from our sight as she stood there at morning light mad with grief, filling your ears with complaints and groans.

You took no heed, for you were snatching me away, using my lusts to put an end to them and chastising her too-carnal desire with the scourge of sorrow. Like all mothers, though far more than most, she loved to have me with her, and she did not know how much joy you were to create for her through my absence. She did not know, and so she wept and wailed,

---

[40] *Blessed Cyprian*: Cyprian was the awe-inspiring Bishop of Carthage, consecrated there in either 248 or 249. With the outbreak of the Decian persecution, Cyprian was first exiled and then martyred in 258, his bones interred and later venerated not far from where ships sent sail into the Mediterranean Sea (some manuscripts show this place of martyrdom to be the same spot as Cyprian's family villa). For North African Christians, he was their monumental hero, a symbol of orthodoxy and strength in the face of pagan persecutors. From a prominent Carthaginian family, Cyprian surely reminded Augustine of his later self: well educated, rhetorically successful as a "pleader in the courts", an adult convert to Christianity, priest, bishop, and defender of the faith, especially in terms of ecclesial unity. On his work *On Baptism Against the Donatists* (written in 400) Augustine gives Cyprian no faint praise, asking of him: "For who can be ignorant that the primacy of his apostleship is to be preferred to any episcopate whatever?" (Book 2.2).

and these cries of pain revealed what there was left of Eve in her, as in anguish she sought the son whom in anguish she had brought to birth.[41] Yet when she had finished blaming my deception and cruelty, she resumed her entreaties for me, and returned to her accustomed haunts, while I went to Rome.

Chapter 9

Illness in Rome; Manichean contacts

16. For me too a scourge was waiting there, in the guise of a bodily illness that brought me to death's door loaded with all the sins I had committed against you, against myself and against other people, evil deeds many and grievous over and above the original sin that binds all of us who die in Adam.[42] For no single one of them had you pardoned me in Christ: he had not broken down the barrier of enmity[43] I had piled up against you by my sins, for how could the crucifixion of a phantom do that for me?[44] And that was all I thought he was. The more illusory for me was his death in the flesh, the more real was the death of my soul. But in truth his bodily death was real; it was my unbelieving soul that was living on illusion. My fever worsened. I was on my way to perdition; for where should I

---

[41] *Eve in her . . . brought to birth*: See Genesis 3:16. It is helpful to keep in mind how throughout the *Confessions* Monica can play a threefold role, each at various times: Eve, the archetypal genesis of all the living; the biological mother of Augustine; as well as the symbol of Mother Church.

[42] *original sin . . . who die in Adam*: See 1 Corinthians 15:22. This is the first substantive use of "original sin" (*peccatum originale*) in Christianity to describe the fallen and rebellious condition of all of Adam's children.

[43] *For no single one of them . . . he had not broken down the barrier of enmity*: See Ephesians 2:14–16.

[44] *crucifixion of a phantom do that for me*: As a Manichee, Augustine's Christology at this point would have been docetic (from the Greek word *dokeo*, "to appear"), in that in Christ God only appeared to have passable flesh capable of vulnerability and suffering. This is no doubt why the Manichees regarded Jesus as a "phantom" whose death in fact achieved nothing. Notice how Augustine effectively contrasts the "death" of Manichean theology with the true "life" paradoxically realized only at Calvary.

have gone, if I had departed at this time? Inevitably to the fire and torments[45] my deeds deserved, according to your just ordinance.

Meanwhile my mother, who knew nothing of this, persevered in praying for me; she was far away, but you are present everywhere, so you heard her in that land where she was, and took pity on me where I was. I recovered my bodily health, though I remained sick in my sacrilegious heart. Even in that dire peril I had no desire for your baptism; better had been my state in boyhood when I begged for it from my loving mother, as I have recalled and confessed already. But I had meanwhile grown up into my disgraceful condition, and like one demented had fallen into the habit of mocking your healing prescriptions, though it was you who now had saved me from dying in that state and so incurring a twofold death.[46] If a blow like that had struck my mother's heart, she would never have recovered. I can find no words to express how intensely she loved me: with far more anxious solicitude did she give birth to me in the spirit than ever she had in the flesh.

17. I cannot see, therefore, how she could possibly have been healed if so terrible a death had overtaken me, and transfixed her too in the tenderest depths of her loving heart. Where would her passionate prayers have gone, those prayers so frequently, so ceaselessly offered?[47] Nowhere, surely, if not into your keeping; and would you, O God of all mercy,[48] spurn the broken, humbled heart[49] of a chaste and temperate widow who was untiring in her acts of charity,[50] attentive to the needs of your saints and faithful in serving them? Never a day would pass but she was careful to make her offering at your altar. Twice a day, at morning and evening, she was unfailingly present in your church, not for gossip or old wives' tales but so that

---

[45] *fire and torments*: See Matthew 25:41.

[46] *twofold death*: See Revelation 20:6, 14; 21:8.

[47] *prayers so frequently, so ceaselessly offered*: See 1 Thessalonians 5:17.

[48] *God of all mercy*: See 2 Corinthians 1:3.

[49] *spurn the broken, humbled heart*: See Psalm 50:19(51:17).

[50] *untiring in her acts of charity*: 1 Timothy 5:10.

she might hearken to your words, as you to her prayers. Could you, then, whose grace had made her what she was, disdain those tears and rebuff her plea for your aid, when what she tearfully begged from you was not gold or silver, not some insecure, ephemeral advantage, but the salvation of her son? No, Lord, that would have been unthinkable; rather you were present, you heard her, and you acted: it was done as you had predestined that it should be. Could you have deceived her in those visions and assurances you had given her, those I have already recorded and others not mentioned, to which she held fast in her faithful heart and which she regularly in prayer presented for your attention, as pledges bearing your own signature?[51] Perish the thought! Though you forgive us all our debts, you deign by your promises to make yourself our debtor, for your merciful love abides for ever.[52]

Chapter 10

18. This is why you restored me from my sickness; you saved your handmaid's son,[53] and gave me back my bodily health for the time being, preserving me so that you might endow me with better and more dependable health later.

At this time I joined the company of the so-called Saints in Rome,[54] who were deceived themselves and deceivers of others; for I was mixing not only with their Hearers, one of whom was the man in whose house I had been ill and had recovered, but also with those whom they call the Elect. It still seemed to me that it is not we who sin, but some other nature within us that is responsible. My pride was gratified at being exculpated by this theory: when I had done something wrong it was pleasant to avoid having to confess that I had done it, a

---

[51] *Could you have deceived ... pledges bearing your own signature*: See Colossians 2:14.

[52] *your merciful love abides for ever*: See Psalm 117(118):1.

[53] *handmaid's son*: See Psalm 85(86):16; 115:7(116:16).

[54] *Saints in Rome*: that is, the Manichees in Rome who provided Augustine with his initial lodging and community of like-minded searchers.

confession that would have given you a chance to heal this soul of mine that had sinned against you.[55] On the contrary, I liked to excuse myself and lay the blame on some other force that was with me but was not myself. But in truth it was all myself. My impious ideas had set up a division, pitting me against myself,[56] and my sin was the more incurable for my conviction that I was not a sinner.

It was a detestable wrong, almighty God, to prefer the lie that you were suffering defeat in me for my destruction to the truth that I was being mastered by you for my salvation. You had not yet set a guard over my mouth or a chaste gate at my lips to keep my heart from straying into evil talk, and from making excuses for itself in its sins as it consorted with evildoers;[57] and so I continued to associate with their Elect. By now I had given up hope of making any progress in that false doctrine, so I held onto the teachings half-heartedly and without giving them much thought, simply because I had resolved to make do with them in default of anything better.

Appeal of Academic skepticism

19. In fact, though, a suspicion had arisen in my mind that another class of philosophers, known as Academics, were more likely to be right.[58] These men had recommended universal

---

[55] *sinned against you*: See Psalm 40:5 (41:4). As we shall soon see, Manichean anthropology allowed Augustine to continue in his sinfulness, providing him with a way of seeing how his truest self was incapable of evil, while his fallen self on earth was simply too mired in heavy matter to be reformed.

[56] *pitting me against myself*: See Matthew 12:26. Again, more than the fallen and thus divided soul of Saint Paul (for example, see Romans 7:15–16) and Saint James (for example, see James 1:8), Manichaeism posited two separate selves at war with each other until the final conflagration; in the meantime the lower self was exculpated for any vicious actions.

[57] *guard over my mouth . . . consorted with evildoers*: See Psalm 140(141):3–4.

[58] *Academics, were more likely to be right*: On his way from Manichaeism to Catholicism, Augustine briefly entertains the insights of academic skepticism (introduced to him no doubt through the writings of his beloved Cicero), against which he writes his next work, *Contra Academicos* (*Against the Skeptics*), in 386

doubt, announcing that no part of the truth could be understood by the human mind. Adopting the commonly held view of them I too believed that they had seen clearly in this matter, though I did not yet understand their real intention. I did not neglect to restrain my host from what I considered his excessive credulity with regard to the fabulous statements of which Manichean books are full, yet I was more comfortable in friendly association with Manichees than with others not of that heresy. No longer did I defend it with my original vehemence, yet familiar acquaintance with these people, of whom Rome harbors a fair number, made me lazy about seeking anything else. This was especially the case because I had despaired of the possibility that anything true could be discovered in your Church, O Lord of heaven and earth,[59] creator of all things, both seen and unseen.[60] The Manichees had turned me away from the Church, and I thought it contemptible to believe that you bore the appearance of human flesh and were confined to our bodily shape and our members.[61] When I wanted to think about my God I did not know how to think otherwise than in terms of bodily size, for whatever did not answer to this description seemed to me to be nothing at all. This misapprehension was the chief and almost sole cause of the error I could not avoid.

20. Consistently with this I believed that there was a similar substance of evil as well, a dark, deformed mass; this was either gross, and called earth, or ethereal and rarefied like an airy body, which the Manichees picture as a malevolent mind

---

while preparing for baptism. The form of skepticism Augustine knew argued that one should always strive to keep an open mind and never assent to anything that is not absolutely knowable and sure. Like Socrates, its adherents saw the good life consisting in rational inquiry (Gk., *skepsis*) and self-examination. This is different than the modern skepticism of a Descartes where reality by its very nature is unsteady and unknowable.

[59] *Lord of heaven and earth*: See Matthew 11:25.

[60] *creator of all things, both seen and unseen*: See Colossians 1:16.

[61] *bore the appearance of human flesh . . . our members*: See Genesis 1:26–27. The Incarnation of the Christ is still very much a scandalous doctrine for the carnally minded Augustine.

creeping about through the earth. Some kind of reverence on my part forced me to believe that a good God could not have created any evil nature, so I mentally constructed two masses opposed to each other: both were infinite, but the evil one I conceived rather more narrowly, the good on a larger scale.[62] From this tainted premise other sacrilegious ideas followed. When my mind attempted to speed back once more to the Catholic faith I was repelled, because the Catholic faith is not what I thought it was. Further, it seemed to me more reverent, O God, God to whom your own merciful dealings with me confess,[63] to believe that you were at any rate infinite on all other sides, even though I was forced to admit that you were finite on that one side where the mass of evil opposed you, than to hold that you were limited on every side by the form of a human body. Since in my ignorance I thought that evil was not only a substance, but even a bodily substance (for I did not know how to envisage a mind except as an ethereal body spread out through space), it seemed to me better to believe that you had not created any evil than to believe that what I thought of as the nature of evil could have proceeded from you.

I even thought that our Savior himself, your only-begotten Son, had been detached from the mass of your huge, brilliant substance for our salvation; so fixed was I in this worthless notion that I believed nothing else of him but what I could picture in terms of it. In consequence I held that a nature of this kind could not have been born of the Virgin Mary without becoming intermingled with flesh; yet a nature such as I pictured it could not be so intermingled without being defiled. I was therefore afraid to believe in One who was born in the flesh, lest I should be forced to believe him defiled by the flesh. Your spiritually-minded faithful will gently and lovingly laugh

---

[62] *good God . . . on a larger scale*: Here is a classic example of the inconsistencies of Manichean doctrine: although both deities are uncaused and infinite, the good god was thought to be somehow more amplified, powerful, and (hopefully) victorious.

[63] *God . . . dealings with me confess*: See Psalm 106(107):8 and recurrently.

at me if they read these confessions of mine; all the same, that is what I was like.

Chapter 11

21. Moreover, I did not consider that your scriptures could be defended on those points where the Manichees had censured them; but there certainly were times when I longed to discuss these one by one with somebody who had studied those books thoroughly, to find out his view of them. While still at Carthage I had been influenced in a preliminary way by the lectures of a certain Elpidius who disputed with the Manichees face-to-face, for he drew arguments from the scriptures which could not easily be gainsaid.[64] The Manichees' reply seemed feeble to me, and they were understandably disinclined to bring it out openly, preferring to give it to us in private. They alleged that the New Testament writings had been falsified by some unknown persons bent on interpolating the Christian faith with elements of the Jewish law; but they produced no incorrupt exemplars themselves.

But most of all it was those massive substances that weighed me down as I thought in terms of bodies; it was as though they pinned me fast and choked me as under their weight I gasped for the pure and unpolluted air of your truth, but found myself unable to breathe it.

Chapter 12

Augustine teaches in Rome

22. I now set myself to work hard at teaching rhetoric in Rome, the task for which I had come. My first move was to

---

[64] *Elpidius . . . not easily be gainsaid*: Elpidius was a North African Arian theologian whose success in debating Manichees was renown. In *Letter* 242 (sometime after 395) we read how Elpidius hoped to gain Augustine for the Arian cause, to recruit him to teach that the Father was of a higher substance than the Son, but Augustine, of course, replies by explaining how the Father and the Son are of the same being (*homoousios*) and concludes by promising Elpidius prayers for his conversion to the one true faith.

gather students together at my house, and I began to make a name for myself among them, and more widely through them. But what did I then discover, but that abuses prevailed in Rome which I had not been obliged to contend with in Africa? It was obviously true that acts of vandalism by young hooligans did not occur there, but, I was told, "A crowd of these young men conspire together, and in order to avoid paying their fees to their teacher suddenly leave him for another. They betray their good faith, and because they hold wealth so dear they account justice cheap."[65] My heart was filled with hatred for these youths, but it fell short of *perfect hatred*,[66] for I probably hated what I might suffer at their hands more than the crimes they might commit against anyone else. Still, people of this type are depraved and break faith with you[67] by setting their hearts on the fleeting baubles of this passing life and the filthy lucre that sullies the hand that grasps it.[68] They embrace an elusive world while despising you who abide for ever, you who call them back again and forgive the wanton human soul that returns to you. Today I hate such people for being depraved and twisted, but I will love them insofar as they may be corrected, and may come to prefer the education to the money, and prefer even to the education you yourself, O God, who are truth and overflowing wealth of goodness that deceives not, and pure, inviolate peace. But at that time, when harm from these bad students threatened me, my desire to avoid it for my own sake was stronger than any desire that they should become good for yours.

---

[65] *avoid paying their fees . . . account justice cheap:* While the bigger cities may have yielded a professor larger fees, there was much more scandal of this type as well. For example, at the same time Augustine experiences this financial fraud, both Palladas, a Greek rhetorician in Alexandria, and Libanius, an orator in Antioch, complain that students would leave the lecture hall before class ended so they could dodge paying.

[66] *perfect hatred:* Psalm 138(139):22.

[67] *depraved and break faith with you:* See Psalm 72(73):27.

[68] *filthy lucre . . . grasps it:* See Titus 1:7; 1 Peter 5:2.

Chapter 13

He wins a teaching post in Milan

23. A message had been sent from Milan to Rome, addressed to the prefect of the city, asking for a master of rhetoric. A pass had also been issued, authorizing the person chosen to use the official post-horses. Against the background of unsatisfactory student behavior I therefore canvassed support among citizens drunk on Manichean nonsense, in the hope that after prescribing a subject for a trial discourse the prefect Symmachus would recommend and dispatch me.[69] My real reason for going was to get away from the Manichees, though this was not apparent either to them or to me at the time.

He arrives in Milan and meets Ambrose

So I came to Milan and to Bishop Ambrose, who was known throughout the world as one of the best of men.[70] He was a

[69] *prefect Symmachus . . . dispatch me*: Quintus Aurelius Symmachus (ca. 340–402) was urban prefect of Rome, 384–385, when this request from Milan, now the imperial see, came. Augustine is being elevated to the official imperial rhetor—the emperor's "speech writer" and minister of propaganda—testifying not only to how illustrious he had become, but also to how ensconced in the pagan scene he was. For Symmachus was the leading rhetorician of his day, and in 382 when the emperor Gratian removed all pagan images from the Roman temples, denied funds for the Vestal Virgins in Rome, and curtailed all non-Christian public festivals, Symmachus was chosen by the Senate to appeal to the emperor's nostalgic love for Rome and its ancient ways. Symmachus was never allowed to deliver this initial speech, but after Gratian was assassinated the following year (383), Symmachus approached his successor, Valentinian II, with the same request for restoring the ancient customs, but this time Bishop Ambrose intervened and won the day. The correspondence between Symmachus and Ambrose reveals the deeply engrained hostilities between the fourth-century Christian and pagan aristocracies; see Symmachus' *Relation* III, as well as Ambrose's *Letters* 17 and 18 on restoring the pagan Altar of Victory in the Senate house.

[70] *Bishop Ambrose . . . best of men*: Aurelius Ambrosius (c. 337–397) was born and raised in a Christian family in Trier, where his father was the leading praetorian prefect of all of Gaul. Ambrose himself entered upon a political career

devout worshiper of you, Lord, and at that time his energetic preaching provided your people with choicest wheat and the joy of oil and the sober intoxication of wine. Unknowingly I was led by you to him, so that through him I might be led, knowingly, to you.

This man of God welcomed me with fatherly kindness and showed the charitable concern for my pilgrimage that befitted a bishop. I began to feel affection for him, not at first as a teacher of truth, for that I had given up hope of finding in your Church, but simply as a man who was kind to me. With professional interest I listened to him conducting disputes before the people, but my intention was not the right one: I was assessing his eloquence to see whether it matched its reputation. I wished to ascertain whether the readiness of speech with which rumor credited him was really there, or something more, or less. I hung keenly upon his words, but cared little for their content, and indeed despised it, as I stood there delighting in the sweetness of his discourse. Though more learned than that of Faustus it was less light-hearted and beguiling; but such criticism concerns the style only, for with regard to the content there was no comparison. While Faustus would wander off into Manichean whimsy, this man was teaching about salvation in a thoroughly salutary way. But salvation is far from sinners,[71] and a sinner I was at that time. Yet little by little, without knowing it, I was drawing near.

---

and by 372 had become the governor of Liguria with Milan as his capital. In 374 when the Bishop of Milan, Auxentius, a follower of Arian Christology (subordinating the Son to the Father), died, the Arians challenged his succession in the hopes of ensuring that a like-minded Arian would replace him. The dispute reached such a fever pitch within the cathedral that Ambrose and his men were called so as to prevent rioting. At some point in this imbroglio, the crowd began to chant, "Ambrose, Bishop", "Ambrose, Bishop", and as one known for his keen sense of justice, Ambrose was found acceptable to both Catholic and Arian parties alike, and within a week's time, he was baptized, ordained, and consecrated the Bishop of Milan.

[71] *salvation is far from sinners*: See Psalm 118(119):155.

Chapter 14

24. I was taking no trouble to learn from what Ambrose was saying, but interested only in listening to how he said it, for that futile concern had remained with me, despairing as I did that any way to you could be open to humankind. Nonetheless as his words, which I enjoyed, penetrated my mind, the substance, which I overlooked, seeped in with them, for I could not separate the two. As I opened my heart to appreciate how skillfully he spoke, the recognition that he was speaking the truth crept in at the same time, though only by slow degrees. At first the case he was making began to seem defensible to me, and I realized that the Catholic faith, in support of which I had believed nothing could be advanced against Manichean opponents, was in fact intellectually respectable. This realization was particularly keen when once, and again, and indeed frequently, I heard some difficult passage of the Old Testament explained figuratively; such passages had been death to me because I was taking them literally.[72] As I listened to many such scriptural texts being interpreted in a spiritual sense I confronted my own attitude, or at least that despair which had led me to believe that no resistance whatever could be offered to people who loathed and derided the law and the prophets. However, I did not yet consider the Catholic way the one to follow simply because it too could have its learned proponents, men who were capable of refuting objections with ample argument and good sense; nor did I yet consider the Manicheanism I professed was to be condemned because I had

---

[72] *Old Testament explained . . . taking them literally*: See 2 Corinthians 3:6. One of the first practical details of doctrine that Ambrose's preaching gave the intellectually eager Augustine was how to understand Scripture rightly. The Manichees ridiculed the Old Testament because they thought *all* passages were historical and literal; through Ambrose's method of preaching, however, Augustine came to see how many passages and images of Scripture are to be understood allegorically, conveying deeper truths that can be understood only in a spiritual sense. Allegory thus taught Augustine that Scripture means much more than what can be captured simply on the page. It is significant that the great orator's mind is beginning to wake up to the beauty and consistency of Christianity by first learning how to understand words rightly.

observed that the party of the defense could make out an equally good case. The Catholic Church appeared to me unconquered, but not so clearly as to appear the conqueror.

25. I then expended much mental effort on trying to discover if I could in any way convict the Manichees of falsehood by some definite proofs. If only I had been capable of envisaging a spiritual substance, all their elaborate constructions would have fallen to pieces at once and been thrown out of my mind; but this I could not do. All the same, as I gave more and more thought to the matter and made comparisons, I judged that many philosophers had held far more probable views on this physical world and on whatever in nature comes within reach of our senses. Accordingly I adopted what is popularly thought to be the Academic position, doubting everything and wavering: I decided that I ought to leave the Manichees, since at this period of uncertainty it was not right for me to continue as a member of a sect to which I judged some philosophers superior; but I flatly refused to entrust the cure of my soul's sickness[73] to philosophers who were strangers to the saving name of Christ. I resolved therefore to live as a catechumen in the Catholic Church, which was what my parents had wished for me, until some kind of certainty dawned by which I might direct my steps aright.

[73] *cure of my soul's sickness:* See Matthew 9:35; Luke 9:1.

Book VI

Milan, 385:
Progress, Friends, Perplexities

Chapter 1

1. O you who have been my hope since my youth[1] where were you when I sought you? How was it that you had gone so far away?[2] Had you not created me and marked me out *from the four-footed beasts, and made me wiser than the birds in the sky?*[3] Yet I was walking a dark and slippery path, searching for you outside myself I had sunk to the depth of the sea,[4] I lost all faith and despaired of ever finding the truth.

Monica comes to Milan

Steadfast in her fidelity, my mother had by this time rejoined me, for so completely did she trust in you that she had not feared to follow me over land and sea. Indeed, amid the perils of the voyage it was she who kept up the spirits of the sailors, though in the ordinary way it is to them that inexperienced and frightened travelers look for reassurance. She, however, had dared to promise them that they would come safely to port, because you had yourself made this promise to her in a dream.[5] She found me, by contrast, beset by mortal danger as

---

[1] *have been my hope since my youth:* See Psalm 70(71):5.

[2] *you had gone so far away:* See Psalm 9:22(10:1).

[3] from the four-footed beasts ... birds in the sky: Job 35:11.

[4] *depth of the sea:* See Psalm 67:23(68:22).

[5] *safely to port ... in a dream:* The trip between Carthage and Rome's port city of Ostia was a common journey, about 350 miles. There is a story in Plutarch's *Cato the Elder* (§27.1) about Cato's hiding recently picked figs in his tunic, and when he allows them to fall onto the floor of the Roman Senate, all were amazed at how fresh they were, to which Cato responded that is because the enemy was

I despaired of discovering the truth. When I told her that I was no longer a Manichee, though not a Catholic Christian either,[6] she was overjoyed, but not as though this news had taken her by surprise. She was already confident with regard to my wretched condition to this extent, that while she constantly wept over me in your sight as over a dead man, it was over one who though dead could still be raised to life again; she offered me to you upon the bier of her meditation, begging you to say to this widow's son, *Young man, arise, I tell you,*[7] that he might live again and begin to speak, so that you could restore him to his mother. Accordingly, when she learned that what she tearfully begged of you every day had been partially granted, inasmuch as I had now been delivered from falsehood, even if I had not yet found the truth, there was no wild excitement or agitation in her heartfelt joy. So certain was she that you, who had promised her everything, would grant what was still lacking, that she told me very tranquilly and with full confidence that in Christ she believed she would see me a faithful Catholic before she departed from this life.

So much she said to me; but to you, the fount of all mercy, she redoubled her prayers and tears, imploring you to make haste to my help[8] and enlighten my darkness.[9] She hurried all the more eagerly to church and hung upon Ambrose's preaching, in which she found a spring of water leaping up to eternal life.[10] She revered that man as an angel of God,[11] for she realized that it was thanks to him that I had meanwhile

---

that close, "only three days away", and therefore, famously, "Carthage must be destroyed."

[6] *no longer a Manichee . . . Christian either:* By 385 Augustine had renounced the Manichees and was reading more and more philosophy, bits of Aristotle, Cicero, and the skeptics (see *Conf.* V.10.19, pp. 120–21) as well as the "books of the Platonists", as we shall read below (see *Conf.* VII.9.13).

[7] Young man, arise, I tell you: Luke 7:14.

[8] *imploring you to make haste to my help:* See Psalm 69:2(70:1).

[9] *enlighten my darkness:* See Psalm 17:29(18:28).

[10] *spring of water . . . eternal life:* See John 4:14.

[11] *She revered that man as an angel of God:* See Galatians 4:14. Augustine spends time introducing some rather intimate details of Monica's soul as a segue into

been brought to my present point of wavering; and she fore-
saw with certainty that I would have to pass through a still
more dangerous condition—a crisis, as the physicians call it—on
my way from sickness to health.

Chapter 2

2. In Africa she had been accustomed to make offerings of
pottage, bread and wine at the tombs of the martyrs. When
she attempted to do the same here, she was prevented by the
doorkeeper; but as soon as she learned that it was the bishop
who had forbidden the practice she complied in so devoted
and obedient a spirit that I marveled at the attitude she had
so readily adopted: criticizing her own custom rather than sitting in judgment on his prohibition. And no wonder, for her
mind was not enslaved to any habit of wine-bibbing, nor did
addiction to wine incite her to hatred of the truth, as is the
case with many men and women who are as disgusted by any
commendation of sobriety as are drunkards when offered
watered-down wine. With my mother it was otherwise: she
would bring her basket containing the festive fare which it
fell to her to taste first and then distribute; but she would then
set out no more than one small cup, mixed to suit her abstemi-
ous palate, and from that she would only sip for courtesy's sake.
If it happened that there were many shrines of the dead to be
honored in this manner she would carry round this same single cup and set it forth in each place. She thus served to her
fellow-worshipers extremely sparing allowances of wine which
was not only heavily diluted but by this time no more than
lukewarm. What she sought to promote at these gatherings
was piety, not intemperance.[12]

---

the person of Bishop Ambrose, because she is not only his earthly mother; her
faith represents "Mother Church", of whom Ambrose is the visible head.

[12] *make offerings . . . not intemperance*: This ancient custom of feasting at the
tombs of one's beloved dead was one of North African Christianity's favorite
ways of celebrating. A pagan custom originally, the *refrigerium* (from a term "to
refresh or cool", meaning here "to revive" the memory of the dead) could include

Once she had ascertained, however, that Ambrose, illustrious preacher and exemplar of piety as he was, had forbidden the celebration of these rites even by those who conducted them with restraint, lest any opportunity might be given to drunkards to indulge in excess, and also because the custom resembled the cult of ancestors and so was close kin to the superstitious practices of the pagans, she most willingly gave it up. She had now seen the wisdom of bringing to the martyrs' shrines not a basket full of the fruits of the earth, but a heart full of more purified offerings, her prayers. In consequence she was now able to give alms to the needy, and it was also possible for the sacrament of the Lord's Body to be celebrated at these shrines—and fittingly, since it was in imitation of his passion that the martyrs offered themselves in sacrifice and were crowned.

All the same, O Lord my God—and in your presence I speak truly from my heart on this matter—it seems to me unlikely that my mother would have yielded easily over the abolition of this custom had it been forbidden by anyone other than Ambrose, whom she highly revered. It was above all for the part he played in my salvation that she esteemed him; and he for his part held her in like esteem for her deeply religious way of life. Her spiritual fervor[13] prompted her to assiduous good works[14] and brought her constantly to church; and

---

celebration of the Mass, or it could simply refer to a "funeral meal" in which relatives and friends gathered at a beloved's tomb to pray, eat, and drink. Excesses inevitably arose, and while many bishops sought to turn such feasting into charitable outreach for the poor, who could also come and receive sustenance (i.e., agape meals), many bishops simply condemned the practice. Augustine's own Bishop Aurelius had recently sought to repress such scandal (see Augustine's *Letter* 22, dated between about 391 and 393), and such abuses forced Ambrose to be among the first to condemn the practice (see *On Elias* §62), a censure a North African like Monica would struggle to understand but to which she would eventually assent. Such a practice does indicate how the cult of the relics arose in Christianity, the Church militant always tangibly mindful of the faithfully departed as she gathers on earth to receive the Lord's Body and Blood.

[13] *Her spiritual fervor:* See Romans 12:11.
[14] *prompted her to assiduous good works:* See 1 Timothy 5:10; 6:18.

accordingly when Ambrose saw me he would often burst out in praise of her, telling me how lucky I was to have such a mother. Little did he know what a son she had: I was full of doubts about all these things and scarcely believed it possible to find the way of life.

Chapter 3

Bishop Ambrose

3. Not yet had I begun to pour forth my groans to you in prayer, begging you to help me; rather was my mind intent on search- ing and restlessly eager for argument. Now I regarded Ambrose as a fortunate man as far as worldly standing went, since he enjoyed the respect of powerful people; it was only his celi- bacy which seemed to me a burdensome undertaking. I had not begun to guess, still less experience in my own case, what hope he bore within him, or what a struggle he waged against the temptations to which his eminent position exposed him, or the encouragement he received in times of difficulty, or what exquisite delights he savored in his secret mouth, the mouth of his heart, as he chewed the bread of your word.

Nor was he aware of my spiritual turmoil or the perilous pit before my feet.[15] There were questions I wanted to put to him, but I was unable to do so as fully as I wished, because the crowds of people who came to him on business impeded me, allowing me little opportunity either to talk or to listen to him. He was habitually available to serve them in their needs, and in the very scant time that he was not with them he would be refreshing either his body with necessary food or his mind with reading. When he read his eyes would travel across the pages and his mind would explore the sense, but his voice and tongue were silent.[16] We would sometimes be present, for he

---

[15] *perilous pit before my feet:* See Matthew 15:14.

[16] *habitually available ... voice and tongue were silent:* The three things that initially strike Augustine upon first encountering Ambrose are his (1) celibacy,

did not forbid anyone access, nor was it customary for anyone
to be announced; and on these occasions we watched him reading silently. It was never otherwise, and so we too would sit
for a long time in silence, for who would have the heart to
interrupt a man so engrossed? Then we would steal away, guess-
ing that in the brief time he had seized for the refreshment of
his mind he was resting from the din of other people's affairs
and reluctant to be called away to other business. We thought
too that he might be apprehensive that if he read aloud, and
any closely attentive listener were doubtful on any point, or
the author he was reading used any obscure expressions, he
would have to stop and explain various difficult problems that
might arise, and after spending time on this be unable to read
as much of the book as he wished. Another and perhaps more
cogent reason for his habit of reading silently was his need to
conserve his voice, which was very prone to hoarseness. But
whatever his reason, that man undoubtedly had a good one.

4. This meant, however, that no opportunity at all was given
me to find out what I longed to know from your holy oracle,
Ambrose's heart. At most, I could only put a point to him
briefly, whereas my inner turmoil was at such a feverish pitch
that I needed to find him completely at leisure if I were to
pour it all out, and I never did so find him. Nonetheless I
listened to him *straightforwardly expounding the word of truth*[17]
to the people every Sunday, and as I listened I became more
and more convinced that it was possible to unravel all those

---

(2) habitual availability in serving others, and (3) silent reading. These are certainly all qualities he never encountered in the successful pagan rhetoricians
and leaders he knew who (1) despised celibacy as an enervating futility, (2) would
have looked down upon a man of Ambrose's talents consorting constantly with
the unwashed masses, and (3) read so as to hear the flourish of their own voices
(given how ancient manuscripts did not usually contain spaces between words—
vellum is expensive!—reading silently was also a sign of intelligence and literary
mastery). Notice how all three qualities bespeak an inner strength, now attractive to Augustine, which were once to him empty and nonsensical: Christians
see great strength in the cross of celibacy, in serving the most vulnerable, and in
the still silence of prayerful study.

[17] straightforwardly expounding the word of truth: 2 Timothy 2:15.

cunning knots of calumny in which the sacred books had been entangled by tricksters who had deceived me and others. I came to realize that your spiritual children, whom you had brought to a new birth by grace from their mother, the Catholic Church, did not in fact understand the truth of your creating human beings in your image[18] in so crude a way that they believed you to be determined by the form of a human body. Although I had not even a faint or shadowy notion[19] of what a spiritual substance could be like, I was filled with joy, albeit a shamefaced joy, at the discovery that what I had barked against for so many years was not the Catholic faith but the figments of carnal imagination. I had been all the more foolhardy and impious in my readiness to rant and denounce where I ought to have inquired and sought to learn.

O God, most high, most deep, and yet nearer than all else, most hidden yet intimately present, you are not framed of greater and lesser limbs; you are everywhere, whole and entire in every place, but confined to none. In no sense is our bodily form to be attributed to you, yet you have made us in your own image, and lo! here we are, from head to foot set in our place!

Chapter 4

Augustine finds some enlightenment

5. Since I did not know how your image could exist in us I would, given the chance, have knocked at the door[20] and proposed my question about how the doctrine was to be believed, instead of opposing it with insults as though it had

---

[18] *creating human beings in your image*: See Genesis 1:26–27; 9:6; Sirach 17:1. This is a stellar example of how Catholic preaching helped Augustine overcome the crude anthropomorphism of the Manichees: to be made in God's "image" does not necessarily mean that God has a body, but that at a deeper level we reflect his goodness, love, reason, and personal communion. It was this sense of being able to read allegorically that not only freed Augustine of so many errors but also helped him to see the reasonableness and truth of Christianity.

[19] *faint or shadowy notion*: See 1 Corinthians 13:12.

[20] *knocked at the door*: See Matthew 7:7.

been believed in the absurd way I had assumed. The anxiety which gnawed at my inner self to determine what I could hold onto as certain was the more intense in proportion to my shame at remembering how long I had been deluded and beguiled by assurances that falsehoods were certain, and had in my headstrong, childish error babbled about such very dubious things as though they were proven. Later on it became clear to me that these tenets were false; but at the time I was at least certain of this, that while they were uncertain I had for a time held them to be certain, and had been arguing blindly in the objections I raised against your Catholic Church. I had not yet come to accept her teachings as true, but at least I now knew that she did not teach the doctrines to which I had gravely objected.

Thus it was that I was put to shame and forced to turn about.[21] I rejoiced to find that your one and only Church, the body of your only Son,[22] that Church within which I had been signed with Christ's name in my infancy,[23] did not entertain infantile nonsense or include in her sound teaching any belief that would seem to confine you, the creator of all things, in any place however vast and spacious, in any place that would hem you in on every side after the manner of human bodies.

6. Another thing that brought me joy was that the ancient writings of the law and the prophets were now being offered to me under quite a different aspect from that under which they had seemed to me absurd when I believed that your holy people

---

[21] *put to shame and forced to turn about*: See Psalm 6:10.

[22] *one and only Church . . . your only Son*: See Colossians 1:18, 24.

[23] *Church . . . in my infancy*: Augustine here admits to his being initiated into the catechumenate as a young boy but not baptized, a common practice in fourth-century Africa, as mentioned. At some point in his early years, Monica would have presented him to the local clergy, and a priest would have consecrated the young Augustine for Christ by tracing the sign of the cross on his forehead, prayed over him by the laying on of his hands, and would have had him take a little salt on his tongue, claiming it for pious use, in particular (cf. *Conf.* I.11.17, p. 19). While this ritual would have rendered Augustine a Christian, he was still considered to be "only" a catechumen and thus not a full member of the Church, as baptism is how one is adopted into the Body of Christ (see *Sermon* 301A, *Commentary on John* 11.4).

held such crude opinions; for the fact was that they did not. I delighted to hear Ambrose often asserting in his sermons to the people, as a principle on which he must insist emphatically, *The letter is death-dealing, but the spirit gives life*.[24] This he would tell them as he drew aside the veil of mystery[25] and opened to them the spiritual meaning of passages which, taken literally, would seem to mislead. He said nothing which offended me, even though I still did not know whether what he said was true. In my heart I was hanging back from any assent, dreading a headlong fall, and nearly died by hanging instead. I longed to become as certain of those things I could not see as I was that seven and three make ten. I was not so demented as to think that even this simple truth was beyond comprehension; but I wanted to have the same grasp of other things, both material entities not immediately present to my senses and spiritual realities of which I did not know how to think in any but a materialistic way. The possibility of healing was, ironically, within my reach if only I had been willing to believe, because then I could with a more purified mind have focused my gaze on your truth, which abides for ever[26] and is deficient in nothing. But just as someone who has suffered under a bad physician may often be afraid to entrust himself to a good one, so it was in my soul's case. It could be healed only by believing, yet it shirked the cure for fear of believing what was false. It struggled in your hands,[27] though it is you who have prepared the healing remedies of faith and spread them over the ills of the world, enduing them with marvelous potency.

Chapter 5

7. Against this background, however, I now began to prefer Catholic doctrine. True, some of its propositions were not

---

[24] The letter is death-dealing, but the spirit gives life: 2 Corinthians 3:6.

[25] *veil of mystery*: See 2 Corinthians 3:14–16.

[26] *your truth, which abides for ever*: See Psalm 116(117):2.

[27] *struggled in your hands*: See Daniel 4:32(35). [Notice how Augustine's numbering of David varies from modern editions.]

demonstrated rationally, either because there might be no one present to whom they could be demonstrated or because they were not demonstrable at all; but I came to see that in commanding that certain things must be believed without demonstration the Church was a good deal more moderate and very much less deceitful than those parties who rashly promised knowledge and derided credulity, but then went on to demand belief in a whole host of fabulous and absurd myths which certainly could not be demonstrated.

So it was, Lord, that you began little by little to work on my heart with your most gentle and merciful hand, and dispose it to reflect how innumerable were the things I believed and held to be true, though I had neither seen them nor been present when they happened. How many truths there were of this kind, such as events of world history, or facts about places and cities I had never seen; how many were the statements I believed on the testimony of friends, or physicians, or various other people; and, indeed, unless we did believe them we should be unable to do anything in this life. With what unshakable certainty, moreover, did I hold fast to the belief that I had been born of my particular parents, yet I could not have known this without believing what I had heard.

So you persuaded me that the truly blameworthy people were not those who believed in your scriptures, the scriptures which you had established with such authority throughout almost all nations, but those who refused to believe in them; and it was to these people that I should beware of listening if by chance any of them might challenge me by asking, "How do you know that those books were provided for the human race by the Spirit of the one, real and most truthful God?" [28] It was precisely

---

[28] *How do you know . . . most truthful God?* Canonical development was still an issue in Augustine's earlier years. What books belonged to the Christian scriptures and which did not? By ca. 130 the four Gospels and thirteen letters of Saint Paul were firmly in place, but Saint Athanasius (in his famed festal letter of 367) was the first to provide an exact list of the New Testament canon as we have it today. A Roman council under Pope Damasus in 382 gave a list of both Old and New Testament books, and Augustine himself preached at the Council

this fact that most commended itself to belief, because not one of the slanderous disputes to be found in the works of philosophers who disagreed among themselves, in any of the vast number of books I had read, had ever been able to wrench away from me the belief that you exist, whatever may be your nature (and of this I was ignorant) and that the course of human affairs concerns you.

8. This conviction was sometimes strong in me, sometimes feeble; but I always believed in your existence and your care for us, even though I did not know what to think about your essential nature, or conceive what way could lead me, or lead me back, to you. It was because *we were weak*[29] and unable to find the truth by pure reason that we needed the authority of the sacred scriptures; and so I began to see that you would not have endowed them with such authority among all nations unless you had willed human beings to believe in you and seek you through them.

Having already heard many parts of the sacred books explained in a reasonable and acceptable way, I came to regard those passages which had previously struck me as absurd, and therefore repelled me, as holy and profound mysteries. The authority of the sacred writings seemed to me all the more deserving of reverence and divine faith in that scripture was easily accessible to every reader, while yet guarding a mysterious dignity in its deeper sense. In plain words and very humble modes of speech it offered itself to everyone, yet stretched the understanding of those who were *not shallow-minded*.[30] It welcomed all comers to its hospitable embrace, yet through narrow openings[31] attracted a few to you—a few, perhaps, but

---

of Hippo in 393, which also approved the canonical list of books as it has since come down to us (in 392 Augustine persuaded Bishop Aurelius to hold a yearly synod and thereby began to revitalize the Church in North Africa).

[29] we were weak: Romans 5:6. Augustine here realizes the inability of human reason alone to discern the two linchpin truths of Christianity: the Trinity (God's "essential nature") and the Incarnation (the "way" that thus "leads back" to God).

[30] not shallow-minded: Sirach 19:4.

[31] *narrow openings*: See Matthew 19:24; cf. Matthew 7:13.

far more than it would have done had it not spoken with such noble authority and drawn the crowds to its embrace by its holy humility.

All the while, Lord, as I pondered these things you stood by me; I sighed and you heard me; I was tossed to and fro and you steered me aright. I wandered down the wide road of the world, but you did not desert me.

Chapter 6

Hollowness of his secular ambitions; the drunken beggar

9. I was hankering after honors, wealth and marriage, but you were laughing at me.[32] Very bitter were the frustrations I endured in chasing my desires, but all the greater was your kindness in being less and less prepared to let anything other than yourself grow sweet to me. Look at my heart, Lord, you who have willed me to remember this and confess to you. You freed my soul from the close-clinging, sticky morass of death; let it now cling to you.[33] How wretched it was! You probed its wound to the raw, to persuade it to leave all else behind[34] and be converted to you[35] who are above all things,[36] without whom nothing whatever would exist—be converted to you and find healing.[37]

I recall how miserable I was, and how one day you brought me to a realization of my miserable state.[38] I was preparing to

---

[32] *you were laughing at me*: See Psalm 2:4; 36(37):13.

[33] *cling to you*: See Psalm 62:9(63:8); 72(73):28.

[34] *leave all else behind*: See Luke 5:11, 28.

[35] *be converted to you*: See Psalm 21:28(22:27); 50:15(51:13).

[36] *who are above all things*: See Romans 9:5.

[37] *be converted to you and find healing*: See Isaiah 6:10; Matthew 13:15.

[38] *I recall ... miserable state*: Recounted here is most probably a panegyric Augustine delivered for Valentinian II and the Milanese court in November 384. These periodic encomiums aimed at flattering the emperor and swaying public opinion to wherever the emperor wanted it. The sad irony, Augustine realizes, is that for the imperial rhetorician, such an event should be the highlight of his career, but he never felt more alone and disgusted with himself.

deliver a eulogy upon the emperor in which I would tell plenty of lies with the object of winning favor with the well-informed by my lying; so my heart was panting with anxiety and seething with feverish, corruptive thoughts. As I passed through a certain district in Milan I noticed a poor beggar, drunk, as I believe, and making merry. I groaned and pointed out to the friends who were with me how many hardships our idiotic enterprises entailed. Goaded by greed, I was dragging my load of unhappiness along, and feeling it all the heavier for being dragged. Yet while all our efforts were directed solely to the attainment of unclouded joy, it appeared that this beggar had already beaten us to the goal, a goal which we would perhaps never reach ourselves. With the help of the few paltry coins he had collected by begging this man was enjoying the temporal happiness for which I strove by so bitter, devious and roundabout a contrivance. His joy was no true joy, to be sure, but what I was seeking in my ambition was a joy far more unreal; and he was undeniably happy while I was full of foreboding; he was carefree, I apprehensive. If anyone had questioned me as to whether I would rather be exhilarated or afraid, I would of course have replied, "Exhilarated"; but if the questioner had pressed me further, asking whether I preferred to be like the beggar, or to be as I was then, I would have chosen to be myself, laden with anxieties and fears. Surely that would have been no right choice, but a perverse one? I could not have preferred my condition to his on the grounds that I was better educated, because that fact was not for me a source of joy but only the means by which I sought to curry favor with human beings: I was not aiming to teach them but only to win their favor;[39] and this was why you broke my bones[40] with the rod of your discipline.[41]

---

[39] *I noticed a poor beggar, drunk . . . to win their favor*: This chance encounter with the drunken beggar sends Augustine into deep recollection. Every human person by nature desires to be happy, and in very strong and visceral language, Augustine points us back to his restless heart: at least the drunken beggar has found some momentary lapses of rest, however transient and artificial. Furthermore, while still having something to look forward to, at least the inebriate knew

10. I have no patience with anyone who would say to my soul, "But it makes a difference what a person is happy about; that beggar was enjoying his intoxication, you longed to bask in glory." What kind of glory was that, Lord? No glory that was to be found in you;[42] for just as his was no true joy, so mine was no true glory, and it turned my head more fatally. He would sleep off his intoxication that same night, whereas I had slept with mine and risen up again, and would sleep and rise with it again ... how many days! I know that it does indeed make a difference what one is joyful about, and the joy of faithful hope is incomparably distant from that empty enjoyment; but even as things were then there was a vast distance between us: he was the happier, not only inasmuch as he was flooded with merriment while I was torn with cares, but also because he had earned his wine by wishing good-day to passers-by, while I was seeking a swollen reputation by lying.

I spoke fully to my friends on these lines, and often in similar circumstances took stock of my reactions. It grieved me that I should be like this, and I took it badly, and this in itself increased my grief. If some good fortune did smile upon me, I felt it not worthwhile to seize it, because almost before I had hold of it, away it would fly.

Chapter 7

Alypius

11. Those of us who lived as friends together sighed deeply over these experiences, and I discussed them most especially

---

his drunken state was not the goal of all human living; Augustine, on the other hand, had spent years deceiving himself that joy could be found in material success and imperial glory. Yet here he is at the height of his career with nothing by which to escape his wretchedness. That being said, he does confess to not wanting such a life of drunken degradation but seems hard-pressed to admit why.

[40] *you broke my bones*: See Psalm 52:6(53:5).

[41] *rod of your discipline*: See Psalm 22(23):4.

[42] *No glory that was to be found in you*: See 1 Corinthians 1:31.

and intimately with Alypius and Nebridius.[43] Alypius and I
had been born in the same town, where his parents were leading citizens. He was younger than I, and had been among my
students when I began to teach in our town. He studied under
me again at Carthage and held me in high esteem, because I
seemed to him good and learned, while I for my part was fond
of him on account of his great nobility of character, which
was unmistakable even before he reached mature years. However, the whirlpool of Carthaginian immoral amusements sucked
him in; it was aboil with frivolous shows, and he was ensnared
in the madness of the circuses. At the time when he was being
wretchedly tossed about in it, I as a professor of rhetoric had
opened a school and was teaching publicly, but he did not
attend my courses on account of a quarrel which had arisen
between me and his father. I had discovered that he loved the
circuses with a passion likely to be his undoing, and I was
extremely anxious because he seemed to me bent on wasting
his excellent promise, if indeed he had not already done so. I
had, however, no opportunity to restrain him by any kind of
pressure, either out of goodwill as a friend or by right as his
teacher, for I presumed that his attitude to me was the same as
his father's, though in fact he was not like that. Accordingly
he disregarded his father's wishes and took to greeting me when
we met; he also began to frequent my lecture hall, where he
would listen awhile, then go away.

12. I did not tackle him about his reckless addiction to worthless shows, or attempt to save him from ruining his fine intelligence on them, because it slipped my memory; but you, Lord,
guide the courses of all your creatures, and you had not forgotten

[43] *Alypius and Nebridius*: We already met Nebridius (see *Conf.* IV.3.6, pp. 78–
79) and are now introduced to his very dear friend Alypius, truly Augustine's
"other self". Also born in Thagaste, a student of Augustine's, an aficionado of
the less than edifying theater, he likewise became a Manichee, was then baptized with Augustine in Milan, and then eventually elected Bishop of Thagaste
in the spring of 395. A stalwart and significant contributor to ecclesiastical affairs
in North Africa, Alypius' last diplomatic journey to Rome can be placed in 427–
428, but we are unsure when he died thereafter.

this man who one day would be set over your children as dispenser of your mysteries. You brought about his correction through my agency, but without my knowledge, so that it might be clearly recognized as your work. One day when I was sitting in my usual place with my students around me he came, greeted me, sat down and applied his mind to the subject we were studying. I chanced to have a text in my hands, and while I was expounding it an apt comparison with the circuses occurred to me, which would drive home the point I was making more humorously and tellingly through caustic mockery of people enslaved by that craze. You know, our God, that I did not think at the time about curing Alypius of this bane. Yet he took my illustration to himself, believing that I had used it solely on his account; and what another person might have regarded as a reason for being angry with me this honest young man regarded rather as a reason for being angry with himself and loving me more ardently. Long ago you had told us, weaving the advice into your scriptures, *Offer correction to a wise man, and he will love you for it.* Yet I had not corrected him myself. You make use of all of us, witting or unwitting, for just purposes known to you, and you made my heart and tongue into burning coals with which to cauterize a promising mind that was wasting away, and heal it.[44]

If anyone is insensitive to your merciful dealings, let such a person silently withhold your praise, but from the marrow of my being those same dealings cry out in confession to you;[45] for after hearing my words he wrenched himself away from that pit in which he had been willfully sinking, and finding incredible pleasure in his blindness. With a strong resolve of temperance he shook his mind free, and all the filth of the circuses dropped away from him. Never again did he go there. Then he overcame his father's opposition to his taking me for his teacher; his father gave in and gave him leave.

[44] *burning coals . . . heal it*: See Psalm 139:11(140:10).
[45] *If anyone is insensitive to your merciful dealings . . . cry out in confession to you*: See Psalm 106(107):8.

Once he had begun to study with me again, he became entangled in the same superstition as I, for he loved the display of continence put up by the Manichees, believing it to be real and authentic. In fact it was insane and seductive. It captivated precious souls[46] who were still too ignorant to penetrate the depth of virtue and liable to be deceived by the superficial appearance of a virtue that was but feigned and faked.

Chapter 8

13. He had been drawn toward a worldly course by his parents' siren song, and he was unwilling to abandon it, so he had gone to Rome ahead of me to study law, and there he was assailed by an entirely unexpected craving for gladiatorial entertainments. This came about in a way no one could have foreseen. He shunned such displays and loathed them; but some of his friends and fellow-students, returning from their midday meal, happened to find the stadium open to them and, as is the way with close friends, drew him in by force, despite his vehement protests and struggles. It was one of the days for cruel and murderous sport, and he kept telling them, "You may drag my body into that place and fix me there, but can you direct my mind and my eyes to the show? I will be there, and yet be absent, and so get the better both of you and of the performance."[47] They heard what he said but took him along with them all the same, wishing perhaps to know if he could make good his claim. When they arrived and settled themselves

---

[46] *captivated precious souls*: See Proverbs 6:26.

[47] *You may drag my body . . . and so get the better of you and of the performances*: This tension between body and soul receives different interpretations and uses throughout Augustine's life, especially here in the *Confessions*: at this point in Augustine's narrative, body and soul wage war against each other, the soul aiming to remain aloof from the massacres of the games, with the body content to remain mired in the chaos and gore. This hostile dualism is reminiscent of Augustine's Manichean phase: body and soul are enemies, the virtuous moral agent (Alypius' soul) is depicted as above the reprobate body, which consents to the bloodshed, and the minority (Alypius) finds itself pitted against larger society (Alypius' friends). This is precisely how the Manichees saw themselves and the world.

in what seats they could find, the whole place was heaving with thoroughly brutal pleasure. He kept the gateways of his eyes closed, forbidding his mind to go out that way to such evils. If only he could have stopped his ears too! At a certain tense moment in the fight a huge roar from the entire crowd beat upon him. He was overwhelmed by curiosity, and on the excuse that he would be prepared to condemn and rise above whatever was happening even if he saw it, he opened his eyes, and suffered a more grievous wound in his soul than the gladiator he wished to see had received in the body.[48] He fell more dreadfully than the other man whose fall had evoked the shouting; for by entering his ears and persuading his eyes to open the noise effected a breach through which his mind—a mind rash rather than strong, and all the weaker for presuming to trust in itself rather than in you, as it should have done[49]— was struck and brought down. As he saw the blood he gulped the brutality along with it; he did not turn away but fixed his gaze there and drank in the frenzy, not aware of what he was doing, reveling in the wicked contest and intoxicated on sanguinary pleasure. No longer was he the man who had joined the crowd; he was now one of the crowd he had joined, and a genuine companion of those who had led him there. What more need be said? He watched, he shouted, he grew hot with excitement, he carried away with him a madness that lured him back again not only in the company of those by whom he had initially been dragged along but even before them, dragging others.[50]

---

[48] *overwhelmed by curiosity . . . received in the body:* Curiosity is condemned as the vice disallowing true intellectual focus, flitting about with whatever tickles one's mind (cf. *Conf.* III.3.5, note 7, pp. 53–54).

[49] *a mind rash . . . all the weaker for presuming to trust in itself rather than in you:* See Judith 6:15. [See Judith 6:19 in modern editions, noting again how the numbering in Augustine's edition of Judith differs.]

[50] *company of those . . . dragging others:* A very strong theme throughout the *Confessions* is the importance of friendship in forming one's moral character. Augustine knew well how neither vice nor virtue is fostered in isolation, but that we all (to some extent) become like those with whom we spend time and in whom we find the deepest desires of our own heart.

Nonetheless you rescued him from his plight with your mighty and most merciful hand, and taught him to rely not on himself but on you;[51] but this was long afterward.

Chapter 9

14. The foregoing episode was stored up in his memory and contributed to his future healing, as also did another. Once when he was still a student and attending my classes at Carthage, he was in the market-place at midday, thinking over the passage he had to declaim, as is customary in scholastic training. You allowed him to be arrested by the temple-guards as a thief; and I think, our God, that you did so for no other reason than to ensure that this youth, who was destined to be such a great man, should learn even at this early stage that in judicial hearings one person ought not to be condemned too easily through the rash gullibility of another.

This is what happened. He was walking up and down alone in front of the lawcourt with his tablets and pen when a certain young student (the real thief) secretly brought an axe and, without Alypius being aware of it, gained access to the leaden gratings over the part of the market assigned to the silversmiths, and began to hack away the lead. The silversmiths below heard the sound of the axe, and softly discussed what to do; then they sent men to arrest anyone they might find. Hearing their voices the thief fled, leaving the axe behind because he was afraid of being caught with it in his possession. But Alypius, who had not seen him go in, observed him come out and take to his heels, and, wishing to know the reason, went into the place, picked up the axe, and stood there holding it, considering the matter in some surprise. The men who had been sent came and found him, alone and holding the very tool which had alerted them by its noise. They seized him and dragged him off, boasting to a crowd of bystanders in the

---

[51] *rely not on himself but on you:* See Proverbs 3:5; Isaiah 57:13.

market-place that they had caught the thief red-handed. Then they led him away to stand trial.[52]

15. But his lesson had gone far enough. You promptly came to the defense of his innocence, O Lord, you who were the sole witness of it.[53] As he was being led off either to imprisonment or to corporal punishment there chanced to meet them a certain architect who had prime responsibility for public buildings. The guards were glad that he in particular should have met them, because they were often suspected by him of having themselves stolen any items which were missing from the market-place, and now they thought that he would at last realize who had committed these thefts. However, this man had frequently seen Alypius at the house of a certain senator whom he used often to visit to pay his respects. He recognized him at once, took him by the hand and drew him aside from the throng, inquiring the reason for this calamity. When he heard what had happened, and heard all the bystanders making a commotion and uttering angry threats, he ordered Alypius to come away with him.

They arrived at the home of the youth who had committed the crime. At the gate was a youngster naive enough to blurt out the whole truth without worrying about the consequences for his master; and he was the slave who had been in attendance on his master in the market-place. Alypius remembered this and told the architect, who showed the axe to the child and asked him whose it was. "Ours," he promptly replied, and on being questioned further revealed the rest of the story.

The case thus shifted to that household, and the crowds who had already begun to jeer at Alypius were balked, while

---

[52] *Once when he was . . . led him away to stand trial*: This third story of Alypius (the first earlier at *Conf.* V.7.11 and his openness to learning; the second in the amphitheatre at *Conf.* VI.8.13) once again provides an insight into his character development, treating his curiosity from another perspective. These stories make more sense within the *Confessions* when we remember they were composed in part to provide Paulinus of Nola a picture of who Alypius was and how he came to prominence in the Church.

[53] *O Lord, you who were the sole witness of it*: See Wisdom 1:6; Jeremiah 29:23.

the man who would one day be the dispenser of your word and the judge of many a case in your Church departed more experienced and better informed.

Chapter 10

16. I had caught up with him in Rome, and since a very strong bond of friendship kept him close to me, he set out for Milan in my company; for he did not want to leave me, and he also hoped to make some use of the legal expertise he had acquired, though this was in response to his parents' wishes rather than his own. Three times already he had acted as assessor, and aroused the amazement of others by his integrity, though for his part he found it still more amazing that they could value gold above honor.[54]

His character was put to the test not only by the lure of covetousness but also by the sting of intimidation. In Rome he served as Assessor to the Chancellor of the Italian Treasury. Now there was at this time a certain very powerful senator who had placed many people under an obligation by his favors, and dominated others by instilling terror. He sought to gain permission for some course of action not permitted by the law, as his influence usually enabled him to do; but Alypius withstood him. A bribe was offered; Alypius laughed heartily. Threats were made, but he spurned them. Everyone marveled at the rare soul which neither sought to make a friend nor feared to make an enemy of this great man, who was widely famed for the innumerable means at his disposal either to do others a good turn or to harm them. The judge to whom Alypius stood as counsel had himself no wish to grant the petition but dared not openly refuse; he therefore

[54] *acted as assessor . . . value gold above honor*: This story obviously wants to show us the progress Alypius has made in withstanding temptation. Since a part of Alypius' job as assessor of the Roman Treasury was to assist in overseeing all forms of government finances, and as Augustine notes, his mettle in not taking bribes or colluding in financial improprieties made him stand out, misunderstood to all those on the proverbial take.

threw the responsibility for the decision onto Alypius, alleg-
ing that he was prevented by his counsel from granting the
request, though the truth was that if he had done so Alypius
would have left the court.

Almost the only source of temptation for him lay in literary
studies, for he had the opportunity to have books copied for
his own use at palace prices; but after considering the claims
of justice he changed his mind for the better, judging that equity,
which forbade him so to act, had more to recommend it than
the privilege of office, which enabled him to. This was a tri-
fling matter, but anyone who is trustworthy in a small thing is
trustworthy in a great one too, and that saying uttered by your
Truth can never be without force: *If you have not proved trustworthy over dishonest money, who will give you what is real? And
if you have not been trustworthy over what belongs to another,
who will give you any of your own?*[55]

This is what he was like, this man so closely united with
me, the friend who concurred with me as we debated the right
way to live.

Nebridius

17. Nebridius[56] too shared our aspirations and was tossed to
and fro along with us, for he was an ardent fellow-seeker of
the happy life and an exceedingly keen researcher into the
most difficult questions. He had left behind his home terri-
tory near Carthage, left Carthage itself where he had spent
most of his time, left his father's fine estate,[57] his home and
his mother (who did not attempt to follow him), and come
to Milan for no other purpose than to live with me and share
in our fiercely burning zeal for truth and wisdom. So then
there were three gaping mouths, three individuals in need,

[55] *If you have not proved ... any of your own?* Luke 16:11–12.
[56] *Nebridius*: We met Nebridius earlier (see *Conf.* IV.3.6, note 6, pp. 78–79).
Of all Augustine's friends, Nebridius was the most urbane and well-off, most
often referred to as *dulcis*, Augustine's sweet companion.
[57] *left behind his home ... his father's fine estate*: See Matthew 19:29.

gasping out their hunger to one another and looking to you to give them their food in due time.[58] By your merciful providence our worldly behavior always brought bitter disappointments, but whenever we sought to discern the reason why we should suffer them, we met with only darkness. So we would turn away, moaning, "How long are we to go on like this?" We were perpetually asking this question, but even as we asked it we made no attempt to change our ways, because we had no light to see what we should grasp instead, if we were to let go of them.

Chapter 11

Perplexities and plans: philosophy and the problem of continence

18. For my own part I was reflecting with anxiety and some perplexity how much time had elapsed since my nineteenth year, when I had first been fired with passion for the pursuit of wisdom, resolving that once I had found it I would leave behind all empty hopes and vain desires and the follies that deluded me.[59] Yet here I was in my thirtieth year sticking fast in the same muddy bog through my craving to enjoy the good things of the present moment, which eluded and dissipated me. "Tomorrow," I had been saying to myself, "tomorrow I will find it; it will appear plainly and I will grasp it. . . .

"Faustus will be coming and he will explain everything. . . .

"Fine fellows, you Academics! So nothing that we need for living our lives can be known with certainty? Nonsense! Let us seek energetically and not give up hope. The passages which used to seem ridiculous in the Church's holy books are not so ridiculous after all, but can be understood in a different and quite acceptable way. I will plant my feet on that step where my parents put me as a child, until self-evident truth comes to light.

---

[58] *give them their food in due time*: See Psalm 103(104):27; 144(145):15.
[59] *the pursuit of wisdom . . . and the follies that deluded me*: See Psalm 39:5(40:4).

"But where is it to be sought? When, even? Ambrose is not available and we have no time to read. Where are we even to look for the right books? Where and when are we to buy them? From whom borrow them?[60]

"Let us plan our day and reserve definite periods of time in the interest of our souls' salvation. A great hope has dawned, for the Catholic faith does not teach what we thought it did when we found fault with it in our vanity; its learned exponents reject as impious any suggestion that God is confined within the shape of a human body. Can we, then, hesitate to knock[61] where other truths may be opened? Our pupils occupy our morning hours, but what are we doing with the rest? Why do we not get on with it?

"Ah, but in that case, when are we to pay court to our important friends, whose patronage we need? When prepare the lessons we sell to our students? When refresh ourselves and relax our minds from concentrating on these problems?

19. "Devil take the lot of them; let us get rid of all these empty, meaningless occupations and devote ourselves solely to the quest for truth. Life is a wretched business and death unpredictable; suppose it takes us by surprise: in what condition shall we depart? Where shall we then have the chance to learn what we have neglected here? Shall we not rather suffer punishment for our negligence?

"But what if death cuts off all anxious searching, along with the power of thought itself, and puts an end to it all? Perhaps we should consider that?

"No, perish the thought! It cannot be so. It is not meaningless, not without purpose, that the eminent and lofty authority of the Christian faith is spread throughout the world.[62] Such

---

[60] *Faustus will be coming . . . borrow them:* Cryptically and cogently are all the stages of Augustine's conversion chronicled: "Faustus" the Manichee, the "Academics", and his study of philosophy, and, finally, "Ambrose" and his final embrace of the Christian faith.

[61] *knock:* See Matthew 7:7–8.

[62] *authority . . . throughout the world:* Such universality for Augustine is a sign that the Catholic Church is the one true Church. It is fitting that the mystical

great and wonderful provision would not have been made for us from above if bodily death meant the destruction of the soul's life as well. Why are we so slow, then, to abandon worldly ambition and apply ourselves singlemindedly to the search for God and a life of happiness?[63]

"Wait a little, for those things are very pleasant too; they hold no slight sweetness. We should not be too ready to shrug them off, for to return to them later would be ignoble. Consider what a fine thing it is for a person to win a reputation. What prize could be more desirable? We have plenty of influential friends: without setting our sights unduly high, one may expect at least a governorship to come one's way. And one might marry a wife who is reasonably well off, and so will not be a heavy expense, and let this be the limit of one's ambitions. Many great men have been dedicated to the pursuit of wisdom in company with their wives, and one would do well to imitate them."

20. All the while, as I talked to myself like this and the wind blew now from this quarter, now from that, hurling my heart hither and thither, time was slipping by. I put off being *converted to the Lord* and from day to day[64] pushed away from me the day when I would live in you, though I could not

---

extension of Christ's own body on earth not be named after a mere man or a limited geographical locale. In a sermon to his people, the Bishop of Hippo makes this point, playing off the Greek etymology of "Catholic" by stressing this ubiquity: "As a Catholic keeps a firm grip on the whole; *holon*, you see, means whole, and that's why the Church is called Catholic, because it is throughout the whole. Was it ever called *Katamerike*, and not Catholic? *Meros*, you see, means part, *holon* means whole; the Church is called Catholic from a Greek word, meaning 'according to the whole'" (*Sermon* 162A). The Donatist belief that Christ's true Church dwells only in North Africa under their own rules and regulations consumed much of Augustine's pastoral and theological energies.

[63] *abandon worldly ambition . . . life of happiness*: The stirrings of monastic *otium*, true Christian leisure, are already taking root in Augustine's heart. Beginning something similar to a monastic community had been a long-time desire of his, to live with like-minded brethren in the pursuit of study and the attainment of God's own life (*deificari in otio*, "to be deified in leisure", as he wrote to Nebridius in 389; see *Letter* 10.9). We shall soon see the beginnings of such a life in the community at Cassiciacum outside Milan (see *Conf.* IX.3.5, p. 230) as Augustine and companions prepare for baptism.

[64] *I put off being converted . . . from day to day*: See Sirach 5:7.

postpone a daily dying in myself. Though I was so enamored
of a happy life I feared to find it in its true home, and fled
from it even as I sought it. For I thought I would be exceedingly miserable if deprived of a woman's embrace, and gave no
thought to the medicine prepared by your mercy[65] for the healing of this infirmity,[66] since I had no experience of it and
believed that continence must be achieved by one's own
strength, a strength of which I was not conscious in my own
case. I was too stupid to realize that, as scripture testifies,[67] no
one can be continent except by your gift. Yet you would certainly have given me the gift if I had beaten[68] upon your ears
with my inward groans and cast my care upon you[69] with res-
olute faith.

Chapter 12

21. Alypius, however, dissuaded me from taking a wife. He
repeatedly played on the fact that once I had done so it would
be impossible for us to live together in carefree leisure and
devote ourselves to philosophy as we had long desired, and
still desired, to do. With regard to this matter he was himself,
even now as a grown man, thoroughly chaste, indeed remarkably so, perhaps because he had had an initial experience of
sexual intercourse in early adolescence, but had not continued in it; he had been hurt and had felt ashamed, and thereafter lived in complete continence. I opposed his view,
reminding him of the examples of people who, though married, had cultivated wisdom and found favor with God,[70] and

[65] *could not postpone a daily dying in myself . . . your mercy*: At this point Augustine is enamored by the Christian way of life, a life of Christ-like sacrifice and
study in particular, but still does not yet understand that such a life can be lived
only through relying on God's grace and through the indwelling of Jesus' own
life within the sanctified soul.

[66] *healing of this infirmity*: See Psalm 102(103):3; Matthew 4:23.

[67] *I was too stupid . . . as scripture testifies*: See Wisdom 8:21.

[68] *you would certainly have given me the gift if I had beaten*: See Matthew 7:7.

[69] *cast my care upon you*: See Psalm 54:23(55:22).

[70] *found favor with God*: See Hebrews 13:16.

had faithfully kept their friends and loved them dearly. Not that I could myself match their nobility of mind: I was shackled by weakness of the flesh and was dragging along with me a chain forged of deadly sweetness, fearing to be freed from it and beating away his words of sound advice as though from a touchy wound, for that advice was a hand that might have set me free. Worse still, the serpent[71] was speaking through me even to Alypius, attempting to bind him too and using my tongue to scatter sweet snares in his path[72] to trap those honorable, nimble feet.

22. He was in no sense overcome by lust for pleasure like mine; what lured him toward a tentative desire for marriage was curiosity. It came about like this. He looked on with astonishment that I, for whom he had no small regard, was so deeply mired in the sticky morass of sensual pleasure that whenever the subject came up for discussion between us I declared that I was utterly incapable of living a celibate life, and defended myself in the face of his obvious astonishment by pointing out the vast difference between that hasty, furtive experience of his, which by now he scarcely remembered and could therefore easily disdain with no trouble at all, and the delights of my habitual way of life. If only the honorable name of matrimony were conferred upon these pleasures, I told him, he would have no right to be astonished that I felt unable to despise the way I lived. He replied that he was most interested to know what this element was, without which my life, which to him appeared so attractive, would be to me a punishment. His mind, free from that fetter, was amazed at my servitude, and through amazement was drawn toward a hankering to experience it. He might have found his way into the same experience and perhaps have fallen from there into the very servitude which had provoked his amazement, for what he was bent upon was a pact with death,[73] and anyone who

---

[71] *Serpent:* See Genesis 3:1.

[72] *snares in his path:* See Psalm 141:4(142:3).

[73] *pact with death:* See Wisdom 1:16; Isaiah 28:18.

falls in love with danger will fall into it.[74] Neither of us considered, except feebly, what the glory of wedlock could be in terms of guiding the course of a marriage and bringing up children. It was my habitual attempt to sate an insatiable concupiscence that for the most part savagely tormented me and held me captive, while for him it was wonder that dragged him along toward captivity.[75]

Such was our condition until you, O Most High, who forsake not our clay,[76] mercifully came to aid our misery in marvelous, hidden ways.

Chapter 13

Projected marriage

23. Insistent pressure was on me to marry a wife. Already I was asking for it myself, and a marriage was being arranged for me, thanks especially to my mother's efforts. She expected to see me washed in the saving waters of baptism after marriage, and she rejoiced to see me being daily shaped toward this end, observing that her prayers were beginning to be answered and your promises with regard to my faith fulfilled. In the light of my request and her own desire she besought you daily, with powerful, heartfelt cry, to show her in a vision something of my future marriage; but you never consented. She did have some illusory, fantastic dreams, brought on by the activity of her own human spirit as she busied herself about this matter, and these she related to me, but without the confidence she usually showed when you revealed something to her: to these dreams she attached little importance. She

---

[74] *anyone who falls in love with danger will fall into it*: See Sirach 3:27.

[75] *captivity*: Sensitive to how the Enemy works on individuals, Augustine realizes that his "captivity" is not Alypius' and that Alypius' is not his. Whereas Augustine is quite honest in admitting how he is allured by the sins of the flesh, Alypius is instead enticed by a curiosity that knows no bounds, precisely what the Beloved was warning against in 1 John 2:16.

[76] *our clay*: See Genesis 2:7.

claimed that by something akin to the sense of taste, a faculty she could not explain in words, she was able to distinguish between your revelations to her and the fantasies of her own dreaming soul.

All the same, the pressure on me was kept up, and an offer for a certain girl was made on my behalf; but she was about two years below marriageable age. I liked her, though, so we decided to wait.[77]

Chapter 14

Dream of an ideal community

24. Many of my friends and I were greatly exercised in mind as we talked together and shared our loathing of the annoying upheavals inseparable from human life; and we almost made up our minds to live a life of leisure, far removed from the crowds. We would set up this place of leisurely retirement in such a way that any possessions we might have would be made available to the community and we would pool our resources in a single fund. The sincerity of our friendship should ensure that this thing should not belong to one person and that to another: there would be one single property formed out of many; the whole would belong to each of us, and all things would belong to all. It seemed to us that about ten people would be able to live like this in the same community and that there would be some exceptionally rich men among us, particularly our fellow-townsman Romanianus; he had been very well known to me since childhood and had now been drawn to the

---

[77] *two years below marriageable age*: We know from the *Code of Justinian* (I.22), a codex of civil laws composed during 529–534, that the marriageable age of girls was set then at twelve years old. This young girl may therefore have been only ten years old, but while we do not know the age of this young bride-to-be, obviously the ways of ancient Rome are not ours today (as Augustine was here thirty-one years old). We do know, however, that it was social snobbery and Monica's insistence that Augustine would move up the social ladder only if he married a girl of the proper classes, an heiress who could introduce the promising rhetorician into the upper echelons of the empire.

court by the serious complexities of his business affairs.[78] He was the most enthusiastic of all for this project, and his persuasion carried special weight inasmuch as he was far more wealthy than the rest. We agreed that two of us should be appointed as officials each year to see to necessary provisions, so that the others could be undisturbed.

But some of us were already married and others hoped to be, and as soon as we began to consider whether our womenfolk would consent to these arrangements the whole elaborate plan fell apart, came to pieces in our hands and had to be discarded. The sequel was sighs and groans and the redirection of our steps into the broad paths of the world,[79] because though our hearts were full of schemes, your design lasts for ever.[80] In the light of that design of yours you laughed at our plans while preparing your own, for you meant to give us our food in due time; you were to open your hand and fill our souls with your blessing.[81]

Chapter 15

Dismissal of Augustine's common-law wife; his grief

25. Meanwhile my sins were multiplying, for the woman with whom I had been cohabiting was ripped from my side, being regarded as an obstacle to my marriage. So deeply was she engrafted into my heart that it was left torn and wounded and trailing blood.[82] She had returned to Africa, vowing to you

[78] *Romanianus . . . business affairs*: Romanianus of Thagaste was the benefactor of Augustine and not only assisted him in financial matters, paying for his schooling in Carthage, but was also there to console Augustine when his father, Patricius, dies (see *Against the Skeptics* 2.2.3). To convert him from Manichaeism, Augustine dedicated his *On True Religion* to him, introduced him to Paulinus of Nola (see *Letter* 27.4), and invited him into his close circle of study. Romanianus was baptized in 396 and seems to be living still after 408, but this is almost all the biographical information we have for him.

[79] *broad paths of the world*: See Matthew 7:13.

[80] *your design lasts for ever*: See Proverbs 19:21; Psalm 32(33):11.

[81] *open your hand and fill our souls with your blessing*: See Psalm 144(145):15–16.

[82] *So deeply was she engrafted . . . wounded and trailing blood*: If ever there is doubt whether Augustine loved the mother of his son, let these lines be proof

that she would never give herself to another man, and the son
I had fathered by her was left with me. But I was too unhappy
to follow a woman's example: I faced two years of waiting before
I could marry the girl to whom I was betrothed, and I chafed
at the delay, for I was no lover of marriage but the slave of
lust. So I got myself another woman, in no sense a wife, that
my soul's malady might be sustained in its pristine vigor or
even aggravated, as it was conducted under the escort of inveterate custom into the realm of matrimony.[83]

The wound inflicted on me by the earlier separation did
not heal either. After the fever and the immediate acute pain
had dulled, it putrefied, and the pain became a cold despair.

Chapter 16

26. Praise be to you, glory be to you,[84] O fount of all mercy!
As I grew more and more miserable, you were drawing nearer.
Already your right hand was ready to seize me and pull me
out of the filth, yet I did not know it. The only thing that
restrained me from being sucked still deeper into the whirlpool of carnal lusts was the fear of death and of your future
judgment, which throughout all the swings of opinion had never
been dislodged from my heart. With my friends Alypius and
Nebridius I argued about the fate of the good and the wicked:

---

that he was devastated when she departed. This, of course, does not exculpate
his selfish decision to send her away, a choice he may have regretted his entire
life, but such "upward mobility" at the cost of others as collateral damage along
the way was, again, a despicable part of Roman aristocratic life.

   [83] *got myself another woman . . . custom into the realm of matrimony:* Again, this
is evidence that Rome's ways are not ours today, as in the eyes of most of his
contemporaries, it would have been commendable of Augustine to take a woman
if even as the object of his sexual outlet; he is obviously still far from understanding the transformative nature of the fullness of the Christian life. Yet even
devout Christians struggled to understand this, as the seventeenth canon of the
First Council of Toledo in the year 400, while forbidding a married man to take
a concubine, does allow unmarried men to do so in good conscience. Common
law marriages, as Augustine himself enjoyed for fourteen years, were the norm
for centuries, a practice and life that was not converted overnight.

   [84] *Praise be to you, glory be to you:* See 1 Chronicles 29:11–12.

I maintained that, as I saw it, Epicurus would have won the debate had I not believed that after death life remains for the soul, and so do the consequences of our moral actions; this Epicurus refused to believe.[85] I posed this question: if we were immortal, and lived in a state of perpetual bodily pleasure without any fear of losing it, why should we not be happy? Would there be anything else to seek? I did not know that it was symptomatic of my vast misery that I had sunk so low, and was so blind, as to be incapable of even conceiving the light of a goodness, a beauty, which deserved to be embraced for its own sake, which the bodily eye sees not, though it is seen by the spirit within. Nor did I in my wretchedness consider what stream it was whence flowed to me the power to discuss even these distasteful things with my friends and still find sweetness in our talk, or whence came my inability to be happy, even in the sense in which I then understood happiness, without my friends, however lavishly supplied I might be with carnal luxuries. I loved these friends for their own sake, and felt myself loved by them for mine.

Oh, how tortuous were those paths! Woe betide the soul which supposes it will find something better if it forsakes you! Toss and turn as we may, now on our back, now side, now belly—our bed is hard at every point, for you alone are our rest. But lo! Here you are;[86] you rescue us from our wretched meanderings and establish us on your way;[87] you console us and bid us, "Run:[88] I will carry you, I will lead you and I will bring you home."[89]

---

[85] *Epicurus refused to believe:* Epicurus (ca. 340–270 B.C.), the eponymous founder of Epicureanism, argued that the soul perished along with the body. Enjoyment of this world is all that mattered, and we should therefore quit fearing the gods and goddesses, do not think about death, and (ironically, as opposed to how Epicureanism has come down to us) limit our desires to the basics so as not to be disappointed by the paucity of this world.

[86] *Here you are:* See Psalm 138(139):8.

[87] *establish us on your way:* See Psalm 31(32):8; 85(86):11.

[88] *Run:* See 1 Corinthians 9:24.

[89] *I will carry you . . . bring you home:* See Isaiah 46:4. Augustine is finally beginning to understand the power of grace, as he understands that while he may need to prepare himself to run, it is the Lord who will carry him home.

Book VII

Neo-Platonism Frees Augustine's Mind

Chapter 1

1. By now my misspent, impious adolescence was dead, and I was entering the period of youth, but as I advanced in age I sank ignobly into foolishness, for I was unable to grasp the idea of substance except as something we can see with our bodily eyes. I was no longer representing you to myself in the shape of a human body, O God, for since beginning to acquire some inkling of philosophy I always shunned this illusion, and now I was rejoicing to find a different view in the belief of our spiritual mother, your Catholic Church.[1] Yet no alternative way of thinking about you had occurred to me; and here was I, a mere human, and a sinful one at that, striving to comprehend you, the supreme, sole, true God.[2]

Materialistic notions of God insufficient

From the core of my being I believed you to be imperishable, inviolable and unchangeable, because although I did not understand why or how this could be, I saw quite plainly and with full conviction that anything perishable is inferior to what is imperishable, and I unhesitatingly reckoned the inviolable higher than anything subject to violation, and what is constant and

[1] *By now . . . your Catholic Church*: Although Augustine is now free of crudely imaging God as one of his bodily creatures, he still cannot conceive of an immaterial order of reality. He similarly admits that his true mother is the Church, and this optimistic opening of Book VII sets us on a path of the final integration of theology and philosophy, of faith and reason, in Augustine's spiritual sojourn.

[2] *supreme, sole, true God*: See John 17:3.

unchanging better than what can be changed.[3] My heart cried out in vehement protest against all the phantom shapes that thronged my imagination, and I strove with this single weapon to beat away from the gaze of my mind the cloud of filth that hovered round me, but hardly had I got rid of it than in another twinkling of an eye[4] it was back again, clotted together, invading and clogging my vision, so that even though I was no longer hampered by the image of a human body, I was still forced to imagine something corporeal spread out in space, whether infused into the world or even diffused through the infinity outside it. This was still the case even though I recognized that this substance was imperishable, inviolable and immutable (necessarily so, being superior to anything perishable, subject to violation or changeable); because anything to which I must deny these spatial dimensions seemed to me to be nothing at all, absolutely nothing, not even a void such as might be left if every kind of body—earthly, watery, aerial or heavenly—were removed from it, for though such a place would be a nothingness, it would still have the quality of space.

2. Whatever was not stretched out in space, or diffused or compacted or inflated or possessed of some such qualities, or at least capable of possessing them, I judged to be nothing at all. Yet in so thinking I was gross of heart[5] and not even luminous to myself; for as my eyes were accustomed to roam among material forms, so did my mind among the images of them, yet I could not see that this very act of perception, whereby I formed those images, was different from them in kind. Yet my mind would never have been able to form them unless it was itself a reality, and a great one.

---

[3] constant and unchanging . . . can be changed: For Plato, to be real is to be immutable: something has reality, worth, or value only insofar as it refuses change. Therefore, one can never know mutable things, because they are in constant flux; only truly unchanging reality is ultimately real and alone knowable (as opposed to mere "opinion", which Plato does say one can have with regard to material things).

[4] twinkling of an eye: See 1 Corinthians 15:52.

[5] gross of heart: See Matthew 13:15; Acts 28:27.

Hence I thought that even you, Life of my life, were a vast reality spread throughout space in every direction: I thought that you penetrated the whole mass of the earth and the immense, unbounded spaces beyond it on all sides, that earth, sky and all things were full of you, and that they found their limits in you, while you yourself had no limit anywhere. Since material air—I mean the atmosphere above the earth—posed no barrier to the sun's light, which was able to penetrate and pass through it, filling it entirely without bursting it apart or tearing it, I assumed that not only the material sky, air and sea, but even the material earth, were similarly traversable by you, penetrable and open in all their greatest and tiniest parts to your presence, which secretly breathes through them within and without, controlling all that you have made.

I held this view only because I was unable to think in any other way; it was false, because on that showing a larger part of the earth would contain a larger portion of you, and a smaller a lesser portion, and all things would be full of you in such a way that an elephant's body would contain a larger amount of you than a sparrow's, because it is bigger and takes up more space. You would be distributed piecemeal throughout the elements of the world, with greater parts of yourself present where there is plenty of room, and smaller parts in more cramped places. Obviously this is not the case. You had not yet illumined my darkness.[6]

Chapter 2

3. I had a sufficient argument, Lord, against those self-deceived deceivers who, though so talkative, were dumb because your word did not sound forth from them. Yes, I had a sufficient argument, one which Nebridius had been wont to propose ever since our days in Carthage, which left us all shaken who heard it. Those so-called powers of darkness, whom they always postulate as a horde deployed in opposition to you: what would

---

[6] *illumined my darkness*: See Psalm 17:29(18:28).

they have done to you if you had refused to fight? If the reply is that they could have inflicted some injury on you, it would imply that you are subject to violation and therefore destructible. If, on the other hand, it is denied that they had power to injure you, there would have been no point in fighting. Yet the fighting is alleged to have been so intense that some portion of yourself, a limb perhaps, or an offspring of your very substance, became entangled with hostile powers and with the natures of beings not created by you, and was by them so far corrupted and changed for the worse that its beatitude was turned to misery, and it could be rescued and purified only with help; and this portion is supposed to be the soul, enslaved, defiled, corrupt, and in need of aid from your Word, which must necessarily be free, pure and unscathed if it is to help, and yet, since it is of the same nature as the soul, must be equally corrupt itself!

It follows that if they admitted that, whatever you are, you are incorruptible (your substance, that is, by which you exist), this whole rigmarole would be shown up as untrue and to be rejected with loathing; but if they alleged that you are corruptible, their position would already be false and no sooner stated than to be condemned. The foregoing argument was therefore quite sufficient, and I ought to have squeezed these people from my gullet and vomited them out, for no escape was left them from the horrible sacrilege of heart and tongue they were committing by thinking and speaking of you in this fashion.

Chapter 3

The problem of evil

4. I declared and firmly believed that you, our God, our true God, who made not only our souls but our bodies too, and not only our souls and bodies but people everywhere and all things, are subject to no defilement or alteration, and are in all respects unchangeable; yet even so I was still convinced

that the cause of evil had not been clarified or disentangled.[7] Nonetheless I saw that, whatever it might be, I must beware of looking for it in such a way as to be forced into believing that the immutable God was changeable, lest I become myself the very thing I was trying to trace. Accordingly I conducted my search without anxiety, certain that those whom I now wholeheartedly shunned were not speaking the truth, because I saw that through their inquiry into the origin of evil they had waxed full of malice,[8] more ready to claim that your substance was vulnerable to evil than that their own perpetrated it.

5. I strained to see for myself the truth of an explanation I had heard: that the cause of evil is the free decision of our will, in consequence of which we act wrongly and suffer your righteous judgment; but I could not see it clearly. I struggled to raise my mental gaze from the depths, but sank back again; I strove repeatedly, but again and again sank back. I was as sure of having a will as I was of being alive, and this it was that lifted me into your light. When I wanted something, or did not want it, I was absolutely certain that no one else but I was wanting or not wanting it, and I was beginning to perceive that the root of my sin lay there. Any involuntary act I regarded as something I suffered rather than as something I did, and I judged it to be a penalty rather than a fault, being quick to acknowledge that I was not unjustly punished in this way, since I held you to be just. But then I was forced to ask further, "Who made me? Was it not my God, who is not merely good, but Goodness itself? Whence, then, did I derive this

---

[7] *I declared . . . clarified or disentangled*: See John 17:3. Clearly no longer a Manichee, Augustine has by now come to affirm the goodness of all creation and realizes that the one and same God who creates spiritual realities desires material creation as well, something a dualist could never admit. Yet, given God's simultaneous goodness and power, how do we explain evil in the world? If God were only good but not all-powerful, like the Manichean god, evil is easily accounted for; if God were all-powerful but just a little puckish, again, evil is explained. Augustine, however, knows that neither of these is an option for a Christian, and so the search for the cause and nature of evil continues.

[8] *waxed full of malice*: See Sirach 9:3; Romans 1:29.

ability to will evil and refuse good? Is it in me simply so that I should deserve the punishment I suffer? Who established that ability in me, who planted in me this bitter cutting,[9] when my whole being is from my most sweet God? If the devil is responsible, where did the devil come from? If he was a good angel who was transformed into a devil by his own perverted will, what was the origin of this evil will in him that turned him into a devil, when an angel is made entirely by the supremely good creator?"

I was pushed down again by these thoughts and nearly choked; but never was I sucked into that pit of error where no one confesses to you, because people would rather hold that you suffer evil than that we commit it.

Chapter 4

6. My efforts were directed toward discovering more of the truth, on the basis of the discovery already made that what is indestructible is better than anything liable to be destroyed. Accordingly I confessed that, whatever you might be, you must be indestructible. No intelligence has ever conceived of anything better than you, or ever will, for you are the supreme and all-surpassing good; but since the indestructible is most truly and certainly to be esteemed above what is destructible, as I already knew, it followed that you must be indestructible, because otherwise my mind would have been able to attain something better than my God.

From this point, then, where I saw that the indestructible must be superior to what can be destroyed, I should have begun my inquiry by trying to understand where evil resides: that is, whence springs the corruption to which your nature is totally immune. For corruption can touch our God in no way whatever: neither by will, nor by necessity, nor by any unexpected misfortune. He is God, and what he wishes for himself is good, and he is himself the very nature of goodness, whereas to be

---

[9] *bitter cutting*: See Hebrews 12:15.

corrupted is not good.[10] Nor are you forced unwillingly into anything, because your will is not greater than your power: it could be greater only if you were greater than yourself, for God's will and God's power are identical with God himself. And what unexpected chance can overtake you, who know everything? No nature exists, except because you know it. What need is there to prove at length why that substance which is God cannot be corruptible? If it were, it would not be God.

Chapter 5

7. So I was seeking the origin of evil, but seeking in an evil way, and failing to see the evil inherent in my search itself. I conjured up before my mind's eye[11] the whole of creation: all the things in it that we can see, such as earth and sea and stars and trees and living things that are mortal, and all that we do not see in it, such as the heavenly firmament overhead and all the angels and all its spiritual inhabitants; and my imagination gave form to them also, and arranged them in their due places as though they had been corporeal. And I envisaged your creation as one huge mass in which all were arrayed according to bodily kinds, both those things which were really bodily in nature and the bodies I had myself attributed to spirits. I pictured it as enormous, not of such size as it really was, of course, for that I could not know, but as large as my fancy stretched, yet finite on all sides. I imagined you, Lord, who are infinite in every possible respect, surrounding and penetrating it in its every part, like a sea extending in all directions through immense space, a single unlimited sea which held within itself a sponge as vast as one could imagine but still finite, and the sponge soaked in every fibre of itself by the boundless sea.

[10] *He is God . . . to be corrupted is not good*: This examination of God's nature proves important in solving the problem of evil because Augustine is coming to understand that being and goodness are synonymous: all that exists is good, and whatever evil is, it cannot be said *to be*.

[11] *I conjured up before my mind's eye*: See Psalm 15(16):8.

This was how I pictured your creation filled with your infinite being, and I reflected, "Look, this is God, and these are the things God has created. God is good, and though he is far more wonderful than they in every respect, still he who is good has created them good; see too how he surrounds and pervades them. Where, then, is evil; where does it come from and how did it creep in? What is its root, its seed? Or does it not exist at all? But in that case, why do we fear and avoid something that has no reality? If we say that our fear is meaningless, then the fear itself is undeniably evil, for it goads and tortures our heart to no purpose, and so the evil is all the greater inasmuch as the object of our fear is non-existent, yet we fear all the same. Either the evil we fear exists, or our fear itself is the evil. So where does it come from, if the good God made all things good?[12] He is the greater good, to be sure, the supreme good, and the things he has made are lesser goods; nonetheless creator and creatures are all good. Whence, then, comes evil? Was something bad in the material he used, so that though he formed it and disposed it in order he left in it some element that was not turned to good? But why? Did he lack the power so to convert and change it all that no evil would remain, he who is omnipotent? In any case, why would he have chosen to use it for making things, rather than using this same almighty power to destroy it entirely? Or could it have existed against his will? Or again, if matter was eternal, why did he allow it to exist so long, from infinite ages past, and then at last decide to make things out of it?[13] Or, if he suddenly decided to act, surely he, being almighty, could have acted in such a way that it should cease to be, and he alone should exist, he, the complete, true, supreme, infinite Good? Or, supposing that it was unseemly for him who is good not to

---

[12] *God made all things good*: See Genesis 1:31.

[13] *if matter was eternal . . . make things out of it?* The eternity of matter was a cosmological solution to those ancient philosophers without a doctrine of God's creating out of nothing (*creatio ex-nihil*; cf. *Conf.* XI.5.7, note 38, p. 334), but Augustine here is unwilling to grant matter or evil any independence apart from the divine will, as that would be incompatible with God's omnipotence.

fashion and build something good as well, ought he not to have done away with all the bad material and destroyed it, and himself originated some good matter instead, which he could use to create everything? If he were able to construct good things only with the help of material he had not himself constructed, he would not be omnipotent."

Such thoughts as these was I turning over in my miserable soul, weighed down as it was by the gnawing anxieties that flowed from my fear that death might overtake me before I had found the truth. Faith in your Christ, our Lord and Savior, as I found it in the Catholic Church, still persisted steadfastly in my heart, though it was a faith still in many ways unformed, wavering and at variance with the norm of her teaching. Yet my mind did not abandon it, but drank it in ever more deeply as the days passed.

Chapter 6

He finally rejects astrology

8. It was some time since I had rejected the misleading divinations and impious ravings of astrologers. On this score too let your merciful dealings themselves sing praise to you from the innermost depths of my soul,[14] O my God! In my obstinacy you took care of me by providing me with a friend: you it was, you and no other, for who else calls us back from our every death-dealing error but the Life that cannot die, the Wisdom who enlightens our needy minds but needs no borrowed light itself, the Wisdom who governs the whole world, even to the fluttering leaves on the trees? Obstinately indeed had I struggled against the shrewd old man, Vindicianus,[15] and against Nebridius, a youth of wonderful insight. The former had declared with emphasis, the latter admittedly with more hesitation, but frequently, that the art of foretelling the future is

[14] *sing praise to you . . . depths of my soul*: See Psalm 106(107):8.
[15] *Vindicianus*: See *Conf.* IV.3.5.

bogus, that human guesswork is often lucky, and that when people talk a great deal many truths about future events are likely to be uttered, not because the speakers know but because they stumble upon them by not keeping their mouths shut. So you provided for me a friend who was keen to consult astrologers, but not well versed in their lore. Having sought answers from them out of curiosity, as I have indicated, he already knew a certain amount, which he had heard, he said, from his father. Little did he know how efficacious it was to prove in giving the lie to that superstition.

His name was Firminus.[16] He had been educated in the liberal arts and was a well-spoken man, and since he regarded me as a dear friend he consulted me about certain of his business affairs of which he had high hopes, inquiring how I interpreted his birth horoscope, as they call it. Now I was already inclined toward Nebridius' view of the practice; however, I did not refuse to offer an interpretation or say what came into my mind, doubtful though I was; but I remarked that I was almost persuaded that divination was absurd and meaningless.

Then he told me that his father had been an avid student of books dealing with such matters, and had had a friend who was equally a devotee. As the two men collaborated in research and discussion they became more and more ardently enthusiastic for this nonsense. If even dumb animals in their households were due to produce young, these men would record the exact moments of birth and note the position of the stars at the time, on the pretext of collecting experimental data for what claimed to be a science. Firminus went on to say that he had heard his father tell how, when his mother was pregnant with him, Firminus, a certain slave-girl in the house of his father's friend was expecting a baby at the same time. This fact could not escape the girl's master, who took the utmost care to calculate even the whelping-times of his dogs. So while one man

---

[16] *Firminus*: We later hear of an exchange of letters between the Bishop of Hippo and this Firminus, but nothing between them remains; we only know of Firminus from this discussion on astrology and horoscopes in the *Confessions*.

was observing and counting with meticulous precision the days, hours and smaller fractions of hours in his wife's case, the other was doing the same in respect of his maid-servant.

The two women gave birth simultaneously, forcing them to assign exactly the same horoscope, even in the finest detail, to both babies, the one to his son, the other to his slave. It happened like this. As the women went into labor the two friends sent word to each other to let each know what was happening at the other's house, and held messengers in readiness who would announce to each the birth of the child as soon as it occurred. It was easy for them to arrange for instantaneous announcement, since each was master in his own domain. So, Firminus related, the two sets of messengers were dispatched, and met at a point exactly halfway between the two houses, which meant that neither of the friends could assign a different position of the stars, or record any different moment of time. Yet Firminus was born in easy circumstances among his own relatives, and pursued quite a brilliant career in the world making money and advancing in rank, while that slave-boy went on serving his masters, with no alleviation whatever of the yoke his status imposed on him. Firminus, who knew him, testified to the fact.

9. As soon as I heard this story, which, in view of the narrator's character, I believed, my obstinate resistance was completely overcome and dropped away. I attempted first of all to rescue Firminus himself from his curiosity about the occult by pointing out to him that if, after inspecting his birth horoscope, I had to make a prediction that accorded with the facts, I would have to say that I read in it that his parents were of excellent standing among his kinsfolk, that his family was a noble one in his home town, and that having been born a gentleman he would receive a good education in the liberal arts; whereas if the slave had consulted me about the indications of his birth horoscope—and his had been precisely the same—I would have to say, if my answer was to match reality, that what I saw in it was a family of the lowest class, a servile status, and all the rest of those very different conditions which marked off his

lot from the other man's. The realization that after inspecting the same data I would either have to make divergent predictions in order to give a true answer, or else make the same prediction in the two cases and thereby speak falsely, was to me most certain evidence that when true predictions were offered by diviners who studied horoscopes, such things were the product of luck, not skill; but when false predictions were made, they resulted not from the practitioner's lack of skill, but from his luck letting him down.[17]

10. Approaching the subject from this aspect and pondering these points, I now turned my attention to the case of twins.[18] I hoped to attack and refute and make a laughing-stock of the demented people who make a living by astrology, and I wanted to make sure that none of them would be in a position to retort that either Firminus had lied to me or his father had lied to him. At the birth of twins, then, it usually happens that both are delivered from the womb with only a short interval of time between them; and however great the influence this space of time may be alleged to have in the course of nature, it cannot be measured by human observation and certainly cannot be registered in the charts which an astrologer will later study with a view to making a true forecast. And true it will not be, because anyone who had examined the one same birth horoscope that applied to Esau and Jacob would have been obliged to foretell the same fate for both of them, whereas in fact their destinies were different. The astrologer would therefore have been wrong; or, if he spoke truly and foretold different things for each, he would have done so on the basis of the same data. He could speak the truth only by chance, then, not by skill.

[17] *false predictions . . . luck letting him down:* See *Conf.* IV.3.5, note 14, p. 77, on Vindicianus.

[18] *turned my attention to the case of twins:* Twins amazed Augustine, as their often divergent lives showed how biology and thus "fate" proved nothing. If the trajectory of one's life was determined by the constellations at the time of one's birth, twins should therefore have identical lives, but this is often not the case, evidenced, for example, by the lives of Jacob and Esau.

For in truth it is you, Lord, who are at work, you, the supremely just ruler of the universe, though those who consult astrologers and those who are consulted know it not. By your secret inspiration you make each inquirer hear what befits him, as your unfathomable judgment shall justly assess our souls' secret deserving. Let no human being challenge you, "What is this?" or "Why that?" Let him not ask; no, let him not ask, for he is but human.

Chapter 7

Still searching

11. So it was that you, my helper,[19] had already freed me from those bonds, but I was still trying to trace the cause of evil, and found no way out of the difficulty. Yet you allowed no flood of thoughts to sweep me away from the faith whereby I believed that you exist, that your essence is unchangeable, that you care for us humans and judge our deeds, and that in your Son, Christ our Lord, and in the holy scriptures which the authority of your Catholic Church guarantees,[20] you have laid down the way for human beings to reach that eternal life which awaits us after death. These beliefs were unaffected, and persisted strong and unshaken in me as I feverishly searched for the origin of evil.

What agonizing birth-pangs tore my heart, what groans it uttered, O my God! And there, unknown to me, were your hearkening ears, for as I labored hard in my silent search the mute sufferings of my mind reached your mercy as loud cries. You alone knew my pain, no one else; for how little of it could

[19] *my helper*: See Psalm 17:3(18:2); 29:11(30:10); 58:18(59:17); 62:8(63:7).

[20] *scriptures . . . authority of your Catholic Church guarantees*: Authority was primarily scriptural for Augustine, as here is where God's own dictates could be found and trusted despite any human doubt or dissension. Yet the Catholic Church is what in turn ratifies the authority of Scripture and subsequent tradition, as he will write against the Manichees at about this time of the *Confessions*: "I would not believe the Gospel unless the authority of the Catholic Church so moved me" (*Answer to the Letter of Mani Known as the Foundation* 5.6).

I express in words to my closest friends! Could their ears have caught all the tumult that raged in my soul, when even I had neither time enough nor eloquence to articulate it? Yet even as my heart roared its anguish my clamor found its way to your hearing, and all my longing lay before you, for the light of my eyes was not there at my command:[21] it was within, but I was outside; it occupied no place, but I had fixed my gaze on spatially positioned things, and so I found in them nowhere to rest. Nor did they welcome me or afford me the chance to say, "This is enough, now all is well," nor did they even release me to return to where I could well have found what was enough. I was nobler than they, but lowlier than you; and as long as I was subject to you my true joy was your very self, and you had subjected to me all those things which you created below me. The happy mean, the central region where I would find salvation, was to preserve your image in me, serving you and subduing my body; but because I was rearing up against you in my pride, charging head-high against the Lord and crassly presuming on my own strength,[22] even those inferior things gained the upper hand and pressed me down, so that nowhere could I find respite or relief. When I looked outward they crowded upon me thick and fast; when I tried to think the images of these material things blocked my path of return, as though demanding, "Where are you off to, you unworthy, degraded fellow?" All this had sprung from my wounded condition, for you humbled this proud man with a wounding blow.[23] My swollen pride got in the way and kept me from you, and my face was so puffy that my eyes were closed.

[21] *my heart roared its anguish . . . at my command*: See Psalm 37:9–11(38:8–10).

[22] *happy mean . . . my own strength*: See Job 15:26. Creatures cannot, of course, give the soul "rest", as we have seen again and again. Because the true state of the human soul is the "happy mean" between lesser creatures and God, Augustine here describes sin as the (literal) "perversion" of the soul's turning downward to love creatures inordinately, thereby diminishing its divine image in being like God. In *To Simplicianus* 1.2.18, Augustine defines sin as a "disorder or perversity, that is, an aversion to the more preferable creator, and a conversion to the inferior creatures."

[23] *humbled this proud man with a wounding blow*: See Psalm 88:11(89:10).

Chapter 8

12. But you, Lord, abide for ever[24] and will not for ever be angry with us,[25] for you have taken pity on us who are earth and ashes;[26] and so it was pleasing in your sight[27] to give new form to my deformity. You goaded me within to make me chafe impatiently until you should grow clear to my spiritual sight. At the unseen touch of your medicine my swelling subsided, while under the stinging eye-salve[28] of curative pain the fretful, darkened vision of my spirit began to improve day by day.

Chapter 9

He reads "the books of the Platonists"

13. You wanted to show me first and foremost how you thwart the proud but give grace to the humble,[29] and with what immense mercy on your part the way of humility was demonstrated to us when your Word was made flesh and dwelt among men and women;[30] and so through a certain man grossly swollen with pride you provided me with some books by the Platonists, translated from the Greek into Latin.[31] In them I read

[24] *you, Lord, abide for ever*: See Psalm 101:13(102:12).

[25] *will not for ever be angry with us*: See Psalm 84:6(85:5); 102(103):9.

[26] *taken pity on us who are earth and ashes*: See Job 42:6; Sirach 17:31.

[27] *it was pleasing in your sight*: See Psalm 18:15(19:14); Daniel 3:40.

[28] *eye-salve*: See Revelation 3:18.

[29] *thwart the proud but give grace to the humble*: See Proverbs 3:34; James 4:6; 1 Peter 5:5.

[30] *Word was made flesh and dwelt among men and women*: See John 1:14.

[31] *books by the Platonists, translated from the Greek into Latin*: In moving to Milan, Augustine would have been immersed in the Platonism of the day, and in Ambrose, he would have come to understand how Christians can use Platonic insights to help open up the Scriptures. Augustine comes into direct contact with the source of this intellectual movement, the "books of the Platonists", most certainly the *Enneads* of Plotinus (named after the Greek word for nine due to their style of arrangement of six books of nine long sections, or enneads). Plotinus is known as the founder of Neoplatonism (ca. A.D. 205–270), and his student Porphyry collected and edited his master's teaching sometime around

(not that the same words were used, but precisely the same doctrine was taught, buttressed by many and various arguments)
that *in the beginning was the Word, and the Word was with God;
he was God. He was with God in the beginning. Everything was
made through him; nothing came to be without him. What was made
is alive with his life, and that life was the light of humankind. The
Light shines in the darkness, and the darkness has never been able to
master it*; and that the human soul, even though it bears *testimony about the Light*, is not itself the Light, but that God, the
Word, is *the true Light, which illumines every human person who
comes into this world*; and that he was in this world, *a world made
by him, but the world did not know him*. But that *he came to his
own home, and his own people did not receive him; but to those who
did receive him he gave power to become children of God: to those,
that is, who believe in his name*[32]—none of this did I read there.

14. I also read in them that God, the Word, was born not
of blood nor man's desire nor lust of the flesh, but of God;[33]
but that *the Word was made flesh and dwelt among us*,[34] I did
not read there. I certainly observed that in these writings it
was often stated, in a variety of ways, that the Son, being *in
the form of God* the Father, *deemed it no robbery to be equal
to God*, because he is identical with him in nature. But that *he
emptied himself and took on the form of a slave, and being made in
the likeness of men was found in human form*, that *he humbled*

---

300 and wrote some mystical-philosophical works, which we know Augustine
read as well. The Latin edition of Plotinus' *Enneads*, which Augustine read, were
translated by the fourth-century Roman orator Marius Victorinus, the famed orator and Christian convert whom we shall soon meet (see *Conf.* VIII.2.3–2.5,
pp. 197–201).

[32] in the beginning was the Word ... who believe in his name: John 1:1–12.
Platonic philosophy gave Augustine the framework to understand all the spiritual and powerful attributes of God: his incorporeity, his self-subsisting life, and
his unmatched goodness. However, what the pagan Greek mind could not at all
provide were the harder truths of the Incarnation: the divine's freely taking on
flesh, God's entrusting himself to creatures and his consequent rejection, the
death of crucified divinity, and the humble service and unconditional forgiveness given to creatures.

[33] *Word, was born not of blood ... but of God*: See John 1:13.

[34] the Word was made flesh and dwelt among us: John 1:14.

*himself and was made obedient to the point of death, even death on
a cross, which is why God raised him from the dead, and gave
him a name above every other name, so that at the name of Jesus
every knee should bow, in heaven, on earth, or in the underworld,
and every tongue confess that Jesus Christ is Lord, in the glory of
God the Father,*[35] of this no mention was made in these books.

I did read in them that your only-begotten Son, coeternal
with you, abides before all ages and above all ages, and that
of his fullness[36] our souls receive, to become blessed thereby,
and that by participation in that Wisdom which abides in
itself[37] they are made new in order to become wise; but that
at the time of our weakness he died for the wicked,[38] and that
you did not spare even your only Son, but delivered him up
for us all,[39] these things are not to be found there. For you
have *hidden these matters from the sagacious and shrewd, and
revealed them to little ones,*[40] so that those who toil under heavy
burdens may come to him and he may give them relief, because
he is gentle and humble of heart.[41] He will guide the gentle
aright and teach the unassuming his ways,[42] for he sees our
lowly estate and our labor, and forgives all our sins.[43] As for
those who are raised on the stilts of their loftier doctrine, too
high to hear him calling, *Learn of me, for I am gentle and humble of heart, and you shall find rest for your souls,*[44] even if they

---

[35] *that the Son, being in the form of God* ... *in the glory of God the Father:*
Philippians 2:6–11.

[36] *of his fullness:* John 1:16.

[37] *Wisdom which abides in itself:* See Wisdom 7:27.

[38] *at the time of our weakness he died for the wicked:* Romans 5:6.

[39] *you did not spare even your only Son, but delivered him up for us all:* See Romans
8:32.

[40] *hidden these matters* ... *revealed them to little ones:* Matthew 11:25.

[41] *those who toil under heavy burdens* ... *he is gentle and humble of heart:* See
Matthew 11:28.

[42] *He will guide the gentle aright and teach the unassuming his ways:* See Psalm
24(25):9.

[43] *he sees our lowly estate and our labor, and forgives all our sins:* See Psalm
24(25):18.

[44] *Learn of me, for I am gentle and humble of heart,* ... *find rest for your
souls:* Matthew 11:29.

know God, they do not honor him as God or give him thanks; their thinking has been frittered away into futility and their foolish hearts are benighted, for in claiming to be wise they have become stupid.[45]

15. In consequence what I also read there was the story of their exchanging your glorious, imperishable nature for idols and a variety of man-made things, for the effigy of a perishable human or of birds or animals or crawling creatures;[46] these are the food of the Egyptians, for the sake of which Esau bartered away his dignity as the first-born,[47] just as your first-born people turned back to Egypt in their hearts,[48] worshiping a beast's head instead of you,[49] and abasing their souls, made in your image, before the image of a calf munching hay.[50]

These things I found there, but I did not eat that food; for it was pleasing in your sight, Lord, to take away from Jacob the shame of his subordination and cause the elder to serve the younger,[51] so you called the Gentiles into your inheritance. And I had come to you from the Gentiles. I set my heart upon the gold which at your bidding your people had brought out of Egypt, because wherever it was, it belonged to you. So you told the Athenians through your apostle that in you we live and move and have our being, and that indeed some of their own authorities had said this,[52] and unquestionably those books I read came from there. I disregarded the idols of the Egyptians, to which they paid homage with gold that belonged to you, for they perverted the truth of God into a

---

[45] *their foolish hearts are benighted, . . . they have become stupid:* See Romans 1:21–22.

[46] *exchanging your glorious, imperishable nature . . . crawling creatures:* See Romans 1:23.

[47] *Esau bartered away his dignity as the first-born:* See Genesis 25:33–34.

[48] *first-born people turned back to Egypt in their hearts:* See Acts 7:39.

[49] *worshiping a beast's head instead of you:* See Exodus 32:1–6.

[50] *image of a calf munching hay:* See Psalm 105(106):20.

[51] *elder to serve the younger:* See Genesis 25:23; Romans 9:12.

[52] *in you we live and move and have our being, . . . authorities had said this:* See Acts 17:28.

lie, worshiping a creature and serving it rather than the creator.[53]

Chapter 10

He attempts Platonic ecstasy, but is "beaten back"

16. Warned by these writings that I must return to myself, I entered under your guidance the innermost places of my being; but only because you had become my helper[54] was I able to do so. I entered, then, and with the vision of my spirit, such as it was, I saw the incommutable light[55] far above my spiritual ken, transcending my mind: not this common light which every carnal eye can see, nor any light of the same order but greater, as though this common light were shining much more powerfully, far more brightly, and so extensively as to fill the universe. The light I saw was not this common light at all, but something different, utterly different, from all these things. Nor was it higher than my mind in the sense that oil floats on water or the sky is above the earth; it was exalted because this very light made me, and I was below it because by it I was made. Anyone who knows truth knows it, and whoever knows it knows eternity. Love knows it.[56]

---

[53] *perverted the truth of God into a lie, worshiping a creature . . . the creator*: See Romans 1:25. In Exodus 3:21–22 and Exodus 12:35–36, Moses tells the chosen people to take the riches of the Egyptians because in their obstinacy against the Lord, they made poor use of them, and if used for the true covenant, they would take on a new importance and beauty. This is Augustine's analogy of the Christian use of pagan philosophy: what may be true and helpful in the hands of the Greeks becomes even more brilliant and fitting when used for the service of Christ. This "spoiling the Egyptians" is first found in Irenaeus and Origen, but Augustine uses it most often (for example, see *On Diverse Questions* 53, *Commentary on the Psalms* 104.28, and *Against Faustus* 71).

[54] *you had become my helper*: See Psalm 29:11(30:10).

[55] *incommutable light*: See John 1:9.

[56] *it was exulted . . . Love knows it*: This is the second of three moments of ecstasy in the *Confessions*. Whereas the first moment used Alypius at the games to illustrate how the soul waged war against the body and how an aloof moral agent acts in opposition to the inevitability of evil in this world (representing

O eternal Truth, true Love, and beloved Eternity, you are my God, and for you I sigh day and night.[57] As I first began to know you you lifted me up[58] and showed me that while that which I might see exists indeed, I was not yet capable of seeing it. Your rays beamed intensely upon me, beating back my feeble gaze, and I trembled with love and dread. I knew myself to be far away from you in a region of unlikeness, and I seemed to hear your voice from on high: "I am the food of the mature; grow then, and you will eat me. You will not change me into yourself like bodily food: you will be changed into me."[59] And I recognized that you have chastened man for his sin and caused my soul to dwindle away like a spider's web,[60] and I said, "Is truth then a nothing, simply because it is not spread out through space either finite or infinite?" Then from afar you cried to me, "By no means, for *I am who am*."[61]

I heard it as one hears a word in the heart, and no possibility of doubt remained to me; I could more easily have doubted that I was alive than that truth exists, truth that is seen and understood through the things that are made.

Augustine's Manichean phase at *Conf.* VI.8.13, pp. 145–47), this second moment of ecstasy represents the Platonic phase of his odyssey in that the soul's desire to see truth is defeated by carnal custom, the body still an impediment to ultimate reality. Here the philosopher is "alone to the Alone" (Plotinus, *Enneads* VI.9.9), and community has no real place in such a pursuit of truth.

[57] *for you I sigh day and night*: See Psalm 1:2; Jeremiah 9:1; Psalm 41:4(42:3).
[58] *you lifted me up*: See Psalm 26(27):10.
[59] *I am the food . . . you will be changed into me*: Often in the *Confessions* Augustine metaphorically uses the imagery of eating to describe one's encounter with the truth (cf., *Conf.* III.1.1; IV.1.1; X.6.8; XIII.18.23), but this is the most strongly Eucharistic line: meeting Jesus does not change him but transforms us; the consumed changes but is not changed. This is the central theme of Augustine's theology of the Eucharist, to become the Body of Christ by receiving the Body of Christ, e.g., "What you receive is what you yourselves are" (*Sermon* 229A.2) and, again, the exhortation "Be what you can see and receive what you are" (*Sermon* 272).
[60] *you have chastened man for his sin . . . like a spider's web*: See Psalm 38:12(39:11).
[61] *I am who am*: Exodus 3:14.

Chapter 11

New light on the problem of evil

17. Contemplating other things below you, I saw that they do not in the fullest sense exist, nor yet are they completely non-beings: they are real because they are from you, but unreal inasmuch as they are not what you are.[62] For that alone truly is, which abides unchangingly. As for me, my good is to hold fast to God,[63] for if I do not abide in him, I shall not be able to in myself; whereas he, abiding ever in himself, renews all things.[64] You are my Lord, for you need no goods of mine.[65]

Chapter 12

18. It was further made clear to me that things prone to destruction are good, since this destructibility would be out of the question if they were either supremely good or not good at all; because if they were supremely good, they would be indestructible, whereas if they were not good at all, there would be nothing in them that could be destroyed. Destruction is obviously harmful, yet it can do harm only by diminishing the good. It follows, then, that either destruction harms nothing, which is impossible, or that all things which suffer harm are being deprived of some good; this conclusion is beyond cavil. If, however, they lose all their good, they will not exist at all, for if they were to continue in existence without being any longer subject to destruction, they would be better, because

[62] *yet are they completely non-beings . . . they are not what you are*: Since all creation teeters between God and nonbeing, insofar as a creature turns to God it is real, but if it turns away, it enters the shadowy regions of nonbeing. For Augustine, all creation imitates the Son's turn to the Father to receive all it is; such conversion informs creation, and in this way, all creation can tell us something of its Creator.

[63] *hold fast to God*: See Psalm 72(73):28. Again, holding fast to God, cleaving to the Creator, emerges as the central metaphor of how Augustine describes the Christian life.

[64] *renews all things*: See Wisdom 7:27.

[65] *You are my Lord, for you need no goods of mine*: See Psalm 15(16):2.

permanently indestructible; and what could be more outrageous than to declare them better for having lost everything
that was good in them? Hence if they are deprived of all good,
they will be simply non-existent; and so it follows that as long
as they do exist, they are good.

Everything that exists is good, then; and so evil, the source
of which I was seeking, cannot be a substance, because if it
were, it would be good. Either it would be an indestructible
substance, and that would mean it was very good indeed, or it
would be a substance liable to destruction—but then it would
not be destructible unless it were good.

I saw, then, for it was made clear to me, that you have made
all good things, and that there are absolutely no substances
that you have not made. I saw too that you have not made all
things equal. They all exist because they are severally good
but collectively very good, for our God has made all things
exceedingly good.[66]

Chapter 13

19. For you evil has no being at all, and this is true not of
yourself only but of everything you have created, since apart
from you there is nothing that could burst in and disrupt the
order you have imposed on it. In some parts of it certain things
are regarded as evil because they do not suit certain others;
but these same things do fit in elsewhere, and they are good
there, and good in themselves. All these things that are at
odds with each other belong to the lower part of creation that
we call earth, which has its own cloudy, windy sky, as befits it.

---

[66] exceedingly good: Genesis 1:31; Sirach 39:21. The Neoplatonic insights
into (1) immateriality and (2) that all that exists is essentially good give Augustine his mature view of evil: it is a *privatio boni*, a privation of the good. Against
the Manichees it is neither a separate substance nor an active force. It is a parasite that cannot thus by definition be a subsistent nature, nor can it be an
efficient cause but a deficient one. Evil "exists" only insofar as goodness crum-
bles and wanes. Therefore, there can be no substantially evil being, because a
substantial privation would literally be no-thing. Augustine must still describe
what evil is (see *Conf.* VIII.10.24, pp. 219–20).

Far be it from me ever to say, "These things ought not to be"; because even if I could see these things alone, and longed, certainly, for something better, it would already be incumbent on me to praise you for them alone; for on earth the dragons and all the depths proclaim you worthy of praise, as do the fire, hail, snow, ice and stormy winds that obey your word, the mountains and hills, fruit-bearing trees and all cedars, wild beasts and tame, creeping creatures and birds on the wing. Earth's kings and all its peoples, rulers and the world's judges, young men and maidens, old men and youths, all praise your name.[67] But since in heaven too your creatures praise you, our God, let all your angels tell your praises on high, let all your powers extol you, sun and moon, all stars and the light, the empyrean and the waters above the heavens: let them too praise your name.[68] No longer was I hankering for any elements to be better than they were, because I was now keeping the totality in view; and though I certainly esteemed the higher creatures above the lower, a more wholesome judgment showed me that the totality was better than the higher things on their own would have been.

Chapter 14

20. There is no wholesomeness[69] for those who find fault with anything you have created, as there was none for me when many of the things you have made displeased me. Since my soul did not dare to find my God displeasing, it was unwilling to admit that anything that displeased it was truly yours. This was why it had strayed away into believing in a duality of substances, but there it found no rest, and only mouthed the opinions of others. Turning back again it had made for itself a god extended through infinite space, all-pervasive, and had thought this god

[67] *on earth the dragons and all the depths . . . all praise your name*: See Psalm 148:7–12.

[68] *in heaven too your creatures praise you, . . . let them too praise your name*: See Psalm 148:1–5.

[69] *There is no wholesomeness*: See Psalm 37:4(38:3).

was you, and had set him up in its heart;[70] so it became yet again a temple for its own idol and an abomination in your sight. But when you cradled my stupid head and closed my eyes to the sight of vain things[71] so that I could absent me from myself awhile, and my unwholesome madness was lulled to sleep, then I awoke in you and saw you to be infinite, but in a different sense; and that vision in no way derived from the flesh.[72]

Chapter 15

21. I turned my gaze to other things and saw that they owe their being to you and that all of them are by you defined, but in a particular sense: not as though contained in a place, but because you hold all things in your Truth as though in your hand; and all of them are true insofar as they exist, and nothing whatever is a deceit unless it is thought to be what it is not. I saw, further, that all things are set not only in their appropriate places but also in their proper times, and that you, who alone are eternal, did not set to work after incalculable stretches of time, because no stretches of time, neither those which have passed away nor those still to come, would pass or come except because you are at work and you abide eternally.

Chapter 16

22. Drawing on my own experience I found it unsurprising that bread, which is pleasant to a healthy palate, is repugnant to a sick one, and that diseased eyes hate the light which to the unclouded is delightful. Villains find even your justice disagreeable, and snakes and maggots far more so, yet you have created these things good, and fit for the lower spheres of your world. Indeed, the villains themselves are fit only for these

---

[70] *had set him up in its heart*: See Ezekiel 14:7.

[71] *vain things*: See Psalm 118(119):37.

[72] *that vision in no way derived from the flesh*: This is a salutary reminder that bad theology is really a form of idolatry. Augustine realizes that he must dethrone these erroneous intellectual idols if he is ever to understand and adore God rightly.

lower regions in the measure that they are unlike you, but for the higher when they come to resemble you more closely.

I inquired then what villainy might be, but I found no substance, only the perversity of a will twisted away from you, God, the supreme substance, toward the depths—a will that throws away its life within[73] and swells with vanity abroad.

Chapter 17

Fresh attempt at mounting to God; he attains That Which Is

23. I found it amazing that though I now loved your very self, and not some figment of imagination in place of you, I could not continue steadfastly in the enjoyment of my God. I was drawn toward you by your beauty but swiftly dragged away from you by my own weight, swept back headlong and groaning onto these things below myself; and this weight was carnal habit. Nonetheless the memory of you stayed with me, and I had no doubt whatever whom I ought to cling to, though I knew that I was not yet capable of clinging, because the perishable body weighs down the soul, and its earthly habitation oppresses a mind teeming with thoughts.[74] I was fully persuaded that your invisible reality is plainly to be understood through created things, your everlasting power also, and your divinity;[75] for I had been trying to understand how it was possible for me to appreciate the beauty of material things in the sky or on earth, and why the power to make sound judgments about changeable matters was readily available to me, so that I could say, "This thing ought to be like this, but that other different";

[73] *perversity of a will twisted*: See Sirach 10:10.

[74] *perishable body weighs down the soul, . . . mind teeming with thoughts*: See Wisdom 9:15. While Neoplatonism is far from Gnosticism (Plotinus wrote vigorously against them; *Enneads* II.9), there can still at times be found a certain mistrust of the human body, especially in trying to understand its relationship with the soul and the positive nature of individuality, which the body makes possible.

[75] *invisible reality is plainly to be understood . . . and your divinity*: See Romans 1:20.

and in seeking the reason why I was able to judge as I did I realized that above my changeable mind soared the real, unchangeable truth, which is eternal.

Thus I pursued my inquiry by stages, from material things to the soul that perceives them through the body, and from there to that inner power of the soul to which the body's senses report external impressions. The intelligence of animals can reach as far as this.

I proceeded further and came to the power of discursive reason, to which the data of our senses are referred for judgment. Yet as found in me even reason acknowledged itself to be subject to change, and stretched upward to the source of its own intelligence, withholding its thoughts from the tyranny of habit and detaching itself from the swarms of noisy phantasms. It strove to discover what this light was that bedewed it when it cried out unhesitatingly that the Unchangeable is better than anything liable to change; it sought the fount whence flowed its concept of the Unchangeable—for unless it had in some fashion recognized Immutability, it could never with such certainty have judged it superior to things that change.

And then my mind attained to *That Which Is*, in the flash of one tremulous glance. Then indeed did I perceive your invisible reality through created things,[76] but to keep my gaze there was beyond my strength. I was forced back through weakness and returned to my familiar surroundings, bearing with me only a loving memory, one that yearned for something of which I had caught the fragrance, but could not yet feast upon.

Chapter 18

He realizes the need for Christ the Mediator

24. Accordingly I looked for a way to gain the strength I needed to enjoy you, but I did not find it until I embraced the mediator between God and humankind, the man Christ

---

[76] *perceive your invisible reality through created things*: See Romans 1:20.

Jesus,[77] who also is God, supreme over all things and blessed
for ever.[78] Not yet had I embraced him, though he called out,
proclaiming, *I am the Way and Truth and the Life*,[79] nor had I
known him as the food which, though I was not yet strong enough
to eat it, he had mingled with our flesh; for the Word became
flesh so that your Wisdom, through whom you created all things,[80]
might become for us the milk adapted to our infancy.[81] Not yet
was I humble enough to grasp the humble Jesus as my God, nor
did I know what his weakness had to teach. Your Word, the
eternal Truth who towers above the higher spheres of your creation, raises up to himself those creatures who bow before him;
but in these lower regions he has built himself a humble dwelling[82] from our clay,[83] and used it to cast down from their pretentious selves those who do not bow before him, and make a
bridge to bring them to himself. He heals their swollen pride
and nourishes their love, that they may not wander even further away through self-confidence, but rather weaken as they
see before their feet the Godhead grown weak[84] by sharing our
garments of skin,[85] and wearily fling themselves down upon
him, so that he may arise and lift them up.

Chapter 19

25. I took a different view at the time, regarding Christ my
Lord as no more than a man, though a man of excellent

---

[77] *mediator between God and humankind, the man Christ Jesus*: See 1 Timothy 2:5.

[78] *who also is God, supreme over all things and blessed for ever*: See Romans 9:5.

[79] I am the Way and Truth and the Life: John 14:6.

[80] *you created all things*: See Colossians 1:16.

[81] *might become for us the milk adapted to our infancy*: This is something no
strict Platonist could ever imagine: the perfect and the eternal becomes lowly
for the sake of transient creatures. For Plato, the mutable and lower realities
must strive upward in order to unite with the perfect forms, but only in Christianity does Perfection long to participate downward in his own fragile creation
so as to elevate others to himself.

[82] *humble dwelling*: See Proverbs 9:1.

[83] *from our clay*: See Genesis 2:7.

[84] *Godhead grown weak*: See 1 Corinthians 1:25.

[85] *by sharing our garments of skin*: See Genesis 3:21.

wisdom and without peer. I was the more firmly persuaded of this because he had been born of a virgin and made plain to us by his own example that disdain for temporal goods is a condition for winning immortality; and it seemed to me that through God's solicitude for us in this respect Christ's teaching had acquired incomparable authority. But I could not even begin to guess what a mystery was concealed in the Word made flesh. All I had understood from the facts about him handed down in the scriptures—as, for instance, that he ate, drank, slept, walked, experienced joy and sorrow and spoke to the people—was that his flesh was united to your Word only in conjunction with a human soul and a human consciousness. This must be obvious to anyone who has recognized the immutability of your Word, as I had insofar as I was able, and on this score I had no doubt. It is characteristic of the instability of our soul or mind that it can move its bodily limbs at one moment and not move them at another, can be affected now by some emotion and now again be unaffected, can give expression to wise sentiments at one time and at another remain silent. If these actions were reported of him falsely it would lay the entirety of the scriptures open to suspicion of lying, and then these writings would afford no possibility of saving faith to the human race. In fact, however, the scriptures are trustworthy; and so I acknowledged Christ to be a perfect man: not a human body only, nor a body with a human soul but lacking intelligence. Yet I held that this same man was to be preferred to others not because he was Truth in person, but on account of the outstanding excellence of his human nature and his more perfect participation in wisdom.

Alypius thought that Catholics believed God to be clothed in flesh in such a way that there was in Christ nothing else but godhead and flesh; he did not think their preaching assigned to him a human soul or a human consciousness. Being firmly convinced that the actions Christ was remembered to have performed would have been impossible in the absence of a principle of created, rational life, Alypius was little disposed to Christian faith; but later on he recognized this error to be that of the Apollinarian heretics, and so he came to rejoice with Catholics in their faith and to acquiesce in it.[86]

For my own part I admit that it was later still that I learned how sharply divergent is Catholic truth from the falsehood of Photinus with respect to the teaching that the Word was made flesh.[87] Indeed the discrediting of heretics serves to throw into high relief the mind of your Church and the content of sound doctrine;[88] for it was necessary for heresies to emerge in order to show up the people of sound faith among the weak.[89]

Chapter 20

Christ the Way

26. But in those days, after reading the books of the Platonists and following their advice to seek for truth beyond corporeal forms, I turned my gaze toward your invisible reality, trying to

[86] *Alypius was little disposed to Christian faith . . . to acquiesce in it*: The heresy misleading Alypius here was Apollinarianism (named after Apollinarius of Laodicea, ca. 310–390), which taught that since only the divine Logos could be the savior of humanity, there was no need for the man Jesus Christ to have a human intellect or human soul. In this way Apollinarius aimed to stress the unity of the divine nature dwelling (only) in the flesh of Jesus as well as to answer any objections (mainly by the Arians) of Christ's intellectual or spiritual development. An early friend of Saint Athanasius, Apollinarius' later views on this matter, wherein the divine indwelling left no room for the fullness of humanity in Christ (i.e., robbing him of a human soul), led to his being condemned at various times in Rome (374–380) as well as at the First Council of Constantinople (381).

[87] *falsehood of Photinus . . . the Word was made flesh*: Photinus became Bishop of Sirmium (in today's Serbia) in 344. He taught a form of Trinitarian modalism, rejecting the real distinction of divine persons in the Trinity. Augustine thus critiques Photinus for denying the preexistence of the Logos, thus rendering Jesus Christ as some sort of superhuman endowed by the Father with divine gifts. Deposed from his see in 351, he was officially condemned at the First Council of Constantinople.

[88] *content of sound doctrine*: See 1 Timothy 1:10; 2 Timothy 4:3–4; Titus 1:9; 2:1.

[89] *necessary for heresies to emerge . . . sound faith among the weak*: See 1 Corinthians 11:19.

understand it through created things,[90] and though I was
rebuffed I did perceive what that reality was which the darkness of my soul would not permit me to contemplate. I was
certain that you exist, that you are infinite but not spread out
through space either finite or infinite, and that you exist in
the fullest sense because you have always been the same,[91]
unvarying in every respect and in no wise subject to change.
All other things I saw to have their being from you,[92] and for
this I needed but one unassailable proof—the fact that they
exist. On these points I was quite certain, but I was far too
weak to enjoy you. Yet I readily chattered as though skilled in
the subject, and had I not been seeking your way in Christ
our Savior[93] I would more probably have been killed than
skilled. For I had already begun to covet a reputation for wisdom, and though fully punished I shed no tears of compunc-
tion; rather was I complacently puffed up with knowledge.
Where was that charity which builds[94] on the foundation of
humility that is Christ Jesus?[95] And when would those books
have taught it to me? I believe that you willed me to stumble
upon them before I gave my mind to your scriptures, so that
the memory of how I had been affected by them might be
impressed upon me when later I had been brought to a new
gentleness through the study of your books, and your fingers
were tending my wounds; thus insight would be mine to

[90] *invisible reality, trying to understand it through created things*: See Romans 1:20.
Remember that Augustine maintained that Plato deservedly "achieved the most
outstanding reputation, overshadowing the rest of ancient philosophy", enjoying a rightful "claim to fame by bringing philosophy to perfection by joining
together" both its contemplative and active demands (*City of God* VIII.4). Known
to Augustine, Plato's *Timaeus* anticipates Saint Paul by also arguing that the
visible world is an iconic pattern of the truly real world of forms and that study
of visible reality inevitably leads the mind upward to true knowledge.

[91] *you have always been the same*: See Psalm 101:28(102:27); Hebrews 1:12.
Neoplatonism allowed Augustine to understand better the immaterial order of
reality as well as how God is absolute unity and immutability.

[92] *All other things I saw to have their being from you*: See Romans 11:36.

[93] *Christ our Savior*: See Titus 1:4.

[94] *puffed up with knowledge . . . charity which builds*: See 1 Corinthians 8:1; 13:4.

[95] *on the foundation of humility that is Christ Jesus*: See 1 Corinthians 3:11.

recognize the difference between presumption and confession, between those who see the goal but not the way to it and the Way to our beatific homeland, a homeland to be not merely descried but lived in. If I had first become well informed about your holy writings and you had grown sweet to me through my familiarity with them, and then I had afterward chanced upon those other volumes, they might perhaps have torn me loose from the strong root of piety, or else, if I had held firm in the salutary devotion I had absorbed, I might have supposed that it could be acquired equally well from those books, if everyone studied them and nothing else.

Chapter 21

Augustine discovers Saint Paul

27. It was therefore with intense eagerness that I seized on the hallowed calligraphy of your Spirit, and most especially the writings of the apostle Paul. In earlier days it had seemed to me that his teaching was self-contradictory, and in conflict with the witness of the law and the prophets,[96] but now as these problems melted away your chaste words[97] presented a single face to me, and I learned to rejoice with reverence.[98]

So I began to read, and discovered that every truth I had read in those other books was taught here also, but now inseparably from your gift of grace, so that no one who sees can boast as though what he sees and the very power to see it were not from you—for who has anything that he has not received?[99] So totally is it a matter of grace that the searcher is not only invited to see you, who are ever the same,[100] but healed as well, so that he can possess you. Whoever is too far off to see

[96] *in conflict with the witness of the law and the prophets*: See Matthew 5:17; 7:12; Luke 16:16.
[97] *problems melted away your chaste words*: See Psalm 11:7(12:6).
[98] *learned to rejoice with reverence*: See Psalm 2:11.
[99] *for who has anything that he has not received?* See 1 Corinthians 4:7.
[100] *who are ever the same*: See Psalm 101:28(102:27); Hebrews 1:12.

may yet walk in the way that will bring him to the place of seeing and possession; for even though a person may be delighted with God's law as far as his inmost self is concerned, how is he to deal with that other law in his bodily members which strives against the law approved by his mind, delivering him as prisoner to the law of sin dominant in his body?[101] You are just, O Lord;[102] but we have sinned, and done wrong, and acted impiously,[103] and your hand has lain heavy upon us.[104] With good reason were we assigned to that ancient sinner who presides over death,[105] for he had seduced our will into imitating that perverse will of his by which he refused to stand fast in your truth.[106]

What is a human wretch to do? Who will free him from this death-laden body, if not your grace, given through Jesus Christ our Lord,[107] whom you have begotten coeternal with yourself and created at the beginning of all your works?[108] In him the ruler of this world found nothing that deserved death,[109] yet slew him all the same; and so the record of debt that stood against us was annulled.[110]

None of this is to be found in those other books. Not in those pages are traced the lineaments of such loving kindness, or the tears of confession, or the sacrifice of an anguished spirit offered to you from a contrite and humbled heart,[111] or the

---

[101] *law in his bodily members . . . sin dominant in his body:* See Romans 7:22–23.

[102] *You are just, O Lord:* See Tobit 3:2; Psalm 118(119):137.

[103] *we have sinned, and done wrong, and acted impiously:* See Daniel 3:27, 29; 1 Kings 8:47.

[104] *your hand has lain heavy upon us:* See Psalm 31(32):4.

[105] *ancient sinner who presides over death:* See Hebrews 2:14.

[106] *he had seduced our will . . . stand fast in your truth:* See John 8:44.

[107] *Who will free him from this death-laden body . . . Jesus Christ our Lord:* See Romans 7:24–25.

[108] *coeternal with yourself and created at the beginning of all your works:* See Proverbs 8:22.

[109] *ruler of this world found nothing that deserved death:* See Luke 23:14–15; John 14:30.

[110] *record of debt that stood against us was annulled:* See Colossians 2:14.

[111] *loving kindness . . . contrite and humbled heart:* See Psalm 50:19(51:17). The same principles that confounded Neoplatonism in trying to come to terms with

salvation of a people, or a city chosen to be your bride,[112] or the pledge of the Holy Spirit,[113] or the cup of our ransom. Not there is anyone heard to sing, *Shall not my soul surrender itself to God? For my salvation comes from him. He is my very God, my Savior, my protector, and I shall waver no more.*[114] No one there hearkens to a voice calling, *Come to me, all you who struggle.* They are too scornful to learn from him, because he is gentle and humble of heart,[115] and you have hidden these things from the sagacious and shrewd, and revealed them to little ones.[116]

It is one thing to survey our peaceful homeland from a wooded height but fail to find the way there, and make vain attempts to travel through impassable terrain, while fugitive deserters marshaled by the lion and the dragon[117] obstruct and lurk in ambush; and quite another to walk steadily in the way that leads there, along the well-built road opened up by the heavenly emperor, where no deserters from the celestial army dare commit robbery, for they avoid that way like torment.[118]

In awe-inspiring ways these truths were striking deep roots within me as I read the least of your apostles;[119] I had contemplated your works and was filled with dread.[120]

---

the Incarnation (see *Conf.* VII.9.13–14) are precisely the places where it fails to understand human salvation as well: love, lowliness, humility, and service of the least.

[112] *city chosen to be your bride:* See Revelation 21:2.

[113] *pledge of the Holy Spirit:* See 2 Corinthians 5:5; 1:22.

[114] *Shall not my soul surrender itself to God? . . . I shall waver no more:* Psalm 61:2–3(62:1–2).

[115] *he is gentle and humble of heart:* See Matthew 11:28–29.

[116] *you have hidden these things . . . revealed them to little ones:* See Matthew 11:25.

[117] *fugitive deserters marshaled by the lion and the dragon:* See Psalm 90(91):13.

[118] *It is one thing . . . for they avoid that way like torment:* Neoplatonism may understand the end, but it is ill-equipped to explain the way—that is, while every creed and philosophy Augustine entertained had a promising vision of salvation and final human wholeness, only Catholic doctrine could offer him the sure means by which to reach this rest.

[119] *least of your apostles:* See 1 Corinthians 15:9.

[120] *contemplated your works and was filled with dread:* See Habakkuk 3:2.

Book VIII

Conversion

Chapter 1

1. In a spirit of thankfulness let me recall the mercies you lavished on me, O my God; to you let me confess them.[1] May I be flooded with love for you until my very bones cry out, "Who is like you, O Lord?"[2] Let me offer you a sacrifice of praise, for you have snapped my bonds.[3] How you broke them I will relate, so that all your worshipers who hear my tale may exclaim, "Blessed be the Lord, blessed in heaven and on earth, for great and wonderful is his name."[4]

Your words were now firmly implanted in my heart of hearts, and I was besieged by you on every side.[5] Concerning your eternal life I was now quite certain, though I had but glimpsed it like a tantalizing reflection in a mirror;[6] this had been enough to take from me any lingering doubt concerning that imperishable substance from which every other substance derives its being. What I now longed for was not greater certainty about you, but a more steadfast abiding in you. In my daily life everything seemed to be teetering, and my heart needed to be cleansed of the old leaven.[7] I was attracted to the Way, which is our Savior himself, but the narrowness of the path daunted me and I still could not walk in it.[8]

---

[1] *mercies you lavished on me, O my God; . . . let me confess them*: See Psalm 85(86):13; Isaiah 63:7.

[2] *bones cry out, "Who is like you, O Lord?"*: See Psalm 4(35):10.

[3] *snapped my bonds*: See Psalm 115(116):16–17.

[4] *Blessed be the Lord, . . . name*: See Psalm 134(135):6; 75:2(76:1); 8:2(1).

[5] *I was besieged by you on every side*: See Isaiah 29:2.

[6] *reflection in a mirror*: See 1 Corinthians 13:12.

[7] *old leaven*: See 1 Corinthians 5:7–8.

[8] *narrowness of the path daunted me and I still could not walk in it*: See Matthew 7:14.

You inspired in me the idea that I ought to go to Simplicianus,[9] and even I could see the sense of this. I regarded him as your good servant, a man from whom grace radiated. Moreover I had heard how from his youth he had lived for you in complete dedication, and since he was an old man by now I assumed that after following your way of life for long years and with such noble zeal he must be rich in experience and deeply learned. And so indeed he was. I hoped, therefore, that if I could discuss my perplexities with him, he would bring out from his storehouse[10] appropriate advice as to how a man in my condition might walk in your way.

2. Surveying the full assembly of the Church I observed that people's lifestyles varied.[11] For my own part I was irked by the secular business I was conducting, for no longer was I fired by ambition, and prepared on that account to endure such heavy servitude in the hope of reputation and wealth, as had formerly been the case. Those prospects held no charm for me now that I was in love with your tender kindness and the beauty of your house;[12] but I was in tight bondage to a woman.[13] The apostle did not forbid me to marry, although he did propose a better choice, earnestly wishing that everyone might live as he did

---

[9] *Simplicianus:* Simplicianus (d. 400) succeeded Ambrose as bishop of Milan in 397. While there are numerous exchanges of letters between Simplicianus and Ambrose, he also appears often in Augustine's works (e.g., *Letter* 37, *City of God* 10.29, *On the Gift of Perseverance* §52) and is even the recipient of Augustine's first work as a bishop, addressing many fine points of proper scriptural exegesis, free will, and salvation (*To Simplicianus*).

[10] *Storehouse:* See Matthew 13:52.

[11] *Surveying the full assembly . . . observed that people's lifestyles varied:* Attempting to live apart from God depersonalizes, while true praise perfects and makes the creature more fully alive and thus individuated. Augustine here realizes that apart from the Church he is less the person he could be in Christ, and the diversity of God's people strikes him in contrast to the faceless pursuits of the world.

[12] *beauty of your house:* See Psalm 25(26):8.

[13] *I was in tight bondage to a woman:* Carnal custom dies hard: Augustine has now procured for himself another live-in lover, even while mulling over Paul's exhortation to celibacy. Still unaware of the power of grace, chastity and continence are delayed.

himself;[14] but I was too weak for that and inclined to an easier course. For this reason alone I was vacillating, bored and listless amid my shriveled cares because I was forced to adapt myself to other aspects of conjugal life to which I had pledged and constrained myself, though they were little to my liking. From the lips of your Truth I had heard that *there are eunuchs who have castrated themselves for love of the kingdom of heaven,* but the saying continues, *Let anyone accept this who can.*[15]

How foolish are they who know not God! So many good things before their eyes, yet *Him Who Is* they fail to see.[16] I was trapped in that foolishness no longer, for I had left it behind by hearkening to the concerted witness of your whole creation, and had discovered you, our creator, and your Word, who dwells with you and is with you the one sole God, through whom you have created all things.[17] But there are impious people of another type, who do recognize God yet have not glorified him as God, nor given him thanks.[18] Into that error too I had formerly blundered, but your right hand grasped me,[19] plucked me out of it and put me in a place where I could be healed, for you have told us that *reverence for God—that is wisdom,*[20] and warned us, *Do not give yourself airs for wisdom,* because *those who believed themselves wise have sunk into folly.*[21] I had found a precious pearl, worth buying at the cost of all I had;[22] but I went on hesitating.

---

[14] *apostle did not forbid me to marry . . . might live as he did himself*: See 1 Corinthians 7:7–8.

[15] there are eunuchs . . . Let anyone accept this who can: Matthew 19:12.

[16] *How foolish are they who know not God! . . . they fail to see*: See Wisdom 13:1.

[17] *your Word, who dwells with you . . . through whom you have created all things*: See John 1:1–3.

[18] *who do recognize God yet have not glorified him as God, nor given him thanks*: See Romans 1:21.

[19] *your right hand grasped me*: See Psalm 117:36(118:35).

[20] reverence for God—that is wisdom: Job 28:28.

[21] Do not give yourself airs for wisdom . . . wise have sunk into folly: Proverbs 26:5; Romans 1:22.

[22] *found a precious pearl, worth buying at the cost of all I had*: See Matthew 13:46; 19:21.

Chapter 2

Conversation with Simplicianus

3. Accordingly I made my way to Simplicianus. When Ambrose, then bishop, had been baptized, Simplicianus had stood as father to him, and Ambrose regarded him with affection as a father indeed. To him I described the winding paths of my wayward life. When I mentioned that I had read certain Platonist books, translated into Latin by Victorinus, who had formerly been a rhetorician in Rome but had, as I had heard, died a Christian, Simplicianus told me how fortunate I was not to have stumbled on the writings of other philosophers, works full of fallacies and dishonesty that smacked of the principles of this world,[23] whereas those Platonist writings conveyed in every possible way, albeit indirectly, the truth of God and his Word.

Story of Victorinus' conversion

He went on to reminisce about this Victorinus with the object of inculcating in me that humility of Christ which is hidden from the sagacious but revealed to little ones.[24] He knew him intimately in Rome, and he told me a story about Victorinus which I will not pass over in silence, since it powerfully redounds to the praise of your grace and moves me to confession, this story of a deeply learned old man.[25]

---

[23] *works full of fallacies . . . that smacked of the principles of this world*: See Colossians 2:8.

[24] *hidden from the sagacious but revealed to little ones*: See Matthew 11:25.

[25] *Victorinus . . . learned old man*: Marius Victorinus was a leading fourth-century Latin rhetorician and Neoplatonic philosopher. Known also as Victorinus Afer, we know he came from North Africa to Rome to serve the emperor, duly honored with a statue in the Roman Forum. Around 355, he converted to the Catholic faith and used his latter years defending pro-Nicene insistence on the constubstantiality of the Father and the Son against the Arians, who wanted to make the Son of God a lesser being than the Father. He also translated his rich theology into hymns explicating the Church's Trinitarian doctrines. Although we can date these works between 359 and 363, we unfortunately remain unaware

Thoroughly conversant with all the liberal arts, Victorinus had also read widely and with discrimination in philosophy and had taught many a noble senator; in recognition of his distinction as a teacher a statue had been erected to him in the Roman forum, which was a very high honor in the eyes of worldly people, and one he well deserved. Until this period of his life he had been a worshiper of idols and shared the abominable superstitions which at that time blew like an ill wind through almost the whole of the Roman nobility, who were agog for Pelusium and for

> Anubis, dog-voiced god, and monstrous deities
> of many a hue, who warred in days gone by
> against Minerva, Neptune, Venus....[26]

These gods Rome had once vanquished, but now worshiped, and the elderly Victorinus with his terrible thunders had habitually defended their cults; yet he was not ashamed to become a child of your Christ and be born as an infant from your font, bending his neck to the yoke of humility[27] and accepting on his docile brow the sign of the ignominious cross.[28]

4. O Lord, Lord, who bade your heavens stoop, who touched the mountains and set them smoking,[29] by what means did you make your hidden way into that man's breast? The story as Simplicianus told it to me was this. Victorinus was in the habit of reading holy scripture and intensively studying all the

---

of when Marius Victorinus died. He is used here obviously as a goad, encouraging Augustine to take the same Way.

[26] *Anubis, dog-voiced god, . . . against Minerva, Neptune, Venus*: from Virgil, *Aeneid* 8.819–20, on the shield of Aeneas. As the easternmost metropolis of Egypt, Pelusium (known by the Israelites as the city of Sin), was the east's entryway into Egypt, a symbol, therefore, of international conquest. Virgil's Aeneas and his travels to found Rome was, of course, the anchor of every Latin boy's education.

[27] *bending his neck to the yoke of humility*: See Sirach 51:34; Jeremiah 27:12; Matthew 11:29.

[28] *sign of the ignominious cross*: See Galatians 5:11.

[29] *O Lord, Lord, who bade your heavens stoop, . . . set them smoking*: See Psalm 143(144):5.

Christian writings, which he subjected to close scrutiny; and he would say to Simplicianus, not openly but in private, intimate conversation, "I am already a Christian, you know." But the other always replied, "I will not believe that, nor count you among Christians, until I see you in Christ's Church." Victorinus would chaff him: "It's the walls that make Christians, then?" He would often talk like this, claiming that he was a Christian. Simplicianus often responded in the same way, and Victorinus would frequently repeat his joke about walls.[30]

The fact was that he was sorely afraid of upsetting the proud demon-worshipers who were his friends, fearing that the weight of their resentment might come storming down on him from the peak of their Babylonian grandeur, as though from lofty cedars on Lebanon not yet felled by the Lord.[31] But later he drank in courage from his avid reading and came to fear that he might be disowned by Christ before his holy angels if he feared to confess him before men and women.[32] In his own eyes he was guilty of a great crime in being ashamed of the holy mysteries instituted by your humble Word, while feeling no shame at the sacrilegious rites of proud demons, whose likeness he had been proud to assume himself. Accordingly he threw off the shamefacedness provoked by vanity and became modest in the face of truth: suddenly and without warning he said to Simplicianus, who told this tale, "Let us go to church: I want to become a Christian."

Hardly able to contain his joy, Simplicianus went with him. He was initiated into the first stage of the catechumenate, and not long afterward he gave in his name, asking for rebirth in baptism. Rome stood amazed, while the Church was

[30] *"It's the walls that make Christians, then?"* . . . *his joke about walls*: This is one of the most quotable lines of the *Confessions*, and one most needed: Simplicianus concedes that Victorinus holds Christian doctrine correctly, but to be a true Christian, one has to get to the gathering Body of Christ and to the sacraments. Christianity is not a religion of abstract spirit but particular and incarnate Truth. The walls, in fact, do make a difference.

[31] *cedars on Lebanon not yet felled by the Lord*: See Psalm 28(29):5.

[32] *disowned by Christ . . . if he feared to confess him before men and women*: See Mark 8:38.

jubilant.[33] The proud looked on and fumed with anger; they ground their teeth in impotent fury;[34] but as for your servant, the Lord God was his hope, and he had no eyes for vanities or lying follies.[35]

5. Eventually the time came for him to make his profession of faith. Custom decrees that those who are approaching your grace in baptism make their profession in the presence of the baptized community of Rome, standing on a raised platform and using a set form of words which has been entrusted to them and committed to memory.[36] Simplicianus told me that Victorinus had been offered by the priests the option of making his statement more privately, for it was customary to offer this concession to people who were likely to lose their nerve through shyness, but that he had chosen rather to proclaim his salvation before the holy company. What he taught in rhetoric was not salvation, he said, yet he had professed that publicly enough. If he was not afraid to address crowds of crazy people in his own words, how much less ought he to fear your peaceable flock as he uttered your word?

As he climbed up to repeat the Creed they all shouted his name to one another in a clamorous outburst of thanksgiving—everyone who knew him, that is; and was there anyone present

[33] *Rome stood amazed, while the Church was jubilant*: Here are the two main competitors of the fourth century: Rome and the Church. Having grown bashful in his later years, Victorinus has the option of undergoing the Rites of Initiation in private but foregoes all pride to be with all of God's people, thus symbolizing the lowliness of God's own descent and the consequent joy of all those around him.

[34] *proud looked on and fumed . . . ground their teeth in impotent fury*: See Psalm 111(112):10.

[35] *Lord God was his hope, and he had no eyes for vanities or lying follies*: See Psalm 39:5(40:4).

[36] *set form of words which has been entrusted to them and committed to memory*: This is the *traditio symboli*, the "handing over" of the Catholic Creed, as entrusting the Church's main beliefs to memory was an integral part of adult baptism; Bishop Ambrose saw this part of the baptismal rite as necessary to make the Church's truths "the heart's ongoing meditation and ever-present guard" (*Explanation of the Creed* §10–11). Augustine surely is drawing our attention to the new use of new words: the grandiloquence of ancient rhetoric has proven moribund, while the lowliness of liturgical language now proves life-giving.

who did not? Then in more subdued tones the word passed from joyful mouth to joyful mouth among them all: "Victorinus, Victorinus!" Spontaneous was their shout of delight as they saw him, and spontaneous their attentive silence to hear him. With magnificent confidence he proclaimed the true faith, and all the people longed to clasp him tenderly to their hearts. And so they did, by loving him and rejoicing with him, for those affections were like clasping hands.

Chapter 3

6. O God, who are so good, what is it in the human heart that makes us rejoice more intensely over the salvation of a soul which is despaired of but then freed from grave danger, than we would if there had always been good prospects for it and its peril slighter? You too, merciful Father, yes, even you are more joyful over one repentant sinner than over ninety-nine righteous people who need no repentance.[37] And we likewise listen with overflowing gladness when we hear how the shepherd carries back on exultant shoulders the sheep that had strayed,[38] and how the coin is returned to your treasury as neighbors share the glee of the woman who found it,[39] while the joy of your eucharistic assembly wrings tears from us when the story is read in your house of a younger son who *was dead, but has come back to life, was lost but is found.*[40] You express your own joy through ours, and through the joy of your angels who are made holy by their holy charity; for you yourself are ever the same,[41] and all transient things, things which cannot abide constantly in their mode of being, are known to your unchanging intelligence.

[37] *more joyful over one repentant sinner . . . people who need no repentance*: See Luke 15:4–7.

[38] *shepherd carries back . . . sheep that had strayed*: See Luke 15:4–6; Psalm 118(119):176.

[39] *coin is returned to your treasury . . . glee of the woman who found it*: See Luke 15:8–9.

[40] was dead, but has come back to life, was lost but is found: Luke 15:24, 32.

[41] *you yourself are ever the same*: See Psalm 101:28(102:27).

7. What is going on in our minds, then, that we should be more highly delighted at finding cherished objects, or having them restored to us, than if we had always kept them safe? Other instances bear this out, and all our experience shouts its corroboration, "Yes, truly this is so." A victorious emperor celebrates his triumph. He would not have been victorious had there been no war, and the more imperiled he has been in battle, the more elated he is in his triumph. Or a storm batters mariners and threatens them with shipwreck. Every face pales at the prospect of death, but sky and sea grow calm, and the sailors' joy is as intense as lately was their fear. Or someone we love falls sick. His pulse betrays the gravity of his condition, and all who long for his recovery are equally tormented in their minds. Then he takes a turn for the better, and although he is not yet walking with his pristine vigor there is already such joy as never there was when in earlier days he strode about well and strong.[42]

Even the natural pleasures of human life are attained through distress, not only through the unexpected calamities that befall against our will but also through deliberate and planned discomfort. There is no pleasure in eating and drinking unless the discomfort of hunger and thirst have preceded them. Drunkards eat somewhat salty food to induce a searing, parched sensation, which will be deliciously quenched by a drink. Then again, custom requires that after betrothal brides shall not be handed over immediately, lest after marriage a man hold cheap the woman for whom he did not as a bridegroom have to sigh and wait.

---

[42] *there is already such joy . . . well and strong*: With a patently Platonic stamp, Augustine here is arguing that most earthly pleasures are spurious because they are merely absences of pain, whereas a true good will be appreciated simply for what it is. God alone can be enjoyed in and of himself, while all other legitimate pleasures must be directed toward and speak to us of God. This is an instance of the classical Augustinian distinction between *uti* and *frui*, between the enjoyment of something (*frui* in Latin) and the use of something (*uti*): God alone can be enjoyed without reference to anything else, while all other loves must be "used" in such a way that God is realized as the measure and standard of their worth and pleasure.

8. This law holds for shameful, demeaning pleasure, but the same is true for what is permitted and lawful, the same for the most sincere and honorable friendship, and the same for that young man who had died but come back to life, had perished but was found. In every case greater sorrow issues in greater joy. How can this be, O Lord my God, when you are yourself your own eternal joy, and all around you heaven rejoices in you eternally? Why is it that our part of creation swings between decay and growth, pain and reconciliation? Perhaps because this is the proper mode of being for these things and with this alone you endowed them when from highest heaven to the lowest places of the earth, from the dawn of the ages to their end, from angel to tiny worm, from the first stirring of change to the last, you assigned all classes of good things and all your righteous works to their appropriate places, and activated them at their proper times?

Ah, how high you are in the heights of heaven,[43] how deep in the depths! From no place are you absent, yet how tardily do we return to you!

Chapter 4

9. Come, Lord, arouse us and call us back, kindle us and seize us, prove to us how sweet you are in your burning tenderness; let us love you and run to you.[44] Are there not many who return to you from a deeper, blinder pit than did Victorinus, many who draw near to you and are illumined[45] as they welcome the light, and in welcoming it receive from you the power to become children of God?[46] Yet if they are less well known to the populace, even people who do know them find less joy in their conversion, because whenever joy is shared among many, even the gladness of individuals is increased, for all are

[43] *how high you are in the heights of heaven*: See Psalm 112(113):4–5; Isaiah 33:5.

[44] *let us love you and run to you*: See Song of Solomon 1:2–3.

[45] *many who draw near to you and are illumined*: See Psalm 33:6(34:5).

[46] *welcome the light . . . power to become children of God*: See John 1:9, 12.

affected by the common enthusiasm and they catch the flame from one another. Moreover, the fact that these converts are generally known ensures that they become for many an author-itative example pointing toward salvation; they forge ahead of crowds that will follow. That is why many who have made the journey before them rejoice particularly, with an eye to others besides these lone individuals.

Forbid it, Lord, that rich personages should ever be more welcome in your tabernacle than the poor, or the nobility than lowly folk,[47] when your own preferential choice fell upon the weak things of this world in order to shame the strong, upon lowly things, contemptible things and nonentities, as though they really were, to set at nought the things that are.[48] Nevertheless the least of your apostles,[49] through whose tongue you sent those words re-echoing, loved to be called not by his former name, "Saul," but "Paul," to commemorate that glorious victory when the proconsul Paulus,[50] his pride beaten down by the apostle's arms, was brought under Christ's lenient yoke to become a common subject of the great King. The enemy is more thoroughly trounced in a person over whom he had a more powerful hold, or through whom he had a hold over a greater number of others; and stronger is his grip over those who on pretext of nobility are proud, stronger too his hold over many another on pretext of their authority.

The higher, then, the value set on the soul of Victorinus, which the devil had captured as an impregnable stronghold, and on Victorinus' tongue, which the devil had wielded like a huge, sharp weapon to destroy many, the greater was the

[47] *rich personages . . . the poor, or the nobility than lowly folk*: See Deuteronomy 1:17; 16:19; Sirach 42:1; Acts 10:34; James 2:1–9.

[48] *choice fell upon the weak . . . set at nought the things that are*: See 1 Corinthi-ans 1:27–28; Romans 4:17. Augustine is beginning to savor the great paradox of Christianity and make room for it in his developing worldview: the Christian God is found not in the strong but in the lowly, not in the self-sufficient but in the humble, not in power but in weakness.

[49] *least of your apostles*: See 1 Corinthians 15:9.

[50] *"Saul," but "Paul," . . . proconsul Paulus*: See Acts 13:7–12.

gladness with which your children rightly rejoiced on seeing the powerful foe bound by our King[51] and his weaponry seized, cleaned, and made fit to serve in your honor as equipment useful to the Master for every good purpose.[52]

Chapter 5

Augustine longs to imitate him, but is hindered by lustful habit

10. On hearing this story I was fired to imitate Victorinus; indeed it was to this end that your servant Simplicianus had related it. But he added a further point. When in the reign of the Emperor Julian a law was passed which forbade Christians to teach literature and rhetoric, Victorinus willingly complied, for he preferred to abandon his school of talkativeness rather than forsake your word, through which you impart eloquence to the tongues of speechless babes.[53] In my eyes he appeared not so much heroic as all the happier for having taken this step, since it afforded him the opportunity to be at leisure for you. I ached for a like chance myself, for it was no iron chain imposed by anyone else that fettered me, but the iron of my own will. The enemy had my power of willing in his clutches, and from it had forged a chain to bind me. The truth is that disordered lust springs from a perverted will; when lust is pandered to, a habit is formed; when habit is not checked,

---

[51] *powerful foe bound by our King:* See Matthew 12:29.

[52] *cleaned, and made fit . . . to the Master for every good purpose:* See 2 Timothy 2:21.

[53] *Emperor Julian . . . tongues of speechless babes:* See Wisdom 10:21. The emperor Julian in question here is better known as Julian the Apostate (361–363), who, once having gained the purple, renounced his Christianity and attempted to restore the ancient pagan deities and rites of Rome. He withdrew imperial favor from the Church and mandated Rome's return to religious eclecticism (in the *Tolerance Edict* of 362), strictly forbidding Christian teachers to teach Latin literature and rhetoric, claiming they were forced to expound on authors and themes in which they could not truly believe. After spending his energies combating the Catholic faith, Julian died from a spear wound in battle in the East, uttering (famously but surely apocryphally), *"Vicisti, Galillaee"*— "Galilean, you have won!"

it hardens into compulsion.[54] These were like interlinking rings forming what I have described as a chain, and my harsh servitude used it to keep me under duress.

A new will had begun to emerge in me, the will to worship you disinterestedly[55] and enjoy you, O God, our only sure felicity; but it was not yet capable of surmounting that earlier will strengthened by inveterate custom. And so the two wills fought it out—the old and the new,[56] the one carnal, the other spiritual—and in their struggle tore my soul apart.

11. I thus came to understand from my own experience what I had read, how the flesh lusts against the spirit and the spirit strives against the flesh.[57] I was aligned with both, but more with the desires I approved in myself than with those I frowned upon, for in these latter I was not really the agent, since for the most part I was enduring them against my will rather than acting freely.[58] All the same, the force of habit that fought against me had grown fiercer by my own doing, because I had come willingly to this point where I now wished not to be. And who has any right to object, when just punishment catches up with a sinner?

I had grown used to pretending that the only reason why I had not yet turned my back on the world to serve you was that my perception of the truth was uncertain, but that excuse was no longer available to me, for by now it was certain. But I was still entangled by the earth and refused to enlist in your service,[59] for the prospect of being freed from all these encumbrances frightened me as much as the encumbrances themselves ought to have done.

---

[54] *disordered lust springs from a perverted will . . . hardens into compulsion*: The psychology of sin is key to Augustine's pastoral care, here and throughout his life; he sees how a perverted will that loves creatures inordinately develops habitual vices, enslaving it through disordered compulsions and addictions, and in turn a deformed character is formed.

[55] *will to worship you disinterestedly*: See Job 1:9.

[56] *old and the new*: See Ephesians 4:22, 24; Colossians 3:9–10.

[57] *flesh lusts against the spirit and the spirit strives against the flesh*: See Galatians 5:17.

[58] *enduring them against my will rather than acting freely*: See Romans 7:16–17.

[59] *entangled by the earth and refused to enlist in your service*: See 2 Timothy 2:4.

12. I was thus weighed down by the pleasant burden of the world in the way one commonly is by sleep, and the thoughts with which I attempted to meditate upon you[60] were like the efforts of people who are trying to wake up, but are overpowered and immersed once more in slumberous deeps. No one wants to be asleep all the time, and it is generally agreed among sensible people that being awake is a better state, yet it often happens that a person puts off the moment when he must shake himself out of sleep because his limbs are heavy with a lassitude that pulls him toward the more attractive alternative, even though he is already trying to resist it and the hour for rising has come; in a similar way I was quite sure that surrendering myself to your love would be better than succumbing to my lust, but while the former course commended itself and was beginning to conquer, the latter charmed and chained me. I had no answer to give as you said to me, *Arise, sleeper, rise from the dead: Christ will enlighten you,*[61] and plied me with evidence that you spoke truly; no, I was convinced by the truth and had no answer whatever except the sluggish, drowsy words, "Just a minute," "One more minute," "Let me have a little longer." But these "minutes" never diminished, and my "little longer" lasted inordinately long.[62]

To find my delight in your law as far as my inmost self was concerned was of no profit to me when a different law in my bodily members was warring against the law of my mind, imprisoning me under the law of sin which held sway in my lower self. For the law of sin is that brute force of habit whereby the mind is dragged along and held fast against its will, and deservedly so because it slipped into the habit willingly. In my

[60] *commonly is by sleep, . . . meditate upon you:* See Psalm 62:7(63:6).

[61] Arise, sleeper, rise from the dead: Christ will enlighten you: Ephesians 5:14.

[62] *"Just a minute," "One more minute," . . . my "little longer" lasted inordinately long:* Sin tries to convince the soul moving more desirous of Christ that it cannot live without the evil habits it has over the years developed, and as the Enemy detects one moving closer to true freedom, he calls out all the more forcefully, "Just one more . . . one more lie, one more night of debauchery, one more uncharitable word or deed", and so on.

wretched state, who was there to free me from this death-doomed body, save your grace through Jesus Christ our Lord?[63]

Chapter 6

Conversation with Ponticianus

13. Now I will relate how you set me free from a craving for sexual gratification which fettered me like a tight-drawn chain, and from my enslavement to worldly affairs: I will confess to your name, O Lord,[64] my helper and redeemer.

I continued to attend to my accustomed duties, but with mounting anxiety. I longed for you every day and spent as much time in your church as could be spared from my business, under the weight of which I was groaning. With me was Alypius, who since his third stint as assessor[65] had been without legal advisory work, and was now looking round for clients to whom he might once more sell his counsel, just as I was trying to sell the art of speaking, insofar as it ever can be imparted by teaching.

Nebridius, however, yielding to our friendly persuasion, had consented to act as assistant teacher to Verecundus, a citizen and schoolmaster of Milan who was very well known to us all.[66] This man had most earnestly desired reliable help from someone of our company, for he stood in sore need of it, and he had reinforced his insistent plea by appealing to his close association with us. Nebridius was not, therefore, attracted to this post by ambition for the advantages it might bring him, for he could have done better by the profession of literature,

---

[63] *In my wretched state, . . . Jesus Christ our Lord?* See Romans 7:24–25.

[64] *I will confess to your name . . . my helper and redeemer:* See Psalm 53:8(54:6).

[65] *Alypius, who since his third stint as assessor:* See *Conf.* VI.10.16.

[66] *Verecundus, a citizen and schoolmaster . . . was very well known to us all:* Verecundus was a wealthy Milanese citizen, a teacher of rhetoric, and quite generous to Augustine and his circle. We know that while he was married to a Christian most of his life, he himself converted only on his deathbed (see *Conf.* IX.3.5, p. 230).

had he willed; he undertook it simply as a kindly service because, being such a very gentle and accommodating friend, he was unwilling to set our request aside. He carried out his duties with the utmost discretion, taking care not to attract the attention of persons whom the world regarded as important. He thus steered clear of any mental disturbance they might have caused him, for he wanted to keep his mind free and disengaged for as much of his time as he possibly could, with a view to research and to reading or listening to anything connected with wisdom.

14. On a certain day when Nebridius was absent (I forget why), something happened. A man named Ponticianus, who held an important post at court, came to our house to visit Alypius and me; being an African he was our compatriot, and he wanted something or other from us.[67] We sat down together and talked. His eye happened to light upon a book that lay on a gaming table nearby; he picked it up, opened it and found it to be the letters of the apostle Paul. This was certainly unexpected, for he had supposed it to be the kind of thing I exhausted myself in teaching. But then he smiled, looked up at me and offered his congratulations, surprised by his sudden discovery that those writings, and those alone, were under my eye. He was himself a baptized Christian and made a practice of prostrating himself in church before you, our God, in frequent and prolonged prayers. When I remarked that I was applying myself to intensive study of those scriptures, he began to tell us about the monk Antony of Egypt, whose name was illustrious and held in high honor among your servants, though

---

[67] *Ponticianus . . . wanted something or other from us*: A fellow African, Ponticianus served originally at the Court of Trier under Valentinian (364–375) and sought with three others (*contubernales*) to live a sort of quasi-monastic life while still working in the world. Now in Milan, he seized the opportunity of seeing some letters of Saint Paul in the possession of Augustine and Alypius to tell them of the attraction of desert asceticism and the life of the great desert hero Saint Antony (as written by Saint Athanasius and translated into Latin by Evagrius of Antioch as early as 371). Monastic life was even strewn throughout the West, Augustine himself admitting that he did not even know of the monastery within the environs of Milan.

we had never heard it until this moment. When Ponticianus learned this he dwelt more fully on the subject, enlightening us about the great man; he was astonished at our ignorance. But we were stupefied as we listened to the tale of the wonders you had worked within the true faith of the Catholic Church, especially as they were most firmly attested by recent memory and had occurred so near to our own times. So all of us were amazed: we because they were so tremendous, and he because we had never heard of them.

15. His discourse led on from this topic to the proliferation of monasteries, the sweet fragrance rising up to you from the lives of monks, and the fecund wastelands of the desert. We had known nothing of all this. There was even a monastery full of good brothers at Milan, outside the city walls, under Ambrose's care, yet we were unaware of it.

Story of conversion of two court officials at Trier

Ponticianus went on talking and developing the theme, while we listened, spellbound. So it came about that he told us that one day when the court was at Trier he and three of his colleagues went out for a walk in the gardens abutting on the walls, while the emperor was occupied with the morning show at the circus. Now it happened that as they strolled about they split into pairs, one companion staying with Ponticianus while the other two went off by themselves. In their wandering these latter chanced upon a cottage where some servants of yours were living, men poor in spirit, the kind of people to whom the kingdom of heaven belongs.[68] There they found a book which contained The Life of Antony. One of them began to read it. His admiration and enthusiasm were aroused, and as he read he began to mull over the possibility of appropriating the same kind of life for himself, by renouncing his secular career to serve you alone. (He belonged to the ranks of so-called administrative

---

[68] poor in spirit, the kind of people to whom the kingdom of heaven belongs: See Matthew 5:3.

officers.) Then quite suddenly he was filled with a love of holiness and a realistic sense of shame and disgust with himself;[69] he turned his gaze toward his friend and demanded, "Tell me: where do we hope all our efforts are going to get us? What are we looking for? In whose cause are we striving? Does life at court promise us anything better than promotion to being Friends of the Emperor? And once we are, will that not be a precarious position, fraught with perils? Will it not mean negotiating many a hazard, only to end in greater danger still? And how long would it take us to get there? Whereas I can become a friend of God[70] here and now if I want to."

Even as he spoke he was in labor with the new life that was struggling to birth within him. He directed his eyes back to the page, and as he read a change began to occur in that hidden place within him where you alone can see; his mind was being stripped of the world, as presently became apparent. The flood-tide of his heart leapt on, and at last he broke off his reading with a groan as he discerned the right course and determined to take it. By now he belonged to you. "I have already torn myself away from the ambitions we cherished, and have made up my mind to serve God," he told his friend. "I am going to set about it this very moment and in this place. If you have no stomach to imitate me, at least don't stand in my way." The other replied that he would bear him company, both in the noble reward and in the glorious combat. And both of them, now enlisted in your service, began to build their tower, knowing the cost full well: they abandoned all their possessions and followed you.[71]

Meanwhile Ponticianus was walking with his companion through other parts of the garden. In search of their friends they arrived at the place, and on finding them there urged

[69] *suddenly he was filled with a love of holiness . . . and disgust with himself*: See Psalm 4:5(4).

[70] *I can become a friend of God*: See James 2:23; Judith 8:22. [Only the Latin version of Judith 8:22 calls Abraham *amicus Dei*, a "friend of God".]

[71] *they abandoned all their possessions and followed you*: See Luke 14:28; Matthew 19:27; Luke 5:11, 28.

them to return, for it was growing late. They, however, told their story, announcing the plan on which they had resolved and describing how the will to take this course had arisen within them and grown firm; and they begged their friends at least to place no obstacles in their way, if they had no mind to join them. Ponticianus and his companion shed tears on their own account, as he related, even though they were in no way altered from the men they had been. They offered devout congratulations to their friends and commended themselves to their prayers; then they went back to the palace, dragging heavy hearts along the ground, while their friends stayed in the cottage with hearts set on heaven. Both were engaged to be married, and when their fiancées later heard of their decision, they likewise dedicated their virginity to you.

Chapter 7

16. Ponticianus went on with his story; but, Lord, even while he spoke you were wrenching me back toward myself, and pulling me round from that standpoint behind my back[72] which I had taken to avoid looking at myself. You set me down before my face,[73] forcing me to mark how despicable I was, how misshapen and begrimed, filthy and festering. I saw and shuddered. If I tried to turn my gaze away, he went on relentlessly telling his tale, and you set me before myself once more, thrusting me into my sight that I might perceive my sin and hate it.[74] I had been aware of it all along, but I had been glossing over it, suppressing it and forgetting.

17. But now self-abhorrence possessed me, all the harsher as my heart went out more ardently to those young men, and I heard of the blessed impulsiveness with which they had without reserve handed themselves over to you for healing. By contrast with them I felt myself loathsome, remembering how many of my years—twelve, perhaps—had gone to waste, and I with

---

[72] *pulling me round from that standpoint behind my back*: See Jeremiah 2:27.

[73] *You set me down before my face*: See Psalm 49(50):21.

[74] *perceive my sin and hate it*: See Psalm 35:3(36:2).

them, since my nineteenth year when I was aroused to pursue wisdom by the reading of Cicero's *Hortensius*. I had been putting off the moment when by spurning earthly happiness I would clear space in my life to search for wisdom; yet even to seek it, let alone find it, would have been more rewarding than discovery of treasure or possession of all this world's kingdoms, or having every bodily pleasure at my beck and call. I had been extremely miserable in adolescence, miserable from its very onset, and as I prayed to you for the gift of chastity I had even pleaded, "Grant me chastity and self-control, but please not yet." [75] I was afraid that you might hear me immediately and heal me forthwith of the morbid lust which I was more anxious to satisfy than to snuff out. So I had wandered off into the crooked paths [76] of a sacrilegious superstition, not because I had any certainty about it but because I preferred it to other beliefs—not that I was investigating these in any spirit of reverence: rather was I opposing them with malicious intent.

18. I had been telling myself that my reason for putting off day after day [77] the decision to renounce worldly ambition and follow you alone was that I could as yet see no certain light by which to steer my course. But the day had dawned when I was stripped naked in my own eyes and my conscience challenged me within: "Where is your ready tongue now? You have been professing yourself reluctant to throw off your load of illusion because truth was uncertain. Well, it is certain now, yet the burden still weighs you down, while other people are given wings on freer shoulders, [78] people who have not worn themselves out with research, nor spent a decade and more reflecting on these questions."

[75] *"Grant me chastity and self-control, but please not yet."* This again is one of the *Confessions'* more memorable quips; Augustine knows what he needs to save his soul, but he cannot bring himself to desire such transformation just yet. He well understands the role of personal desires and honesty in prayer when evaluating one's own growth in the Spirit.

[76] *I had wandered off into the crooked paths*: See Sirach 2:16.

[77] *putting off day after day*: See Sirach 5:8.

[78] *wings on freer shoulders*: See Psalm 54:7(55:6).

My conscience gnawed away at me in this fashion, and I was fiercely shamed and flung into hideous confusion while Ponticianus was relating all this. Having brought the conversation to a close and settled his business with us, he returned to his place, and I to myself.

Was anything left unsaid in my inner debate? Was there any whip of sage advice I left unused to lash my soul into coming with me, as I tried to follow you? It fought and resisted, but could find no excuse. All its arguments had been used up and refuted, but there remained a dumb dread: frightful as death seemed the restraining of habit's oozy discharge, that very seepage which was rotting it to death.

Chapter 8

Struggle in the garden

19. Within the house of my spirit the violent conflict raged on, the quarrel with my soul that I had so powerfully provoked in our secret dwelling, my heart,[79] and at the height of it I rushed to Alypius with my mental anguish plain upon my face. "What is happening to us?" I exclaimed. "What does this mean? What did you make of it? The untaught are rising up and taking heaven by storm,[80] while we with all our dispassionate teachings are still groveling in this world of flesh and blood![81] Are we ashamed to follow, just because they have taken the lead, yet not ashamed of lacking the courage even to follow?" Some such words as these I spoke, and then my frenzy tore me away from him, while he regarded me in silent bewilderment. Unusual, certainly, was my speech, but my brow, cheeks and eyes, my flushed countenance and the cadences of my voice expressed my mind more fully than the words I uttered.

[79] *secret dwelling, my heart*: See Matthew 6:6.
[80] *taking heaven by storm*: See Matthew 11:12.
[81] *this world of flesh and blood*: See 1 Corinthians 15:50; Matthew 16:17; Galatians 1:16.

Adjacent to our lodgings was a small garden. We were free to make use of it as well as of the house, for our host, who owned the house, did not live there. The tumult in my breast had swept me away to this place, where no one would interfere with the blazing dispute I had engaged in with myself until it should be resolved. What the outcome would be you knew, not I. All I knew was that I was going mad, but for the sake of my sanity, and dying that I might live, aware of the evil that I was but unaware of the good I was soon to become. So I went out into the garden and Alypius followed at my heels; my privacy was not infringed by his presence, and, in any case, how could he abandon me in that state? We sat down as far as possible from the house. I was groaning in spirit[82] and shaken by violent anger because I could form no resolve to enter into a covenant with you, though in my bones I knew that this was what I ought to do,[83] and everything in me lauded such a course to the skies. It was a journey not to be undertaken by ship or carriage or on foot,[84] nor need it take me even that short distance I had walked from the house to the place where we were sitting; for to travel—and more, to reach journey's end—was nothing else but to want to go there, but to want it valiantly and with all my heart, not to whirl and toss this way and that a will half crippled by the struggle, as part of it rose up to walk while part sank down.

20. While this vacillation was at its most intense many of my bodily gestures were of the kind that people sometimes want to perform but cannot, either because the requisite limbs are missing, or because they are bound and restricted, or paralyzed through illness, or in some other way impeded. If I tore out my hair, battered my forehead, entwined my fingers and clasped them round my knee, I did so because I wanted to. I might have wanted to but found myself unable, if my limbs had not been mobile enough to obey. So then, there were plenty

---

[82] *groaning in spirit*: See John 11:33.

[83] *in my bones I knew that this was what I ought to do*: See Psalm 34(35):10.

[84] *It was a journey not to be undertaken by ship or carriage or on foot*: See *Conf.* I.18.28.

of actions that I performed where willing was not the same thing as being able; yet I was not doing the one thing that was incomparably more desirable to me, the thing that I would be able to do as soon as I willed, because as soon as I willed— why, then, I would be willing it! For in this sole instance the faculty to act and the will to act precisely coincide, and the willing is already the doing. Yet this was not happening. My body was more ready to obey the slightest whim of my soul in the matter of moving my limbs, than the soul was to obey its own command in carrying out this major volition, which was to be accomplished within the will alone.

Chapter 9

21. How did this bizarre situation arise, how develop? May your mercy shed light on my inquiry, so that perhaps an answer may be found in the mysterious punishments meted out to humankind, those utterly baffling pains that afflict the children of Adam. How then did this bizarre situation arise, how develop? The mind commands the body and is instantly obeyed; the mind commands itself, and meets with resistance. When the mind orders the hand to move, so smooth is the compliance that command can scarcely be distinguished from execution; yet the mind is mind, while the hand is body. When the mind issues its command that the mind itself should will something (and the mind so commanded is no other than itself), it fails to do so. How did this bizarre situation arise, how develop? As I say, the mind commands itself to will something: it would not be giving the order if it did not want this thing; yet it does not do what it commands.

Evidently, then, it does not want this thing with the whole of itself, and therefore the command does not proceed from an undivided mind.[85] Inasmuch as it issues the command, it

---

[85] *undivided mind*: The divide in Augustine's will is no longer between two minds or between two separate wills as his former Manichaeism would have posited, but now between two loves in one and the same heart. Augustine admits that he does not really and wholeheartedly desire to be God's and God's alone,

does will it, but inasmuch as the command is not carried out, it does not will it. What the will is ordering is that a certain volition should exist, and this volition is not some alien thing, but its very self. Hence it cannot be giving the order with its whole self. It cannot be identical with that thing which it is commanding to come into existence, for if it were whole and entire, it would not command itself to be, since it would be already.

This partial willing and partial non-willing is thus not so bizarre, but a sickness of the mind, which cannot rise with its whole self on the wings of truth because it is heavily burdened by habit. There are two wills, then, and neither is the whole: what one has the other lacks.

Chapter 10

22. Some there are who on perceiving two wills engaged in deliberation assert that in us there are two natures, one good, the other evil, each with a mind of its own. Let them perish from your presence, O God,[86] as perish all who talk wildly and lead our minds astray.[87] They are evil themselves as long as they hold these opinions, yet these same people will be good if they embrace true opinions and assent to true teaching, and so merit the apostle's commendation, *You were darkness once, but now you are light in the Lord.*[88] The trouble is that they want to be light not in the Lord but in themselves, with their notion that the soul is by nature divine, and so they have become denser darkness still, because by their appalling arrogance they have moved further away from you, the true Light,

---

and such internal fragmentation alienates Augustine from his truest self because he has not (yet) given all he is over to the One who handed himself over freely for him. He wills Christ, but he also senses how he does not want Jesus to get too close (described as nonwilling), a double-mindedness he later describes as a self-imposed loneliness and sickness of the mind.

[86] *Let them perish from your presence, O God:* See Psalm 67:3 (68:2).

[87] *as perish all who talk wildly and lead our minds astray:* See Titus 1:10.

[88] You were darkness once, but now you are light in the Lord: Ephesians 5:8.

who enlighten everyone who comes into the world.[89] I warn
these people, Take stock of what you are saying, and let it
shame you; but once draw near to him and be illumined, and
your faces will not blush with shame.[90]

When I was making up my mind to serve the Lord my God[91]
at last, as I had long since purposed, I was the one who wanted
to follow that course, and I was the one who wanted not to. I
was the only one involved. I neither wanted it wholeheartedly nor turned from it wholeheartedly. I was at odds with
myself, and fragmenting myself. This disintegration was occur-
ring without my consent, but what it indicated was not the
presence in me of a mind belonging to some alien nature but
the punishment undergone by my own.[92] In this sense, and
this sense only, it was not I who brought it about, but the sin
that dwelt within me[93] as penalty for that other sin committed with greater freedom; for I was a son of Adam.

23. Moreover, if we were to take the number of conflicting
urges to signify the number of natures present in us, we should
have to assume that there are not two, but many. If someone
is trying to make up his mind whether to go to a Manichean
conventicle[94] or to the theater, the Manichees declare, "There
you are, there's the evidence for two natures: the good one is

[89] *true Light, who enlighten everyone who comes into the world*: See John 1:9.

[90] *be illumined, and your faces will not blush with shame*: See Psalm 33:6(34:5).

[91] *serve the Lord my God*: See Deuteronomy 6:13; Matthew 4:10; Jeremiah 30.9.

[92] *belonging to some alien nature but the punishment undergone by my own*: No longer able to blame his vices conveniently on some separated other self, Augustine comes to see how the alienation experienced in sin is the punishment of one's own turning from the Good. Whereas divine conversion brings unity and integrity within the self, running from God brings disintegration and thus pain-ful isolation not only from God but from others and, most ironically, from one's own self as well. A helpful etymology is to see how, to Augustine's Latin mind, the word for "devil", *diabolus*, literally means "the one who divides and scatters" (*dia* is the Greek prefix "to disperse", and *ballo* is the verb "to throw", from which we get English words like "ball" and "ballistics").

[93] *sin that dwelt within me*: See Romans 7:17, 20.

[94] *Manichean conventicler*: a meeting house for the Manichees situated often-times secretly in urban centers, allowing Manichaeism to survive well after its official condemnation.

dragging him our way, the bad one is pulling him back in the other direction. How else explain this dithering between contradictory wills?" But I regard both as bad, the one that leads him to them and the one that lures him back to the theater. They, on the contrary, think that an inclination toward them can only be good.

But consider this: suppose one of our people is deliberating, and as two desires clash he is undecided whether to go to the theater or to our church, will not our opponents too be undecided what attitude to take? Either they will have to admit that it is good will that leads a person to our church, just as good as that which leads to theirs the people who are initiated into their sacred rites and trapped there—and this they are unwilling to admit; or they will conclude that two evil natures and two bad minds are pitted against each other within one person, in which case their habitual assertion of one good and one evil nature will be erroneous; or, finally, they will be brought round to the truth and no longer deny that when a person is deliberating there is but one soul, thrown into turmoil by divergent impulses.

24. When, therefore, they observe two conflicting impulses within one person, let them stop saying that two hostile minds are at war, one good, the other evil, and that these derive from two hostile substances and two hostile principles. For you are true, O God, and so you chide and rebuke them and prove them wrong. The choice may lie between two impulses that are both evil, as when a person is debating whether to murder someone with poison or a dagger; whether to annex this part of another man's property or that, assuming he cannot get both; whether to buy himself pleasure by extravagant spending or hoard his money out of avarice; whether to go to the circus or the theater if both performances are on the same day—and I would even add a third possibility: whether to go and steal from someone else's house while he has the chance, and a fourth as well: whether to commit adultery while he is about it. All these impulses may occur together, at exactly the same time, and all be equally tempting, but they cannot all be acted upon

at once. The mind is then rent apart by the plethora of desirable objects as four inclinations, or even more, do battle among themselves; yet the Manichees do not claim that there are as many disparate substances in us as this.

The same holds true for good impulses. I would put these questions to them: Is it good to find delight in a reading from the apostle? To enjoy the serenity of a psalm? To discuss the gospel? To each point they will reply, "Yes, that is good." Where does that leave us? If all these things tug at our will with equal force, and all together at the same time, will not these divergent inclinations put a great strain on the human heart, as we deliberate which to select? All are good, but they compete among themselves until one is chosen, to which the will, hitherto distracted between many options, may move as a united whole. So too when the joys of eternity call us from above, and pleasure in temporal prosperity holds us fast below, our one soul is in no state to embrace either with its entire will. Claimed by truth for the one, to the other clamped by custom, the soul is torn apart in its distress.[95]

Chapter 11

25. Such was the sickness in which I agonized, blaming myself more sharply than ever, turning and twisting in my chain as I strove to tear free from it completely, for slender indeed was the bond that still held me. But hold me it did. In my secret heart you stood by me, Lord, redoubling the lashes of fear and shame in the severity of your mercy, lest I give up the struggle

---

[95] *the soul is torn apart in its distress:* Whereas earlier evil was explained in terms of its being, Augustine decidedly arguing that ontologically evil must be understood to be a no-thing, here he explains the reality of evil as rational creatures freely choosing lower over higher goods, as there is (are) no evil being(s). The fallen soul is thus depicted as simultaneously yearning for the truest joys of heaven as well as the fleeting goods of earth. Sin thus arises when I choose a lower good (e.g., my third bowl of pasta) over a higher good (e.g., my health, the habitual fostering of temperance, the fair distribution of food, etc.), as Augustine would argue we never choose anything *qua* evil but only as a perceived good.

and that slender, fragile bond that remained be not broken after all, but thicken again and constrict me more tightly. "Let it be now," I was saying to myself. "Now is the moment, let it be now," and merely by saying this I was moving toward the decision. I would almost achieve it, but then fall just short; yet I did not slip right down to my starting-point, but stood aside to get my breath back. Then I would make a fresh attempt, and now I was almost there, almost there ... I was touching the goal, grasping it ... and then I was not there, not touching, not grasping it. I shrank from dying to death and living to life, for ingrained evil was more powerful in me than new-grafted good. The nearer it came, that moment when I would be changed, the more it pierced me with terror. Dismayed, but not quite dislodged, I was left hanging.

26. The frivolity of frivolous aims, the futility of futile pursuits,[96] these things that had been my cronies of long standing, still held me back, plucking softly at my garment of flesh and murmuring in my ear, "Do you mean to get rid of us? Shall we never be your companions again after that moment ... never ... never again? From that time onward so-and-so will be forbidden to you, all your life long." And what was it that they were reminding me of by those words, "so-and-so,"[97] O my God, what were they bringing to my mind? May your mercy banish such memories far from me! What foul deeds were they not hinting at, what disgraceful exploits! But now their voices were less than half as loud, for they no longer confronted me directly to argue their case, but muttered behind my back and slyly tweaked me as I walked away, trying to make me look back. Yet they did slow me down, for I could not bring myself to tear free

[96] *frivolity of frivolous aims, the futility of futile pursuits*: See Ecclesiastes 1:2; 12:8.

[97] *murmuring in my ear . . . "so-and-so,"*: As Augustine's sins cry out defending his dependency upon them, one cannot help but hear the end of C.S. Lewis' *The Great Divorce* [(New York: Touchstone, [1946] 1996), p. 99] as a good angel begs the man to give up his sins at his earthly life's final moment, but sin reaches up to the man's ear to warn him: "He can kill me. One fatal word from you and he *will*! Then you'll be without me for ever and ever. It's not natural. How could you live? You'd be only a sort of ghost, not a real man as you are now."

and shake them off and leap across to that place whither I was summoned, while aggressive habit still taunted me: "Do you imagine you will be able to live without these things?"

27. The taunts had begun to sound much less persuasive, however; for a revelation was coming to me from that country toward which I was facing, but into which I trembled to cross. There I beheld the chaste, dignified figure of Continence. Calm and cheerful was her manner, though modest, pure and honorable her charm as she coaxed me to come and hesitate no longer, stretching kindly hands to welcome and embrace me, hands filled with a wealth of heartening examples. A multitude of boys and girls were there, a great concourse of youth and persons of every age, venerable widows and women grown old in their virginity, and in all of them I saw that this same Continence was by no means sterile, but the fruitful mother of children[98] conceived in joy from you, her Bridegroom. She was smiling at me, but with a challenging smile, as though to say, "Can you not do what these men have done, these women? Could any of them achieve it by their own strength, without the Lord their God? He it was, the Lord their God, who granted me to them. Why try to stand by yourself, only to lose your footing? Cast yourself on him and do not be afraid: he will not step back and let you fall. Cast yourself upon him trustfully; he will support and heal you." And I was bitterly ashamed, because I could still hear the murmurs of those frivolities, and I was still in suspense, still hanging back. Again she appealed to me, as though urging, "Close your ears against those unclean parts of you which belong to the earth[99] and let them be put to death. They tell you titillating tales, but have nothing to do with the law of the Lord your God."[100]

All this argument in my heart raged only between myself and myself. Alypius stood fast at my side, silently awaiting the outcome of my unprecedented agitation.

---

[98] *fruitful mother of children*: See Psalm 112(113):9.

[99] *unclean parts of you which belong to the earth*: See Colossians 3:5.

[100] *nothing to do with the law of the Lord your God*: See Psalm 118(119):85.

Chapter 12

28. But as this deep meditation dredged all my wretchedness up from the secret profundity of my being and heaped it all together before the eyes of my heart, a huge storm blew up within me and brought on a heavy rain of tears. In order to pour them out unchecked with the sobs that accompanied them I arose and left Alypius, for solitude seemed to me more suitable for the business of weeping. I withdrew far enough to ensure that his presence—even his—would not be burdensome to me. This was my need, and he understood it, for I think I had risen to my feet and blurted out something, my voice already choked with tears. He accordingly remained, in stunned amazement, at the place where we had been sitting. I flung myself down somehow under a fig-tree and gave free rein to the tears that burst from my eyes like rivers, as an acceptable sacrifice to you.[101] Many things I had to say to you, and the gist of them, though not the precise words, was: "O Lord, how long?[102] How long? Will you be angry for ever? Do not remember our age-old sins."[103] For by these I was conscious of being held prisoner. I uttered cries of misery: "Why must I go on saying, 'Tomorrow ... tomorrow'? Why not now? Why not put an end to my depravity this very hour?"

"Pick it up and read"

29. I went on talking like this and weeping in the intense bitterness of my broken heart.[104] Suddenly I heard a voice from a house nearby—perhaps a voice of some boy or girl, I do not know—singing over and over again, "Pick it up and read, pick it up and read."[105] My expression immediately altered and I

---

[101] *acceptable sacrifice to you*: See Psalm 50:19(51:17).

[102] *O Lord, how long?* See Psalm 6:4(3).

[103] *How long? Will you be angry for ever? Do not remember our age-old sins*: See Psalm 78(79):5, 8.

[104] *weeping in the intense bitterness of my broken heart*: See Psalm 50:19(51:17).

[105] *I heard a voice ... "Pick it up and read, pick it up and read"*: At the decisive moment of his conversion, the great rhetorician is brought to truth by a voice so

began to think hard whether children ordinarily repeated a ditty like this in any sort of game, but I could not recall ever having heard it anywhere else. I stemmed the flood of tears and rose to my feet, believing that this could be nothing other than a divine command to open the Book and read the first passage I chanced upon; for I had heard the story of how Antony had been instructed by a gospel text. He happened to arrive while the gospel was being read, and took the words to be addressed to himself when he heard, *Go and sell all you possess and give the money to the poor: you will have treasure in heaven. Then come, follow me.*[106] So he was promptly converted to you by this plainly divine message. Stung into action, I returned to the place where Alypius was sitting, for on leaving it I had put down there the book of the apostle's letters. I snatched it up, opened it and read in silence the passage on which my eyes first lighted: *Not in dissipation and drunkenness, nor in debauchery and lewdness, nor in arguing and jealousy; but put on the Lord Jesus Christ, and make no provision for the flesh or the gratification of your desires.*[107] I had no wish to read further, nor was there need. No sooner had I reached the end of the verse than the light of certainty flooded my heart and all dark shades of doubt fled away.

Conversion of Augustine and Alypius; Monica's joy

30. I closed the book, marking the place with a finger between the leaves or by some other means, and told Alypius what had happened. My face was peaceful now. He in return told me what had been happening to him without my knowledge. He

---

lowly and nondescript that one cannot even discern if it is coming from a boy or from a girl. Augustine is humbled enough to perceive the chant, *Tolle, lege, tolle, lege*—"Pick up and read, pick up and read"—and in some act of sortilege, in which a reader randomly turns to a book's page (here probably a scroll of Romans), Augustine is given a line from Paul which perfectly summarizes his old lifestyle while exhorting him to a new way of living.

[106] Go and sell ... come, follow me: Matthew 19:21.

[107] Not in dissipation ... or the gratification of your desires: Romans 13:13–14.

asked to see what I had read: I showed him, but he looked further than my reading had taken me. I did not know what followed, but the next verse was, *Make room for the person who is weak in faith.*[108] He referred this text to himself and interpreted it to me. Confirmed by this admonition he associated himself with my decision and good purpose without any upheaval or delay, for it was entirely in harmony with his own moral character, which for a long time now had been far, far better than mine.

We went indoors and told my mother, who was overjoyed.[109] When we related to her how it had happened she was filled with triumphant delight and blessed you, who have power to do more than we ask or understand,[110] for she saw that you had granted her much more in my regard than she had been wont to beg of you in her wretched, tearful groaning. Many years earlier you had shown her a vision of me standing on the rule of faith;[111] and now indeed I stood there, no longer seeking a wife or entertaining any worldly hope, for you had converted me to yourself. In so doing you had also converted her grief into a joy[112] far more abundant than she had desired, and much more tender and chaste than she could ever have looked to find in grandchildren from my flesh.[113]

---

[108] Make room for the person who is weak in faith: Romans 14:1.

[109] *my mother, who was overjoyed*: Here the unnamed mother plays two roles: literally Monica, the biological mother, who has prayed for this moment for decades, as well as metaphorically Mother Church, who now receives Augustine with gratitude and jubilation.

[110] *who have power to do more than we ask or understand*: See Ephesians 3:10.

[111] *Many years earlier . . . a vision of me standing on the rule of faith*: See Conf. III.11.19.

[112] *converted her grief into a joy*: See Psalm 29:12(30:11).

[113] *far more abundant than she had desired . . . grandchildren from my flesh*: Monica now finds more joy in Augustine's newly embraced chastity, which she must have known was concomitant with his embracing Christ and his Church, than she had in the possibility of more grandchildren.

Book IX

Death and Rebirth

Chapter 1

1. O Lord, I am your servant, I am your servant and your hand-maid's son. You burst my bonds asunder, and to you will I offer a sacrifice of praise.[1] May my heart and tongue give praise to you, and all my bones cry out their question, "Who is like you, O Lord?"[2] Yes, let them ask, and then do you respond and say to my soul, "I am your salvation."[3]

But who am I, what am I? Is there any evil I have not committed in my deeds, or if not in deeds, then in my words, or if not in words, at least by willing it? But you, Lord, are good and merciful,[4] and your right hand plumbed the depths of my death, draining the cesspit of corruption in my heart, so that I ceased to will all that I had been wont to will, and now willed what you willed.[5] But where had my power of free decision been throughout those long, weary years, and from what depth, what hidden profundity, was it called forth in a moment, enabling me to bow my neck to your benign yoke and my shoulders to your light burden,[6] O Christ Jesus, my helper and redeemer?[7] How sweet did it suddenly seem to me to shrug off

---

[1] *O Lord, I am your servant . . . sacrifice of praise*: See Psalm 115(116):16–17; 85(86):15–16.

[2] *my bones cry out their question, "Who is like you, O Lord?"*: See Psalm 34(35):10.

[3] *say to my soul, "I am your salvation"*: See Psalm 34(35):3.

[4] *you, Lord, are good and merciful*: See Exodus 34:6; Psalm 85(86):15.

[5] *willed what you willed*: See Matthew 26:39; Mark 14:36.

[6] *bow my neck to your benign yoke and my shoulders to your light burden*: See Matthew 11:30.

[7] *O Christ Jesus, my helper and redeemer*: See Psalm 18:15(19:14). Augustine finally realizes that the Word he wished to articulate as a rhetorician and the Truth he sought to know as a philosopher were all along not things but the man Jesus Christ.

those sweet frivolities, and how glad I now was to get rid of them—I who had been loath to let them go![8] For it was you who cast them out from me, you, our real and all-surpassing sweetness. You cast them out and entered yourself to take their place, you who are lovelier than any pleasure, though not to flesh and blood, more lustrous than any light, yet more inward than is any secret intimacy, loftier than all honor, yet not to those who look for loftiness in themselves. My mind was free at last from the gnawing need to seek advancement and riches, to welter in filth and scratch my itching lust. Childlike, I chattered away to you, my glory, my wealth, my salvation, and my Lord and God.

Chapter 2

Augustine decides to renounce his career

2. I believed it to be pleasing in your sight that I should withdraw the service of my tongue from the market of speechifying, so that young boys who were devoting their thoughts not to your law,[9] not to your peace, but to lying follies and legal battles, should no longer buy from my mouth the weapons for their frenzy; but I thought it better to retire unobtrusively rather than make an abrupt and sensational break. Fortunately there were now only a few days left before the vintage holidays and I decided to put up with this delay. I would then resign in the

---

[8] *How sweet did it suddenly seem to me to shrug off. . . loath to let them go!* Although Augustine may have spent most of his later years combating the belief of the British monk Pelagius (ca. 350 through ca. after 430), that the human person can make himself perfect if he simply desires and acts toward holiness resolutely enough (Augustine emphasizing the radical indispensability of God's grace for *every* good thought and deed), he does realize that the human person must nonetheless act freely in cooperation with God, and here he is finally coming to terms with the stark reality that his life was not going to become Christ's until he let go of all his disordered loves and vice-filled pursuits.

[9] *I should withdraw the service of my tongue . . . your law*: See Psalm 118(119):70, 77. His recent conversion has made Augustine ever more sensitive to the duplicity of training the young in the power of rhetoric.

regular way, but return no more to offer myself for sale, now that you had redeemed me.[10]

Our plan was therefore kept between ourselves and you, and not made known to other people outside our own company. We had agreed that it should not be divulged to all and sundry, even though as we climbed up from the valley of weeping[11] singing our pilgrim-song,[12] you had armed us with sharp arrows and burning coals[13] with which to fight the guileful tongues of any who opposed our project while pretending to promote it, and devoured us as they might food on pretense of liking.

3. With the arrows of your charity you had pierced our hearts, and we bore your words within us like a sword penetrating us to the core. The examples of your servants, whom you had changed from murky to luminous beings, from dead to living men, were crowding in upon our thoughts, where they burned and consumed the heavy torpor that might have pulled us down again. So powerfully did they ignite us that every breath of guileful opposition blew our flame into fiercer heat, rather than extinguishing us.

We could be certain, however, that there would be some who would admire the course we had resolved to follow, since you had spread the knowledge of your holy name throughout the world.[14] It therefore seemed like boastfulness to refuse to wait for a holiday period so close at hand, and instead to quit a professional post where I was in the public eye in such a fashion that, as everyone's attention was drawn to what I was doing, and they noted how little time was left before the first

---

[10] *I would then resign . . . you had redeemed me*: Augustine resigned from his post in Milan sometime in the fall of 386, waiting for the annual imperial holiday (the *feriae vindemiales*, which that year would have fallen between late August to mid-October) that aimed to give city dwellers a brief respite from the hot Italian days and farmers the time to harvest their autumnal crops. Most European academic calendars continue to follow this rhythm.

[11] *valley of weeping*: See Psalm 83:7(84:6).

[12] *singing our pilgrim-song*: Psalm 119–33(120–34).

[13] *sharp arrows and burning coals*: See Psalm 119(120):3–4.

[14] *spread the knowledge of your holy name throughout the world*: See Ezekiel 36:23.

day of the holidays, which I had nevertheless chosen to fore-stall, they might have plenty to say about it, concluding that I merely wished to look important. And what was the point of arousing conjecture and contention over my state of mind, and letting this good thing that had come our way provide an occasion for slanderous gossip?[15]

4. It happened by coincidence that in that same summer my lungs had begun to fail under the severe strain of teaching, making it difficult for me to draw breath and giving proof of their unhealthy condition by pains in my chest. My tone was husky and I could not manage any sustained vocal effort. These symptoms had worried me when they first appeared, because they were forcing upon me the necessity of either giving up my professorial career or, if there was any prospect of my being cured and recovering my strength, at least of taking some rest. But now that a wholehearted desire to be still and see that you are the Lord[16] had arisen within me and grown strong, as you know, my God, I began even to rejoice that a genuine excuse lay to hand which I could use to appease those parents who for their children's sake were unwilling ever to allow me freedom. Full of this joy I endured the interval of time until it had run its course—it lasted perhaps twenty days or so—yet this took fortitude, because the desire for gain that had customarily helped me to sustain the heavy burden of work had now left me, and had not patience taken its place I should have been crushed by the load.

It may be that someone among your servants, my brethren in the faith, will judge that I sinned in this matter by allowing myself to remain even for an hour in a professorial chair of lying[17] once my heart was fully intent on your service. I will

---

[15] *quit a professional post . . . slanderous gossip:* See Romans 14:16. Augustine is perhaps worried that once colleagues and students find out he is retiring out of Catholic conviction, they will feel judged and he will look like an opportunist, since he did not leave (what he now considers) such a scandalous career the second he converted in the garden.

[16] *be still and see that you are the Lord:* See Psalm 45:11(46:10).

[17] *chair of lying:* See Psalm 1:1.

not argue. But have you not pardoned this sin, most merciful Lord, along with all the rest of my hideous, dismal sins, in the water of baptism, and forgiven me?[18]

Chapter 3

5. Verecundus was racked with anxiety over this good thing that had befallen us, because he saw himself being distanced from our fellowship by the bonds that unbreakably held him.[19] He was not yet a Christian, and though his wife was a believer, it was precisely she who trammeled him most rigidly and restrained him from the path on which we had set out; for he declared that he was unwilling to be a Christian in any way other than that from which he was debarred. In spite of this he kindly suggested that as long as we were there we should stay on his estate. At the resurrection of the just you will surely reward him, Lord,[20] since you have granted him already his allotted place among the just;[21] for later on, when we had gone to Rome, he was overtaken by an illness, in the course of which he became a believing Christian in our absence, and in that state departed this life. So it was that you showed mercy not only to him but to us as well, sparing us the unbearable grief of being forced to recall his outstanding kindliness toward us while at the same time regarding him as an outsider to your flock. Thanks be to you, our God! We belong to you. You prove it by the exhortations and consolations you provide for us.

---

[18] *not pardoned this sin . . . forgiven me*: The distinction between serious sins (as Augustine here worries his scandal of remaining an imperial employee may have been) and less serious offenses is well known by Augustine, encountered surely at 1 John 5:16–17, where the beloved apostle distinguishes between deadly (i.e., mortal) sin and a sin that is not deadly (what became known in contradistinction as "venial" sin).

[19] *Verecundus . . . bonds that unbreakably held him*: We met Verecundus earlier (see *Conf.* VIII.6.13, p. 208), but here Augustine is commenting on how Verecundus' marriage and position in the world would disallow him from joining these early companions' hopes at a monastic way of life, if that hope should ever come to fruition.

[20] *At the resurrection of the just you will surely reward him, Lord*: See Luke 14:14.

[21] *his allotted place among the just*: See Psalm 124(125):3.

Because you are faithful to your promises you are even now rewarding Verecundus for that country house of his at Cassiciacum, where we found rest in you from the hurly-burly of the world. In exchange for his estate you now endow him with the delights of your verdant paradise for ever, since you pardoned him for his earthly sins by setting him on the mountain of rich pasture, your mountain, the mount of plenty.[22]

6. Verecundus was therefore full of anxiety at the time of which I speak, whereas Nebridius shared our joy. While not yet a Christian he, like us, had fallen into a pit of very dangerous error,[23] believing that the flesh of your Son, who is the Truth, was mere make-believe;[24] but he was beginning to emerge from this error, and was in the position of one who, though not yet initiated into any of the rites of your Church, was a most ardent seeker of the truth.

But not very long after our conversion and rebirth in baptism, when he too was a believing Catholic, when he was serving you in perfect chastity and continence among his own people in Africa, when his whole household had become Christian through his example, you released him from the flesh.

---

[22] *exhortations and consolations you provide for us ... mount of plenty*: See Psalm 67:16(68:15). After Augustine reads Paul and desires to cling solely to Christ, he resigns his post and now gathers friends to join him at Verecundus' estate twenty or so miles northeast of central Milan. The rural village was then known as Cassiciacum (today, in all probability, Cassiago di Brianza, where an inscription with the name Verecundus has been located), and the palatial country manor was loaned out to Augustine; Monica; his son, Adeodatus; his brother, Navigius; two cousins, Lastidianus and Rusticus; two students, Trygetius and Licentius; as well as his boon companion Alypius, from the late summer of 386 up until the Easter Vigil (April 24) of 387. At Cassiciacum, this group would have joined in daily prayer, spiritual reflection, and preparation for those who were to be baptized, and Augustine himself even wrote four treatises in dialogue style: *Against the Skeptics*, *On the Happy Life*, *On Order*, and the *Soliloquies*, a term he actually invented to capture his own internal (*solus*, the self) dialogue (*loquor*, to speak in Latin).

[23] *fallen into a pit of very dangerous error*: See Psalm 7:16(15).

[24] *believing that the flesh of your Son, who is the Truth, was mere make-believe*: This seems to be a form of Docetism we encountered earlier, the belief that Jesus only appeared to have flesh and therefore only seemed to experience the human condition (see *Conf.* V.9.16, note 44, p. 117).

And now he lives in Abraham's bosom.[25] Whatever that may be, whatever the gospel word "bosom" may mean, there my Nebridius is living, to me a friend most tenderly loved, to you, Lord, a freedman adopted as your son; yes, there he lives on. Where else could such a soul be at home? He is alive in that place about which he used to ask me so many questions, ignorant and paltry fellow that I am. No longer does he bend his ear to my mouth; rather does he lay the mouth of his spirit to your fountain and avidly slake his thirst as he drinks your wisdom to the uttermost of his capacity, in happiness without end. Yet I cannot believe that he is so inebriated as to forget me, since you, Lord, from whom he drinks, are mindful of us.

Such, then, was our situation. On the one hand we sought to console Verecundus who, though saddened by our conversion, continued to be our friend, urging him to be faithful to his own calling, namely married life; on the other we waited for Nebridius to follow us. He was very close to doing so, indeed on the point of making his decision, when the days of waiting expired at last. Slow and tedious they had seemed, so sharp was my longing for leisured freedom in which to sing with every fibre of my being, *To you my heart tells its love: I have sought your face, O Lord, for your face will I seek.*[26]

Chapter 4

To Cassiciacum with his mother, son, and friends

7. At last the day arrived which was to set me free in fact from the profession of rhetor, as I was free already in spirit. And so it was done; you detached my tongue from that bond whence you had already delivered my heart, and I blessed you as I joyfully set out for the villa with all my company. The evidence of what I did there in the way of literary work is to be found in the books that record disputations held between

[25] *Abraham's bosom:* See Luke 16:22.
[26] To you my heart tells its love ... your face will I seek: Psalm 26(27):8.

those there present, and deliberations alone with myself in your sight; it was work unquestionably devoted by now to your service, but still with a whiff of scholastic pride about it, like combatants still panting in the interval. What I wrote to Nebridius, who was absent, my letters to him testify.

When could I ever find time enough to record all your generous favors to us during that period—especially now that I am hurrying on to greater matters still? My memory harks back to our sojourn there, and it is my delight, Lord, to acknowledge before you what inward goads you employed to tame me, how you laid low the mountains and hills of my proud intellect and made of me an even plain, how you straightened my winding ways and smoothed my rugged patches,[27] and how you also brought my heart's brother, Alypius, to submit to the name of your only-begotten Son, our Lord and Savior Jesus Christ. At first he disdained to admit it into our writings, for he wanted them to give off the tang of those lofty cedars of Lebanon, felled though these now were by the Lord,[28] rather than the scent of plants grown in your Church and efficacious against snakebite.

He lives with the psalms

8. How loudly I cried out to you, my God, as I read the psalms of David, songs full of faith, outbursts of devotion with no room

---

[27] *you straightened my winding ways and smoothed my rugged patches*: See Isaiah 40:4; Luke 3:4–5.

[28] *Alypius, to submit to the name of your only-begotten Son . . . by the Lord*: See Psalm 28(29):5. In wishing to avoid the name of Jesus Christ, Alypius seems to want to keep his spiritual journey strictly on the philosophical level, "disdaining" perhaps a more popular Christian piety, assenting only to what can be rationally understood. Augustine, on the other hand, knows the deeper mysteries cannot be accessed by the light of natural reason unassisted. Faith must complement intellect. Similar to Augustine not long ago, Alypius thus has not yet seen that the lofty cedars of Lebanon (philosophical propositions) are humbled by a lowlier plant that can save one's life (here from snakes, *serpentibus*), surely an allusion to some more mundane herb as a metaphor for life-restoring theology.

in them for the breath of pride![29] Uncouth I was in real love for you, a catechumen on holiday in a country house with another catechumen, Alypius; but my mother kept us company, woman in outward form but endowed with virile faith, uniting the serenity of an elderly person with a mother's love and Christian devotion. How loudly I began to cry out to you in those psalms, how I was inflamed by them with love for you and fired to recite them to the whole world, were I able, as a remedy against human pride! Yet in truth they are sung throughout the world, and no one can hide from your burning heat.[30] I felt bitterly angry with the Manichees, though my indignation was tinged with pity, because they knew nothing of this remedy and ranted against the very antidote which might have healed them. I could wish that they had been somewhere nearby, without my knowing it, and had gazed upon my face and listened to my voice as I read the fourth psalm in that place of peace. *When I called on him he heard me, the God of my vindication; when I was hard beset you led me into spacious freedom. Have mercy on me, Lord, and hearken to my prayer:*[31] would that they had heard what these words of the psalm did

---

[29] *psalms of David . . . breath of pride*: The Psalms for our author are *the* prayerful songs of Christ's Church. He spent the years 392 to 418 periodically preaching and thus commenting on the Psalms, eventually his longest written work (more than double the length of his massive *City of God*). He gave such importance to the Psalms because he really saw how, unlike other parts of Scripture, they could change the affections by bringing the reader into the presence of the "whole Christ" (*totus Christus*), who was Christ the head crying out in and on behalf of the body he has taken to himself, his Church. Crying out in one voice, then, the psalmist mysteriously captures how the faithful come to see "we are Christ" (for example, see *Commentary on the Psalms* 26[2]2; 49.2; 100.3) as they hear their incarnate Head cry out on their behalf. The Psalms are ultimately Christ's book of song for Augustine, as we encounter throughout the "great exchange"—the Son exchanging his humanity for our divinity. Accordingly, when Augustine sang any psalm, he understood that Jesus is now so humbly one with needy humanity that the incarnate Son goes with us as one of us to the Father to cry out psalms of lament, so unashamedly one with us sinners that he prays with us our psalms of contrition, so joyfully joined with us so as to extol the Father with psalms of praise, while at other times also to be worshipped by us as our God.

[30] *no one can hide from your burning heat*: See Psalm 18:7(19:6).

[31] When I called on him . . . hearken to my prayer: Psalm 4:2(1).

to me, but heard without my knowledge, lest they think that it was for their benefit that I uttered words of my own, interspersed with yours! I would surely not have spoken, or not in the same vein, had I felt myself exposed to their ears and eyes; and even if I had, they would not have taken those words I uttered for what they were, the intimate expression of my mind, as I conversed with myself and addressed myself in your presence.

9. I shuddered with awe, yet all the while hope and joy surged up within me at your mercy, Father.[32] It all found an outlet through my eyes and voice when your good Spirit turned to us, saying, *How long will you be heavy-hearted, human creatures? Why love emptiness and chase falsehood?*[33] I, certainly, had loved emptiness and chased falsehood, and you, Lord, had already glorified your Holy One,[34] raising him from the dead and setting him at your right hand, whence he could send the Paraclete, the Spirit of Truth[35] from on high, as he had promised.[36] He had sent him already, but I did not know it. Yes, he had sent the Spirit, for already he had been glorified in his resurrection from the dead[37] and ascension to heaven. Before that time the Spirit was not given, because Jesus had not been glorified.[38] This is why the prophecy cries out, *How long will you be heavy-hearted? Why love emptiness and chase falsehood? Be sure of this: the Lord has glorified his Holy One.*[39] It demands, *How long?* It cries, *Be sure of this;* yet for so long I had been anything but sure, and had loved emptiness and chased falsehood, and so I trembled as I heard these words, for they are

---

[32] *hope and joy surged up within me at your mercy, Father*: See Psalm 30:7–8(31:6–7).

[33] How long will you be heavy-hearted ... chase falsehood? Psalm 4:3(2).

[34] *you, Lord, had already glorified your Holy One*: See Psalm 4:4(3).

[35] *Paraclete, the Spirit of Truth*: See John 14:16–17.

[36] *from on high, as he had promised*: See Luke 24:49.

[37] *he had been glorified in his resurrection from the dead*: See Romans 6:9; 7:4; 1 Corinthians 15:20.

[38] *Spirit was not given, because Jesus had not been glorified*: See John 7:39.

[39] How long will you be heavy-hearted? ... Lord has glorified his Holy One: Psalm 4:3–4(2–3).

addressed to the kind of person I remembered myself to have been. In the fables which I had taken for truth there was emptiness and falsehood; loud and strong I bewailed many an episode among my painful memories. Oh, that they could have heard me, those who still love emptiness and chase falsehood! They might perhaps be so shaken as to spew it out, and then you would hear them when they cried to you,[40] because he who for us died a true death in the flesh now intercedes with you on our behalf.

10. Then I read, *Let your anger deter you from sin,*[41] and how these words moved me, my God! I had already learned to feel for my past sins an anger with myself that would hold me back from sinning again. With good reason had I learned this anger, since it was no alien nature from a tribe of darkness that had been sinning through me, as they maintain who, though not angry with themselves, are accumulating a fund of anger that will overwhelm them on the day of anger, the day when your righteous judgment is to be revealed.[42]

For me, good things were no longer outside, no longer quested for by fleshly eyes in this world's sunlight. Those who want to find their joy in externals all too easily grow empty themselves. They pour themselves out on things which, being seen, are but transient,[43] and lick even the images of these things with their famished imagination. If only they would weary of their starvation and ask, *Who will show us good things?*[44] Let us answer them, and let them hear the truth: *The light of your countenance has set its seal upon us, O Lord.* We are not ourselves that Light which illumines every human being,[45] but by you we are illumined, so that we who were once darkness

[40] *you would hear them when they cried to you:* See Psalm 4:4(3).

[41] Let your anger deter you from sin: Psalm 4:5(4).

[42] *day of anger, the day when your righteous judgment is to be revealed:* See Romans 2:5.

[43] *pour themselves out on things which, being seen, are but transient:* See 2 Corinthians 4:18.

[44] Who will show us good things? Psalm 4:6(5).

[45] light of your countenance ... *illumines every human being:* See John 1:9.

may become light in you.[46] Ah, if only they could see the eternal reality within! I had tasted it,[47] and was frantic at my inability to show it to them; if only they would bring to me those hearts of theirs which lived in their outward-gazing eyes, outside and away from you; if only they would say, *Who will show us good things?* There within, where I had grown angry with myself, there in the inner chamber where I was pierced with sorrow,[48] where I had offered sacrifice, slaying my old nature[49] and hoping in you as I began to give my mind to the new life,[50] there you had begun to make me feel your sweetness and had given me *joy in my heart.*[51]

As I read these words outwardly and experienced their truth inwardly I shouted with joy, and lost my desire to dissipate myself amid a profusion of earthly goods, eating up time as I was myself eaten by it; for in your eternal simplicity I now had a different *wheat and wine and oil.*[52]

11. The next verse wrung a cry from the very depths of my heart: *In peace!* Oh, *In Being itself!* What did it say? *I will rest and fall asleep.* Yes, for who shall make war against us when that promise of scripture is fulfilled, *Death is swallowed up into victory?*[53] In truth you are Being itself, unchangeable, and in you is found the rest that is mindful no more of its labors, for there is no one else beside you, nor need our rest concern itself

---

[46] *by you we are illumined . . . darkness may become light in you:* See Ephesians 5:8. Augustine's theory of participation helps to make sense of how creatures can be intimately involved in God's life without altering the divine nature: all beings may depend wholly upon God for their existence and all their natural properties, but he does not depend on them. So we often get these kinds of expressions: we are illumined by a Light who itself needs no illumination. God is every positive attribute per se, while we participate in them according to our various natures: God is light, rational souls are illumined; God is goodness, all other beings are good; and so on.

[47] *I had tasted it:* See Psalm 33:9(34:8).

[48] *inner chamber where I was pierced with sorrow:* See Psalm 4:5(4).

[49] *slaying my old nature:* See Ephesians 4:22; Colossians 3:9.

[50] *give my mind to the new life:* See Colossians 3:10; 2 Corinthians 4:16.

[51] joy in my heart: Psalm 4:7.

[52] wheat and wine and oil: Psalm 4:8(7).

[53] Death is swallowed up into victory: 1 Corinthians 15:54.

with striving for a host of other things that are not what you are; rather it is you, *you, Lord, who through hope establish me in unity.*[54]

I read on and on, all afire, but I could find no way to help those deaf, dead folk among whom I had once been numbered. I had been a lethal nuisance, bitter and blind and baying against honey-sweet scriptures distilled from heaven's honey, scriptures luminous by your light;[55] but now to think of the enemies of that scripture[56] caused me anguish.

12. How shall I ever remember all that happened during that holiday? But one thing I cannot forget and will not omit, a harsh chastisement you laid on me, which was followed with amazing swiftness by your mercy. At that time you tortured me with a toothache, and when it had grown so severe that I could not speak, the thought entered my heart that I should urge all my own people who were there to pray for me to you, the God of every kind of healing.[57] I wrote this on a wax tablet and gave it to one of them to read out to the rest. The moment we knelt down and begged this favor from you, the pain vanished. What was that pain? Where did it go? I must admit that I was terrified, my Lord and my God,[58] for I had never in all my life experienced anything like it. It came home to me most deeply that this was a sign of your powerful will, and I rejoiced in my faith as I praised your name;[59] yet this

[54] *you, Lord, who through hope establish me in unity*: Psalm 4:10(8).

[55] *honey-sweet scriptures . . . luminous by your light*: See Psalm 118(119):103, 105.

[56] *enemies of that scripture*: See Psalm 138(139):21.

[57] *you tortured me with a toothache . . . God of every kind of healing*: Throughout Augustine's preaching and writing, he rarely shies away from sharing an intimate detail or two, and this and the following section provide a good example: the young man growing into middle age is waking up to the fragility of the human body, first suffering from a toothache and then from chest pains (see *Conf.* IX.5.13). Is this merely medical recall, or is there a lesson intended for his readers? Perhaps— the body and soul are one, and when the body aches, the mind finds deep contemplation and study difficult, if not impossible.

[58] *my Lord and my God*: See John 20:28.

[59] *rejoiced in my faith as I praised your name*: See Psalm 144(145):2; Sirach 51:15.

same faith did not allow me to be complacent about my past sins, which had not yet been forgiven me through baptism.

Chapter 5

13. When the holidays were over I announced my retirement. The citizens of Milan would have to provide another word-peddler for their students, because I had made up my mind to give myself to your service, and in any case I was unequal to that profession now that I had difficulty in breathing and pains in the chest. I wrote to the holy man Ambrose, your bishop, notifying him of my past errors and present intention, and asking his advice as to which of your books in particular I ought to read, the better to prepare myself for so great a grace and render me more fit to receive it. He recommended the prophet Isaiah, I think because he more plainly than all others foretold the gospel and the call of the Gentiles. The first part I read of this book was incomprehensible to me, however, and, assuming that all the rest would be the same, I put it off, meaning to take it up again later, when I was more proficient in the word of the Lord.

Chapter 6

They return to Milan and are baptized

14. The time arrived for me to give in my name for baptism, so we left the country and moved back to Milan. Alypius had decided to join me in being reborn in you, and was already clothed with the humility[60] that befitted your mysteries. He was also extremely courageous in subduing his body, even to the point of walking barefoot on the icy soil of Italy, a thing few dared to do. We associated the boy Adeodatus with us as well, my son according to the flesh, born of my sin.[61] Very fair had you fashioned

---

[60] *clothed with the humility*: See Colossians 3:12.

[61] *Adeodatus . . . born of my sin*: We were briefly introduced to Adeodatus already (see *Conf.* IV.2.2, note 7, p. 75). Born in Carthage in 372 he is not

him. He was then about fifteen, but surpassed many educated
men of weighty learning. I am acknowledging that these were
your gifts, O Lord my God, creator of all things,[62] who are more
than powerful enough to give fair form to our deformities, for
nothing did I contribute to that boy's making except my fault. It
was you, and you alone, who had inspired us to instruct him in
your truth as he grew up, and so it is your own gifts that I acknowledge to you. There is a book of ours entitled *The Teacher*, in
which he converses with me. You know that all the thoughts
there attributed to my interlocutor were truly his, although he
was only about sixteen years old. Many other things even more
wonderful did I observe in him. The brilliance he evinced filled
me with awe, for who else but you could be the artificer of such
prodigies? Very soon you took him away from this life on earth,
but I remember him without anxiety, for I have no fear about
anything in his boyhood or adolescence; indeed I fear nothing
whatever for that man. We included him in the group as our
contemporary in the life of your grace, to be schooled along with
us in your doctrine.

And so we were baptized, and all our dread about our earlier
lives dropped away from us.[63] During the days that followed I
could not get enough of the wonderful sweetness that filled me
as I meditated upon your deep design for the salvation of the
human race. How copiously I wept at your hymns and canticles,
how intensely was I moved by the lovely harmonies of your
singing Church! Those voices flooded my ears, and the truth
was distilled into my heart until it overflowed in loving devotion; my tears ran down, and I was the better for them.

---

fourteen or fifteen years old and proves to be an eager philosophical interlocutor
with his father, as evidenced by his role in the early dialogues (Augustine here
citing *On the Teacher*, in which Adeodatus plays a major role). He was baptized
with his father by Bishop Ambrose, was present when his grandmother Monica
died, and he sailed back to Africa with Augustine but died there sometime in or
around 389. From what, we are never told.

[62] *O Lord my God, creator of all things:* See 2 Maccabees 1:24.

[63] *we were baptized . . . earlier lives dropped away from us:* a curiously anticlimatic,
singular reference to Augustine's baptism at the Easter Vigil, April 24, 387.

Chapter 7

Use of hymns in liturgy

15. Not long since, the faithful of the church in Milan had begun to find mutual comfort and encouragement in the liturgy through the practice of singing hymns, in which everyone fervently joined with voice and heart.[64] It was about a year earlier, or not much more, that Justina, mother of the boy-emperor Valentinian, had been persecuting your faithful Ambrose, in the interests of the Arian heresy by which she had been led astray.[65] His God-fearing congregation, prepared to die with their bishop, your servant, stayed up all night in the church. Your maidservant, my mother, was among them, foremost in giving support and keeping vigil, and constant in

---

[64] *faithful of the church in Milan . . . joined with voice and heart*: Along with Saint Hilary of Poitiers (ca. 300–ca. 367/368) just before him, Ambrose is considered the father of Latin church song. The hymns we have (most probably) from Ambrose convey not only beauty but also doctrinal accuracy; many lines were aimed directly against Arian heresy. These hymns reveal Ambrose's classical training as well, all following a scheme of eight four-line stanzas in iambic dimeter. He also developed a congregational response to many psalms during Mass, the "antiphonal" chant thus introduced into common liturgy, and is acknowledged for composing the unmatchable *Te Deum*, intoning it at Augustine's baptism.

[65] *Arian heresy by which she had been led astray*: Augustine now clearly finds himself squarely within the struggle between the Arian court and the Catholic Church; the empress Justina (ca. 340–ca. 391) acted as the viceroy for her son Valentinian II (371–392), who was raised to the Western throne when only four years old (when Valentinian I died on military campaign, the army acclaimed his son *Augustus* so as to keep any other more powerful leader from challenging their desired stronghold on government affairs). Justina was an obstinate Arian who used the opportunity of her Catholic husband's death and her son's innocence to inculcate him against Ambrose's Catholicism in the hope of usurping all the Church's property for herself. In a move that smacks as much from political intrigue as from religious conviction, Justinian invited Ambrose to come and baptize him at his court in Vienne; the emperor was however soon found hanging, and while his enemies circulated the motive of his cowardice in the face of opposition from his military, other sources speak of how he was killed by those faithful to the charismatic general Arbogast, whom he had just publicly dismissed. Having his corpse conveyed to Milan, Ambrose preached his funeral homily and praised him for his courageous conversion to the Catholic faith (see Ambrose's *Consolation on the Emperor Valentinian*).

her life of prayer. As for us, we were still cold, not being yet warmed by the fire of your Spirit, yet we too were stirred as alarm and excitement shook the city.

It was then that the practice was established of singing hymns and psalms[66] in the manner customary in regions of the East, to prevent the people losing heart and fainting from weariness. It has persisted from that time until the present, and in other parts of the world also many of your churches imitate the practice: indeed, nearly all of them.

Discovery of the bodies of two saints

16. At this same time you revealed in a vision to the aforementioned Ambrose, your bishop, where the bodies of the martyrs Gervasius and Protasius were hidden.[67] You had for many years treasured them, incorrupt and concealed in a secret place of your own, until the right moment came when you could bring them out into the open to check a certain person's ferocity—a woman's rage only, yet a queen's. When they had been exposed to the light of day and dug up, and were being transported with due honor to the Ambrosian basilica, some people hitherto tormented by unclean spirits were restored to health[68] as confession was wrung from these same demons. But that was not all. A certain citizen of Milan, very well known in the city, who had been blind for several years, became aware of the riotous joy of the people and inquired the reason for it;

---

[66] *singing hymns and psalms:* See Colossians 3:16.

[67] *revealed in a vision to the aforementioned Ambrose . . . martyrs Gervasius and Protasius were hidden:* According to the most reliable *acta*, Bishop Ambrose desired to consecrate his cathedral against the Arians in a special way and so wanted to inter there the remains of Milan's patron saints, the proto-martyrs Gervasius and Protasius, who went to their deaths under the emperor Marcus Aurelius (161–180). Through some sort of vision, Ambrose was led in early 386 to dig under the Church of Sts. Felix and Nabor, where he thus found the martyr's skeletons, their heads duly severed. June 19 is their feast day, commemorating the day Ambrose had their relics translated into the basilica now bearing his name, *Sant'Ambrogio*.

[68] *tormented by unclean spirits were restored to health:* See Luke 6:18.

on hearing what was happening he leapt up and asked his guide to take him there. He was led to the basilica and begged to be admitted, so that he might touch with his handkerchief the funeral bier of your holy ones, whose death was precious in your sight.[69] He did so, and applied the handkerchief to his eyes: they were immediately opened. The consequences of this were the wide diffusion of the story, fervent praise offered to you, and a change of mind on the part of our enemy, for although she was not brought to the healthy state of believing, her persecuting fury was at least curbed. Thanks be to you, O my God!

From what point, by what path, have you led my memory to this, so that I can include in my confession to you these great happenings, which I had forgotten and passed over? Yet at that time, though the fragrance of your ointments blew so freely abroad, we did not run after you;[70] and that was why I wept the more abundantly later on when your hymns were sung: once I had gasped for you, but now at last I breathed your fragrance, insofar as your wind can blow through our house of straw.

Chapter 8

Monica's story

17. You gather like-minded people to dwell together,[71] and so you brought into our fellowship a young man named Evodius,

---

[69] *touch with his handkerchief the funeral bier of your holy ones, . . . precious in your sight*: See Psalm 115(116):16. Augustine had a great devotion to the cult of the saints and often preached how Christ's miraculous power was experienced through their relics. As the Bishop of Hippo, he preached over five hundred homilies in honor of the saints, giving, however, more deference and admiration to those martyred. Saints for Augustine were living reminders of the way Jesus can orient a life and a person's loves single-heartedly toward heaven, examples of humble imitation, courageous sacrifice, and eternal joy.

[70] *fragrance of your ointments blew so freely abroad, we did not run after you*: See Song of Solomon 1:3.

[71] *gather like-minded people to dwell together*: See Psalm 67:7(68:6).

who was from our home town.[72] While serving as an administrative officer in the Special Branch he had been converted to you before we were; he was then baptized and abandoned his secular career to enlist in your service. We stayed together, and made a holy agreement to live together in the future. In search of a place where we could best serve you, we made arrangements to return as a group to Africa. And while we were at Ostia on the Tiber my mother died.[73]

I am passing over many things because time is short: accept my confessions and thanks for mercies without number, O my God, though I offer them in silence. But I will not pass over anything that my soul brings forth concerning that servant of yours who brought me forth from her flesh to birth in this temporal light, and from her heart to birth in light eternal. I will speak not of her gifts, but of the gifts with which you endowed her; for she did not fashion herself or bring herself up: you created her, and not even her father or mother knew what kind of child would be born from them. She was brought up to reverence you,[74] schooled by the crook of your Christ,[75] the shepherd's care of your only Son, in a faithful family that was a sound limb of your Church. She used to speak less, though, of

---

[72] *Evodius, who was from our home town*: Evodius (ca. 360/370–ca. 425) was, like Augustine, born in Thagaste and embarked upon an imperial career, but came to Christianity much earlier. He and Augustine seem here to have met up sometime after Milan but before Augustine's return to Africa, so probably in the summer of 387 in Rome. For Evodius plays a significant part in the two dialogues written from this time, *On the Greatness of the Soul* and *On Free Will* (both late 387, early 388). Evodius was eventually made the Bishop of Uzalis, a tiny town outside Carthage, while he and Augustine stayed in seemingly good touch most of their adult (and episcopal) lives, as evidenced in Augustine, *Letters* 158–64 and 169.

[73] *while we were at Ostia on the Tiber my mother died*: This would be sometime in mid-387, Monica being fifty-six years old when she died. Augustine and his retinue were now at the Roman port town of Ostia awaiting safe passage back to North Africa to begin their new life together as convicted Catholics and prayerful ascetics. While we know Augustine's day of death was August 28, the Church fittingly celebrates Monica on August 27, but in truth we do not know the exact date of her birth into heaven.

[74] *brought up to reverence you*: See Psalm 5:8(7); 118(119):138.

[75] *crook of your Christ*: See Psalm 22(23):4.

her mother's discipline than of the training she received from a certain aged servant who had carried her father in his childhood, as is often the way with little girls who carry smaller children on their backs. In consideration of this, and of her advanced age and excellent character, the servant was held in high respect by her master and mistress in this Christian household. The care of her master's daughters was therefore entrusted to her, and she carried out her duty conscientiously, drastic with a holy severity in controlling them as occasion required, discreet and sensible in teaching them. An example of this was her refusal to allow them so much as a drink of water outside the hours when they were sufficiently provided for at their parents' table, even if they were burning with thirst. She was taking precautions against the development of harmful habits, and made the point with her wise counsel: "It is water that you are drinking now, because wine is not within your reach; but the day will come when you are married and find yourselves in charge of storerooms and cellars, and then water will not seem good enough; yet the habit of tippling will be too strong for you." By this policy of advising the girls and exercising authority over them she reined in their childish greed and imposed a reasonable measure on their very thirst, with the result that they lost even the desire for what was unbecoming.

18. In spite of this, something had stealthily snared your handmaid, as she told me, her son—a furtive fondness for wine: for whenever, in accord with custom, her parents sent this responsible daughter of theirs to draw wine from the cask by dipping a cup in through an opening near the head, she would take a tiny sip by brushing it with her lips before pouring it into the decanter. Repugnance prevented her from taking more, for she was acting not from any real craving for drink, but from a certain exuberance of youthful naughtiness, which is apt to erupt in playful behavior, and is usually curbed when it appears in children by the authority of their elders.[76] But by

---

[76] *snared your handmaid, as she told me, her son . . . authority of their elders*: Augustine refuses to whitewash Monica as a saint and applies the same honest

adding to that modest allowance daily modest allowances—for one who allows himself license in little things is ruined little by little[77]—she had fallen at length into the habit of avidly quaffing near goblets-full of wine.

What had become of the wise old woman and her stern prohibition? Would anything have been efficacious against that sly sickness, had your medicine not been watching over us, Lord? Father, mother and guardians may all be absent, but you are present, you who created us and called us and even through those set over us work for our good and the saving of souls. How did you work then, O my God? How did you cure her, how bring her back to health? Did you not elicit a hard, sharp reproof from another soul, and use it like a surgeon's knife drawn from your hidden, providential resources to cut away that diseased tissue in a single sweep? The maid who usually accompanied her to the cask was one day quarreling with her young mistress—a thing that sometimes happens—and flung an accusation against her when the two of them were alone, calling her in the most bitterly insulting language a wine-swiller. This shaft went home, and my mother took heed to her disgraceful conduct, condemned it and threw it off at once.

Just as flattering friends pervert, so quarrelsome foes may often correct us, though you requite them not for what you effect through their means but for their intention. That angry maid meant to upset her little mistress, not heal her, so she spoke up in private, either because the quarrel happened to break out in a place and at a time when they were alone, or because she might have exposed herself to danger if it emerged that she had delayed so long in reporting the matter. But you, Lord, are the ruler of all things in heaven and on earth, and as

---

confession to her life as he does to his own: she too struggled with fallen desires and subsequent addictions, here a creeping craving for wine. Another intersection of their lives to which our author no doubt wants to draw our attention is how both were cured by the voice of a child and one(s) counted insignificant by the powerful of society—for Augustine, a children's ditty; for Monica, the rebuff of a slave girl.

[77] *who allows himself license in little things is ruined little by little*: See Sirach 19:1.

worldly events flow on their tumultuous way you dispose them in due order, diverting the course of that deep torrent to serve your purposes. Through one unwholesome soul you brought wholesomeness to another, so that no one who takes note of this episode may ascribe it to his own power if another person, who, in his opinion, stands in need of correction, is put right by some word of his.

Chapter 9

19. She was thus nurtured in an atmosphere of purity and temperance, and was subjected by you to the authority of her parents rather than by them to yours. When she attained full marriageable age she was entrusted to a husband; she served him as her lord,[78] but she made it her business to win him for you[79] by preaching you to him through her way of life, for by her conduct you made her beautiful in her husband's eyes, as a person to be respected, loved and admired. So gently did she put up with his marital infidelities that no quarrel ever broke out between them on this score, for she looked to you to show him mercy, knowing that once he came to believe he would become chaste.[80] Although he was outstandingly generous, he was also hot-tempered, but she learned to offer him no resistance, by deed or even by word, when he was angry; she would wait for a favorable moment, when she saw that his mood had changed and he was calm again, and then explain her action, in case he had given way to wrath without due consideration. There were plenty of women married to husbands of gentler temper whose faces were badly disfigured by traces of blows, who while gossiping together would complain about their husbands' behavior; but she checked their talk, reminding them in what seemed to be a joking vein but with serious import that from the time they had heard their marriage contracts

---

[78] *entrusted to a husband; she served him as her lord*: See Ephesians 5:22; 1 Peter 3:6.

[79] *she made it her business to win him for you*: See 1 Peter 3:1.

[80] *knowing that once he came to believe he would become chaste*: See 1 John 3:3.

read out they had been in duty bound to consider these as legal documents which made slaves of them. In consequence they ought to keep their subservient status in mind and not defy their masters. These other wives knew what a violent husband she had to put up with, and were amazed that there had never been any rumor of Patricius striking his wife, nor the least evidence of its happening, nor even a day's domestic strife between the two of them; and in friendly talk they sought an explanation.[81] My mother would then instruct them in this plan of hers that I have outlined. Those who followed it found out its worth and were happy; those who did not continued to be bullied and battered.

20. By persevering in devoted service, and by patience and gentleness, she won over her mother-in-law, who had initially been provoked against her by the whispering of mischievous maids, but now of her own accord informed her son of the servants' meddling tongues that had troubled the domestic peace between herself and her daughter-in-law, and demanded that those responsible be punished. Minded to obey his mother, to enforce discipline in the household and to ensure concord between his relatives, he punished those reported to him with beatings, as she who had reported them judged fit; and she promised that anyone who in the future should say anything malicious to her concerning her daughter-in-law, with a view to currying favor, might hope for a like recompense from her. Since no one dared to do so again, the two lived in a remarkably sweet atmosphere of mutual goodwill.

21. There was another great gift with which you had endowed this bondswoman of yours, in whose womb you created me, O

---

[81] *had never been any rumor of Patricius striking his wife . . . they sought an expla-nation:* Throughout his writings, one never gets the sense Augustine was all too fond of his father. He respected him and never slanders him, but he never strives to paint a very positive picture of him either. Here, for example, the best he can muster is the fact that Patricius never laid an angry hand on his wife (and, presumably, his children either). This sets up the virtues Augustine continues to extol in Monica, namely, her patience, her ability to reconcile opposing parties, and her refusal to gossip and speak of others wrongly.

my God, my mercy,[82] and that was the gift of acting as peace-maker whenever she could if friction occurred between souls at variance. She would hear many a bitter accusation from each against the other, of the kind that lumpy, ill-digested dis-cord is wont to belch forth when someone dyspeptic with hatred spews out acid talk to a present friend concerning an absent enemy; but never would she repeat to one anything the other had alleged, except what would be effective in reconciling them. This would have seemed to me a boon of small account, did I not have sad experience of innumerable hordes of people, inspired by what rampant, grisly gangrene of sin I cannot con-ceive, who not only betray to angry people what their angry enemies have said, but add things unsaid as well, whereas it ought to be easy enough for any who have kindly feelings toward their own kind to avoid provoking or aggravating the enmity of others by reporting malicious gossip, except in cases where they have made sure they can extinguish it again by peaceable speech. Such was she, because you, her intimate teacher, instructed her in the school of her heart.[83]

22. Eventually she won even her husband for you, toward the end of his life on earth, and she had no cause for complaint about anything in him after his baptism that she had tolerated in him while unbaptized.[84] Moreover she was the servant of your servants. Every one of them who knew her found ample reason to praise, honor and love you as he sensed your pres-ence in her heart, attested by the fruits of her holy way of life.[85] She had been married to one man only, had loyally repaid what she owed to her parents, had governed her household in the

[82] *O my God, my mercy*: See Psalm 58:18(59:17).

[83] *school of her heart*: A wonderfully Augustinian image—*in schola pectoris*—the heart as the only place where essential truths can be heard and eternal les-sons be learned. Such internal docility is seemingly what keeps Monica from joining in on the contagion of gossip and uncharitable speech.

[84] *Eventually she won even her husband for you, . . . while unbaptized*: Monica's long-suffering won the day and helped to convert her husband: for sometime before his death in late 370 or early/mid-371, Patricius asked for baptism and died not long thereafter at his home in Thagaste when Augustine was seventeen.

[85] *fruits of her holy way of life*: See Matthew 7:20; 2 Peter 3:11.

fear of God, and earned a reputation for good works. She had brought up children, in labor anew with them[86] each time she saw them straying away from you. Finally, Lord, she took care of all of us who were your servants—for by your gift you permit us to speak—who before her death lived together as companions in you after receiving the grace of your baptism; she took care of us all as though all had been her children, and served us as though she had been the daughter of all.[87]

Chapter 10

Ostia

23. But because the day when she was to quit this life was drawing near—a day known to you, though we were ignorant of it—she and I happened to be alone, through the mysterious workings of your will, as I believe. We stood leaning against a window which looked out on a garden within the house where we were staying at Ostia on the Tiber, for there, far from the crowds, we were recruiting our strength after the long journey, in preparation for our voyage overseas. We were alone, conferring very intimately. Forgetting what lay in the past, and stretching out to what was ahead,[88] we inquired between ourselves in the light of present truth, the Truth which is yourself,[89] what the eternal life of the saints would be like. Eye

---

[86] *brought up children, in labor anew with them*: See Galatians 4:19.

[87] *lived together as companions . . . she had been the daughter of all*: Augustine's theology of marriage has stamped the Catholic Church's understanding of sacred matrimony indelibly. In his many writings on marriage, he argues consistently how three main goods should be present in the union between a Christian man and woman: (1) the sacrament that binds them objectively thus manifesting Christ's love for his Bride, the Church, (2) the shared faithfulness fostered between them day in and day out, as well as (3) the children that are brought about in such loving mutuality—*sacramentum*, *fides*, and *proles* (progeny) being the three typically Augustinian Latin terms.

[88] *Forgetting what lay in the past, and stretching out to what was ahead*: See Philippians 3:13.

[89] *Truth which is yourself*: See John 14:6; 2 Peter 1:12.

has not seen nor ear heard nor human heart conceived it,[90] yet with the mouth of our hearts wide open we panted thirstily for the celestial streams of your fountain, the fount of life which is with you,[91] that bedewed from it according to our present capacity we might in our little measure think upon a thing so great.

24. Our colloquy led us to the point where the pleasures of the body's senses, however intense and in however brilliant a material light enjoyed, seemed unworthy not merely of comparison but even of remembrance beside the joy of that life, and we lifted ourselves in longing yet more ardent toward *That Which Is*, and step by step traversed all bodily creatures and heaven itself, whence sun and moon and stars shed their light upon the earth. Higher still we mounted by inward thought and wondering discourse on your works, and we arrived at the summit of our own minds; and this too we transcended, to touch that land of never-failing plenty[92] where you pasture Israel[93] for ever with the food of truth. Life there is the Wisdom through whom all these things are made,[94] and all others that have been or ever will be; but Wisdom herself is not made: she is as she always has been and will be for ever. Rather should we say that in her there is no "has been" or "will be," but only being, for she is eternal, but past and future do not belong to eternity. And as we talked and panted for it, we just touched the edge of it by the utmost leap of our hearts; then, sighing and unsatisfied, we left the first-fruits of our spirit captive there, and returned to the noise of articulate speech, where a word has beginning and end. How different from your Word, our Lord, who abides in himself, and grows not old, but renews all things.[95]

25. Then we said,

---

[90] *Eye has not seen nor ear heard nor human heart conceived it*: See Isaiah 64:4; 1 Corinthians 2:9–10.

[91] *fount of life which is with you*: See Psalm 35:10(36:9).

[92] *land of never-failing plenty*: See Ezekiel 34:14.

[93] *where you pasture Israel*: See Psalm 79:2(80:1).

[94] *Wisdom through whom all these things are made*: See Proverbs 8:23–31.

[95] *abides in himself, and grows not old, but renews all things*: See Wisdom 7:27.

If the tumult of the flesh fell silent for someone,
and silent too were the phantasms of earth, sea and air,
silent the heavens,
and the very soul silent to itself,
that it might pass beyond itself by not thinking of its own
     being;
if dreams and revelations known through its imagination
     were silent,
if every tongue, and every sign, and whatever is subject to
     transience were wholly stilled for him
—for if anyone listens, all these things will tell him,
"We did not make ourselves;[96]
he made us who abides for ever"[97]—
and having said this they held their peace
for they had pricked the listening ear to him who made them;
and then he alone were to speak,
not through things that are made, but of himself,
that we might hear his Word,
not through fleshly tongue nor angel's voice,
nor thundercloud,[98]
nor any riddling parable,[99]
hear him unmediated, whom we love in all these things,
hear him without them,
as now we stretch out[100] and in a flash of thought
touch that eternal Wisdom who abides above all things;
if this could last,
and all other visions, so far inferior, be taken away,
and this sight alone ravish him who saw it,
and engulf him and hide him away, kept for inward joys,
so that this moment of knowledge—
this passing moment that left us aching for more—

[96] *We did not make ourselves:* See Psalm 99(100):3.
[97] *he made us who abides for ever:* See Sirach 18:1; Psalm 32(33):11; 116(117):2;
Isaiah 40:8; John 12:34.
[98] *thundercloud:* See Psalm 76:18(77:17); Exodus 19:19; John 12:29.
[99] *riddling parable:* See 1 Corinthians 13:12; Numbers 12:6–8.
[100] *we stretch out:* See Philippians 3:13.

should there be life eternal,
would not *Enter into the joy of your Lord*[101]
be this, and this alone?
And when, when will this be?
When we all rise again, but not all are changed?[102]

26. So did I speak, though not in this wise exactly, nor in these same words. Yet you know, O Lord, how on that very day amid this talk of ours that seemed to make the world with all its charms grow cheap, she said, "For my part, my son, I find pleasure no longer in anything this life holds. What I am doing here still, or why I tarry, I do not know, for all worldly hope has withered away for me. One thing only there was for which I desired to linger awhile in this life: to see you a Catholic Christian before I died. And this my God has granted to me more lavishly than I could have hoped, letting me see you even spurning earthly happiness to be his servant. What now keeps me here?"

Chapter 11

Monica's death

27. What I replied I do not clearly remember, because just about that time—five days afterward or not much more—she

---

[101] Enter into the joy of your Lord: Matthew 25:21.

[102] *When we all rise . . . not all are changed?* See 1 Corinthians 15:51. This is what I consider the third moment of ecstasy in the *Confessions*. It is rare to have a vision shared by two creatures together, but Augustine and Monica simultaneously are lifted out of their bodies and out of the created order into some sort of direct union with God. Notice how, unlike the previous two moments of a soul's leaving its body, this moment is decidedly Christian. Unlike the Manichean violence suffered by Alypius between his body and soul and between his virtuous self and the vicious crowd (see *Conf.* VI.8.13), and unlike the weighty hindrance the body proves to the philosopher as he alone seeks the Alone (see *Conf.* VII.10.16), here bodily creatures serve as a translucent ladder on which Monica and Augustine ascend together (true communion of persons is possible only in the Church of Christ) through matter so as to see the truth in and behind all creatures. There is no rupture, no dualism between body and spirit, no opposition between others, but a fluid and joyful ascent where all things are seen to serve the Lord and thus dwell harmoniously forever.

took to her bed with fever. One day during her illness she lapsed
into unconsciousness and for a short time was unaware of her
surroundings. We all came running, but she quickly returned
to her senses, and, gazing at me and my brother as we stood
there, she asked in puzzlement, "Where was I?" We were bewil-
dered with grief, but she looked keenly at us and said, "You
are to bury your mother here." I was silent, holding back my
tears, but my brother said something about his hope that she
would not die far from home, but in her own country, for that
would be a happier way. On hearing this she looked anxious
and her eyes rebuked him for thinking so; then she turned her
gaze from him to me and said, "What silly talk!"[103] Not long
afterward, addressing us both, she said, "Lay this body anywhere, and take no trouble over it. One thing only do I ask of
you, that you remember me at the altar of the Lord wherever
you may be." Having made her meaning clear to us with such
words as she could muster, she fell silent, and travailed as the
disease grew worse.

28. But my thoughts were upon the gifts you implant in the
hearts of your faithful, O invisible God,[104] and the wondrous
fruits they produce. I was rejoicing and thanking you[105] as I
recalled what had earlier been well known to me: her constant preoccupation with the grave she had provided for herself beside the body of her husband. Since they had lived

[103] *"You are to bury your mother here."* . . . *"What silly talk!"* It is difficult for us
traveling and globalized moderns to appreciate how necessary it was for the
ancients to be buried in their familial ground, the place of promise and prosperity, even for the dead. In her rebuke, however, Monica reestablishes her earlier
statement through Christian conviction: simply bury me and do not worry about
ancestral nostalgia or earthly geography. She trusts Jesus will know from where
to raise her! Catholicism is by nature cosmopolitan: *any* place in the cosmos can
be one's polis. So, even though Monica surely had a place prepared next to Patricius' grave in Thagaste, she was buried in Ostia Antica just southwest of Rome.
In 408 the Roman consul Bassius had an inscription placed above where her
body lay, and in 1430 Pope Martin V had her relics moved from the Church of
St. Aurea in Ostia to a church now bearing her name, Saint Monica's (originally the Augustinian Church of St. Tryphon) directly off the Piazza Navona.

[104] *invisible God*: See Colossians 1:15.

[105] *rejoicing and thanking you*: See Colossians 1:3.

together in such harmony, she wanted this blessing also to be
added to their happiness (so inept is the human mind at grasping divine reality), a blessing people would remember: that
when her pilgrimage overseas was done, it had been granted
to her that the earthly remains of husband and wife[106] should
be covered by one same earth. When this frivolous wish had
by your generous goodness left her heart I did not know, and
I was filled with wondering joy that its departure had been
signaled to me in this fashion; although in our conversation
at the window her words, "What still keeps me here?" did not
suggest that she desired to die in her own country. Later I heard
that already during our stay at Ostia she was one day talking
with motherly openness with some of my friends, in my absence,
about contempt for this life and the blessing of death. They
were amazed at such courage in a woman—for it was you who
had given it to her—and asked whether she was not afraid to
leave her body so far from her own city. "Nothing is far from
God," she replied. "There is no danger that at the end of the
world he will not know where to find me and raise me up."

So on the ninth day of her illness, in the fifty-sixth year of
her age, in my thirty-third year, that religious and godly soul
was set free from her body.

Chapter 12

Augustine's grief

29. I closed her eyes, and a huge sadness surged into my heart;
the tears welled up, but in response to a ferocious command
from my mind my eyes held the fount in check until it dried
up, though the struggle was intensely painful for me. But as
she breathed her last the boy Adeodatus burst out crying; he
was restrained by all of us and grew quiet. By this means something boyish in myself, which was sliding toward tears, was
also restrained by the man's voice of my heart, and it too grew

---

[106] *earthly remains of husband and wife:* See Genesis 2:7.

quiet. We judged it unfitting[107] to mark this death by plaintive protests and laments, since these are customarily employed to mourn the misery of the dying, or death as complete extinction. But she neither died in misery nor died altogether. The evidence of her virtues and her sincere faith[108] gave us good reason to hold this as certain.

30. What was it, then, that gave me such sharp inward pain? She and I had grown accustomed to living together; an exceedingly gentle and dear custom it was, and its sudden disruption was like a newly-inflicted wound. I found some solace in her commendation of me, for in that last illness she would at times respond with a caress to some little service I rendered her, calling me a devoted son, and with deep affection would declare that she had never heard from my lips any harsh or rough expression flung against her. But what is that, O my God, who have made us?[109] What common measure is there between the respect with which I treated her and the service she did to me? Being now bereft of her comfort, so great a comfort, my soul was wounded; it was as though my life was rent apart, for there had been but one life, woven out of mine and hers.[110]

31. As soon as we had persuaded the boy to stop weeping, Evodius took up the psalter and began to sing a psalm. All of us in the house joined in: *I will sing to you of your mercy and justice, O Lord.*[111] Many brethren and religious women assembled when they heard what was happening, and while those whose business it was prepared the body for burial, according to

---

[107] *We judged it unfitting*: See 1 Thessalonians 4:12.

[108] *her virtues and her sincere faith*: See 1 Timothy 1:5.

[109] *O my God, who have made us*: See Psalm 99(100):3; Baruch 4:7.

[110] *there had been but one life, woven out of mine and hers*: Friendship emerges once again as the way of understanding personal intimacy forged by the Spirit, as Monica is remembered as the one with whom Augustine had his own life's story inextricably weaved. In the contemporaneous writings from this period, it is really Monica who appears as Augustine's teacher and guide; for example, "in a debate I held on my birthday with friends and put into a little book [viz., *On the Happy Life*], her mental capacity was so clear to me that nothing seemed better suited to true philosophy" (*On Order* II.1.1).

[111] *I will sing to you of your mercy and justice, O Lord*: Psalm 100(101):1.

custom, I withdrew to where I could suitably engage in disputation on subjects appropriate to this occasion with those who
felt I should not be left alone. With this salve of truth I soothed
the agony that was known only to you; they were unaware of it,
and though they listened attentively to my words, they believed
that I felt no pain. Yet in your ears, where none of them could
hear me, I chided myself with weakness for feeling as I did, and
dammed up the flood of grief, so that for a little space it receded
from me; but then a fresh wave swept over me, and though it
was not enough to bring on an outburst of tears or even a change
of expression, I knew myself what I was suppressing in my heart.
And since I was gravely displeased to find how powerfully I could
be affected by these human experiences, which in the due order
of things and as a consequence of our natural condition are bound
to occur, the woe I felt over my woe was yet another woe, and I
was distressed by this double sadness.

32. Now came the moment when the body was borne away.
We followed it, and returned again dry-eyed; for not even in
the course of those prayers we poured out to you when the
sacrifice of our redemption was offered for her beside the grave,
where the body had been laid prior to burial, as is the custom
there—no, not even during those prayers did I weep, but all
day long I was secretly weighed down by sorrow, and in my
mental turmoil I begged you as best I could to heal my hurt.
You did not, and this because, as I believe, you were reminding me that any sort of habit is bondage, even to a mind no
longer feeding on deceitful words.

I thought it a good idea to go and take a bath, because I
had heard that baths derived their name from the Greeks, who
called a bath *balaneion* because it banishes worry from the
mind.[112] *This too I must confess to your mercy, O Father of*

---

[112] *good idea to go and take a bath . . . banishes worry from the mind*: In antiquity
the public bath house was the central place of conviviality and relaxation, so to
navigate their presence there, the early Christians had to devise strategies to
preserve modesty and chastity, but rarely did a bishop condemn their use outright. Augustine proves one of the more moderate Church Fathers on this issue,
providing basic guidelines for the bath's proper use and even allowing consecrated

orphans,[113] *that I bathed, and afterward was quite unchanged, for I had not sweated the bitter sorrow out of my heart. But then I went to sleep, and on awakening felt a good deal better. As I lay in bed alone I remembered some lines by your servant Ambrose, which rang true for me:*

> *Creator God, O Lord of all,*
> *who rule the skies, you clothe the day*
> *in radiant color, bid the night*
> *in quietness serve the gracious sway*
> *of sleep, that weary limbs, restored*
> *to labor's use, may rise again,*
> *and jaded minds abate their fret,*
> *and mourners find release from pain.*[114]

33. Little by little I recovered my earlier thoughts about your handmaid, remembering how devout had been her attitude toward you, and how full of holy kindness, how willing to make allowances, she had been in our regard; and now that I was suddenly bereft of this I found comfort in weeping before you about her and for her, about myself and for myself. The tears that I had been holding back I now released to flow as plentifully as they would, and strewed them as a bed beneath my heart. There it could rest, because there were your ears only, not the ears of anyone who would judge my weeping by the norms of his own pride.

And now, Lord, it is in writing that I confess to you. Let anyone read it who will, and judge it as he will, and if he finds

---

women to go (provided they travel in threes; for example, see *Letter* 211.13). Augustine's (rather fanciful) etymology here again plays off the Greek word "to throw" (see *Conf.* VIII.10.22, note 92, p. 218), as the bath "tosses" out the mind's worries.

[113] Father of orphans: See Psalm 67:6(68:5).

[114] Creator God, O Lord of all, ... mourners find release from pain: This is from Ambrose's famous hymn *Deus, Creator Omnium*, which we read previously at *Conf.* IV.10.15, pp. 88–89. Since he composed it for Vesper prayers at sunset, perhaps recalling Bishop's Ambrose words here at the end of the more autobiographical books was Augustine's way of saying "thanks" one last time for the great Bishop of Milan's courageous sanctity and example.

it sinful that I wept over my mother for a brief part of a single hour—the mother who for a little space was to my sight dead, and who had wept long years for me that in your sight I might live—then let such a reader not mock, but rather, if his charity is wide enough, himself weep for my sins to you, who are Father to all whom your Christ calls his brethren.

Chapter 13

34. But now that my heart is healed of that wound, in which I was perhaps guilty of some carnal affection, I pour out to you tears of a very different kind for this servant of yours, O our God; they come gushing forth from a mind struck by the perils besetting every soul that dies in Adam. True, she had been brought to new life in Christ,[115] and even before her release from the body she so lived that her faith and conduct redounded to the glory of your name. Yet all the same I dare not assert that from the time you brought her to new birth in baptism[116] no word contrary to your commandment escaped her lips.[117] And by the Truth who is your Son[118] we are warned, *If anyone says to his brother, "You fool!"* he will be liable to hellfire,[119] so woe betide anyone, even one whose life is praiseworthy, if you should examine it without mercy![120] But since you are not ruthless in searching out our faults, we trustingly hope for a place in your house. If anyone were to give you an account of his real merits, what else would that be but a list of your gifts? If only humans would acknowledge that they are human, and anyone minded to boast would boast in the Lord![121]

[115] *brought to new life in Christ*: See 1 Corinthians 15:22; Ephesians 2:5.

[116] *new birth in baptism*: See Titus 3:5.

[117] *no word contrary to your commandment escaped her lips*: See Matthew 12:36–37.

[118] *Truth who is your Son*: See John 14:6.

[119] *If anyone says to his brother, "You fool!" he will be liable to hellfire*: See Matthew 5:22.

[120] *if you should examine it without mercy*: See Psalm 129(130):3.

[121] *If anyone were to give you an account of his real merits . . . boast in the Lord!* See 1 Corinthians 1:31; 2 Corinthians 10:17. This is a very Augustinian move: alone we tend toward nothing, but in Christ we can be holy, loving, and eternal.

35. This is why, O God of my heart,[122] my praise,[123] my life, I will for a little while disregard her good deeds, for which I joyfully give you thanks, and pray to you now for my mother's sins. Hear me through that healing remedy who hung upon the tree,[124] the medicine for our wounds who sits at your right hand and intercedes for us.[125] I know that she dealt mercifully with others and from her heart forgave her debtors their debts; do you then forgive her any debts[126] she contracted during all those years after she had passed through the saving waters. Forgive her, Lord, forgive, I beg you,[127] and do not arraign her before you.[128] Let mercy triumph over judgment,[129] for you, whose utterances are true, have to the merciful promised mercy.[130] Since their very power to be merciful was your gift to them in the first place, you will be showing mercy to those with whom you have yourself dealt mercifully, and granting pity to those toward whom you have shown pity first.[131]

I can therefore never boast of what I do, but of what Christ is doing with, in, and through me. Because he dwells in me, it is he who effects my holiness: "Must I exclude my holiness from Christ's? No; I can be certain that when he speaks, he speaks inseparably from his body. Shall even then I dare to say, *I am holy?* If I meant 'holy' in the sense of making others holy and standing in no need of anyone to sanctify me, I should be arrogant to claim it, and a liar; but if I mean 'holy' in the sense of 'made holy' ... then, yes, let Christ's body dare to say it" (*Commentary on the Psalms* 85.4).

[122] *O God of my heart:* See Psalm 72(73):26.

[123] *my praise:* See Psalm 117(118):14; 21:4, 26(22:3, 25); Jeremiah 17:14; Exodus 15:2; Isaiah 12:2; Deuteronomy 10:21.

[124] *healing remedy who hung upon the tree:* See Deuteronomy 21:23; Galatians 3:13.

[125] *who sits at your right hand and intercedes for us:* See Psalm 109(110):1; Romans 8:34.

[126] *forgave her debtors their debts; do you then forgive her any debts:* See Matthew 6:12; 18:35.

[127] *Lord, forgive, I beg you:* See Numbers 14:19.

[128] *do not arraign her before you:* See Psalm 142(143):2.

[129] *Let mercy triumph over judgment:* See James 2:13.

[130] *for you, whose utterances are true, have to the merciful promised mercy:* See Matthew 5:7.

[131] *their very power to be merciful was your gift ... you have shown pity first:* See Exodus 33:19; Romans 9:15.

36. I believe you have already done what I am asking you, but look favorably, Lord, on this free offering of my lips.[132] On the day when her release was at hand[133] she gave no thought to costly burial or the embalming of her body with spices, nor did she pine for a special monument or concern herself about a grave in her native land; no, that was not her command to us. She desired only to be remembered at your altar, where she had served you with never a day's absence. From that altar, as she knew, the holy Victim is made available to us, he through whom the record of debt that stood against us was annulled.[134] He has triumphed over an enemy who does keep a tally of our faults and looks for anything to lay to our charge, but finds no case against him.[135] In him we win our victory. Who will reimburse him for that innocent blood?[136] Who will pay back to him the price he paid[137] to purchase us, as though to snatch us back from him?

To the sacrament of that ransom-price your handmaid made fast her soul with the bonds of faith. Let no one wrench her away from your protection. Let no lion or dragon[138] thrust in between by force or guile; for she will not claim that she has no debts to pay, lest she be convicted by the crafty accuser and fall into his power; she will reply only that her debts have been forgiven by him to whom no one can repay what he paid for us, though he owed us nothing.

Peace

37. May she then rest in peace with her husband. She was married to no other man[139] either before or after him, and in

---

[132] *free offering of my lips*: See Psalm 118(119):108.

[133] *her release was at hand*: See 2 Timothy 4:6.

[134] *record of debt that stood against us was annulled*: See Colossians 2:14–15.

[135] *finds no case against him*: See Luke 23:4; John 14:30; 18:38; 19:4.

[136] *innocent blood*: See Matthew 27:4.

[137] *price he paid*: See 1 Corinthians 6:20; 7:23.

[138] *Let no lion or dragon*: See Psalm 90(91):13.

[139] *May she then rest in peace with her husband . . . married to no other man*: See 1 Timothy 5:9.

serving him she brought forth fruit for you by patience,[140] to win him for you in the end. Inspire others, my Lord, my God,[141] inspire your servants who are my brethren, your children who are my masters, whom I now serve with heart and voice and pen, that as many of them as read this may remember Monica, your servant, at your altar, along with Patricius, sometime her husband. From their flesh you brought me into this life, though how I do not know. Let them remember with loving devotion these two who were my parents in this transitory light, but also were my brethren under you, our Father, within our mother the Catholic Church,[142] and my fellow-citizens in the eternal Jerusalem, for which your people[143] sighs with longing throughout its pilgrimage, from its setting out to its return. So may the last request she made of me be granted to her more abundantly by the prayers of many, evoked by my confessions, than by my prayers alone.

---

[140] *brought forth fruit for you by patience*: See Luke 8:15.

[141] *my Lord, my God*: See John 20:28.

[142] *our mother the Catholic Church*: certainly an echo of that other great North African bishop Cyprian (d. 258): "You cannot have God for your Father if you have not the Church for your mother" (*On The Unity of the Catholic Church* §6).

[143] *fellow-citizens in the eternal Jerusalem, for which your people*: See Hebrews 11:10, 13, 14.

Book X

Memory

Chapter 1

1. Let me know you, O you who know me; then shall I know even as I am known.[1] You are the strength of my soul; make your way in and shape it to yourself, that it may be yours to have and to hold, free from stain or wrinkle.[2] I speak because this is my hope,[3] and whenever my joy springs from that hope it is joy well founded. As for the rest of this life's experiences, the more tears are shed over them the less are they worth weeping over, and the more truly worth lamenting the less do we bewail them while mired in them.[4] You love the truth[5] because anyone who "does truth" comes to the light. Truth it is that I want to do, in my heart by confession in your presence, and with my pen before many witnesses.[6]

Chapter 2

Motives for confession

2. But the abyss of the human conscience lies naked to your eyes, O Lord,[7] so would anything in me be secret even if I

---

[1] *then shall I know even as I am known:* See 1 Corinthians 13:12; 8:2–3; Galatians 4:9.

[2] *free from stain or wrinkle:* See Ephesians 5:27.

[3] *I speak because this is my hope:* See Psalm 115(116):10; 2 Corinthians 4:13.

[4] *the more tears are shed over them . . . the less do we bewail them while mired in them:* Disordered loves invert our priorities by placing lesser over higher goods. As a result, Augustine notes here, the things we spend so much energy worrying about are, in the end, not so important, while the concerns that should motivate our every heart's beat are usually the first things to be put off until tomorrow.

[5] *You love the truth:* See Psalm 50:8(51:6).

[6] *anyone who "does truth" comes to the light . . . before many witnesses:* See John 3:21; Ephesians 4:15.

[7] *lies naked to your eyes, O Lord:* See Sirach 42:18–20; Hebrews 4:13.

were unwilling to confess to you? I would be hiding you from myself, but not myself from you. But now that my groans bear witness that I find no pleasure in myself, you shed light upon me and give me joy, you offer yourself, lovable and longed for, that I may thrust myself away in disgust and choose you, and be pleasing no more either to you or to myself except in what I have from you.[8]

To you, then, Lord, I lie exposed, exactly as I am. I have spoken of what I hope to gain by confessing to you. My confession to you is made not with words of tongue and voice, but with the words of my soul and the clamor of my thought, to which your ear is attuned; for when I am bad, confession to you is simply disgust with myself, but when I am good, confession to you consists in not attributing my goodness to myself, because though you, Lord, bless the person who is just, it is only because you have first made him just when he was sinful.[9] This is why, O my God, my confession in your presence is silent, yet not altogether silent: there is no noise to it, but it shouts by love. I can say nothing right to other people unless you have heard it from me first, nor can you even hear anything of the kind from me which you have not first told me.

Chapter 3

3. What point is there for me in other people hearing my confessions? Are they likely to heal my infirmities?[10] A curious lot they are, eager to pry into the lives of others, but tardy when it comes to correcting their own. Why should they seek

---

[8] *I find no pleasure in myself . . . what I have from you:* This is far from some sort of Buddhist self-denial: for the Christian, the self must always "thrust away" any illusion of autonomy (not to mention loneliness or need to be self-sufficient), as each of the baptized must understand himself no longer as a separate "I" from Christ, but now a "we" dwelling in each of God's children. Augustine here is calling for us not to destroy the self but to see it as inherently relational. Is this not why Jesus taught us to pray incessantly, "*Our* Father"?

[9] *you have first made him just when he was sinful:* See Psalm 5:13(12); Romans 4:5.

[10] *heal my infirmities:* See Psalm 102(103):3; Matthew 4:23.

to hear from me what I am, when they are reluctant to hear from you what they are? And when they hear from me about myself, how do they know that I am speaking the truth, since no one knows what goes on inside a person except the spirit of that person within him?[11] If, on the contrary, they hear from you about themselves, they will be in no position to say, "The Lord is lying." Is hearing the truth about oneself from you anything different from knowing oneself? And can anyone have this self-knowledge and still protest, "It is not true," unless he himself is lying?

Yet charity believes without stint,[12] at least among those who are bonded together by charity,[13] and so I also confess to you, Lord, in such a way that people to whom I can offer no proof may discern whether I confess truthfully. I cannot prove it, but all whose ears are open to me by love will believe me.

4. All the same, my inward healer, make clear to me what advantage there is in doing this. When the confession of my past evil deeds is read and listened to—those evil deeds which you have forgiven and covered over[14] to make me glad in yourself, transforming my soul by faith and your sacrament—that recital arouses the hearer's heart, forbidding it to slump into despair and say, "I can't." Let it rather keep watch[15] for your loving mercy and your gentle grace, through which every weak soul that knows its own weakness grows strong.[16] It is cheering to good people to hear about the past evil deeds of those who are now freed from them: cheering not because the deeds were evil but because they existed once but exist no more.[17]

---

[11] *no one knows what goes on inside a person except the spirit of that person within him*: See 1 Corinthians 2:11.

[12] *charity believes without stint*: See 1 Corinthians 13:7.

[13] *among those who are bonded together by charity*: See Colossians 3:14.

[14] *evil deeds which you have forgiven and covered over*: See Psalm 31(32):1.

[15] *keep watch*: See Song of Solomon 5:2; Matthew 25:1–13.

[16] *your gentle grace . . . every weak soul that knows its own weakness grows strong*: See 2 Corinthians 12:9–10.

[17] *It is cheering to good people to hear about the past evil deeds . . . exist no more*: Only in Christianity can admittance of such past sin elicit joy. Augustine is aware of how his bringing to light all that he has done and experienced should

But then what profit is there, O my Lord, to whom my conscience confesses every day, more secure in the hope of your mercy than in its own innocence—what profit is there, I ask, if through these writings I also confess to other people in your presence not what I have been, but what I still am? The desirability of confessing the past I have recognized and stated; but there are many people who desire to know what I still am at this time of writing my confessions, people who know me without really knowing me, people who have read my works or know me only by hearsay. None of these have laid their ears to my heart, though it is only there that I am whoever I am. They therefore want to hear from my own confession what I am within, where they can venture neither eye nor ear nor mind. They want to hear and are ready to believe me: will they really recognize me? Yes, because the charity that makes them good assures them that I am not lying when I confess about myself; that very charity in them believes me.

Chapter 4

5. But what do they hope to gain, those who want this? Do they wish to congratulate me when they hear how much progress I am making toward you by your gift, and to pray for me when they hear how badly I am dragged back by my own weight? To people like that I will disclose myself, for it is no small gain, O Lord my God, if thanks are offered to you by many people on our account[18] and many pray to you for us. Yes, let a fraternal mind love in me what you teach us to be worthy of love, and deplore in me what you teach us to be deplorable. But let it be

---

be occasion for gratitude. In a mysterious way, such confession is Christ's example at John 20:21, where showing his paschal wounds elicits joy from the apostles (as opposed to sorrow or revenge, as most wounds would). When the Father brings us to himself and heals what has been wounded, we should rejoice and therefore not wallow in shame but let others see the power of God to heal and to raise.

[18] *thanks are offered to you by many people on our account*: See 2 Corinthians 1:11.

a brotherly mind that does this, not the mind of a stranger, not the minds of alien foes who mouth falsehood and whose power wreaks wickedness;[19] let it be a brotherly mind which when it approves of me will rejoice over me, and when it disapproves will be saddened on my account, because whether it approves or disapproves it still loves me. To such people I will disclose myself: let them sigh with relief over my good actions, but with grief over my evil deeds. The good derive from you and are your gift; the evil are my sins and your punishments. Let them sigh with relief over the one and with grief over the other, and let both hymns and laments ascend into your presence from the hearts of my brethren, which are your censers.[20] And then do you, Lord, in your delight at the fragrance which pervades your holy temple, have mercy on me according to your great mercy[21] for the sake of your name.[22] Do not, I entreat you, do not abandon your unfinished work, but bring to perfection all that is wanting in me.[23]

6. So then, when I confess not what I have been but what I am now, this is the fruit to be reaped from my confessions: I confess not only before you in secret exultation tinged with fear[24] and secret sorrow infused with hope, but also in the ears of believing men and women, the companions of my joy and sharers in my mortality, my fellow citizens still on pilgrimage with me, those who have gone before and those who will follow, and all who bear me company in my life. They are your servants and my brethren, but you have willed them to be your children and my masters, and you have ordered me to serve them if I wish to live with you and share your life. This command of yours would mean little to me if it were only

[19] not the mind of a stranger . . . whose power wreaks wickedness: See Psalm 143(144):11.

[20] hymns and laments ascend into your presence from the hearts . . . which are your censers: See Revelation 8:3–4.

[21] have mercy on me according to your great mercy: See Psalm 50:3(51:1).

[22] for the sake of your name: See Matthew 10:22; 24:9; John 15:21.

[23] do not abandon your unfinished work, but bring to perfection all that is wanting in me: See Philippians 1:6.

[24] tinged with fear: See Psalm 2:11.

spoken, and not first carried out in deed as well.[25] So I do likewise, and I do it in deeds and in words; I do it under your outstretched wings[26] and would do it in grave peril, were it not that under those wings my soul is surrendered to you[27] and to you my weakness known. I am a little child, but my Father lives for ever and in him I have a guardian suited to me. He who begot me is also he who keeps me safe; you yourself are all the good I have, you are almighty and you are with me before ever I am with you.

To such people, then, the people you command me to serve, I will disclose myself not as I have been but as I am now, as I am still, though I do not judge myself.[28] In this way, then, let me be heard.

Chapter 5

7. For it is you, Lord, who judge me. No one knows what he himself is made of, except his own spirit within him,[29] yet there is still some part of him which remains hidden even from his own spirit; but you, Lord, know everything about a human being because you have made him. And though in your sight I may despise myself and reckon myself dust and ashes[30] I know something about you which I do not know about myself. It is true that we now see only a tantalizing reflection in a mirror,[31] and so it is that while I am on pilgrimage far from you[32]

---

[25] *This command of yours . . . carried out in deed as well:* See John 13:1–17.

[26] *under your outstretched wings:* See Psalm 16(17):8; 35:8(36:7).

[27] *my soul is surrendered to you:* See Psalm 61:2(62:1).

[28] *I do not judge myself:* See 1 Corinthians 4:3.

[29] *No one knows what he himself is made of, except his own spirit within him:* See 1 Corinthians 2:11.

[30] *I may despise myself and reckon myself dust and ashes:* See Job 42:6; Sirach 10:9; Genesis 18:37.

[31] *see only a tantalizing reflection in a mirror:* See 1 Corinthians 13:12.

[32] *I am on pilgrimage far from you:* See 2 Corinthians 5:6. Again the metaphor of distance is employed: in holiness we allow God to draw near to us; in sinfulness we distance ourselves from God. Ironically, sinners are less than themselves because they are overly present to themselves, while saints are more alive and more themselves because they see themselves in God.

I am more present to myself than to you; yet I do know that you cannot be defiled in any way whatever,[33] whereas I do not know which temptations I may have the strength to resist, and to which ones I shall succumb. Our hope is that, because you are trustworthy, you do not allow us to be tempted more fiercely than we can bear, but along with the temptation you ordain the outcome of it, so that we can endure.[34] Let me, then, confess what I know about myself, and confess too what I do not know, because what I know of myself I know only because you shed light on me, and what I do not know I shall remain ignorant about until my darkness becomes like bright noon before your face.[35]

Chapter 6

Looking for God in creatures

8. I love you, Lord, with no doubtful mind but with absolute certainty. You pierced my heart with your word, and I fell in love with you. But the sky and the earth too, and everything in them—all these things around me are telling me that I should love you; and since they never cease to proclaim this to everyone, those who do not hear are left without excuse.[36] But you, far above, will show mercy to anyone with whom you have already determined to deal mercifully, and will grant pity to whomsoever you choose.[37] Were this not so, the sky and the earth would be proclaiming your praises to the deaf.

But what am I loving when I love you? Not beauty of body nor transient grace, not this fair light which is now so friendly

---

[33] *I do know that you cannot be defiled in any way whatever*: as opposed to his earlier Manichean views where (the good) god could be defiled and disgraced.

[34] *you do not allow us to be tempted more fiercely than we can bear, . . . so that we can endure*: See 1 Corinthians 10:13.

[35] *until my darkness becomes like bright noon before your face*: See Isaiah 58:10; Psalm 89(90):8.

[36] *those who do not hear are left without excuse*: See Romans 1:20.

[37] *will show mercy . . . and will grant pity to whomsoever you choose*: See Romans 9:15; Exodus 33:19.

to my eyes, not melodious song in all its lovely harmonies, not the sweet fragrance of flowers or ointments or spices, not manna or honey, not limbs that draw me to carnal embrace: none of these do I love when I love my God. And yet I do love a kind of light, a kind of voice, a certain fragrance, a food and an embrace, when I love my God: a light, voice, fragrance, food and embrace for my inmost self, where something limited to no place shines into my mind, where something not snatched away by passing time sings for me, where something no breath blows away yields to me its scent, where there is savor undiminished by famished eating, and where I am clasped in a union from which no satiety can tear me away. This is what I love, when I love my God.[38]

9. And what is this?

I put my question to the earth, and it replied, "I am not he"; I questioned everything it held, and they confessed the same. I questioned the sea and the great deep,[39]
and the teeming live creatures that crawl,[40]
and they replied,
"We are not God; seek higher."
I questioned the gusty winds,
and every breeze with all its flying creatures told me,
"Anaximenes was wrong: I am not God."
To the sky I put my question, to sun, moon, stars,
but they denied me: "We are not the God you seek."
And to all things which stood around the portals of my flesh
    I said,

---

[38] *But what am I loving . . . when I love my God*: The history of ancient philosophy is brought into conversation here because one of the first questions asked by the pre-Socratics concerned the ultimate principle of reality (the *arche*) out of which came all other things. Anaximenes of Miletus (d. ca. 528 B.C.), for example, argued that air was the primal substrate out of which all other things, hardened and thus individuated, arose; Heraclitus (d. ca. 475 B.C.) thought it must be fire, Thales (d. ca. 546 B.C.) settled on water, and others on various theories of matter.

[39] *I questioned the sea and the great deep*: See Job 28:14.

[40] *teeming live creatures that crawl*: See Genesis 1:20.

"Tell me of my God.
You are not he, but tell me something of him."
Then they lifted up their mighty voices and cried,
"He made us."[41]
My questioning was my attentive spirit,
and their reply, their beauty.

Then toward myself I turned, and asked myself, "Who are you?" And I answered my own question: "A man." See, here are the body and soul that make up myself, the one outward and the other within. Through which of these should I seek my God? With my body's senses I had already sought him from earth to heaven, to the farthest place whither I could send the darting rays of my eyes; but what lay within me was better, and to this all those bodily messengers reported back, for it controlled and judged the replies of sky and earth, and of all the creatures dwelling in them, all those who had proclaimed, "We are not God," and "He made us." My inner self[42] recognized them all through the service of the outer. I, who was that inmost self, I, who was mind, knew them through the senses of my body; and so I questioned the vast frame of the world concerning my God, and it answered, "I am not he, but he made me."

10. Surely this beauty is apparent to all whose faculties are sound? Why, then, does it not speak the same message to all?

---

[41] *He made us:* See Psalm 99(100):3. Creation's mutability raises the perceptive mind to immutability; beautiful creatures bring the ardent seeker to Beauty itself. Augustine's theology of creation presumes that all creatures imitate the Son in that all things must turn toward the Father to receive existence. In this way all creation comes to be through the Son and his eternal reception of the Father: "Thus the Son as the beginning (cf. John 1:1) implies his being the source of creation as it comes into being from him while still imperfect, while his being the Word implies his conferring perfection on creation by calling it back to himself, so that all things may be given form by adhering to the creator, and by imitating in its own measure the form (i.e., the Son) who adheres eternally and unchangingly to the Father" (*Literal Commentary on Genesis* I.4). In their imitating the Son, then, all creatures can point us to the Father (see *Conf.* XIII.2.3, pp. 409–10).

[42] *My inner self:* See Romans 7:22; 2 Corinthians 4:16; Ephesians 3:16.

Animals, both small and large, see the beauty, but they are not able to question it, for in them reason does not hold sway as judge over the reports of the senses. Human beings have the power to question, so that by understanding the things he has made they may glimpse the unseen things of God;[43] but by base love they subject themselves to these creatures, and once subject can no longer judge. Creatures do not respond to those who question unless the questioners are also judges: not that they change their voice—that is, their beauty—if one person merely sees it, while another sees and inquires, as though they would appear in one guise to the former, and differently to the latter; no, the beauty appears in the same way to both beholders, but to one it is dumb, and to the other it speaks. Or rather, it speaks to all, but only they understand who test the voice heard outwardly against the truth within. Truth tells me, "Neither earth nor sky nor any bodily thing is your God." Their own nature avers it. Do you not see, my soul? Nature is an extended mass, smaller in any one part than in the whole. Even you, my soul, are better than that, for you impart energy to the mass of your body and endow it with life, and no corporeal thing can do that for any other corporeal thing. But your God is to you the life of your life itself.

Chapter 7

11. What is it, then, that I love when I love my God? Who is he who towers above my soul? By this same soul I will mount to him. I will leave behind that faculty whereby I am united to a body and animate its frame. Not by that faculty do I find my God, for horse and mule would find him equally, since the same faculty gives life to their bodies too, yet they are beasts who lack intelligence.[44]

There is another power by which I do more than give life to my flesh: with this I endow with senses the flesh that God has

---

[43] *by understanding the things he has made they may glimpse the unseen things of God*: See Romans 1:20.

[44] *they are beasts who lack intelligence*: See Psalm 31(32):9.

fashioned for me, commanding the eye not to hear and the ear not to see, giving to my organ of seeing and my organ of hearing and to all my other senses what is proper to them in their respective places and for their particular work. Their functions are diverse, but I, the one mind, act through them all. This power too I will leave behind, for horse and mule have it too, since they also have sensory organs throughout their bodies.

Chapter 8

Looking for God in himself: the fields of memory [45]

12. So then, I will leave behind that faculty of my nature, and mount by stages toward him who made me. [46]

Now I arrive in the fields and vast mansions of memory, where are treasured innumerable images brought in there from objects of every conceivable kind perceived by the senses. There too are hidden away the modified images we produce when by our thinking we magnify or diminish or in any way alter the information our senses have reported. There too is everything else that has been consigned and stowed away, and not yet engulfed and buried in oblivion. Sojourning there I command something I want to present itself, and immediately certain things

---

[45] Looking for God in himself: the fields of memory: As Book X unfolds, keep in mind that memory for Augustine is a much more expansive term than how we use it today as the place where we keep past images and experiences. For anyone working out of the Platonic tradition, the memory borders on the divine and the eternal, transcending space and time. It is where all the experiences of one's life's story are held together in a single moment. Furthermore, the memory also bridges the two worlds inhabited by the human person, as the mind applies eternal images to temporal realities. The memory hence enjoys a uniquely special role in Augustinian theology because it is here one is most enabled to behold God. Similarly, Augustine's theology of memory holds a central place in the *Confessions* because it is the memory that enables each of us to tell our life's story.

[46] *So then, I will leave behind that faculty of my nature, . . . him who made me*: As the search for a fuller and fuller understanding of the divine continues, Augustine now sees how he must properly transcend creation, including his own limited mental capabilities, and thus be brought by grace up through creatures to God's very self.

emerge, while others have to be pursued for some time and dug out from remote crannies. Others again come tumbling out in disorderly profusion, and leap into prominence as though asking, "Are we what you want?" when it is something different that I am asking for and trying to recall.[47] With my mental hand I push them out of the way of my effort to remember, until what I want becomes clear and breaks from cover. Then there are remembered items that come to hand easily and in orderly sequence as soon as they are summoned, the earlier members giving way to those that follow and returning to their storage-places, ready to be retrieved next time I need them. All of which happens when I recite anything from memory.

13. Preserved there, classified and distinct, are all those impressions which have been admitted through the entrances proper to each: light, colors and bodily shapes through the eye; all kinds of sound through the ears; various odors through the gateways of the nostrils; flavors through the entrance of the mouth; and through the pervasive sense of touch whatever is felt as hard or soft, hot or cold, smooth or rough, heavy or light, external to the body or inside it. The huge repository of the memory, with its secret and unimaginable caverns, welcomes and keeps all these things, to be recalled and brought out for use when needed; and as all of them have their particular ways into it, so all are put back again in their proper places.

The sense-impressions themselves do not find their way in, however; it is the images of things perceived by the senses that are available there to the person who recalls them. Who can tell how these images are fashioned, obvious though it may be through which senses they were captured and stowed away within? For when I am sitting quietly in the dark I can bring up colors in my memory if I wish, and distinguish white from black and any others I select. No sounds burst in to intrude on these images acquired through my eyes, which I am considering, though

---

[47] *trying to recall*: The phenomenon of forgetting is a humorous riddle, Augustine musing on how if something *really* fell into oblivion, how is it then ever later recalled?

sounds too are present there, lying hidden and stored in a place by themselves. I can summon them equally well, if I wish, and find them present at once, and though my tongue and throat are silent I sing as much as I like. Images of color, which are just as truly present, do not thrust themselves in on my song or interrupt it while I am enjoying this other treasure, which has flowed into me through my ears. Similarly I can recall at will anything drawn in and hoarded by way of my other senses. I can distinguish the scent of lilies from violets even though I am not actually smelling anything, and honey from grape-juice, smooth from rough, without tasting or feeling anything: I am simply passing them in review before my mind by remembering them.

14. This I do within myself in the immense court of my memory; for there sky and earth and sea are readily available to me, together with everything that I have ever been able to perceive in them, apart from what I have forgotten. And there I come to meet myself. I recall myself, what I did, when and where I acted in a certain way, and how I felt about so acting. Everything is there which I remember having experienced for myself or believed on the assertion of others. Moreover, I can draw on this abundant store to form imaginary pictures which resemble the things I have myself experienced, or believed because my own experience confirmed them, and weave these together with images from the past, and so evoke future actions, occurrences or hopes; and on all these as well I can meditate as though they were present to me. In that same enormous recess of my mind, thronging with so many great images, I say to myself, "That's what I will do!" And the action I have envisaged follows. "Oh, if only this or that could be! Pray God this or that may not happen!" I say to myself, and even as I say it the images of all these things of which I speak pass before me, coming from the same treasure-house of memory. If they were not there, I would be quite unable to conjure up such possibilities.

15. This faculty of memory is a great one, O my God, exceedingly great, a vast, infinite recess. Who can plumb its depth?

This is a faculty of my mind, belonging to my nature, yet I cannot myself comprehend all that I am. Is the mind, then, too narrow to grasp itself, forcing us to ask where that part of it is which it is incapable of grasping? Is it outside the mind, not inside? How can the mind not compass it?

Enormous wonder wells up within me when I think of this, and I am dumbfounded. People go to admire lofty mountains, and huge breakers at sea, and crashing waterfalls, and vast stretches of ocean, and the dance of the stars, but they leave themselves behind out of sight. It does not strike them as wonderful that I could enumerate those things without seeing them with my eyes, and that I could not even have spoken of them unless I could within my mind contemplate mountains and waves and rivers and stars (which I have seen), and the ocean (which I only take on trust), and contemplate them there in spaces just as vast as though I were seeing them outside myself.[48] But I did not suck them into myself when I looked at them with my eyes, for it was not these things themselves that entered me, but only the images of them; and I know which impressions were made on me through which of my bodily senses.

Chapter 9

16. The immense spaces of my memory harbor even more than these, however. Here too are all those things which I received through a liberal education and have not yet forgotten; they are stored away in some remote inner place, which yet is not really a place at all. However, in this case it is not images of the realities that I harbor, but the realities themselves; for everything I know about literature, or skill in debate, or how many kinds of questions can logically be formulated, lodges indeed in my memory, but not like an image which remains after I have turned away from some object perceived externally, nor

---

[48] *Enormous wonder . . . as though I were seeing them outside myself*: Why do so many people stand in awe at visible creation, as beautiful as it is, but never stop deeply enough to marvel at the vastness and profoundness of their own souls? Perhaps this is *the* question the *Confessions* wishes to ask each of us.

like the trace of a sound that has faded, by means of which a voice that has penetrated my ears can still be recalled as though audible when it is audible no longer, nor like a fleeting scent that is blown away by the wind after affecting our nostrils, but leaves an image of itself in the memory which we can savor again later by remembering it, nor like food, which is certainly no longer present as a flavor in the stomach but can still be tasted in the memory, nor like anything which is felt by bodily touch and can still be touched by our memory when the object is no longer in contact with our bodies. None of these objects is admitted into the memory in its own right; only the images of them are captured with astonishing speed, put away in wonderful compartments, and brought out again in a wonderful way when we recall them.

Chapter 10

17. When I hear that there are three classes of questions—namely, whether something exists, what it is, and what qualities belong to it[49]—I do, to be sure, retain images of the sounds by which these words are composed; and I know that those sounds were borne upon the breeze with some noise, but have now fallen silent. But through no bodily sense whatever have I made contact with the realities themselves, for I have never seen these realities anywhere except in my own mind. What I have stowed away in my memory is not the images of these things but the things themselves. Let them say how they found their way into me if they can, for when I check every physical gateway in myself I find none by which they can have entered. My eyes tell me, "If those things were colored, it was we who reported them"; my ears declare, "If they made some sound, we gave you the information"; my nostrils say, "If there was a smell to them, we let them through"; my sense of taste replies,

---

[49] *three classes of questions . . . what qualities belong to it*: As creation exists because it imitates the Son's reception of the Father, each creature likewise manifests a triadic structure reflecting the Triune life of God—that is, each creature reveals a trinity: it exists, *what* it is, and *how* it fits into the overall order of the cosmos.

"If they had no flavor, don't ask me"; touch says, "If they had no bodily substance, I did not handle them, and if I did not handle them, I told you nothing." From what source and by what route did they enter my memory? I do not know, for when I learned them I did not take them on trust from some stranger's intelligence but recognized them as present in my own, and affirmed them as true, and entrusted them to my memory for safekeeping so that I could bring them out again when I wished. This means that they were there even before I learned them, but not remembered. Where and why did I recognize them and say, "Yes, that's how it is; that is true," when these things were stated? Surely because they were already in my memory, but so remote, so hidden from sight in concealed hollows, that unless they had been dug out by someone who reminded me, I would perhaps never have been able to think about them.[50]

Chapter 11

18. We are therefore led to conclude that when we learn things which are not imbibed through the senses as images, but are known directly in their own reality inside the mind, as they are in themselves, and without the intervention of images, we are collecting by means of our thought those things which the memory already held, but in a scattered and disorderly way. By applying our minds to them we ensure that they are stacked ready-to-hand in the memory, where they may be easily available for habitual use, instead of lying hidden, dispersed and neglected, as hitherto. How many things of this kind are

---

[50] *they were already in my memory, but so remote . . . never have been able to think about them:* So perhaps forgetting is not placing something into nothingness, but simply misplacing it for a time. Forgetting, I think, amazes Augustine because it symbolically captures both the beauty and the frustration of an eternal creature living in time. Behind this inquiry is the paradox of Plato's *Meno:* How can one recognize something as true, if one never had had contact with that truth before? For Plato, all education is really a form of recollection, as particular truths in this world only trigger glimpses of the perfectly real the soul knew rightly before it fell into the body. As a Christian, Augustine refuses to believe in the preexistence of the soul and so must locate the source of truth elsewhere, namely, in the soul's proper encounter with God and the world.

carried in my memory! Such things have been found and placed ready-to-hand in the way I have described, and so it is said that we have learned them and now we know them. If I have ceased to recall them for a fair stretch of time, they sink back again and slip away into distant caverns, and then they need to be pulled from the same places (for there is no other home for them) as though newly thought out, and herded together to become knowable once more: that is to say they need to be collected again, which is why we call this activity cogitating, or collecting one's thoughts. *Cogo* is related to *cogito* as *ago* is to *agito* and *facio* to *factito*. The mind, however, has claimed this verb as properly applicable to itself, so that only what is "collected," within the mind, what is "herded together" there, and there only, is properly said to be "thought."[51]

Chapter 12

19. The memory also stores countless truths and laws of mathematics and mensuration, no single one of which was impressed upon it by bodily sense, for they have no color, sound or smell, nor have they been tasted or handled. I heard the sound of the words that indicated these truths when they were under discussion, but the sounds are one thing and the truths themselves something else. The words sound one way in Greek and differently in Latin, but the truths are neither Greek nor Latin, nor spoken entities of any kind.[52] I have seen a draughtsman's geometric lines, and even though they are infinitely fine, like a spider's thread, the mathematical lines they represent are something quite different, not the images of those lines which

[51] *Cogo is related to* cogito ... properly said to be "thought": The professional rhetorician continues to open up a word's meaning, here linking the verb "to think" or "cogitate", *cogitare*, from the Latin verb "to gather together", *cogere*.

[52] *sound of the words ... spoken entities of any kind*: Augustine provided the field of semiotics, the study of signs and language, with many of its foundational principles. Worked out mainly in his works on how to explicate Scripture properly (e.g., *On Dialect, On the Teacher, On Christian Doctrine*), Augustine distinguishes between the words (*signa, verba*) used and the realities (*res*) that such words attempt to convey.

my fleshly eye has observed. Everyone knows these truths, without a physical representation of any kind being involved. One recognizes them within oneself. With all my bodily senses I have apprehended the numbers of things as we count them; but the principle of number is something entirely different, and without it we could not think mathematically at all. This principle is not an image of the things counted, and therefore has a much more real existence. Let anyone who cannot see it laugh at me, but allow me to pity him for laughing.

Chapter 13

20. Not only do I retain all these things in my memory: I can also keep in my memory the way in which I learned them. I have heard many completely erroneous arguments urged against them, and these too I retain in my memory. Erroneous they were, yet my memory is not in error as I recall them. Further, I can remember discriminating between the truth and those erroneous arguments against it, and I see that my discrimination between them today is distinct from the discrimination I often practiced at various times in the past when I thought about them. So I remember that I have often understood these matters, and I also store in my memory what I discern and understand now, so that later on I may remember that I understood it today. It follows that I have the power to remember that I remembered, just as later, if I recall that I have been able to remember these things now, I shall undoubtedly be recalling it through the faculty of memory.

Chapter 14

21. The same memory also records emotions previously experienced in the mind, not in the same way as the mind experienced them at the time, but in the mode proper to the power of memory. I remember having been happy, without feeling happy now; I recall my past sadness but feel no sadness in so doing; I remember having been afraid once, but am not frightened as I remember; I summon the memory of how I once

wanted something, but without wanting it today. Sometimes the opposite emotion is present: I can happily remember some sadness I suffered which is now over and done with, or sadly recall lost happiness. There is nothing strange about this where the previous experience was one that simply involved the body, for the mind is one thing and the body another;[53] it is therefore unremarkable if in my mind I joyfully recall some former bodily pain. Mind and memory, however, are one and the same. This is why when we instruct someone to remember a point we say, "Be sure to bear that in mind"; and when we forget we say, "I didn't have my mind on it" or "It slipped my mind." So we call memory itself "mind." This being the case, how does it happen that when I happily recall my past sadness, my mind is experiencing joy while my memory is of sorrow, and yet while the mind is happy in the joy it contains, the memory is not saddened by the sadness in it? Does the memory not belong to the mind? Who would maintain that? It is truer to say that the memory is like the mind's stomach,[54] while joy and sorrow are like delicious or bitter food. When they are committed to memory they are transferred to the stomach, as it were, and can be kept there, but cannot be tasted. It is absurd to think the operations of memory and stomach are really alike, yet they are not in all respects dissimilar.

22. But now suppose I produce something else from my memory: I state that there are four passions that disturb the

---

[53] *mind is one thing and the body another*: Later scholars have tended to use lines like this to make Augustine out to be antibody. As an intelligent Christian, however, he can never deprecate matter, but he does at times use less than helpful phrases to discuss the characteristics proper to the human mind and those proper to the human body. He knows his flesh is his dear and eternal friend throughout eternity ("*caro amica mea*" [*Sermon* 14.15]) and that the torments of one's body will, at Christ's Resurrection, be turned into ornaments (playing cleverly off the move from *tormentum* to *ornamentum* in a typical Latin flourish; see *Sermon* 240.3). In this section, his two points are thus simply that (1) the body and mind have separate and distinguishable characteristics and that (2) he will be using mind (*mens*) and memory (*memoria*) interchangeably in what follows.

[54] *memory is like the mind's stomach*: a wonderfully earthy image and one that will (in the next paragraph) be even more exploited, likening human recall to how cattle regurgitate their stomach's contents.

soul—desire, joy, fear and sadness; for purposes of disputation I state whatever analysis of them I have formulated by dividing each according to species and genus; I find in my memory what I am to say and it is from there that I produce my statement; yet when I run through these passions from memory I suffer no emotional disturbance from any of them. Before they were recalled and brought out for inspection they were there: that is why they could be fetched by the act of remembrance. Perhaps, then, these things are produced from the memory in the same way that cattle can bring food back from the stomach for chewing the cud. But in that case why does the disputant (that is, the person who remembers) not taste the sweetness of joy or the bitterness of grief in the mouth of his thought? Or is this precisely the point of difference between two activities, the point where the analogy breaks down? Who indeed would discuss these passions if every time we mentioned sadness or fear we were forced to mourn or feel frightened? And yet we would be in no position to discuss them unless we found in our memory not just the sound of their names, as images derived from sense-impressions, but the very notions of the things themselves. These we have received through no gateway of the flesh; the mind itself has become aware of them by undergoing its emotions and has committed them to memory, or else the memory has retained them of its own accord, though they were not expressly entrusted to it.

Chapter 15

23. It is not easy to say whether this process occurs with the help of images or not. I speak of a stone, or the sun, when these objects are not present to my senses, and unquestionably the images of them are available in my memory. I name a bodily pain: it is not present to me, because nothing is hurting; but unless the image of it resided in my memory I would not know how to speak of it, nor would I be able in an argument to distinguish it from pleasure. I name bodily health when I am myself in a healthy condition; in this case the object itself is present

to me, yet if its image were not also retained in my memory, I would be quite unable to recall what the sound of its name signified; and similarly sick people would not know the meaning of any statement about health if the same image were not retained by the power of memory, even though the thing itself is lacking in their bodies.[55]

When I speak of "numbers"—ideal numbers in the light of which we count—it is not the images of them that are present in my memory but the numbers themselves. I speak of "the image of the sun," and this is precisely what is in my memory, for what I recall is not an image of that image, but the primary image itself: it is this which springs to mind immediately in my act of remembering. I name "memory," and recognize what I am naming; but where can this act of recognition take place, except in the memory? Does this mean that memory is present to itself through its image, and not in itself?[56]

Chapter 16

24. Now when I name "forgetfulness" and similarly recognize the thing I am naming, whence comes my recognition, if not from an act of remembering? I do not mean recognition of the sound of its name, but of the thing signified, for if I forgot that, I would be unable to recognize the meaning of the word. So when I remember "memory," memory itself immediately makes itself available; but when I remember "forgetfulness," both memory and forgetfulness are promptly present: memory since by means of it I remember, and forgetfulness since that

[55] *if its image were not also retained in my memory . . . the thing itself is lacking in their bodies*: Another paradox of memory is that we can recall images and states of things mentally without actually effecting those same realities. Again, this is not a dualist, anti-incarnational anthropology but simply the admittance that the mind can entertain the realities the body cannot.

[56] *Does this mean that memory . . . and not in itself?* For Plato, the realm of mathematics is the first true reality the soul encounters as it makes its way upward out of the material order (see *Republic* VI.509D–513E). Augustine's point echoes this: we can intellectually count without actually having to picture or image the number of material things counted.

is what I am remembering. But what else is forgetfulness but loss of memory? How then can it be present so that I can remember it, when its very presence deprives me of the power to remember? What we remember, we retain in our memory. If we did not remember forgetfulness, we would never recognize the reality which is being referred to when we hear its name; hence forgetfulness is retained by the memory. It must be present, otherwise we would forget it, yet when it is present we forget! Are we to understand, then, that forgetfulness is not in itself present in the memory when we remember it, but present only through its image, since if it were immediately present in its reality it would make us forget, not remember? In the end, who can fathom this matter, who understand how the mind works?

25. This much is certain, Lord, that I am laboring over it, laboring over myself, and I have become for myself a land hard to till and of heavy sweat.[57] We are not in this instance gazing at the expanses of the sky or calculating the distances between stars or the weight of the earth: the person who remembers is myself; I am my mind.[58] It is not surprising that whatever is not myself should be remote, but what can be nearer to me than I am to myself? Yet here I am, unable to comprehend the nature of my memory, when I cannot even speak of myself without it. How am I to explain it, when I am quite certain that I remember forgetting? Am I to say that something I remember is not in my memory? Or am I to say that forgetfulness is in my memory for the very purpose of preventing me from forgetting? Either alternative is completely absurd.

Is there a third possibility?[59] I might say that when I remember "forgetfulness" it is only the image of forgetfulness that is

---

[57] *land hard to till and of heavy sweat*: See Genesis 3:17, 19.

[58] *I am my mind*: As we have seen, it is primarily the mind's ability to gather and understand reality (the particularly human process Augustine is calling "memory") that gives one's life coherence and meaning.

[59] *Is there a third possibility?* Moving quickly, Augustine has already provided three options into how forgetting is possible: (1) simply, that what has been forgotten has dropped out of the memory; (2) a principle called "forgetfulness" is

held in my memory, not forgetfulness itself. But what right have I to make that assertion, in view of the fact that when an image of something is imprinted upon the memory, the thing itself must have been present first, so that the image can be derived from it and imprinted? That is how I remember Carthage; that is how I remember all the places where I have been and the faces of people I have met, and that is how I remember all the information reported by my other senses, and the health or pain of my own body: when these objects were to hand my memory abstracted from them images which I would be able to contemplate as truly present and review in my mind, when later I remembered those objects in their absence. It would follow, then, that if "forgetfulness" is kept in the memory not in its own reality but by means of its image, it would need to have been present so that its image could be abstracted. But when it was present, how did it inscribe its image in my memory, when its very presence blotted out even what it found already registered there?

Nonetheless in some way, some way which is incomprehensible and defies explanation, I am certain that I do remember forgetfulness—that very forgetfulness beneath which what we remember is submerged.

Chapter 17

26. O my God, profound, infinite complexity, what a great faculty memory is, how awesome a mystery! It is the mind, and this is nothing other than my very self. What am I, then, O my God? What is my nature? It is teeming life of every conceivable kind, and exceedingly vast. See, in the measureless plains and vaults and caves of my memory, immeasurably full of countless kinds of things which are there either through

---

something coexistent with memory, and "here" all forgotten things are in fact stored; and (3), like (2), this databank called "forgetfulness" is not *really* a separate reality in the mind but only an image of it. This is the position he now sets out to explain.

their images (as with material things), or by being themselves present (as is the knowledge acquired through a liberal education), or by registering themselves and making their mark in some indefinable way (as with emotional states which the memory retains even when the mind is not actually experiencing them, although whatever is in the memory must be in the mind too)—in this wide land I am made free of all of them, free to run and fly to and fro, to penetrate as deeply as I can, to collide with no boundary anywhere. So great is the faculty of memory, so great the power of life in a person whose life is tending toward death!

What shall I do, then, O my God, my true life? I will pass beyond this faculty of mine called memory, I will pass beyond it and continue resolutely toward you, O lovely Light.[60] What are you saying to me? See, I am climbing through my mind to you who abide high above me; I will pass beyond even this faculty of mine which is called memory in my longing to touch you from that side whence you can be touched, and cleave to you in the way in which holding fast to you is possible. For animals and birds also have memories; they would not otherwise return to their accustomed lairs and nests, rather than randomly to others, and indeed they would never be able to grow accustomed to anything without memory. I will therefore pass beyond memory and try to touch him who marked me out from the four-footed beasts and made me wiser than the birds in the sky;[61] yes, I will pass beyond even my

[60] *I will pass beyond this faculty of mine called memory, ... O lovely Light*: See Ecclesiastes 11:7. Following Plotinus on this point (see *Enneads* V.1.3), Augustine argues that there is no intervening nature between the human soul's highest faculty (located in the memory) and God himself—that is, "since the human person participates in wisdom according to the inner man, as such he is in the image of God in such a way that he is formed without the interposition of any other nature. Therefore nothing is more closely united to God, for man knows and lives and exists and thus is unsurpassed among created beings" (*On Eighty-Three Varied Questions*, 86). Later he argues that the divine image in the human soul, of all God's creatures, "has received God's direct imprint and there is no other nature interposed between him and itself" (*On the Trinity* XI.5.8).

[61] *four-footed beasts and made me wiser than the birds in the sky*: See Job 35:11.

memory that I may find you ... where? O my true good, O
sweetness that will never fail me, that I may find you ... where?
If I find you somewhere beyond my memory, that means that
I shall be forgetful of you. And how shall I find you, once I
am no longer mindful of you?

Chapter 18

27. A woman had lost a coin; she searched for it with a lamp,[62]
and unless she had had some memory of it she would not have
found it, for when it was found, how could she have known
that this was it, if she did not remember it? I remember losing
many things myself, and looking for them and finding them,
and this is how I know, because when I was searching for one
or another of them, and someone said to me, "Perhaps this is
it?" or "Is that it?" I went on saying, "No, that's not it," until
what I was looking for was offered to me. Unless I had remembered that thing, whatever it was, I would not have found it
even when it was handed to me, because I would not have
recognized it. This is what always happens when we look for
something we have lost and then find it. If some article chances
to drop out of view, but not out of memory, such as any kind
of visible object, the image of it persists within us and the
thing is sought until it comes to light again; and when it has
been found it is recognized by comparison with this inward
image. We do not say that we have found the lost object unless
we recognize it, and we cannot recognize it if we do not remember it. The thing had disappeared from our sight, but was held
in our memory.

Chapter 19

28. What follows? When the memory itself loses some item,
as for instance when we forget something and try to remember, where are we to search in the end but in the memory
itself? And if some other thing is offered us there, we brush it

---

[62] *A woman had lost a coin; she searched for it with a lamp*: See Luke 15:8.

aside, until the thing we are looking for turns up. When it does, we say, "That's it!" which we would not be in a position to say if we did not recognize the object, and we could not recognize it if we did not remember it. Yet we had undoubtedly forgotten. Is this the explanation: that the thing had not fallen out of the memory entirely? Can it be that the part which was retained gave a clue to the part which had vanished, because the memory was aware that some item was absent from the full complement it was used to turning over and, feeling itself to be lame and lacking something that normally belonged to it, demanded that the missing element be restored? Suppose we see with our eyes or consider in our mind a certain person known to us, but cannot remember his name, and try to recall it. Any other name that presents itself will seem quite irrelevant to him, because we are not used to associating him with that, and so we reject it. Then at last the right one comes up, and this fits satisfactorily with our habitual knowledge of the person. From where does it emerge, if not from the memory itself? This must be the case, because even if someone else reminds us, we recognize it again only because it springs from our memory: we do not believe what we are told as though this were a piece of fresh information, but remember and agree that what we have just been told is correct. If it has been entirely blotted out from the mind, we do not remember even when reminded. If we remember that we have forgotten something, we have not forgotten it entirely. But if we have forgotten altogether, we shall not be in a position to search for it.

Chapter 20

Universal desire for happiness

29. How then am I to seek you, Lord? When I seek you, my God, what I am seeking is a life of happiness. Let me seek you that my soul may live,[63] for as my body draws its life from my

---

[63] *Let me seek you that my soul may live:* See Psalm 68:33 (69:32); Isaiah 55:3.

soul, so does my soul draw its life from you.[64] How, then, am
I to seek a life of happiness? It is not mine until I can say,
"This is all I want; here is happiness." I must know how to
seek it. Should it be by way of remembering, as though it were
something I have forgotten but am still aware of having forgotten? Or by thirsting for a life still strange to me, either
because I have never known it or because I have so completely forgotten that I do not even remember that I have forgotten? What is a life of happiness? Surely what everyone wants,
absolutely everyone without exception? But if they all want it
so badly, where did they come to know it? Where have they
seen it, that they are so enamored of it? Evidently we possess
it in some fashion.[65] A person who possesses it is happy in
one way, actually happy; in a different manner others are made
happy by hoping for happiness. These latter possess happiness
in a less perfect way than the former, who are happy in the
reality itself, but they are better off than people who are happy
neither in possessing the reality nor in hoping for it. Yet even
these would not so strongly desire happiness unless they possessed it in some degree, and there can be no doubt that they
do desire it. In some mysterious way they must know it, therefore, and hence truly possess it through some kind of cogni-
zance. What I am attempting to find out is whether this resides
in the memory, because if it does, that must mean that we
were happy once upon a time—though whether each of us
was happy individually, or we were all happy in the man who
committed the first sin, in whom we all died and from whom

[64] *my body draws its life from my soul, so does my soul draw its life from you*: This
is the order of the Augustinian cosmos: body, soul, God.

[65] *How, then, am I to seek a life of happiness? . . . we possess it in some fashion*:
In one paragraph, Augustine unites Plato's emphasis on memory, Aristotle's claim
that the human search for happiness is a universal and indispensable reality (which
Augustine would have read through Cicero's *Hortensius*, fragment 36), with the
Christian teaching that all humanity is present in Adam and Eve. How could
every human soul desire beatitude if every human soul has not somehow "already"
experienced it? We must all have had some sort of acquaintance with it, otherwise we would not desire it.

we are all born to misery,[66] I am not now inquiring. I am simply posing the question: Does the life of happiness exist in the memory? We should not love it if we had no acquaintance with it.[67] When we hear the word we all acknowledge that what we want is the reality behind the name, for the sound in itself holds no attraction for us. If a Greek hears it mentioned in Latin, he does not find it delightful, because he does not understand what has been said; we, on the contrary, are delighted, just as he would be if he heard it in Greek, because the reality itself is neither Greek nor Latin. Greek-speakers, Latin-speakers and peoples of every other tongue are all athirst with longing to gain it. This proves that it is known to everyone, and if they could all be asked in some common tongue whether they wish to be happy, they would undoubtedly all reply that they do. This affirmation would not be possible if the reality spoken of were not held in their memories.

Chapter 21

30. Do they retain it in their memories in the same way as someone remembers Carthage after visiting it? No: the happy life is not seen with the eye, since it is not a corporeal object. Perhaps in the way we remember numbers, then? No, for a person who has knowledge of these does not still seek to gain it; but while we have knowledge of the happy life and therefore love for it, we still long to obtain it in order to be happy. Then in the way we remember eloquence, perhaps? No again. It is true that on hearing the word "eloquence" even people who are not yet eloquent remember the reality, and many of them desire to make it their own; this proves that some knowledge of

[66] *the man who committed the first sin, . . . from whom we are all born to misery*: See 1 Corinthians 15:22.

[67] *Does the life of happiness exist . . . if we had no acquaintance with it*: Augustine's sense of humanity's real and collective communion in our protoparents, Adam and Eve, was strong and runs throughout his thought in sometimes surprising ways. Here, for example, his argument for the universal thirst for happiness rests on his theory that in Adam every human soul throughout the millennia was brought into existence with some primordial taste of Eden.

eloquence is in them, but that is only because they have been exposed through the medium of their bodily senses to eloquence in others, and have appreciated it and desire to be similarly eloquent (though to be sure they would not appreciate it unless some knowledge of it were in them already, and they would not want it for themselves if they had no appreciation of it). But we do not experience the happy life in other people through any kind of bodily sense. Are we aware of it, then, in the way that we remember enjoyment? This may be the case, for even when sad I remember my earlier enjoyment, as I can remember leading a happy life even when I am miserable, yet I have never made contact with my enjoyment through any bodily sense: I have never seen, heard, smelled, tasted or touched it; in my mind alone I experienced being happy, and the knowledge of it stuck fast in my memory, so that I am able to remember it, sometimes with contempt and at other times with longing for the various things which I recall having enjoyed. I was formerly flooded with a kind of joy in depraved actions which I now recollect with loathing and disgust. Sometimes, though, it was good and honorable things that I enjoyed, and when I recall these I am stirred by desire for them, even if perhaps they are no longer present, and then it is in sadness that I recollect my earlier joy.

31. So where and when did I experience my life of happiness, so as to remember, love and desire it? This desire is not confined to me alone, nor to me and a few others; absolutely all of us want to be happy. Unless we had some sure knowledge of it, our wills would not be so firmly set on gaining it. But how can this be? If two men are asked whether they wish to undertake military service, it may happen that one of them will reply that he does, and the other that he does not, whereas if they are asked whether they wish to be happy, each of them will immediately say without hesitation that this is what he longs for; and in fact the choice of military service by the one and the refusal of it by the other are directed to no other end than happiness. Is this, perhaps, because one person finds enjoyment in one way and another differently? Thus all agree that

they want to be happy, just as they would, if questioned, all agree that they want to enjoy life, and they think that a life of happiness consists of this enjoyment. One person pursues it in this way, another in that, but all are striving for the same goal, enjoyment. And since no one can claim never to have enjoyed anything, enjoyment is discovered in the memory and recognized there when the life of happiness is mentioned.

Chapter 22

32. Far be it, Lord, far be it from the heart of your servant who confesses to you, far be it from me to think that enjoyment of any and every kind could make me happy. A joy there is that is not granted to the godless,[68] but to those only who worship you without looking for reward, because you yourself are their joy. This is the happy life, and this alone: to rejoice in you, about you and because of you.[69] This is the life of happiness, and it is not to be found anywhere else. Whoever thinks there can be some other is chasing a joy that is not the true one; yet such a person's will has not turned away from all notion of joy.

Chapter 23

33. We cannot therefore assert without qualification that everyone wants to be happy, because people who are unwilling to find joy in you, in which alone the happy life consists, obviously do not want the happy life. Perhaps, though, all men and women do want it, but by reason of the struggle of flesh against spirit and spirit against flesh, which hinders them from doing what they want to do,[70] they fall back on what their strength permits, and make do with that? But is this because

---

[68] *A joy there is that is not granted to the godless*: See Isaiah 48:22.

[69] *This is the happy life, and this alone: to rejoice in you, . . . because of you*: With all his talk of happiness, this is as close to a definition of beatitude Augustine comes to providing: rejoicing in God.

[70] *struggle of flesh against spirit and spirit against flesh, . . . doing what they want to do*: See Galatians 5:17.

they do not want that other thing, for which strength is lacking, ardently enough to find the necessary strength? I think so, because when I ask everybody which they prefer: joy over the truth or joy over what is false,[71] they are as unhesitating in their reply that they prefer to rejoice over the truth as in their declaration that they want to be happy. Now the happy life is joy in the truth; and that means joy in you, who are the Truth,[72] O God who shed the light of salvation on my face,[73] my God.

Everyone wants this happy life, this life which alone deserves to be called happy; all want it, all want joy in the truth. I have met plenty of people who would gladly deceive others, but no one who wants to be deceived. Where else, then, did they come to know this happy life, except where they also came to know about truth? Since they do not wish to be deceived, they must love truth; and when they love the happy life, which is nothing else but joy in the truth, they are unquestionably loving truth also; but they could not be loving the truth unless there was some knowledge of it in their memories. Why, in that case, do they not rejoice over it? Why are they not happy? Because they are more immediately engrossed in other things which more surely make them miserable than that other reality, so faintly remembered, can make them happy. For a little while yet there is light for human beings; let them walk in it, yes, let them walk, lest the darkness close over them.[74]

34. Why, though, does "truth engender hatred," why does a servant of yours who preaches the truth make himself an enemy

---

[71] *joy over the truth or joy over what is false:* See 1 Corinthians 13:6. If happiness is rejoicing in God, perhaps some do not desire to be happy, as some do not wish to place their life in God's. To get out of this aporia, Augustine next argues that happiness is sometimes rightly and sometimes wrongly defined, depending ultimately on what one loves and therefore what one seeks in life.

[72] *you, who are the Truth:* See John 14:6.

[73] *O God who shed the light of salvation on my face:* See Psalm 26(27):1; 41:12(42:11); 42(43):5.

[74] *while yet there is light . . . let them walk, lest the darkness close over them:* See John 12:35.

to his hearers,[75] if the life of happiness, which consists in rejoicing over the truth, is what they love? It must be because people love truth in such a way that those who love something else wish to regard what they love as truth and, since they would not want to be deceived, are unwilling to be convinced that they are wrong. They are thus led into hatred of truth for the sake of that very thing which they love under the guise of truth. They love truth when it enlightens them, but hate it when it accuses them.[76] In this attitude of reluctance to be eceived and intent to deceive others they love truth when it veals itself but hate it when it reveals them. Truth will therefore take its revenge: when people refuse to be shown up by it, truth will show them up willy-nilly and yet elude them. Yes, this is our condition, this is the lot of the human soul, this is its case, as blind and feeble, disreputable and shabby, it attempts to hide, while at the same time not wishing anything to be hidden from it. It is paid back in a coin which is the opposite to what it desires, for while the soul cannot hide from truth, truth hides from the soul. Nonetheless, even while in this miserable state it would rather rejoice in truth than in a sham; and so it will be happy when it comes to rejoice without interruption or hindrance in the very truth, upon which depends whatever else is true.

Chapter 24

In memory he knows God

35. How widely I have ranged through my memory seeking you, Lord, and I have not found you outside it; for I have discovered nothing about you that I did not remember from the time I learned to know you. From that time when I learned about you I have never forgotten you, because wherever I have

---

[75] *a servant of yours who preaches the truth . . . an enemy to his hearers*: See John 8:40; Galatians 4:16.

[76] *They love truth when it enlightens them, but hate it when it accuses them*: See John 3:20; 5:35.

found truth I have found my God who is absolute Truth, and once I had learned that I did not forget it. That is why you have dwelt in my memory ever since I learned to know you, and it is there that I find you when I remember and delight in you. These are my holy delights, and they are your gift to me, for in your mercy you look graciously upon my poverty.

Chapter 25

36. But whereabouts in my memory do you dwell, Lord, in which part of it do you abide? What kind of couch have you fashioned for your repose, what manner of temple have you built yourself there? You have honored my memory by making it your dwelling-place, but I am wondering in what region of it you dwell. As I remembered you I left behind those parts of it which animals also possess, because I did not find you there amid the images of material things. I came to those regions of memory to which I had committed my emotional states, but I did not find you there either. Then I arrived at that place in my memory where my mind itself is enthroned, for indeed the mind must reside there, since it can remember itself; yet not even there were you to be found. Just as you are not any corporeal image, nor any of the emotions that belong to a living person, such as we experience when we are joyful or sad, when we desire or fear something, when we remember or forget or anything similar, so too you are not the mind itself: you are the Lord and God of the mind, and though all these things are subject to change you abide unchangeably[77] above them all. And yet you have deigned to dwell in my memory from the first day that I learned to know you. What am I doing, inquiring which place in it is your place, as though there were really places there? Most certain it is that you do dwell in it, because I have been remembering you since I first learned to know you, and there I find you when I remember you.

---

[77] *you abide unchangeably*: See Psalm 101:27(102:26).

Chapter 26

37. If that is so, where did I find you in order to make acquaintance with you at the outset? You could not have been in my memory before I learned to know you. Where then could I have found you in order to learn of you, if not in yourself, far above me? "Place" has here no meaning: further away from you or toward you we may travel, but place there is none. O Truth, you hold sovereign sway over all who turn to you for counsel, and to all of them you respond at the same time, however diverse their pleas. Clear is your response, but not all hear it clearly. They all appeal to you about what they want, but do not always hear what they want to hear. Your best servant is the one who is less intent on hearing from you what accords with his own will, and more on embracing with his will what he has heard from you.

Chapter 27

38. Late have I loved you, Beauty so ancient and so new,
late have I loved you!
Lo, you were within,
but I outside, seeking there for you,
and upon the shapely things you have made I rushed
    headlong,
I, misshapen.
You were with me, but I was not with you.
They held me back far from you,
those things which would have no being
were they not in you.
You called, shouted, broke through my deafness;
you flared, blazed, banished my blindness;
you lavished your fragrance, I gasped, and now I pant for you;
I tasted you, and I hunger and thirst;
you touched me, and I burned for your peace.[78]

---

[78] *Late have I loved you, . . . you touched me, and I burned for your peace*: This is the most celebrated prayer in the *Confessions*, but as intentionally beautiful as

Chapter 28

39. When at last I cling to you[79] with my whole being there will be no more anguish or labor for me,[80] and my life will be alive indeed, because filled with you. But now it is very different. Anyone whom you fill you also uplift, but I am not full of you, and so I am a burden to myself. Joys over which I ought to weep do battle with sorrows that should be matter for joy, and I know not which will be victorious. But I also see griefs that are evil at war in me with joys that are good, and I know not which will win the day. This is agony, Lord, have pity on me! It is agony! See, I do not hide my wounds; you are the physician and I am sick; you are merciful, I in need of mercy. Is not human life on earth a time of testing?[81]

Who would choose troubles and hardships? You command us to endure them, but not to love them.[82] No one loves what he has to endure, even if he loves the endurance, for although

---

Augustine composed it, he also structured it didactically, taking his reader through his own search for God, as beginning (wrongly) in the things outside of him, only to discover God was already within. Furthermore, this initial experience of the divine is what causes further desire, further seeking, an interplay of already holding but still ardently desirous, already knowing but still seeking more. Perhaps with this first line in mind, "so ancient and so new", Saint Jerome wrote Augustine late in 418 and conveyed how "you are known throughout the world; Catholics honor and esteem you as the one who has established *the ancient Faith anew*" (*Letter* 195); emphasis added.

[79] *When at last I cling to you*: See Psalm 62:9(63:8).

[80] *with my whole being there will be no more anguish or labor for me*: See Psalm 89(90):10.

[81] *Is not human life on earth a time of testing?* See Job 7:11, Old Latin.

[82] *You command us to endure them, but not to love them*: This distinction between use (*uti*) and enjoyment (*frui*) was introduced earlier (see *Conf.* VIII.3.7, note 42, p. 202). All created reality is to be used to draw us closer to God, but God alone can be enjoyed. In other words, without denying its goodness or dignity, Augustine argues that no creature is an absolute end in and of itself; all creatures must be icons unto the divine. This is not to separate, say, love of neighbor and love of God but to place them properly together: in loving God we will necessarily love our neighbor, but if we seek to "love" neighbor only, not only do we fail to love God, we shall one day see that the "love" we had for our neighbor was all along only a form of self-indulgent concupiscence.

he may rejoice in his power to endure, he would prefer to have nothing that demands endurance. In adverse circumstances I long for prosperity, and in times of prosperity I dread adversity. What middle ground is there between the two, where human life might be free from trial? Woe and woe again betide worldly prosperity, from fear of disaster and evanescent joy! But woe, woe, and woe again upon worldly adversity, from envy of better fortune, the hardship of adversity itself, and the fear that endurance may falter. Is not human life on earth a time of testing without respite?

Chapter 29

"Give what you command"

40. On your exceedingly great mercy rests all my hope. Give what you command, and then command whatever you will.[83] You order us to practice continence. A certain writer tells us, *I knew that no one can be continent except by God's gift, and that it is already a mark of wisdom to recognize whose gift this is.*[84] By continence the scattered elements of the self are collected and brought back into the unity from which we have slid away into dispersion; for anyone who loves

---

[83] *Give what you command, and then command whatever you will*: According to Augustine (see *The Gift of Perseverance* 20.53), when the British monk Pelagius (d. ca. 420) read this very line in the *Confessions*, he set out to combat what he perceived as morose fatalism running throughout Augustine's theology. Pelagianism began as a lay, aristocratic movement stressing human freedom and effort in attaining the fullness of the Christian life. This particular line would have been offensive because, according to Pelagius, God cannot command what is not already within human power, nor does God condemn that which is humanly unavoidable. Consequently, Pelagius came to deemphasize any sense of original sin, the need for grace, or the transformative power of Jesus Christ—instead stressing humanity's innate goodness and even perfection if we only chose to avoid Adam's bad example and freely imitate Christ's good example. Augustine is at his bleakest and most cantankerous when dialoguing with (what he perceived to be an) overly optimistic Pelagius.

[84] *I knew that no one can be continent except by God's gift, ... recognize whose gift this is*: Wisdom 8:21.

something else along with you, but does not love it for your sake, loves you less.[85] O Love, ever burning, never extinguished, O Charity, my God, set me on fire! You command continence: give what you command, and then command whatever you will.

Chapter 30

Concupiscence of the flesh: sense of touch[86]

41. Quite certainly you command me to refrain from concupiscence of the flesh and concupiscence of the eyes and worldly pride.[87] You commanded me to abstain from fornication, and recommended a course even better than the marital union you have sanctioned;[88] and because you granted me the grace, this was the course I took even before I was ordained as a dispenser of your sacrament.

Yet in my memory, of which I have spoken at length, sexual images survive, because they were imprinted there by former habit. While I am awake they suggest themselves feebly enough, but in dreams with power to arouse me not only to pleasurable sensations but even to consent, to something closely akin to the act they represent. So strongly does the illusory image in my mind affect my body that these unreal figments influence me in sleep in a way that the reality could never do

[85] *for anyone who loves something else along with you, . . . loves you less*: Love of God and loving all else in God unites the self and provides coherence to all the heart's desires; loving wrongly scatters the self and renders a life incoherent.

[86] Concupiscence of the flesh: sense of touch: The five senses of touch, taste, smell, hearing, and sight are now taken up and put in conversation with the three warnings of 1 John 2:16 to use one's portals to the outside world correctly against concupiscence of the flesh, of the eyes, and against pride. Augustine knows that it is through the body's senses our loves are formed, rightly or wrongly.

[87] *refrain from concupiscence of the flesh and . . . of the eyes and worldly pride*: See 1 John 2:16.

[88] *You commanded me to abstain from fornication, . . . marital union you have sanctioned*: See 1 Corinthians 7:38. Augustine is now resolutely intent on consecrated chastity and possible ecclesial service as a priest.

while I am awake.[89] Surely this cannot mean that I am not myself while asleep, O Lord my God? Yet the moment of passing from wakefulness to sleep or back again certainly marks a great change in me. What becomes then of my reason, which enables me to resist these suggestions in waking hours, and remain unshaken if the actions themselves intrude upon my attention? Is reason shut down along with my eyelids? Is it lulled to sleep with the body's senses? Surely not, for how can it happen that often we do resist even in dreams, remembering our commitment and standing firm in complete chastity, giving no consent to these seductions? There is, notwithstanding, so wide a difference between the two states that even when the opposite occurs we return to peace of conscience on awakening, for the very difference between sleep and waking is obvious enough to convince us that we did not really do the disgraceful thing, even though we are sorry that it was in some sense done in us.

42. Is your hand not powerful enough[90] to heal all my soul's ills,[91] all-powerful God, and by a still more generous grace to extinguish unruly stirrings even in my sleep? Yes, Lord, you will heap gift after gift upon me, that my soul may shake itself free from the sticky morass of concupiscence and follow me to you. As for those foul obscenities in my dreams, where bestial imagination drives the flesh to the point of polluting itself, grant that this soul of mine, through your grace rebellious against itself no more, may not even consent to, still less commit them. You are the Almighty, able to do more than we ask or understand,[92] and it is no great task for you

---

[89] *So strongly does the illusory image in my mind . . . reality could never do while I am awake:* Now intent on a life oriented toward God without exception or excuse, Augustine takes even the dreams over which he has no control to prayer. He understands that free will and intention distinguishes a moral action from an action that simply occurs within or to us, yet his shame is not, however, lessened here as he recalls how disgraceful images from his past still at times trouble him.

[90] *Is your hand not powerful enough:* See Numbers 11:23.

[91] *to heal all my soul's ills:* See Psalm 102(103):3.

[92] *You are the Almighty, able to do more than we ask or understand:* See Ephesians 3:20.

to make provision that nothing of this kind shall arouse the least sensual pleasure—not even such slight titillation as may be easily restrained—in a person of chaste intention while he is asleep, and this even in the prime of life.

But now that I have declared what I still am in this area of my sinfulness, speaking to my good Lord and exulting with trepidation[93] in what your gift has achieved in me, while deploring my unfinished state, my hope is that you will bring your merciful dealings in me to perfection, until I attain that utter peace which all that is within me and all my outward being will enjoy with you, when death shall be swallowed up in victory.[94]

Chapter 31

Taste

43. During the day there is another trouble—and would that the day's troubles were limited to this![95] By eating and drinking we repair the daily wear and tear on our bodies, until such time as you consign both food and belly to destruction.[96] Then you will put an end to our penury with wondrous abundance, and clothe this corruptible flesh in everlasting incorruptibility.[97] For the present, however, this necessity is pleasant to me, and I fight against the pleasure in order not to be captivated by it.[98] By fasting I wage a daily warfare, and habitually force my body to obey me,[99] yet the painfulness of this is outweighed by pleasure, for hunger and thirst are pains of a sort,

---

[93] *exulting with trepidation*: See Psalm 2:11.

[94] *death shall be swallowed up in victory*: See 1 Corinthians 15:54.

[95] *the day's troubles were limited to this*: See Matthew 6:34.

[96] *you consign both food and belly to destruction*: See 1 Corinthians 6:13.

[97] *clothe this corruptible flesh in everlasting incorruptibility*: See 1 Corinthians 15:53.

[98] *I fight against the pleasure in order not to be captivated by it*: A Christian's love of created goods must always be informed by the love of God. If not, fallen creation tends to hold us captive and keep our minds and hearts from soaring heavenward.

[99] *force my body to obey me*: See 1 Corinthians 9:26–27.

which like a fever burn and even kill unless we have recourse to the medicine of food; and since this is ready-to-hand through your comforting provision, whereby earth and water and sky are at the service of our weakness, what could be a calamity for us becomes instead an occasion of enjoyment.

44. You have taught me to take food at mealtimes as though it were medicine. But when I pass from uncomfortable need to tranquil satisfaction, the snare of concupiscence lies waiting for me in the very passage from one to the other; for this transition itself is pleasurable, yet there is no other route for us to take if we are to arrive where necessity forces us to go. Preservation of health is our justification for eating and drinking, but perilous partiality comes hot on its heels, and indeed often tries to run ahead, and so becomes the real motive for what I profess to do (and hope I am doing) in the interests of health. The same standard does not apply to both, for what suffices to maintain health appears meager to appetite, and it is frequently hard to tell whether proper care for the body indicates that further support is needed, or deceitful, pleasure-seeking greed is demanding what will gratify it. At this uncertainty the wretched soul cheers up and marshals excuses in its own defense, glad to take advantage of the ambiguity about what temperate preservation of health requires, and cloaks its self-indulgence under the pretense that health is being prudently provided for.

Every day I strive to withstand these temptations. I call upon your right hand and submit my perplexity to you, because as yet I do not know where I stand in this matter.

45. I hear the voice of my God commanding us, *Let not your hearts become gross with gluttony and drunkenness.*[100] In my case, drunkenness is far away, and by your mercy it will not come near me. Gluttony is a different matter: sometimes it creeps up on your servant, and only your mercy will drive it away. For no one can be continent except by your gift. When

---

[100] Let not your hearts become gross with gluttony and drunkenness: Luke 21:34.

we pray you grant us many things; whatever good we had before we prayed was ours because we received it from you; and even the grace to recognize this afterward is received from you as gift. I have never been a drunkard myself, but I have known drunkards turned sober by you. It is your doing, then, that those who have never been drunkards are not so, and your doing again that those who have been should not be permanently addicted, and finally your doing that both sorts know whose work this is.

I have also heard you telling us: *Go not after your unruly desires, and hold back from indulgence.*[101] Another admonition too I have heard from your Spirit, and this I greatly love: *If we eat we shall be none the better for it, and if we abstain, none the worse;*[102] this means that the one choice will not make me rich, nor the other miserable. Again, there is another saying that I have heard: *Whatever circumstances I am in, I have learned to be content with them; I know how to have enough and to spare, and also how to endure privation. I am capable of anything in him who strengthens me.*[103] And the man who made that claim was a soldier of the heavenly army, not mere dust as we are.

But dust we are, Lord,[104] and remember that from this dust you made us,[105] and that our race, once lost, was found again.[106] I love Paul for saying what he did in response to the breath of your Spirit, but not even he could have spoken so by his own powers, for he was made of the same dust; but, he declared, *I am capable of anything in him who strengthens me.* Strengthen me too, that I may be capable, give what you command, and then command whatever you will. Paul acknowledges that he

[101] *Go not after your unruly desires, and hold back from indulgence:* Sirach 18:30.

[102] *If we eat we shall be none the better for it, and if we abstain, none the worse:* 1 Corinthians 8:8.

[103] *Whatever circumstances I am in, ... I am capable of anything in him who strengthens me:* Philippians 4:11–13.

[104] *dust we are, Lord:* See Psalm 102(103):14.

[105] *from this dust you made us:* See Genesis 3:19.

[106] *our race, once lost, was found again:* See Luke 15:24, 32.

has received everything from you, and his boasting is boasting only in the Lord.[107] I have heard another man making a similar request to mine: *Take gluttony away from me*, he prays.[108] These texts make it clear, O holy God, my God, that when what you command is done, it is by your gift.

46. You have taught me, my good Father, that *to the pure all things are pure*,[109] but that *it is bad for anyone to eat in a way that gives scandal*.[110] You have taught that everything you have created is good, and *nothing is to be rejected, provided it is received with thankfulness*,[111] that *food does not commend us to God*,[112] that *no one should take us to task in the matter of food or drink*,[113] and that *a person who eats should not despise one who abstains, nor should a person who abstains pass judgment on another who eats*.[114] All this I have learned, and I give thanks and praise to you, my God, my teacher, for knocking at the door of my ears[115] and shedding your light into my heart. Pluck me free from all temptation. It is no uncleanness in food that I fear, but the uncleanness of greed. I know that Noah was given permission to eat any kind of flesh meat that was serviceable as food,[116] that Elijah was sustained with meat,[117] and that John, for all his marvelous grace of abstinence, was not defiled by animal food when he made use of locusts.[118] On the contrary, I am aware that Esau was led astray by craving for

---

[107] *Paul acknowledges . . . his boasting is boasting only in the Lord*: See 1 Corinthians 1:31; 2 Corinthians 10:17.

[108] *Take gluttony away from me, he prays*: Sirach 23:6.

[109] *to the pure all things are pure*: Titus 1:15.

[110] *it is bad for anyone to eat in a way that gives scandal*: Romans 14:20.

[111] *nothing is to be rejected, provided it is received with thankfulness*: 1 Timothy 4:4.

[112] *food does not commend us to God*: 1 Corinthians 8:8.

[113] *no one should take us to task in the matter of food or drink*: Colossians 2:16.

[114] *a person who eats . . . pass judgment on another who eats*: Romans 14:3.

[115] *knocking at the door of my ears*: See Revelation 3:20.

[116] *Noah was given permission to eat any kind of flesh meat that was serviceable as food*: See Genesis 9:2–3.

[117] *Elijah was sustained with meat*: See 1 Kings 17:6.

[118] *John, . . . made use of locusts*: See Matthew 3:4.

lentils,[119] that David condemned himself for his intemperate thirst for water[120] and that our King himself was tempted not by meat but by bread.[121] So too your people deserved rebuke in the desert not because they wanted meat, but because their hunger for food led them to murmur against the Lord.[122]

47. Beset by these temptations I struggle every day against gluttony, for eating and drinking are not something I can decide to cut away once and for all, and never touch again, as I have been able to do with sexual indulgence. The reins that control the throat must therefore be relaxed or tightened judiciously; and is there anyone, Lord, who is not sometimes dragged a little beyond the bounds of what is needful? If there is such a person, he is a great man, so let him tell out the greatness of your name.[123] I am not he, for I am a sinful man;[124] yet I will tell out the greatness of your name nonetheless; and may he who has overcome the world[125] intercede for my sins,[126] and count me among the frailer members of his body,[127] because your eyes rest upon my imperfections and in your book everyone will find a place.[128]

Chapter 32

Smell

48. I am not much troubled by sensuality in regard to pleasant smells: if they are absent, I do not seek them, if present, I do

---

[119] *Esau was led astray by craving for lentils*: See Genesis 25:34.

[120] *David condemned himself for his intemperate thirst for water*: See 2 Samuel 23:15–17.

[121] *our King himself was tempted not by meat but by bread*: See Matthew 4:3.

[122] *your people deserved rebuke in the desert . . . led them to murmur against the Lord*: See Numbers 11:1–20.

[123] *let him tell out the greatness of your name*: See Psalm 68:31(69:30); Revelation 15:4; Luke 1:46.

[124] *I am a sinful man*: See Luke 5:8.

[125] *he who has overcome the world*: See John 16:33.

[126] *intercede for my sins*: See Romans 8:34.

[127] *frailer members of his body*: See Romans 12:5; 1 Corinthians 12:22.

[128] *in your book everyone will find a place*: See Psalm 138(139):16.

not reject them, and I am prepared to do without them at all times. Or so it seems to me, though I may perhaps be deceived; for whatever discernment there is in me is shrouded by dismal darkness and hidden from my sight, so that when my mind questions itself about its powers it can scarcely trust any reply it receives.[129] What lies within is generally obscured unless brought to the light by experience. In this life, which is said to be one long temptation,[130] no one should be complacent, for we cannot tell whether someone who has perhaps made progress from a bad state to a better may not also degenerate from that better state to something worse. There is but one hope, one reliance, one solid promise, and that is your mercy.

Chapter 33

Hearing

49. In earlier days the pleasures of the ear enthralled me more persistently and held me under their spell, but you broke my bonds and set me free. Nowadays I do admittedly find some peaceful contentment in sounds to which your words impart life and meaning, provided the words are sung sensitively by a tuneful voice; but the pleasure is not such as to hold me fast, for when I wish I can get up and go. These melodies, however, demand a place of some dignity in my heart, along with the ideas that are their life and in whose company they gain admittance, and I do not find it easy to determine what place is suitable for them. At times it seems to me that I am paying them more honor than is their due, because I am aware that our minds are more deeply moved to devotion by those holy words when they are sung, and more ardently inflamed to piety, than would be the case without singing. I realize that all the

[129] *I am not much troubled by sensuality in regard to pleasant smells . . . scarcely trust any reply it receives*: In his usual honest tenor, Augustine never claims to understand himself fully, but he is sure that there is not much danger in the enticements brought about by pleasant odors.

[130] *this life, which is said to be one long temptation*: See Job 7:1.

varied emotions of the human spirit respond in ways proper to themselves to a singing voice and a song, which arouse them by appealing to some secret affinity.[131] Yet sensuous gratification, to which I must not yield my mind for fear it grow languid, often deceives me: not content to follow meekly in the wake of reason, in whose company it has gained entrance, sensuous enjoyment often essays[132] to run ahead and take the lead. And so in this respect I sin inadvertently, and only realize it later.

50. On occasion, however, I stray into excessive rigor in my exaggerated caution against such a mistake. While this mood lasts I would dearly like all those sweet and tuneful strains which accompany David's psalter to be banished from my ears, and indeed from the ears of the Church. It seems safer to me that we should follow the example of Athanasius, bishop of Alexandria, of which I have been frequently reminded: he permitted the reader of the psalm so slight an inflection of the voice that he seemed to be proclaiming it rather than singing.[133]

[131] *I realize that all the varied emotions of the human spirit . . . appealing to some secret affinity*: Shortly after his baptism in 387, Augustine began *On Music*. Within this discussion of hearing, he raises the warning that certain types of music can strike affinities with the lower parts of the soul, thereby enticing our more animalistic passions. He, of course, never records having witnessed the frenzy of teenagers moshing or thrashing about to hardcore punk music, but he certainly would have understood it.

[132] *sensuous enjoyment often essays*: that is, to attempt or to put to the test.

[133] *follow the example of Athanasius, bishop of Alexandria, . . . proclaiming it rather than singing*: The customs of Bishop Ambrose of Milan are contrasted with the more severe practices of Bishop Athanasius (ca. 295–373) in Alexandria, Egypt, who forbad any elaborate melodizing because it might detract from the focus demanded by worship. This was not, however, uniform throughout the Alexandrian see. We have a wonderful story from the *Apophthegmeta Patrum* about a monk who comes back to his abbot in the Nitrian desert after having run an errand to Alexandria and, having witnessed the beauty of liturgical song and chant there, wishes to introduce it into the monastery. A follower of Athanasius, Abbot Pombo strongly rebukes the young monk, exclaiming: "Woe to us, my son! Is this the day monks turn away from enduring nourishment and surrender themselves to singing? What kind of contrition and tears can come from singing? What enlightenment can a monk achieve by raising his voice like mooing cattle? ... We have come to the desert not to sing melodies and to make rhythms, to shake our hands and stomp our feet—our only duty is to pray to

All the same, I remember the tears I shed at the Church's song in the early days of my newly-recovered faith, and how even today I am moved not by the singing as such but by the substance of what is sung, when it is rendered in a clear voice and in the most appropriate melodies, and then I recognize once more the value of this custom.

Thus I vacillate between the danger of sensuality and the undeniable benefits. Without pretending to give a definitive opinion I am more inclined to approve the custom of singing in church, to the end that through the pleasures of the ear a weaker mind may rise up to loving devotion. Nonetheless when in my own case it happens that the singing has a more powerful effect on me than the sense of what is sung, I confess my sin and my need of repentance, and then I would rather not hear any singer. Such is my condition: weep with me, and weep for me, you who feel within yourselves that goodness from which kind actions spring! Any of you who do not have these feelings will not be moved by my experience. But do you hear me, O Lord my God: look upon me and see,[134] have mercy and heal me,[135] for in your eyes I have become an enigma to myself, and herein lies my sickness.

Chapter 34

Sight

51. If we are to conclude the account of these temptations of the flesh[136] that still beat upon me as I groan and long to have my heavenly tent put on over this earthly one,[137] I must confess in the tender, brotherly hearing of your temple my

---

God in fear and in trembling, with tears and sighing, with devotion and vigilance, modesty and a *humble* voice."

[134] *look upon me and see*: See Psalm 79:15(80:14).

[135] *have mercy and heal me*: See Psalm 6:3(2); 12:4(13:3); 24(25):16–17; 102(103):3; Matthew 4:23.

[136] *temptations of the flesh*: See 1 John 2:16.

[137] *heavenly tent put on over this earthly one*: See 2 Corinthians 5:2.

weakness with regard to one more sense that remains to be discussed: over-indulgence of the eyes. Beautiful things and varied shapes appeal to them, vivid and well-matched colors attract; but let not these captivate my soul. Rather let God ravish it; he made these things exceedingly good,[138] to be sure, but he is my good, not they. Every day, all through the hours that I am awake, colors and shapes impinge upon me, and never is any respite from them allowed me, as it is from the sound of song, or sometimes from all sounds, when silence reigns. Light is the queen of colors and bathes everything we see, and wherever I am in the daytime it flows all around me, and caresses me even while I am doing something else and not thinking about it. So insistently does it make its way in that if it is suddenly withdrawn, we long to get it back, and if we are deprived of it for any length of time, we feel depressed.

52. O Light, Tobit saw you when despite the blindness of his carnal eyes he pointed out the path of life to his son, and strode unerringly ahead, borne by the feet of charity.[139] Isaac saw you, though his bodily eyes were dimmed and closed by age, when true insight was granted him in blessing his sons, notwithstanding his inability to tell one from the other as he uttered his blessing.[140] Jacob saw you when, likewise blinded by advanced age, he beheld by the radiant vision of his heart the tribes of the people that was to be, prefigured in his sons; and when, stretching out crossed hands in a gesture full of mystery, he laid them on his grandsons, Joseph's children, not in the way indicated by their father, who saw only the externals, but as he himself judged to be right by the vision that guided him within.[141] All these enjoyed the same Light, the Light that is one in itself and unites all who see and love it.

---

[138] *he made these things exceedingly good*: See Genesis 1:31.

[139] *Tobit saw you . . . and strode unerringly ahead, borne by the feet of charity*: See Tobit 4:2–20.

[140] *Isaac saw you . . . he uttered his blessing*: See Genesis 27:1–40.

[141] *Jacob saw you . . . vision that guided him within*: See Genesis 48:3; 49:28.

The case is different with earthly light,[142] of which I was speaking. This imparts to the life of this world a seductive zest, dangerous to those whose love for it is blind. Yet once they have learned to praise you for light as well as for your other gifts, Creator God, O Lord of all, they take it up in a hymn to your glory, instead of being sapped by it in somnolence of spirit, and this is how I would wish to act. I resist alluring sights lest my feet, those feet with which I walk in your way, become entangled, and to you I lift the invisible eyes of my spirit that you may pluck my feet from the snare.[143] I know that you will pluck them free again and again, for enmeshed they often are. I am repeatedly caught in the traps scattered on every side, but you will never fail to free me, for you neither grow drowsy nor fall asleep, who guard Israel.[144]

53. How many things craftsmen have made, things without number, employing their manifold skills and ingenuity on apparel, footwear, pottery and artifacts of every conceivable kind, on pictures too, and various images; and how far they have in these matters exceeded what is reasonably necessary or useful, or serves some pious purpose! All of them increase the temptations to which our eyes are subject. People pursue outside themselves what they are making, but forsake the One within by whom they were made, and so destroy what they were made to be by driving it out of doors.

O my God, for me you are loveliness itself; yet for all these things too I sing a hymn and offer a sacrifice of praise[145] to you who sanctify me, because the beautiful designs that are born in our minds and find expression through clever hands derive from that Beauty which transcends all minds, the Beauty

---

[142] *case is different with earthly light*: It is normal for Augustine to distinguish between the invisible and internal from the external and sensible. Here it is light, but he does the same with all the senses as well. We shall encounter his patent phrases "inner ear" (see *Conf.* XI.6.8, p. 335; XIII.29.44, p. 452) as well as an "inner eye" (see *Conf.* XII.20.29, p. 388).

[143] *to you I lift the invisible eyes of my spirit that you may pluck my feet from the snare*: See Psalm 24(25):15.

[144] *you neither grow drowsy nor fall asleep, who guard Israel*: See Psalm 120(121):4.

[145] *I sing a hymn and offer a sacrifice of praise*: See Psalm 115(116):17.

to which my own mind aspires day and night. Those who create beauty in material things, and those who seek it, draw from that source their power to appreciate beauty, but not the norm for its use. The norm is there, and could they but see it they would need to search no further. They could save their strength for you[146] rather than dissipate it on enervating luxuries.

As for me, I say all these things and recognize their truth, yet still I snag my steps on these beautiful objects; but you pluck me free, Lord, you pluck me free because my eyes are fixed on your mercy.[147] I am miserably caught, but you mercifully extricate me, sometimes without my being aware of it, when I am only lightly entangled, but sometimes painfully because I am already stuck fast.

Chapter 35

Concupiscence of the eyes

54. There is still another temptation, one more fraught with danger. In addition to the concupiscence of the flesh, which lures us to indulge in the pleasures of all the senses, and brings disaster on its slaves who flee far from you,[148] there is also concupiscence of the mind, a frivolous, avid curiosity. Though it works through these same senses it is a craving not for gratification of the flesh but for experience through the flesh. It masquerades as a zeal for knowledge and learning. Since it is rooted in a thirst for firsthand information about everything, and since the eyes are paramount among the senses in acquiring information, this inquisitive tendency is called in holy scripture *concupiscence of the eyes*.[149] Sight is, properly speaking, the eyes' business, but we use the word also of our other senses in their cognitive function. Thus we do not say, "Listen for anything red," or "Smell how shiny!" or "Taste how brilliant

---

[146] *They could save their strength for you:* See Psalm 58:10(59:9).

[147] *my eyes are fixed on your mercy:* See Psalm 25(26):3.

[148] *slaves who flee far from you:* See Psalm 72(73):27.

[149] concupiscence of the eyes: 1 John 2:16.

this is!" or "Feel the brightness of that!" For all such objects we speak of seeing. Yet we do say not only, "See how it shines," which the eyes alone can report; we also say, "Let's see how this sounds ... See how fragrant ... See what this tastes like ... Just look how hard that is!" So, as I have pointed out, general sense-experience is called lust of the eyes, because when the other senses explore an object in an effort to collect knowledge, they claim for themselves, by a certain analogy, the office of seeing, in which the eyes unquestionably hold the primacy.

55. From this consideration the distinction more clearly emerges between two kinds of activity on the part of the senses: pleasure-seeking and curiosity; for sensuality pursues the beautiful, the melodious, the fragrant, the tasty and the silky, whereas curiosity seeks the opposite to all these, not because it wants to undergo discomfort but from lust to experience and find out. What sensual pleasure is to be had in viewing a mangled corpse which sickens you?[150] Yet if there is one lying anywhere, people congregate in order to experience ashen-faced horror. At the same time they are frightened that it may give them nightmares! Anyone would think they had been forced to look at the thing while awake, or had been persuaded to do so by some rumor of its beauty. The same holds for the other senses, but it would be tedious to pursue the point through them all.

To satisfy this morbid craving monstrous sights are exhibited at shows. From the same motive efforts are made to scrutinize the secrets of the natural world that lie beyond our sight;

---

[150] *viewing a mangled corpse which sickens you*: In the *Republic*, Plato uses the example of Leonitus' inability to look away from a freshly executed corpse (the first "gaper's delay" recorded in Western literature) to distinguish the three parts of the soul: the senses that want to look, the mind that detects this as debauched, and, in the middle, the passions that either give in to the senses or else seek a way to strategize so as not to look (see *Republic* IV.439E–441C). Here, Augustine's point is that there is no harm in seeking pleasure rightly, because it can draw the virtuous seeker upward to God, whereas curiosity has, by definition, no order or purpose and leaves the mind scattered and directionless. As he concludes this paragraph, we see that even the religious share in this struggle: choosing God for God's own sake or for just some experience of God.

knowledge of these is of no profit, yet people want to know them simply for the sake of knowing. The same motive prompts some to seek perverted knowledge through magical practices. In religion itself people tempt God from the same motive, demanding signs and wonders[151] not for any salutary purpose but simply because they crave experience.

56. In this vast thicket full of snares and perils there are many temptations that I have by now lopped off and cleared out of my heart, as you have enabled me, O God of my salvation;[152] yet when dare I claim, with so many of these things besetting our daily life with their din—when dare I claim that by no such sight am I ever drawn to gaze, ever trapped into frivolous fascination? Theatrical shows, admittedly, have no hold on me now, nor do I care to trace the movements of the stars, nor has my mind ever sought answers through necromancy; I hate all unhallowed rites. But with what contrivances does the enemy work to persuade me to ask some sign of you, O Lord my God, to whom I owe humble and single-hearted service! I beg you through our King and through Jerusalem, our single-hearted, chaste homeland, that as consent to such suggestions is far from me, so may it be far always, and farther still. When I entreat you for the salvation of someone, the object of my prayer is quite different. You grant me, and will continue to grant me, the grace to follow you freely, whatever you choose to do.

57. Be that as it may, the many minute, contemptible things that solicit our curiosity every day are past counting, as are our frequent falls. How often do we begin by putting up with gossips in order not to upset the vulnerable, and then gradually come to listen avidly? When a hound in pursuit of a hare is part of a show at the circus I will not watch, but when it happens in the country and I chance to be passing, the chase may distract me from some deep thought and attract me to

---

[151] *people tempt God from the same motive, demanding signs and wonders:* See Luke 11:16; John 4:48.

[152] *O God of my salvation:* See Psalm 17:47(18:46); 37:23(38:22).

itself. It is not the swerving of my horse's body that alters my course, but the inclination of my own heart; and unless you promptly show me my weakness and command me to use the spectacle as a means of lifting my mind to you by some suitable reflection, or else to disregard the whole thing and pass on, I stand foolishly gaping. Even when I am sitting at home, why does a lizard catching flies, or a spider binding them when they blunder into its web, often have me gazing intently? Does the fact that these animals are so small make any difference to the situation? True, I pass from watching them to praising you, wonderful creator and dispenser of all that is, but it is not in that frame of mind that I begin to watch. To get up without delay is one thing, not to fall in the first place is another.[153]

My life is full of such weaknesses, and my sole hope is your exceedingly great mercy. When our heart becomes a bin for things like this, stuffed with a load of idle rubbish, our prayers are often interrupted and disturbed by it, and though the pleading of our heart is addressed to your ears, worthless thoughts intrude from who knows where to cut short the great business on which we are engaged in your presence.[154]

Chapter 36

The third great temptation: pride

58. Are we to regard this as a trivial fault? Can there be for us any route back to hope other than your mercy, of which we have proof already because you have begun to change us?

---

[153] *To get up without delay is one thing, not to fall in the first place is another*: Advanced as he is becoming in the spiritual life, Augustine is still amazed how distracted he can become. At least now, he finds some solace; he allows grace to lift those distractions rather speedily into divine contemplation again.

[154] *When our heart . . . we are engaged in your presence*: This long section on the senses and their powers is really an examination of the "outer man", which conveys creatures to the soul. Augustine is not here being prudish but prudent. He wants to leave no love, no pull on his soul, unexamined, and that begins by cataloging and seeking to understand sensible goods first.

You know how much you have changed me, for you began by healing me of the itch to justify myself, so that you could be compassionate to all my other iniquities as well, heal all my ailments, rescue my life from decay, crown me in pity and mercy and overwhelmingly satisfy my desire with good things.[155] You crushed my pride by inspiring in me reverential fear, and you made my neck submissive to your yoke.[156] And now I wear it, and find it benign, as you have promised and as you have made it. Indeed it was so before, when I was afraid to take it on me, but I did not know it then.

59. Is it possible, Lord—this I ask of you who alone hold sway without trace of pride, because you alone are the true Lord[157] who owe fealty to no other—is it possible that the third category of temptation[158] has left me in peace, or ever can leave me in peace throughout my life in this world? This is the temptation to want veneration and affection from others, and to want them not for the sake of some quality that merits them, but in order to make such admiration itself the cause of my joy. It is no true joy at all, but leads only to a miserable life and shameful ostentation. This tendency is one of the chief impediments to loving you and revering you with chaste fear,[159] and therefore you thwart the proud but give your grace to the humble;[160] you thunder at this world's ambitions till the foundations of the mountains shudder.[161]

The enemy of our true happiness therefore lies in wait for those of us who by reason of our official positions in human society must of necessity be loved and honored by our fellows. On every side he scatters popular plaudits to trap us, so

---

[155] heal all my ailments . . . satisfy my desire with good things: See Psalm 102(103):3.
[156] made my neck submissive to your yoke: See Matthew 11:30.
[157] you alone are the true Lord: See Isaiah 37:20.
[158] third category of temptation: See 1 John 2:16.
[159] loving you and revering you with chaste fear: See Psalm 18:10(19:9).
[160] you thwart the proud but give your grace to the humble: See James 4:6; 1 Peter 5:5.
[161] you thunder at this world's ambitions till the foundations of the mountains shudder: See Psalm 17:14, 8(18:13, 7).

that as we eagerly collect them we may be caught unawares, and abandon our delight in your truth to look for it instead in human flattery.[162] So the affection and honor we receive come to be something we enjoy not for your sake but in your stead, and in this way that enemy who decided to set up his throne in the far recesses of the north[163] wins cronies in his own likeness, not to live with him in loving concord but to be tormented in his company, slaves in darkness and cold of him who imitates you in his perverse, distorted fashion.

But as for us, Lord, remember that we are your little flock:[164] keep us as your own.[165] Spread your wings and let us flee to shelter beneath them. Be yourself our glory: let us be loved on your account, and let it be your word in us that is honored. Whoever touts for human praise that you reprehend will find no human champion when you judge, nor be reprieved when you condemn. It may not be the case that a sinner is praised for his cherished plans, or a wrongdoer commended;[166] even so, if a person is lauded for some gift that you have given him, and he derives more joy from being praised than for possessing the gift which earns the praise, he too is accepting praise which in your sight is a sham. Even the one who extols him is better off than the one so esteemed, for the former at least appreciates God's gift in a human being, whereas the other prizes what humans give him more than the gift of God.

---

[162] *On every side . . . in human flattery*: Blaise Pascal, introduced above as a student of Augustine's thought (see *Conf.* V.3.3, note 10, p. 103)—emphasizing the heart over rational proof—drew from Augustine to argue that the powerful of the world seek plaudits and flattery as diversions because they temporarily relieve them from thinking introspectively. This is, according to Pascal, why all seek to be the king, "because people are continually trying to divert him and procure him every kind of people. A king is surrounded by people whose only thought is to divert him and stop him thinking about himself, because, king though he is, he becomes unhappy as soon as he thinks about himself" (*Pensées* §139).

[163] *set up his throne in the far recesses of the north*: See Isaiah 14:13–15.

[164] *we are your little flock*: See Luke 12:32.

[165] *keep us as your own*: See Isaiah 26:13.

[166] *sinner is praised for his cherished plans, or a wrongdoer commended*: See Psalm 9:24(10:3).

Chapter 37

60. We are put to the test by these temptations every day, Lord, unceasingly are we tempted; and the crucible in which we are assayed is the human tongue.[167] In this respect too you lay upon us the injunction to continence: so give what you command, and then command whatever you will. You know how my heart groans to you[168] over this, and how my eyes stream with tears; for there is a dangerous infection here, and how far I am clear of it is not easy for me to discern. I am sorely afraid about my hidden sins,[169] which are plain to your eyes[170] but not to mine. In other areas of temptation I have some shrewdness in self-examination, but in this matter almost none. Where sensual desires or idle curiosity are concerned I can measure my progress in self-restraint by going without these pleasures either voluntarily or because opportunity for indulgence is lacking. In that situation I question myself as to whether I am more troubled by their absence, or less. The same applies to riches. People seek wealth in order to use it in the furtherance of one of the three concupiscences, or two of them, or all three; and anyone who lacks the insight to be certain whether he can despise wealth while still possessing it can test himself by getting rid of it. But what of praise? Are we to lead evil lives in order to be rid of it and so test our ability? Should we live in such an abandoned and brutal fashion that everyone who knows us will hate us? Can one imagine a crazier idea than this? If a good life characterized by noble works inevitably and rightly entails being commended, neither the good life nor the resultant commendation can be renounced. Yet only when something pleasant has been withdrawn can I be sure of my ability to live without it, either contentedly or perhaps with reluctance.

61. What then am I to confess to you, Lord, with regard to this kind of temptation? What indeed, except that I do enjoy

---

[167] *We are put to the test . . . assayed is the human tongue*: See Proverbs 27:21.
[168] *You know how my heart groans to you*: See Psalm 37:9(38:8).
[169] *I am sorely afraid about my hidden sins*: See Psalm 18:13(19:12).
[170] *plain to your eyes*: See Sirach 15:20.

being praised? But I take more delight in truth itself than in any eulogy; for if I were asked which I would prefer: to be a thief and crooked in every respect yet praised for it by other people, or to be steadfast and absolutely firm in the truth, but reviled by all, I know which I would choose. All the same I must admit that, though I would not wish the satisfaction I take in anything good about myself to be enhanced by someone else's approbation, yet it is enhanced; and, what is more, criticism diminishes it.

And when this wretchedness on my part troubles me, an excuse sidles into my mind, the validity of which only you know, O God, for it leaves me perplexed. You have enjoined upon us not only continence, which means restraining our love from certain objects, but also justice, which requires us to bestow it on certain others; and you have willed that our charity should be directed not to you alone but also to our neighbor. Now, the idea often occurs to me that when I take pleasure in being spoken highly of by someone of good understanding, what I am pleased about is the progress, or the promise, shown by my neighbor, while on the contrary I am saddened by my neighbor's misfortune when I hear him finding fault with something good, or something he does not understand. In fact I am saddened at times by the adulation I receive when qualities of mine which I do not myself much like are eulogized, or even when good points which are of only slight importance are rated more highly than they deserve. I am reluctant, then, to have a person who speaks highly of me holding a different opinion from my own on the subject of myself; but how am I to know whether this reaction springs from concern for the other person's welfare? Might it not just as well be due to the fact that I get increased satisfaction from good features I like in my own character when they find favor with another person too? After all, it is no compliment to me if my opinion of myself does not commend itself to others, since this implies either that qualities displeasing to me are being applauded, or that features which I find less attractive are being accorded higher honor. Am I not justified, then, in saying that in this matter I do not know where I stand?

62. You are Truth, and in you I see that if I am touched by the high opinion others hold of me, it should be not for my own sake but so that my neighbor may profit thereby. And whether this is the case, I do not know. In this respect I know myself less clearly than I know you. I beg you to reveal myself to me as well, O my God, so that I may confess the wounded condition I diagnose in myself to my brethren, who will pray for me.

Let me try again, and question myself more carefully. If I am anxious that my neighbor shall profit by praising me, why am I less concerned when some other person is unjustly criticized than when I am myself? Why does an affront offered to myself bite more deeply than one flung at another person in my hearing, given that the injustice of it is the same in either case? Do I really not know the answer? Is there nothing left to say, but that I am deluding myself[171] and not acting truthfully[172] with heart and tongue in your sight? Remove this madness far from me, Lord, lest my own mouth supply me with the sinners's oil to ooze over my head.[173]

Chapter 38

63. Needy and poor am I,[174] but I am the better for recognizing it and lamenting it in secret, and seeking your mercy until my shortcomings are made good and my imperfect self brought to perfection in a peace which the gaze of the arrogant will never descry. But words proceed from the mouth, and actions are observed by other people, and this is fraught with peril, because a hankering for praise will garner every little tribute of approval it can beg, to bolster some fancied pre-eminence of its own. This is a real temptation to me, and even when I am accusing myself of it, the very fact that I am accusing myself

[171] *I am deluding myself*: See Galatians 6:3.

[172] *not acting truthfully*: See John 3:21; 1 John 1:6.

[173] *lest my own mouth supply me with the sinners's oil to ooze over my head*: See Psalm 140(141):5.

[174] *Needy and poor am I*: See Psalm 108(109):22.

tempts me to further self-esteem. We can make our very contempt for vainglory a ground for preening ourselves more vainly still, which proves that what we are congratulating ourselves on is certainly not contempt for vainglory; for no one who indulges in it can be despising it.

Chapter 39

64. Within our own hearts too, yes, deep within, is another wicked temptation of the same class. Some there are who are complacent about themselves although they are not liked by others, or even actively disliked; and such people may make no attempt to be likeable. But self-satisfied though they are, they are very displeasing to you, not only because they make a virtue out of what is not good, but also because they arrogate your good gifts to themselves, or perhaps acknowledge them as yours but claim them as their due, or again recognize them as the gifts of your grace, but hug the grace to themselves, grudging it to others and refusing to share the joy.

You see the fear in my heart, hemmed in as I am by all these dangers and struggles, and many another like them. It is not that I have ceased to inflict these wounds on myself; rather I am conscious that ever and anew you are healing them.

Chapter 40

Summary of all his discoveries

65. O Truth, is there any road where you have not walked with me, teaching me what to avoid and what to aim at, whenever I referred to you the paltry insights I had managed to attain, and sought your guidance? I surveyed the external world as best I could with the aid of my senses and studied the life my body derives from my spirit, and my senses themselves. Then I moved inward to the storehouse of my memory, to those vast, complex places amazingly filled with riches beyond

counting; I contemplated them and was adread.[175] No single one of them could I have perceived without you, but I found that no single one of them was you. But what of myself, the discoverer, I who scanned them all and tried to distinguish them and evaluate each in accordance with its proper dignity? Some things I questioned as my senses reported them, others I felt to be inextricably part of myself; I classified and counted the very messengers, and in the ample stores of memory I scrutinized some items, pushed some into the background and dragged others into the light: what, then of me? No, I was not you, either, not even I as I did all this: the faculty, that is, by which I achieved it, not even that faculty in me was you; for you are that abiding Light[176] whom I consulted throughout my search. I questioned you about each thing, asking whether it existed, what it was, how highly it should be regarded; and all the while I listened to you teaching me and laying your commands upon me.

It is still my constant delight to reflect like this; in such meditation I take refuge from the demands of necessary business, insofar as I can free myself. Nowhere amid all these things which I survey under your guidance do I find a safe haven for my soul except in you; only there are the scattered elements of my being collected, so that no part of me may escape from you.

From time to time you lead me into an inward experience quite unlike any other, a sweetness beyond understanding. If ever it is brought to fullness in me, my life will not be what it is now, though what it will be I cannot tell. But I am dragged down again by my weight of woe, sucked back into everyday

[175] *I contemplated them and was adread*: See Habakkuk 3:2.
[176] *you are that abiding Light*: See John 1:9; 8:12; 9:5; 12:46; 1 John 1:5. As Augustine reviews the mental processes he undertook throughout Book X, he moves us from external sensible goods inward to the goods of the human soul, and further yet still upward to God, who ultimately unites this movement. It proves to be God, depicted here as the Light, who guides, and in so doing not only makes this journey possible but also guides it from without to within to above.

things and held fast in them; grievously I lament, but just as grievously am I held. How high a price we pay for the burden of habit! I am fitted for life here where I do not want to be, I want to live there but am unfit for it, and on both counts I am miserable.

Chapter 41

66. So now under the three headings of temptation I have taken stock of the sickly state to which my sins have reduced me, and I have called upon your right hand for saving help.[177] I have seen your blazing splendor, but with a wounded heart; I was beaten back, and I asked, "Can anyone reach that?" I was flung far out of your sight.[178] You are the Truth,[179] sovereign over all. I did not want to lose you, but in my greed I thought to possess falsehood along with you, just as no one wants to tell lies in such a way that he loses his own sense of what is true. That was why I lost you, for you did not consent to be possessed in consort with a lie.

Chapter 42

The Mediator, priest and victim

67. Whom could I find to reconcile me to you? Should I go courting the angels? With what prayer or by what rites could I win them to my cause? Many have there been who tried to make their way back to you and, finding themselves insufficient by their own powers, had recourse to such means as these, only to lapse into a fancy for visions that tickled their curiosity. They were deservedly deluded for they sought you in arrogance, thrusting out their chests in their haughty knowledge instead of beating them in penitence; and so they attracted to

---

[177] *So now under the three headings . . . saving help*: See Psalm 59:7(60:5); 102(103):3; 107:7(108:6); Matthew 4:23.

[178] *I was flung far out of your sight*: See Psalm 30:23(31:22).

[179] *You are the Truth*: See John 14:6.

themselves the spiritual powers of the air[180] as their true kin,
fit accomplices and allies of their pride. These spirits used
magical powers to beguile their clients, who were seeking a
mediator to purge them of their impurities, but found none;
for there was no one there but the devil, disguised as an angel
of light.[181] Being without a fleshly body himself, he strongly
appealed to the pride of fleshly humans. They were mortal
and sinful, whereas you, Lord, to whom they sought, though
proudly, to be reconciled, are immortal and without sin. What
we needed was a mediator to stand between God and men[182]
who should be in one respect like God, in another kin to
human beings, for if he were manlike in both regards, he would
be far from God, but if Godlike in both, far from us; and
then he would be no mediator.[183] By the same token that
spurious mediator, by whose means pride was deservedly duped
in keeping with your secret decree, does have one thing in
common with human beings, namely sin; and he appears to
have something else in common with God because, not being
clad in mortal flesh, he is able to flaunt himself as immortal.
But in fact since death is the wage sin earns[184] he has this in
common with humans, that he lies under sentence of death
as surely as they do.

Chapter 43

68. In your unfathomable mercy you first gave the humble certain pointers to the true Mediator, and then sent him, that by

[180] *spiritual powers of the air*: See Ephesians 2:2.

[181] *devil, disguised as an angel of light*: See 2 Corinthians 11:14. From Augustine's discussion of mediation in *City of God* X, we learn the bad angels are distinguished from the good by the fact that they want to usurp praise for themselves,
whereas the latter rejoice in bringing the gratitude and praise of humans upward
to God, who alone is worthy of adoration.

[182] *mediator to stand between God and men*: See 1 Timothy 2:5.

[183] *if he were manlike . . . he would be no mediator*: As Book X ends and we
come to understand memory as the place where we move from without to within
to above, it is fitting that we end with a discourse on Christ the high priest, the
Mediator between heaven and earth, between sensible signs and invisible realities.

[184] *death is the wage sin earns*: See Romans 6:23.

his example they might learn even a humility like his. This Mediator between God and humankind, the man Christ Jesus,[185] appeared to stand between mortal sinners and the God who is immortal and just: like us he was mortal, but like God he was just. Now the wage due to justice is life and peace; and so through the justice whereby he was one with God he broke the power of death[186] on behalf of malefactors rendered just,[187] using that very death to which he willed to be liable along with them. He was pointed out to holy people under the old dispensation that they might be saved through faith in his future passion,[188] as we are through faith in that passion now accomplished. Only in virtue of his humanity is he the Mediator; in his nature as the Word he does not stand between us and God, for he is God's equal,[189] God with God,[190] and with him one only God.

69. How you loved us, O good Father, who spared not even your only Son, but gave him up for us evildoers![191] How you loved us, for whose sake he who deemed it no robbery to be your equal was made subservient, even to the point of dying on the cross![192] Alone of all he was free among the dead,[193] for he had power to lay down his life and power to retrieve it.[194] For our sake he stood to you as both victor and victim, and victor because victim;[195] for us he stood to you as priest

---

[185] *This Mediator between God and humankind, the man Christ Jesus*: See 1 Timothy 2:5.

[186] *he broke the power of death*: See 2 Timothy 1:10.

[187] *on behalf of malefactors rendered just*: See Romans 4:5.

[188] *old dispensation that they might be saved through faith in his future passion*: See Romans 4:5; 1 Timothy 2:4.

[189] *he is God's equal*: See Philippians 2:6.

[190] *God with God*: See John 1:1.

[191] *O good Father, who spared not even your only Son, but gave him up for us evildoers*: See Romans 8:32.

[192] *deemed it no robbery to be your equal . . . point of dying on the cross*: See Philippians 2:6, 8.

[193] *free among the dead*: See Psalm 87:6(88:5).

[194] *he had power to lay down his life and power to retrieve it*: See John 10:18.

[195] *he stood to you as both victor and victim, and victor because victim*: See Hebrews 9:28.

and sacrifice, and priest because sacrifice,[196] making us sons
and daughters to you instead of servants[197] by being born of
you to serve us. With good reason is there solid hope for me
in him, because you will heal all my infirmities[198] through
him who sits at your right hand and intercedes for us.[199] Were
it not so, I would despair. Many and grave are those infirmities, many and grave; but wider-reaching is your healing power.
We might have despaired, thinking your Word remote from
any conjunction with humankind, had he not become flesh
and made his dwelling among us.[200]

70. Filled with terror by my sins and my load of misery I
had been turning over in my mind a plan to flee into solitude, but you forbade me, and strengthened me by your words.
To this end Christ died for all, you reminded me, *that they who
are alive may live not for themselves, but for him who died for
them.*[201] See, then, Lord: I cast my care upon you[202] that I
may live, and I will contemplate the wonders you have
revealed.[203] You know how stupid and weak I am:[204] teach
me and heal me.[205] Your only Son, in whom are hidden all

---

[196] *he stood to you as priest and sacrifice, and priest because sacrifice*: See Hebrews
7:27.

[197] *making us sons and daughters to you instead of servants*: See Galatians 4:7.

[198] *you will heal all my infirmities*: See Psalm 102(103):3.

[199] *through him who sits at your right hand and intercedes for us*: See Romans
8:34.

[200] *had he not become flesh and made his dwelling among us*: See John 1:14. Christ's
conjoining God and humanity is a matter both of divine lowliness (*kenosis*) as
well as human greatness (*theosis*). Christians become divinely transformed by
imitating the Son's humility: "Do you wish to lay hold of the loftiness of God?
First catch hold of God's lowliness. Deign to be lowly, to be humble, because
God has deigned to be lowly and humble on the same account, yours, not his
own. So catch hold of God's humility, learn to be humble, don't be proud. Confess your infirmity, lie there patiently in the presence of the doctor. When you
have caught hold of his humility, you start rising up with him" (*Sermon* 117.17).

[201] To this end Christ died for all ... may live not for themselves, but for him
who died for them: 2 Corinthians 5:15.

[202] *I cast my care upon you*: See Psalm 54:23(55:22).

[203] *I will contemplate the wonders you have revealed*: See Psalm 118(119):17–18.

[204] *You know how stupid and weak I am*: See Psalm 68:6(69:5).

[205] *teach me and heal me*: See Psalm 24(25):5; 6:3(2).

treasures of wisdom and knowledge,[206] has redeemed me with his blood. Let not the proud disparage me,[207] for I am mindful of my ransom. I eat it, I drink it,[208] I dispense it to others, and as a poor man I long to be filled[209] with it among those who are fed and feasted. And then do those who seek him praise the Lord.[210]

[206] *Your only Son, in whom are hidden all treasures of wisdom and knowledge:* See Colossians 2:3.

[207] *Let not the proud disparage me:* See Psalm 118(119):22.

[208] *I eat it, I drink it:* See John 6:55, 57; 1 Corinthians 10:31; 11:29. Here the Eucharist is represented as the antidote to pride: as an ordained priest, Augustine is charged to dispense it; as a sinful Christian, he longs to receive it.

[209] *as a poor man I long to be filled:* See Luke 16:21.

[210] *those who seek him praise the Lord:* See Psalm 21:27(22:26).

Book XI

Time and Eternity

Chapter 1

1. Eternity belongs to you, O Lord, so surely you can neither be ignorant of what I am telling you, nor view what happens in time as though you were conditioned by time yourself.[1]

Why then am I relating all this to you at such length? Certainly not in order to inform you. I do it to arouse my own loving devotion toward you, and that of my readers, so that together we may declare, *Great is the Lord, and exceedingly worthy of praise.*[2] I have said already, and will say again, that it is out of love for loving you that I do this, even as we pray for things though Truth tells us that *Your Father knows what you need before you ask him.*[3] We confess to you our miseries and the mercies you have shown us in your will to set us free completely, as you have begun to do already; and by so confessing to you we lay bare our loving devotion. Our hope is that we may cease to be miserable in ourselves and may find our beatitude in you; for you have called us to be poor in spirit, to be meek, to mourn,

---

[1] *Eternity belongs to you, O Lord, . . . conditioned by time yourself*: In confessing his life in God, Augustine sees that while memory makes the recalling of such a narrative possible, it is time through which he must cross. Analysis of memory (Book X) thus leads to the contemplation of time (Book XI) because memory comes into being only as the soul traverses forward (just as the future comes into being only as the soul looks ahead), and it is this traversing which Augustine will call "time". Book X ended with Jesus Christ introduced as Mediator, and since the Eternal has now broken into time, time must next be treated and, in so doing, Augustine shows us how sequence leads to duration, movement to rest, time to eternity.

[2] Great is the Lord, and exceedingly worthy of praise: Psalm 47:2(48:1); 95(96):4; 144(145):3, echoing the *Confessions'* opening line.

[3] Your Father knows what you need before you ask him: Matthew 6:8.

to hunger and thirst for righteousness, to be merciful and pure-hearted, and to be peacemakers.[4]

See, then, how long a tale I have told you, as best I could and as I truly wanted to, because you first willed that I should confess to you, my Lord and God, for you are good and your mercy endures for ever.[5]

Chapter 2

Augustine prays for understanding of the scriptures

2. My pen serves me as a tongue,[6] but when will it find eloquence enough to recount all those exhortations and threats, all that encouragement and guidance, by which you led me to this position where I must preach the word and administer the sacrament to your people?[7] Furthermore, even had I skill to relate it all in order, the dripping moments of time are too precious to me.[8] I have long burned with desire to meditate

---

[4] *our beatitude in you; for you have called us to be . . . peacemakers*: See Matthew 5:3–9.

[5] *my Lord and God, for you are good and your mercy endures for ever*: See Psalm 117(118):1–4.

[6] *My pen serves me as a tongue*: See Psalm 44:2(45:1).

[7] *I must preach the word and administer the sacrament to your people*: Augustine was ordained a priest in 391 by Bishop Valerius of Hippo (d. 396). Having arrived back in Africa to begin the foundations of their anticipated monastic community on some land Augustine inherited around Thagaste (in 388), he traveled to interview a candidate for the monastery in Hippo. In *Sermon 355* (preached in 426) Augustine notes that because he sensed his rising popularity, "I wouldn't go near a place where I knew there was no bishop". So, thinking he would be safe in Hippo, he set out; but once the people heard the famous convert was coming to Hippo, they surrounded him at Sunday Mass while praying in the back of the cathedral and begged Valerius to ordain him a priest. Valerius was a Greek speaker and advanced in years who had a deuce of a time preaching in Latin, let alone understanding the dialect spoken by his rustic parishioners (see *Commentary on Romans* §13); with the Donatists growing, Valerius no doubt saw in the accomplished Augustine a very helpful accomplice indeed.

[8] *dripping moments of time are too precious to me*: a rare instance of gleaning some facts about daily Roman life. Augustine would have kept time with a water clock (a clepsydra—literally, a water thief), which measured a set amount of time by the drips of water. Such a method of timekeeping was common in law

on your law,[9] that there I may confess to you both what I know
and what I still find baffling, your dawning light in me and
the residual darkness that will linger until my weakness is swallowed up by your strength. I am chary of frittering away on
anything else the hours I find free from such needful activities
as bodily refreshment, mental concentration, the duties I owe
to the people and others which I do not owe but render
nonetheless.

3. O Lord my God, hear my prayer,[10]
may your mercy hearken to my longing,[11]
a longing on fire not for myself alone
but to serve the brethren I dearly love;
you see my heart and know this is true.
Let me offer in sacrifice to you the service of my heart and
    tongue,
but grant me first what I can offer you;
for I am needy and poor,[12]
but you are rich unto all who call upon you,[13]
and you care for us though no care troubles you.
Circumcise all that is within me from presumption
and my lips without from falsehood.[14]
Let your scriptures be my chaste delight,
let me not be deceived in them
nor through them deceive others.
Hearken, O Lord, have mercy, my Lord and God,[15]

---

courts and places of debate in which each party had an agreed amount of time
to make his case.

[9] *long burned with desire to meditate on your law:* See Psalm 1:2.

[10] *O Lord my God, hear my prayer:* See Psalm 60:2(61:1).

[11] *may your mercy hearken to my longing:* See Psalm 9B:38(10:17).

[12] *I am needy and poor:* See Psalm 85(86):1.

[13] *you are rich unto all who call upon you:* See Romans 10:12.

[14] *Circumcise all that is within me from presumption and my lips without from
falsehood:* See Exodus 6:12.

[15] *Hearken, O Lord, have mercy, my Lord and God:* See Jeremiah 18:19; Psalm
26(27):7.

O Light of the blind, Strength of the weak—
who yet are Light to those who see and Strength to the strong—
hearken to my soul,
hear me as I cry from the depths,[16]
for unless your ears be present in our deepest places
where shall we go[17] and whither cry?
Yours is the day, yours the night,[18]
a sign from you sends minutes speeding by;
spare in their fleeting course a space for us
to ponder the hidden wonders of your law:
shut it not against us as we knock.[19]
Not in vain have you willed so many pages to be written,
pages deep in shadow, obscure in their secrets;
not in vain do harts and hinds seek shelter in those woods,
to hide and venture forth,
roam and browse, lie down and ruminate.
Perfect me too, Lord, and reveal those woods to me.[20]
Lo, your voice is joy to me,
your voice that rings out above a flood of joys.
Give me what I love;
for I love indeed, and this love you have given me.
Forsake not your gifts, disdain not your parched grass.
Let me confess to you all I have found in your books,
Let me hear the voice of praise,[21]
and drink from you,
and contemplate the wonders of your law[22]
from the beginning when you made heaven and earth
to that everlasting reign when we shall be with you in your
   holy city.

---

[16] *hear me as I cry from the depths*: See Psalm 129(130):1.

[17] *where shall we go*: See Psalm 138(139):7–8.

[18] *Yours is the day, yours the night*: See Psalm 73(74):16.

[19] *as we knock*: See Matthew 7:7–8; Luke 11:9–10.

[20] *Perfect me too, Lord, and reveal those woods to me*: See Psalm 28(29):9.

[21] *Let me hear the voice of praise*: See Psalm 25(26):7.

[22] *contemplate the wonders of your law*: See Psalm 118(119):18.

4. Have mercy on me, Lord, and hearken to my longing;[23] for I do not think it arises from this earth, or concerns itself with gold or silver or precious stones, with splendid raiment or honors or positions of power, with the pleasures of the flesh or with things we need for the body and for this our life of pilgrimage; for all these things are provided for those who seek your kingdom and your righteousness.[24] Look and see, O my God, whence springs my desire. The unrighteous have told me titillating tales, but they have nothing to do with your law, O Lord;[25] and see, that law is what stirs my longing. See, Father, have regard to me and see and bless my longing, and let it be pleasing in your merciful eyes[26] that I find grace before you,[27] so that the inner meaning of your words may be opened to me as I knock at their door.[28] I beg this grace through our Lord Jesus Christ, your Son, the man at your right hand,[29] the Son of Man whom you have made strong to stand between yourself and us as mediator.[30] Through him you sought us when we were not seeking you,[31] but you sought us that we might begin to seek you. He is the Word through whom you made all things,[32] and me among them, your only Son through whom you called your believing

---

[23] *Have mercy on me, Lord, and hearken to my longing:* See Psalm 26(27):7; 9B:38(10:17).

[24] *for those who seek your kingdom and your righteousness:* See Matthew 6:33.

[25] *unrighteous have told me titillating tales, . . . your law, O Lord:* See Psalm 118(119):85.

[26] *let it be pleasing in your merciful eyes:* See Psalm 18:15(19:14).

[27] *that I find grace before you:* See Daniel 3:40.

[28] *as I knock at their door:* See Matthew 7:7–8; Luke 11:9–10.

[29] *Lord Jesus Christ, your Son, the man at your right hand:* See Psalm 79:18(80:17).

[30] *unrighteous have told me titillating tales . . . to stand between yourself and us as mediator:* See 1 Timothy 2:5. The unrighteous spewing "titillating tales" are, of course, the Manichees, while the law of the Lord (a possible allusion to the truth of the Old Testament) whets Augustine's desire for holiness, fulfilled only in the Person of Jesus Christ, presented here as the only Mediator strong enough to bridge heaven and earth, divinity and humanity.

[31] *Through him you sought us when we were not seeking you:* See Romans 10:20.

[32] *He is the Word through whom you made all things:* See John 1:1–3.

people to be your sons by adoption,[33] and me among them;
through him, then, do I make my plea to you, through him
who sits at your right hand to intercede for us,[34] for in him
are hidden all treasures of wisdom and knowledge.[35] And they
are what I seek in your books. Moses wrote of him; Christ
told us so himself,[36] and he is the Truth.

Chapter 3

"In the Beginning God made heaven and earth"

5. Let me listen, so that I may understand how you made heaven
and earth in the beginning.[37] Moses wrote that statement; he
wrote it and went away, and made his passover, his passing
from you to you; and so he is not here face-to-face with me
now. If he were, I would take hold of him and ask him and in
your name implore him to open these mysteries to me. I would
bend my bodily ears to the sounds that broke from his mouth,

---

[33] *your sons by adoption*: See Galatians 4:5. As Augustine grew in his knowledge of Saint Paul, so did his emphasis on salvation in Christ as a matter of
divine adoption, becoming daughters and sons in the Son. He saw in this adop-
tive process that the creature is elevated and thus participates in God's own self:
"God wants to make you a god; not by nature, of course, like the one whom he
begot, but by his gift and by his adoption. For just as he was made a participant
in your mortality through humanity, so through his exalting you he makes you a
sharer in his immortality" (*Sermon* 166.4).

[34] *through him who sits at your right hand to intercede for us*: See Romans 8:34.

[35] *in him are hidden all treasures of wisdom and knowledge*: See Colossians 2:3.

[36] *Moses wrote of him; Christ told us so himself*: See John 5:46. Like all Church
Fathers, Augustine believed that Moses was the author of Genesis.

[37] *you made heaven and earth in the beginning*: Here the "beginning" is not a
thing or a concept, but a Person. It is important in following Augustine's theology of Genesis 1:1 to know that the "beginning" in *whom* God creates is the
Son. Augustine will read Scripture Christologically whenever possible, and in
using John 1 to interpret Genesis 1, he claims that the principle or archetype in
whom the Father creates is the Son, finding the Trinity in the opening passage
of Scripture: "[T]he Father is found in the name of 'God' and the Son in the
name 'beginning', who here is not the 'beginning' of the Father but who is the
'beginning' for all of creation ... and as the Spirit of God was being borne over
the water (Genesis 1:2), we acknowledge the complete commemoration of the
Trinity" (*Literal Commentary on Genesis* I.6).

though if he spoke Hebrew, those sounds would knock in vain at the door of my perception, for nothing of what was said would reach my mind, whereas if he spoke Latin, I would know what he was saying. But how would I know whether he spoke the truth? If I were to ascertain that too, could it be on his assertion? No; undoubtedly within myself, in that inner habitation of my thought, the truth that is neither Hebrew nor Greek nor Latin nor any vernacular would speak to me without bodily organ of mouth or tongue, and without any clatter of syllables would tell me, "He is speaking the truth"; and then with instant certainty I would say to that man who served you, "What you say is true."

But since I cannot question him, who spoke truthfully because you, O Truth, had filled him, I beg you yourself, O Truth, my God, to pardon my sins, and as you granted that servant of yours the grace to say those things, grant also to me the grace to understand them.

Chapter 4

6. Heaven and earth plainly exist, and by the very fact that they undergo change and variation they cry out that they were made. If anything was not made, yet exists, there is no element in it that was not present earlier; for change and variation imply that something is made that was not previously there. Heaven and earth further proclaim that they did not make themselves: "We are, because we have been made; we did not exist before we came to be, as though to bring ourselves into being." And their visible existence is the voice with which they say this. It was you who made them, Lord: you are beautiful, so it must have been you, because they are beautiful; you who are good must have made them, because they are good; you who are, because they are. Yet not in the same way as you, their creator, are they beautiful and good, nor do they exist as you exist; compared with you they have neither beauty nor goodness nor being. We know this, and we thank you for the knowledge, yet compared with your knowledge ours is but ignorance.

Chapter 5

God creates in his Word

7. But how did you make heaven and earth? What tool did you employ for so vast an enterprise? You cannot have gone to work like a human craftsman, who forms a material object from some material in accordance with his imaginative decision. Whatever design his mind's eye conjures up within, the mind has power to impose upon the material, but where would he get this power, if you had not made his mind? He merely stamps a form on matter already in existence and in possession of its being, such as clay or stone or wood or gold or any other stuff of the kind. And whence would these derive their existence, unless you had established them in being?[38] You made the craftsman's body; you made the mind which exercises control over his limbs; you made the material he needs to fashion anything; you made the skill that equips him to master his art and visualize within his mind the plan to which he will give outward expression. You made the perceptive senses which can interpret the design in the mind and transfer it to the material to produce the thing he is making, and then report back to the mind on what has been made, so that the craftsman may test it against the truth that rules him within himself, to ensure that it is made properly. All these things praise you, the creator of them all.

But you, how do you make them? How did you make heaven and earth, O God? You certainly did not use either heaven or earth as your workshop when you made heaven and earth, nor did you work in the air or in the waters, because these too belong to heaven and earth; nor can you have made the whole universe anywhere within the whole universe, because there was no place in it where such work could be done before it

---

[38] *would these derive their existence, unless you had established them in being*: A doctrine never made explicitly clear in Scripture, although alluded to (see 2 Maccabees 7:28; Romans 4:17; Hebrews 11:3), creation from nothing (*creatio ex-nihil*) is by Augustine's time a standard cosmological assumption for Christian thinkers.

was made and given its being. Nor did you hold in your hand some material from which to fashion heaven and earth, for where would you have obtained any material you had not made, in order to use it for making something else? Is there anything that exists at all, if not because of you?

Clearly, then, you spoke and things were made. By your word you made them.[39]

Chapter 6

8. But how did you speak? Surely not in the same way as you did when a voice came from the cloud, saying, *This is my beloved Son?*[40] That utterance came and went; it had a beginning and an end. Its syllables made themselves heard and then faded away, the second following the first, the third following the second, and so on in due order until the last one followed the others, and silence fell after the last. From this it is self-evident that your voice made itself heard through the movement of a created thing, which was the temporal instrument of your eternal will. Then these words of yours, in their temporal expression, would be reported by the outward ear to the mind of any discerning listener whose inner ear was attuned to your eternal Word. The mind would then compare the words sounding in time with your silent Word in eternity, and say, "These are something different, totally different. They are far below me and have no being, since they are fleeting and

---

[39] *Clearly, then, you spoke and things were made. By your word you made them*: See Psalm 32(33):9, 6.

[40] *But how did you speak?...This is my beloved Son:* There is a difference between the Father's "speaking" in the Son so as to create and the Father's speaking to the Son as he rose from the Jordan as the incarnate Christ (see Matthew 3:17), or as he came down the mountain at the Transfiguration (see Matthew 17:5; Luke 9:35). In the latter, the Father used created intermediaries to move the air and to produce the sound that, by definition, must have both a beginning and an end. On the other hand, in Genesis 1:1 the Father does not speak in time, because there was not yet time. The speaking of creation was coterminous with time; the speaking to Christ was in time. The first was expressed existentially, the second temporally. Neither is to be confused with the very Word itself (the Logos of John's Prologue), as is made clear in the next section.

ephemeral; but the Word of my God is above me and abides for ever."[41] It seems, then, that if you made use of audible, evanescent words to say that heaven and earth should come to be, and that was how you made heaven and earth, there must have been some material thing in existence before you made heaven and earth, so that such a voice might use the creature's temporal movements to make itself audible in time. But no material thing did exist before heaven and earth; or, if there was such a thing, you undoubtedly must have made it without using transitory speech, since you meant to use it as the vehicle of that transitory utterance in which you would say that heaven and earth should come to be. Whatever that thing was from which such an utterance might be produced, it could not have existed at all unless you had made it. So what word did you speak to bring into being that material object, from which those other words were to proceed?

Chapter 7

This Word is eternal

9. You are evidently inviting us to understand that the word in question is that Word who is God, God with you who are God;[42] he is uttered eternally, and through him are eternally uttered all things. This does not mean that one thing was said, and then, when that was finished, another thing, so that everything could be mentioned in succession; no, all things are uttered simultaneously in one eternal speaking. Were this not so, time and change would come into it, and there would be neither true eternity nor true immortality. I know this, my God, and I give you thanks for it. I know, and I confess to you, Lord,[43] and everyone who is grateful for assured truth knows it with me, and blesses you. We know this, Lord, we know it,

---

[41] *the Word of my God is above me and abides for ever*: See Isaiah 40:8.

[42] *God with you who are God*: See John 1:1.

[43] *I know, and I confess to you, Lord*: See Matthew 11:25–27; Luke 10:21–22.

because insofar as a thing is no longer what it once was, or is now what it once was not, that thing is dying or rising to new life; but in your Word there is no cessation or succession, for all is truly immortal and eternal. Thus in that Word who is coeternal with yourself you speak all that you speak simultaneously and eternally, and whatever you say shall be comes into being. Your creative act is in no way different from your speaking. Yet things which you create by speaking do not all come to be simultaneously, nor are they eternal.[44]

Chapter 8

The eternal Word is "the Beginning"

10. Why is this, I ask, O Lord my God? I do understand to some degree, but I do not know how to articulate it, except like this: everything which begins to exist and then ceases to exist does so at the due time for its beginning and cessation decreed in that eternal Reason where nothing begins or comes to an end. This eternal Reason is your Word, who is "the Beginning" in that he also speaks to us. The gospel records that he claimed this by word of mouth, making his claim audible to people's outward ears that they might believe him and seek him within themselves and find him in the eternal Truth where he, our sole teacher,[45] instructs apt disciples. There it is that I

---

[44] *things which you create by speaking . . . nor are they eternal*: All created words come into existence and out of existence; all created words have particular durations, conveying limited and particular meaning; and created words mediate truthful claims. Yet only the Word, the Second Person of the Trinity, is eternal without beginning or end, who does not come into being but in whom all other beings are brought to be. Augustine concludes this section by pointing to how God does not create all things simultaneously but out of the "rational seeds" of creation. This was originally a Stoic claim that out of *rationes seminales* (Gk., *logoi spermatikoi*)—life-giving principles—God created all things in potency and allowed various circumstances and epochs to draw out the actual creature that was already held there in seed. Such a theory, common among the Church Fathers, allowed creation to be understood as indeed complete (cf. Genesis 2:1), but also allowed for unforeseen creatures to arise over long stretches of time.

[45] *our sole teacher*: See Matthew 23:8.

hear your voice, O Lord, the voice of one who speaks to me, because anyone who truly teaches us speaks to us directly, whereas one who is no true teacher does not speak to us, though speak he may. After all, can anyone teach us, other than stable Truth? When some changeable creature advises us, we are but led to that stable Truth, where we truly learn as we stand still and listen to him, and are filled with joy on hearing the Bridegroom's voice,[46] and surrender ourselves once more to him from whom we came. He is "the Beginning" for us in the sense that if he were not abidingly the same, we should have nowhere to return to after going astray. When we turn back from our errant ways it is by acknowledging the truth that we turn back, and he it is who teaches us to acknowledge it, because he is "the Beginning" who speaks to us.

Chapter 9

11. In this Beginning you made heaven and earth, O God. You made them in your Word, your Son, your Power, your Wisdom,[47] your Truth, wonderfully speaking and in a wondrous way creating. Who can understand this? Who explain it? What is this light that shines through the chinks of my mind and pierces my heart, doing it no injury? I begin to shudder yet catch fire with longing: I shudder inasmuch as I am unlike him, yet I am afire with longing for him because some likeness there is. Wisdom it is, none other than Wisdom, that shines through my darkness, tearing apart the cloud that envelops me; yet I fall away from it and am plunged into obscurity once more, lost in the murk and rubble that are my punishment, for so wasted away is my strength to the point of destitution[48] that I cannot even support the good that I have, until you, O Lord, who are mercifully disposed toward all my sins, heal all my ailments too.

---

[46] *filled with joy on hearing the Bridegroom's voice*: See John 3:29.

[47] *your Son, your Power, your Wisdom*: See 1 Corinthians 1:24.

[48] *for so wasted away is my strength to the point of destitution*: See Psalm 30:11 (31:10).

And I know you will, for you will rescue my life from decay, crown me in pity and mercy, and overwhelmingly satisfy my desire with good things; and my youth will be renewed like an eagle's.[49] We are already saved, but in hope, and in patience we look forward to the fulfillment of your promises.[50]

Let everyone who has the aptitude listen to your spoken word within; for my part I will begin with confidence from your word in scripture, and cry out, *How magnificent are your works, O Lord! In wisdom you have created all things.*[51] This wisdom is no other than the Beginning, and in that Beginning you have made heaven and earth.

Chapter 10

"What was God doing before that?" Meaningless question

12. People who ask us, "What was God doing before he made heaven and earth?" are obviously full of their stale old nature.[52]

---

[49] *you will rescue my life from decay . . . my youth will be renewed like an eagle's:* See Psalm 102(103):3–5.

[50] *We are already saved, but in hope . . . fulfillment of your promises:* See Romans 8:24–25.

[51] How magnificent are your works, O Lord! In wisdom you have created all things: Psalm 103(104):24.

[52] *People who ask us . . . full of their stale old nature:* The Manichees are probably meant here, since in his *Commentary on Genesis: A Refutation of the Manichees* (I.24), Augustine mentions that they would mock Catholics and taunt them with the question of God's whereabouts and intentions before creation. This is utterly erroneous (Augustine calls the question *nefas*, profane and impious) because it seeks a cause greater than God's will, as if God created because he was after or in need of something. For Augustine, the only answer we can give to why God created is simply because God is good (and wanted to share such goodness) and because God wanted to (not because he had to). In short, the divine nature is free from all jealousy and limitation. Since nothing can be neither greater nor antecedent to God's will, one can never ascribe an external motivation to God's actions but, as only the "friends of God" can understand, anything God does, he does because he is love. The quip we are about to hear regarding God's creating hell for those who continue to ask such questions (see *Conf.* XI.12.14) is surely Augustine's tongue-in-cheek warning to the Manichees who render God's will knowable, inevitable, and not wholly good.

"If he was at leisure," they say, "and not making anything, why did he not continue so thereafter and for ever, just as he had always done nothing prior to that? If some change took place in God, and some new volition emerged to inaugurate created being, a thing he had never done before, then an act of will was arising in him which had not previously been present, and in that case how would he truly be eternal? God's will is not a created thing; it exists prior to the act of creation, because nothing would be created unless the creator first willed it. Now, God's will belongs to the very substance of God. But if some element appears in God's substance that was previously not there, that substance cannot accurately be called eternal. On the other hand, if God's will that creation should occur is eternal, why is creation not eternal as well?" [53]

Chapter 11

13. People who take that line do not yet understand you, O Wisdom of God and Light of our minds. They do not yet understand how things which receive their being through you and in you come into existence; they strive to be wise about eternal realities, but their heart flutters about between the changes of past and future found in created things, and an empty heart it remains. [54] Who is to take hold of it and peg it down, that it may stand still for a little while and capture, if only briefly, the splendor of that eternity which stands for ever, and compare it with the fugitive moments that never stand still, and find it incomparable, and come to see that a long time is not

[53] *if God's will that creation should occur is eternal, why is creation not eternal as well?* Creation is not begotten from God but made "externally" out of nothing, as we examined above. Against pagan principles (most probably with Porphyry in mind), Augustine has to defend the Father's begetting of the Son with the creating of the world *ad extra*. Creation is not eternal, because it is "made", implying posteriority and a decrease in dignity (e.g., we humans are always prior to and greater than anything we make), whereas the Son is eternal and equal to the Father because he is "begotten not made", as Augustine knew the Creed had definitively pronounced (see *Conf.* XII.7.7, p. 370 below, on the three types of causality).

[54] *their heart flutters . . . and an empty heart it remains:* See Psalm 5:10(9).

long except in virtue of a great number of passing moments which cannot all run their course at once? They would see that in eternity nothing passes, for the whole is present, whereas time cannot be present all at once. Can they not see that whatever is past has been pushed out of the way by what was future, and all the future follows on the heels of the past, and the whole of both past and future flows forth from him who is always present, and is by him created?[55] Who shall take hold of the human heart, to make it stand still and see how eternity, which stands firm, has neither future nor past, but ordains future and past times? Has my hand the strength for this, or my mouth the persuasiveness to achieve such a thing?

Chapter 12

14. However, I will set about replying to the questioner who asks, "What was God doing before he made heaven and earth?" But I will not respond with that joke someone is said to have made: "He was getting hell ready for people who inquisitively peer into deep matters"; for this is to evade the force of the question. It is one thing to see the solution, and something different to make fun of the problem. So I will not give that reply. I would rather have answered, "What I do not know, I do not know," than have cracked a joke that exposed a serious questioner to ridicule and won applause for giving an untrue answer. Instead I will state that you, our God, are the creator of every created thing; and, if we take "heaven and earth" to cover all that is created, I boldly make this assertion: Before God made heaven and earth, he was not doing anything; for if he was

---

[55] *Can they not see . . . is by him created?* All creatures flow in and out of the present, which, Augustine is preparing to teach us, is all there is. Eternity is a dynamic and an ever-present "now", whereas the created "now" is simply the fleeting fulfillment of the past and the foreshadowing of the future. For God there is no "then" or "will be", but only now, whereas God's creatures must learn to train their hearts to make sense of what they have just lived through while also preparing for what lies ahead. This is how the heart "stands still", as Augustine puts it: in realizing that the only thing that really exists is, with God, the now.

doing or making something, what else would he be doing but creating? And no creature was made before any creature was made. I wish I could know everything that I desire to know to my own profit with the same certainty with which I know that.

Chapter 13

15. If any giddy-minded person wanders off into fantasy about epochs of time before creation, and finds it amazing that you, God almighty, who are the creator of all things, you who are the architect of heaven and earth and hold everything in your hand, should through measureless ages have been at rest before undertaking this huge task, such a person should wake up and realize that his amazement is misplaced. How could measureless ages have passed by if you had not made them, since you are the author and creator of the ages?[56] Or what epochs of time could have existed, that had not been created by you? And how could they have passed by, if they had never existed? If there was a "time" before you made heaven and earth, how can it be said that you were not at work then, you who are the initiator of all times? For of course you would have made that time too; there could not have been any passing times before you created times. If, therefore, there was no time before heaven and earth came to be, how can anyone ask what you were doing then? There was no such thing as "then" when there was no time.

16. Nor can it be said that you are "earlier in time" than all eras of time, for that would mean that there was some kind of time already in existence before you. You have precedence over the past by the loftiness of your ever-present eternity, and you live beyond all the future, because future times are future, but as soon as they have arrived they will be past, whereas you are ever the same, and your years fail not.[57] Your years do not

---

[56] *you are the author and creator of the ages*: See Hebrews 1:2.

[57] *Nor can it be said that you are "earlier in time" . . . your years fail not*: See Psalm 101:28(102:27); Hebrews 1:12. Augustine would accordingly have us banish all questions that drag God into time: "Where was God *when* . . .?" or, "Does

come and go. Our years pass and new ones arrive only so that all may come in turn, but your years stand all at once, because they are stable: there is no pushing out of vanishing years by those that are coming on, because with you none are transient. In our case, our years will be complete only when there are none left. Your years are a single day,[58] and this day of yours is not a daily recurrence, but a simple "Today," because your Today does not give way to tomorrow, nor follow yesterday. Your Today is eternity, and therefore your Son, to whom you said, *Today have I begotten you,*[59] is coeternal with you. You have made all eras of time and you are before all time, and there was never a "time" when time did not exist.

Chapter 14

Time, a creature of God—what is it?

17. There was therefore never any time when you had not made anything, because you made time itself. And no phases of time are coeternal with you, for you abide, and if they likewise were to abide, they would not be time. For what is time? Who could find any quick or easy answer to that? Who could even grasp it in his thought clearly enough to put the matter into words? Yet is there anything to which we refer in conversation with more familiarity, any matter of more common experience, than time? And we know perfectly well what we mean when we speak of it, and understand just as well when we hear someone else refer to it. What, then, is time? If no one asks me, I know; if I want to explain it to someone who asks me, I do not know.[60] I can state with confidence,

---

God know who *will ...?*" are misleading. Those who seek God know that God *is* present and that God *is* faithful, and that seems to be the spiritual lesson contained on this otherwise intensely philosophical treatise on time.

[58] *Your years are a single day:* See Psalm 89:4(90:3); 2 Peter 3:8.

[59] Today have I begotten you: Psalm 2:7; Acts 13:33; Hebrews 1:5; 5:5.

[60] *I do not know:* We have seen over and over how our author is not afraid to admit his sin as well as his ignorance, and here is one of the most beautifully

however, that this much I do know: if nothing passed away, there would be no past time; if there was nothing still on its way, there would be no future time; and if nothing existed, there would be no present time.

Now, what about those two times, past and future: in what sense do they have real being, if the past no longer exists and the future does not exist yet? As for present time, if that were always present and never slipped away into the past, it would not be time at all; it would be eternity. If, therefore, the present's only claim to be called "time" is that it is slipping away into the past, how can we assert that this thing *is*, when its only title to being is that it will soon cease to be? In other words, we cannot really say that time exists, except because it tends to non-being.[61]

Chapter 15

18. Nonetheless we speak of a long time or a short time, and we do so only of time past or time in the future. For example, we call a hundred years ago a long time in the past, and likewise a hundred years hence a long time in the future; but we call—say—ten days ago a short time past, and ten days hence a short time in the future. But on what grounds can something that does not exist be called long or short? The past no longer exists and the future does not exist yet. We ought not, therefore, to say, "That is a long time," but, when speaking of the past, we should say, "That was long," and of the future, "That will be long."

---

honest lines of all the *Confessions*, one to which we can all relate. We know exactly what time is—until someone asks us to define it. We habitually use abstract concepts as if we knew what they meant, but when pressed, we are usually ill-suited to provide a coherent explanation. There are certainly hints of Plotinus' own admitted intellectual limitations here as well (cf. *Enneads* 3.7.1).

[61] *we cannot really say that time exists, except because it tends to non-being:* This is as close as Augustine comes to venturing to providing a definition of time at this early stage of his thinking. He labels it the "tendency toward non-being" (*tendit non esse*), drawing our attention to how time is the creaturely movement into the present (the past) and out of the present (the future).

O my Lord, my light,[62] will your truth not deride us humans for speaking so? This long time in the past: was it long when it was already past, or earlier than that, when it was still present? If the latter, yes, then it might have been long, because there was something to be long; but if it was already past it no longer existed, and therefore could not have been long, since it was not in existence at all. We ought not, therefore, to say, "That era in the past was a long one," for we shall not find anything that was long, for since that point at which it became past time it has no longer had any being. Rather, we ought to say, "That era of time was long while present," because while it was present it was long. It had not yet passed away and so passed out of existence, and so there was something there which could be long. But when it passed away it ceased to be long at that very point when it ceased to be at all.

19. Now, human mind, let us consider whether present time can be long, as you seem to think it can, since you have been granted the power to be aware of duration and to measure it.[63] Answer my questions, then. Is the present century a long period of time? Before you say yes, reflect whether a hundred years can be present. If the first of them is running its course, that year is present, but ninety-nine others are future and therefore as yet have no being. If the second year is running its course, one year is already past, another is present, and the remainder are still to come. In the same fashion we may represent any one of the intervening years of the century as present, and always the years that preceded it will be past, and those that follow it future. Evidently, then, a hundred years cannot be present.

Well then, consider whether the one current year at least can be present. If we are in the first month of it, the other months are in the future; if we are in the second, the first

---

[62] *O my Lord, my light:* See Micah 7:8; Psalm 26(27):1.

[63] *let us consider whether present time can be long . . . aware of duration and to measure it:* The little bit of Aristotle our author knew may be behind this connecting time with the activity of the soul, as Aristotle's treatise on time (see *Physics* IV.10.217b29–218a30) understands time to be the rational soul's awareness of the succession of ever-changing "nows".

month is already past and the rest do not yet exist. Even the current year, then, is not present in its totality, and if it is not present in its totality, the year is not present; for a year consists of twelve months, and while any one of them is current that one is present, but the others are either past or future.

But we must go further, and notice that the current month is not in fact present, because only one day of it is: if we are on the first day, the rest are future; if on the last, the others are past; if on any day in the middle, we shall be midway between past and future days.

20. Look where this leaves us. We saw earlier that present time was the only one of the three that might properly be called long, and now this present time has been pared down to the span of a bare day. But let us take the discussion further, because not even a single day is present all at once. It is made up of night hours and day hours, twenty-four in all. From the standpoint of the first hour all the rest are still future; the last hour looks to all those already past; and any one we pick in between has some before it, others to follow. Even a single hour runs its course through fleeing minutes: whatever portion of it has flown is now past, and what remains is future. If we can conceive of a moment in time which cannot be further divided into even the tiniest of minute particles, that alone can be rightly termed the present; yet even this flies by from the future into the past with such haste that it seems to last no time at all. Even if it has some duration, that too is divisible into past and future; hence the present is reduced to vanishing-point.

What kind of time, then, can be referred to as "a long time"? Future time, perhaps? Then we must not say, "That is a long time," because there is as yet nothing to be long; we will have to say, "That will be long." But when will it be so? If at the point of speaking that period is still in the future, it will not be long, because nothing yet exists to be long; if, however, at the moment when we speak it has begun to exist by emerging from the nonexistent future, and so has become present, so that there is something in existence to be long, then this present time proclaims itself incapable of being long for the reasons already discussed.

Chapter 16

21. All the same, Lord, we are conscious of intervals of time, and we compare them with each other and pronounce some longer, others shorter. We also calculate by how much this period of time is longer or shorter than that other, and we report that the one is twice or three times as long as the other, or that it is the same length. But when we measure periods of time by our awareness of them, what we measure is passing time. Could anyone measure past periods that no longer exist, or future periods that do not yet exist? Only someone who is bold enough to claim that what has no being can be measured. So then, while time is passing it can be felt and measured, but once past it cannot, because it no longer exists.

Chapter 17

22. I am asking questions, Father, not making assertions: rule me, O my God, and shepherd me.[64] For who would make so bold as to tell me that there are not really three tenses or times—past, present and future—as we learned as children and as we in our turn have taught our children, but that there is only present, since the other two do not exist? Or is the truth perhaps that they do exist, but that when a future thing becomes present it emerges from some hiding-place, and then retreats into another hiding-place when it moves from the present into the past? Where, otherwise, did soothsayers see future events, if they do not yet exist? What has no being cannot be seen. Nor would people who tell stories about the past be telling true tales if they had no vision of those past events in their minds; and if the events in question were non-existent, they could not be seen. The future and the past must exist, then?[65]

---

[64] *rule me, O my God, and shepherd me*: See Psalm 22(23):1; 27(28):9.

[65] *The future and the past must exist, then?* Here is the dilemma: if "past" and "future" actually exist, where do they exist? Human convention (and what all Latin instructors have drilled into their students) divides reality into three tenses—past, present, and future—but Augustine is wrestling with how to understand

Chapter 18

23. Allow me, Lord, to press the question further: O my hope,[66] do not let me lose the thread. If future and past things do exist, I want to know where they are. If this is not yet within my compass, I do know at any rate that, wherever they are, they are not there as future or past, but as present. For if in that place too future things are future, they are not there yet; and if there too past things are past, they are there no longer. Clearly, then, wherever they are and whatever they are, they can only be present. Nonetheless, when a true account is given of past events, what is brought forth from the memory is not the events themselves, which have passed away, but words formed from images of those events which as they happened and went on their way left some kind of traces in the mind through the medium of the senses. This is the case with my childhood, which no longer exists: it belongs to past time which exists no longer, but when I recall it and tell the story I contemplate the image of it which is still in my memory.[67]

Whether something similar occurs in the prediction of future events, in that the seer has a presentiment of images which exist already, I confess, O my God, that I do not know. But this I undoubtedly do know, that we often plan our future actions beforehand, and that the plans in our mind are present to us, though the action we are planning has as yet no being, because it is future. When we set about it, and begin to do what we were planning, then the action will have real being, because then it will be not future but present.

how "past" and "future" exist when he is only really conscious of an ever-fleeting present.

[66] O my hope: See Psalm 70(71):5.

[67] it belongs to past time which exists no longer . . . still in my memory: Here is the way out of Augustine's problem: he begins to realize that the existence of the "past" is nothing other than the present recall of prior experiences, while the "future" exists only as the present anticipation and application of such past experiences. He uses this insight in the next paragraph to explain how he can then look forward to the sun's rising and believe it will happen tomorrow morning because he has kept it present in his memory.

24. However the mysterious presentiment of future events may be explained, only what exists can be seen. But what already exists is not future but present. Therefore when it is claimed that future events are seen, it is not that these things are seen in themselves, because they have as yet no existence, being still future. It may be, however, that their causes, or signs of them, are seen, because these already exist; hence they are not future but present to the people who discern them, and from them future events may take shape in the mind and can be foretold. These ideas in the mind also exist already, and can be inwardly contemplated by people who predict the future.

Let me take an example from a wealth of such occurrences. I watch the dawn, and I give advance notice that the sun is about to rise. What I am looking at is present; what I foretell is future. Not that the sun is future, of course—no, that exists already, but its rising is future; it has not yet happened, yet unless I could imagine the sunrise in my mind, as I do now while I speak of it, I would be unable to forecast it. The dawn, which I am watching in the sky, is not the sunrise, but only precedes it; and similarly the picture I have in my mind is not the sunrise either. But these two realities are present and open to observation, so that the future event can be announced before its time.

We must conclude, then, that future events have no being as yet, and if they have no being yet, they do not exist, and if they do not exist, it is absolutely impossible for anyone to see them. But they can be predicted on the basis of other things which are already present and hence can be seen.

Chapter 19

25. You are the king of your creation; tell me, then: how do you instruct people's minds about the future? You did so teach the prophets. What method can you adopt for teaching what is future, when to you nothing is future at all? Would it be better to say that you teach what is present but has a bearing on the future? Yes, because what does not exist obviously cannot be

taught. This method of yours is far above the reach of my mind; it is too much for me[68] and of myself I cannot see it, but I will see it with your help, when you grant me this gift, O gracious light of my secret eyes.[69]

Chapter 20

26. What is now clear and unmistakable is that neither things past nor things future have any existence, and that it is inaccurate to say, "There are three tenses or times: past, present and future," though it might properly be said, "There are three tenses or times: the present of past things, the present of present things, and the present of future things." These are three realities in the mind, but nowhere else as far as I can see, for the present of past things is memory, the present of present things is attention, and the present of future things is expectation. If we are allowed to put it that way, I do see three tenses or times, and admit that they are three. Very well, then, let the phrase pass: "There are three tenses or times: past, present and future," as common usage improperly has it: let people go on saying this. I do not mind, nor will I put up any opposition or offer correction, provided we understand what we are saying, and do not assert that either the future or the past exists now. There are few things, in fact, which we state accurately; far more we express loosely, but what we mean is understood.

Chapter 21

27. I said just now that we measure periods of time as they pass, so as to declare this interval twice as long as that, or this equal to that, and report anything else about segments of time that our measurements have revealed. It follows, then, that we measure these intervals of time as they are passing by, as I remarked, and if anyone asks me, "How do you know that?" I must be allowed to reply, "I know it because we do in fact

---

[68] *far above the reach of my mind; it is too much for me*: See Psalm 138(139):6.
[69] *light of my secret eyes*: See Ecclesiastes 11:7; Psalm 37:11(38:10).

measure them; but what does not exist we cannot measure, and past and future do not exist." But how can we measure present time, when it has no extension? We can only hope to measure it as it passes by, because once it has passed by there will be no measuring; it will not exist to be measured.

But when it is measured, where does it come from, by what path does it pass, and whither go? Where from, if not from the future? By what path, if not the present? Whither, if not into the past? It comes, then, from what is not yet real, travels through what occupies no space, and is bound for what is no longer real. But what are we trying to measure, if not time that does have some extension? We speak of "half as long," "double the time," "three times as long," "equal in length," and make similar statements about time only in reference to extended time, or duration. Where then is this duration which will give us a chance to measure passing time? In the future, whence it has come to pass us by? But we do not measure what does not yet exist. In the present, perhaps, through which it passes on its way? But where there is no extension we cannot measure. In the past, then, to which it has gone? But we cannot measure what no longer exists.

Chapter 22

28. My mind is on fire to solve this most intricate enigma. O Lord, my God, my good Father, through Christ I beg you not to shut against me the door to these truths, so familiar yet so mysterious. Do not slam the door in the face of my desire, nor forbid me entrance to that place where I may watch these things grow luminous as your mercy sheds its light upon them, Lord. To whom should I put my questions about them? And to whom should I confess my stupidity with greater profit than to you, who do not weary of my intense, burning interest in your scriptures? Give me what I love; for I love indeed, and this love you have given me. Give this to me, Father, for you truly know how to give good gifts to your children;[70] give me this gift, for

---

[70] *you truly know how to give good gifts to your children:* See Matthew 7:11.

I have only just begun to understand, and the labor is too much for me[71] until you open the door.[72] Through Christ I implore you, in the name of that holy of holies, let no noisy person stand in my way. I too have believed, and so I too speak.[73] This is my hope, for this I live: to contemplate the delight of the Lord.[74] See how old you have made my days;[75] they are slipping away and I know not how.[76]

We speak of one time and another time, of this period of time or that; we ask, "How long did that man speak?" or "How long did he take to do it?" We say, "What a long time it is since I saw so-and-so," and "This syllable has twice the length of that short one." We say these things and listen to them, we are understood and we understand. They are perfectly plain and fully familiar, yet at the same time deeply mysterious, and we still need to discover their meaning.

Chapter 23

*Movements of the heavenly bodies are not time itself,
but only markers of it*

29. I was once told by a certain learned man that the movements of the sun, moon and stars themselves constitute time.[77] I did not agree with him. Why, in that case, should not the

[71] *labor is too much for me:* See Psalm 72(73):16, Old Latin.

[72] *until you open the door:* See Matthew 7:7–8; Luke 11:9–10.

[73] *I too have believed, and so I too speak:* See Psalm 115(116):10.

[74] *This is my hope . . . the delight of the Lord:* See Psalm 26(27):4.

[75] *how old you have made my days:* See Psalm 38:6(39:5), Old Latin.

[76] *they are slipping away and I know not how:* Like all creatures, time will corrupt if distant from Christ. Apart from God, things grow old and decrepit, whereas clinging to Christ alone rejuvenates. Through Jesus, we thus enter Eternity, the holy of holies, and thus grow younger, a symbolic contrast Augustine uses often, stating how all those born in original sin are born old (*veteres nascuntur*—for example, see *Letter* 190.5.16; *Sermon* 376A.1), while Christ communicates unending vitality and youth.

[77] *movements of the sun, moon and stars themselves constitute time:* The first main argument of Book XI (15.20–21.27) established that in truth only the present exists, and we now turn to the second central point (23.30–24.31), namely, that

movements of all corporeal things constitute time? Suppose the luminaries of heaven were to halt, but a potter's wheel went on turning, would there not still be time by which we could measure those rotations, and say either that all of them took the same time, or (if the speed of the wheel varied) that some were of longer duration, others shorter? And when we said this, would we too not be speaking within time; and in the words we used, would there not be some long syllables and some short; and why could that be said of them, unless because some of them had taken a longer time to pronounce than others?

Through this small thing, O God, grant our human minds insight into the principles common to small things and great. The stars and the other luminaries in the sky are there to mark our times and days and years. Yes, granted; but as I would not assert that the revolution of that little wooden wheel itself constituted a day, so my learned informant on the other hand had no business to say that its gyrations did not occupy a space of time.

30. I want to know the essence and nature of time, whereby we measure the movement of bodies and say, for instance, that one movement lasts twice as long as another. Now I have a question to ask. Taking the word "day" to apply not only to the period of sunlight on earth—day as opposed to night, that is—but to the sun's whole course from the east and back to the east again, in the sense that we say, "So many days elapsed," meaning to include the nights, and not reckoning the nights as extra time over and above the days; taking it, then, that the movement of the sun in its circular course from the east back to the east completes a day, this is my question: is it the movement itself that constitutes a day? Or the time it takes? Or both? If the movement constitutes a day, then it would still be one day if the sun were to achieve its circuit in an interval of time equivalent to a single hour. If it is the time it takes, there would not be a day if the space between one sunrise and the next were as short as an hour; the sun would have

---

time is in no way dependent upon the movement of the celestial spheres. Time may mark such motion but itself is not that movement.

to go round twenty-four times to make up a day. If both were required—a complete circuit of the sun and the customary duration of this—we could not call it a day if the sun traveled through its whole circuit in the space of an hour, nor could we if the sun stopped and as much time elapsed as it usually takes to run its whole course from morning to morning.

My question now is not, therefore, what is it that we call a day, but what is time itself, the time whereby we would be able to measure the sun's revolution and say that it had been completed in only half the usual time, if the circuit had occupied only that space of time represented by twelve hours? We could compare the two periods in terms of time and say that one was twice the length of the other, and this would still be possible even if the sun sometimes took the single period, and sometimes the double, to circle from the east and back to the east again. Let no one tell me, then, that time is simply the motion of the heavenly bodies. After all, at the prayer of a certain man the sun halted so that he could press home the battle to victory.[78] The sun stood still, but time flowed on its way, and that fight had all the time it needed to be carried through to the finish.

I see, therefore, that time is a kind of strain or tension. But do I really see it? Or only seem to see? You will show me, O Light, O Truth.

Chapter 24

31. Are you commanding me to agree with someone who says that time is the motion of a body? You do not so command me. No corporeal object moves except within time: this is what I hear; this is what you tell me. But that a corporeal object's movement is itself time I do not hear; this you do not say. When a body moves, I measure in terms of time how long it is in motion,

---

[78] *at the prayer of a certain man the sun halted . . . press home the battle to victory*: See Joshua 10:12–13. If time were the movement of the celestial bodies, time would have ceased when the sun stood still for Joshua and his troops (a particularly thorny scriptural passage during the Galileo affair), a position Augustine finds untenable.

from the moment when it begins until its motion ceases. If I did not notice when it began, and it continues to move without my seeing when it stops, I cannot measure the time, except perhaps the interval between the moment when I began to watch and that when I ceased to observe it. If my observation is prolonged, I can only say that the process went on for a long time; I cannot say exactly how long, because when we add a definite indication of a length of time we do so by reference to some agreed standard. "This is as long as that," we say; or "This is twice as long as that other," or something similar. If, on the other hand, we have been able to note the position of some corporeal object when it moves (or when parts of it move, if, for example, it is being turned on a lathe), and we have observed its starting-point and its point of arrival, then we are able to state how much time has elapsed while the movement of the object was effected from the one place to the other, or how long it has taken to revolve on its axis.

Therefore if the motion of an object is one thing, and the standard by which we measure its duration another, is it not obvious which of the two has the stronger claim to be called time? Moreover, if the motion is irregular, so that the object is sometimes moving and sometimes stationary, we measure not only its motion but also its static periods in terms of time, and say, "Its stationary periods were equivalent in length to its phases of motion," or "It was stationary for two or three times as long as it was in motion," or whatever else our calculation has ascertained or estimated roughly—more or less, as we customarily say. Clearly, then, time is not the movement of any corporeal object.

Chapter 25

32. I confess to you, Lord,[79] that even today I am still ignorant of what time is; but I praise you, Lord, for the fact that I know I am making this avowal within time, and for my realization that within time I am talking about time at such length,

---

[79] *I confess to you, Lord*: See Psalm 9:2(1); Matthew 11:25; Luke 10:21.

and that I know this "length" itself is long only because time has been passing all the while. But how can I know that, when I do not know what time is? Or perhaps I simply do not know how to articulate what I know? Woe is me, for I do not even know what I do not know!

Behold me here before you, O my God; see that I do not lie.[80] As I speak, this is the true state of my heart. You, you alone, will light my lamp, O Lord; O my God, you will illumine my darkness.[81]

Chapter 26

Perhaps time is tension of our consciousness[82]

33. Am I not making a truthful confession to you when I praise you for my ability to measure time? But this must mean, O my God, that though I can measure it, I do not know what I am measuring! I measure the movement of a body in terms of time, but surely I am by that same calculation measuring time itself? Would it be possible for me to measure a body's motion, to calculate how long it lasts and how long the object takes to travel from here to there, without also measuring the time within which the motion occurs? With what, then, do I measure time itself? Do we measure a longer time by the standard of a shorter, as we use the cubit to measure the span of a cross-beam? That indeed

---

[80] *Behold me here before you, O my God; see that I do not lie:* See Galatians 1:20.

[81] *you alone, will light my lamp, O Lord; O my God, you will illumine my darkness:* See Psalm 17:29(18:28).

[82] *Perhaps time is tension of our consciousness:* This counts as the third main division of Book XI (26.33–27.36). Here Augustine wants to establish that (and how) time is best understood as the soul's distension, and that what we call "past" and "future" exist only as psychological states but cannot be found apart from such mental activities. He learned from his guide here, Plotinus (see *Enneads* 3.7.11), that time is a *diastesis*—a spreading out—of the soul. Augustine accordingly latinized this Greek term and invented the term *distentio* here to give him the concept he needed to express the soul's movement back to the "past" through memory and forward to the "future" through anticipation.

seems to be how we measure the quantity of a long syllable by that of a short syllable, and decide that the former is twice as long. Similarly we measure the length of poems by the length of their lines, and the length of the lines by the length of the feet, and the length of each foot by the length of its syllables, and the length of a long syllable by that of a short syllable. We do not reckon by the number of pages—that would be to impose a spatial, not a temporal standard—but by the pronunciation as voices recite them and die away. We declare, "That is a lengthy poem, for it consists of so many lines; the lines are long, since each is composed of so many feet; the feet are long, since each extends over so many syllables; and a syllable is long, when it is twice the quantity of a short one."

But the mensuration of time by these methods yields no result that is absolute, since it may happen that the sound of a shorter line, spoken with a drawl, actually lasts longer than that of a longer one hurried over. The same holds for the whole poem, a foot, and a syllable.

I have therefore come to the conclusion that time is nothing other than tension: but tension of what, I do not know, and I would be very surprised if it is not tension of consciousness itself. What am I measuring, I beg you to tell me, my God, when I say in imprecise terms, "This is longer than that," or even, precisely, "This is twice that"? That I am measuring time, I know; but I am not measuring future time, because it does not yet exist, nor present time, which is a point without extension, nor past time, which exists no more. What, then, am I measuring? Time as it passes by, but not once it has passed? That was what I said earlier.

Chapter 27

34. Stick to it, now, my mind, and pay close attention. God is our ally;[83] and he made us, not we ourselves.[84] Mark where truth brightens to the dawn!

[83] *God is our ally:* See Psalm 61:9(62:8).
[84] *he made us, not we ourselves:* See Psalm 99(100):3.

Suppose now that a physical voice begins to sound ... and goes on sounding ... and is still sounding ... and now stops. Now there is silence, and that voice is past and is a voice no longer. Before it sounded forth it was a future thing, so it could not be measured because it did not yet exist; neither can it be now, because it exists no more. Perhaps, then, it could be measured while it was sounding forth, because something did then exist that could be measured? But at that time it was not standing still; it was but a fleeting thing that was speeding on its way. Was it therefore any more measurable while sounding than before or after? Only as something transient was it extended over a period of time whereby it might be measured—only as transient, because the present moment has no duration. If it is argued that the sound could, nevertheless, be measured while it lasted, consider this: another voice begins to sound and is still sounding in a continuous, steady tone. Let us measure it, then, while it is sounding, for once it has fallen silent it will be a thing of the past, and nothing measurable will then exist. By all means let us measure it now, and state how long it lasts.

Ah, but it is still sounding, and there is no way of timing it except from its beginning, when the sound originated, to its end, when it ceases. Obviously we measure any interval of time from some inception to some ending. Hence the sound of a voice which has not yet finished cannot be measured in such a way that anyone can say how long or how short it is, nor can it be declared to be of the same length as something else, or half the length, or twice the length, or anything of the kind. But once finished, it will not exist. So by what criteria will it then be subject to measurement?

All the same we do measure periods of time, not periods which as yet have no being, nor those which have ceased to be, nor those which have no duration, nor those which have no terminus. We measure neither future nor past nor present nor passing time. Yet time we do measure.

35. Take the line, *Deus, creator omnium*.[85] This line consists of eight syllables, short and long alternating. The four short ones—the first, third, fifth and seventh—are thus half the length of the four long ones—the second, fourth, sixth and eighth. Each of these latter lasts twice as long as each of the former; I have only to pronounce the line to report that this is the case, insofar as clear sense-perception can verify it. Relying on this unmistakable evidence of my ear I measure each long syllable by the criterion of a short one, and perceive that it is twice the quantity. But the syllables make themselves heard in succession; and if the first is short and the second long, how am I to hold on to the short one, how am I to apply it to the long one as a measuring-rod in order to discover that the long one has twice the quantity, when the long one does not begin to sound until the short one has ceased? Am I to measure the long one while it is present? Impossible, because I cannot measure something unfinished. But its completion is its passing away, so what now exists for me to measure? Where is the short syllable I was going to use as a standard? What has become of the long one I want to measure? Both have made their sound, and flown away, and passed by, and exist no more; yet I do my calculation and confidently assert that insofar as the testimony of my trained ear can be trusted, the short is half the long, the long twice the short; and obviously I am speaking about a space of time. I can only do this because the syllables have passed away and are completed. Evidently, then, what I am measuring is not the syllables themselves, which no longer exist, but something in my memory, something fixed and permanent there.

36. In you, my mind, I measure time. Do not interrupt me by clamoring that time has objective existence, nor hinder yourself with the hurly-burly of your impressions. In you, I

[85] Deus, creator omnium: Saint Ambrose's hymns continue to accompany him (cf. *Conf.* IV.10.15, pp. 87–88, and *Conf.* IX.12.32, p. 258).

say, do I measure time. What I measure is the impression which passing phenomena leave in you, which abides after they have passed by: that is what I measure as a present reality, not the things that passed by so that the impression could be formed. The impression itself is what I measure when I measure intervals of time. Hence either time is this impression, or what I measure is not time.

What about when we measure silences, and say that this silent pause lasted as long as that sound? Do we not strain our thought to retain the feeling of a sound's duration, as though it were still audible, so as to be able to estimate the intervals of silence in relation to the whole space of time in question? Without any articulate word or even opening our mouths we go over in our minds poems, their lines, a speech, and we assess their developmental patterns and the time they occupied in relation to one another; and our estimate is no different from what it would have been if we had been reciting them aloud.

Suppose a person wishes to utter a fairly long sound, and has determined beforehand in his own mind how long it is to be. He must have first thought through that period of time in silence and committed the impression of it to memory; then he begins to utter the sound, which continues until it reaches the predetermined end. Or rather, it does not "continue," because the sound is evidently both something already heard and something still to be heard, for the part of it already completed is sound that has been, but the part that remains is sound still to be. Thus it is carried through as our present awareness drags what is future into the past. As the future dwindles the past grows, until the future is used up altogether and the whole thing is past.

Chapter 28

37. But how can a future which does not yet exist dwindle or be used up, and how can a past which no longer exists grow? Only because there are three realities in the mind

which conducts this operation. The mind expects, and attends, and remembers, so that what it expects passes by way of what it attends to into what it remembers. No one, surely, would deny that the future is as yet non-existent? Yet an expectation of future events does exist in the mind. And would anyone deny that the past has ceased to be? Yet the memory of past events still lives on in the mind. And who would deny that the present has no duration, since it passes in an instant? Yet our attention does endure, and through our attention what is still to be makes its way into the state where it is no more. It is not, therefore, future time which is long, for it does not exist; a long future is simply an expectation of the future which represents it as long. Nor is the past a long period of time, because it does not exist at all; a long past is simply a memory of the past which represents it as long.

38. Suppose I have to recite a poem I know by heart. Before I begin, my expectation is directed to the whole poem, but once I have begun, whatever I have plucked away from the domain of expectation and tossed behind me to the past becomes the business of my memory, and the vital energy of what I am doing is in tension between the two of them: it strains toward my memory because of the part I have already recited, and to my expectation on account of the part I still have to speak. But my attention is present all the while, for the future is being channeled through it to become the past. As the poem goes on and on, expectation is curtailed and memory prolonged, until expectation is entirely used up, when the whole completed action has passed into memory.

What is true of the poem as a whole is true equally of its individual stanzas and syllables. The same is true of the whole long performance, in which this poem may be a single item. The same thing happens in the entirety of a person's life, of which all his actions are parts; and the same in the entire sweep of human history, the parts of which are individual human lives.

Chapter 29

Our time and God's eternity

39. Because your mercy is better than many a life[86] I confess that my life is no more than anxious distraction; but in my Lord, the Son of Man, your right hand upholds me.[87] He stands as mediator between you, the one God, and us, the many,[88] who are pulled many ways by multifarious distractions.[89] In him your right hand holds me fast, so that I may grasp that for which I have been grasped myself, and may be gathered in from dispersion in my stale days to pursue the One, forgetting the past and stretching undistracted not to future things doomed to pass away, but to my eternal goal. With no distracted mind but with focused attention I press on to the prize of our heavenly calling,[90] to that place where I yearn to hear songs of praise[91] and contemplate your delight,[92] which neither comes, nor slips away.

Now as my years waste away amid groaning[93] you are my solace, Lord, because you are my Father, and you are eternal. But I have leapt down into the flux of time where all is confusion to me. In the most intimate depths of my soul my thoughts are torn to fragments by tempestuous changes until that time when I flow into you, purged and rendered molten by the fire of your love.

[86] *your mercy is better than many a life*: See Psalm 62:4(63:3).

[87] *your right hand upholds me*: See Psalm 17:36(18;35); 62:9(63:8).

[88] *He stands as mediator between you, the one God, and us, the many*: See 1 Timothy 2:5.

[89] *who are pulled many ways by multifarious distractions*: We again see that the mediation of Christ unifies: life in Jesus thus gathers together not only one's life's experiences, but also the otherwise evanescent moments of the "now". As Mediator, Christ lifts and unifies the ever-flowing present moments into the one eternal now.

[90] *press on to the prize of our heavenly calling*: See Philippians 3:12–14.

[91] *yearn to hear songs of praise*: See Psalm 25(26):7.

[92] *contemplate your delight*: See Psalm 26(27):4.

[93] *my years waste away amid groaning*: See Psalm 30:11(31:10).

Chapter 30

40. I will stand still,[94] then, and find firm footing in you, in your Truth who is shaping me to himself, and no longer will I tolerate the questions of people who, sickly under sin's punishment, crave more than they can take in. "What was God doing before he made heaven and earth?" they ask. "Why did it enter his head to make something, when he had never made anything before?" Grant them, Lord, the grace to think clearly what they are saying, and to realize that the word "never" has no meaning where time does not exist. If God is said never to have done something, that simply means that he did not do it at any time.[95] Let such people see, then, that there cannot be any time apart from creation, and stop talking nonsense.[96] Let them even stretch their minds to what lies ahead[97] and understand that you exist before all ages of time, because you are the eternal creator of all times, and that no time is coeternal with you, nor any creature whatsoever, even if any was created outside time.

Chapter 31

41. How deep is that mystery hidden in the secret recesses of your being, O Lord, my God! And how far from it have the consequences of my sins hurled me! Heal my eyes, that I may rejoice with you in your light.

---

[94] *I will stand still*: See Philippians 4:1; 1 Thessalonians 3:8.

[95] *If God is said never to have done something, . . . he did not do it at any time*: As time's Creator, God is neither subject to nor inside time, and, therefore, he can never be said to do anything within temporal conditions. There is no "was" or "will be" for God. Since God is the Eternal Now, those made in his image come to be evermore like him, the more they learn to imitate this divine living in the now. Sin, on the other hand, leads us astray by having us dwell on the past or to make us think that God is encountered only in some distant future. I wonder if this is not the lesson Augustine the pastor wants us to take away from Book XI: we have learned that the now is the only temporal reality, so find God precisely where you are right now and stop thinking the past was, or the future will be, somehow more graced with his holy presence.

[96] *stop talking nonsense*: See Psalm 143(144):8.

[97] *stretch their minds to what lies ahead*: See Philippians 3:13.

It could be said with certainty that if there is anywhere a person whose mind is so richly endowed, whose knowledge and foresight are so vast, that he knows all past and all future things in the same way that I know a song that is very familiar to me, such a mind is wonderful, so amazing as to fill us with awe, since nothing that has happened and nothing still to come throughout the ages is hidden from it, even as nothing in the song I am singing is hidden from me, whatever portions of it have passed away since its opening, and whatever parts remain before its end. But far be it from us to suppose that you, the creator of the universe, creator of souls and bodies, know all things future and past in this fashion! Perish the thought! Far, far more wonderful is your mode of knowing, and far more mysterious. When a person is singing words well known to him, or listening to a familiar song, his senses are strained between anticipating sounds still to come and remembering those sung already; but with you it is quite otherwise. Nothing can happen to you in your unchangeable eternity, you who are truly the eternal creator of all minds. As you knew heaven and earth in the beginning, without the slightest modification in your knowledge, so too you made heaven and earth in the beginning without any distension in your activity.

Let anyone who understands this praise you, and anyone who does not understand it praise you no less. Oh, how high and glorious you are, who make the humble-hearted your home![98] You help the downtrodden to their feet,[99] and they do not fall, for their high dignity is yourself.

[98] *who make the humble-hearted your home*: See Psalm 137(138):6; Daniel 3:87; Isaiah 57:15.

[99] *You help the downtrodden to their feet*: See Psalm 144(145):14; 145(146):8.

Book XII

Heaven and Earth

Chapter 1

1. The words of your holy scripture have knocked at the door of my heart, O Lord, and in this poverty-stricken life of mine my heart is busy about many things concerning them.[1] The penury of human understanding is apt to lead to excessive wordiness, for to seek requires more talking than to find, to ask takes longer than to obtain, and the hand that knocks puts in more effort than the hand that receives. But we cling to your promise: who shall rob it of its force? If God is for us, who is against us?[2] *Ask, and you will obtain; seek, and you will find; knock, and the door will be opened to you. For everyone who asks, obtains, and the seeker will find, and to the one who knocks the door will be opened:*[3] these are your promises; and who need fear to be deceived by the promises of Truth himself?

Chapter 2

"Heaven's heaven" is the spiritual creation

2. My lowly tongue lauds your sublime majesty,[4] for you have made heaven and earth: this heaven which I see, and the earth on which I tread, and this frame of clay I carry—you made them all. But where, Lord, is that *heaven's heaven* of

---

[1] *my heart is busy about many things concerning them:* See Luke 10:40–42.

[2] *If God is for us, who is against us?* See Romans 8:31.

[3] Ask, and you will obtain ... the door will be opened: Matthew 7:7–8; Luke 11:9–10; see John 16:24.

[4] *My lowly tongue lauds your sublime majesty:* See Romans 14:11.

which we hear in the psalm: *Heaven's heaven is for the Lord;*
but he has assigned the earth to humankind?[5] Where is that
heaven we cannot see, in comparison with which all we can
see is but earth? This whole material world has been endowed
with beauty of form even in its furthest parts, the lowest of
which is our earth (though not uniformly throughout, for
the material world is not the same or wholly present
everywhere); yet compared with *heaven's heaven* the heaven
that overarches our earth is itself no better than earth. And
not without good reason are those two vast realities—our
earth and our sky—to be regarded as mere lowly earth beside
that unimaginable heaven which is for the Lord, not for
humankind.[6]

Chapter 3

Formless matter, the abyss

3. This earth was, moreover, neither visible nor organized; it
was an abyss of inconceivable depth over which no light
dawned, because it had no form. This is why you commanded your writer to record that *darkness loured over the abyss,*[7]

---

[5] Heaven's heaven is for the Lord; but he has assigned the earth to humankind: Psalm 113(115):16. As the *Confessions* now turn to examine how time has
been created from the Eternal One, Book XII opens by looking at the "heaven's
heaven" (*caelum caeli*) of Psalm 113. After his treatise on time (Book XI), Augustine next turns us to the first timeless creature, the *caelum caeli* where (some)
angelic creatures have never turned away from God and where the souls of the
just dwell.

[6] *two vast realities . . . not for humankind*: The typical method throughout Book
XII is to approach creation by way of outermost extremes: the heaven's heaven,
which represents the highest creature (pictured as the "ceiling" of creation), and
formable earth (the "basement"), from which all visible reality is molded.

[7] darkness loured over the abyss: Genesis 1:2. Augustine focused often on
the pages of Genesis. He wrote three explicit commentaries on Genesis: the
earliest was (as you might by now expect) *On Genesis Against the Manichees*
(388–389), then the *Unfinished Literal Interpretation of Genesis* (393), and *On
the Literal Interpretation of Genesis* (ca. 400–415). He also takes questions raised
in Genesis at significant length here at Books XI–XIII in the *Confessions* (397–
401), the *City of God* XI–XIII (413–427), as well as in parts of *Questions on the*

for what does that mean, except complete absence of light? If light had existed, where would it have been, if not over-head, lifted on high and shedding its radiance from there over everything? So if there was as yet no light, what else can the presence of darkness signify but the mere absence of light? Over it all, then, there was darkness, simply because over it all there was no light, just as there is silence where there is no sound. What does it mean to say that silence reigns, if not that sound is absent? Have you not yourself taught this soul which confesses to you, Lord, have you not taught me[8] that before you imparted form and distinction to that formless matter there was nothing—no color, no shape, no body, no spirit? Yet not nothing at all, no, not that either, for there was some kind of formlessness with no differentiation.[9]

Chapter 4

4. What could this be called? How could the meaning of that statement be conveyed to slower minds, except by some famil-iar expression? Nowhere in the world can anything be found more akin to total formlessness than "earth" or "the deep." Lying so far below us, they are less distinctive than other, radi-ant, lofty objects and all resplendent things. I am therefore justified, I think, in assuming that when the earth is said to be *invisible and unorganized*, this is a convenient way of making clear to people what formless matter is, the matter which you

---

Heptateuch and Against the Adversaries of the Law and the Prophets (both dated 419–420).

[8] *Lord, have you not taught me:* See Psalm 70(71):17.

[9] *there was some kind of formlessness with no differentiation:* See Wisdom 11:18. The concept of a formless substrate "with no differentiation" out of which all else would come was first devised by Aristotle and his notion of pure potency, traditionally referred to as "prime matter". Prime matter is not a discernable object, not a "that which", but a "that-by-which". In other words, prime matter is not some material thing but a that-by-which all material things come. Augustine needs this primal substrate to account for how things can at all be formed and, therefore, how substantial change is possible.

had created undifferentiated in order to make from it the world in all its form and distinction.

Chapter 5

5. When our thought looks for something to grasp in this, or for something the senses can apprehend, it says to itself, "There is no intelligible reality here, such as life or justice, because 'matter' belongs to bodily things; but there is no reality perceptible to the senses either, because in something *invisible and unorganized* there is nothing that can be seen or perceived." If human speculation runs on these lines, it would be well advised to aim at knowledge by way of unknowing, or be content with an ignorance that is yet a kind of knowledge.

Chapter 6

6. But for my own part, Lord, if I am to confess to you with tongue and pen all that you have taught me about this primal matter ... in earlier days I heard it mentioned but failed to understand what it was, when people who were equally devoid of understanding told me about it, and I pictured it to myself under innumerable forms of all kinds, which is to say that I was not thinking of it as it truly was at all. My mind passed in review disgusting, hideous forms, distortions of the natural order, certainly, but forms nonetheless. I dubbed "formless" not something that really lacked all form, but what had a kind of form from which, if it were to appear, my gaze would turn away as from something weird and grotesque, and liable to upset weak human sensibility very badly. But what I thus imagined was not formless in the sense that it lacked all form, but formless only by comparison with other things of fairer form; and clear thinking was beginning to convince me that I must eliminate the last vestiges of form entirely if I wished to gain a notion of what true formlessness would be.[10] And this I could not do. I

---

[10] *wished to gain a notion of what true formlessness would be:* Augustine did not have the word he is searching for here until much later. To describe this primal,

would have found it easier to deem anything that entirely lacked form non-existent, than to conceive of something midway between form and nothingness, neither formed existence nor nothingness, formless and all but non-existent.

Hence my intellect gave up asking questions of my imagination, filled as this was with pictures of formed corporeal things which it could shuffle and vary at will; and I turned my attention to the bodily things themselves, and more carefully examined their mutability. They cease to be what they formerly were, and begin to be what they were not, and I came to suspect that this transition from one form to another involves passing through formlessness, rather than through absolute non-being; but I was anxious to know, and not merely suspect.

So, as I was saying, if my voice and my pen are to confess to you everything that you have disentangled for me concerning this problem, how many of my readers will have enough stamina to take it in? Still, that is no reason for my heart to withhold honor from you, or to stop singing your praises for all that it understands but cannot record here. The mutability of mutable things itself gives them their potential to receive all those forms into which mutable things can be changed. And what is this mutability? A soul? A body? The form of a soul or of a body? No; I would call it "a nothing-something" or "an-is-that-is-not," if such expressions were allowed. And yet it must have had some kind of being, to be capable of receiving those visible and organized forms.[11]

---

unformed creature, he coined (as he did so often) the Latin term *formabilitas*, or "the-ability-to-be-formed" (*Literal Commentary on Genesis* V.5.16). Very cleverly, then, the absolutely *first* creature for Augustine is not a thing to which one could point, but it is the "possibility of being formed", as before creation this reality did not exist since the uncreated cannot be formed or changed in any way.

[11] *call it "a nothing-something" . . . visible and organized forms*: Again, formability cannot be a no-thing; it must therefore be a "thing-out-of-which" all other things come. What Augustine is straining to explain here is that the lowest, most mutable creature is not some-thing, but neither is it a no-thing; it is the reality accounting for the changeableness of creation or, as he will define it below, nothing other than "the capacity to receive form" (see *Conf.* XII.8.8, p. 371).

Chapter 7

7. And whence would it have any kind of being, if not from you, from whom derive all things[12] which to any degree have being? They are far from you, not by any spatial distance, but in the measure that they are unlike you; for it is you, Lord, you who vary not from one time to another, who are never inconsistent in your action from one time to another, but are Being-Itself, ever unchanging, ever the selfsame. *Holy, Holy, Holy, Lord God almighty* you it is who have created something out of nothing, and created it in that Beginning who is from your very self, in your Wisdom, born of your own substance. Not from your own substance did you make heaven and earth: if you had, they would have been equal to your only-begotten Son and hence to yourself, and it would in no way have been right for them to be equal to you, these things which were not from your substance.[13] Apart from yourself nothing existed from which you might make them, O God, undivided Trinity and threefold Unity, and therefore you made heaven and earth out of nothing—heaven and earth, a great thing and a small thing, because you are omnipotent and your goodness led you to make all good things, a mighty heaven and a tiny earth. You were; but nothing else was, from which you might make heaven and earth, two realities: one near to yourself, the other bordering on nothingness; one, to which you alone would be superior, the other, than which nothing would be lower.[14]

[12] *would it have any kind of being, if not from you, from whom derive all things*: See Romans 11:36; 1 Corinthians 8:6.

[13] *Lord God almighty you it is who have created something out of nothing . . . not from your substance*: There are three ways of bringing something new about: (1) begetting, in which persons bring about those equal in nature to themselves; (2) generating or manufacturing, in which prior existing creatures are artificially put together; and (3) creating, which technically only God can do, as only God can bring something *wholly* novel about. Creatures are therefore not equal to God, because they are posterior and are made from another substance, whereas the Son is equal to the Father because he is eternally begotten.

[14] *Apart from yourself nothing existed . . . nothing would be lower*: This is a good instance of how Augustine conceives of the created cosmos, from top to bottom:

Chapter 8

8. But *heaven's heaven* was for you, Lord.[15] As for the earth, which you have given to us mortals to gaze upon and touch, it was not like the earth we see and touch today. It was *invisible and unorganized*, an abyss over which no light dawned; or, rather, it was a darkness overwhelming the abyss, which means it out-darkened the darkness of the deepest ocean. The abyss we know, the deep ocean of waters now visible, admits even in its most unfathomable depths some semblance of light which is perceptible to the fish and slithering creatures[16] that live down on the ocean floor; but the primal abyss was almost nothingness, for it was still totally without form, although it did exist, since it had the capacity to receive form. For you, Lord, made the world from formless matter, and that formless matter that was almost nothing at all you made from nothing at all, intending to create from it all the great things which fill us humans with wonder.

Truly marvelous is this material heaven which you established as a vault separating water from water when on the second day, after creating light, you said, *Let there be a vault,*[17] and so it came to be. You called the vault "sky," for it was to be the heaven or sky overarching our earth and sea. (These you were to make when on the third day you gave visible form to the formless matter you had made before there were any days.) You had indeed made a heaven before any day existed, but that was *heaven's heaven* far above this sky of ours; we know this because it was *in the beginning* that you *created heaven and earth.*[18] The *earth* here referred to, which you had already made, was the formless matter, invisible,

---

the heaven of heaven, which is wholly near to God, being itself, and formability, which is as close to nonbeing as one could possibly imagine.

[15] heaven's heaven *was for you, Lord*: See Psalm 113(115):16.

[16] *deep ocean of waters now visible . . . fish and slithering creatures*: See Genesis 1:20–22.

[17] *Let there be a vault*: Genesis 1:6.

[18] *in the beginning that you* created heaven and earth: Genesis 1:1.

unorganized and deeper than the deepest darkness; and from this invisible, unorganized earth, from this thing that was almost nothing, you were to make all these things of which our changeable world consists in its inconsistency. Its very mutability, so evident to us, makes possible our awareness and demarcation of passing times, because this is what the rolling seasons are—the changes that occur in creatures as various forms proliferate and develop. But the aforementioned invisible earth is the matter underlying all forms.

Chapter 9

There was no time there

9. This is the reason why the Spirit who instructed your servant, Moses, says nothing about time and is silent on the subject of days when he records that you made heaven and earth in the beginning. It is clear that this *heaven's heaven* which you made in the beginning is some kind of intellectual creation. Participating in your eternity, though in no sense coeternal with you, O Trinity, this intellectual creation largely transcends its mutability through the intense bliss it enjoys in contemplation of you, and by holding fast to you[19] with a constancy from which it has never fallen since its first creation, it is independent of the spinning changes of time.[20]

Not even primal formlessness, however, the invisible and unorganized earth, is mentioned in the counting of the days. Where there is no form, neither is there order, and nothing comes or passes away; and where this does not happen there are certainly no days, nor any variation between successive periods of time.

[19] *holding fast to you*: See Psalm 72(73):28.

[20] *spinning changes of time*: Being in time is not necessarily destructive for Augustine, but the heaven's heaven is so united with Eternity, it has never known the vicissitudes of the temporal order. Creatures on pilgrimage, therefore, will have to be united with God only partially until they reach this unchanging homeland. This, as Augustine makes clear in other works, is the role of the virtues and the Church's sacraments.

Chapter 10

10. O Truth, illumination of my heart,
let not my own darkness speak to me!
I slid away to material things, sank into shadow,
yet even there, even from there, I loved you.
Away I wandered, yet I remembered you.
I heard your voice behind me,[21] calling me back,
yet scarcely heard it for the tumult of the unquiet.
See now, I come back to you,
fevered and panting for your fountain.
Let no one bar my way,
let me drink it and draw life from it.
Let me not be my own life:
evil was the life I lived of myself;
I was death to me; but in you I begin to live again.
Speak to me yourself, converse with me.
I have believed your scriptures,
but those words are full of hidden meaning.

Chapter 11

11. Loud and clear have you spoken to me already in my inward
ear, O Lord, telling me that you are eternal, and to you alone
immortality belongs,[22] because no alteration of form, no motion,
changes you. Nor does your will vary with changing times, for
a will that can be sometimes one thing, sometimes another, is
not immortal. In your sight[23] this is clear to me, but I beg you
that it may grow clearer still, and in that disclosure I will prudently stand firm beneath your wings.

Again, Lord, loud and clear have you spoken to me in my
inward ear, to tell me that you have made all natures and substances which are not what you are and yet have being; that

[21] *I heard your voice behind me*: See Ezekiel 3:12; Isaiah 30:21. Augustine's prayers
are full of images of a dialogue, an internal conversation between God and the
self.

[22] *to you alone immortality belongs*: See 1 Timothy 6:16.

[23] *In your sight*: See Psalm 18:15(19:14).

alone is not from you which has no being. You have told me also that if our will moves away from you, who are, toward anything which less truly is, that movement is transgression and sin, but no one's sin either harms you or disturbs the order of your reign at any point, first or last. In your sight this is clear to me, but I beg you that it may grow clearer still, and in that disclosure I will prudently stand firm beneath your wings.

12. Loud and clear have you spoken to me once more in my inward ear, to tell me that no creature is coeternal with you, not even a created being whose entire pleasure is in you alone. Drinking deeply from you in unswerving fidelity, such a creature shows no trace of mutability at any point, for it is bound fast by the whole strength of its love to you, who are always present to it; and having nothing to expect in the future, nor any memories to relegate to the past, it is neither affected by change nor a prey to distended consciousness. How blessed is such a creature, if any such there be! Its beatitude is to hold fast to your beatitude, its blessedness to have you as its everlasting guest and enlightener. Nothing can I find that I would more readily call *heaven's heaven, which belongs to the Lord* than this your household, which contemplates your entrancing beauty, never tiring, never turning aside to any other joy. This pure mind builds up your family of holy, spiritual beings, united in perfect concord on the foundation of peace; it is the mind of all the citizens of your holy city in that heaven above the heaven we see.[24]

13. If a soul has been on a long journey,[25] how can it know whether it yet thirsts for you, whether yet its tears have become its daily bread as every day it hears the taunt, *Where is your God?*[26] How can it know whether yet it has but one plea to

---

[24] *your holy city in that heaven above the heaven we see:* See Ephesians 2:19; 4:3. Slowly the pieces of the picture are coming together: the heaven's heaven, which Book XII examines, will be revealed as the Church, as that unfallen and collective praise where God and creatures enjoy, finally, perfect harmony.

[25] *If a soul has been on a long journey:* See Luke 15:13. The soul that confesses is a pilgrim soul, not yet one with God fully but not wholly absent from him either.

[26] *Where is your God?* Psalm 41:3, 4, 11(42:2, 3, 10).

make to you, that it may dwell in your house all the days of its life?[27] And what is its life, but yourself?[28] And what are your days but your eternity; what else are they but your years that fail not, because you are ever the same?[29] Your household has never journeyed to any far country, and though it is not coeternal with you, yet by holding fast to you unceasingly and without wavering it suffers none of the vicissitudes of time; from this let any soul capable of grasping it learn how far above all temporal change are you, the eternal. In your sight this is clear to me, but I beg you that it may grow clearer still, and in that disclosure I will prudently stand firm beneath your wings.

14. It is quite evident now that in the alterations to which creatures of the last and lowest degree are subject there is some kind of formlessness. Who, except someone who wanders amid the foolish notions of his own mind and is whirled about by his fantasies, who, I ask, except such a person, will tell me that when all form is diminished and reduced to nothing, and all that remains is the formlessness through which a being passed as it was changed from one form into another, any temporal succession can still be found? Such a thing is entirely impossible, because there is no time where there is no variation or movement, and no variation where no form exists.

Chapter 12

Summary of foregoing remarks on spiritual and material creation

15. In the light of these considerations, O my God, I observe insofar as you enable me and urge me to knock, and open to

---

[27] *it may dwell in your house all the days of its life*: See Psalm 26(27):4.

[28] *what is its life, but yourself?* Life and death are analogous terms for Christians, as life is ultimately union with God, whereas the death to be feared is separation and aversion from God. In turning his confession to the heaven of heaven, Augustine is orienting his readers' eyes to see that life begins even now, by freely joining ourselves to the unmediated presence of the Eternal dwelling in the unfragmented body of his angels and saints.

[29] *your years that fail not, because you are ever the same*: See Psalm 101:28(102:27).

my knocking,[30] that you made two kinds of creatures which are unaffected by the passage of time, although neither is coeternal with you. One was so formed that without any slackening in its contemplation, without any intervening period of change, and without suffering any mutation in itself in spite of its mutability, it finds its total fulfillment in your eternal immutability. The other was created so formless that it lacked all capacity to be changed from one form to another, whether of motion or of rest, and so become subject to time.

But you did not leave it to its formlessness, because these two things I have mentioned, heaven and earth, were what you made before all days, in the beginning. *The earth was invisible and unorganized, and darkness loured over the abyss.*[31] These words suggest formlessness, so that the truth may gradually lay hold on the minds of those who are unable to think of an absolute privation of all form without pushing the idea to nothingness. From this formlessness were to be made another heaven and the visible, organized earth, and the beauty of fully formed water, and whatever else would thereafter constitute our world. In the making of this world a succession of days is mentioned, because the nature of these things is such that temporal succession is needed in their case to bring about ordered modifications of motion or form.

Chapter 13

16. This, then, is the view I take at present, O my God, when I hear your scripture declare, *In the beginning God made heaven and earth; but the earth was invisible and unorganized, and darkness loured over the abyss,* without mentioning that you made them on any particular day in a series. I take this view provisionally for two reasons: first, on account of *heaven's heaven,* that intellectual heaven where it is the prerogative of intelligence to know all at once, not partially, nor in riddles, nor as

---

[30] *urge me to knock, and open to my knocking:* See Matthew 7:7–8; Luke 11:9–10.
[31] The earth was invisible and unorganized, and darkness loured over the abyss: Genesis 1:2.

reflected in a mirror, but totally, in open manifestation, face-to-face;[32] not needing to know one thing, then another, but knowing all at once, as I have said, without any succession of time; and secondly on account of the invisible and unorganized earth, where also there was no succession of time, for succession implies that one thing is followed by another, and where there is no form there cannot be any question of one thing, then another.[33]

My present view, then, is that it was on account of these two realities—the one formed from the very first and the other formless through and through, the one a heaven, but a heaven above our heavens, the other an earth, but an earth invisible and unorganized—on account of these two it was that your scripture states, without mentioning days, *In the beginning God made heaven and earth*; for it immediately adds a line to show what "earth" it means. And by recording that on the second day a vault was established and called "heaven" or "sky,"[34] it indicates of what heaven it had been speaking before it began to count the days.

Chapter 14

Some people disagree with me about the
spiritual and material creation

17. How amazing is the profundity of your words! We are confronted with a superficial meaning that offers easy access to the unlettered; yet how amazing their profundity, O my God, how amazingly deep they are! To look into that depth makes

---

[32] *as reflected in a mirror . . . face-to-face*: See 1 Corinthians 13:12.

[33] *not needing to know one thing . . . then another*: Conceiving of binary opposites again assists Augustine's reading of Genesis: the heaven's heaven and the "invisible and unorganized earth" frame the entire cosmos and are similar in that neither is susceptible to time or alteration—the first creature being above change, the latter being change itself.

[34] *on the second day a vault was established and called "heaven" or "sky,"*: See Genesis 1:7–8.

me shudder, but it is the shudder of awe, the trembling of love. I regard with intense hatred all who attack the scriptures;[35] if only you would slay them with your double-edged sword,[36] that they might be enemies no longer! How dearly would I love them to be slain in that respect, that they might live to you!

There are others, however, who, so far from carping at the Book of Genesis, speak highly of it. "The Spirit of God, who caused those verses to be written by his servant, Moses," these people declare, "did not intend to convey that meaning. No, he did not intend us to understand them in the way you have explained, but differently, according to our interpretation." You must be the judge, you, the God of us all, as I reply to them as follows.[37]

Chapter 15

18. You will surely not claim that everything Truth told me so loudly in my inward ear concerning the eternity of the creator was false? Can it be untrue that his substance varies not one whit throughout time, and that his will is not separate from his substance? From that I infer that he does not first will something, then something else; whatever he wills, he wills once only and all together and eternally, not in repetitive fashion, nor this today and that tomorrow, nor willing later what he did not will previously, nor going back later on what he wanted earlier. A will like that is subject to change, and anything changeable is not eternal; but our God is eternal.[38]

---

[35] *I regard with intense hatred all who attack the scriptures*: See Psalm 138(139):21–22.

[36] *slay them with your double-edged sword*: See Psalm 149·6; Hebrews 4:12.

[37] *There are others . . . as I reply to them as follows*: The legitimacy of reading Scripture allegorically is now being defended. Augustine's guiding hermeneutic in how to approach Scripture is essentially one of charity. He can very easily hold many varying interpretations of a single passage together without contradiction, and he can even allow those with whom he disagrees to maintain a valid interpretation, knowing all along that ultimately God will prove to be the judge of whose reading and application is correct.

[38] *our God is eternal*: See Psalm 47(48):14.

Another thing that he imparts to my inward ear is that our
expectation of future events turns into direct attention to them
when they come to pass, and this attention becomes memory
when they have passed away. Now it is obvious that any awareness which varies like this is mutable, and nothing mutable is
eternal, whereas our God is eternal.[39]

These are the truths I gather, and by combining them I discover that my God, the eternal God, did not bring creation
into being by some new act of will, nor is his knowledge subject to any impermanence.

19. Well, my opponents, what have you to say to that? Are
these statements incorrect? "No," they say. What does that
mean? You surely are not going to accuse me of error when I
claim that every formed nature, and all matter capable of
receiving form, is from him alone who is supremely good, and
supremely exists? "We do not dispute that either," they reply.
What is your objection, then? Would you deny that there is
a sublime order of creation which by pure love clings so closely
to the true God, the truly eternal God, that, even though
not coeternal with him, it never loosens its grip or slips away
from him into any temporal succession or the vicissitudes of
time, but rests in utterly real contemplation of him alone?
You, O God, show yourself to anyone who loves you according to your bidding, and are wholly sufficient to him,[40]
so that such a one turns not aside from you or to himself.
This order of creation is God's house,[41] neither terrestrial nor
some massive celestial building, but a spiritual structure which
shares your eternity, and is unstained for ever. You have established it to last for ever, and your ordinance will not pass

---

[39] *Another thing that he imparts . . . our God is eternal*: This paragraph brings
Books X and XI into conversation with Book XII: future realities can legiti-
mately be anticipated because the memory retains what time sweeps away. This
makes our awareness of contingent events mutable and less than perfect, as compared to the Eternal, who has perfect knowledge of all things because he sees
them precisely as now.

[40] *You, O God, show yourself . . . and are wholly sufficient to him*: See John
14:8–9, 21.

[41] *This order of creation is God's house*: See Psalm 26(27):4.

away.[42] Yet it is not coeternal with you, for it did have a beginning: it was created.

20. Before its creation we find no mention of time, for wisdom is known to be the eldest of all created things.[43] The wisdom here referred to is obviously not the Wisdom who is fully coeternal with you, his Father, who are our God, and equal to you;[44] no, not that Wisdom through whom all things were created,[45] not that Beginning in whom you made heaven and earth. The wisdom of which I speak is a created wisdom, the intellectual order of being which by contemplating the Light becomes light itself. Wisdom it is called, but it is a created wisdom, and as there is a vast difference between Light as source and that which is lit up by another, the difference is just as great between Wisdom that creates and the wisdom that has been created. A comparable gulf exists between the justice that justifies us and the justice created in us by that act of justification, which is why even we are said to be "your justice" in the words of a certain servant of yours: *so that in him we might become the justice of God.*[46] Well then, the first of all creatures was wisdom understood in this way, created wisdom, which is the rational, intelligent mind of your chaste city.[47] That city on high is our mother, and she is free[48] and eternal

---

[42] *You have established it to last for ever, and your ordinance will not pass away:* See Psalm 148:6.

[43] *wisdom is known to be the eldest of all created things:* See Sirach 1:1–5. Following the ancient Hebraic literature, Augustine approaches wisdom here not as the coeternal Son of God (although the Christ is, of course, "the power and wisdom of God" [1 Corinthians 1:24]), but as the first of creation upon which God patterns all his activities in time and in which all rational creatures who grow in wisdom participate.

[44] *his Father, who are our God, and equal to you:* See Philippians 2:6.

[45] *not that Wisdom through whom all things were created:* See Colossians 1:16.

[46] *so that in him we might become the justice of God:* 2 Corinthians 5:21.

[47] *mind of your chaste city:* This city is the spotless and saintly bride, the *ecclesia perfecta,* in heaven who is simultaneously and mysteriously also the *ecclesia permixta,* the body of saint and sinner, on earth. This is a relationship Augustine was forced to work out especially in his struggle with the Donatists, who expected a visibly perfect and pure Church while on earth.

[48] *That city on high is our mother, and she is free:* See Galatians 4:26.

in heaven[49]—and what heaven can that be, if not the *heaven's heaven* which praises you, *heaven's heaven* which belongs to the Lord?[50] We find no mention of time prior to this wisdom, since what was created before all else necessarily precedes time, which is also a creature; but it is preceded by the eternity of the creator himself. From him came its origin: not a temporal beginning, for time did not yet exist, but the dawn of its creation.

21. It therefore derives its being from you, our God, in such a way that it is entirely different from you; it is not Being-Itself. Not only before it came to be, but even in its life, we find no time, because it has the capacity to look upon your face always[51] and never turns its gaze away. Accordingly no change or variation affects it; but all the same it contains within it a potential for change which would cause it to darken and grow cold, did it not cling to you with immense love, shining with your light like noonday never dimmed and burning with your fire.

O lightsome house, so fair of form, I have fallen in love with your beauty, loved you as the place where dwells the glory of my Lord,[52] who fashioned you and claims you as his own. My pilgrim-soul sighs for you, and I pray him who made you to claim me also as his own within you, for he made me too. Like a lost sheep I have gone astray,[53] but on the shoulders of my shepherd, your builder, I hope to be carried back to you.[54]

22. Now, my opponents, you whom I was addressing, those of you at least who believe that Moses was God's trusty servant and that his books are the utterance of the Holy Spirit, what have you to say? Does such a house of God exist, not indeed coeternal with God, yet in its own way eternal in

---

[49] *eternal in heaven*: See 2 Corinthians 5:1.

[50] *what heaven can that be . . . heaven's heaven which belongs to the Lord*: See Psalm 148:4; 113(115):16.

[51] *look upon your face always*: See Matthew 18:10.

[52] *the place where dwells the glory of my Lord*: See Psalm 25(26):8.

[53] *Like a lost sheep I have gone astray*: See Psalm 118(119):176.

[54] *on the shoulders of my shepherd . . . I hope to be carried back to you*: See Luke 15:4–5.

heaven,[55] in which you will look in vain for temporal succession, because nothing of the kind is to be found there? For any creature which finds its good in always holding fast to God[56] transcends all distension of being and all the fleeting passage of time. "Yes, it does exist," they say.

Which point, then, do you allege to be false out of those which my heart cried out to my God as it listened to his praises resounding within it? Do you dispute my statement that there was unformed matter, and that where no form existed there was no order? But where there was no order, neither could there be any succession of periods of time. Yet this thing that was almost nothing derived from him insofar as it was not quite nothing, because whatever is, whatever in any fashion exists, is from him. "We do not dispute this either," they say.

Chapter 16

Augustine's response to those who disagree

23. In your presence, O my God, I want to discuss some matters with those who acknowledge as true what your Truth never ceases to tell me within my own mind. As for the people who will not concede this, they may bark as much as they please until they deafen themselves; I will merely attempt to persuade them to be quiet, and so open a way by which your word may reach them. If they refuse and rebuff me, I beg you, my God, not to answer me with silence.[57] Speak to me yourself within my heart in truth, for you alone speak so.[58] Then I will get rid of those people who blow into the dust only to stir up earth and get it into their eyes; then let me retire to

---

[55] *Does such a house of God exist . . . eternal in heaven*: See 2 Corinthians 5:1.
[56] *holding fast to God*: See Psalm 72(73):28.
[57] *I beg you, my God, not to answer me with silence*: See Psalm 27(28):1.
[58] *Speak to me yourself within my heart in truth, for you alone speak so*: While creatures must speak to us from some external distance, God alone can speak to us from within.

my private room[59] and sing my songs of love to you, giving vent to my inarticulate groans[60] as I walk my pilgrim way, remembering Jerusalem and lifting up my heart toward her.[61] To her would I stretch out, to Jerusalem my homeland, Jerusalem my mother,[62] and to you who are her ruler, her illuminator, Father, guardian and husband, her chaste, intense delight, her unshakable joy: to you who are the fullness of good things beyond all telling, and all good things at once, because you are the one supreme and true Good. Let me not waver from my course before you have gathered all that I am, my whole disintegrated and deformed self, into that dearly loved mother's peace, where are lodged the first-fruits of my spirit, and whence I draw my present certainty, that so you may reshape me to new form, new firmness, for eternity, O my God, my mercy.[63]

To those, however, do I address myself in the following lines, who do not decry all these true statements as errors, but respect your holy scripture, written through the agency of holy Moses, and attribute to it, as we do, the loftiest normative authority, but who contradict us nonetheless on certain points. Do you, our God, stand as arbiter between my confessions and their contradictions.

Chapter 17

24. "Although your assertions are true," they say, "it was not those two realities that Moses had in mind when in response to the revealing Spirit he said, *In the beginning God made heaven and earth.* By the name *heaven* he did not mean to indicate the

---

[59] *let me retire to my private room*: See Matthew 6:6.

[60] *my inarticulate groans*: See Romans 8:26.

[61] *lifting up my heart toward her*: The liturgical phrase of "lifting up my heart" (*sursum corde*) is aimed at bringing the reader into Book XII's vision of creation as a cosmic offertory.

[62] *Jerusalem my mother*: See Galatians 4:26. The New Jerusalem is the Catholic Church, where the otherwise "disintegrated and deformed" self can become whole and beautiful, forms of *integer* and *forma* in Latin, among Augustine's favorite images for what the Church gives her children. Highlighting Jerusalem as a caring Mother only solidifies the ecclesial emphasis found here.

[63] *O my God, my mercy*: See Psalm 58:18(59:17).

spiritual or intellectual creation which unceasingly contemplates the face of God,[64] nor did he indicate formless matter by the name *earth*." [65]

What, then?

"What we say is what the author meant," they reply. "We can explain what he enunciated in those words."

And what is that?

"By *heaven and earth* he intended to signify this whole visible world in brief and comprehensive terms first of all," they say, "so that afterward, by means of a series of days, he could enumerate one by one all those things which it pleased the Holy Spirit to have mentioned separately in this way. The race to whom he was speaking was crude and of carnal disposition; they were the kind of people to whom he judged it impossible to convey an idea of any works of God other than visible ones."

With regard to the invisible and unorganized earth and the dark abyss, from which in the next verse the whole array of visible things familiar to all of us are shown to be created and assigned to their places, these objectors agree that it is not unreasonable to understand this as formless matter.

25. What now of another opinion, which holds that the terms *heaven* and *earth* are used by anticipation to mean this same formless, confused matter? It can be called by these names because from it were created and perfected our visible world, with all its assortment of beings so plainly evident, this world

---

[64] *the face of God*: See Matthew 18:10.

[65] In the beginning . . . *formless matter*: Having admitted that the opening words of Genesis reveal a great "profundity" (see *Conf.* XII.14.17, p. 377), Augustine now turns to four other ways "heaven and earth" have been understood. Whereas his view is that by "heaven" Moses meant to include all spiritual or intellectual realities who are incessantly turned toward God (i.e., blessed angels), and by "earth" Moses meant that initially formless matter from which all things come, the first divergent doctrine is that "this whole visible world" was immediately created as "formless matter" with the Holy Spirit drawing out particular named creatures over the next six days. This is a position, Augustine admits, that is helpful for those of "crude and carnal" disposition, needing the very concrete and sensible words provided by the days of the week provided by Genesis.

which in customary speech is often called "heaven and earth." [66]

Another view again is that both invisible and visible nature are quite appropriately styled *heaven and earth*,[67] and that under these two names is comprised the entire universe which God made in his Wisdom, that is, in the Beginning. According to this opinion the terms *heaven* and *earth* are used by anticipation to indicate the still formless matter which is common to all things, both invisible and visible; this usage is justified because all these creatures were made not from God's own substance but out of nothing; they are not Being-Itself like God and a certain mutability is inherent in all of them, whether they abide, as does the eternal house of God, or suffer change, as do the human soul and body. From this primal matter, still formless but undoubtedly capable of receiving form, heaven and earth were to be made, that is, both invisible and visible creation in their formed state. Under this double name, however, are included both the *invisible and unorganized earth* and the *darkness louring over the abyss*, but with this distinction: the invisible and unorganized earth is understood to be corporeal matter before it received the distinguishing qualities of form, while the darkness louring over the deep stands for spiritual matter before its impetuous flux was restrained and it was illumined by wisdom. So runs the theory: what are we to make of it?

26. Anyone so minded might advance yet another opinion,[68] namely that when we read *In the beginning God made*

[66] *What now of another opinion . . . often called "heaven and earth"*: This second option takes "heaven and earth" together as the confusion of unformed and undifferentiated matter. This group takes "heaven and earth" in the sense most of us use it in a daily sense: the visible world above and the visible earth below.

[67] *Another view . . . appropriately styled* heaven and earth: The third possible doctrine maintains that "heaven and earth" comprise all of creation, not only visible but invisible realities as well. This group's advancement is in its right understanding that God brought all of reality, not out of his own self, but out of nothing.

[68] *Anyone so minded might advance yet another opinion*: This fourth interpretation reads "heaven and earth" as the unformed state of all things (*informem inchoationem rerum*), which, when formed, will then be called "heaven and earth". Some contemporary commentators see in this position the anticipation of some

heaven and earth, the words do not refer to invisible and visible natures already perfect and formed, but to the still unformed seeds of things, the matter capable of being formed and created, because in it were potentially present, though mingled confusedly, and not yet distinguished by qualities and forms, all those things which are now distributed in their various ranks, the spiritual and the corporeal creation which we now call, respectively, heaven and earth.

Chapter 18

The author's intention must be sought, in charity

27. Having listened to all these divergent opinions and weighed them, I do not wish to bandy words, for that serves no purpose except to ruin those who listen.[69] The law is an excellent thing for building us up provided we use it lawfully, because its object is to promote the charity which springs from a pure heart, a good conscience and unfeigned faith,[70] and I know what were the twin precepts on which our Master made the whole law and the prophets depend.[71] If I confess this with burning love, O my God, O secret light of my eyes,[72] what does it matter to me that various interpretations of those words are proffered, as long as they are true?[73] I repeat, what does it

---

evolutionary theories. This fourth position of the continual commencement of originally unformed things is subtly different from what Sister Boulding has translated, the term "seeds" not being in the original Latin. The *rationes seminales* of *Conf.* XI.7.9, note 44 (p. 337) provide a different concept than does the mere substrate of "unformed inchoateness" indicated here.

[69] *ruin those who listen*: See 2 Timothy 2:14.

[70] *The law is an excellent thing . . . a pure heart, a good conscience and unfeigned faith*: See 1 Timothy 1:4–5, 8.

[71] *the twin precepts on which our Master made the whole law and the prophets depend*: See Matthew 22:40.

[72] *O my God, O secret light of my eyes*: See Psalm 37:11(38:10).

[73] *as long as they are true*: As mentioned, Augustine always seeks to let his guiding principle in intellectual matters be charity. Here he admits that in figuring out the richness and depths of Genesis, there can be various possible interpretations, and it does not matter from where they come or who holds them, as

matter to me if what I think the author thought is different from what someone else thinks he thought? All of us, his readers, are doing our utmost to search out and understand the writer's intention, and since we believe him to be truthful, we do not presume to interpret him as making any statement that we either know or suppose to be false. Provided, therefore, that each person tries to ascertain in the holy scriptures the meaning the author intended, what harm is there if a reader holds an opinion which you, the light of all truthful minds, show to be true, even though it is not what was intended by the author, who himself meant something true, but not exactly that?

Chapter 19

28. True it is, Lord, that you made heaven and earth. And it is true that your Wisdom, in whom you made all things,[74] is the Beginning. It is also true that this visible world consists of the great regions we call heaven and earth, and that these names, "heaven" and "earth," can be used as a brief, compendious phrase to connote all the natural things made and created within them. Again, it is true that every changeable thing suggests to us the notion of a certain formlessness, whereby that creature can receive form, or can be changed and transformed into something else. It is true that any being which holds fast to immutable form with such constancy that, though changeable in itself, it does not change, is not subject to variations of time. It is also true that formlessness, which is close to nothingness, cannot experience any passage of time either. It is true that a substance from which something else is made can by a certain convention of speech be given proleptically the name of the thing which is to issue from it: hence the

---

long as they are true. Because Pope Benedict XVI is steeped in the Augustinian ways of looking at things (he wrote his first dissertation on Augustine's ecclesiology and his second on Bonaventure's theology of history), it should not surprise us to hear how often Pope Benedict calls for those in the academy to proceed by way of "intellectual charity".

[74] *your Wisdom, in whom you made all things:* See Psalm 103(104):24.

formless matter from which heaven and earth were made could have been called "heaven and earth." It is true that, out of all formed creatures, nothing is nearer to formlessness than earth and the deep. It is true that you, from whom all things come,[75] made not only what is created and formed, but also matter with the potential to be created and formed. It is true that anything which is formed from what is unformed is formless first, and then formed.

Chapter 20

29. All these valid points of view are available to people who entertain no doubts about their truth because you have granted them the grace to discern these matters with the inner eye, and they believe unwaveringly that your servant Moses spoke in a truthful spirit.[76] On the basis of these agreed truths, then, one person picks out one meaning to explain the words, *In the beginning God made heaven and earth*, and says, "This means that in his Word, coeternal with himself, God made both intelligible and sensible creation, or spiritual and corporeal." Another chooses differently: "*In the beginning God made heaven and earth* means that in his Word, coeternal with himself, God made the whole vast bulk of this corporeal world, together with all the array of natures known to us which it contains." Another adopts a different interpretation again: "*In the beginning God created heaven and earth* means that in his Word, coeternal with himself, he made the formless matter underlying his spiritual and material creation." Another view is taken by

---

[75] *you, from whom all things come*: See Romans 11:36; 1 Corinthians 8:6.

[76] *Moses spoke in a truthful spirit*: Augustine's own doctrine (that by "heaven and earth" we are first to understand all unfallen intellectual and unformed material creation) is once more firmly stated before he again parades the four differing doctrines we just rehearsed at *Conf.* XII.17.24–25. Here, however, his emphasis is on how to understand the term "in the beginning". He argues that his own position fits in well with the first three possible interpretations, namely, that "in the beginning" (*in principio*) refers to the Son, who is the Principle (the *Arche* of John 1:1) in whom the Father creates. Only the fourth reading reduces "the beginning" to a simple chronological phrase, i.e., the "very inception" of God's choosing to create.

the one who says, "*In the beginning God made heaven and earth* means that in his Word, coeternal with himself, God made the formless matter of his corporeal creation; contained within it in a still confused state were the heaven and earth which in this vast world we now perceive as distinct and formed." Yet another takes the view that "*In the beginning God made heaven and earth* simply means that at the very inception of his making and working God made that formless matter which contained heaven and earth in a confused state, and from it they now stand forth plain to see, together with all that is in them."

Chapter 21

30. The situation is the same with regard to our understanding of the words that follow. Confronted by all the true interpretations I have listed, each of us chooses differently to explain the next verse, *The earth was invisible and unorganized, and darkness loured over the abyss.* One says, "It means that God's corporeal creation was still only the formless matter whence corporeal things would come; it was still devoid of order and lacked light." Another makes a different choice: "*The earth was invisible and unorganized, and darkness loured over the abyss* means that this totality which is called heaven and earth was still formless, dark matter, but from it the corporeal heaven and the corporeal earth would emerge, together with all the beings within them which our corporeal senses recognize." Another prefers the explanation: "*The earth was invisible and unorganized, and darkness loured over the abyss* means that this totality, here called heaven and earth, was still unformed, dark matter, but from it were to be made the intelligible heaven (elsewhere called *heaven's heaven*[77]) and the earth, that is, the whole of corporeal nature, including our material sky; thus the entire creation, both invisible and visible, would be made from it." Another selects the interpretation which says, "*The earth was invisible and unorganized, and darkness loured over the abyss*

[77] heaven's heaven See Psalm 113(15) 6.

suggests that scripture did not assign the names 'heaven' and 'earth' to that unformed matter, but the formlessness, it says, was there, and it called this formlessness an invisible, unorganized earth and a dark abyss. From this formless matter it had already told us that God made heaven and earth, that is, his spiritual and corporeal creation." Another holds that "*The earth was invisible and unorganized, and darkness loured over the abyss* means that the formlessness was already a kind of matter, from which, as scripture has told us in the preceding verse, God made heaven and earth, that is, the entire corporeal mass of the world, divided into two great regions, an upper and a lower, together with all the familiar, everyday creatures within them."

Chapter 22

31. It may be that someone will attempt to undermine the last two positions mentioned by arguing as follows: "If you will not allow that this formless matter should seem to be given the name 'heaven' and 'earth,' you will have to admit that there must have been something which God had not made, something from which he was going to make heaven and earth; for scripture does not relate that God made this prime matter, unless we take it to be covered by the phrase 'heaven' and 'earth,' or 'earth' alone, when we are told, *In the beginning God made heaven and earth.* Although when the following verse states that *the earth was invisible and unorganized*, the writer may have chosen so to designate formless matter, we have no right to understand 'earth' in this verse any differently from the earth which God is said to have made in the preceding verse: *he made heaven and earth.*"

When the proponents of the two views we put last on our list (or of one or the other of them) hear this objection, they will reply, "We certainly do not deny that this primal matter was made by God. From God come all things that are exceedingly good,[78] and just as we declare what is created and formed

---

[78] *From God come all things that are exceedingly good*: See Genesis 1:31.

to be better, so too we acknowledge that what has the potential to be created and formed is less good, but good all the same. Now scripture does not record that God made this formless matter, but neither does it record that he made many other things—the cherubim and seraphim,[79] for instance, and the other ranks which the apostle specifically mentions: *thrones, sovereignties, authorities and powers;*[80] and it is self-evident that God made all these. Moreover, if the words, *he made heaven and earth,* are taken to be a complete statement, what are we to say of the waters over which the Spirit of God hovered? For if they are to be understood as included when 'earth' is named, how can the same word, 'earth,' mean formless matter, when the waters we see are so fairly formed? Or, if we do accept that 'earth' means formless matter, why does scripture say that out of this same formlessness a vault was fashioned and called 'sky,' without saying that the waters were made? They are not still formless and invisible, these waters that we watch flowing and formed so fair. Or, if it is alleged that they received their form only when God said, *Let the water below the vault be gathered into one place,*[81] so that this gathering itself would be their endowment with form, what is to be said of the waters above the vault?[82] They could not have been worthy of so honorable a station if they were still unformed,

---

[79] *neither does it record that he made many other things—the cherubim and seraphim:* See Genesis 3:24; Isaiah 37:16; 6:2, along with other invisible realities, Augustine realizes that Genesis never explicitly mentions angels in its roll call of creatures (most Church Fathers relied on Psalm 148 and Daniel 3 for the creation of angels). Yet, in his inestimable way, he later on sees very cleverly how the first moment of creation must include angels, interpreting Genesis 1:3 as the initial moment of angelic refulgence and illumination as they turn to God, and then the darkness that is "separated" and not "created" (Genesis 1:4) is the moment when the fallen angels turn away from the Lord's brilliance (see *City of God* XI.9; *Literal Commentary on Genesis* I.3.7). In reading Genesis 1:3–4 in this way, Augustine can account for (1) the creation of angels, (2) for that initial light that is not dependent upon the sun (not created until Genesis 1:14–15), as well as (3) the presence of a fallen angel lurking in Eden come Genesis 3.

[80] *thrones, sovereignties, authorities and powers:* Colossians 1:16.

[81] *Let the water below the vault be gathered into one place:* Genesis 1:9.

[82] *waters above the vault:* See Genesis 1:7.

yet scripture says nothing of any word spoken to give form to them. We must conclude, then, that if Genesis is silent about God's making something, still a healthy faith and clear intellect are in no doubt that God did make it.[83] No sane teaching will presume to claim that because we hear those waters mentioned in Genesis, but find no mention of their being made, we should on those grounds suppose them coeternal with God. Why then should we not by the same token understand, under Truth's tutelage, that formless matter too—the formless matter which this verse of scripture calls an *invisible and unorganized earth* and a *dark abyss*—was made by God out of nothing and is therefore not coeternal with him? And should we not understand it thus even though the account has omitted to say when formless matter was made?"

Chapter 23

32. I have listened to these arguments and examined them insofar as my weakness permits—the weakness I confess to you, my God, though you know it—and I observe that two kinds of disagreement may arise when something is announced by truthful informants through signs. One is when the dispute is about the facts themselves, the other when it concerns the intention of the person who announces them. It is one thing to seek the truth about the making of the created universe, and another to inquire what Moses, that most excellent servant in your household of faith,[84] wished his reader or hearer to understand from his words.[85] With regard to the former, I will have no truck with any who think they know things which

---

[83] *We must conclude . . . that God did make it*: Augustine acknowledges the complementary roles played by faith and reason in scriptural interpretation.

[84] *Moses that most excellent servant in your household of faith*: See Hebrews 3:5.

[85] *It is one hing . . . to understand from his words*: The biblical exegete for whom Augustine has absolutely no patience either selfishly holds on to what is obviously untrue or maintains that the author of Genesis erred in recording the truth. This simply cannot be true: for Augustine, all Scripture is absolutely true in everything it says, but then precisely *how to understand* that truth is another matter.

are in fact untrue. With regard to the latter, neither will I have anything to do with those who think that Moses could have said what is untrue.[86] But as for those who feed on your truth in the wide pastures of charity,[87] let me be united with them in you, and in you find my delight in company with them. Let us approach the words of your book together, and there seek your will as expressed through the will of your servant, by whose pen you have dispensed your words to us.[88]

Chapter 24

33. A great variety of interpretations, many of them legitimate, confronts our exploring minds as we search among these words to discover your will. Is there any one of us who is so sure of having found it that he can declare with as much confidence that Moses meant this or that in his narrative, as that so-and-so is true, whether Moses meant that or something different? For see, my God: I am your servant;[89] I have dedicated this writing to you as my sacrificial confession, and I pray that by your mercy I may fulfill my vows to you;[90] see now with how much confidence I assert that you made all things, invisible and visible, in your immutable Word. But am I prepared to state so confidently that Moses intended nothing else but

[86] *With regard to the former . . . what is untrue*: The former group seems to be heretical Christians or Jewish scholars who read Genesis differently than the Catholic interpretation Augustine is here working out, while the latter are most likely Gnostics like Marcion or Mani who discount Genesis as full of lies and therefore not worthy of being read and certainly not to be believed.

[87] *feed on your truth in the wide pastures of charity*: See Ephesians 3:18–19.

[88] *Let us approach the words of your book together . . . you have dispensed your words to us*: A popular Protestant caricature is that the Church Fathers withheld Scripture from nonclerics, disallowing the laity from reading the Bible. This simply is not true. Notwithstanding questions of literacy rates in the fourth and fifth centuries, Augustine always speaks of the Scripture's meaning "for us", meaning him and his congregation. He is sure that the united community of the faithful is capable of ascertaining the truth and often exhorts those who could read to take up the Scriptures ("*tolle, lege*", as he himself did while a layman, well before priestly ordination!) and therein to meet the living Lord.

[89] *my God: I am your servant*: See Psalm 115(116):16.

[90] *by your mercy I may fulfill my vows to you*: See Psalm 115(116):18.

this when he wrote, *In the beginning God made heaven and earth*? In your truth I see that this is certain, but I do not see with equal certainty into his mind, so as to be sure that he was thinking this when he wrote the words. It is possible that when he wrote, *In the beginning*, he meant simply "at the very outset of the creative process." Again, he could have wished us to understand "heaven and earth" in this context not as any already formed and perfect nature, whether spiritual or corporeal, but as both kinds in an inchoate and still unformed condition. I see indeed that, whichever of these was being stated, it could have been stated truly; but I do not see which of them was in his mind when he wrote the words. I have no doubt, however, that whether his mental gaze was directed to one of these meanings, or to some other which I have not recorded, a man of such stature will have seen what was true and expressed it fittingly.[91]

Chapter 25

34. Let no one henceforth try to pick a quarrel with me[92] by telling me, "Moses did not mean what you say; he meant what I say." If instead the objector had asked, "How do you know that Moses intended the meaning that you get out of his words?" I would be obliged to meet the challenge calmly, and I would perhaps reply on the lines I have already indicated, or somewhat more fully if he proved stubborn. But when he says, "He did not mean what you say, but what I say," yet does not deny that what each of us says is true, then, O life of the poor, O my God, in whose tender embrace there is no contradiction, then rain down gentleness into my heart, that I may patiently

[91] *I have no doubt . . . what was true and expressed it fittingly*: Throughout this section, Augustine demonstrates a sophisticated understanding of authorial intention related to the inspired Scripture. While his hermeneutic of charity allows him to admit that he may not know what Moses had intended to convey, he is confident that Moses knew the truth and fittingly communicated what God intended. In the end, Augustine's confidence in ascertaining the truth is not located in understanding the mind of Moses, but the mind of God.

[92] *Let no one henceforth try to pick a quarrel with me*: See Galatians 6:17.

put up with such people, who say this to me not because they are godlike and have seen what they assert in the heart of your servant, but because they are proud, and without having grasped Moses' idea they are infatuated with their own, not because it is true but because it is theirs. Were this not the case they would look with equal favor on a valid opinion held by someone else, just as I am favorably disposed to what they say when they talk good sense, not because the exegesis is theirs but because it is true. Indeed, once it is true, it is no longer their property. If they love it because it is true, then it belongs to me as well as to them, because it is a common bounty for all lovers of truth.

But when they contend that Moses did not mean what I say, but what they say, I reject their claim and have no time for it, because even if what they say is correct, so reckless an assertion is a mark of presumption, not of knowledge; it is the fruit of no vision but of conceit.[93]

This is why we must tremble before your judgments, O Lord, for your Truth is not mine, nor his, nor hers, but belongs to all of us whom you call to share it in communion with him, at the same time giving us the terrible warning not to arrogate truth to ourselves as private property, lest we find ourselves deprived of it.[94] For anyone who appropriates what you provide for all to enjoy, and claims as his own what belongs to all, is cast out from this commonwealth, cast out to what is truly his own, which is to say from the truth to a lie; for anyone who lies is speaking from what is his own.[95]

35. Pay heed, O God, most excellent judge, you who are very Truth, pay heed to what I am going to say to this man

---

[93] *But when they contend . . . no vision but of conceit*: So while Augustine can admit he may not know, he won't allow others to act in the same presumptuous manner that he is intent on avoiding.

[94] *lest we find ourselves deprived of it*: See 1 Timothy 6:5.

[95] *For anyone who appropriates . . . for anyone who lies is speaking from what is his own*: See John 8:44. God gives the gift of truth to all people and not for the private possession of any. Augustine here interprets those with private and exclusionary live as people who defy the reality that truth is an ecclesial, communal possession.

who contradicts me; pay heed, for I say it in your presence
and in that of my brethren, who make lawful use of the law
for the promotion of charity;[96] pay heed, and mark what I
shall say to him, if this finds favor with you. The brotherly,
irenic reply I will offer him is this: "If we both see that what
you say is true, and we both see that what I say is true, where
do we see it? I certainly do not see it in you, nor do you in me;
we both see it in the immutable truth itself which towers above
our minds.[97] Since, then, we do not argue about that light of
the Lord our God, why should we argue about the thought in
the mind of our neighbor? We cannot see that, for it is not
available to us in the way that unchangeable truth offers itself
to us to be seen; even if Moses himself appeared to us and
said, 'This is what was in my mind,' we still should not see his
thought; we would only believe him. Let us not *go beyond what
is written, inflated with pride and playing one off against another*.[98] Rather let us love the Lord our God with our whole heart,
our whole soul and our whole mind, and our neighbor as ourselves.[99] Unless we believe that Moses meant whatever he did
mean in his books with an eye to those twin commandments
of charity, we shall make the Lord out to be a liar,[100] by attributing to our fellow-servant a purpose which is at odds with
the Lord's teaching. Since, then, so rich a variety of highly
plausible interpretations can be culled from those words, consider how foolish it is rashly to assert that Moses intended one
particular meaning rather than any of the others. If we engage

[96] *who make lawful use of the law for the promotion of charity*: See 1 Timothy
1:8, 5.

[97] *we both see it in the immutable truth which towers above our minds*: See *Conf.*
X.26.37, p. 296.

[98] go beyond what is written, inflated with pride and playing one off against
another: 1 Corinthians 4:6.

[99] *let us love the Lord our God . . . and our neighbor as ourselves*: See Matthew
22:37–39; Mark 12:30–31; Luke 10:27.

[100] *Unless we believe that Moses . . . we shall make the Lord out to be a liar*: See
1 John 1:10; 5:10. Here is the real reason we believe in the inerrancy of sacred
Scripture: since the Holy Spirit is the true author, to disregard anything in the
Bible as false (as opposed to looking for a deeper intended truth) is to make not
Moses but God out to be a liar.

in hurtful strife as we attempt to expound his words, we offend against the very charity for the sake of which he said all those things."

Chapter 26

"If I had been Moses"

36. All the same, O my God, you who lift up my lowliness, who are rest amid my labor, who hear my confessions and forgive my sins,[101] you command me to love my neighbor as myself, and in view of that precept I cannot believe that Moses, your devotedly faithful servant, received a meaner gift than I would have hoped and desired should be given to me, had I been born at the time he was and put by you in precisely the same place, so that my heart and tongue might dispense those writings which would benefit all nations so long afterward, and would by their eminent authority, acknowledged throughout the world, subjugate all erroneous, proud doctrines. I would have wanted, had I been Moses at that time—well, we all come from the same lump of clay after all,[102] and is any human being anything, except because you are mindful of him?[103]—as I say, if I had been in his place then, and the task of writing the Book of Genesis had been laid upon me, I would have wished that such a gift of eloquence should be given me, and such skill in weaving words, that readers unable to understand how God creates would not reject what I said as too difficult for them, while those who could already understand it, whatever might be the true idea they had arrived at by their own reasoning, should not find that their idea had been overlooked in your servant's few words. Finally I would hope to have written in such a way that if anyone else had in the light of truth seen some other valid meaning, that too should not be excluded,

---

[101] *forgive my sins:* See Matthew 6:15; Mark 11:25.

[102] *we all come from the same lump of clay after all:* See Romans 9:21.

[103] *is any human being anything, except because you are mindful of him?* See Psalm 8:5(4).

but present itself as a possible way of understanding in what I had said.

Chapter 27

How fruitful are these verses of Genesis!

37. A spring wells up in quite a small space, yet by means of its branching streams it is a source of richer fertility, and waters wider tracts of countryside, than can any one of the derivative streams alone, far though this may flow from its parent fount.[104] So too the steward you entrusted[105] with the telling of your story confined his message within a small compass, yet this narrative, destined to supply a theme for many messengers of the word, is a spring whence rivers of limpid truth gush forth. Everyone draws for himself whatever truth he can from it about these questions, each a different point, and then hauls his discovery through the meandering channels of his own discourse, which are somewhat longer.

On reading or hearing the scriptural words some people think of God in the guise of a man, or as some huge being possessed of immense power, who arrived at a sudden new decision to make heaven and earth outside himself, as though located at a distance from him, and made them like two vast solid structures, above and below, within which everything would be contained. And when they hear, God said, "Let there be ..." whatever it is, and this thing came to be, they think his words began and ended, echoing through a space of time and then

---

[104] *A spring wells up in quite a small space ... far though this may flow from its parent fount*: This is an apt metaphor for how Augustine conceives of theology: beginning from a small yet powerful statement in Scripture, the source of all Catholic thinking, the theologian develops that truth and allows it to flow out in new ways and in a new idiom so as not only to water the already fertile Christian mind but also convert those still outside its lifegiving waters. This is why a theologian must strive to remain always a steward: his task is to explicate and unfold the truth already given in Scripture, not artificially add opinions and fads from the outside.

[105] *So too the steward you entrusted*: See Titus 1:7.

fading away, and that as soon as they were finished the object God had ordered to exist sprang into existence. And many similar notions fill their minds, derived from life in the flesh, to which they are accustomed. Such people are still children with their carnal outlook,[106] but while their weakness is cradled in scripture's humble mode of discourse as though in their mother's arms, their faith is being built up for salvation, since they hold it as certain and firmly believe that God made all those natural things which their senses observe all round them in amazing variety. If any one of these people should disdain this mode of expression as not grand enough, and in his feeble pride lean out of the nest where he was reared—alas, he will fall, poor wretch! Have pity on him, Lord God, lest passers-by trample on the unfledged squab; send your angel to put him back in the nest, that he may survive until he is ready to fly.

Chapter 28

38. There are others for whom these words are no longer a nest. For them they are shady thickets in which they espy hidden fruit; they fly to and fro joyfully, chattering as they search it out, and plucking it. When they read or hear these words they perceive that all past and future eons of time are transcended by your steadfast permanence, O eternal God, but that nonetheless there is no creature subject to time which you have not made. Your will is identical with yourself, and you made all things by no change of will whatever, without the emergence of any volition which had not previously been present.[107] You made them all, not from your own substance, in that image of

---

[106] *derived from life in the flesh . . . their carnal outlook*: See 1 Corinthians 3:1–3; 2:14. Like Saint Paul, Augustine often uses "carnal" and "flesh" to represent a mind or an ethic that remains totally earthbound; neither are vilifying matter or that which is truly bodily. All sin is spiritual, the body only an accomplice.

[107] *Your will is identical with yourself . . . without the emergence of any volition which had not previously been present*: See Titus 1:7. God's will to create does not imply change in God's nature, as the divine attributes and operations of God are not "parts" of God but essentially identical with the divine nature. God, for example, does not love or show mercy; God is love and mercy. God's will in

yourself that gives form to all things, but out of nothing, as formless matter quite unlike yourself, which was yet destined to be formed through your image by returning to you, the One, in proportion to the capacity of each, as imparted to it according to its kind.[108] Thus they would become exceedingly good,[109] whether they remain closely grouped about you or, arrayed in ever-widening circles through time and space, they bring about changes or themselves beautifully evolve. All these things do such people perceive, and they rejoice over them in the light of your truth, to the limited degree possible here below.

39. Another interpreter concentrates on the words, *In the beginning God made* . . . , and prefers to think of Wisdom as the Beginning, because Wisdom also speaks to us.[110] Another again concentrates on the same words, but understands "beginning" to mean the first stage in the creation of things, and so takes *In the beginning God made* . . . to mean simply, "He first made. . . ."

Among those who understand *In the beginning* . . . to be a statement that you made heaven and earth in Wisdom, one will hold that when the text says "heaven and earth" it is the formless matter with the potential to be created into heaven and earth that is so designated; another will take the words to mean natures already formed and distinct; another will read there that one nature, the spiritual, was already formed, and called "heaven," but that by the name "earth" we should understand the other, unformed nature of corporeal matter.

As for those who take the names "heaven and earth" to signify the still unformed matter from which heaven and earth were to be formed, even they do not agree. One understands

---

history accordingly only shows who God is from before time and not his reaction to something that just appeared as new or urgent to him.

[108] *You made them all . . . according to its kind:* In imitating the Image of God, the Son (see Colossians 1:15), all creatures are informed with their own nature and all attributes proper to their natures. This produces a rich diversity in that single turn toward God, thereby allowing all creation to speak to us of God and his goodness in creating.

[109] *exceedingly good:* See Genesis 1:31.

[110] *Wisdom as the Beginning, because Wisdom also speaks to us:* See John 8:25.

the formless matter to be that from which both intelligible and sensible creatures would come; another thinks that it means that from which would emerge only this vast corporeal mass perceptible to our senses, enfolding in its huge bosom all these natures so evident and accessible to us.

Nor is there unanimity among those who believe that in this text it is creatures already deployed and assigned to their places that are referred to as "heaven and earth," for one takes it to mean both invisible and visible creation, but another the visible creation only, in which we look up at a luminous sky from a dark earth, and all the beings within them.

Chapter 29

40. Anyone, however, who takes *In the beginning God made . . .* to mean nothing more than "He first made . . ." has no coherent way of understanding "heaven and earth" except as the primal matter from which heaven and earth were to be formed, which is to say the primal matter of the whole universe, of all creation both intelligible and corporeal; for if this person argues that "heaven and earth" means the universe already formed, we have the right to ask him, "If God made that first, what did he make next?" Our disputant will not find anything else subsequent to the whole universe, and so he will be disconcerted by the question, "How can that be 'first,' if nothing else came after it?"

If, though, he means that God made first a formless, and then a formed universe, there is nothing contradictory in his position, provided he is able to distinguish between what precedes in virtue of eternity, what precedes in time, what has precedence in the order of choice, and what has a purely logical priority.

In virtue of eternity: in the way that God precedes all things.
In time: as the flower appears before the fruit.
In the order of choice: the fruit takes precedence over the flower.
By logical priority: the sound precedes the song.

Among these four kinds of priority which I have enumerated the first and the last are very difficult to understand, but the two middle ones are quite easy.

Rare indeed, and exceedingly arduous for us, Lord, is contemplation of your eternal being which, though immutable in itself, makes mutable creatures, and is in this sense prior to them.

Then again, whose mind is so acute as to discern without great labor how the sound must be prior to the song, because song is formed sound? While it is possible for something to exist in an unformed state, what does not exist cannot be formed. In this sense, matter is prior to what is made out of it. This does not mean that matter enjoys any power to make that thing—rather it is made itself—nor that it has any priority in time, for we do not first utter unformed sounds, tunelessly, and then later shape them to the form of a song. Nor do we work on them as we might make a chest out of wood, or some vessel out of silver; these materials are, of course, anterior even in time to the forms of objects made from them. But this is not the case with a song. When someone is singing we hear sound and song both at once; it is not as though formless noise were heard first and then given the form of the song. If some kind of sound is audible in advance, it dies away, and then there will be nothing of it left which you could take up again and compose into a song by employing your musical skill. The song, therefore, happens in its sound, and this sound is the matter of the song. This very sound is what is formed so as to become song. And therefore, as I was saying, the matter, sound, has priority over the form that is sung, but not a priority in the sense of having power to create, for the sound is not the composer of what is to be sung; it is merely made available to the mind of the singer by the bodily organ he uses when he sings. Neither has the sound any temporal priority, for it is uttered simultaneously with the song. Nor has it any precedence in the order of choice, for no one would think sound more excellent than song, since the song is not mere sound, but sound endowed with beautiful form. But the sound does have logical priority, because it is not the song that is given form to make it into sound, but the sound which is formed to turn it into song.

This example may help anyone who can follow the argument to understand that primal matter was made first and called "heaven and earth" because from it heaven and earth were made. We must understand, though, that "first" does not mean earlier in time, because it is the forms of things that give rise to time, whereas matter was formless; but once time exists, we can observe within time both matter and form. Yet nothing can be told with regard to formless matter without our seeming to attribute to it a temporal priority, although in terms of value it is of the lowest rank, things endowed with form being unquestionably better than what is unformed; and certainly it is preceded by the eternity of its creator. And rightly, so that the matter from which something was to be made should itself be made from nothing.

Chapter 30

Conclusion: the one Truth, many human approaches

41. Amid this profusion of true opinions let Truth itself engender concord; may our God have mercy upon us[111] and grant us to make lawful use of the law for the purpose envisaged by his commandment, pure charity.[112] In that perspective, if anyone asks me which of them is what Moses, your servant, intended, these writings are no true confession of mine unless I confess to you, "I do not know." Yet I do know that these opinions are valid (I do not speak here of the carnal-minded, of whom I have said as much as I thought necessary; the words of your book, teaching lofty truths in humble guise and many things in small compass, do not frighten them, those promising children). But let all of us who, as I acknowledge, discern rightly and speak truly on these texts, love one another and

---

[111] *may our God have mercy upon us*: See Psalm 66:2 (67:1).
[112] *grant us to make lawful use of the law . . . pure charity*: See 1 Timothy 1:8, 5.

likewise love you,[113] our God, the fount of truth, if truth is really what we thirst for, and not illusions. Let us also honor this same servant of yours whom you filled with your Spirit and entrusted with the promulgation of your scripture, by believing that when he wrote these things he had in mind what you revealed to him to be the best of all meanings in the light of truth, and with respect to the profit it would yield.

Chapter 31

42. Accordingly when anyone claims, "He meant what I say," and another retorts, "No, rather what I find there," I think that I will be answering in a more religious spirit if I say, "Why not both, if both are true? And if there is a third possibility, and a fourth, and if someone else sees an entirely different meaning in these words, why should we not think that he was aware of all of them, since it was through him that the one God carefully tempered his sacred writings to meet the minds of many people, who would see different things in them, and all true?"

Of this I am certain, and I am not afraid to declare it from my heart, that if I had to write something to which the highest authority would be attributed, I would rather write it in such a way that my words would reinforce for each reader whatever truth he was able to grasp about these matters, than express a single idea so unambiguously as to exclude others, provided these did not offend me by their falsehood. It would therefore be overhasty to conclude that Moses did not enjoy the same favor from you, O my God, and I am unwilling to think so. I am convinced that when he wrote those words what he meant and what he thought was all the truth we have been able to discover there, and whatever truth we have not been able to find, or have not found yet, but which is nonetheless there to be found.[114]

---

113 *let all of us . . . love one another and likewise love you:* See Deuteronomy 6:5; Matthew 22:37–39; Mark 12:30–31; Luke 10:27; 1 John 4:7.

114 *Of this I am certain . . . nonetheless there to be found:* The Church is progressively becoming aware of the fullness of God's truth. Here Augustine makes

Chapter 32

43. Finally, Lord, what if human vision is incomplete? Does that mean that anything you intended to reveal by these words to later generations of readers—you who are God, not flesh and blood[115]—was hidden from your good Spirit, who will, I pray, lead me into the right land?[116] Is this not the case even if the man through whom you spoke to us had perhaps only one of the true meanings in mind? If he did, by all means let that one which he intended be taken as paramount.[117] But as for us, Lord, we beg you to point out to us either that sense which he intended or any other true meaning which you choose, so that whether you take occasion of these words to make plain to us the same thing that you showed him, or something different, you still may feed us and no error dupe us.[118]

Mark how much we have written about so few words, O Lord my God, how remarkably much! If we continue in this style, where shall we find sufficient energy or time to cover all your books? Grant me, then, to make my confession to you more briefly as I comment on them, and to select one meaning only, one that is inspired by you as true, certain and good, even if many suggest themselves in those places where indeed

---

the striking claim that Moses' apprehension of the truth, a gift from God, was fuller still than the Church has yet been able to ascertain. This, again, is the task of the theologian: to continue to mine all the truth still buried in the gemstones of Scripture.

[115] *you who are God, not flesh and blood*: See Matthew 16:17; 1 Corinthians 15:20.

[116] *lead me into the right land*: See Psalm 142(143):10.

[117] *Is this not the case . . . be taken as paramount*: Augustine implicitly qualifies his claim (see *Conf.* XII.30.42, p. 404) regarding Moses' ability to know the fullness of God's truth. Here he allows that even if Moses is unaware of the full diversity of true interpretations, the intention Moses had in mind should be given preeminent place.

[118] *But as for us, Lord, we beg you . . . you still may feed us and no error dupe us*: Our author's exegetical pragmatism is obvious: Augustine pleads to God that, in the event that Moses' intention eludes him, God would reveal another true interpretation by which the Church can be nourished.

many may. For this is the assurance on which I make my confession: that if I manage to expound the sense intended by the writer who served you, that will be correct and the best course I could take, and that I must endeavor to do; but if I do not succeed in that, I may at least say what your Truth wills to reveal to me through the words of Moses, since it was your Truth who communicated to him also whatever he willed.[119]

[119] *that will be correct and the best course . . . whatever he willed*: Augustine concludes by stressing how the "correct" and "best" interpretation is one that apprehends the intention of the divinely inspired human author. However, in the instance that he is unable to discern this meaning, he requests that God will reveal to him a true interpretation from the same Truth that inspired Moses.

Book XIII

The Days of Creation, Prophecy of the Church*

Chapter 1

1. Upon you I call, O God, my mercy,[1] who made me and did not forget me when I forgot you. Into my soul I call you, for you prepare it to be your dwelling by the desire you inspire in it. Do not forsake me now when I call upon you, who before ever I called on you forestalled me[2] by your persistent, urgent entreaties, multiplying and varying your appeals that I might hear you from afar, and turn back, and begin to call upon you who were calling me. You have blotted out all the evils in me that deserved your punishment, Lord, not requiting me for the work of my hands, by which I defected from you to my own unmaking, and you have anticipated all my good actions, rewarding the work of your own hands that made me;[3] for before ever I was, you were; I did not even exist to receive your gift of being; yet lo! now I do exist, thanks to your goodness. Over all that I am, both what you have made me and that from which you made me, your goodness has absolute precedence. You had no need of me. Am I so valuable as to be a help to you, my Lord and my God? Did you will me to serve

---

* The Days of Creation, Prophecy of the Church: Reminiscent of T.S. Eliot's line that "in my beginning is my end" (Four Quartets), the Confessions now clarify that the end reveals what was already in the beginning: a unified story striving for wholeness and proper praise. Now, however, we see how Augustine's was never the tale of an isolated individual or of a single author, but the story of Christ's Church. Christian redemption is the story of a collected people once present in Adam who turned away from God, and in God's descent in Christ all were regathered and brought lovingly back into unity with God and each other. This ongoing process is the Church, the subject of Book XIII.

[1] O God, my mercy: See Psalm 58:18(59:17).

[2] you forestalled me: See Psalm 58:11(59:10).

[3] the work of your own hands that made me: See Psalm 17:21(18:20); 118(119):73.

you so that you might be spared fatigue in your work, or because
your power might be diminished if my homage were wanting
to it? Nor did you will me to pay cult to you as I would cul-
tivate the earth, as though you feared to stay uncultivated for
want of cult from me! No, you command me to serve you and
worship you that it may be well with me of your bounty, who
have granted me first to exist, that I may enjoy well-being.[4]

Chapter 2

Why did God create?

2. Solely by your abundant goodness has your creation come
to be and stood firm, for you did not want so good a thing to
be missing.[5] It could be of no profit to you, nor equal to yourself as though proceeding from your own substance,[6] yet there
was the possibility of its existing as your creation. What advance
claim did heaven and earth have upon you, when you made
them in the Beginning? Let your spiritual and corporeal creation speak up and tell us what rights they had. In your Wisdom you made them,[7] so that on your Wisdom might depend
even those inchoate, formless beings, whether of the spiritual

[4] *who have granted me first to exist, that I may enjoy well-being*: Augustine's anthropology coheres with his cosmology. Humanity receives not only the gift of existence from God, but of goodness as well. We see how the Lord is always working
on both levels of nature and supernature, longing not only to give us human life
but a share in his own divine life as well. As Augustine will preach just a few
years after writing Book XIII here, echoing the *Confessions* opening: "To what
hope the Lord has called us, what we now carry about with us, what we endure,
what we look forward to, is well known.... We carry mortality about with us,
we endure infirmity, we look forward to divinity. For God wishes not only to
vivify, but also to deify us. When would human infirmity ever have dared to
hope for this, unless divine truth had promised it?" (*Sermon* 23B1).

[5] *you did not want so good a thing to be missing*: As we have already seen (see
Conf. XI.10.12, note 53, p. 340) and as we shall see again (see *Conf.* XIII.4.5,
pp. 411–12), God created because he was free from all restraint and simply wanted
to share the relationality and love realized perfectly in the Trinity.

[6] *equal to yourself as though proceeding from your own substance*: See Philippians
2:6.

[7] *In your Wisdom you made them*: See Psalm 103(104):2.

or the corporeal order, beings plunging into excess or straying into far-off regions of unlikeness to yourself.[8] Even in its unformed state the spiritual was of higher dignity than any formed corporeal thing, and a corporeal being, even unformed, had more dignity than if it had had no existence at all. Thus these formless things would have depended on your Word even had they not by that same Word been summoned back to your unity and received form, and become, every one of them, exceedingly good[9] because they are from you, the one supreme Good. What prior entitlement had they to exist even as formless things, when they could not exist at all except by your creation?[10]

3. As for corporeal matter, did that have some pre-emptive claim upon you to exist at least in an invisible and unorganized state? No: how could it, when it could not even be, except because you made it? Since it did not exist, it could have acquired no right to existence that could be urged in your presence. And what of the inchoate spiritual creation: did it earn the right at least to exist as dark and wavering like the deep ocean, but utterly unlike yourself? Only through the same Word that gave it being could it be converted to him who made it and become light at his illumination, not indeed as his equal but by being shaped and conformed to him who, being in the form of God, is equal to you.[11] For just as, in the case of a

---

[8] *plunging into exces or straying into far off regions f unlikeness to yourself*: See Luke 15:13

[9] *received form, and become, every one of them, exceedingly good*: See Genesis 1:31.

[10] *What prior entitl ment . . . could not exi t at all except by your creation?* All creation is dependent on God for its be ng and thus receives God's gifts for no other reason than divine generosity. No hing created, therefore, has a claim on God, in terms f either its exis ence o any other property not deemed by God.

[11] *Only through the same Word . . . being in the form of God, is equal to you*: See Romans 8:29; Philippians 2:6. We have seen this Augustinian insight earlier (see *Conf.* X 6 9, note 41, p. 271): creation exists because it imitates the Son's reception of the Father. In "turning" in and with the Son to the Father, each creature receives both existence as well as its proper essence, and in this way all things cry out the Word's divine beauty and goodness in whom they are

corporeal creature, to be is not the same thing as to be beautiful (otherwise it would be impossible for it to be ugly), so too for a created spirit to live is not the same thing as to live in accord with wisdom, for otherwise it would be infallibly wise. But such a creature's good is to hold fast to you always,[12] lest by turning away it lose the light it acquired by its conversion, and slip back into the old life, dark and abysmal. We ourselves, who in respect of our souls are also your spiritual creatures, were once turned away from you who are our Light; in that earlier life we were darkness,[13] and even now we labor in our residual gloom, until in your only Son we become your righteousness;[14] for that righteousness is like God's high and holy mountains, while your judgments, which were all the being we then had, are like the deep.[15]

Chapter 3

Not for any deserving on the creature's side

4. Among your first acts of creation you said, "Let there be light," and light was made.[16] It seems to me reasonable to refer this to your spiritual creation, which was already alive in some

---

made. While this "conversion and formation" is not conscious, it is existentially necessary for all creatures: "In each existent's unique conversion and formation it imitates God the Word, the Son of God who is always cohering to the Father with the fullness of similitude and the equality of essence, by which he and the Father are one. However, if an existent does not imitate this form of the Word, if it turns away from the creator, it remains unformed and imperfect.... A creature, each in its own manner, is thus formed by adhering to the creator, imitating the form always and unchangeably adhering to the Father, the one by whom that creature immediately is what he is" (*Literal Commentary on Genesis* I.4).

[12] *such a creature's good is to hold fast to you always:* See Psalm 72(73):28.

[13] *you who are our Light; in that earlier life we were darkness:* See Ephesians 5:8.

[14] *in your only Son we become your righteousness:* See 2 Corinthians 5:21.

[15] *that righteousness is like God's high and holy mountains ... like the deep:* See Psalm 35:7(36:6).

[16] *Among your first acts of creation you said, "Let there be light," and light was made:* Genesis 1:3.

fashion and capable of receiving your illumination. But just as it had in no way deserved well of you or earned the right to be alive like that, neither had it any claim on you to be illumined. Its unformed state would not have been pleasing to you, had it not also become light; but this could not happen merely in virtue of its existence, for it needed to contemplate the Light which would shed radiance upon it, and hold fast to that.[17] It would thus be indebted to your free grace both for its initial life and for its life in the beatitude which it won by changing for the better in being converted to you, who can change neither for better nor for worse. You alone are, because you alone exist in utter simplicity, for with you to live is the same thing as to live in blessedness, since you yourself are beatitude.

Chapter 4

5. What, then, would have been lacking to that Good which is your very self, even if these things had never come to be at all, or had remained in their unformed state? It was no need on your part that drove you to make them. Out of your sheer goodness you controlled them and converted them to their form; it was not as though your own happiness stood in need of completion by them. Their imperfection is displeasing to you who are perfect in the sense that you will them to be perfected and so become pleasing to you, not in the sense that you are yourself imperfect and look to reach your own perfection by helping them to theirs. Your good Spirit[18] hung poised above the waters,[19] but the waters did not support him,

---

[17] *your spiritual creation . . . hold fast to that*: Not all of creation is meant here: whereas all creation must unconsciously "turn" to the Father in the Son, the conversion of rational creatures must be free and conscious (what Plotinus would have known as the movement from the *epistrophe* of all creation to the *metanoia* of rational souls only); by cleaving to God in contemplation, higher, spiritual creation (angels and human persons) receives not only God's gifts of sheer existence and goodness, but also may share in God's divine beatitude.

[18] *Your good Spirit*: See Psalm 142(143):10.

[19] *hung poised above the waters*: See Genesis 1:2.

as though he needed them to rest upon. When your Spirit is said to rest upon people,[20] it means that he causes them to rest in himself. Rather did your unassailable, immutable will, sufficient in itself unto itself, brood over the life you had made, over the creature for which life is not the same as beatitude, for it is alive even in its own dark turbulence; but it has the prospect of being converted to him who made it, that so it may live more and more fully on the fount of life, and in his light see light,[21] and so be perfected, illumined, and beatified.

Chapter 5

God's Spirit. Third Person of the Trinity

6. Ah, now I have found what I was looking for! In symbolic form a Trinity now dawns clear for me, the Trinity which is yourself, my God. You, Father. made heaven and earth in that Beginning who originates our wisdom, that is to say in the Wisdom who is your Son, coequal and coeternal with yourself. And already we have spoken at length of heaven's heaven,[22] and of the invisible and unorganized earth, and spoken too of the abyss, dark with the unstable flux of spiritual formlessness and destined so to remain until it should be converted to him from whom it drew such life as it had. But once illuminated by him it was transformed into a life so beautiful that it became the heaven overarching that other heavenly vault to be established later between upper and lower waters.[23] I understood already that the name "God" signified the Father who made these things, and the name "Beginning" the Son in whom he made them; and believing as I did that my God is a Trinity, I sought for a Trinity among his

[20] *When your Spirit is said to rest upon people*: See Numbers 11:25; Isaiah 11:2; 1 Peter 4:14.

[21] *on the fount of life, and in his light see light*: See Psalm 35:10(36.9).

[22] *heaven's heaven*: See Psalm 113(115):16.

[23] *that other heavenly vault to be established later between upper and lower waters*: See Genesis 1:6.

holy utterances.[24] And there was your Spirit poised above the waters! Here, then, is the Trinity who is my God: Father, Son and Holy Spirit, creator of the whole created universe.[25]

Chapter 6

7. But then why was it . . . O truth-speaking Light, I bring my heart to you lest it beguile me with empty thoughts: dispel its darkness and tell me, I beg you, through Charity, our mother, I beg you, tell me, why was it that only after naming heaven, and the invisible and unorganized earth, and the darkness over the deep, did your scripture mention your Spirit, last of all? Was it because he had to be introduced in such a way that he could be described as poised overhead? This could not be said of him unless something else was mentioned first, over which your Spirit could hover. He could not be poised above Father or Son, nor could he be rightly said to hang poised at all, if there was nothing over which he could hover. Some object

[24] *my God is a Trinity, I sought for a Trinity among his holy utterances*: Augustine is unique in arguing that whereas most early Patristic theology on the nature of the Trinity concentrated chiefly on the equality of the Father and the Son (thus deemed *homoousios*, consubstantial, against Arius at the Council of Nicaea in 325), the discussion in these early centuries still involved the Holy Spirit even though he was not explicitly mentioned. How so? Augustine argues that "the Holy Spirit is a kind of inexpressible communion or fellowship of Father and Son, and perhaps he is given this name just because the same name can be applied to the Father and the Son. He is properly called what they are in common, seeing that both Father and Son are both *holy* and both Father and Son are *spirit*. So to signify the communion of them both by a name which applies to them both, the gift of both is called the Holy Spirit" (*On the Trinity* V.11.12). In one sentence, then, Augustine seeks to exonerate earlier theologians from not being more deliberate about the Spirit as consubstantially divine as well as present in the consistent tradition of the Church that both Son and Spirit are *homoousios* with the Father.

[25] *there was your Spirit . . . creator of the whole created universe*: Having discussed the Son as the "beginning" of Genesis 1:1, Augustine must still treat the Holy Spirit's role in creation. As the Father imparts existence and as the Son communicates form and beauty, the Spirit's role is to order all things in the cosmos into a harmonious and structured whole. Look therefore in his discussion of the Spirit for images of unity, ordering, and governing.

therefore had to be mentioned first, and only then could he be referred to, since it was not fitting for him to be presented in any way other than as hovering like this. But why could he not be introduced otherwise?

Chapter 7

8. Anyone with enough mental agility should here follow your apostle, who tells us that *the love of God has been poured out into our hearts through the Holy Spirit who has been given us.*[26] But then, minded to instruct us on spiritual matters,[27] the apostle points out a way of loftiest excellence, the way of charity;[28] and he kneels before you[29] on our behalf, entreating you to grant us some understanding of the charity of Christ, which is exalted above all knowledge.[30] This is why the Spirit, who is supereminent Love, was said to be poised above the waters at the beginning.

To whom should I speak, and how express myself, about the passion that drags us headlong into the deep, and the charity that uplifts us through your Spirit, who hovered over the waters? To whom should I say this, and in what terms? These are not literally places, into which we plunge and from which we emerge: what could seem more place-like than they, yet what is in reality more different? They are movements of the heart, they are two loves. One is the uncleanness of our own spirit, which like a flood-tide sweeps us down, in love with restless cares; the other is the holiness of your Spirit, which bears us upward in a love for peace beyond all care, that our hearts may be lifted up to you,[31] to where your Spirit is poised above the waters, so that once our soul has crossed

[26] *the love of God has been poured out ... through the Holy Spirit who has been given us:* Romans 5:5.

[27] *minded to instruct us on spiritual matters:* See 1 Corinthians 12:1.

[28] *the apostle points out a way of loftiest excellence, the way of charity:* See 1 Corinthians 12:31.

[29] *he kneels before you:* See Ephesians 3:14.

[30] *the charity of Christ, which is exalted above all knowledge:* See Ephesians 3:19.

[31] *that our hearts may be lifted up to you:* See Colossians 3:1–2.

over those waters on which there is no reliance we may reach all-surpassing rest.[32]

Chapter 8

9. An angel was swept away; the human soul was swept away; and they had shown that all spiritual creatures would have been engulfed in darkness, had you not said at that first moment, *Let there be light*,[33] and brought light into being; and had not every obedient intelligence in your heavenly city clung fast to you and found its rest in your Spirit, who unchangingly broods over everything subject to change. Otherwise the very heaven above our heaven would have been a dark abyss in itself, whereas now it is light in the Lord.[34] When spirits slide away from you they are stripped of their vesture of light and exposed in their native darkness, and then their unhappy restlessness amply proves to us how noble is each rational creature you have made, for nothing less than yourself can suffice to give it any measure of blessed rest, nor indeed can it be its own satisfaction. For it is you, Lord, who will light up our darkness.[35] From you derives our garment of light, and in you our darkness will be bright as noon.[36]

Give me yourself, O my God, give yourself back to me. Lo, I love you, but if my love is too mean, let me love more passionately. I cannot gauge my love, nor know how far it fails, how much more love I need for my life to set its course straight into your arms, never swerving until hidden in the covert of your face.[37] This alone I know, that without you all to me is misery, woe outside myself and woe within, and all wealth but penury, if it is not my God.

---

[32] *those waters on which there is no reliance we may reach all-surpassing rest*: See Psalm 123(124):5.

[33] *Let there be light*: Genesis 1:3.

[34] *it is light in the Lord*: See Ephesians 5:8.

[35] *For it is you, Lord, who will light up our darkness*: See Psalm 17:29(18:28).

[36] *From you derives our garment of light, and in you our darkness will be bright as noon*: See Isaiah 58:10.

[37] *hidden in the covert of your face*: See Colossians 3:3; Psalm 30:21(31:20).

Chapter 9

10. It cannot be denied, surely, that the Father too was borne aloft over the waters, and the Son? If the expression means poised in a place, after the manner of a body, then the Holy Spirit was not poised there either; but if it means that the eminence of unchangeable Godhead is far above all that is changeable, then certainly the one God, Father, Son and Holy Spirit, was poised above the waters. Why, then, was this stated of your Spirit only? Why of him alone, as though he were in a place, when it is no place; and why only of him who alone is said to be your Gift?[38]

Because, I think, in your Gift we find rest, and there we enjoy you. Our true place is where we find rest. We are borne toward it by love, and it is your good Spirit[39] who lifts up our sunken nature from the gates of death.[40] In goodness of will is our peace.[41] A body gravitates to its proper place by its own weight.[42] This weight does not necessarily drag it downward, but pulls it to the place proper to it: thus fire tends upward, a stone downward. Drawn by their weight, things seek their rightful places. If oil is poured into water, it will rise to the surface, but if water is poured onto oil it will sink below the oil: drawn by their weight, things seek their rightful places. They are not at rest as long as they are disordered, but once brought to order they find their rest. Now, my weight is my love, and wherever I am carried, it is this weight that carries me. Your Gift sets us afire and we are borne upward; we catch his flame and up we

---

[38] *your Spirit . . . your Gift*: See Acts 2:38. As the eternal bond of Love between the Lover (the Father) and the Beloved (the Son) the Holy Spirit's names will always signify relationship. Here, for example, he is Gift because the very name implies a Giver (the Begetting Father) and a Receiver (the Begotten Son).

[39] *your good Spirit*: See Psalm 142(143):10.

[40] *the gates of death*: See Psalm 9:14–15(13).

[41] *In goodness of will is our peace*: See Luke 2:14.

[42] *A body gravitates to its proper place by its own weight*: Lovers are drawn toward the objects of their love, as a gravity draws a body to its proper place. By identifying love as his "weight", Augustine shows that love carries him into God's presence, the eternal rest of love that is the proper place of every creature.

go. In our hearts we climb those upwardpaths,[43] singing the songs of ascent. By your fire, your beneficent fire, are we enflamed, because we are making our way up to *the peace of Jerusalem. For I rejoiced when I was told,* "We are going to the Lord's house." [44] There shall a good will find us a place, that we may have no other desire but to abide there for ever.[45]

Chapter 10

11. How blessed is that creature which knew no different lot! Indeed, it might itself have been something very different, had not your Gift, the Spirit who broods over all that is mutable, raised it up without the least delay, from the moment it was made, and summoned it with the words, *Let there be light.* And light it became. In our case there are distinct periods of time, for we were darkness once, and then we became light.[46] Not so for that creature: what it would have been, had it not been illumined, was announced, and announced in such a way that it might seem to have once been all darkness and chaotic flux; but this was to show why it was made capable of becoming something different, enlightened by conversion to the Light that never fails.[47]

Let anyone grasp this who can, or else let him seek understanding from you. Why should he pester me, as though I had the power to illumine anyone coming into this world?[48]

Chapter 11

12. Can anyone comprehend the almighty Trinity? Everyone talks about it—but is it really the Trinity of which they talk?

---

[43] *In our hearts we climb those upward paths:* See Psalm 83:6(84:5).
[44] the peace of Jerusalem ... *"We are going to the Lord's house":* Psalm 121(122):6, 1.
[45] *abide there for ever:* See Psalm 60:8(61:7).
[46] *we were darkness once, and then we became light:* See Ephesians 5:8.
[47] *the Light that never fails:* See Sirach 24:6.
[48] *illumine anyone coming into this world:* See John 1:9.

Rare indeed is the person who understands the subject of his discourse, when he speaks of that. People argue and wrangle over it, yet no one sees that vision unless he is at peace.

I wish they would turn their attention to the triad they have within themselves. It is, to be sure, a triad far distant from the Trinity, but I propose it as a topic on which they may exercise their minds, by way of experiment and in order to make clear to themselves how great the difference is. The triad I mean is being, knowledge and will. I am, and I know, and I will.[49] Knowingly and willingly I exist; I know that I am and that I will; I will to be and to know. Let anyone with the wit to see it observe how in these three there is one inseparable life: there is one life, one mind and one essence. How inseparable they are in their distinctness! Yet distinction there is. Everyone has himself readily available for inspection; let each, then, scrutinize himself, and see what he can find, and tell me.

But when he has verified this unity between his powers, he must not suppose that what he has discovered is that which exists immutably above our creaturely minds, that which unchangeably is and unchangeably knows and unchangeably wills. Do these three coexistent acts constitute the Trinity? Or are all three found in each Person, so that each is this triple reality? Or are both these propositions true, the simplicity and the complexity being reconciled in some way beyond our comprehension, since the Persons are defined by their mutual relationships yet infinite in themselves?[50] Thus

---

[49] *The triad I mean is being, knowledge and will. I am, and I know, and I will:* Triune relations prove a distant analogy to the triad of being, knowledge, and will that constitute the human being. Yet here is the beginning of a search that lasted most of Augustine's life, wondering how the human soul is the image of God. This is the purpose of the latter books of *On the Trinity*, and the final answer proffered there is the triune soul (memory, intellect, and will) is most alive and most an icon of the divine when in union—remembering, knowing, and loving—Father, Son, and Holy Spirit.

[50] *the Persons are defined by their mutual relationships yet infinite in themselves:* One of the first to meditate deeply on the implications of the Trinity, Augustine sees how each of the three divine Persons is "defined by their mutual

the Godhead exists and is known to itself and is its own all-sufficient joy without variation for ever, Being-Itself in the manifold greatness of its unity. Who can find any way to express this truth? Who dare make any assertion about it?[51]

Chapter 12

Allegorical interpretation of Gn 1. Day One: Light[52]

13. But let my faith go further, and say to the Lord my God, "Holy, holy, holy,[53] Lord my God, in your name, Father, Son and Spirit, were we baptized, and in your name, Father, Son and Holy Spirit, we administer baptism,"[54] for among us too

---

relationships", what later medieval theologians will call subsistent relationships. Since each of us human persons instantiates his own humanity, relationships between humans are accidental, affecting only who we are circumstantially (e.g., my father dies and I remain). However, since there is only one divine nature, the three Persons sharing divinity wholly and perfectly, each Person of the Trinity is constituted wholly by relationship with the other two. The Father is who he is because he begets the Son, thus wholly dependent upon the Son in order to be Father; the Son is Son because he is defined totally by his being begotten; and the Spirit's personal identity is eternally established by being the union of the Father and the Son. It is ironically challenging to realize that the Persons of the Trinity must rely more upon each other for their unique identity than we humans do on one another. Gazing upon the Trinity we might therefore learn that in growing less autonomous and more dependent upon another is a hint of the divine life.

[51] *Thus the Godhead exists . . . Who dare make any assertions about it?* A discourse on the Trinity makes eminent sense when we recall that Book XIII is dedicated to the Church and how unity can be made from the many. The Trinity's life is the pattern as well as the goal of the Church, as the "one" and the "many", where unity and alterity are perfectly reconciled. The examination now turns to the unity of creation as evidenced by the divisions of each day.

[52] *Day One: Light*: The six days of creation are now taken up in turn, interpreted allegorically so as to see their deeper meanings. The "let there be light" of the first day is thus understood as God's call for those in his Church to move from ignorance to understanding, from slavery into the true freedom of God's own children.

[53] *say to the Lord my God, "Holy, holy, holy*: See Isaiah 6:3; Revelation 4:8.

[54] *in your name, Father, Son and Holy Spirit, we administer baptism*: See 1 Corinthians 1:15; Matthew 28:19.

has God in his Christ created a heaven and an earth: the spiritual and the carnal members of his Church.[55] Before our earth was formed by his teaching it was invisible and unorganized,[56] and we were shrouded in the darkness of ignorance, because you castigated humankind for its sin[57] and your judgments are deep as a chasmic abyss.[58] But your mercy did not forsake us in our misery, for your Spirit hovered over the water; and you said, *Let there be light; repent, for the kingdom of heaven is near, repent, and let there be light.*[59] And because our souls were deeply disquieted within themselves we remembered you, O Lord, from our muddy Jordan; we called you to mind in that mountain which, though lofty as yourself, was brought low for us.[60] Disgusted with our darkness, we were converted to you, and light dawned. See now, we who once were darkness are now light in the Lord.[61]

Chapter 13

14. But as yet we know this only by faith, not by anything we see;[62] for we have been saved indeed, but in hope, and hope that is seen is hope no longer.[63] Deep still calls unto deep, but now in the roar of your waterfalls.[64] Paul himself, even Paul, who says, *Not as spiritual persons could I speak to you, but only as carnal,*[65] even he does not consider himself to have laid

[55] *the spiritual and the carnal members of his Church*: See 1 Corinthians 3:1.

[56] *Before our earth was formed by his teaching it was invisible and unorganized*: See Genesis 1:2.

[57] *you castigated humankind for its sin*. See Psalm 38:12(39:11).

[58] *your judgments are deep as a chasmic abyss*· See Psalm 35:7(36:6).

[59] *Let there be light; repent* . . . *and let there be light*: Genesis 1:3; Matthew 3:2; 4:17.

[60] *our souls were deeply disquieted* . . . *brought low for us*: See Psalm 41:6–7(42:5–6).

[61] *we who once were darkness are now light in the Lord*: See Ephesians 5:8.

[62] *we know this only by faith, not by anything we see*: See 2 Corinthians 5:7.

[63] *hope that is seen is hope no longer*: See Romans 8:24.

[64] *Deep still calls unto deep* . . . *in the roar of your waterfalls*: See Psalm 41:8(42:7).

[65] *Not as spiritual persons could I speak to you, but only as carnal*: 1 Corinthians 3:1. A *homo spiritualis* for Augustine is a person who is "spiritualized", not in the sense of denying his embodiment or the goodness of matter, of course,

hold on his salvation already, but, forgetting what lies behind him, he stretches out to what lies ahead,[66] groaning and oppressed[67] because his soul is athirst for the living God, like a parched deer running to springs of water and panting, "When shall I reach it?"[68] He longs to have his heavenly habitation put on over his earthly vesture;[69] and he calls to those deeper in the abyss than himself, *Conform yourselves no longer to the standards of this world, but allow yourselves to be reformed by the renewal of your minds,* and *Do not be childish in your outlook; be babes in your innocence of evil, but mature in mind;* and again, *You stupid Galatians! Who has bewitched you?*[70] But he calls to them no longer in his own voice. In your voice he calls to them, for you sent your Spirit from heaven[71] through Christ who ascended on high[72] and threw open your floodgates that your gifts might cascade upon us and your rushing river bring joy to your city.[73]

For him does Paul, the Bridegroom's friend,[74] sigh with longing, for to him has Paul dedicated the first-fruits of his spirit, but still he groans within himself as he awaits the

---

but one who is able to grasp spiritual truths rightly. Spiritual truths are not simply religious doctrines for Augustine (although they are that); they are also sophisticated cosmological and philosophical truths, like the ones he has been working out regarding creation. To grasp such truths is a gift of the Holy Spirit, obtainable only within the Body of Christ, the Church.

[66] *forgetting what lies behind him, he stretches out to what lies ahead*: See Philippians 3:13.

[67] *groaning and oppressed*: See 2 Corinthians 5:4.

[68] *like a parched deer running to springs of water and panting, "When shall I reach it?"* See Psalm 41:2–3 (42:1–2).

[69] *He longs to have his heavenly habitation put on over his earthly vesture*: See 2 Corinthians 5:2.

[70] *Conform yourselves ... bewitched you*: Romans 12:2; 1 Corinthians 14:20; Galatians 3:1.

[71] *you sent your Spirit from heaven*: See Wisdom 9:17.

[72] *through Christ who ascended on high*: See Psalm 67:19 (68:18).

[73] *your rushing river bring joy to your city*: See Psalm 45:5 (46:4).

[74] *For him does Paul, the Bridegroom's friend*: See John 3:29. The nuptial imagery throughout is rich: whereas the first life-giving union of Adam and Eve bred disobedience and consequent death, the eternal union of Christ and his Bride the Church bring forth divinely adopted sons and daughters.

adoption that will set his whole self free.[75] For Christ he yearns, for he is a member of the bride, but on Christ's behalf he is jealous, for he is the Bridegroom's friend. Not for his own rights is he jealous, but for Christ's; not in his own voice but in the thunder of your waterfalls he calls out to that deeper abyss, alert with jealous fear lest, as once the serpent seduced Eve by his wiles, she too may lose the purity of her singleminded devotion to our Bridegroom, your only Son.[76]

What, then, is this fair light? A light by which we shall see him as he is,[77] a light to put an end to the tears that have become bread to me, daily, nightly, as I hear the unceasing taunt, "Where is your God?"[78]

Chapter 14

15. And I too ask, "Where are you, my God?" But this is where you are. I find a little respite[79] in you when I pour out my soul in rising above myself with a shout of joy and praise, the clamor of a pilgrim keeping festival.[80] Yet still my soul is sad, because it slips back and becomes an abyss once more, or rather, it feels itself to be still in the depths.[81]

But my faith takes it to task, that faith which you have kindled, lamp-like, on my nocturnal path: "Why so sorrowful, my soul, why do you disquiet me? Trust in the Lord; his word is a

[75] *Paul dedicated the first-fruits of his spirit . . . the adoption that will set his whole self free:* See Romans 8:23.

[76] *as once the serpent seduced Eve . . . our Bridegroom, your only Son:* See 2 Corinthians 11:3.

[77] *we shall see him as he is:* See 1 John 3:2.

[78] *as I hear the unceasing taunt, "Where is your God?"* See Psalm 41:4(42:3).

[79] *I find a little respite:* See Job 32:20.

[80] *clamor of a pilgrim keeping festival:* See Psalm 41:5(42:4).

[81] *Yet still my soul is sad . . . feels itself to be still in the depths:* Augustine's created will inevitably reflects the metaphysical dynamics of creation itself, teetering between God, the fullness of being, and the nothingness from which he was drawn. Virtue and charity convert us upward toward perfection; sin and aversion from God plunge us further downward into the abyss.

lamp for your feet.[82] Keep your hope high and persevere until night, nurturer of the wicked, shall pass away, until the Lord's anger shall pass.[83] We too were once children of his wrath;[84] once darkness,[85] we carry that residual gloom in bodies marked for death because of sin,[86] but hope on until day dawns and shadows disperse.[87] Hope in the Lord. In the morning I shall stand in his presence and contemplate him,[88] and I will praise him for ever."

In the morning I will stand and see my God, who sheds the light of salvation on my face,[89] who will breathe life even into our mortal bodies through the Spirit who dwells in us[90] and has been mercifully hovering over the dark chaos of our inner being. By this we have received, even on our pilgrim way, the pledge[91] that we are children of the light already. Saved only in hope we may be,[92] but we are at home in the light and in the day. No longer are we children of the night or of darkness,[93] as once we were. But you alone distinguish between us and the night-born in this present uncertainty where human knowledge falters, for you test our hearts, and call light "day" and darkness "night."[94] Who but you can tell them apart? Yet what do we possess that we have not received from you, since from the one same lump you have formed us for honorable service, and others for common use?

---

[82] *my soul, why do you disquiet me . . . his word is a lamp for your feet*: See Psalm 41:6, 12(42:5, 11); 118(119):105.

[83] *until the Lord's anger shall pass*: See Isaiah 26:20.

[84] *We too were once children of his wrath*: See Ephesians 2:3.

[85] *once darkness*: See Ephesians 5:8.

[86] *marked for death because of sin*: See Romans 8:10.

[87] *hope on until day dawns and shadows disperse*: See Song of Solomon 2:17.

[88] *In the morning I shall stand in his presence and contemplate him*: See Psalm 5:5(3).

[89] *I will stand and see my God, who sheds the light of salvation on my face*: See Psalm 42(43):5.

[90] *who will breathe life even into our mortal bodies through the Spirit who dwells in us*: See Romans 8:11.

[91] *the pledge*: See 2 Corinthians 1:22; 5:5.

[92] *Saved only in hope we may be*: See Romans 8:24.

[93] *No longer are we children of the night or of darkness*: See 1 Thessalonians 5:5.

[94] *call light "day" and darkness "night."* See Genesis 1:4–5; Psalm 16(17):3.

Chapter 15

Day Two: The vault of scripture[95]

16. Moreover you alone, our God, have made for us a vault overhead in giving us your divine scripture.[96] The sky will one day be rolled up like a book, but for the present it is stretched out above us like the skin of a tent,[97] for your divine scripture has attained an even nobler authority now that the mortal writers through whom you provided it for us have died. And you know, Lord, you know[98] how you clothed human beings in skins when they became mortal in consequence of their sin.[99] That is why you are said to have stretched out the vault that is your book, stretched out like the skin of a tent those words of yours so free from discord, which you have canopied over us through the ministry of mortal men. The firm authority inherent in your revelation, which they have passed on to us, is by their very death spread more widely over all the world below, for in their lifetime it had not been raised so high or extended so far. At that time you had not yet stretched out the sky like a tent, nor had you caused their death to become resoundingly famous far and wide.

17. Let us contemplate the heavens, the work of your fingers, O Lord;[100] clear away that cloud you have spread

[95] Day Two: The vault of scripture: Whereas the first day had to do with the metaphor of light, the second day revolves around Scripture as something rolled out for rational creatures to read as well as a protective shelter against mortality (represented by the skins of animal clothing worn by Adam and Eve as a consequence of the Fall). As astrologers gaze into the skies to understand deeper realities, Christians should be so gazing onto the pages of Scripture.

[96] *you alone, our God, have made for us a vault overhead in giving us your divine scripture*: See Genesis 1:7.

[97] *The sky ... it is stretched out above us like the skin of a tent*: See Psalm 103(104):2.

[98] *you know, Lord, you know*: See Tobit 3:16; 8:9; John 21:15–17.

[99] *how you clothed human beings in skins ... in consequence of their sin*: See Genesis 3:21.

[100] *the heavens, the work of your fingers, O Lord*: See Psalm 8:4(3).

beneath them, hiding them from our eyes. There is the witness you have borne to yourself, and to little ones it imparts wisdom.[101] Out of the mouths of infants and sucklings evoke perfect praise, O my God.[102] We know no other books with the like power to lay pride low[103] and so surely to silence the obstinate contender who tries to thwart your reconciling work by defending his sins. Nowhere else, Lord, indeed nowhere else do I know such chaste words,[104] words with such efficacy to persuade me to confession, to gentle my neck beneath your kindly yoke[105] and invite me to worship you without thought of reward. Grant me understanding of your words, good Father, give me this gift, stationed as I am below them, because it is for us earth-dwellers that you have fashioned that strong vault overhead.

18. Above this vault are other waters,[106] and these, I believe, are immortal, immune to earthly decay. Let them praise your name,[107] let them praise you, your angelic peoples above the heavens, who have no need to look up at the vault and learn by reading your word in it; for they behold your face unceasingly[108] and there read without the aid of time-bound syllables the decree of your eternal will. They read it, they make it their choice, they love it; they read it always, and what they read never passes away, for in their act of choosing and loving they read the unchangeable constancy of your purpose. Their book is never closed, their scroll never rolled up,[109] for you are their book and are so eternally, because you have assigned them their place above the vault you strongly framed

---

[101] *to little ones it imparts wisdom*: See Psalm 18:8(19:7).
[102] *Out of the mouths of infants and sucklings evoke perfect praise, O my God*: See Psalm 8:3(2).
[103] *with the like power to lay pride low*: See Ezekiel 30:6.
[104] *nowhere else do I know such chaste words*: See Psalm 11:7(12:6).
[105] *to gentle my neck beneath your kindly yoke*: See Matthew 11:29–30.
[106] *Above this vault are other waters*: See Genesis 1:7.
[107] *Let them praise your name*: See Psalm 148:4–5.
[108] *they behold your face unceasingly*: See Matthew 18:10.
[109] *their scroll never rolled up*: See Isaiah 34:4.

over the weakness of your lower peoples.[110] Into that vault we look up, there to recognize the mercy which manifests you in time, you who have created time; *for your mercy is heaven-high, O Lord, and your faithfulness reaches to the clouds.*[111] Clouds are wafted away, but heaven abides. Preachers of your word are wafted away out of this life into another, but your scripture remains stretched above your people everywhere until the end of the world. Then will even sky and earth be swept away,[112] but your utterances will stand unmoved, because though the tent is folded and the grass where it was pitched withers with all its verdure, your Word abides for ever.[113] Not as he is, but tantalizingly, as though veiled by cloud and mirrored in his heaven,[114] does this Word appear to us now, for though we are the beloved of your Son, it has not yet appeared what we shall be.[115] He peeps through the trellis of our flesh, and coaxes us, and enkindles our love until we run after him, allured by his fragrance.[116] *But when he appears, we shall be like him, because we shall see him as he is.*[117] Our seeing then, Lord, will be the vision of you as you are, but this is not granted to us yet.

---

[110] *you are their book . . . the weakness of your lower peoples*: God is ultimately the true book, the sacred canon being a manifestation of God calibrated to creatures so as to elevate and transform them into godliness.

[111] *for your mercy . . . your faithfulness reaches to the clouds*: Psalm 35:6(36:5).

[112] *Then will even sky and earth be swept away*: See Matthew 24:35.

[113] *the grass where it was pitched withers . . . your Word abides for ever*: See Isaiah 40:6–8. Notice the progression of permanence, showing why God himself is the ultimate word: creation tells us something of God, as do Christian preachers, as do the Scriptures themselves, then the very utterances of God, and then the Word himself.

[114] *mirrored in his heaven*: See 1 Corinthians 13:12.

[115] *it has not yet appeared what we shall be*: See 1 John 3:2. Our union with God is not yet total. Rather, God is remaking us and drawing us closer to him so that we may one day be granted the full vision of God. We shall be thus made like God when this occurs, and, as Augustine comments elsewhere on 1 John, then "there shall be one Christ loving himself" (*Homilies on the First Epistle of John* 10.3).

[116] *He peeps through the trellis . . . allured by his fragrance*: See Song of Solomon 2:9; 1:3.

[117] *But when he appears . . . we shall see him as he is*: 1 John 3:2.

Chapter 16

19. As you exist in all fullness, so too do you alone possess the fullness of knowledge: you unchangeably exist, unchangeably know and unchangeably will. Your essence knows and wills unchangeably; your knowledge is and wills unchangeably; your will is and knows unchangeably. It therefore does not seem fitting to you that the unchangeable Light should be known by the changeable being it illumines in the same way as it knows itself. This is why my soul is like an arid land before you,[118] for as it cannot illumine itself from its own resources, neither can it slake its thirst from itself. So truly is the fount of life with you, that only in your light will we see light.[119]

Chapter 17

Day Three: Bitter sea, dry land, fruitfulness[120]

20. Who else gathered people brewing bitterness into a single mass? All of them are bent on the same quest for earthly, temporal happiness; this is the object of all they do, though the waves of care that toss them to and fro are endlessly varied. Who called them together if not you, Lord, who commanded that the waters be gathered into a single mass and dry land emerge,[121] athirst for you? To you even the sea belongs, for

---

[118] *my soul is like an arid land before you:* See Psalm 142(143):6.

[119] *the fount of life with you, that only in your light will we see light:* See Psalm 35:10(36:9).

[120] Day Three: Bitter sea, dry land, fruitfulness: Out of the "brewing bitterness" of pre- and non-Christian religions, God is forming an *ecclesia*, a people called out of the "raging sea" into the Church, the barque of salvation. The Mediterranean-born Augustine saw in the tempestuous sea a fitting metaphor for this world: "for the sea is used as a symbol of this world, harsh in saltiness and battered by storms. In this sea the perverse and depraved lusts of human beings have made them like fishes devouring each other" (*Commentary on the Psalms* 64.9).

[121] *Lord, who commanded that the waters be gathered into a single mass and dry land emerge:* See Genesis 1:9.

you made it and your hands formed the dry earth.[122] It is not the bitter brine of those conflicting wills that earns the name "sea," but their gathering; for you control even the unruly urges of our souls, and set limits to their onrush, boundaries where their surging waves must break.[123] Thus your sway over all things imposes order, and you create "sea."[124]

21. But you have other souls in view as well, souls athirst for you,[125] whose very different aim marks them out clearly from the surrounding sea. Their thirst you quench from the sweet waters of your secret fountain, that the earth too may yield its increase.[126] And yield it does: at the command of its Lord and God the soil of our souls grows fertile in works of mercy according to its kind.[127] We fructify in love of our neighbors[128] by assisting them in their bodily needs, for, having seed of similar kind within ourselves, we learn compassion from our own weakness.[129] So we are impelled to succor the needy in the way we would wish to be relieved ourselves, were we in the same distress. This means not only the easy provision that could be likened to seed-bearing grass; we may also be called upon to supply the stout, oak-like protection of a fruit-bearing

[122] *To you even the sea belongs . . . your hands formed the dry earth*: See Psalm 94(95):5.

[123] *set limits to their onrush, boundaries where their surging waves must break*: See Job 38:10–11.

[124] *your sway over all things imposes order, and you create "sea"*: As land is collected together and thus saved from the bitter seas, God longs to gather all peoples together, joined by the divine thirst their unquiet hearts produce.

[125] *souls athirst for you*: See Psalm 62:2(63:1).

[126] *the earth too may yield its increase*: See Psalm 84:13(85:12).

[127] *at the command of its Lord . . . according to its kind*: See Genesis 1:12.

[128] *We fructify in love of our neighbors*: See Matthew 22:39; Mark 12:31. This is the difference between smaller and greater goods. Whereas smaller goods (e.g., material objects) diminish as distributed, great goods, like charity and mercy, actually increase when shared.

[129] *by assisting them in their bodily needs . . . we learn compassion from our own weakness*: Augustine contrasts the conflicting wills of people whose aims are temporal with those concerned with eternity, showing that when the Church draws from God's resources, there is more than enough to care for the needs of others. The Church's needs are met in abundance by caring for the needs of others— i.e., great goods are magnified when sacrificed.

tree, which in its benign strength can lift an injured person clear of the grasp of a powerful oppressor, and furnish protective shade by the unshakable firmness of just judgment.

Chapter 18

Day Four: Lamps of wisdom and knowledge[130]

22. And so I pray you, Lord: as you cause joy and strength to spring and grow, even so let the truth spring up: let it sprout from the earth, and let righteousness look down from heaven,[131] and let luminaries be set in the firmament.[132] Let us break our bread for the hungry and bring the homeless poor under our roof, let us clothe the naked and not spurn our own kin.[133] When these fruits are burgeoning on earth, take heed and see that it is good. Then may swift dawn break for us, so that rising from this lowly crop of active works to the delights of contemplation, we may lay hold on the Word of Life above,[134] and appear like luminaries for the world, firmly set in the vault that is your scripture. There you school us to mark the distinction between realities of the mind and sensible things, as between day and night, or between souls devoted to the life of the mind and others preoccupied with sensible matters. No longer then is it you alone who in the secret recesses of your own judgment separate light from darkness, as before that vault was made; for now that your grace is manifested throughout the world your spiritual children too, set in the vault and plainly visible, may shine upon the earth,

[130] Day Four: Lamps of wisdom and knowledge: As God formed the celestial luminaries on the fourth day, here he longs to impart his own brilliance into those now gathered into his Body, enabling them to become the light of the world.

[131] *let the truth spring up . . . let righteousness look down from heaven*: See Psalm 84:12 (85:11).

[132] *let luminaries be set in the firmament*: See Genesis 1:14.

[133] *Let us break our bread for the hungry . . . clothe the naked and not spurn our own kin*: See Isaiah 58:7–8.

[134] *Word of Life above*: See Philippians 2:15–16; 1 John 1:1.

separate day from night, and mark distinct periods of time.[135] This is because old things have passed away now and all is made new;[136] our salvation is nearer now than when we first believed; night is far gone and day is breaking.[137] You crown the year with your blessing,[138] sending laborers into your harvest[139] where others have toiled over the sowing.[140] Different workers you send to sow new crops, which will be reaped at the end.[141]

Accordingly you grant our requests when we pray to you, and bless the passing years of a just person, but your years do not pass,[142] and in your unchanging eternity you are preparing a barn for the harvest of our fleeting years.

You lavish your heavenly blessings on the earth at due times, as determined by your eternal counsel; [23.] for to one person is granted the gift of speaking with wisdom, like the greater light you made, for the benefit of those who find their joy in the brilliant transparency of truth as in the light of early morning; to another is given through the grace of the same Spirit an ability to put the knowledge he has into words, and this is like the lesser light; to another is granted gifts of healing, to another miraculous powers, to another prophecy, to another discernment between spirits, and to yet another various tongues. All these are like stars. All of them are the work of one and the same Spirit, who allots appropriate gifts to different people as he wills, and causes stars to shine out clearly for the benefit of all.[143]

---

[135] *separate light from darkness . . . mark distinct periods of time*: See Genesis 1:14–18.

[136] *old things have passed away now and all is made new*: See 2 Corinthians 5:17.

[137] *our salvation is nearer . . . night is far gone and day is breaking*: See Romans 13:11–12.

[138] *You crown the year with your blessing*: See Psalm 64:12(65:11).

[139] *sending laborers into your harvest*: See Matthew 9:38.

[140] *where others have toiled over the sowing*: See John 4:38.

[141] *Different workers you send to sow . . . reaped at the end*: See Matthew 13:39.

[142] *your years do not pass*: See Psalm 101:28(102:27).

[143] *You lavish your heavenly blessings . . . for the benefit of all*: See 1 Corinthians 12:7–11.

As for knowledge expressed in apt words, comprising all those sacred signs[144] which wane and wax like the moon, and the other gifts which in their diversity I likened to stars, all these differ so greatly from the glorious wisdom in which the aforesaid day rejoices that they are but rulers of the night. Nonetheless they are necessary for those people to whom your very prudent servant could speak only as carnal, not as spiritual persons,[145] whereas among the mature he speaks wisdom.[146] A sensual person is like a small child in Christ, in need of milk until he is robust enough to eat solid food and his eyes have the strength to stand exposure to the sun. Meanwhile, however, he does not live in a night devoid of all illumination, but must be content with the light of moon and stars.

These things you teach us with consummate wisdom in your book, which is the vault[147] you provide for us, O our God, so that they may all become plain to us through contemplation of your wonders. Still, though, we must discern them through signs, and transient phases, and passing days and years.

Chapter 19

24. "But first you must wash, get yourselves clean, purge the wickedness from your souls and take it out of my sight, that dry land may appear. Learn to do good, champion the orphan and defend the rights of the widow, that your earth may yield nourishing crops and fruit-bearing trees, and then come back and let us discuss matters," says the Lord,[148] "so that there may be lights in the vault of heaven to shed their radiance on earth."[149]

---

[144] *As for knowledge . . . comprising all those sacred signs*: See 1 Corinthians 13:2.

[145] *only as carnal, not as spiritual persons*: See 1 Corinthians 3:1.

[146] *among the mature he speaks wisdom*: See 1 Corinthians 2:6.

[147] *in your book, which is the vault*: Augustine continues to speak of Scripture metaphorically as the "vault".

[148] *"But first you must wash . . . come back and let us discuss matters," says the Lord*: See Isaiah 1:16–18.

[149] *so that there may be lights in the vault of heaven to shed their radiance on earth*: The Church is a place of both discipleship as well as dogma, not only enacting

Remember the rich man in the gospel who was seeking guidance from a good teacher as to what he ought to do to win eternal life. Let that good teacher (whom he believed to be a man and no more, whereas Christ is good because he is God)— let that good teacher tell him that if he wishes to attain to life, he must keep the commandments, steer clear of bitter malice and wickedness, refrain from killing, adultery and theft, and never tell lies against anyone. Then dry land will have a chance to appear and bear the fruits of honor toward his mother and father and love for his neighbor. *I have done all this*, the young man says.[150] Then where do these rampant thorns come from, if your land is fruitful? Go and root out the wild clumps of avarice, sell your possessions, get yourself rich fruit by giving to the poor, for you will have treasure in heaven. If you want to be perfect, follow the Lord in the company of those to whom he speaks wisdom,[151] he who knows which gifts to assign to the day and which to the night, so that you may know too, and there may be lights in the vault of heaven to shine for you as well. This will not happen unless your heart is there; and that in turn will not happen unless your treasure is deposited there,[152] as you have heard from your good teacher.

But the barren earth was saddened,[153] and thorns choked the word.[154]

25. As for you, race of the elect,[155] weaklings in the world's esteem,[156] who have left all to follow the Lord, march after

---

God's care for the world, but in so doing, interpreting Scripture rightly for all ages.

[150] *the rich man in the gospel . . . the young man says*: See Matthew 19:16–22; Mark 10:17–22; Luke 18:18–23.

[151] *in the company of those to whom he speaks wisdom*: See 1 Corinthians 2:6.

[152] *This will not happen . . . unless your treasure is deposited there*: See Matthew 6:21. The Gospel invites all to a life beyond mere obedience; the Gospel is an invitation to the freedom of children, to union with God through his Mystical Body, the Church.

[153] *the barren earth was saddened*: See Luke 18:23.

[154] *thorns choked the word*: See Matthew 13:7, 22.

[155] *race of the elect*: See 1 Peter 2:9.

[156] *weaklings in the world's esteem*: See 1 Corinthians 1:27.

him and rout the strong,[157] march after him, you beautiful feet.[158] Shine in the firmament that the heavens may proclaim his glory.[159] Separate the light of the mature, who yet are not angels, from the darkness of the little ones, who yet are not to be despaired of; shine over the whole earth, and let the day, radiant with its sun, tell out the word of wisdom to the day, and the night, steeped in moonlight, proclaim the word of knowledge[160] to the night.[161] Let moon and stars lend brightness to the night, but let not the night overwhelm them with its darkness, for they do illumine it, in its measure.

As though God were once more commanding, *Let there be lights in the vault of heaven,*[162] there came a sudden noise from on high as though a violent wind were sweeping through, and tongues like fire appeared, separating and coming to rest on each one of them.[163] So they became luminaries in the vault of heaven, endowed with the word of life.[164] Run everywhere, you holy fires, you fires so beautiful, for you are the light of the world, and your place is not under a meal-tub.[165] He to whom you have given yourselves is exalted, and now he has exalted you. Run, then, and make him known to all nations.[166]

---

[157] *As for you . . . march after him and rout the strong:* See 1 Corinthians 1:7.

[158] *march after him, you beautiful feet:* See Isaiah 52:7; Romans 10:15.

[159] *the heavens may proclaim his glory:* See Psalm 18:2 (19:1).

[160] *proclaim the word of knowledge:* See 1 Corinthians 12:8.

[161] *tell out the word of wisdom to the day . . . to the night:* See Psalm 18:3 (19:2).

[162] *Let there be lights in the vault of heaven:* Genesis 1:14.

[163] *there came a sudden noise . . . coming to rest on each one of them:* See Acts 2:2–3.

[164] *luminaries in the vault of heaven, endowed with the word of life:* See Philippians 2:15–16; 1 John 1:1.

[165] *you are the light of the world, and your place is not under a meal-tub:* See Matthew 5:14–15.

[166] *Run everywhere . . . make him known to all nations:* See Matthew 28:19. Augustine's allusion to Pentecost here illustrates how he sees the Church as God's unceasing spiritualization of and re-creating action in the world. The Church is to light the world, entrusted with the luminous message that Christ has been raised and has now raised creation for deifying union with God.

Chapter 20

Day Five: Sea creatures represent signs and sacraments[167]

26. Let the sea conceive and bring forth your works, and let the waters produce living things that crawl;[168] for you have become God's spokesmen, separating worth from dross.[169] Through you he was able to say, *Let the waters bring forth living things that crawl* (not "living souls," which the dry land alone was to produce, but crawling things), *and birds to fly above the earth;*[170] for these aquatic creatures represent your holy signs, O God. Amid the waves of this world's temptations they swarmed, thanks to the efforts of your saints, to the end that the Gentiles might be stamped with your name in baptism. Among them were also some prodigious and wonderful feats,[171] suggested by the massive whales. The birds represent the voices of your messengers, who flew above the earth and close to the sky which is your book, for this book was the authority set over them, and wherever they might travel they always stayed beneath it. Never a word, never an utterance of theirs, but the rumor of it was heard as their sound echoed throughout the world and their words to the ends of the earth,[172] because you, Lord, caused them to multiply by your blessing.

27. Am I to be charged with lying or with causing confusion, by failing to draw a distinction between the luminous comprehension of these mysteries in the vault of heaven, and the

---

[167] Day Five: Sea creatures represent signs and sacraments: The creatures of the sea represent the sacraments as they rest below the world's storms; and the birds of the air represent Christ's evangelists as they fly above the earth, contemplating Scripture and conveying its words to the world.

[168] *Let the sea conceive and bring forth your works . . . produce living things that crawl*: See Genesis 1:20–22.

[169] *you have become God's spokesmen, separating worth from dross*: See Jeremiah 15:19.

[170] Let the waters bring forth living things that crawl . . . and birds to fly above the earth: Genesis 1:20.

[171] *Among them were . . . wonderful feats*: See Acts 2:11.

[172] *Never a word, never an utterance . . . to the ends of the earth*: See Psalm 18:4(19:3).

corporeal works achieved far below in the waves of the sea? It is true that the characteristics of certain things are fixed and finalized, and not subject to development over successive generations, and among these are the splendors of wisdom and knowledge; but these same realities work themselves out in the sphere of bodily things in a great variety of forms which constantly increase and multiply through your blessing, O God. You have made kindly provision for the learning processes of us mortals, so prone to weariness, by arranging that our minds should attain to understanding as one single truth is figuratively expressed and enunciated in many different ways through the variations to which corporeal things are subject. The waters it was that produced these things, but in response to your creative word. It was the needs of peoples estranged from your eternal truth that produced them, but only at the preaching of your gospel, for though it was the waters themselves that threw up these prodigies, in the sense that the bitter weariness of those waters occasioned them, they emerged only at your bidding.

28. All these things of your making are lovely, and lo, you who made them are more lovely still, unutterably more. If Adam had not fallen away from you, that briny sea would not have gushed from him, the deeply curious and stormily swollen and unstable flux that is the human race. And then there would have been no need for the deeds performed and the words spoken by your stewards[173] amid the pounding waves, words and deeds material and sensible, yet fraught with sacramental power.

This is what the creeping things and birds suggest to me at present, for even though people have been baptized and initiated, and have submitted to these material sacraments, they would proceed no further, did their souls not rise to a new level of spiritual life, and move on from elementary doctrine toward maturity.[174]

---

[173] *deeds performed . . . by your stewards*: See 1 Corinthians 4:1.

[174] *have been baptized and initiated . . . elementary doctrine toward maturity*: See Hebrews 6:1–3. Initial salvation comes by way of the sacraments, while continual sanctification comes by way of contemplation.

Chapter 21

Day Six: Animals, the "living soul"[175]

29. What now emerges, then, are neither living things that crawl, nor anything from the depths of the sea: at your command the land, which stands clear from the bitter sea, throws up a *living creature*.[176] This creature no longer stands in need of baptism as the pagans do, and as it did itself while sunk beneath the waters, for since you ordained baptism as the means of entry into the kingdom of heaven no one can get in by any other way.[177] Nor does this creature demand prodigious miracles to prompt it to faith; it is not like people who refuse to believe unless they see signs and wonders,[178] for already it is believing earth, clearly demarcated from the waves of the sea and their bitter unbelief; and tongues serve as a sign to unbelievers, not to the faithful.[179]

Neither does this dry land, which you have established upon the waters,[180] need those flying creatures which the waters produced at your command. Send your word to the land through your messengers: we recount their works, yet it is you who work in them,[181] enabling their work to give rise to a living soul.

[175] Day Six: Animals, the "living soul": The sixth day is particularly important: all of humanity appeared in Adam on the sixth day, and, fittingly, the New Adam has come in the sixth age to redeem all of humanity. Here the day is accordingly interpreted as the living soul, the soul of all living humanity.

[176] living creature: Genesis 1:24.

[177] you ordained baptism . . . no one can get in by any other way: See John 3:5. While we may have wondered why Augustine did not use the occasion of his own baptism (see *Conf.* IX.6.14, pp. 239–40) to elaborate on this mystery of Christian initiation, his writings on baptism are profound and numerous. Above all, he stresses the irrevocable "newness" that the Spirit's life-giving waters bestow, stressing charity as indispensable to bringing to fruition what was planted in the soul when plunged into the baptismal font of Christ's own death and Resurrection.

[178] people who refuse to believe unless they see signs and wonders: See John 4:48.

[179] tongues serve as a sign to unbelievers, not to the faithful: See 1 Corinthians 14:22.

[180] this dry land, which you have established upon the waters: See Psalm 135(136):6.

[181] it is you who work in them: See Philippians 2:13.

The land indeed produces it, in the sense that it is the land's need that occasions your preachers' efforts there, just as it was the sea's need that occasioned their summoning from it living things that crawl and birds to fly beneath the vault of heaven. The land needs these no longer, though at that table which you have prepared in the presence of believers[182] it eats a fish[183] raised up from the deep, raised up for the very purpose of watering the parched land.

Although birds are the sea's progeny, they flock over the land,[184] for though human unbelief was the reason why the evangelists' voices were originally needed, believers are daily encouraged and blessed by them too. Nonetheless it is from the land that the living soul takes its rise, because only believers profit by so restraining themselves from attachment to this world[185] that each soul, once dead through trying to live in death-dealing depravity,[186] may live instead for you,[187] who to a pure heart are life-giving delight.

30. No longer must your ministers work with the methods they used amid the waters of unbelief, announcing their message and conveying their meaning through miracles and signs and symbolic expressions. The attention of ignorant people is attracted by such things and gives birth to a wondering fear of the unknown that lies behind these signs; for since Adam's children have forgotten you, and now hide from your presence[188] and become the abyss, no other access to faith is open

---

[182] *that table which you have prepared in the presence of believers:* See Psalm 22(23):5.

[183] *it eats a fish:* Just as in Augustine's day proclamation of the Word preceded the sacrifice of the altar, here too preaching gives way to the holy table's "fish" (remember, the Greek *icthus* is an anagram for Christ: i=*iesus*; c=*christus*; th=*theos*, or God; u=*uious*, son; s=*soter*, savior), which paradoxically comes up from the sea (i.e., taken from humanity) to water the otherwise dry earth.

[184] *birds are the sea's progeny, they flock over the land:* See Genesis 1:22.

[185] *believers profit by so restraining attachment to this world:* See James 1:27.

[186] *each soul, once dead through trying to live in death-dealing depravity:* See 1 Timothy 5:6.

[187] *may live instead for you:* See 2 Corinthians 5:15.

[188] *Adam's children have forgotten you, and now hide from your presence:* See Genesis 3:8.

to them. But now it is on land that stands clear from the eddying deep that your ministers must work, and there make themselves an example to the faithful[189] by living alongside them and arousing them to imitation.

Thus it comes about that believers do not merely listen, but listen with a view to acting on what they hear, when they are bidden, *Seek God, and your soul will live*,[190] and so the earth will bring forth a living creature; and again, *Shape yourselves no longer to the standards of this world*,[191] but restrain yourselves from it. The soul that dies by craving lives by avoiding what it craved. Restrain yourselves from the monstrous savagery of pride, from the luxurious inertia of self-indulgence, and from sham pretension to knowledge,[192] so that wild beasts may become gentle, domestic animals responsive and snakes harmless. These animals symbolize the impulses of the soul; but arrogant self-importance and wallowing in lust and poisonous curiosity are the impulses of a soul that is dead, though not dead in such a way as to be motionless. It dies by forsaking the fountain of life,[193] and thus is welcomed by this passing world and shaped to it:

31. But the fountain of eternal life is your Word, O God, which passes not,[194] and so it is by your word that we are dissuaded from drifting away. *Shape yourselves no longer to the standards of this world*, we are warned. Through this fount of life the land can produce a living being; that is to say, by your word, delivered through your evangelists, it is enabled to bring forth a soul that restrains itself from excesses by imitating those who imitate your Christ.[195] To act so is to act *according to its*

---

[189] *make themselves an example to the faithful*: See 1 Thessalonians 1:7.

[190] Seek God, and your soul will live: Psalm 68:33(69:32).

[191] Shape yourselves no longer to the standards of this world: Romans 12:2.

[192] *Restrain yourselves . . . from sham pretension to knowledge*: See 1 Timothy 6:20.

[193] *soul that is dead, though not . . . motionless. It dies by forsaking the fountain of life*: See Jeremiah 2:13. Death is not a motionless state but, rather, an averting from God and consequent conforming to the world.

[194] *the fountain of eternal life is your Word, O God, which passes not*: See John 1:1; 4:14; 6:69; Matthew 24:35.

[195] *imitating those who imitate your Christ*: See 1 Corinthians 4:16; 11:1.

kind,[196] for friendship prompts us to emulation,[197] as Paul suggests when he urges, *Adapt yourselves to me, as I have adapted myself to you.*[198]

The wild beasts in this living soul will thus become good and gentle in their conduct, as you have commanded us to be: *Be gentle in all you do, and you will be loved by everyone.*[199] The domestic animals will be good too, discovering that when they have eaten they do not suffer from excess, and when they have not eaten they feel none the worse.[200] The snakes will be good, not dangerous and liable to hurt people but astute and wary,[201] given to exploring the nature of this world of time to whatever degree is necessary that through created things eternity may be glimpsed and understood.[202] These animals are the servants of reason and are truly alive when they are held back from fatally dissipating themselves, and tamed to goodness.

Chapter 22

Humanity in God's image and likeness

32. Our attachment to this world brought us to death's door by evil living; but see, O Lord, our God and creator, once the soul has controlled its hankering for worldly things, and has begun to revive by living a good life, and that word which you spoke through your apostle has become a reality in it: *Shape yourselves no longer to the standards of this world*, something else follows, for you immediately added, *but allow yourselves to be reformed by the renewal of your minds.* You do not say, "reformed

---

[196] according to its kind: Genesis 1:21.

[197] *for friendship prompts us to emulation:* See Ecclesiastes 4:4, Old Latin.

[198] Adapt yourselves to me, as I have adapted myself to you: Galatians 4:12.

[199] Be gentle in all you do, and you will be loved by everyone: Sirach 3:19(17).

[200] *when they have eaten they do not suffer from excess, . . . feel none the worse:* See 1 Corinthians 8:8.

[201] *snakes will be good, not dangerous . . . but astute and wary:* See Genesis 3:1; Matthew 10:16–17.

[202] *through created things eternity may be glimpsed and understood:* See Romans 1:20.

according to your kind," as though imitating some neighbor who had gone ahead, or taking some better person as the norm for your lives. No, for you, O God, did not say, "Let there be man, according to his kind," but *Let us make man according to our image and likeness,*[203] for you meant us to discern your will for ourselves. Such was your steward's aim[204] in urging, *Allow yourselves to be reformed by the renewal of your minds, that you may be able to discern what is God's will, what is good and pleasing to him and perfect,*[205] for while he had begotten children through the gospel[206] he did not want them to remain for ever babies whom he must feed on milk and care for like a nurse.[207] This is why you do not say, "Let there be man," but, *Let us make . . .*; nor do you say, "according to his kind," but, *according to our image and likeness.*[208]

A person thus made new considers your truth and understands it. He does not need some other human being to explain it to him so that he may imitate his own kind; you explain it to him, so that he can discern for himself what is your will, what is good and pleasing to you and perfect. And since he now has the capacity to understand, you teach him to contemplate the Trinity in Unity, the Unity that is Trinity. This is why after the plural expression, *Let us make man,* the singular is implied by the next verse, *So God made man in his own*

---

[203] Let us make man according to our image and likeness: Genesis 1:26.

[204] *your steward's aim:* See 1 Corinthians 4:1, the image of the theologian as steward again.

[205] Allow yourselves to be reformed . . . what is good and pleasing to him and perfect: Romans 12:2.

[206] *begotten children through the gospel:* See 1 Corinthians 4:15.

[207] *babies whom he must feed on milk and care for like a nurse:* See 1 Corinthians 3:1–2; 1 Thessalonians 2:7.

[208] *This is why you do not say, "Let there be man,"* . . . *according to our image and likeness:* God's desire for humanity is make each of us like himself. This is possible, however, because we were first made in his divine image, and in sending his Son, the Father longs to restore that divine icon within each of our souls: "Just as a coin, you see, if it's rubbed with earth, loses the emperor's image, so the human mind, if it is rubbed with earthly lusts, loses God's image. However, along comes Christ, the master of the mint, to strike the coins afresh . . . and he will show you that God is looking for his image" (*Sermon* 229W).

image,[209] and after the plural *according to our image and like-ness* the singular is suggested by *in the image of God he created him*. In this way man is renewed in the knowledge of God in accordance with the image of his creator.[210] He becomes a Spirit-filled person, fit to judge of any matters that call for judgment, though he himself is not subject to the judgment of his fellows.

Chapter 23

33. "Judging everything" means that human beings have domin-ion over the fish of the sea and the birds in the sky and all domestic animals and wild beasts, and the whole earth, and all reptiles that crawl there.[211] They exercise it through their intelligent minds, which give them insight into whatever con-cerns the Spirit of God. Were this not the case, human beings, for all their high dignity, would not understand; they would be on a level with senseless beasts and become like them.[212]

This is why in your Church, O God, persons gifted with the Spirit judge of spiritual things in virtue of the grace you have given her,[213] for we are of your craftsmanship, created for good

---

[209] So God made man in his own image: Genesis 1:27.

[210] *man is renewed . . . in accordance with the image of his creator*: See Coloss-ians 3:10. Later, Augustine will make clear that God desires to bring the human person toward a divine "likeness", not through humanity's own natural powers, of course, but through the "likeness" provided in the Son's Incarnation: "the human person was made not entirely equal to God, as he was not born from him but created by him ... that is, he is not made equal by an equivalence but approaches it by a certain likeness" (*On the Trinity* VII.6.12). It this union with Christ and his Holy Spirit that thus spiritualizes the human person, enabling him to participate in the divine life, bestowing upon him the divine attributes of charity, mercy, incorruptibility, immortality, and so on. Augustine here stresses the ability to judge rightly for those who have been filled with the Spirit. In becoming like God, they see rightly the things of God as well as show them-selves to be lords over brute creation as well as obedient masters over their own lives.

[211] *human beings have dominion over . . . the whole earth, and all reptiles that crawl there*: See Genesis 1:26.

[212] *on a level with senseless beasts and become like them*: See Psalm 48:13 (49:12).

[213] *persons gifted with the Spirit judge . . . in virtue of the grace you have given her*: See 1 Corinthians 3:10.

works.[214] Judgment is exercised not only by the holders of spiritual authority but by those also who are subject to them in the Spirit, for it is in this sense that you have created humanity male and female in the sphere of your spiritual grace: in respect of bodily sexuality male and female here have no significance, any more than do differences between Jew and Greek, slave and free.[215] Spirit-filled persons, then, whether they rule or obey, judge in the light of the Spirit,[216] but not in respect of the splendors of wisdom ablaze in the vault of heaven,[217] for it would be presumptuous to pass judgment on an authority so sublime. Nor do they judge your book itself, because to that we submit our intellects, even if something in it is less than luminous, holding it certain that what is impenetrable to our gaze is nonetheless spoken rightly and with truth; for even a person who is already in the Spirit, already made new in the knowledge of God in accordance with the image of our creator,[218] must be a doer of the law,[219] not a judge of it.

Nor, again, can such a person judge of the distinction between spiritual and carnal people. These are known in your sight, our God, but are not yet clearly distinguished in ours by the criterion of any deeds, which might enable us to tell them by their fruits.[220] You, Lord, know them already, and have drawn your distinction and issued your call, before ever you made the firmament.

Nor, finally, does such a person, however spiritual, judge of the mudbound races of this world, for what business of his are

---

[214] *we are of your craftsmanship, created for good works:* See Ephesians 2:10.

[215] *in respect of bodily sexuality male and female . . . slave and free:* See Galatians 3:28. Grace is not bestowed according to natural attributes, so in one sense "male" and "female" have no significance when it comes to meriting supernatural gifts.

[216] *Spirit-filled persons, then, whether they rule or obey, judge in the light of the Spirit:* See 1 Corinthians 2:15.

[217] *splendors of wisdom ablaze in the vault of heaven:* See Genesis 1:15, 17.

[218] *a person who is already in the Spirit, . . . in accordance with the image of our creator:* See Colossians 3:9–10.

[219] *must be a doer of the law:* See James 4:11.

[220] *might enable us to tell them by their fruits:* See Matthew 7:20.

outsiders,[221] when he cannot know which of them will forsake the sea for your sweet grace, and which will remain in that unendingly bitter godlessness?

34. This is why human beings whom you have created in your image did not receive dominion over the luminaries set in the heavenly vault, nor over the hidden heaven itself, nor over the day and the night which you called into being before you established the vault, nor over the amassed waters known as sea. But they were entrusted with dominion over the fish of the sea and the birds in the sky and all domestic cattle, and over the whole land and all the reptiles that crawl upon it. They judge and approve what they find done rightly, but condemn anything they find amiss; and this they do through the celebration of those rites whereby people whom your mercy has sought out in the vast ocean are initiated; or at the solemn rite which makes present the fish raised up from the deep and devoutly eaten by the faithful; or by preaching, which through exegesis, discussion and argument attempts to make plain the meaning of your words, while subjecting itself always to the authority of your book as though winging its way beneath the sky; and through blessing and invoking you, so that as these sounds break from our mouths and make themselves heard, the populace may answer, "Amen."[222] That all these explanations have to be delivered through the spoken word is due to the needs of that abyss which is this world and the blindness of the flesh, for when people cannot see the truth under consideration, it must be dinned into their ears. Although the birds flock over the land, they originate from the waters, and we can see why.

A person endowed with the Spirit also exercises judgment by approving what he finds proper and rebuking anything he finds amiss in the activities and conduct of the faithful. He

---

[221] *does such a person, however spiritual, judge . . . for what business of his are outsiders*: See 1 Corinthians 5:12.

[222] *the populace may answer, "Amen"*: Creation gives way to liturgy with the entire cosmos praising God (each in its own way) with a resounding "Amen". Such liturgy, however, is made possible by expositing Scripture "from below", that is, always in submission to the biblical text.

commends their almsgiving as he would fruitful soil; and he judges favorably the affections tamed to gentleness that characterize a living soul, its chastity, fasting,[223] and devout reflection on the experiences of the senses. In short, he can be said to exercise judgment in areas where he also has authority to correct what is wrong.

Chapter 24

"Increase and multiply"

35. But now to something puzzling: what sort of mystery have we here?[224] You bless human beings, O Lord, commanding them to increase and multiply and fill the earth.[225] Are you giving us some kind of hint here? Do you not mean us to understand something? You did not confer the same blessing on the light, which you named "day," or on the vault of the sky, or on its luminaries, or on stars, earth or sea: why not? I would have said that you, our God, who created us according to your image, willed to lavish this blessing on humankind exclusively; yes, that is what I would have said, were it not that you gave it equally to the fish and the sea monsters, bidding them swarm and fill the waters of the sea, and commanding the birds also to flock over the land.[226] Or again I might have said that this blessing was restricted to those classes of creatures which give birth and propagate themselves, if I had found it also applied to shrubs and bushes and land animals. But the fact is that the command, *Increase and multiply*,[227] is not addressed

---

[223] *the affections tamed to gentleness that characterize a living soul, its chastity, fasting*: See 2 Corinthians 6:5–6.

[224] *"Increase and multiply" ... what sort of mystery have we here?* See Sirach 39:26. This command to multiply is unique to human persons, though its fullest meaning is not immediately clear. Augustine ruminates on this phrase at length.

[225] *O Lord, commanding them to increase and multiply and fill the earth*: See Genesis 1:28.

[226] *you gave it equally to the fish and the sea monsters, . . . birds also to flock over the land*: See Genesis 1:22.

[227] Increase and multiply: Genesis 1:22, 28.

to vegetation or trees, or to beasts or reptiles, although all these keep up their numbers and conserve their species by giving birth, as do fish and birds and humans.

36. What am I to say, then, O my Light, O Truth? That this is without significance, and idly so expressed? That is unthinkable, most careful Father: far be it from a servant of your word to say such a thing.[228] If I do not understand what you mean to convey by this saying, let better men make better use of it—people more intelligent than I, in the measure of the wisdom you have granted to each of them.[229] But may my confession too be pleasing in your sight when I confess that I do not believe, Lord, that you spoke in these terms to no purpose. I will not pass over in silence the meaning that comes to my mind when this passage is read, for it is true in itself, and I do not see what is to stop me responding sensitively to figurative expressions in your books.

Now I know that something may be signified in a variety of ways through material means, yet understood in only one way by the mind, or, conversely, understood in multiple ways by the mind, although signified in only one way materially. An example is love of God and our neighbor: it is simple in itself, but in what a variety of mysterious ways, in what tongues without number, and in any one tongue through what innumerable modes of speech is it given tangible expression! This corresponds to the way in which the offspring of the waters increases and multiplies.

Then consider another example, you who read this: observe that scripture offers us a single truth, couched in simple words, when it tells us, *In the beginning God made heaven and earth.* But is it not interpreted in manifold ways? Leaving aside fallacious and mistaken theories, are there not divergent schools of true opinion? This corresponds to the increase and multiplication of human progeny.

---

[228] *What am I to say, . . . to say such a thing:* Every scriptural word and beat conveys some divine truth that only the careful and the prayerful will discover.

[229] *in the measure of the wisdom you have granted to each of them:* See Romans 12:3; 1 Corinthians 3:5.

37. So then, if we consider the nature of creatures as they are in themselves, not allegorically but literally, the command, *Increase and multiply*, is appropriate to all those which are propagated from seed. If, however, we take it for granted that the statement is figurative—and I am inclined to think that this was what scripture intended, for it cannot have confined this blessing to the offspring of sea creatures and humans without good reason—then we do indeed find things multiplying everywhere: among both spiritual and corporeal creatures, represented by heaven and earth; among souls both righteous and unjust, described as light and darkness; among the sacred writers through whom the law was mediated, described as the vault fixed firm between upper waters and lower; in the throng of peoples brewing bitterness, who are called "sea"; in the zeal of devout souls, represented by dry land; in the works of mercy appropriate to this present life,[230] described as self-seeding plants and fruit-bearing trees; in spiritual gifts bestowed for the good of all,[231] symbolized by the celestial luminaries; in impulses trained to temperance, described as the "living soul."

In all these instances we discover multiplication, increase and growth, but we do not find anything able to increase and multiply in the way that one truth may be articulated in various modes, or one articulation understood in many different senses; this we find only amid signs displayed by corporeal things and concepts of the mind. Deep-seated carnality and its needs suggest that we take the offspring of the waters to represent signs displayed materially; but the fecundity of our human reason leads us to interpret the breeding of humans as a symbol of truths processed by the intelligence. And we believe that this, Lord, is why your command, *Increase and multiply*, was issued to each of these two; for I assume that by this blessing you granted us the faculty and the power both to articulate in various forms something we have grasped in a single way in our minds, and

---

[230] *in the works of mercy appropriate to this present life*: See 1 Timothy 4:8.
[231] *spiritual gifts bestowed for the good of all*: See 1 Corinthians 12:7.

to interpret in many different senses something we have read, which, though obscure, is couched in simple terms.[232]

Thus the waters of the sea are filled, for it takes a variety of signs to stir them; and so too do human generations populate the land whose aridity bespeaks its thirst for knowledge, the land where reason holds sway.

Chapter 25

God assigns them their food

38. I also want to say what the following verses of your scripture bring to mind, Lord my God. I will say it without scruple, because I shall be speaking the truth that is in me by your inspiration, since you have willed me to say what these words mean to me. I do not believe I could speak truthfully under inspiration from anyone other than you, since you are the Truth, whereas all human beings are liars.[233] Thus anyone who tells lies is speaking from what is his own;[234] and in order to speak the truth, I must speak from what is yours.

Well now, you gave us *for food every seeding plant that grows on earth, and every tree that bears fruit yielding seed.*[235] These you gave not to us alone but also to all birds in the sky and land animals and serpents, but you did not give them to the fish or the huge whales. This accords with what we were saying earlier: that these fruits of the earth symbolize and represent in

---

[232] *we believe that this, Lord, is why your command,* Increase and multiply, *is couched in simple terms:* Augustine finally rests upon a figurative interpretation of the command "increase and multiply". This command symbolizes both the capacity of the human intellect to communicate in various ways a single apprehension of the truth as well as to derive multiple senses from Scripture. Thus "increase and multiply" conveys God's command for men and women to apply the full power of their intellects to the multivalent meanings found throughout God's Scriptures.

[233] *you are the Truth, whereas all human beings are liars:* See John 14:6; Psalm 115(116):11.

[234] *anyone who tells lies is speaking from what is his own:* See John 8:44.

[235] *for food every seeding plant ... bears fruit yielding seed:* Genesis 1:29–30.

allegorical terms the works of mercy produced by fertile soil to meet the needs of this present life. The charitable Onesiphorus was soil of this type, and you showed mercy to his household because he often relieved Paul's hardships and was not ashamed to consort with a prisoner.[236] Other brethren did the same and bore similar fruit by supplying from Macedonia what Paul needed.[237] But how disappointed he was over certain other trees which failed to bear him the fruit they owed: *The first time I offered my defense*, he says, *no one stood by me. One and all, they left me in the lurch: may it not be held against them.*[238] For we owe food to those who dispense intelligent teaching to others from their own penetration into divine mysteries, and on this score it is due to them as human beings. We owe it to them also as "living creatures," in that they offer themselves as an example to be followed in every kind of self-restraint. Finally we owe it to them as to birds, in that flocks of blessings fly from them over the land; indeed, *their sound echoed throughout the world.*[239]

Chapter 26

39. Only those who find this food delicious are nourished by it; people whose god is their belly[240] do not enjoy it. As for those who supply the food, it is not what they give that is the fruit, but the intention with which they give. I can plainly see the source of that man's joy who served God, and not his own belly;[241] I see it, and with all my heart I rejoice with him. True, he had received the gifts which the Philippians

---

[236] *Onesiphorus . . . relieved Paul's hardships and was not ashamed to consort with a prisoner*: See 2 Timothy 1:16.

[237] *Other brethren . . . bore similar fruit by supplying from Macedonia what Paul needed*: See 2 Corinthians 11:9.

[238] The first time I offered my defense . . . may it not be held against them: 2 Timothy 4:16.

[239] their sound echoed throughout the world: Psalm 18:5(19:4).

[240] *people whose god is their belly*: See Philippians 3:19.

[241] *that man's joy who served God, and not his own belly*: a reference to Paul; see Romans 16:18.

had sent him through Epaphroditus,[242] but all the same I can see the real source of his joy. What brings him joy feeds him. He is speaking the truth when he tells them, *I am splendidly joyful in the Lord to see you putting forth new shoots of care for me. You used to show your care, but then you wearied.* Long-drawn-out weariness had left them too withered and shriveled to bear fruit in good works, so now Paul rejoices on their account, in that fresh green shoots are appearing, rather than on his own, in having his poverty relieved. He therefore continues, *I am not suggesting that I lack anything. Whatever circumstances I am in, I have learned to be content with them; I know how to endure privation, but I also know how to have enough and to spare. I have been thoroughly initiated into the art of withstanding plenty and hunger, abundance and penury. I am capable of anything in him who strengthens me.*[243]

40. Whence, then, springs your joy, great Paul? What brings you joy, and what nourishes you, a man made new in the knowledge of God, modeled on the image of your creator,[244] a creature truly alive in your heroic continence, a winged tongue uttering mysteries?[245] All these types of living beings are entitled to eat the food in question, as we know. What is your food, then? Joy! Let me hear your next words: *All the same, you did well to share with me in my trouble.*[246]

This is what he rejoices over, and on this he feeds, that they have acted well, not that his own distress has been alleviated. *When I was hard beset you led me into spacious freedom,*[247] he says to you, because he has learned to withstand both abundance and penury in you, who strengthen him.

---

[242] *received the gifts which the Philippians had sent him through Epaphroditus*: See Philippians 4:18.

[243] I am not suggesting that I lack anything ... in him who strengthens me: Philippians 4:11–13.

[244] *a man made new in the knowledge of God, modeled on the image of your creator*: See Colossians 3:9–10.

[245] *a winged tongue uttering mysteries*: See 1 Corinthians 14:2.

[246] All the same, you did well to share with me in my trouble: Philippians 4:14.

[247] When I was hard beset you led me into spacious freedom: Psalm 4:2(1).

For you know yourselves, Philippians, he continues, *that in the early days of my mission, when I set out from Macedonia, no church entered into partnership with me in the business of disbursements and receipts except yourselves alone, for you sent contributions even to Thessalonica, once and then a second time, to defray my expenses.*[248] Now he rejoices in their resumption of these good works and delights over the new growth they are showing, as though over a once-fertile field brought back into good heart.

41. Are we to understand from his words, *You sent to defray my expenses,* that their settling of his money affairs was his motive for such joy? No, not that. How do we know it was not? Because he himself goes on to say, *Not that I seek your gift: all I seek is the fruit accruing to you.*[249] From you, my God, I have learned to distinguish between gift and fruit.[250] The gift is the actual thing given by the person who supplies these necessary goods: it may be cash, food, drink, clothing, shelter, assistance of some kind. But the fruit is the good, upright will of the giver. Our good Master does not simply say, *Anyone who welcomes a prophet;* he specifies: *inasmuch as he is a prophet.* And he says not simply, *Anyone who welcomes a just person,* but adds, *inasmuch as he is a just person.* Only so will the one receive a prophet's reward and the other the reward of a just person. Again, he says not only, *Anyone who gives a cup of cold water to one of my little ones,* but adds, *simply because he is a disciple,* and then goes on to promise, *I tell you, he will not miss his reward.*[251] The gift consists in welcoming the prophet, welcoming the just person, and handing a cup of cold water to a disciple; but the fruit consists in doing it

---

[248] For you know yourselves, Philippians ... to defray my expenses: Philippians 4:15–16.

[249] Not that I seek your gift: all I seek is the fruit accruing to you: Philippians 4:17.

[250] *From you, my God, I have learned to distinguish between gift and fruit:* Here Augustine observes the difference between material goods and virtue. Paul's joy is that the Church in Philippi demonstrates the growth and ripening of spiritual fruits in their generosity and care for him by way of the Christians in Thessalonica. Augustine uses this to underscore the difference between temporal and eternal goods.

[251] Anyone who welcomes a prophet ... I tell you, he will not miss his reward: Matthew 10:41–42.

precisely because the other is a prophet, or a just person, or a disciple. Elijah was fed by a widow who knew that she was feeding a man of God and did it for that reason, and so she sustained him with fruit; but the food brought him by the raven was no more than a gift:[252] not the spirit of Elijah but only the outer man was fed, the outer man who could have died for lack of such food.

Chapter 27

42. I would say, therefore, what I believe to be true in your sight, Lord, with regard to uninstructed and unbelieving persons, the kind who need preliminary rites and spectacular miracles if they are to be initiated into faith and won over, the people who, as we have said, are typified by fishes and whales. When such people welcome your servants, offering them bodily refreshment or any kind of timely assistance in their daily lives, but do so without knowing why it should be done or what is implied, they do not truly feed their guests, nor are the guests fed by them, because no holy or upright will prompts the hosts' actions, nor do your servants yet find in the gifts received any fruit over which to rejoice. So true is it that our spirit feeds on what gives it joy. This is why the fishes and whales are not permitted to eat the foods which spring up only from soil already marked out and emergent from the bitter waves of the sea.

Chapter 28

"God saw that it was exceedingly good" (against the Manichees)

43. And you looked upon all the things you have made, O God, and lo, they are exceedingly good;[253] we too look upon

---

[252] *Elijah was fed by a widow . . . was no more than a gift*: See 1 Kings (= 3 Kings) 17:6–16.

[253] *you looked upon all the things you have made*, O God, *and lo, they are exceedingly good*: See Genesis 1:31.

them, and even in our eyes they are exceedingly good. In every successive act of creation you had commanded some class of creature to be, and it came into being, and you saw that each was good. Seven times, according to my count, does scripture relate that you looked on what you have made and found it good; but this eighth time you looked on all your works together, and lo, not merely are they good, but taken as a whole they are exceedingly good. Severally good, they are exceedingly good all together. Every beautiful body conveys the same message, for a body consisting of beautiful limbs is far more beautiful than its component parts individually, because though each one has its own loveliness, it is only through their exquisite coordination that the whole organism attains its perfection.

Chapter 29

44. I now applied my mind to discover whether you really did look upon your works seven or eight times when you found them pleasing, and I discovered in your act of seeing no element of temporality which would explain to me how you could have looked so many times at what you had made. I therefore appealed to you: "Surely, Lord, this scripture of yours is true, since you are its author and you are truthful—indeed, Truth itself?[254] Why, then, do you tell me that there is no element of time in your seeing, whereas your scripture tells me that day after day you saw that your work was good? I was even able to count these occasions, and find out how many times you looked at your creatures."

You reply to me, because you are my God, and you speak loudly in your servant's inner ear, bursting through my deafness;[255] you cry out to me, "Listen, human creature: what my scripture says, I myself say, but whereas scripture says it in terms of time, my Word is untouched by time, because he subsists with me eternally, equal to myself. What you see through my

---

[254] *Lord, this scripture of yours is true, since you are . . . Truth itself*: See John 3:33; 14:6.

[255] *You reply to me, . . . bursting through my deafness*: See Conf. X.27.38.

Spirit, I see, just as what you say through my Spirit, I say. You see these things in terms of time, but I do not see in time, nor when you say these things in temporal fashion do I speak in a way conditioned by time."[256]

Chapter 30

45. I heard your answer, O Lord my God, and from this truth I sucked out a drop of sweetness. I understood why some people do not find your creatures pleasing; they hold that you were driven by necessity when you built such things as the heavens and the constellations, and that these had already been created somewhere else and by some other power. You, they say, merely assembled them, fitted and welded them together when you were laboriously constructing the ramparts of the world after vanquishing your enemies, to barricade them in and ensure that they would never again rebel against you. Other things, such as all the animals and the minutest life-forms and everything that clings to the soil by its roots, they do not believe you made or even put together at all; a hostile intelligence, some other nature not created by you and working against you, spawned and shaped them in the lower regions of the world. People who allege this are mad, because they do not contemplate your works through your Spirit, nor recognize you in them.

Chapter 31

46. It is different for people who see creation through your Spirit, for you are seeing it through their eyes. Thus when such people see that these things are good, you are seeing that they are good; whatever created things please them for your sake, it is you who are arousing their delight in these things; and anything that gives us joy through your Spirit gives you joy in

---

[256] *You see these things in terms of time, . . . I speak in a way conditioned by time*: Augustine resolves an apparent tension in Scripture that the divine nature is above time: Scripture chooses to describe God temporally because Scripture's interlocutors are inevitably conditioned by time, and so God condescends to communicate in terms and images intelligible to temporal creatures.

us. Yet scripture asks, *Who knows the reality of anyone, except that person's own inward spirit? So too no one knows the reality of God except God's own Spirit. But we,* says scripture, *we have not received the spirit of this world, but the Spirit which is of God, that we may know what gifts have been bestowed on us by God.*[257]

Plainly I am bound to say that no one knows the reality of God except the Spirit of God. How, then, can we too know the gifts that God has given us? This is the answer that comes to me: if we know something through his Spirit, it is still true to say that *no one knows* it *except God's own Spirit*; for just as it could rightly be said to people who spoke in the Spirit of God, *It is not you who are speaking,*[258] so too is it rightly said to those who know anything in the Spirit of God, "It is not you who are knowing this." With equal justice could it be said to people who contemplate creation in the Spirit of God, "It is not you who are seeing this." If, then, seeing something in God's Spirit, they perceive it to be good, it is evidently not they, but God, who sees that it is good.[259]

One point of view, therefore, is that of someone who thinks a good thing evil; of such people mention has been made already. Another approach is to see that it is good, as many do who find your good creation pleasant, but fail to find you within it, and look for their enjoyment in creation itself rather than in you. Different from both is the attitude of one who sees it

---

[257] *Who knows the reality of anyone, ... what gifts have been bestowed on us by God:* 1 Corinthians 2:11–12.

[258] *It is not you who are speaking:* Matthew 10:20.

[259] *God, who sees that it is good:* Seeing reality from God's perspective is a sign obviously of God's life in the human soul, and here it is God who sees in and through us. This is an instance of Augustine's doctrine of deification at work: elevating the human so as to act and think like the divine. It is asking God to grant us the gift of "deified eyes", as Augustine will exhort his congregation later (*Sermon* 126.14). In claiming God himself operates in and through the spiritualized Christian, Augustine can thus at times exhort his congregation to "rejoice and then give thanks that we have become not only Christians, but Christ himself. Do you understand and grasp, brethren, God's grace toward us? Marvel and rejoice: we have become Christ, or if he is the head, we are the members; he and we together are the whole man" (*Homilies on the Gospel of John* 21.8; quoted in the *Catechism of the Catholic Church,* no. 795).

as good in such a way that their God views its goodness through the person's human eyes.[260] This means that God is loved in what he has made. But he could not be loved were it not through the Spirit he has given us, *because the love of God has been poured out into our hearts through the Holy Spirit bestowed upon us.*[261] Through him we see that everything is good which in any degree has being, because it derives from him who has being in no degree at all, but is simply *He Is.*[262]

Chapter 32

Summary of literal exegesis; man and woman

47. Thanks be to you, O Lord. We contemplate heaven and earth, whether this be understood as the upper and lower regions of your material creation, or your spiritual as distinct from your embodied creatures. We see also the adornment of these parts, of which either the whole bulk of the physical world, or the entire created universe, consists, for we see light created and separated from darkness. We behold the vault of heaven, which means either the barrier between the spiritual waters on high and the lower waters which constitute the primordial matter of the world, or else the airy space of sky through which birds freely wander, since this too goes by the name "heaven." Across it they wing their way between the

---

[260] *One point of view . . . God views its goodness through the person's human eyes*: There are three ways of viewing creation: (1) the Manichean view, that creation is evil, (2) the later Neoplatonic view, that creation is good but in no way the economy of salvation, and (3) the Christian view, that creation is good and that God is to be known and loved on account of his making it. These views represent various views of Providence in antiquity.

[261] *because the love of God . . . through the Holy Spirit bestowed upon us*: Romans 5:5.

[262] *Through him we see . . . He Is*: Exodus 3:14. It is only by the Spirit that one can practice this third view of Providence. The Spirit enables us to see and love God in creation because such vision recognizes that the existence and goodness of creation is contingent on God. As Augustine "winds down", this is his way of asking us to trust that our life's stories are trustworthy and that God has always been providentially present to us.

waters which sail overhead in cloudy vapor, bedewing the earth even on fine nights, and the heavy waters that surge on earth. We contemplate the beauty of waters gathered together in the wide expanses of the sea, and the dry land, still bare as it rises from the sea, or endowed with visible, organized form to bring forth plants and trees. We see the lamps shining on high, the sun flooding the day and the moon and stars bringing solace to the night, and all of them serving to indicate periods of time and mark its passage. On every side we see the watery world teeming with fish and whales, and with birds too, because their flight is upborne on air made denser by evaporation from the waters. We regard the fair face of the earth adorned with land animals; and we see humankind, made in your image and likeness, set over all these irrational living creatures in virtue of this same image and likeness to you, which resides in its reason and intelligence. And just as within the human soul one faculty deliberates and takes decisions, while another must be submissive and obedient, so too was woman made physically subordinate to man. Though equal to him by nature in her rational mind and intelligence, with respect to bodily sexuality she was subjected to the male, even as the impulse to action must be submissive in order to conceive from the rational mind the sagacity to act aright.

All these things we see. Severally they are good, and together they are exceedingly good.

Chapter 33

Summary of allegorical exegesis

48. Your creation sings praise to you[263] so that we may love you, and we love you so that praise may be offered to you by your creation. Created things have their beginning and their end in time, their rising and setting, their growth and decline, their beauty of form and their formlessness; and thus they have

---

[263] *Your creation sings praise to you:* See Psalm 144(145):10; Daniel 3:57.

their morning and evening, though sometimes this is hidden, sometimes plainly seen. Inevitably so, because they were made by you out of nothing: not made from you, nor from any matter not of your making, nor from anything pre-existent, but from concreated matter: that is, matter which you created formless at the same instant that you gave it form, without any interval. Although the primal matter of heaven and earth is something other than the form of heaven and earth, you made their matter from nothingness, and their formed condition from unformed matter, and both simultaneously, so that form followed on the heels of matter without the least interruption or lapse of time.

Chapter 34

49. We also scrutinized the text to discover what figurative meaning you intended to suggest in willing these things to happen, or at any rate to be written, in this particular order. And in your Word, your only Son, we saw them severally as good and collectively as exceedingly good; for what we saw was heaven and earth, the Head and the body of the Church[264] which you predestined before time began, when there was neither morning nor evening.

But when you began to give effect in time to your predetermined plan, when you purposed to bring your hidden decrees[265] to light and give form to our unformed state (formless it was because with our sins weighing us down we had been dragged away from you into the darkness of the deep, but your good Spirit[266] was hovering overhead to help us in our time of need), then you justified the godless,[267] marked them out from the wicked, and established the vault of your authoritative scripture between the upper creatures who were docile to you, and the lower who were subject to them.

---

[264] *your Word, your only Son, . . . Head and the body of the Church*: See Colossians 1:18.
[265] *your predetermined plan, . . . to bring your hidden decrees*: See Psalm 50:8(51:6).
[266] *your good Spirit*: See Psalm 142(143):10.
[267] *you justified the godless*: See Romans 4:5.

Then you gathered the great horde of unbelievers into a cohesive mass, which would throw into relief the zealous efforts of the faithful who were to bear fruit for you in works of mercy, even to the point of distributing their worldly goods to the poor[268] and so winning wealth in heaven.

After this you kindled special lamps in the vault; these are your saints, entrusted with the word of life,[269] whose sublime authority was attested by their spiritual gifts.[270] Through them you drew forth sacraments from corporeal matter, palpable miracles and doctrine in harmony with your overarching scripture, all designed to instill faith into unbelieving Gentiles, though apt to shed their benediction upon the faithful as well.

Then you gave form to the believing soul, the soul truly alive because by robust self-control it had reduced its impulses to good order.[271] Its mind was now subject to you alone, and needed no human norm to imitate, for you made it new after your own image and in your likeness, and subordinated its rational activity to the sovereignty of intellect, as woman is to man.

Finally you willed that all your ministers, whose work is necessary in this present life to bring your faithful to maturity, should be provided for in the temporal sphere by these same faithful, whose services will bear fruit for the life to come.

All these things we see to be exceedingly good, because you see them in us, you who have given us the Spirit to enable us to see them, and in them to love you.[272]

---

[268] *distributing their worldly goods to the poor:* See 1 Corinthians 13:3.

[269] *special lamps in the vault . . . entrusted with the word of life:* See Philippians 2:15–16; John 6:69.

[270] *whose sublime authority was attested by their spiritual gifts:* See 1 Corinthians 12:7.

[271] *you gave form to the believing soul, . . . reduced its impulses to good order:* The baptized Church loves rightly, now being conformed to the image and likeness of God.

[272] *All these things we see to be exceedingly good, . . . to love you:* This serves as a nice summary, as the purpose throughout Book XIII has been to underscore how the Spirit enables the Church to love God through creation, beginning with our neighbor.

Chapter 35

Conclusion: rest on the seventh day

50. Give us peace, Lord God, for you have given us all else;[273] give us the peace that is repose, the peace of the Sabbath, and the peace that knows no evening.[274] This whole order of exceedingly good things, intensely beautiful as it is, will pass away when it has served its purpose: these things too will have their morning and their evening.[275]

Chapter 36

51. But the seventh day has no evening and sinks toward no sunset, for you sanctified it that it might abide for ever. After completing your exceedingly good works you rested on the seventh day, though you achieved them in repose; and you willed your book to tell us this as a promise that when our works are finished (works exceedingly good inasmuch as they are your gift to us) we too may rest in you, in the Sabbath of eternal life.

Chapter 37

52. And then you will rest in us, as now you work in us, and your rest will be rest through us as now those works of yours are wrought through us. But you yourself, Lord, are ever working,

---

[273] *Give us peace, Lord God, for you have given us all else*: See Isaiah 26:12; Numbers 6:26.

[274] *give us the peace that is repose, . . . and the peace that knows no evening*: See 2 Thessalonians 3:16.

[275] *This whole order of exceedingly good things . . . will have their morning and their evening*: See Genesis 1:5–31. In this way we see how the six days of creation lead to the eternal sabbath, God's rest here being a metaphor for the Church finally eternally triumphant. That "the world was created for the sake of the Church" (*Shepherd of Hermas* [*Pastor Hermae*], vision 2.4.1; quoted in the *Catechism of the Catholic Church*, no. 760) was standard for the Fathers, and orienting all of creation toward its Creator, Augustine likewise situates and subordinates all things in Christ and his Church.

ever resting. You neither see for a time nor change for a time nor enjoy repose for a time, yet you create our temporal seeing and time itself and our repose after time.

Chapter 38

53. We, therefore, see these things you have made, because they exist, but for you it is different: they exist because you see them. Moreover when we see that they exist, we see it outside ourselves, but when we see that they are good, we see it by inner vision, whereas you see them as created in no other place than where you saw them as non-existent things you willed to create.

Once our heart had conceived by your Spirit we made a fresh start and began to act well, though at an earlier stage we had been impelled to wrongdoing and abandoned you; but you, O God undivided and good, have never ceased to act well. Some of our works are indeed good, thanks to your Gift, but they will not last for ever, and when they are done we hope that we shall rest in your immense holiness. But you, the supreme Good, need no other good and are eternally at rest, because you yourself are your rest.[276]

What human can empower another human to understand these things? What angel can grant understanding to another angel? What angel to a human? Let us rather ask of you, seek in you, knock at your door. Only so will we receive, only so find, and only so will the door be opened to us. Amen.[277]

---

[276] *you yourself are your rest*: Our hearts are restless until we rest in God, who is himself rest; Augustine ends the *Confessions* by asking to be received in the eternal door of God's rest.

[277] *ask of you, seek in you, knock at your door . . . so will the door be opened to us. Amen*: See Matthew 7:7–8.

Contemporary Criticism

The *Confessions*: Augustine's First Treatise on Grace

Joseph T. Lienhard, S.J.
Fordham University

Saint Augustine of Hippo is known to tradition as the Doctor of Grace. During the last twenty years of his life, he wrote tirelessly in defense of God's grace, and of all that grace implied. His writings in those years were not simply abstractions; his theology of grace was rooted in his experience of grace, an overwhelming experience that changed his life forever. Augustine had tried to recount that experience in his *Confessions*. Thus the *Confessions* is Augustine's first treatise on grace, understood as God's freely given gift by which he moves the human will to choose (freely) the good or the better.

Unlike some other converts, Augustine did not immediately set down his conversion story in writing. He did not begin to write the *Confessions* until 397, after he was ordained a bishop, and more than ten years after his experience in the garden at Milan. Many reasons have been proposed for this delay. The one that makes the most sense, though, is that Augustine did not fully understand what had happened to him until he reflected on the Epistle to the Romans in 396. That reflection, which Augustine recorded in a book, *To Simplicianus: On Various Questions*,[1] brought him, for the first time, to a full understanding of his earlier life: that God's Providence had been guiding him throughout his life, and that the "conversion" of 386 was not his decision, but the call of grace. Augustine was finally free to understand his life and to interpret it as a guide to others. Thus, the *Confessions* is his first treatise on grace.

---

[1] See John H. S. Burleigh, *Augustine: Earlier Writings*, Library of Christian Classics (Philadelphia: Westminster, 1953), pp. 376–406.

Augustine and Simplicianus

It was Simplicianus, at the time a priest in Milan, who encouraged Augustine in 396 to reflect on parts of the Epistle to the Romans, and thus was the one who brought Augustine to his first full understanding of the workings of grace. Simplicianus is a somewhat mysterious but fascinating figure in the fourth-century Latin Church, and a figure worth considering briefly for his influence on Augustine and on key figures in Augustine's life.

Simplicianus was born around 324. A fervent Christian even in his early years, he was well educated, and he traveled widely out of interest in theology. Around 354, he was in Rome, and there he was the adviser—spiritual director, we might say—to Marius Victorinus. Augustine recounts the conversion of Marius Victorinus to Christianity in Book VIII of the *Confessions*, surely as an example of the move of a highly educated intellectual and teacher into the Christian faith and the Christian Church, a model for Augustine himself.

As Augustine recounts it, Marius Victorinus was an elderly man when Simplicianus met him in Rome. He was learned and skilled in all the liberal studies; he had read many philosophical works, and he had been the teacher of many noble senators. A statue of him had even been erected in the Roman forum to honor him as a teacher. But, up to his old age, he had remained a pagan, a worshipper of idols; he even defended the whole array of pagan deities with thundering eloquence.

Then, however, Victorinus began to read the Christian scriptures; beyond that, he searched into all sorts of Christian writings. He was convinced of the truth in these writings, and one day he said to Simplicianus privately, "I am already a Christian, you know." Simplicianus answered, "I will not believe that, nor count you among Christians, until I see you in Christ's Church." Victorinus laughed and said, "It's the walls that make Christians, then?" Victorinus liked the joke and repeated it often to Simplicianus. In his heart, he was afraid of offending his friends, who were still pagans. Victorinus eventually realized how wrong it was to be ashamed of the humble rites of the Church while he was proud of the sacrilegious rites of the demons. In a moment of impulse, he said to Simplicianus, "Let us go to church: I want to become a Christian." [2]

When the priest Simplicianus narrated this story to Augustine, a web of relationships began to form among Augustine, Simplicianus, Ambrose, and Marius Victorinus. After his years in Rome, Simplicianus had gone to Milan. When Ambrose was elected bishop, even before he was baptized, Simplicianus instructed him in the faith and helped him during his first few years as bishop. Augustine even calls Simplicianus Ambrose's father in the faith (see *Conf.* VIII.2.3); the books of the Platonists, which Augustine was to read, were translated into Latin by Marius Victorinus, Simplicianus' convert. During his time in Milan, Augustine found Simplicianus easier to converse with than Ambrose, and a friendship developed between them. [3]

Simplicianus himself never wrote anything, [4] but he was a stimulus to others. Ambrose attests [5] that Simplicianus encouraged him to preach about Saint Paul's letters, but Simplicianus' interest in Saint Paul fits into a larger pattern. Beginning around 350, Latin theologians began to show a remarkable interest in interpreting Saint Paul's letters. [6] Marius Victorinus himself wrote commentaries on Galatians, Philippians, and Ephesians. [7] An unknown author, called the Ambrosiaster since the sixteenth century, [8] wrote (in Rome,

----

[2] Saint Augustine, *The Confessions*, ed. David Vincent Meconi, S.J., Ignatius Critical Editions (San Francisco: Ignatius Press, 2012), VIII.2.4, p. 199. Subsequent quotations from this edition will be cited in the text. References are to book, section, and paragraph.

[3] See *City of God* X.29; Paulinus of Milan, *Life of Ambrose* 46.49.

[4] See Gennadius, *On Illustrious Men*, 37.

[5] See Ambrose, *Letter* 7 (written, c. 386).

[6] See Alexander Souter, *The Earliest Latin Commentaries on the Epistles of St. Paul* (Oxford: Clarendon, 1927).

[7] *Marius Victorinus' Commentary on Galatians: Introduction, Translation, and Notes*, ed. and trans. Stephen Andrew Cooper, Oxford Early Christian Studies (Oxford: Oxford University Press, 2005).

[8] The name "Ambrosiaster" means "the incompetent Ambrose", as "poetaster" means "incompetent poet"; the name was invented by Erasmus.

before 384) commentaries on all the Pauline letters except Hebrews.[9] In 386, Jerome, who was living in Bethlehem, wrote on Galatians, Ephesians, Titus, and Philemon.[10] Early in the fifth century, Rufinus of Aquileia translated into Latin (and condensed) Origen's *Commentary on Romans.*[11] At about the same time, Pelagius wrote comments on thirteen Pauline letters.[12] Finally, during his years as a priest in Hippo, Augustine tried to study Romans and Galatians: he wrote *Eighty-Four Questions on Romans* (394),[13] the *Unfinished Commentary on Romans* (395),[14] and the *Explanation of the Letter to the Galatians* (394/395).[15] This burst of interest in the writings of Saint Paul represented not merely a pastoral or scholarly interest in the Apostle, but a new interpretation of Paul, even a discovery of the Paul who passed beyond the law and experienced the full effects of Christian faith and grace.[16]

Saint Augustine's *Confessions* fits into this picture of the rediscovery of Saint Paul. In the famous scene in the garden at

[9] The Latin Church had accepted Hebrews as Paul's by the fourth century.

[10] See Ronald E. Heine, ed., *The Commentaries of Origen and Jerome on St Paul's Epistle to the Ephesians* (Oxford: Oxford University Press, 2002), who translates and compares the two commentaries, with the goal of reestablishing as much of Origen's commentary as possible (it survives only in fragments).

[11] *Origen: Commentary on the Epistle to the Romans*, trans. Thomas P. Scheck, 2 vols., Fathers of the Church 103, 104 (Washington, D.C., 2001, 2002). See also Thomas P. Scheck, *Origen and the History of Justification: The Legacy of Origen's Commentary on Romans* (Notre Dame, Ind.: University of Notre Dame Press, 2008). Augustine read this commentary later in his life; the codex Lyon 483 (fifth cent.) contains annotations on Rufinus' translation of Origen's commentary on Romans that may be in Augustine's own hand. See also Caroline P. Bammel, "Augustine, Origen and the Exegesis of St. Paul", *Augustinianum* 32 (1992): 341–68.

[12] *Pelagius' Commentary on St Paul's Epistle to the Romans: Translated with Introduction and Notes*, trans. Theodore De Bruyn, Oxford Early Christian Studies (Oxford: Oxford University Press, 1993).

[13] *Augustine on Romans*, trans. P. F. Landes (Chico, Calif.: Scholars Press, 1982).

[14] Translation in ibid.

[15] *Augustine's Commentary on Galatians: Introduction, Text, Translation, and Notes*, ed. and trans. Eric Antoine Plumer, Oxford Early Christian Texts (Oxford: Oxford University Press, 2003).

[16] See Hans von Campenhausen, *Fathers of the Latin Church*, trans. Manfred Hoffmann (Repr., Peabody, Mass.: Hendrickson, 1998), pp. 2–3, 184–85.

Milan in Book VIII, it is a copy of the letters of Saint Paul that is lying on the table between Augustine and Alypius. And, when Augustine hears, "Pick it up and read", he rushes back to the table and reads a verse from the Epistle to the Romans. Augustine presents the whole scene in Book VIII as the work of grace upon him; the mysterious voice of the child, the unfamiliar words, the codex falling open to Romans 13:13, and the effect of that verse, "the light of certainty flooded my heart"—it was finally not a decision to be made, but a gift to be received (see *Conf.* VIII.12.29, p. 224).

Simplicianus had prepared Augustine—almost set him up, we might say—to reach this new understanding of his life. Just at the time Augustine became a bishop, Simplicianus wrote him a letter and asked several questions about the Scriptures—five on the Old Testament, and two on the New Testament. Both questions on the New Testament dealt with the Epistle to the Romans—one on chapter 7, on law and grace, and the other on chapter 9, on the election of Jacob and the reprobation of Esau. It is not hard to guess that Simplicianus, who had asked Ambrose to preach on Paul, and who had undoubtedly known of Marius Victorinus' commentaries on Paul, was encouraging Augustine to apply the Epistle to the Romans to his own life—and Augustine did. Of his painfully detailed and even convoluted meditation on Romans 9, Augustine later wrote, "In the solution of this question [Romans 9:10–29], I, indeed, labored in defense of the free choice of the human will; but the grace of God conquered, and finally I was able to understand, with full clarity, the meaning of the Apostle: 'For who singles thee out? Or what hast thou that thou hast not received? And if thou hast received it, why dost thou boast as if thou hadst not received it?' [cf. 1 Corinthians 4:7]."[17]

---

[17] *Saint Augustine: The Retractations*, trans. Mary Inez Bogan, Fathers of the Church Series, no. 60 (Washington, D.C.: Catholic University of America Press, 1968), 2.27, p. 120 (Augustine's *Revisions* is also known as the *Retractations*). Augustine considered the insight he gained while writing the *Questions to Simplicianus* important enough that he referred back to it in *Predestination of the Saints* 4.8 and *The Gift of Perseverance* 20.52.

It was thus while writing the *Questions to Simplicianus*, the first work he wrote as a bishop, that Augustine came to understand fully what had happened to him ten years before, and in fact during his entire life: God's grace had been guiding him, even when he seemed to be moving away from God. He could write, "[W]here was I as I sought you? You were straight ahead of me, but I had roamed away from myself and could not find even myself, let alone you!" (see *Conf.* V.2.2, p. 103).

Freedom and Grace

During the last twenty years of his life, Augustine was to meditate and write at length on the relation of grace and freedom. Before he received the gift of grace, he was not free from God's grace. In fact, he did not understand what true freedom is, or accept it. Augustine's discovery of the truth of freedom—or, to put it more exactly, the truth of the free choice of the will—runs more or less parallel to his experience of grace. Only when he came to accept free choice of the will was he capable of understanding the workings of God's grace.

The great obstacle to Augustine's accepting free choice was materialism: "When I wanted to think about my God I did not know how to think otherwise than in terms of bodily size, for whatever did not answer to this description seemed to me to be nothing at all. This misapprehension was the chief and almost sole cause of the error I could not avoid" (see *Conf.* V.10.19, p. 121). The phrase "the chief and almost sole cause of the error I could not avoid" is worth pondering. Philosophically, Augustine was, at that stage of his life, a materialist. Like many other Roman philosophers, he thought that everything that existed was some form of matter or stuff; even what he might call "spirit" was actually a fine form of matter. Such a belief had far-reaching consequences. As a materialist, Augustine could think of God only "in terms of bodily size" or as "an immense, luminous body" (see *Conf.* V.10.19, p. 121; IV.16.31, p. 99). Evil must therefore be material, derived from some great material principle, as the Manichees taught (see

Conf. V.10.20). Furthermore, the human soul must be material; but, if it is matter, it cannot have free choice, for the only way that matter can move is if it is pushed or set in motion by other matter. Augustine could accordingly blame his evil actions on some force outside himself, or at least outside his true self, for the Manichees had taught him that his body came from the evil Kingdom of Darkness and his soul, his true self, from the good Kingdom of Light. His materialism also explained his fascination with astrology: the course of his life, he was convinced, had been determined by the planets at the time of his birth (see *Conf.* IV.3.4); if he could not change his life, at least he could know what to expect. For years, he believed in astrology and carefully studied the books of the *mathematici*, as the astrologers were called. As a materialist, Augustine was thus trapped in a deterministic world. Materialism even affected his attempts to read the Bible, for he could read it only literally, and not perceive any spiritual sense: the letter is the only thing there is, and the letter can be repulsive (see *Conf.* III.7.12).

The dam broke when Augustine came to understand what a spiritual substance is: an intellectual being that has no extension or quantity, and occupies no space. If God is such a spiritual substance, so is his own mind (see *Conf.* VII.1.2). No longer envisioning God as material, Augustine thus also came to understand that God is absolute Good. Consequently and suddenly, the problem of evil was solved: if God is absolute Existence and absolute Good, then evil is the opposite, the absence of existence. Moreover, if evil is the absence of existence and goodness, the "source" of evil is a prior goodness, a preceding being, and not some autonomous Kingdom of Darkness. Rather, physical evil is the absence of good that should be present, and moral evil is perversity of will (see *Conf.* VII.12.18; VII.16.22). Augustine realizes that the spiritual soul can be the source of its own actions: he himself is the cause of his sinning, and he himself can make the right choices. Scripture likewise can have a spiritual sense (see *Conf.* VI.4.6; VI.5.7), for its meaning can lie beyond the words on the page.

Augustine's discovery of free choice of the will thus prepared him for the events of his Christian life, for only a free, intellectual being can accept the grace of God. As the years go on, however, Augustine will also ponder the limits of freedom: concupiscence, habit, original sin. By the end of his life, he will have reached a profound analysis of the human psyche and its many complexities.

Books and Grace

At important points in the *Confessions*, Augustine encountered books that, often in mysterious and sometimes negative ways, led him to God. In other words, books were often the occasion on which God's grace reached out to help Augustine and guide him along the way of return. It was the book of Paul's letters, of course, that occasioned Augustine's accepting the gift of faith and the call to continence. His encounters with life-changing books, however, began much earlier.

Augustine's first conversion—if it may be called that—occurred when he was a student at Carthage. There, he read a book by Cicero, the *Hortensius* (see *Conf.* III.4.7).[18] The book was an exhortation to a young man to dedicate his life to philosophy, to the pursuit of wisdom. It was the book that perfectly fit Augustine's moment of need, and he did what Cicero urged: with incredible ardor of soul, he sought undying wisdom. Only much later in life did he come to realize that wisdom is a Person—Jesus Christ, the power of God and the wisdom of God (see 1 Corinthians 1:24). Even later in life did he realize that, through a pagan author's book, God had begun to draw Augustine to himself.

Ironically, the first place Augustine looked for wisdom was the Christian Bible. The Latin style of the Bible was admittedly primitive, awkward, and unsophisticated,[19] and Augustine

---

[18] The work is lost.

[19] The version Augustine would have read was the Old Latin, a piecemeal translation; Jerome would later retranslate or rework much of the Latin Bible into a more elegant translation, called the Vulgate.

rejected it (see *Conf.* III.5.9). As a young man, the proud Augustine demanded fine style rather than truth; later, the humble Augustine will accept the truth, even if it is clothed in lowly style.

Augustine also encountered the writings of other pagan philosophers along his way. He read Aristotle's *Ten Categories* (see *Conf.* IV.16.28). The book, in which Aristotle treated of substance and the nine categories of accidents, did not help him understand that God is immaterial. But later in his life, Augustine would use terms from Aristotle's *Ten Categories* to explain his understanding of the Trinity, as he created the new category "substantial relations" for Father, Son, and Holy Spirit. More immediately helpful to Augustine on his intellectual journey were "some books by the Platonists" (see *Conf.* VII.9.13, p. 175), writings by Plotinus and perhaps some by Porphyry, that he read at Milan, and which Marius Victorinus had translated into Latin. In an astounding chapter (see *Conf.* VII.9.13–15), Augustine wrote that he read these books and found there the teachings of the New Testament—but not all of them.

A book that Augustine did not read, but only heard about, was the *Life of Antony* by Saint Athanasius of Alexandria.[20] This book, written around 356 (the year after the great Antony died), was soon translated into Latin and took the western Christian world by storm. Augustine writes of two young men at Trier, both in the service of the emperor, who were instantly converted to the monastic way by reading the *Life of Antony* (see *Conf.* VIII.6.14–15), just as Antony was converted by one verse from Saint Matthew's Gospel[21] and Augustine by one sentence from Saint Paul.[22]

---

[20] Several translations are available, among them *St. Athanasius: The Life of Saint Antony*, trans. Robert T. Meyer, Ancient Christian Writers 10 (Westminster, Md.: Newman, 1950) and *Athanasius: The Life of Antony and the Letter to Marcellinus*, trans. Robert C. Gregg (New York: Paulist Press, 1980).

[21] The passage Antony heard was Matthew 19:21: "If you would be perfect, go, sell what you possess and give to the poor, and you will have treasure in heaven."

[22] God spoke to Augustine through Romans 13:13–14: "[L]et us conduct ourselves . . . not in reveling and drunkenness, not in debauchery and licentiousness,

Long before he opened the book of Saint Paul's letters and read Romans 13:13, Augustine knew of the practice of the *sortes Virgilianae*, or "casting of Virgilian lots", a kind of fortune-telling that used Virgil's *Aeneid* (see *Conf.* IV.3.5, p. 78). The Romans would open the *Aeneid* at random, put a finger on a line, and accept that line as a prophecy of their fate. In the garden at Milan, Augustine did the same thing with the letters of Saint Paul, but with a key difference: he was convinced that he was being guided, not by chance or fate, but by divine Providence, God's grace guiding his life.

The Journey Home to Himself

Two themes join in the *Confessions* to make Augustine's narrative both unique and fascinating. At key points in the work, Augustine alludes to the parable of the prodigal son from Saint Luke's Gospel (see Luke 15:11–32). Obviously, he sees himself in the prodigal son: a young man on a journey, returning to the home and to the father whom he had so willfully and foolishly left. The second theme is a more abstract reprise of the prodigal son: Augustine's conviction that the right path of his journey was from the exterior to the interior, and from the inferior to the superior. When he wrote the *Soliloquies* a few months before his baptism, his own reason had asked him, "What then do you wish to know?" "God and the soul", he answered. "Nothing more?" "Nothing whatsoever." [23] Augustine, who was almost always surrounded by a group of devoted friends, was a man fascinated by his own mind.

Augustine launches the theme of the prodigal son at the end of Book II of the *Confessions*, as he writes of himself at sixteen, "I slid away from you and wandered away, my God; far from your steadfastness I strayed in adolescence, and I became to myself a land of famine" (see *Conf.* II.10.18, p. 49).

---

not in quarreling and jealousy. But put on the Lord Jesus Christ, and make no provision for the flesh, to gratify its desires."

[23] Saint Augustine, *Soliloquies*, trans. Kim Paffenroth (Hyde Park, N.Y.: New City Press, 2000), I.2.7, p. 25.

He ends that sentence with one of his many somewhat mysterious and intriguing phrases: "[A]nd I became to myself a land of famine." The next time Augustine alludes to the prodigal son is when he reads the *Hortensius*; "I began to rise up, in order to return to you", he writes (see *Conf.* III.4.7, p. 56), and not without irony. Here, Augustine reads a pagan philosopher, rejects the Bible, and becomes a Manichee; but still, he had begun to rise up—he was on the way back to God, because God was leading him to undying wisdom, even though he would not understand for many years what was really happening to him. Still, at that moment, he began to rise up and go to his Father.

In the same book, Augustine writes of his days as a teacher of grammar and a Manichee: "I was certainly roving far away from you, and debarred even from the pods I was feeding to pigs" (see *Conf.* III.6.11, p. 60)—that is, teaching the fables of Latin literature was vain, but at least everyone knew that they were fables; but Augustine actually believed the fables of the Manichees. He had little use for his early success as a teacher of eloquence: "I did not guard my strength by approaching you, but left you and set out for a distant land to squander it there on the quest for meretricious gratifications" (see *Conf.* IV.16.30, p. 99; see also V.12.22). By his use of the beautiful parable of the prodigal son, Augustine combined wonder and disgust at his early years with the sense that, even then, he had a true home, although he had turned his back on it.

And then, on a more abstract level, phrases throughout the *Confessions* suggest that, for many years, God was not absent from Augustine; Augustine was rather absent from God and from himself. "I had roamed away from myself", he wrote, "and could not find even myself, let alone you!" (see *Conf.* V.2.2, p. 103). Or, in one of his most intriguing phrases, "I knew myself to be far away from you in a region of unlikeness" (see *Conf.* VII.10.16, p. 180). But God was there all along: "You were more intimately present to me than my inmost being, and higher than the highest peak of my spirit" (see *Conf.* III.6.11, p. 61). And, Augustine could still find his true self:

"Warned by these writings that I must return to myself, I entered under your guidance the innermost places of my being" (see *Conf.* VII.10.16, p. 179).

Conclusion

The *Confessions* is a dialogue with a silent partner. The work begins with the sentence "Great are you, O Lord, and exceedingly worthy of praise" (see *Conf.* I.1.1, p. 3). Throughout the work, Augustine addresses God. God never speaks, but he acts. His action, by which he moves the human will toward himself as the only source of true happiness, is what we call grace.

It was through a meditation on the Epistle to the Romans, which Simplicianus prompted the new bishop to undertake, that Augustine came to a full understanding of what had happened to him. In the course of many years, he had come to know himself, and, in particular, himself as free and responsible. He turned inward, toward his inmost self, and from there he looked up to uncreated and infinite Light. He thus came to understand how that Light had guided him, along a crooked way, in a clear direction, until he realized that God made us for himself. The Augustine of the *Confessions* is Everyman. He writes of his journey, not to amaze us, but to invite us to follow the same path. His message to each reader is this: You too can walk the way I have walked. You too can come to God. For as you walk, God will be leading you, laying out the path before you, guiding you to your truest self, and to himself.

Creation in the *Confessions*

Jared Ortiz
Hope College

Introduction

In the *Confessions*, Augustine lives, speaks, and thinks in terms of creation. Creation lies at the heart of the various struggles of his life; it informs the way he crafts his speech, and it makes up the fundamental rhythms of his thought. For Augustine, creation is not just one doctrine or theme among others, but it is the foundational context for all doctrines and all themes. If we want to understand the *Confessions*, we need to situate it within Augustine's understanding of creation.

This approach is not immediately obvious, but consider the following: the *Confessions* begins with Augustine seeking for a way to understand the distinction between the "Great" "Lord" and the "part of [his] creation",[1] and ends with a discussion of the eternal Sabbath rest prefigured on the seventh day of creation. The last three books are an extended meditation on the literal and figurative meaning of the creation account in Genesis, and the most frequently used phrase in the *Confessions* is "God who made heaven and earth". For Augustine, creation is decisive, and the *Confessions* cannot be understood without taking stock of its fundamental importance.

Augustine's Understanding of Creation

What, then, is Augustine's understanding of creation? And, why is it so important? Augustine's understanding of creation is the Church's understanding, the faith given to the apostles, though this traditional doctrine takes on a characteristically

---

[1] Saint Augustine, *The Confessions*, ed. David Vincent Meconi, S.J., Ignatius Critical Editions (San Francisco: Ignatius Press, 2012), I.1.1. Subsequent quotations from this edition will be cited in the text. References are to book, section, and paragraph.

Augustinian form in the saint's hands. It is so important because, as he understands it, the first article of the Creed contains the whole faith. Get creation wrong, and we get the rest of the faith wrong. But, get creation right, and everything else logically follows. For Augustine, creation provides the conceptual space for properly thinking about the mysteries of God.

Augustine uses the word "creation" to mean various things: sometimes he means the *divine activity* that introduces being from nothing; other times he means *all the things* God has created, all of material and spiritual reality, what I will call "the world". Augustine also uses creation in a broader and deeper sense as *that which defines how he understands* God and the world.[2] Following Saint Paul's teaching that creation reveals God, Augustine exclaims, "By hearkening to the concerted witness of your whole creation, [I] had discovered you, our creator, and your Word" (see *Conf.* VIII.1.2, p. 196).[3] For those who have eyes to see and ears to hear, creation is a revelation that not only sheds light on, but determines our understanding of the Creator, what and how he creates, and how his creation is distinct from and related to him.

For the Christian, God is not a part of the world, but is utterly transcendent to it. This seeming truism, which can be found in any catechism, is not as obvious as it might seem. It certainly was not obvious to the young Augustine. When we want to think about God, we often unwittingly *imagine* him; that is, we make an image of him, and whenever we do, we

---

[2] I am indebted to Msgr. Robert Sokolowski for these distinctions. See his illuminating *The God of Faith and Reason: Foundations of Christian Theology* (Washington, D.C.: Catholic University of America Press, 1995) and "Creation and Christian Understanding", in *Christian Faith and Human Understanding: Studies on the Eucharist, Trinity, and the Human Person* (Washington, D.C.: Catholic University of America Press, 2006), pp. 38–50.

[3] See Romans 1:20: "Ever since the creation of the world his invisible nature, namely, his eternal power and deity, has been clearly perceived in the things that have been made." Augustine alludes to this passage six times in the *Confessions*, four of which occur in Book VII when he comes to the proper distinction between God and the world for the first time. See VII.10.16; VII.17.23 (2x); VII.20.26; X.6.10; XIII.21.31.

reduce him to something *within the horizon of the world*. This is a perennial temptation of human reason. Augustine relates two of these imaginative reductions familiar in his day: when people ask, "What was God doing before he made heaven and earth?" (see *Conf*. XI.10.12, p. 339), and when they think of God "in the guise of a man, or as some huge being possessed of immense power" who creates the world "outside of himself, as though located at a distance from him" (see *Conf*. XII.27.37, p. 398), they are imagining God as a being in the world subject to time and space as we are. Instead of understanding God as the transcendent Source of creation, he is understood as the highest thing *in* creation. This kind of thinking makes creation ultimate; it makes the stuff of the world all there is. But, for the Christian, the world is not ultimate but radically contingent, for God created it from nothing (*ex nihilo*). God is ultimate. He is the fullness of Being, sufficient unto himself, Goodness Itself, perfect and perfectly simple, who, without any change in himself, freely creates from nothing in a radical outpouring of love (see *Conf*. XIII.1.1–2.2; XIII.16.19). This means that God is utterly transcendent and distinct from the world, which, paradoxically, enables him to be intimately present to it (see *Conf*. I.4.4).

God is Being Itself. This is the meaning of "I Am Who I Am",[4] God's revelation of his name to Moses on Mt. Sinai, and God's revelation to Augustine after he had read the Platonists (see *Conf*. VII.10.16). But creatures are created from nothing, which means that they receive their being from Another. Creatures *have* what God *is*. Creatures have being by "participation", by sharing in God's Being, not in the sense that God is divided and creatures are a part of God (this is the Manichean error), but in the sense that God makes creatures to be like him in some way. The more a creature is like God, the more it participates in him, and the closer it is to him. Rational creatures participate most in God—they are an image of God in their rational souls (even if disfigured by sin), and

[4] Exodus 3:14.

they vary in likeness to God depending on love, on the "move-ments of the heart" (see *Conf*. XIII.7.8, p. 414).

In the world, creatures have being in different degrees, and the more creatures there are, the more good there is. God looks at each thing he creates and calls it "good", but when he looks at the whole of creation, he calls it "very good" (see *Conf*. XIII.28.43, p. 452).[5] So, an angel and a dog are better than an angel alone; a man and a rock are better than a man alone. But, God and the world are *not* better than God alone, because God is completely Good in himself. Creation does not add anything to the Goodness or Being of God, because God wholly Is and wholly is Good, even without creation. This does not mean that creation is worthless. On the contrary, God will-ingly chose it to be when it did not have to be; he loves cre-ation into being. In the Christian understanding that Augustine inherited, our existence and the existence of all things in cre-ation are understood as God's good and utterly gratuitous gifts (see *Conf*. I.20.31).

Augustine develops this traditional doctrine in distinctive ways.[6] Through a combination of philosophical reflection and Christian exegesis, Augustine discerns that Father, Son, and Holy Spirit create in a threefold simultaneous act, which he describes under the terms "creation", "conversion", and "for-mation" (*creatio, conversio, formatio*). "In the beginning God created the heavens and the earth"[7]—this refers to the *cre-ation* of formless matter (see *Conf*. XII.8.8). God called this formless matter back to himself through his Word: "Let there be light."[8] This calling back through the Word constitutes the *conversion* of formless matter (utterly unlike God) to sim-ilarity with God (see *Conf*. XIII.2.2). The formless creature simultaneously receives its *form* as whatever it is supposed to

---

[5] Genesis 1:31. The actual quote by Saint Augustine is "exceedingly good".

[6] Augustine discusses creation throughout the *Confessions*, but offers a search-ing exegesis of the Genesis creation narrative in Books XI–XIII, providing a very precise summary in Book XIII.1.1–11.12.

[7] Genesis 1:1.

[8] Genesis 1:3.

be—"and there was light".[9] For rational creatures, "formation" means "illumination", which, for Augustine, means being made in the image and likeness of God and having the capacity to lovingly participate in the Light of God's Wisdom (see *Conf.* XIII.2.3).

This *creatio, conversio, formatio* exegetical pattern is found throughout the *Confessions* and has profound implications for Augustine's understanding of the world. Creation has a kind of "conversion torque", a dynamic orientation toward the Creator, in its very being. This is the meaning of Augustine's most famous line: "[Y]ou have made us and drawn us to yourself, and our heart is unquiet until it rests in you" (see *Conf.* I.1.1, p. 3). To sin is to turn away from God, *aversio* instead of *conversio*, and this undoes our created being—we actually become less. We become dissipated, we lose our *form*, and our constitution trickles away toward that formless abyss out of which we were made. But, through the Incarnation, the Word calls us back to God; we are *converted* and *re-formed* according to his Image. This drama of creation, aversion, and re-creation is Augustine's own story and, as we will see, the story of all creation.

Creation as the Structure of the *Confessions*

Augustine's understanding of creation offers a number of illuminating ways for giving an account of the structure of the *Confessions*. We will look at only one of these, the one that comes out of Augustine's own suggestion of the structure. He says, "The first ten books were written about myself; the last three about holy scripture, from the words: *In the Beginning God created heaven and earth* as far as the Sabbath rest." [10] What is the connection between the two parts? The first ten deal with conversion, while the last three with creation. Augustine understands his own life, especially his conversion, as patterned after God's original

---

[9] Genesis 1:3.

[10] This comment comes from *Revisions* II.6.32, a work written at the end of his life, in which Augustine reviewed and commented on all of his writings.

creative act. The last three books on creation, then, provide the theological and metaphysical underpinnings for the first ten books on conversion.

Augustine's initial division can be refined further. Books I–V tell of Augustine's creation and subsequent aversion and dissipation into created things. Books V–X tell of Augustine's re-creation, his conversion back to God, and re-formation in his Creator. The exegetical pattern that Augustine discerned in the Genesis story—*creatio, conversio, formatio* (including *aversio* and *re-creatio*)—provides a framework for confessing his life. The creation narrative examined in Books XI–XIII offers Augustine, and us, a scriptural mirror through which we can understand our creation and re-creation after the Fall.

Coming to Terms with Creation

In the *Confessions*, Augustine tells the story of his "coming to terms" with creation. The phrase "coming to terms" has a double sense: first, Augustine must learn the actual *terms*, that is, the appropriate metaphysical categories for *thinking* about creation properly; but, second, he must also come to *accept* the fact that he himself is created—he must "come to terms" with this truth in a moral way. There is an intellectual and a moral aspect to Augustine's coming to terms with creation: both his mind and will are engaged. Although we will only be able to deal with a part of this drama—Augustine's struggle with the Manichees and Platonists and the resolution of these struggles in the Catholic Church— our treatment will show how the whole *Confessions* can be understood in light of creation.

After reading Cicero's *Hortensius*, Augustine falls in love with Wisdom and turns to the Scriptures, seeking a path that contained the name of Christ. But, compared with the eloquence of Cicero, the Scriptures strike him as painfully vulgar (see *Conf.* III.5.9). Disappointed, he becomes susceptible to the questions and criticisms of the quasi-Christian Manichees: "[T]hey constantly asked me about the origin of evil, and whether God was confined to a material form with hair and nails, and whether people who practiced polygamy, killed human beings and offered animal sacrifices could be considered righteous" (see *Conf*. III.7.12, pp. 61–62). To these troubling questions, the Manichees offered plausible answers: there are two coeternal principles, Light and Darkness, which are constantly at war. Evil does not come from God (as the Manichees accused the Catholics of teaching), but from a separate evil substance, which has invaded the good and taken it captive. God is not limited to a human shape, but is an "immense, luminous body" (see *Conf*. IV.16.31, p. 99). The human soul is a particle of God, which is trapped in an evil material body. The Hebrew scriptures are objectionable, the New Testament has been corrupted by Judaizers (see *Conf*. V.11.21), and the truth has been given to Mani, in whom the Holy Spirit was personally present (see *Conf*. V.5.8), and who taught that the Manichean Elect mediate between God and humankind (see *Conf*. IV.1.1). These answers have an air of plausibility and, unlike the Catholics who (it was alleged) demanded an uncritical faith, the Manichees promised the truth through reason alone. The Manichean answers directly addressed Augustine's intellectual and moral struggles. Both his struggles and their answers were, at root, about creation.[11]

Manichean theology shows a profound confusion about creation: in short, it blurs the distinction between Creator and creation. For the Manichees, Light and Darkness are, in a sense, two gods who are understood in corporeal terms, infinite extensions of very fine material that are bounded only by one another. God is a divisible thing, for anything with extension can be divided. "When I wanted to think about my God", Augustine says of his thinking while a Manichee, "I did not know how to think otherwise than in terms of bodily size, for whatever did not answer to this description seemed to me to be nothing at all" (see *Conf*. V.10.19, p. 121). The Manichees reduce reality to corporeality.

---

[11] It is no accident that soon after his conversion Augustine wrote a work entitled *On Genesis against the Manichees*.

The world comes about from a cosmic struggle between the two coeternal principles, and is composed of Light trapped in Darkness. There is, therefore, an *identity* between the elements that compose the world and the elements that compose the coeternal principles. This means that, in the Manichean view of things, *there is no ontological distinction between God and the world*. The Manichean God (or gods) remains within the horizon of the world, superior, in a sense, but not transcendent. The flip side of this confusion is that the Manichees exalt creation to the level of God: the Light is trapped in the world, and the human soul is identical to God's divided substance (see *Conf*. IV.15.26). This amounts to a denial that the human person is created, which, for the mature Augustine, is a denial of the most fundamental truth of what it means to be human.

The Manichean confusion about creation has dramatic consequences for their understanding of salvation. Since the human person is a particle of the good God trapped in evil matter, he is essentially good, and evil is not something he does, but something he suffers from an alien source. Thus, there is no free will and no personal sin (see *Conf*. VIII.10.22–23). Each person is an instantiation, and therefore victim, of a cosmic struggle between Light and Darkness. Salvation comes from liberating the Light in the world and in ourselves through participation in the dietary regimen of the Elect whose ritual masticating releases the entrapped Light so it can return to the sun and moon, the repositories for liberated God particles (see *Conf*. III.6.10). The whole saving economy is turned upside down by the Manichees: God does not save the human person from his sin (for there is no sin); rather, the human person saves God from confinement and thereby saves himself. Because matter is evil, salvation means not the redemption of body and soul, but the separation of these incongruous elements. Redemption, for the Manichees, means the dissolution of the person back to his coeternal places of origin.

The Manichean errors begin to loosen their hold when Augustine encounters Faustus, Ambrose, and, most importantly, the Platonist books. Through them, Augustine begins to think about God and the world properly: he comes to recognize the "truth that is seen and understood through the things that are made" (see *Conf.* VII.10.16, p. 180).

With divine help, Augustine is inspired by the Platonist books to attempt an ascent from created things to their Creator.[12] Augustine withdraws from the outer world and enters into his own soul where he "sees" (with an intellectual vision) an "incommutable light far above my spiritual ken, transcending my mind". It is different from the light he sees with his eyes: it is not simply a brighter version of natural light. He sees the light as "above" him, not by space or intensity, but "because this very light made me, and I was below it because by it I was made" (see *Conf.* VII.10.16, p. 179). Creation reveals the truth about God and himself. Augustine learns from the Platonists that God is not the highest thing in the world nor is he identical to it. Rather, God is ontologically distinct from the world, the transcendent Creator of it.

Freed from his errors about creation, the problem of evil also falls into place. Evil is not some independent substance, and neither is God the source of evil. God is good, which means that all he creates is good. Evil, then, is a privation or corruption of that good. And, without a substantial evil to blame his troubles on, Augustine finds he is responsible for the evil in himself.

After reading the Platonists, Augustine turns immediately to Saint Paul and finds there the same truth "but now inseparably from your gift of grace". What the Platonists teach about God and creation is true, but it is not saving knowledge. They see the truth, but they do not draw the right conclusions about what this means, namely, "that no one who sees can boast as though what he sees and the very power to see it were not from you—for who has anything that he has not received?"

---

[12] There are numerous ascents in the *Confessions*: IV.12.18–15.26; VII.10.16; VII.17.23; VII.20.26; IX.10.23–25; X.1.1–27.38; and Books XI–XIII considered together.

(see *Conf*. VII.21.27, p. 191).[13] The Platonists' teaching leads
to pride (see *Conf*. VII.20.26), but Paul's teaching leads to the
humble acknowledgment that the truth and the ability to see
the truth are God's gifts. It is an acknowledgment about the
truth of creation, not only *that* we are created, but of *what it
means* to be created. For Augustine, this can only come about
through the example and grace of Christ.

Christ and Creation

Although Augustine always maintained a certain piety toward
Christ, he struggled with how to understand him, for how one
understands Christ is intimately related to how one understands creation. As a Manichee, Augustine adopted a form of
Docetism, that is, a belief that God did not really become incarnate, but only *appeared* to do so. Augustine believed this
because, as a Manichee, he thought that God and the human
person are both beings in the world and so compete within
the same order of causes. Thus, they cannot be united without being mingled or one canceling out the other (see *Conf*.
V.10.20). Far from being salvific, the Incarnation is the very
problem itself: God trapped in matter. To preserve God's integrity, Augustine became a Docetist.

Augustine could not follow the Platonists either because they
rejected Christ. They saw the need for something to mediate
between the transcendent God and his mutable creation, but
instead of a mediator who was *both* God and man, they fell
into worshipping demonic mediators *in between* God and
humankind (see *Conf*. X.42.67). They could not accept the
Incarnation because, they thought, it would overthrow their
whole understanding of reality. For the Platonist, lower things
depend on higher things for their existence—participation only
works upward—but in the Incarnation God comes down to
participate in our humanity (see *Conf*. VII.18.24). This was
incomprehensible to them, and so they looked for a "link" to

---

[13] Augustine is alluding to 1 Corinthians 4:7.

connect God, who is remote, to man, who strives on his own to ascend (see *Conf.* X.43.69).

Lastly, before Augustine became a Catholic, he adopted what he calls a "Photinian" view of Christ: Christ was not God, but an unparalleled ethical teacher and "man of excellent wisdom" (see *Conf.* VII.19.25, pp. 187–88). Augustine agnostically refused to say how God is related to humankind in the Incarnation, keeping each within a separate sphere.

Augustine converts from Photinianism to Catholicism when he personally encounters Christ, God and man, in the garden at Milan. The conversion is recounted in Book VIII, a book which I think can be fruitfully understood as a kind of "interior view" of the creating and converting Word. As Book VIII progresses, the Word calls Augustine ever closer to himself until, in the garden, Augustine finally "surrenders" to the Word and "enters in".

As Augustine tells it, the examples of Anthony, Victorinus, and the other imitators of Christ (see *Conf.* VIII.2.3–7.18)[14] prepare the ground by exciting his desire for conversion and showing him the Way. His divided will prevents him from imitating them, and he despairs, until, in the midst of weeping, he hears a child's singsong voice: "Pick it up and read, pick it up and read" (see *Conf.* VIII.12.29, p. 223). Interpreting this as a divine command, Augustine picks up the Scriptures and falls upon a passage exhorting him to "put on the Lord Jesus Christ, and make no provision for the flesh or the gratification of your desires."[15] Instantly, "the light of certainty flooded my heart and all dark shades of doubt fled away" (see *Conf.* VIII.12.29, p. 224).

What has happened here? The Word being imitated prepares Augustine to hear the Word speaking through the child's

---

[14] For "imitators of Christ", see 1 Corinthians 11:1: "Be imitators of me as I am of Christ." The language of imitation is, for Augustine, creation language. The Word is the Image of the Father, the perfect Likeness, through whom all things are made in a Trinitarian act of *creatio, conversio, formatio*. All things, then, bear a likeness to God; they imitate God in their created being, because they bear the stamp of the Image and Likeness.

[15] Romans 13:13–14.

words, which leads to the Word of the Scriptures, which leads to the Word made flesh. In each of these temporal events, the unchanging Word beckons Augustine to *conversion*, to increased likeness to Christ and so greater participation in God. When Augustine obeys the Word, he is *illumined*, and the image of God in him begins to be *re-formed* after the pattern of his original creation. Augustine is exhorted to "put on the Lord Jesus Christ", a clear reference to baptism (see *Conf.* IX.6.14, p. 239), which will complete the earthly incorporation into the Word (i.e., the Body of Christ, the Church) and make him a "new creation".[16]

Augustine's description here of how God interacts with the world arises from his understanding of creation. God acts in the world without in any way imposing himself on the events or on Augustine's will: "The divine action is not an action by a worldly agent, it does not insert itself into the sequence of motives and causes."[17] Since God is not a competing cause in the world, he acts in the world without encroaching on the integrity of the world. The events have a natural integrity in which all the actors act of their own volition, and *at the same time* God works through them to bring about his own ends. God does not manipulate Augustine's heart to get him to convert; rather, through grace, he frees it from the external hindrances that divide it so that it can be fully at work while he is fully at work in it. "[F]rom what depth", says Augustine, "was [my free decision] called forth in a moment, enabling me to bow my neck to your benign yolk and my shoulders to your light burden, O Christ Jesus, my helper and my redeemer?" (see *Conf.* IX.1.1, p. 226). Far from denying free will, grace establishes it. For Augustine, grace means greater participation in the divine life, and it comes through Christ, God

---

[16] See 2 Corinthians 5:17.

[17] Frederick Crosson, "Structure and Meaning in St. Augustine's *Confessions*", in *The Augustinian Tradition*, ed. Gareth Matthews (Berkeley: University of California Press, 1999), p. 31. Crosson brilliantly illumines the noncompetition between God and the world and shows how this understanding opens up the meaning of the *Confessions*.

personally present in the world, whose activity in us makes us *more* free.

Augustine probably does not grasp all of this in the garden, but his experience there leads him to the truth that the Church teaches: God is not remote from the world, but is intimately present to it and active in it through his Son. This possibility is opened up by the Platonists' understanding of God and the world that also enables Augustine to understand the Incarnation: Christ is true God and true man (see *Conf.* X.43.68), two integral natures, which find union without conflict or competition in one "Person of Truth" (*persona veritatis*).[18]

The truth of the Incarnation at once radicalizes the distinction between God and the world and reveals a new relationship. It reveals that God can be united to humankind *in a personal way*; God can participate in our human nature without compromising his divinity (see *Conf.* VII.18.24). For this to make sense, we must deepen our understanding of God's transcendence. In turn, the Incarnation also makes possible humanity's personal union with God, which Augustine understands as the transforming of our nature into God's. "I am the food of the mature", God reveals to Augustine; "grow then, and you will eat me. You will not change me into yourself like bodily food: you will be changed into me" (see *Conf.* VII.10.16, p. 180). We are not God, as the Manichees thought, but we are destined to become God *by participation* because God participated in us.

The New Context Creation Establishes

The truth about creation opens up the possibility of understanding the truth about Christ, and therefore salvation, while the truth about Christ completes our understanding of creation. Together, this understanding of God and the world establishes a new context from which all things are understood anew.

---

[18] This translation is taken from Augustine, *Confessions*, trans. F. J. Sheed (Indianapolis, Ind.: Hackett, 1993), VII.19.25; see also p. 188 in this edition.

Readers of the *Confessions* are often struck by how often Augustine quotes and paraphrases Scripture, especially the Psalms. For Augustine, this is not simply pious rhetoric, but his very keen insight that the new context demands a new language. In the world, the language of the world is generally sufficient to communicate about the things of the world. But in the new context, the language of the world is not sufficient to appropriately speak about God, because God is not a part of the world. Augustine finds a way to speak *about* the transcendent God in the Scriptures and *to* him in the Psalms. The Scriptures are the inspired Word of God, and so they are God's speech about himself. The Psalms are the Word of God, which become the prayers of men and women directed back to God. God speaks to God through human beings who adopt the language of God to communicate with their God. The Psalms, as Augustine understands them, are the premier example of *confession*.[19]

Augustine uses the word "confession" in a number of senses. He uses it, as we do, to mean admitting our sins (see *Conf.* X.2.2), but he also takes pains to elevate another meaning, which, for him, is prior and more important: confession understood as praise and thanksgiving (see *Conf.* V.1.1; VIII.1.1). Even if we had never sinned, Augustine suggests, we would still have to offer God a confession of praise because God is, in himself, "exceedingly worthy of praise" (see *Conf.* I.1.1; p. 3). We would also have to give thanks because God created us *ex nihilo*, and this gift calls forth a response of gratitude. All these meanings of confession are a form of sacrifice (see *Conf.* V.1.1; VIII.12.38; XII.24.33), which are offered to God not in words alone, but in deeds and sacraments.

Confession, in this deep sense, leads us right to the heart of Augustine's understanding of life in the new context. Our life is God's utterly gratuitous gift, which must be offered back to him in praise and thanksgiving. For Augustine, this means that we must turn our life into a confession, an acceptable sacrifice

---

[19] In light of this discussion, it is worth reflecting on what Augustine means when he says that time is a psalm (see XI.28.38).

to the Lord. But we cannot do this on our own, for only God can give God an acceptable sacrifice, and so our words and deeds must be taken up sacramentally.

Augustine understands the sacraments of baptism and the Eucharist very much in terms of creation and confession. Baptism is the "sacrament of *conversion*" [20] in which we are incorporated into the Body of Christ and become a "new creation".[21] The bread and wine truly become the Eucharistic Body of Christ, which is the sacrament of ongoing *re-formation* and *conformation* to Christ. These sacraments complete the entering into the Word in this life, thereby beginning our transformation into God to be completed in the next. In the celebration of the Eucharist, the congregation unites itself to the bread and wine on the altar: the Body of Christ (the baptized congregation) offers itself along with and precisely as the perfect sacrifice of the Body of Christ (the Eucharist). The gifts God has given us in creation and elevated in re-creation are offered back to him in the sacrifice of the whole Christ. The *Confessions* itself is just such an offering (see *Conf.* XI.2.3), and this offering is, I would suggest, the deep meaning of confession.

The Church as the Goal of Creation

Augustine's sacrifice of confessions culminates in Book XIII, which, despite its difficulty, is a beautiful and entirely fitting culmination for his endeavor: to "arouse the human mind and affections toward God." [22] Book XIII presents itself as the magisterial summary of a master teacher; though, given the sheer density of Scripture quotes, it would perhaps be more accurate to say that Augustine presents it as an inspired summary of *the* Master Teacher. For twelve books, Augustine has exercised our minds and stretched our hearts; in the last book, he presents the Truth—or, the Truth is presented through him—in its entire splendor. It is, of course, no accident that its subject matter is creation.

[20] *Letter* 98.9.
[21] See 2 Corinthians 5:17.
[22] *Revisions* II.6.32.

Book XIII has two major parts: a straightforward literal exegesis of Genesis 1:1–2 (see *Conf.* XIII.1.1–11.12), which we discussed above, and a spiritual or allegorical exegesis of Genesis 1:1–2:4 (see *Conf.* XIII.12.13–38.53), which interprets the creation story as the story of the Church. The structure of Book XIII suggests that the spiritual meaning completes and fulfills the literal or, more pointedly, that the Church completes and fulfills creation. Importantly, Augustine transitions from the literal to spiritual interpretation with a discussion of baptism, that is, the act by which creation becomes a new creation (see *Conf.* XIII.12.13). For Augustine, "the church is the divine origin and the goal of all things: God created the world for human beings, and human beings for himself, to share his life with them."[23] The Church, at once human and divine, is the way and the goal for creation. For it is in the Church, the Body of Christ, that the world is sacramentally taken up, transformed, and offered back to God as a Eucharistic offering. It is in the Church, animated by the Spirit, that creation finds its voice of praise. Augustine employs both the form and content of his inspired exegesis in Book XIII to convey this deep truth.

For now, the Church lives in "the flux of time where all is confusion", but in the end, she will be "purged and rendered molten by the fire of your love" (see *Conf.* XI.29.39, p. 362). On her earthly pilgrimage, the one ecclesial heart of the Body of Christ is unquiet, but in heaven, "by contemplating the Light", she will become "light itself" (see *Conf.* XII.15.20, p. 380). Then, our restless heart shall find rest. This rest, prefigured in the seventh day of creation, is an eternal Sabbath, a day without end (see *Conf.* XIII.36.51), when God will be our rest (see *Conf.* XIII.38.53), for he has made us and drawn us to himself and our heart is restless until it rests in him (see *Conf.* I.1.1).

---

[23] Robert McMahon, "Book Thirteen: The Creation of the Church as the Paradigm for the *Confessions*", in *A Reader's Companion to Augustine's Confessions*, eds. Kim Paffenroth and Robert P. Kennedy (Louisville: Westminster John Knox Press, 2003), p. 214.

Confession, Prayer, Transformation

Allan Fitzgerald, O.S.A.
Villanova University

Late in his life, Augustine wrote this description of his *Confessions*: "The thirteen books of my *Confessions* praise the just and good God, both for my good and my bad actions, and they raise the human spirit and heart toward him; ... they had that effect on me when they were written, and they do that when they are read."[1] Thus, in 427, Augustine recognized the impact that the *Confessions* had on him and on others. What is there about a story that lifts minds and feelings toward God? It has to be more than a recitation of events, more than a history or an autobiography. It makes more sense to describe the *Confessions* as a prayer that resonates with the words of Scripture, as biblical prayer.[2]

Confession as Prayer

Not too long before his conversion in a Milanese garden, Augustine began to know what it meant to think spiritually: "I had not even a faint or shadowy notion of what a spiritual substance could be like".[3] Returning to himself (see *Conf.* VII.10.16), he realized that he was loved (see *Conf.* VII.17.23), that he wanted to be stronger (see *Conf.* VII.18.24), and that he could (barely) admit his need (see *Conf.* VII.20.26). In the

---

[1] Augustine, *Revisions*, in the *Works of Saint Augustine: a Translation for the 21st Century*, trans. Boniface Ramsey (Hyde Park, N.Y.: New City Press, 2010), II.6.1, p. 114.

[2] See Goulven Madec, "Les *Confessions* comme Prière Biblique", in *Lectures Augustiniennes* (Paris: Institut des Études Augustiniennes, 2001), pp. 111–19.

[3] Saint Augustine, *The Confessions*, ed. David Vincent Meconi, S.J., Ignatius Critical Editions (San Francisco: Ignatius Press, 2012), VI.3.4, p. 135. See, too, *Conf.* VI.4.6 and *Conf.* VII.20.26. Subsequent quotations from this edition will be cited in the text. References are to book, section, and paragraph.

more than ten years between these first steps toward Christian faith and the writing of the *Confessions*, his experience of the Christian communities from Milan to Hippo (passing through Rome, Carthage, and Thagaste in between) brought him into living contact with their faith, their use of the Scriptures, and their prayer.

In the course of the fourth century in the West, increased use of the Psalms in Christian common prayer also led to a shift from an emphasis on profession of faith in God (*confessio fidei*) to praise of God (*confessio laudis*).[4] The Latin for "confession", whether the noun, *confessio*, or the verb, *confiteor*, is used for the human experiences of professing faith, confessing sin, and praising God. Even though it may not be immediately obvious, the confession of sin was, for Augustine, a way to praise God; that meant that, by acknowledging one's sin, a sinner proclaims that God is just and merciful. In some way, the sinner justifies God—or lets God be God—by placing his hope in God's grace, by seeking his pardon, and thus preaching his justice.[5]

From the beginning of the fourth century, once they were granted rights as full citizens in the Roman Empire and began to have their own churches, Christians gathered more often for prayer. They prayed with the Psalms—the prayer book of the Hebrew scriptures, which gives voice to the human experience of God's people. Christians were invited in this way to see their own experiences from within the history of salvation by using the words of God to communicate with God, that is, to see prayer as a conversation that did not begin and that would not end with them.

After Augustine heard how Ambrose explained the Scriptures by differentiating the spirit and the letter (see *Conf.*

---

[4] Augustine is not the first to speak of confession as "confession of praise" as well as of "sin". Hilary and Jerome, both based on Origen, gave this double meaning to confession; see G. Q. A. Meershoek, *Le Latin Biblique d'après Saint Jérôme* (Nijmegen: Dekker & Van der Vegt, 1966), p. 82.

[5] See Allan Fitzgerald, "Ambrose and Augustine: *Confessio as Initium Iustitiae*", *Augustinianum* 40, no. 1 (2000): 173–85.

VI.4.6), he began to read, study, and appropriate these words. To read his *Confessions* is to see how his reading and praying helped him articulate the meaning of his conversion as guided by God. He claims no personal revelation; his journey, rather, engaged the words of God and came to terms with the Word of God.[6] That helped him gain a new understanding of himself and allowed him to do what the psalmist did: confess to God by revealing himself to God and to all.[7]

Grappling with the Scriptures

By looking back at the place Augustine gives the Scriptures in the *Confessions*, this article may also show why this book still interests—even captivates—its readers. This book, in fact, is a lively patchwork of scriptural texts;[8] it invites the reader to take part in the dialogue that Augustine had with his God when he wrote it. It is possible to begin to appreciate how avidly Augustine had read the Bible and how its words began to be his words. Because of the importance of the Word of God to him in the period before his conversion and, even more explicitly, in the years that led to the writing of the *Confessions*, Augustine's account is much more than a merely personal story. Not only was it a way to solidify his relation with God, but it was also a way to engage those who would read it in a similar examination of their inner lives: "When the confession of my past evil deeds is read and listened to ... that recital arouses the hearer's heart, forbidding it to slump into despair and say, 'I can't.' Let it rather keep watch for

---

[6] See Isabelle Bochet, "Interprétation scripturaire et compréhension de soi. Du *De doctrina christiana* aux *Confessiones* de saint Augustin", in *Comprendre et interpréter. Le paradigme herméneutique de la raison* (Paris, Beauchesne, 1993), pp. 21–50, especially p. 37.

[7] See Suzanne Poque, "La prière du Catéchumène Augustin en Septembre 386 (*Confessiones* IX.4.8–11)", in *Congresso Internazionale su S. Agostino nel XVI centenario della Conversione*, vol. 2 (Rome: Institutum Patristicum Augustinianum, 1987), pp. 79–84.

[8] G. Madec, *Lectures Augustiniennes*, p. 116.

your loving mercy and your gentle grace" (see *Conf.* X.3.4, p. 265). And just soon thereafter, we similarly hear, "[T]his is the fruit to be reaped from my confessions: I confess not only before you … but also in the ears of believing men and women…. [Y]ou have ordered me to serve them if I wish to live with you and share your life" (see *Conf.* X.4.6, p. 267).

The Scriptures, in fact, were quite foreign to Augustine in his youth. Early in the *Confessions* he recalled his disdain for their style when he was a student in Carthage: "[W]hen I studied the Bible and compared it with Cicero's dignified prose, it seemed to me unworthy" (see *Conf.* III.5.9, p. 57).[9] His interest in the Bible at that time was stimulated by the reading of the *Hortensius* by Cicero, a book that aroused his passion for wisdom. Since the *Hortensius* lacked the name of Christ, he could not accept it fully, as he says: "No writing from which that name was missing, even if learned, of literary elegance and truthful, could ever captivate me completely" (see *Conf.* III.4.8, p. 57).

In his childhood, there can be little doubt about the importance of the name of Christ—which he had drunk in with his mother's milk (see *Conf.* III.4.8)—even though he does not tell us much. One has to wonder, therefore, how often Augustine the boy went to church with his mother and heard the name of Christ. One has to wonder how he came to value the name of Christ so strongly. What is clear is that his childhood piety had given way to the questioning of a young student. He sees the Scriptures as a book, as a text set before his eyes, as something that he did not value, because it failed to compare with Ciceronian style. Whatever faith he had was not consciously linked to the words of the Bible at that time.[10]

---

[9] See, too, Augustine, *Instructing Beginners in Faith* (Hyde Park: New City Press, 2006), 9.13, p. 76.

[10] See Michael McCarthy, "'We Are Your Books': Augustine, the Bible, and the Practice of Authority", *Journal of the American Academy of Religion* 75, no. 2 (2007): 324–52, for a fascinating discussion of how Augustine's approach to the

Although he did not find the name of Christ in Cicero's writing, he did discover it was used (constantly) by the Manichees, "who seemed to him more intellectually sophisticated"[11] than Christians. Hence, it is not surprising that Augustine turned to the Manichees to satisfy his desire for understanding (see *Conf.* III.6.10). After joining them, his questions about the Scriptures only deepened; their questions about the Scriptures and its apparent contradictions heightened his disdain: "I became more and more convinced that it was possible to unravel all those cunning knots of calumny in which the sacred books had been entangled by tricksters who had deceived me and others" (see *Conf.* VI.3.4, pp. 134–35).

Even so, he recorded a moment, shortly before going to Rome, when the lectures of a certain Elpidius gave him a chance to see that there might be more to the Scriptures than he had first supposed: "While still at Carthage I had been influenced in a preliminary way by the lectures of a certain Elpidius who disputed with the Manichees face to face, for he drew arguments from the scriptures which could not easily be gainsaid" (see *Conf.* V.11.21, p. 123). Later, he will again note that his view of the Scriptures through his experience with the Manichees was challenged. At that time it was the preaching of Ambrose that gave him pause: "As I listened to many such scriptural texts being interpreted in a spiritual sense I confronted my own attitude or at least that despair which had led me to believe that no resistance whatever could be offered to people who loathed and derided the law and the prophets" (see *Conf.* V.14.24, p. 127). After Augustine came to Milan, he read some "books of the Platonists" (*libri platonici*; see *Conf.* VII.9.13, p. 175). He will explain that it was important for

---

Bible as a book to be studied will develop into an ability to read it from within, not study it as an object.

[11] Robert A. Markus, "Life, Culture, and Controversies of Augustine", in *Augustine through the Ages: An Encyclopedia*, ed. Allan D. Fitzgerald, O.S.A. (Grand Rapids, Mich.: W. B. Eerdmans, 1999), p. 498.

him to discover those books before he rediscovered the Scriptures. The books of the Platonists opened him to spiritual thinking, to the immaterial. That meant that he no longer read the Scriptures superficially. Platonism allowed him to see the words and the style differently, but Augustine found things in the Scriptures that he did not find in that philosophy. In Book VII, he explains how much he learned from them—adding how much more he found in the Scriptures. The Word of God showed him what the books of the Platonists did not: how necessary the "truth beyond corporeal forms" (see *Conf*. VII.20.26, p. 189) really was.

His discovery of the books of the Platonists—just as it had happened with the discovery of the *Hortensius*—had led him back to the Scriptures. He realized that he was not just dealing with words on a page, but with the Word who was Christ. Augustine writes, "It was therefore with intense eagerness that I seized on the hallowed calligraphy of your Spirit, and most especially the writings of the apostle Paul. In earlier days it had seemed to me that his teaching was self-contradictory ... but now as these problems melted away your chaste words presented a single face to me, and I learned to rejoice with reverence" (see *Conf*. VII.21.27, p. 191). Because of the preaching of Ambrose, he now had a way to appreciate that the writings of Paul were not just words to be studied.

By the time Augustine gave up his position as rhetorician ("from the market of speechifying"; see *Conf*. IX.2.2, p. 227) and went to Cassiciacum, his knowledge of the Scriptures had grown. He contrasted their authority with that of the Platonic books, noting how the books that conveyed the divine mysteries were the ones that inflamed him.[12] Hence, his conversion was no merely intellectual matter: "[T]he experience of Augustine triggered by the reading of the *books of the*

---

[12] See Augustine, *The Happy Life*, in *Fathers of the Church* 5, trans. Ludwig Schopp (New York: Cima, 1948), 1.4, p. 169: "At the age of 19, when ... I came upon Cicero's book, *Hortensius*, I was inflamed with such enthusiasm for philosophy that I thought of devoting myself to it immediately."

Platonists is not bookish."[13] The Platonists, after all, sought union with the One in a rather generic, impersonal way. Augustine's journey was quite different: "Plotinus never gossiped with the One as Augustine gossips in the *Confessions*."[14] In other words, there was both a deeply Christian quality to Augustine's conversion and a true originality in his *Confessions*.

Rather than having an apparently pure spirituality that subtly mixes Platonist and Christian elements into a new theological synthesis, Augustine presents himself to God as a human being with a name, with deeds that are both good and bad. He is a person in a relationship whose existence is and will be recognizable because of the Other. "With Augustine a new man makes his appearance in the history of consciousness.... [T]he 'I' enters the history of consciousness; the religious relationship takes the form of a dialogue between the 'Thou' and the 'I.'"[15] The Scriptures were thus an integral part of his life and of his reflection—especially because of their interpersonal quality.[16] Not long before he wrote the *Confessions*, Augustine wrote in the treatise *On Christian Doctrine* that, by reading the Scriptures, a studious person would find the double precept of love of God and of neighbor. Augustine continues, "Then it follows that each one will first discover in the [reading of the] Scriptures that he has been enmeshed in the love of this age, that is, of passing things, a love that is far removed from the great love of God and of neighbor that the Scripture prescribes. But then, that fear which reflects on the judgment of God, and that piety which can only believe and accede to the

[13] Goulven Madec, "'In te supra me': Le sujet dans les *Confessiones* de saint Augustine", *Revue de l'Institut catholique de Paris* 28 (1988): 53.

[14] Eric R. Dodds, "Augustine's Confessions", *Hibbert Journal* 26 (1926–1927): 471; cited by P. Brown, *Augustine of Hippo: A Biography* (Berkeley: University of California Press, 2000), p. 160.

[15] Pierre Hadot, *Porphyre et Victorinus* (Paris: Études Augustiniennes, 1968), p. 16.

[16] See Isabelle Bochet, *"Le Firmament de L'Écriture": L'Herméneutique Augustinienne* (Paris: Études Augustiniennes, 2004), p. 53: "The reading of the Scripture only takes on its full sense when it becomes a place of interior dialogue between a person and God."

authority of the sacred books, will force him to lament his own situation." [17]

In other words, the experience of reading the Scriptures made Augustine aware of the problem of being caught up in the things of time and led him back to his true self. When writing the *Confessions*, this same reverence for the Scriptures and for their impact on him is repeated:

> We know no other books with the like power to lay pride low and so surely to silence the obstinate contender who tries to thwart your reconciling work by defending his sins. Nowhere else, Lord, indeed nowhere else do I know such chaste words, words with such efficacy to persuade me to confession, to gentle my neck beneath your kindly yoke and invite me to worship you without thought of reward. Grant me understanding of your words, good Father, give me this gift, stationed as I am below them, because it is for us earth-dwellers that you have fashioned that strong vault overhead (see *Conf.* XIII.15.17). [18]

Hence, only someone who has allowed himself to be instructed by the Scriptures is able to confess in the way Augustine confesses his state both to God and to his fellow human beings. Bochet explains:

> The passage from *praesumptio* to *confessio* is explicitly linked to the reading of the Scripture: more precisely to the reading of the Letters of Paul at the end of Book VII and to the reading of the Psalms in Book IX. This reading is not, obviously, just any reading. It is a reading that had the recognition of the authority of the Scriptures in the background. . . . In addition, it is a reading led by an ardent desire. . . . In that context, Augustine makes the text of the Scriptures his own; he hears it as a divine word that is addressed to him directly and personally. [19]

---

[17] Augustine, *On Christian Doctrine* (New York: Bobbs-Merrill, 1958), II.10, p. 39.

[18] Bochet notes that an explicit description of the passage through the gifts of the Holy Spirit is found in *Sermon* 347.3.3.

[19] Bochet, "Interprétation scripturaire", p. 33 (my translation).

Not only were the Scriptures the real basis for Augustine's conversion, but Augustine saw them as so persuasive that even the Platonists—were they still living—would have assented to their authority.[20]

The Confessions

It may not be possible to determine the exact historical circumstances that led to the writing of the *Confessions*. He wrote it not long after he became Bishop of Hippo. As a tapestry of personal experiences framed in biblical terms and articulated with biblical words, images, and phrases, this book depends greatly on his use, meditation, and appropriation of the Scriptures in the preceding years. The story of his conversion has been transformed—not by turning the facts of his life into fables, but by an appreciation of those facts in relation to the plan of God. Discerning the work of God in his life and writing about it have become more important than any historical detail. Augustine was, undoubtedly, a more perceptive commentator on the meaning of his experience than he could have been as a catechumen.[21]

After he was ordained a priest, his interest will only increase. Thus did he ask Valerius, his bishop, for some time to study the Scriptures—a request based not in some merely personal interest, but in the need he felt to find out how "to exercise this ministry for the salvation of others". He was looking for counsels "by the knowledge and grasp of which a man of God can care for the more ordinary affairs of the Church".[22] At about the same time, writing to Honoratus, a boyhood friend whom he had convinced to join him in becoming a Manichee, he affirms the special place that the Scriptures had for him:

[20] See *On True Religion* 4.7.

[21] See Suzanne Poque, "La prière du Catechumène Augustin en Septembre 386 (*Confessions* IX, iv, 8–11)", in *Congresso Internazionale su S. Agostino nel XVI centenario della Conversione*, vol. 2 (Rome: Institutum Patristicum Augustinianum, 1987), pp. 79–84, especially p. 79.

[22] Augustine, *Letters* (Hyde Park, N.Y.: New City Press, 2001), 21.4, p. 56.

My own conscience, Honoratus, and the God who dwells in pure souls are my witness that in my estimation there is nothing wiser or more pure or more sacred than all those writings that the Catholic Church preserves under the name of the Old Testament.... Believe me, everything in that scripture is profound and from God. There is absolute truth there, and teaching finely adapted to the renewal and restoration of souls and clearly presented in such a way that there is no one who cannot draw from it.[23]

The Bible had become the focus of his work, of his search for truth, of his life—not just as a book with lots of phrases to quote: "I have believed your scriptures, but those words are full of hidden meaning" (see *Conf.* XII.10.10, p. 373). Instead of a piecemeal appreciation of this part of the Scripture, "the ideal reader for Augustine knows the whole book. A truly accomplished investigator of holy scriptures has read and become familiar with them all, even if she or he does not yet understand them."[24]

Thus was the pear theft that he described in Book II become a reflection on the sin of Adam so as to understand and face how his preference for camaraderie led away from the law of God and he became to himself "a land of famine" (see *Conf.* II.10.18, p. 49). The story of the prodigal son allowed him to describe the meaning of his return to Catholic Christianity.[25] This parable becomes a paradigm for Augustine's attitude toward his own experience, as well as for Christian penance and

---

[23] Augustine, *The Advantage of Believing*, in *On Christian Belief* (Hyde Park, N.Y.: New City Press, 2005), 6.13, p. 126.

[24] McCarthy, "'We Are Your Books'", p. 331, note 10, citing *On Christian Doctrine* 2.8.12.

[25] See Luke 15:11–32; also, see A. Fitzgerald, "Arise! A Scriptural Model for Augustine's Conversion", *Angelicum* 64 (1987): 359–75; and L. Verheijen, "The Confessiones: Two Grids of Composition and Reading", in *Augustine: "Second Founder of the Faith"* (Collectanea Agustiniana 1), J.C. Schnaubelt and F. Van Fleteren, eds. (New York: Peter Lang, 1990), 175–201, where he affirms; "In the *Confessions* there are no fewer than nineteen very clear allusions to the parable of the prodigal son", p. 188. See also L.C. Ferrari, "The theme of the Prodigal Son in Augustine's *Confessions*", *Recherches Augustiniennes* 12 (1977): 105–18.

conversion. In this case, too, he shows that the Scriptures consolidate the significance of his own conversion for himself.[26] Similar comments can be made about his use of the stories of the widow of Naim and of the raising of Lazarus.[27]

The Book of Psalms

However, the book of Psalms had a particularly significant place in the process of his conversion: "How loudly I began to cry out to you in those psalms, how I was inflamed by them with love for you" (see *Conf.* IX.4.8, p. 234).[28] They provided him with the language of confession, of praise of God. Reflecting on Psalm 8, Augustine wrote, "Nowhere else, Lord, indeed nowhere else do I know such chaste words, words with such efficacy to persuade me to confession, to gentle my neck beneath your kindly yoke and invite me to worship you without thought of reward" (see *Conf.* XIII.15.17, p. 425). As one example among many, it shows how Augustine's meditation on the Psalms allowed him to write the *Confessions*.[29]

That meditation took place within the Christian community whose prayer book was the psalter. The Psalms, in fact, had a broad range of meanings and could refer to many kinds of events or circumstances—thus integrating those who prayed them into the history of salvation. Such was also Augustine's experience: "The anonymous character of the psalms, just as much as their symbolic language, allowed Augustine to apply

[26] See A. M. La Bonnardière, *Recherches de chronologie augustinienne* (Paris: Institut des Etude Augustiniennes, 1965), p. 180, on the general importance of the Scriptures.

[27] These scriptural texts are discussed in a different context in Fitzgerald, "Arise!", pp. 359–75.

[28] See, too, Luc Verheijen, *Eloquentia Pedisequa. Observations sur le Style des Confessions de s. Augustin* (Nijmegen: Dekker & Van der Vegt, 1949), pp. 66, 79. His experience with the Psalms was where Augustine learned the meaning of *confiteor* and *confessio*.

[29] See Isabelle Bochet, "In Ps. 1–32, un prelude aux *Confessions*?" in *Les Commenataires des Psaumes 1–16*, as in *Bibliothèque Augustinienne* 57A (Paris: Institut des Etudes Augustiniennes, 2009), p. 99; the Scriptures are accessible to the humble rather than to the proud.

them to his conversion experience; but he likewise found a language that could express the universal scope and the meaning of his experience. In addition, taking into account the history of salvation, to which both the psalms and their interpretation by the Church invited him, led Augustine to recognize conversion as a piece of the whole plan of salvation."[30] But Augustine sees the benefit of such a process in terms of the Christian community. Not only does it allow him to articulate his experience in Christian terms, but he is quite explicit about his intentions: "Truth it is that I want to do, in my heart by confession in your presence, and with my pen before many witnesses" (see *Conf.* X.1.1, p. 263).

These examples provide a basis for beginning to notice how Augustine's appropriation of the Scriptures became a way to interpret his own experience.[31] Whether it was his use of the Psalms,[32] his study of Paul,[33] or his understanding of the Gospels,[34] his life was in dialogue with God through his Word. Thus could he say, "Is hearing the truth about oneself from you anything different from knowing oneself?" (see *Conf.* X.3.3). Hence, Augustine is a Christian who does not just tell his story in a clever and engaging way. His familiarity with the Bible allowed him to see his life in biblical terms. When he appropriates the prayer of the Psalms, or recognizes himself in the prodigal son, or sees himself, son of Adam, as saved by Christ,

---

[30] Ibid., p. 87.

[31] See Bochet, *"Le Firmament de L'Écriture"*. The comments of this section of this article depend on pages 91–186 of that book.

[32] See Luc Verheijen, *Eloquentia Pedisequa. Observations sur le Style des Confessions de s. Augustin*; as well as U. Duchrow, "Der Aufbau von Augustins Schriften *Confessiones* und *De trinitate*", *Zeitschrift für Theologie und Kirche* 6 (1965): 338–67; and K. Knauer, *Psalmenzitate in Augustins Konfessionem* (Göttigen, Vandenhoeck and Ruprecht, 1955).

[33] See *Conf.* VIII.5.11: "I thus came to understand from my own experience what I had read, how the flesh lusts against the spirit and the spirit strives against the flesh."

[34] Especially the parable of the prodigal son. See Fitzgerald, "Arise!", pp. 359–75; and Luc Verheijen, "The *Confessions* of Saint Augustine: Two Grids of Composition and Reading", in *The Proceedings of the Patristic Mediaeval and Renaissance Conference* (Villanova: Villanova University Press, 1986), pp. 1–18.

he becomes like a biblical figure, created in the image of God and saved by Jesus Christ. He presents himself, not merely "in the uniqueness of his own experience",[35] but from within the experience of biblical figures. That shifts the focus of his concern beyond himself to what God has done in him by his Word: "I recognized that you have chastened man for his sin and caused my soul to dwindle away like a spider's web, and I said, 'Is truth then a nothing, simply because it is not spread out through space either finite or infinite?' Then from afar you cried to me, 'By no means, for *I am who am*.' I heard it as one hears a word in the heart" (see *Conf.* VII.10.16; italics in original, p. 180).

Conclusion

All through these years, the Scriptures play a central role, helping Augustine to articulate the meaning of his own conversion in a way that would inspire others to do the same. His reading of the Scriptures had moved him to conversion: "I thus came to understand from my own experience what I had read" (see *Conf.* VIII.5.11, p. 206).[36] Augustine had learned to see his story from the point of view of the mystery of salvation in Christ.[37] In approaching the Scriptures first as a seeker and then as a Christian and, finally, as overseer of a Christian community, he also learned that only through the confession of God's mercy, revealed in Christ, does the sinner find the solution for sin and misery. Thus do the *Confessions* give voice to the experience of praising God and of questioning God in biblical terms and images. The Bible became *his*, not in the sense of something memorized or cited, but a part of his very way of thinking, talking, and being.

[35] Madec, "'In te supra me'", p. 52.

[36] Bochet shows clearly that this transformation by the reading of the Scriptures both began prior to his conversion and continued afterwards. See Bochet, "*Le Firmament*", pp. 263–64.

[37] See G. Madec, *Recherches Augustiennes* 10 (1975): 77–85, especially p. 82, for a general commentary on Augustine's relation to Christ. Augustine's concern for the name of Christ on the way toward conversion is frequently expressed (see *Conf.* III.4.8; III.6.10; V.14.25; VI.4.5; IX.4.7).

Augustine's *Confessions* and the
Source of Christian Character*

Christopher J. Thompson
University of St. Thomas

The desire to love deeply—eternally and truthfully—is the splendid prize of every human life and animates our choices from birth to death. Augustine's *Confessions*, written by a forty-something bishop at the peak of his powers, narrates his own journey in love from his birth to "second birth", more specifically, his reception into the Catholic Church.

But his is not a "tell all" tale, so popular nowadays in our contemporary culture of endless talk shows and worldwide blogging. Despite the title, which may suggest otherwise to modern readers, Augustine's "confessions" is not an exercise in catharsis, a chronicle of the intricacies of his own ego. Such self-absorption, such overwrought introspection, would have left the Bishop of Hippo in the same condition it leaves any us who become preoccupied with the labyrinthine ways of our own egos—bored and exhausted. Augustine would be disappointed to think that his efforts leave the reader wanting to know more about Augustine. For as fascinating as I may be to myself, Augustine reminds me, my "self" is not what satisfies.

The point is not to learn about his life, but to learn about the God of his life; his aim is to convey something intensely personal, but not private. This is the thrust of the *Confessions*: authentic autobiography is essentially doxology—God, and God alone, quiets the restless heart. One journeys into the interior life, not in an effort to "know thyself", but to

*Significant portions of this essay were drawn from Chapter IV of my book, *Christian Doctrine, Christian Identity: Augustine and the Narratives of Character* (Lanham, Md.: University Press of America, 2000).

know thyself in God, to know thyself as a creature of God—created in goodness, caught in sin, cured by the redeeming grace of Christ. To narrate one's life along other, perhaps more familiar, lines of one's hopes, dreams, loves, and losses is ultimately to engage in self-defeating "spin". God's love for me, not my love for me, is the only prism through which I honestly confess. God, closer to me than I am to myself, is the reality against which my life, my efforts to love truly, deeply, eternally, is made whole.

For the first time in Christian culture, the *Confessions* makes an argument that the revelation of God, as the Good Creator of all that is and the Redeemer of all who seek salvation, supplies the theological foundations that give intelligible shape to one's interior life. The emphasis is not on Augustine's experience, then, and how it might illuminate Christian doctrine (the modern "turn to the subject" will not be taken for several more centuries); rather, priority is given to the doctrine of the Church and how it illuminates, indeed constitutes, human experience.

This is why the *Confessions* concludes in the manner that it does, so vexing to contemporary scholars who read it with modern lenses, with an analysis of Genesis and the Church. It is the Church's creed that discloses to Augustine the outlines of what it means to be the kind of person narrated in Books I–IX. Jettison the doctrinal affirmations made in those latter chapters, and what is he left with in terms of his "experience"? A witless pastiche of disconnected impulses toward this or that good, this or that evil. What am "I" apart from God's sustaining love? An accidental occasion of perennial neediness, a petty player (to borrow from Shakespeare) whose tale is "told by an idiot, full of sound and fury, signifying nothing" (*Macbeth*, Act 5, scene 5, lines 27–28).

In Augustine's time, there were alternatives to the existential ennui that ensues with the absence of faith in a loving God. He knew that any account of the waywardness of human loving could become vulnerable to rival interpretations, alien to the orthodox faith of the Church—interpretations, it will turn out, that take at face value the seemingly contradictory features of human experience and leave them essentially intact.

The experience of our inclinations to this or that good will not yield to the notion of one, continuous relationship to an all-persistent Love by whom we are created and through whom we find our "rest". Rather, experience points to rival voices, so they will argue. It names a chimera, a "fiction" that masks the fundamental chaos and rupture at the ontological depths of things.

The Manichean Context

It is easier to appreciate this intimate relationship between identity and doctrine when one considers the rival interpretation of human experience proposed by Manichaeism, for Manichaeism will propose a radically different creed, and hence, a radically different conception of what constitutes human experience. Their portrait of human identity is rooted in an altogether different theological paradigm, and Augustine's efforts to dismantle that vision of existence help highlight the fundamental interdependence of theological doctrine and conceptions of human identity.

Briefly stated, Manichees hold to a theological dualism, namely, that at the origin of the cosmos, two principles existed—one good (Light), one evil (Darkness). From an attack initiated by the Evil Principle, good and evil became engaged in a cosmic struggle. As a result of this struggle, the Evil Principle fashioned animated bodies, especially human beings, as a means of keeping a part of the Good Principle trapped.

Their theological story bore cosmological implications as well. As thoroughgoing materialists, the Manichees held that the universe itself was the material extension of these original, "divine" principles. The progressive unfolding of the world, then, consists in the constant struggle between good forces and evil forces whereby the former, though defenseless against the attacks of the latter, seeks to return to its native place. Through procreation, the good "stuff" trapped inside living individuals remains in physical bodies, and thus, through successive procreation and generation, the Evil Principle reigns.

In Manichean cosmology, the world did not originate, as Augustine would eventually come to believe, in the creative act of a supremely good Creator, in which all that is created is good. The order of the world, the coming to be and passing away of creatures, and especially the human being are not the creations of one, supremely loving God.[1] Instead, we are the fallout, the collateral damage of a primordial violence waged at the dawn of the aeons.

The Manichees' habit for reducing "good" and "evil" to purely material categories meant that human experience could not yield evidence of a subject of moral action. The human person is, rather, the mere object of rival forces, the occasion of perennial battles. The "I" is not an enduring subject of actions over time, nor does human experience disclose an integrated self who is the author of good and evil actions. The human creature is, instead, an amalgam of rival forces; he is merely the battleground between dueling, cosmic parties, liberated or saved only to the extent that the "*gnosis*" of one's condition is acknowledged. "It still seemed to me that it is not we who sin," Augustine reports of his earlier time among the Manichees in Rome, "but some other nature within us that is responsible" (see *Conf.* V.10.18, p. 119).

When we engage in evil actions, the Manichees contended, it is due to the causality of the Evil Principle, and thus, such actions are not rightly attributed to what they would identify as our "truer" part. "I liked to excuse myself", he says, "and lay the blame on some other force that was with me but was not myself".[2] The term "Augustine", then, identifies the

---

[1] See Saint Augustine, *The Confessions*, ed. David Vincent Meconi, S.J., Ignatius Critical Editions (San Francisco: Ignatius Press, 2012), XIII.30.45. Subsequent quotations from this edition will be cited in the text. References are to book, section, and paragraph. A brief description is also provided in Augustine's *On the Nature of the Good* §46.

[2] It is not clear how Augustine may have reconciled this position with the apparent confessional formulas articulated at the Bema Festival, of which he

conjunction of opposing primordial forces of good and evil. It names the locus of confrontation and does not name, according to Manichean beliefs, a substantial unity, a true "I". "But in truth", Augustine eventually comes to see, "it was all myself" (see *Conf.* V.10.18, p. 120). Alas, he was one creature, a single character, a *totum ego*. And, it is precisely his defense of this conclusion that drives the argument of the *Confessions*.

When reading from this anti-Manichean vantage, one can begin to appreciate further the systematic significance of the latter books of the *Confessions*. For those books supply elements of the theological critique of the Manichean portrait of human experience. More than this negative function, however, they supply in a positive fashion the theological warrant for such a portrait of Christian personal identity.

Books X–XIII:
Toward an Ontology of Christian Integrity

Having just completed, in Books I–IX, his own narrative of his life up to his reception into the Church, Augustine advances his argument in Book X to a higher level, to a metaconsideration of the capacity on the part of the human person to narrate one's life as such. Notwithstanding the sometimes arduous efforts to recall or to organize one's experience in an intelligible order, he insists that "the person who remembers is myself; I am my mind" (see *Conf.* X.16.25, p. 284). It is the memory of a single, integrated "I", not the divided, bifurcated self that a Manichean sympathizer would propose. This unity of identity among diverse recollections challenges Augustine to look further into the mystery of human consciousness. In Book XI, the interplay between the past, present, and future will become his central preoccupation. For the moment,

---

may have been aware. It should be noted that in naming the Evil Principle as "alien" and "not I" Augustine shifts the paradigm from that of an otherwise evil self with some particle of good trapped inside to that of a good self with an evil, though lesser dimension.

it is enough to recognize that *memoria* is more than simple chronological recall; rather, it is that capacity to situate ourselves within a story of our lives.

Of course, it is the experience of God that is central to the Christian's story, and so Augustine turns to the question of our consideration of Christ. The development at this point in Augustine's thought is subtle but central. Noting the vast power of memory to situate ourselves within a narrative of experience, he tells us that God is not to be identified with that capacity. God is not the mind itself, for "you are the Lord and God of the mind" (see *Conf.* X.25.36, p. 295).

Augustine's "memory" of God, his ability to narrate an account of himself as one taken up in the plan of salvation, is not merely an exercise in historical chronology; it is to move to a more penetrating analysis of the nature of reality itself. It is not a matter of placing God within the horizon of one's experience. It is not a matter of trying to "recall" when God entered as a character among the vast storehouse of characters known as his "experience". Experience itself is to be placed within the prior reality of God. The depth of this insight gives rise to one of the most beautiful and often cited passages of the *Confessions*: "You were with me, but I was not with you. They [the things in my life] held me back far from you, those things which would have no being were they not in you. You called, shouted, broke through my deafness; you flared, blazed, banished my blindness; you lavished your fragrance, I gasped and now I pant for you; I tasted you, and I hunger and thirst; you touched me, and I burned for your peace" (see *Conf.* X.27.38, p. 296). Conversion will not consist in recognizing God in one's life; it will consist in recognizing one's life in God. I do not come to the God of revelation with my experiences; the God of revelation reveals to me the coherence and truth of my experiences.

Book XI continues this effort at the macrolevel, situating all of the created order within the Creative Word, and to maintain this primacy of the Word in spite of our "fallen" tendencies to do otherwise.[3] It is the Word who is the first principle of all creation. As sinful creatures, the task will be to resist the habit of constantly telling the story of our lives in a way that obfuscates our dependency on Christ. This story can only be truthfully told within the Church, the story of the Creative and Redeeming Word, who heals us and makes of our distended ways authentic persons. This is the fullest sense in which the Church's story of God's providential presence to us becomes the normative narrative of all authentic Christian personality. I am not the detritus of some cosmic calamity. Nor am I an abandoned ego, marooned on the shoals of an otherwise meaningless, impenetrable cosmos, prisoner of my own imagination or self-constituting reason. I am an adopted child of a loving God, a God more intimate to me than I am to myself.

Augustine takes up this promise of integrity in Books XII and XIII with an allegorical interpretation of the opening chapters of Genesis. The move is not to direct our attention historically backward to the origins of the world, but deeper into the world as it is now, to a more penetrating insight into the nature of human existence. The opening chapters of Genesis symbolically disclose the structure of our corporate solidarity both with Adam and Eve (as fallen) and Christ (as believers). Having completed the analysis of the subjective and objective conditions of what it means to be a character within the drama of salvation, Augustine turns to Scripture and seeks to find within its pages an outline of the role of the Church. As the Body of Christ, the Church is that community in history which sustains us along our pilgrimage to that "heaven of heaven", the City of God, which was inaugurated before the beginning of time.

---

[3] See "The Theological Dimensions of Time in *Confessiones* XI", in *Collectanea Augustiniana II: Presbyter Factus Sum*, ed. Joseph T. Lienhard, S.J., Earl C. Muller, S.J., and Roland J. Teske, S.J. (New York: Peter Lang, 1993), pp. 187–93. On the creaturely status of time, see Augustine's *Literal Commentary on Genesis* V.5.12.

Books I–IX: A Christian Narrative of Identity

In the more autobiographical books (I–IX), Augustine's concern to defend a conception of Christian identity is no less acute, though it is diffuse and dispersed among the personal anecdotes. Without the interpretive clues of the latter books, however, one risks missing the thrust of his narrative. God is first, and his life is the counterpoint. The many scriptural allusions, the appeals to God, are not mere rhetorical flourishes. They provide the mortar, which holds the bricks of his life, making of his account a single edifice. And so, the anecdotes of Augustine's life are placed within a tapestry of meditations concerning God and his relationship to him. Autobiography is made perfect in prayer.

The problem of moral evil is a constant theme in the first books, though the subject is virtually abandoned in the last three. Book II is the point of departure for the subject, offering an extended meditation upon the now famous theft of pears. For my purposes, it is enough to note that virtually every aspect of the episode described would have riveted the attention of anyone with an awareness of Manichaeism.

In the Manichean mind, there could have been no greater example of complete moral depravity than the theft of pears recorded in Book II. Augustine's extensive reflection on this adolescent prank reveals the Good Shepherd guiding the flock through the labyrinth of moral corruption—not, of course, in an effort to lead the "hearers" back to their dualistic origins but to lead them ahead to the vision of the good Creation, affirmed in the opening chapters of Genesis.

It is not likely due to lingering remorse that Augustine reports the deed, for he has recognized at the end of Book II that God has "melted [his] sins away like ice" (see *Conf.* II.7.15, p. 46). Nor is it enough to say that theft is a serious crime (though it is) and so deserves special attention in the account, for in Book I, Augustine has already admitted that he committed thefts from his parents' cellar (see *Conf.* I.19.30). Obviously, this theft does not have the arresting effect on the flow of the narrative like the theft of pears in Book II. Why the appeal to pears?

Simply stated, the example appears to be a direct appeal to the Manichee. All the elements of a most vicious act are present in this brief paragraph. If Augustine wanted to take up the problem of Christian identity against the Manichees, he could not have selected a more riveting example. In the first place, there is the setting—the cover of darkness, an atmosphere in which, according to Manichean lore, evil forces exercise unchallenged reign. As materialistic dualists, it is not only Light that exercises physical force within the created order.[4]

Perhaps the most significant aspect is the issue of the fruit itself. In Manichean cosmology, parts of the "good" god himself are trapped within the animated substances of the created order. All animated things, in varying degrees, contain elements of the good god, which in turn seek release from the bondage of material evil. Nonhuman animals occupy one of the lowest levels in this hierarchy, while plants—especially figs, dates, fruits, and vegetables—contain the greatest amount of divinity. The general rule of thumb for Manichees regarding the presence of the divine in certain fruits and vegetables is that the more translucent the substance, or the more brilliant its coloring, the more it contained parts of the divine.

To the Manichee, parts of a god were trapped in the stolen fruit and were denied the possibility of redemption—i.e., they were denied the possibility of being eaten by the Elect. For it was only through the discriminating bowels of the Elect that the divine particles could have been released through digestion. Any food that was spoiled, then, would have to seek another route of redemption by returning to the soil, entering a tree, and then passing through an Elect. The worst fate their god could suffer would be to be eaten by a pig, since the pig

---

[4] Darkness itself has its elements of control. In the sixty-fifth chapter of the Manichean *Kephalia*, one reads that among the various effects of Darkness as it "fills the whole world" and "spreads its shadows" is that "all creatures are drawn toward rebellion.... They rebel in their hearts and do wicked and perverse things" (*Kephalia* LXV.161.1–2).

(along with snakes) occupied the lowest level in the hierarchy of reality. Once devoured by a pig, virtually no hope remained for their god who was trapped inside—even in the eschaton such divinity could not be restored to its rightful place. Finally, Augustine carefully informs the reader that even if he and his friends had eaten a few, their pleasure lay in doing what was not allowed (see *Conf.* II.4.9). To a Manichean hearer, the situation was completely hopeless. The god himself had either been left to rot, forced to enter the bowels of a pig, or, equally worse, the bowels of a non-Manichean. There could have been no better example to introduce the problems of human moral depravity.

Having been a Manichee for nine years, Augustine is well versed in this tradition, and all of the above Manichean features are well documented in his earlier works. In *On the Manichean Way of Life*, for example, he tells the story of a Manichean community in Rome who had apparently killed one of their members by force-feeding him. This was done in order to avoid blaspheming against the divinity who remained inside some leftover fruits and vegetables. "I would not have believed it", Augustine notes, "had I not known how sinful you consider it either to give this food to those who are not of the Elect or to get rid of it by throwing it out."[5] In that same work, Augustine explicitly speaks of plucking fruit from a tree, and remarks that "one would undoubtedly be condemned by you ... if he did this intentionally and not accidentally."[6] No Manichean sympathizer would have wandered from Augustine's graphic depiction of the nature of moral evil.

Evil actions, Augustine argues, do not emerge from an alien principle of evil within the self. Rather, an evil character emerges from the development of wicked habits, and these in turn are rooted in our relationship to the original sin of Adam. "[D]isordered lust springs from a perverted will", Augustine claims, and by acquiescence to disordered passion, "a habit is

---

[5] *On The Manichean Way of Life* XVI.52.
[6] *On The Manichean Way of Life* XVI.55.

formed; when habit is not checked it hardens into compulsion" (see *Conf.* VIII.5.10, pp. 205–6). This psychological principle of habit will effectively replace the Manichean materialist principle of evil. The shift is not insignificant in that it recasts the problems of the divided self from a cosmological context to a psychological one, from a consideration of causes extrinsic to an otherwise bifurcated entity, the *object* of cosmic impulses, to an account of the struggle of an integrated (though wounded) person, the singular *subject* of moral action, a single "I", who lives in constant union with an eternally present God.

Note well, though, how it is *not* on the level of the mere description, the mere chronology of experiences, that Augustine exhibits the outlines of authentic Christian character. He knows that a mere description of experience *cannot* be the normative guide, for a description of one's experiences can be told from many perspectives—some of which are hostile to Christian doctrine. For Augustine, it will not be enough to simply tell his experiences; he must narrate them rightly. An account of *Christian* character will take into consideration the doctrine of the Church as the normative guide.

The problem of the inadequacy of experience uninformed by doctrine emerges in Book VIII, in which the details of his dramatic conversion are discussed. With an orthodox psychology on the line, much is at stake in describing the conditions of the struggle properly. Augustine knows that without the further elaboration of the latter books, in which the doctrines underwriting an authentic portrait of Christian identity are developed, the reader might misinterpret the nature of his experience in the garden in Milan. Augustine insists throughout his account that "I was the only one involved" (see *Conf.* VIII.10.22, p. 218). His repeated emphasis on the singularity of human identity is intentional and points to his determination to have his story read rightly.

Augustine suspects that readers might misinterpret his experience, and so he interrupts the flow of the narrative and addresses the issue of a rival interpretation. "Let them perish from your presence, O God," he says concerning those "who on perceiving two wills engaged in deliberation assert that in us there are two natures, one good, the other evil, each with a mind of its own" (see *Conf.* VIII.10.22, p. 217). A Manichee would have held that the competing interests within the creature signal the presence of competing forces, competing principles of activity. Augustine's account of intense deliberations, they would argue, fully confirms their materialist dualism.

By maintaining the position that the human creature is an amalgam of warring parties, Augustine argues, the Manichees tear apart the soul. For if there are as many competing causes as there are inclinations, it would appear that the creature is the amalgam of much more than merely two opposing forces the Manichees identify (see *Conf.* VIII.10.24). Moreover, experience shows that we deliberate and thus give rise to rival inclinations, not merely in conflicts *between* good and evil, but *among* good and evil: to go to the theatre or to church, to assault a man this way or that. What is the Manichee to say when "good" inclinations seem to war with other "good" ones, or evil with evil? By positing as many distinct causes for actions as there are diverse and competing interests, the Manichees destroy the very fabric of moral integrity, the very notion of an "I". To be a human being, Augustine argues, is to be the consistent, enduring subject of one's deliberations and actions. One and the same soul wavers between conflicting interests. The controversy in Augustine's heart is a war *within* a single whole, not *amid* an amalgam of rival forces. Character requires singularity of purpose, simplicity not variety, integrity not diversity.[7]

Yet, it is not simply the continuity of mere *ego* that Augustine seeks to defend. Rather, he seeks to portray an authentically *Christian* character. And so, in the midst of his dramatic account of his conversion in Book VIII, Augustine turns to his detractors and says that they would become renewed if they

[7] For an excellent interpretation of Augustine on this point, see William Mallard, *Language and Love: Introducing Augustine's Religious Thought through the Confessions Story* (University Park, Penn.: Pennsylvania State University Press, 1994), especially pp. 150–62.

held to the true doctrines and assented to the "true teaching, and so merit the apostle's commendation, 'You were darkness, once, but now you are light in the Lord' [Ephesians 5:8]" (see *Conf.* VIII.10.22, p. 217). Here, as in several other places, Augustine muses upon the implications of this passage[8] and gives us hints as to the line of theological argument he will take up in the latter books.

This possibility of being at one time darkness but now "light in the Lord" strikes to the very heart of Augustine's defense of Christian integrity and highlights how the account of his own struggles with sin and conversion are framed within these broader theological concerns. The reference echoes the reflections of Book XIII and gives a foretaste of the meditations to come.[9] The passage from sin to redemption on the part of fallen humanity entails distinct moments of time, he insists, and this means that something of a self endures through the struggle from sin to salvation. That "something" is the created human soul—good from the point of view of its existence, yet wounded by sin. It is this soul, distended yet nonetheless integral, which has an enduring character through the drama of creation and salvation.

It is, moreover, a soul that is "in the Lord", an "I" that is progressively brought by the grace of Christ, the Creative and Redeeming Word, from darkness to light, a subject who resides in the providential care of the Word, the *principium* of creation and mediator of salvation. It is this participation in Christ— Word and Redeemer—that is the fundamental ground of our enduring existence through sin and salvation. The decision to

---

[8] See *Conf.* IX.4.10; XIII.2.3; XIII.8.9; XIII.10.11; XIII.12.13; XIII.14.15.

[9] In Book XIII, one reads of "heaven's heaven", the community of intelligences toward which we are now in pilgrimage. Members of this community do not experience this kind of transition from darkness to light "in the Lord", for they have always been "in the Lord", the Word of Creation and Redemption. It is this community which enjoyed integral creatureliness, a unity that was not lost due to original sin. Unlike ourselves as fallen people who experience "distinct moments of time" between a life in darkness and one "in the Lord", the "heaven's heaven" cleaves to God from the moment of its creation without any experience of distension; see *Conf.* XIII.10.11.

be baptized into Christ is the decision to begin an ongoing transformation toward Christian integrity.

It is finally in this Christological context that Augustine's
defense of Christian identity is brought to fruition. It is in the
Lord that we participate, in the Word who has "made" us and
will "make" us "anew" and give us consolation (see *Conf.* V.2.2,
p. 102). The fact that the Triune God is one, that the Creative Word is the source of our creation, and his Spirit the
means of our redemption helps fill in the Augustinian anthropology in important ways.

In the first place, it marks a paradigmatic shift from the dualistic principles of Manichean theology to the normative quality of Christian experience. The enduring quality of the creature
through darkness to "light in the Lord" is precisely what the
Manichean schema had eliminated. Darkness and Light, one
may recall, are distinct and diametrically opposing entities.
Hence, nothing, according to the Manichees, can change from
darkness to "light in the Lord".

More importantly, by recognizing our participation in Christ,
the kind of Christian integrity Augustine seeks to defend is
not merely the unity of consciousness disclosed by storytell-
ing; rather, the singularity of *Christian* identity rests upon our
relationship with Christ, the *principium* of our being and our
being made whole. It is the doctrine of the Creative and
Redeeming Word that supplies the broadest context in which
human beings understand themselves as enduring characters
within the journey from sin to salvation. It is in Christ and
his Church that the fullness of one's self is brought to light.

The *Confessions* displays how Augustine's notion of Christ
as both the Word (Logos) of creation and the Word Incarnate of Redemption is the condition for authentic Christian
character. In an account of authentic Christian praxis, a person supplies more than the chronology of private experience;
rather, it is a chronology of experience permeated by the action
of God in Christ and his Church. It means any account that
proposes to be Christian must give priority not to the historical unfolding of our private experiences, but to the enduring

presence of God's creative Word, Christ the *principium* of creation (see *Conf.* XI.8.10), Christ the voice of Scripture (see *Conf.* XIII.29.44), Christ the Word made flesh (see *Conf.* VII.18.24), Christ the true mediator (see *Conf.* X.43.68), Christ our Eucharistic food (see *Conf.* VII.10.16), Christ the Bridegroom of the Heavenly Jerusalem (see *Conf.* XIII.13.14). To discover what it is to be a Christian is to discover one's self as taken up within the broader narrative of God's providential plan of which one is a part. It is to discover a theological ontology of subjectivity.

"[A]s my years waste away amid groaning", the man of midlife begins to muse, "you are my solace, Lord, because you are my Father, and you are eternal." He continues, "In the most intimate depths of my soul my thoughts are torn to fragments by tempestuous changes until that time when I flow into you, purged and rendered molten by the fire of your love" (see *Conf.* XI.29.39, p. 362). There, in the Heart of Love, we learn to love—deeply, eternally, truthfully.

CONTRIBUTORS

Allan Fitzgerald, O.S.A., is the director of the Augustinian Institute (since 2009) at Villanova University in Pennsylvania. He has taught in the Department of Theology at Villanova (1972–1997) and in the Augustinian Patristic Institute in Rome (1997–2009). He edited the volume *Augustine through the Ages: An Encyclopedia* (Wm. Eerdmans, 1999) and is the editor of *Augustinian Studies* since 1990. His interests include the history of penance and the life and thought of Augustine of Hippo and of Ambrose of Milan.

Joseph T. Lienhard, S.J., received his degrees from the University of Freiburg, Germany, with works on Paulinus of Nola and Marcellus of Ancyra. From 1975 to 1990 he taught at Marquette University, and since then at Fordham University. He has held visiting professorships at John Carroll University, Boston College, St. Joseph's Seminary, the Pontifical Biblical Institute, and the Pontifical Gregorian University. He is the author, editor, or translator of twelve books, and the author of more than fifty scholarly articles.

David Vincent Meconi, S.J., is currently the assistant professor of patristic theology at Saint Louis University as well as the director of the Undergraduate Studies Program there. He holds degrees from Marquette University, the Pontifical License in Patrology from the University of Innsbruck in Austria, as well as a D.Phil. (Oxon.), in ecclesiastical history from Oxford University. His latest book is *The One Christ: St. Augustine's Theology of Deification* (Catholic University of America Press, 2012). He is the author of numerous monographs, essays, and video series, as well as the editor of *Homiletic and Pastoral Review*.

Jared Ortiz is Assistant Professor of Religion at Hope College in Holland, Michigan. He earned his doctorate in theology from The Catholic University of America where he wrote a dissertation on the role of creation in Augustine's *Confessions*. He has also earned an M.A. from Catholic University as well as an M.A. in Liberal Arts from the St. John's College Graduate Institute.

Christopher J. Thompson holds degrees in theology and philosophy from Creighton University, Saint Louis University, and Marquette University. He serves as the Academic Dean of the Saint Paul Seminary School of Divinity at the University of St. Thomas, in Saint Paul, Minnesota, and writes and teaches on a variety of topics, including Thomistic moral theology, marriage and family, and the environment. He resides in Saint Paul with his wife and three children.

A final word of thanks to those students here at Saint Louis University who helped Father Meconi with so much collecting, proofreading, and praying: **Andrew Chronister, Scott Dermer, Rachel Kondro,** and **Ben Wayman**. Thank you to **Dr. Geoffrey Miller** for his help in researching the "Old Latin" scriptural references. May the Doctor of Grace continue to lead you into Christ's own restful heart.